Lecture Notes in Artificial Intelligence   11876

Subseries of Lecture Notes in Computer Science

More information about this series at http://www.springer.com/series/1244

Preface

The 11th International Conference on Social Robotics (ICSR 2019) was held in Madrid, Spain, during November 26–29, 2019. This book includes the proceedings of the conference, comprising 69 refereed papers, reviewed by the International Program Committee, and presented during the technical sessions of the conference.

The ICSR conference series brings together researchers and practitioners working on the interaction between humans and robots and on the integration of robots into our society. Now in its 11th year, ICSR is the leading international forum for researchers in social robotics. ICSR provides researchers and practitioners the opportunity to present and engage in dialogs on the latest progress in the field of social robotics.

The theme of the ICSR 2019 was "Friendly Robots." Social robots are intended to coexist with humans and engage in relationships that lead them to a better quality of life. The success of these relationships relies on a positive perception of the robots that can be achieved by their behavior through Artificial Intelligence (AI), computational models, or robot embodiments. ICSR 2019 aimed to foster discussion on the development of innovative ideas, novel applications, and relevant studies that contribute to the integration of social robots in our society. ICSR is the premier forum that looks into the potential of these technologies and gives insights to address the challenges and risks.

ICSR 2019 received 92 submissions in total and accepted 69 as full papers, yielding an overall acceptance rate of 75%. Accepted papers were arranged under the topics: perceptions and expectations of social robots; cognition and social values for social robots; verbal interaction with social robots; social cues and design of social robots; emotional and expressive interaction with social robots, collaborative SR, and SR at the workplace; game approaches and applications to HRI; applications in heath domain; robots at home and at public spaces; robots in education; technical innovations in social robotics; and privacy and safety of social robots.

In addition to the technical sessions, ICSR 2019 included six workshops: (i) The Communication Challenges in Joint Action for Human-Robot Interaction, (ii) Perspectives on Human-Aware Navigation, (iii) Self-coaching Tools for Conducting Responsible Research and Innovation with Social Robots, (iv) Quality of Interaction in Socially Assistive Robots, (v) Experimental and Integrative Approaches to Robo-ethics, and (vi) Robots in the Wild: from the Lab, Field and Showrooms to Real-world Experiences in Social Robotics.

ICSR 2019 included three distinguished researchers in social robotics as keynote speakers: Dr. Katsu Yamane, Senior Scientist at Honda Research Institute, USA; Francesco Ferro, CEO and co-founder of PAL Robotics, Spain; and Lola Cañamero, Head of the Embodied Emotion, Cognition and (Inter-)Action Lab in the School of Computer Science at the University of Hertfordshire, UK.

We would like to express our appreciation to the Organizing Committee for putting together an excellent program, to the International Program Committee for their rigorous review of the papers, and most importantly to the authors and participants who enhanced the quality and effectiveness of the conference through their papers, presentations, and conversations.

We are hopeful that this conference will generate many future collaborations and research endeavors, resulting in enhancing human lives through the utilization of social robots and AI.

November 2019

Miguel A. Salichs
Shuzhi Sam Ge
Emilia Barakova
John-John Cabibihan
Alan R. Wagner
Álvaro Castro-González
Hongsheng He

Organization

General Chairs

Miguel Ángel Salichs   Universidad Carlos III Madrid, Spain
Shuzhi Sam Ge   National University of Singapore, Singapore

Program Chairs

Emilia Barakova   Eindhoven University of Technology, The Netherlands
Alan R. Wagner   Pennsylvania State University, USA
John-John Cabibihan   Qatar University, Qatar

Publication Chairs

Álvaro Castro-González   Universidad Carlos III Madrid, Spain
Hongsheng He   Wichita State University, USA

Awards Chairs

Agnieszka Wykowska   Italian Institute of Technology, Italy
Lola Cañamero   University of Hertfordshire, UK

Competitions Chairs

Amit Kumar Pandey   Hanson Robotics, China
Ho Seok AHN   University of Auckland, New Zealand

Workshop Chairs

Luisa Damiano   University of Messina, Italy
José Carlos Castillo   Universidad Carlos III Madrid, Spain

Publicity Chairs

Silvia Rossi   University of Naples Federico II, Italy
Pooyan Fazli   San Francisco State University, USA
Kristiina Jokinen   AI Research Center of AIST Tokyo Waterfront, Japan

Standing Committee

Shuzhi Sam Ge   National University of Singapore, Singapore
Oussama Khatib   Stanford University, USA

Maja Mataric	University of Southern California, Los Angeles, USA
Haizhou Li	A*Star, Singapore
Jong Hwan Kim	Korea Advanced Institute of Science and Technology, Korea
Paolo Dario	Scuola Superiore Sant'Anna, Italy
Ronald C. Arkin	Georgia Institute of Technology, USA

Local Organizing Committee Chairs

| María Malfaz | Universidad Carlos III Madrid, Spain |
| Fernando Alonso | Universidad Carlos III Madrid, Spain |

Program Committee

Kyveli Kompatsiari	Istituto Italiano di Tecnologia, Italy
Suman Ojha	University of Technology Sydney, Australia
Tatsuya Nomura	Ryukoku University, Japan
Markus Vincze	TU Wien University, Austria
Roxana Agrigoroaie	ENSTA ParisTech, France
Zeynep Yucel	Okayama University, Japan
Seiichiro Katsura	Keio University, Japan
Trung Dung Ngo	University of Prince Edward Island, Canada
Víctor H. Andaluz	Universidad de las Fuerzas Armadas ESPE, Ecuador
Azadeh Shariati	Sharif University of Technology, Iran
Norihiro Hagita	ATR, Japan
Kenji Suzuki	University of Tsukuba, Japan
Arturo Cruz-Maya	Softbank Robotics Europe, France
Taras Kucherenko	KTH Royal Institute of Technology, Sweden
Mariacarla Staffa	University of Naples Federico II, Italy
Jaime Rincon	UPV, Spain
Takayuki Kanda	Kyoto University, Japan
Phongtharin Vinayavekhin	IBM, Japan
Mirjam de Haas	Tilburg University, The Netherlands
Xan-Tung Truong	Le Quy Don Technical University, Vietnam
Paulo Novais	Universidade do Minho, Portugal
Hiroyuki Umemuro	Tokyo Institute of Technology, Japan
Marketta Niemelä	VTT Technical Research Centre of Finland Ltd, Finland
Natalia Reich-Stiebert	FernUniversität Hagen, Germany
Davide Carneiro	ESTG/IPP, Portugal
Giulia Perugia	Uppsala University, Sweden
Lynne Baillie	Heriot-Watt University, UK
Kentaro Watanabe	National Institute of Advanced Industrial Science and Technology, Japan
Eiichi Yoshida	AIST, Japan
Ruth Aylett	Heriot-Watt University, UK

Elena Lazkano   UPV/EHU, Spain
Meg Tonkin   University of Technology Sydney, Australia
Alessandra Rossi   University of Hertfordshire, UK
Francesco Rea   Istituto Italiano di Tecnologia, Italy
Minoo Alemi   Islamic Azad University, Tehran-west Branch, Iran
Tom Williams   Colorado School of Mines, USA
Adeline Chanseau   University of Hertfordshire, UK
Kerstin Sophie Haring   University of Denver, USA
Raymond Cuijpers   Eindhoven University of Technology, The Netherlands
Peter McKenna   Heriot-Watt University, UK
Gabriele Trovato   Pontificia Universidad Catolica del Peru, Peru
Hifza Javed   George Washington University, USA
Franziska Kirstein   Blue Ocean Robotics, Denmark
Frank Broz   Heriot-Watt University, UK
Matej Hoffmann   Czech Technical University in Prague, Czech Republic
Graham Wilcock   CDM Interact, Finland
Maya Dimitrova   Institute of Robotics, BAS, Bulgaria
Paul Robinette   MIT, USA
Floris Erich   National Institute of Advanced Industrial Science
                         and Technology, Japan
Ali Meghdari   Sharif University of Technology, Iran
Antonio   Universidad de Castilla-La Mancha, Spain
   Fernández-Caballero
Ismael García-Varea   Universidad de Castilla-La Mancha, Spain
Birgit Lugrin   Universität of Würzburg, Germany
Adriana Tapus   ENSTA ParisTech, France
Kimmo Vänni   Tampere University of Applied Sciences, Finland
Friederike Eyssel   Bielefeld University, Germany
Luke Wood   University of Hertfordshire, UK
Vassilis Kaburlasos   International Hellenic University (IHU), Greece
Tiago Oliveira   Tokio Medical and Dental University, Japan
Jonathan Vitale   University of Technology Sydney, Australia

Reviewers

Ehsan Ahmadi   Sharif University of Technology, Iran
Fernando Alonso Martín   Universidad Carlos III de Madrid, Spain
Ali Amoozandeh Nobaveh   Delft University of Technology, The Netherlands
Antonio Andriella   Institut de Robòtica i Informàtica Industrial,
                         CSIC-UPC, Spain
Olatz Arbelaitz Gallego University of the Basque Country UPV/EHU, Spain
Giovanni Ercolano   University of Naples Federico II, Italy
Enrique Fernández Rodicio Universidad Carlos III de Madrid, Spain
Juan José Gamboa   Universidad Carlos III de Madrid, Spain
Masakazu Hirokawa   University of Tsukuba, Japan
Michael Koller   TU Wien University, Austria

Contents

Verbal Interaction with Social Robots

Social Cues and Design of Social Robots

Game Approaches and Applications to HRI

Applications in Health Domain

Robots at Home and at Public Spaces

Robots in Education

Technical Innovations in Social Robotics

Privacy and Safety of the Social Robots

Perceptions and Expectations of Social Robots

Boundary-Crossing Robots: Societal Impact of Interactions with Socially Capable Autonomous Agents

Kristiina Jokinen[1]([⊠]) and Kentaro Watanabe[2]

[1] AI Research Center, AIST Tokyo Waterfront, Tokyo, Japan
kristiina.jokinen@aist.go.jp
[2] Human Augmentation Research Center, AIST, Chiba, Japan
kentaro.watanabe@aist.go.jp

Abstract. The paper introduces the notion of a Boundary-Crossing Robot which refers to the use of AI research and novel technology in symbiotic interaction with human users, especially in the meaning creation processes that make the world sensible and interpretable in the course of everyday activities. Co-evolution of collaboration is considered from the point of view of social robots with dual characteristics as agents and elaborated computers, and the focus is on the robot's interaction capability. The paper emphasizes important questions related to trust in social encounters with boundary-crossing agents.

Keywords: Human-robot interaction · Boundary-crossing agents · Ethics · Trust

1 Introduction

AI technology has rapidly developed in all areas of society, and the number of autonomous systems aiming at offering more effective and personalized digital services has increased in most service sectors. As the innovative development transforms traditional services into digitalized ones, the need for interactive systems which can interact with humans and explain their actions in a natural manner, has also increased. In particular, possibilities offered by robot companions which can assist humans in their everyday life, support patients and their care-givers, or provide help in restaurants and convenience stores have become notable solutions for challenging situations caused by social and demographic changes in the modern societies. However, an important aspect of their interaction with humans is the dual characteristics of the robot as an elaborated computer as well as a social agent [12]: they can perform quick computations on big data, but also support human-like natural interaction. Social robots do not easily fit in the technical view of a robot as an inanimate tool, as their functioning borders on a more agent-like understanding of human needs and multimodal behaviour. Several ongoing research projects and framework programmes in EU and Japan focus intensively on both of these aspects, with the aim of creating value for the different stake-holders: e.g. ALIZ-E[1] (children in hospitals), Empathic[2] (coaching), ERATO[3] (human like companion), RobotCare[4].

Innovative services are created in interaction by the users and novel technologies, and in such processes, issues concerning natural interaction with the digital technology must be addressed. For instance, in practical care-work, communicating robot agents can be of valuable help and provide useful information to the users, assist novice care givers by instructing them how to do a particular task, or simply act as a companion to work with. In [12, 13, 15] the authors discuss how a robot agent can explicate care-giving practices for care-givers and engage them in interaction that resembles human dialogue. This kind of interaction is a new type of interface where the robot is not just a tool to look for information but an agent to communicate with. Moreover, humanoid robots which can move in a three-dimensional environment and observe human participants' behaviour, can embody an interactive partner which is expected to show sensitivity to social aspects of communication with a human partner: the robot agent could understand people's intentions and emotions, communicate in natural language, and offer companionship and peer-type assistance through their capability to chat, monitor, and present information. The challenge for the robot agents is that such dialogues require rich knowledge of the partners and the context in which the dialogues take place. AI solutions are not only needed to process big data to find meaningful patterns and trends in the databases, but also to equip the agents with knowledge that enables them to communicate in a flexible and natural manner. As argued in [12], the dual characteristics of robots make social robots unique in that their functionality is determined and evaluated by their computing capability as well as by their social competence.

In [10], it is argued that social agents introduce a novel concept of Automated Social Presence, which concerns the extent to which technology makes customers feel the presence of another social entity. In this paper, we elaborate the concept of *Boundary-Crossing Robot (BCR)*, first discussed in the context of social robots in [12], as a new metaphor for designing social robots and their interaction with humans. We thus take the notion of presence even further by suggesting that social robots can be regarded as agents which challenge the prototypical categorisation of actors in the world in two ways: first, they resemble human agents and thus cross the border between agents and non-agents (bordering the philosophical questions of volition, intention, identity etc.) and second, they function in work situations to organise, assist, monitor and attend several people and processes simultaneously, and thus cross the border between a tool and a co-worker (bordering the issues of human capability and its extension by technological means). In the future society, envisaged as the Society 5.0[5] where inanimate objects are connected and able to communicate with each other, BCRs

---

[1] https://fp7alizeproject.wordpress.com/.
[2] http://cordis.europa.eu/project/rcn/212371_en.html.
[3] http://www.jst.go.jp/erato/ishiguro/en/.
[4] Robotic Devices for Nursing Care (http://robotcare.jp/?lang=en).
[5] Society 5.0. https://www.japanindustrynews.com/2019/04/connected-industries-japans-approach-to-industry-4-0-on-the-way-to-society-5-0/.

add a new dimension for human interaction and call for new solutions in decision making and service design. Consequently, we assume that the strategy to analyse affective social robot interactions and assess their functionality for various service domains is to experiment with various types of human-robot interactive applications from the point of view of practical work. To get a better understanding of the issues related to BCRs and their role in the Society 5.0, it is important to explore interactive applications in everyday life situation and study their usefulness and applicability to practical problems. In this way, it is possible to extend the current state of the art in social robotics into various service contexts where novel technologies such as robotics, AI and cloud services can provide a real change and support greater operational efficiency (cf. [34]). This can direct research and development of social robotics towards a society that is good for all.

The paper is organized as follows: in Sect. 2 we briefly discuss the concepts related to human-robot interaction and dialogue modelling in general. In Sect. 3, we present the concept of Boundary-Crossing Robot, i.e. interactive intelligent agents which cross the traditional conceptual categories of inanimate and animate agents and can be seen as partners in the process of co-creating the world around us. In Sect. 4 we briefly discuss societal aspects and acceptance of social robots in the Society 5.0. Finally, we conclude and provide future views in Sect. 5.

2 Co-creating Interaction

Social interaction governs the individual's behaviour and especially the meaning creation processes that make the world sensible and interpretable in the course of everyday activities. Conversational interactions are considered cooperative activities through which the interlocutors build common ground (see [1, 4, 5, 11, 29, 32] among others). Cooperation assumes the interlocutors' basic willingness to engage in conversations and negotiate about issues important to them and to the activity they are currently performing. (From this point of view, communication about conflicting goals also requires cooperation, namely minimum willingness to assert one's own view and continue interaction.) According to the Constructive Dialogue Modelling (CDM) framework [11], we assume that communication includes certain enablements, i.e. the agents pay attention to communicative signals that indicate if the partner is in contact and able to perceive the speaker's intention to communicate, and if the partner has understood the message. Then, the speaker produces some reaction which, according to the principles of cooperation, conveys new information in relation to the partner's utterance as well as indicates their emotional and affective state. In this way, the participants interactively create a common ground, i.e. shared knowledge of the conversations and their individual contributions to it. The process presupposes that the participants have an ability to understand differences in the partner's knowledge and points of view, i.e. it relates to the Theory of Mind [37]. Through such dynamic creation of the common ground, the participants can express their goals, negotiate interpretation of the important concepts, and build understanding of each other's intentions. The participants also create shared experience and mutual understanding of the situation. The notion of *grounding* is often used to refer to the dynamics of conversation and to the construction of a shared context within which the participants co-create their understanding of the world and each other's intentions [5, 11, 32]. It should be noticed that in robotics, symbol grounding usually denotes the process of linking concepts and words to the physical world, while in dialogue modelling, the notion refers to the linking of the content of the participant's utterance to the common ground.

Dialogue management for social robots deals with interaction models that allow the robot to understand human utterances and produce meaningful communication [11, 16, 21, 22]. In the future, it can be expected that the robot agents can also learn new concepts, actions and action sequences through interaction [28], by manipulating objects and grounding their knowledge to the physical world and the communicative context. Such learning capability can be regarded as part of the functionality of Boundary-Crossing Robots which can observe and learn suitable actions and appropriate behaviour from long-term interactions with the humans. However, such behaviour also brings forward many ethical and privacy issues which need to be taken into consideration. For instance, in [17] some issues concerning long-term relations in human-robot interactions are discussed. In case of various recognition techniques, one of the main questions is the reliability of the results and their interpretation. Although detecting and recognizing a face may simply amount to confirming an objective fact whether the face is in the database of familiar users or not, interpretation of various user behaviors, such as emotional state, personality, or level of understanding, depends on the context and the training material on which the models are built. Technology that relies on the use of such models depends on the correctness of the models, whereas usability of the technology depends on the user's trust that the underlying model provides a correct interpretation. While technology can be improved by bigger and more comprehensive data modelling, the issues of trust are harder to determine objectively, and often elude downright definition in terms of features that are crucial for eliciting trust in the autonomous agents. Rather, trust seems to be learnt through interaction that accords with the human user's expectations of appropriate and affordable interaction. The user simply has confidence in the robot's capability to provide information and to perform physical tasks. In the process of accepting social robots as companions, trust and reliability are pertinent preconditions that extend the boundaries of agenthood and responsibility towards trustworthy BCRs.

An important part of dialogue modelling is the context. The context can vary from linguistic utterances to a conversational context and to wider contexts of culture and individual history. Cultural habits and traditions affect the way in which people interact and interpret each other's behaviour and what is socially acceptable behaviour. For instance, in Western cultures it is not necessary to share information about one's private life with a care-giver, whereas in Eastern cultures, the care-giver's involvement in the personal issues of the cared-for person often measures the depth of care [14]. Cultural differences have been much studied with animated agents [2, 6], and comparative studies such as [35] will be meaningful for clarifying cross-cultural differences about BCRs.

In Society 5.0, the context for BCRs also includes the communicating nodes and sensors in the IoT-based network [30]. By interacting with the robots, human users can have access to a large repertoire of actions, activities and knowledge that is available in the cloud, ranging from professional information (shared e.g. by care givers in elder care facilities or teachers and parents at school) to personal information (usually shared voluntarily among friends). Consequently, social robots should be able to assess the type of information: if it is considered sensitive and if it can be safely delivered in the given context of communication. We refer to [14] for an extensive discussion on privacy, ethics, and data protection on social robot interactions.

Context is important when considering how users will accept new technologies. The robot can elicit more personal engagement in human partners but needs different capabilities for different users: e.g. autistic children tend to engage with a robot care-taker more easily than a human one due to the robot's less social appearance and behaviour [3], while adults allow more intimate interactions and share personal experiences with a robot which lacks the social evaluative attitude towards the person's story [33].

3 Boundary-Crossing Robots

We take Activity Theory by [7] as a starting point to study the impact of complex technological devices in society. In this approach, an important role is assigned to agents who cross boundaries to new work situations and habits. Such boundary-crossing agents can bridge the gap between technology developers and technology users and facilitate interaction and mutual intelligibility between the various perspectives. We share the view that it is important to learn new ways to interact with mul-timodal, affective and social robot agents, but also maintain that such robot agents themselves operate as boundary-crossing agents. In the current digitalisation of the society, research on affective human-robot interaction will pave the way to a new kind of interactive agents, the *Boundary-Crossing Robots*, regarded as a specific case of the boundary-crossing agents discussed in Activity Theory [7]. As mentioned earlier, BCRs have dual characteristics as sophisticated computer tools and cooperative communicating agents, and advanced AI technologies, including dialogue models, speech and language processing, cognitive science and machine learning are pertinent for their development. They can cross boundaries in several ways, but in this paper, we consider two types of boundary-crossings: one that relates to conceptual boundaries in the categorization of agents, the other to new concepts of working and co-workers.

3.1 Conceptual Boundaries

According to Media Equation Hypothesis, the users can bond with robots and interact in a natural manner since people's interactions with computers and new media are "fundamentally social like interactions in real life" [27]. For instance, humans tend to apply rather natural turn-taking patterns when interacting with a social robot, although the robot's non-verbal behaviour as such does not necessarily follow human natural behaviour. On the other hand, the robot's human-like appearance is known to have impact on the interaction and the participants' social behaviour. For instance, industrial robots are not designed to elicit affection or social effects, so social gazing patterns in industrial robot's behaviour do not create emotional effects in the user (yet can support floor management and make the user feel more responsible for the task [8]). It is obvious that human-like appearance as such does not guarantee agenthood; this is a complex phenomenon which requires that the robot is perceived as exhibiting human-like behaviour as well, i.e. the robot's social competence should conform to its appearance.

The interaction between humans and intelligent agents is a large research area where both statistical and rule-based approaches are used to manage the relevant phenomena. Concerning affective and natural interaction management, important features for the design of friendly, context-sensitive social robot agents deal with those that would make the robot's perception more sensitive to the user' needs as well as making the robot's own behavior more expressive using the whole repertoire of communicative signals available for human communicators. The view of an autonomous system as an intelligent agent is thus related to *affordance*, the concept originally discussed by [9] and introduced in dialogue modelling by [11]: the system's communicative competence affords natural language interaction and lends itself to the intuitive use of the system.

Studies to enable affordable behavior in social agents contribute to the state of the art in interaction technology, deeper understanding of human behavior, and usability of the applications by the users [31]. These issues are also relevant in facilitating acceptability of such applications by the users, and they thus support development of service sectors where intelligent interactive agents create new solutions to changing needs.

Such interactive applications will have implications to the famous Uncanny Valley hypothesis [24]. This hypothesis states that the artefact's increasing human-likeness will, at some point close to real resemblance, cause the user's acceptance of the artefact suddenly to drop. The Uncanny Valley phenomenon is explained on the basis of category boundaries [23]: when humans encounter atypical phenomena or feel they cross the boundaries of everyday life, they experience uncomfortable feelings. However, such uncomfortable feelings can be overcome by more regular encounters with the untypical object. Considering a humanoid robot which is not a typical member of either the classes "human" or "robot", it may cause uncomfortable feelings because of being perceived as something strange in the borderline of normal life. In order to accommodate humanoid, communicating robots into the existing world, a new category needs to be created for them. If encounters with the untypical object become more regular, it does not elicit uncomfortable feelings anymore, and a boundary-crossing agent is being developed. Autonomous and communicating robots will thus become more acceptable if the audience have more interactions with them, besides increased social communication capability. They will become Boundary-Crossing Robots.

As an example of a robot which crosses a conceptual boundary, we present AIBO, a dog-type robot developed by Sony, and one of the limited cases of mass-produced social robots. AIBO crossed the border of being part of the family. The question how AIBO was accepted by its owners, especially in Japan, became prominent when Sony stopped the maintenance and parts supply of AIBO, and several hundred AIBO robot dogs received mass funerals in Buddhist temples [19]. On the other hand, Japan has a tradition to have similar religious rituals for objects, e.g. for dolls used for a long time, and AIBO was treated in a similar manner: it was regarded as a member of the family.

In fact, the relationship between a robot dog and its human owner is a research topic in the new AIBO generation[6] which focuses on a cute robot dog developing relationships with people through its learning capability, recognition of familiar faces and thus shaping its personality in various interactions like with a pet dog. The earlier discussed privacy and ethical issues of course apply to AIBO, too, but separately from these considerations, AIBO seems to cross boundaries between real pet animals and pet robot dogs.

3.2 Co-worker Boundaries

Another line of discussion concerns the robot's acceptability in society as a co-worker or a companion. The EU Barometer[7] seven years ago (2012) showed the citizens' rather negative attitudes towards robots "stealing our jobs" and their oddness as automatic agents which can provide cooking instructions, serve as receptionists at shops and banks, perform accurate surgery, walk the dog, take care of elderly people, read bed-time stories to children. A recent version of the same survey (see Footnote 7) (2017) shows that the attitudes have changed towards more positive opinions of robots as the opportunities for them to be realised have grown to be part of everyday life.

As an example of a robot crossing boundaries as a co-worker, we can mention Pepper, developed by Softbank Robotics. While Pepper is used in various service settings, the application of Pepper in Hamazushi, a sushi restaurant chain is considered as an effective use case in practice[8]. Pepper in a Hamazushi restaurant works as a receptionist, wearing the restaurant uniform. It lets customers input their number and request for a table, and then issues a number ticket, welcoming them verbally. According to the article, Pepper is better than a tablet, because just having a tablet at the table is too tasteless. Having Pepper at the restaurant, service workers can also focus on serving customers. With an adequate role, Pepper has become a member of restaurant workers.

The Pepper case emphasizes the importance of assigning a suitable competence role to the social robot in the work environment. For instance, although Pepper has speech recognition, this is used only to the limit of enabling the robot to work meaningfully with the human co-workers and the management. The role and competence of social robots should thus be determined from the viewpoint of total service operations which require adequate service design to take into account social robots as service agents in a service system, cf. discussion in Sect. 2 about the importance of context in interaction modelling. Interestingly, service design for better use of social robots is not much studied compared to a large number of studies concerning human-robot interaction design. The impact of BCRs can be well investigated from the multi-stakeholder perspectives related to the agents. In order to create better experience for customers and other stakeholders, further research is needed on service design including social robots.

---

[6] https://us.aibo.com/.

[7] https://ec.europa.eu/digital-single-market/en/news/attitudes-towards-impact-digitisation-and-automation-daily-life.

[8] https://dot.asahi.com/dot/2018120300014.html (in Japanese).

4 Connected Companions and Society 5.0

Human-centered society is the vision for Society 5.0, launched by the Japanese government as an ambitious view of the society being connected and operated by IT. The exact plan of how to achieve that in the future and provide harmonious symbiosis between humans and robots is not specified, but it can be expected that the dual characteristics of robot agents as elaborated computers with multiple sensors and socially competent interaction will play a substantial role in the realization.

When exploring the ways in which social robots can transform into BCRs and act as helpful co-workers and support human well-being, we may be able to sketch at least some aspects of how Society 5.0 can be developed simultaneously with the category change of the robot from a tool to an agent. However, such change is not only triggered by the robot's physical appearance or superior interaction capability, but by the robot being perceived as a meaningful partner which fulfils an important role among the human partners in specified situations through their (possibly limited) functionality. The studies of AIBO and Pepper show that they can be accepted as part of the social context, and moreover, they are real examples, not science fiction. Social robots can thus embody interactions between humans and AI technologies and provide means to co-create innovative services in Society 5.0. In this case, the BCRs can be said to cross borders in the technological development and evolution from Information Society to Super Smart Society, supporting societal transformation from Industry 4.0 to Society 5.0.

5 Conclusions and Future Work

Long periods characterized by rapid changes will create a need for new paradigms and frameworks to study, understand and manage the contextualization of actors in societies, cultures, and markets. In these situations, it is important to learn new approaches, as well as to build new tools and develop alternative uses for existing ones. In particular, this is important if the users do not feel comfortable with new technologies and services.

To describe the changes in society and the rapid development of interactive social robot technology, we presented the concept of Boundary-Crossing Robot which concerns the interaction of human users with AI technology. BCRs function as facilitators in the dynamically developing situations by helping the users to re-categorize their environment and create meaningful processes and services that support their everyday activities. As discussed above, BCRs tend to challenge earlier categorizations of the world by extending the limits of agenthood and by providing useful assistants with a well-defined role which challenge the notion of a cooperative co-worker. Moreover, societal changes call for BCRs to leverage development from one stage to another. In all border crossings, however, it is important that BCRs elicit the user's trust in them as a competent partner, enabling the human to complete the tasks successfully within the designed functionality of the BCR.

Impact of BCRs on society is not yet systematically studied. Successful implementation of social robots creates entities which cross borders on both conceptual and practical levels, and given the examples discussed in the text, we have grounds to believe that technologies related to social and affective robotics, cloud services and machine learning techniques can indeed support greater operational efficiency for various service areas in society and create new solutions for human everyday activities. Interactive and attentive robot agents can be expected to be in the core of Society 5.0. to bring through full utilization of technological innovations based on IoT, AI, and Big Data.

Future research concerns both practical and theoretical investigations of BCRs. On the practical side, it is essential to explore various interactive robot agents which afford flexible communication with various users and emphasize natural dialogue models based on the agents' multimodal and expressive behaviour. It is also important to experiment with their applicability, trustworthiness, and usability to engage human users, especially in interactions which offer new services but may simultaneously cross borders of the human cognitive limits. Finally, long-term relation between humans and BCRs in Society 5.0 needs to be studied further. This line of work facilitates the users to become acquainted with various types of social robots and agent technologies, as well as gain deeper understanding of human capabilities with the opportunities and challenges embedded in the development of AI to advance a society that is good for all.

Acknowledgment. This study is based on the results obtained from a project commissioned by the New Energy and Industrial Technology Development Organization (NEDO) and partly supported by JSPS KAKENHI Grant Number JP19H04416.

References

1. Allwood, J.: Linguistic Communication as Action and Cooperation. Gothenburg Monographs in Linguistics, vol. 2. University of Gothenburg, Göteborg (1976)
2. Aylett, R., Paiva, A., Vannini, N., Enz, S., Andre, E., Hall, L.: But that was in another country: agents and intercultural empathy. In: Proceedings of the 8th International Conference on Autonomous Agents and Multiagent Systems (AAMAS), Budapest, Hungary (2009)
3. Billard, A., Robins, B., Nadel, J., Dautenhahn, K.: Building robota, a mini-humanoid robot for the rehabilitation of children with autism. RESNA Assist. Technol. J. **19**, 37–49 (2006)
4. Brennan, S., Chen, X., Dickinson, C., Neider, M., Zelinsky, G.: Coordinating cognition: the costs and benefits of shared gaze during collaborative search. Cognition **106**, 1465–1477 (2008)
5. Clark, H.H., Schaefer, E.F.: Collaborating on contributions to conversation. Lang. Cogn. Process. **2**, 19–41 (1987)
6. Endrass, B., Andre, E., Rehm, M., Nakano, Y.: Investigating culture-related aspects of behavior for virtual characters. In: Proceedings of the 12th International Conference on Autonomous Agents and Multiagent Systems (AAMAS) (2013)
7. Engeström, Y.: Activity theory as a framework for analyzing and redesigning work. Ergonomics **43**(7), 960–974 (2000)
8. Fischer, K., Lohan, K.S., Nehaniv, C., Lehmann, H.: Effects of different kinds of robot feedback. In: Herrmann, G., Pearson, M.J., Lenz, A., Bremner, P., Spiers, A., Leonards, U. (eds.) ICSR 2013. LNCS (LNAI), vol. 8239, pp. 260–269. Springer, Cham (2013). https://doi.org/10.1007/978-3-319-02675-6_26

9. Gibson, J.: The Ecological Approach to Visual Perception. Houghton Mifflin, Boston (1979)
10. Gonzalez-Jimenez, H.: Taking the fiction out of science fiction: (Self-aware) robots and what they mean for society, retailers and marketers. Futures **98**, 49–56 (2018)
11. Jokinen, K.: Constructive Dialogue Modelling – Speech Interaction with Rational Agents. Wiley, Chichester (2009)
12. Jokinen, K.: Dialogue models for social robots. In: Proceedings of the International Conference on Social Robotics (ICSR 2018), Qingdao, China (2018)
13. Jokinen, K., Nishimura, S., Watanabe, K., Nishimura, T.: Human-robot dialogues for explaining activities. In: D'Haro, L.F., Banchs, R.E., Li, H. (eds.) 9th International Workshop on Spoken Dialogue System Technology. LNEE, vol. 579, pp. 239–251. Springer, Singapore (2019). https://doi.org/10.1007/978-981-13-9443-0_20
14. Jokinen, K., et al.: Privacy and sensor information in the interactive service applications for elder people. In: Proceedings of 7th National Conference of Servicology, Tokyo (2019)
15. Jokinen, K., Nishimura, S., Fukuda, K., Nishimura, T.: Dialogues with IoT companions - enabling human interaction with intelligent service items. In: Proceedings of the 2nd International Conference on Companion Technology (ICCT 2017). IEEE (2017)
16. Jokinen, K., Wilcock, G.: Multimodal open-domain conversations with the Nao Robot. In: Mariani, J., Rosset, S., Garnier-Rizet, M., Devillers, L. (eds.) Natural Interaction with Robots, Knowbots and Smartphones: Putting Spoken Dialogue Systems into Practice, pp. 213–224. Springer, New York (2014). https://doi.org/10.1007/978-1-4614-8280-2_19
17. Jokinen, K., Wilcock, G.: Towards long-term relations in social robot interactions. In: Proceedings of HRI Workshop on Social Human-Robot Interaction of Human-care Service Robots, Daegu Korea (2019)
18. Kanda, T., Hirano, T., Eaton, D., Ishiguro, H.: Interactive robots as social partners and peer tutors for children: a field trial. Hum.-Comput. Interact. **19**(1–2), 61–84 (2004)
19. Knox, E., Watanabe, K.: AIBO robot mortuary rites in the Japanese cultural context. In: Proceedings of IEEE/RSJ International Conference on Intelligent Robots and Systems (IROS), pp. 2020–2025 (2018)
20. Leite, I., Martinho, C., Paiva, A.: Social robots for long-term interaction: a survey. Int. J. Soc. Robot. **5**(2), 291–308 (2013)
21. Montemayor, J.: From pets to Storykit: creating new technology with and intergenerational design team. In: Proceedings of the Workshop on Interactive Robots and Entertainment (WIRE), Pittsburgh (2000)
22. Montemerlo, M., Pineau, J., Roy, N., Thrun, S., Verma, V.: Experiences with a mobile robotic guide for the elderly. In: Proceedings of AAAI National Conference on Artificial Intelligence (2002)
23. Moore, R.: A Bayesian explanation of the 'Uncanny Valley' effect and related psychological phenomena (2014). http://www.ncbi.nlm.nih.gov/pmc/articles/PMC3499759/
24. Mori, M.: The Uncanny Valley. Energy, **7**(4), 33–35. English translation by Karl F. MacDorman and Takashi Minato (1970)
25. Paléologue, V., Martin, J., Pandey, A.K., Chetouani, M.: Semantic-based interaction for teaching robot behavior compositions using spoken language. In: Ge, S.S., et al. (eds.) ICSR 2018. LNCS (LNAI), vol. 11357, pp. 421–430. Springer, Cham (2018). https://doi.org/10.1007/978-3-030-05204-1_41
26. Pollack, M.E.: Intelligent technology for an aging population: the use of AI to assist elders with cognitive impairment. AI Mag. **26**(2), 9–24 (2005)
27. Reeves, N., Nass, C.: The Media Equation: How People Treat Computers, Television, and New Media Like Real People and Places. Cambridge University Press, New York (1996)

28. Senft, E., Baxter, P., Kennedy, J., Lemaignan, S., Belpaeme, T.: Supervised autonomy for online learning in human-robot interaction. Pattern Recogn. Lett. **99**, 77–86 (2017)
29. Sidner, C., Rich, C., Shayganfar, M., Bickmore, T., Ring, L., Zhang, Z.: A robotic companion for social support of isolated older adults. In: Proceedings of the 10th Annual ACM/IEEE International Conference on Human-Robot Interaction, Extended Abstracts, p. 289 (2015)
30. Smith, I.G. (ed.): The Internet of Things 2012: New Horizons. IERC-Internet of Things European Research Cluster. Halifax, U.K (2012)
31. Tay, B., Jung, Y., Park, T.: When stereotypes meet robots: the double-edge sword of robot gender and personality in human–robot interaction. Comput. Hum. Behav. **38**, 75–84 (2014)
32. Traum, D.R., Allen, J.F.: Discourse obligations in dialogue processing. In: Proceedings of the 32nd Annual Meeting of ACL, pp. 1–8. Morristown, NJ, USA (1994)
33. Van Doorn, J., et al.: Domo Arigato Mr. Roboto: emergence of automated social presence in organizational frontlines and customers' service experiences. J. Serv. Res. **20**(1), 43–58 (2017)
34. Watanabe, K., Mochimaru, M.: Expanding impacts of technology-assisted service systems through generalization: case study of the Japanese service engineering research project. Serv. Sci. **9**(3), 250–262 (2017)
35. Watanabe, K., Niemelä, M.: Aging and technology in Japan and Finland: comparative remarks. In: Toivonen, M., Saari, E. (eds.) Human-Centered Digitalization and Services. TSS, vol. 19, pp. 155–175. Springer, Singapore (2019). https://doi.org/10.1007/978-981-13-7725-9_9
36. Wilcock, G., Jokinen, K.: Advances in Wikipedia-based interaction with robots. In: ICMI Workshop Multi-modal, Multi-Party, Real-World Human-Robot Interaction, pp. 13–18 (2014)
37. Wimmer, H., Perner, J.: Beliefs about beliefs: representation and constraining function of wrong beliefs in young children's understanding of deception. Cognition **13**, 103–128 (1983)

Effects of Previous Exposure on Children's Perception of a Humanoid Robot

Gabriella Lakatos[1(✉)], Luke Jai Wood[1], Abolfazl Zaraki[2],
Ben Robins[1], Kerstin Dautenhahn[3], and Farshid Amirabdollahian[1]

[1] University of Hertfordshire, Hatfield AL10 9AB, UK
g.lakatos@herts.ac.uk
[2] University of Reading, Reading RG6 6AH, UK
[3] University of Waterloo, Waterloo, ON N2L 3G1, Canada

Abstract. The study described in this paper investigated the effects of previous exposure to robots on children's perception of the Kaspar robot. 166 children aged between 7 and 11 participated in the study in the framework of a UK robotics week 2018 event, in which we visited a local primary school with a number of different robotic platforms to teach the children about robotics. Children's perception of the Kaspar robot was measured using a questionnaire following a direct interaction with the robot in a teaching scenario. Children's previous exposure to other robots and Kaspar itself was manipulated by controlling the order of children's participation in the different activities over the event. Effects of age and gender were also examined. Results suggest significant effects of previous exposure and gender on children's perception of Kaspar, while age had no significant effect. Important methodological implications for future studies are discussed.

Keywords: Robot perception · Child-robot interaction · Assistive robots

1 Introduction

The study detailed in this paper was part of a UK Robotics week 2018 event, in which the University of Hertfordshire's Adaptive Systems Research Group members visited a local primary school with several different robotic platforms to teach the children about robotics. In total 175 children took part in the event, involving six classes in the school, 166 of which were involved in the study. Among other activities, every child had the opportunity to (a) program the Kaspar robots [1, 2] using Scratch [3], (b) teach the Kaspar robot via a semi-autonomous human-robot-interaction, (c) learn how to use 3D CAD software (SketchUp) [4] at a basic level, (d) learn about the principles of 3D printing and (e) see how Artificial Intelligence algorithms on a small 3D printed 18 DOF hexapod robot, called Scampi, affected the autonomous behaviours of the robot.

The study we present in this paper is focusing on one specific aspect of this event, namely on how children's exposure to the different activities affects their perception of the Kaspar robot, along with other factors such as age and gender.

© Springer Nature Switzerland AG 2019
M. A. Salichs et al. (Eds.): ICSR 2019, LNAI 11876, pp. 14–23, 2019.
https://doi.org/10.1007/978-3-030-35888-4_2

2 Background and Motivation

The child sized humanoid robot, Kaspar, was built by the Adaptive Systems Research Group at the University of Hertfordshire to help children with Autism Spectrum Disorder (ASD) with their communication and social interaction skills. The robot possesses some distinct advantages when working with children with ASD. Kaspar's simple, minimally expressive features and the predictability of its behaviour make the interaction easy and enjoyable for them [1]. Kaspar has been successfully used in a number of long term studies - with positive developmental and therapeutic outcomes - involving more than 230 children over the years [5, 6]. However, the use of Kaspar should not be restricted to children with ASD. In fact, as Kaspar is getting increasingly used in different environments such as schools, it is also being considered as an educational tool for typically developing (TD) children. Recent evidence suggested that Kaspar could be used in robot-mediated interviews as well, showing that children respond to it in a similar way as to a human interviewer and pointing towards the prospect of using robots when human interviewers may face challenges [7, 8].

Although many robots are specifically designed to be used with children (e.g. for therapeutic and educational purposes), studies investigating attitudes, perception and preferences about robots are still generally focusing on adults [9–11]. As Woods et al. suggested [10], if robots are to be successfully used within activities involved in the education, children's perception of robots should be at the center of the research. Even so, very few studies have examined specifically children's perception of robots before [12]. In a previous study Woods et al. [10] tested children's perceptions of 5 different robots with regards to physical attributes, emotional traits and personality via a questionnaire study using a large sample of TD children. Results of this study indicated that children distinguished between emotions and behaviour when judging robots based on their images. Children judged human-like robots as aggressive, but animal-like and human-machine robots as friendly (supporting the Uncanny Valley [13]). However, as the authors also recognized, reliance on images of the robots could make it difficult to relate to the actual robot behaviour [10]. Hence, it is essential to expose children to real robots when measuring their perception of robots.

To our knowledge there has been only one study comparing the perception of robots of TD children (N = 46) and children with ASD (N = 18). This study involved Kaspar [11], and used a specifically designed "matching pictures game" to measure children's perception of robots. Pictures featured 6 social robots to be matched to one of the following categories: machines, humans, animals and toys. In addition, the authors measured the preference for a certain robot by ranking. Findings suggested that both groups of children perceived robots mainly as toys, although a big percentage of children with ASD, especially boys, also perceived robots as machines. According to the findings the best preferred robot by both groups of children (Keepon) had exaggerated cartoon-like features [11]. With regards to Kaspar, however, results of this study were somewhat controversial. While children with ASD rated Kaspar both high and low ranked, TD children rated Kaspar mainly low ranked, which the authors explained by the phenomenon of Uncanny Valley. However, again, it is important to note that pictures do not give any impression of a robot's size, or its movement and interaction capabilities, and while children are clearly attracted to a cartoon-like robot, the range of interactions supported by these robots also have to be taken into consideration.

This is why in the current study we investigated children's perception of the Kaspar robot using a short questionnaire following a direct interaction with Kaspar in a simple teaching scenario. Additionally, we varied children's previous exposure to Kaspar and other robots before this interaction. Interestingly - to our knowledge - no studies have methodically examined the effects of previous exposure on the perception of social robots before, even though it can have important implications for the design of HRI experiments. In the current study, children either (a) participated in the teaching scenario without any previous exposure to Kaspar and other robots, (b) were previously exposed to an activity with Scampi, a robot substantially different to Kaspar, or (c) were previously exposed to both Scampi and Kaspar. Our hypothesis here was that prior exposure to Kaspar improves the perception of the robot.

3   Methods

3.1   Participants

One hundred and sixty-six (N = 166) children (83 male, 83 female) took part in the study, aged between 7 and 11 (49 children from Year 3, 59 children from Year 4 and 58 children from Year 5). Participants were randomly assigned to one of the three experimental conditions that manipulated their exposure order to the activities with the different robots, while maintaining age- and gender-balanced distributions.

3.2   Experimental Procedure

Children in each class were broken down into three groups. Each of these groups focused on a different activity for eighty minutes before having a break then rotating to the next activity until all of the children had taken part in all of the activities.

This research was approved by the University of Hertfordshire's ethics committee for studies involving human participants, protocol numbers: acCOM SF UH 02069 and cCOM/SF/UH/02080. Informed consent was obtained in writing from all parents of the children participating in the study.

A description of each of the activities is as follows (see also Fig. 1):

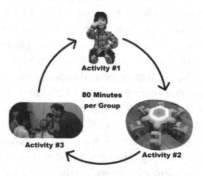

Fig. 1. Children spent eighty minutes on each activity before rotating to the next activity.

Activity #1 - Programming the Kaspar Robot
In this activity children were working in pairs. Each pair had access to a Kaspar robot, which they were able to program via Scratch [3]. A researcher and a school teacher assisted the children in programming the Kaspar robot to display five different emotions [14]. The children learned about the basic principles of how robots can be programmed. Details of this work can be found in a previous publication [14].

Activity #2 – Observing Scampi
In this activity the children were taught about the principles of Artificial Intelligence (AI). The children saw a number of demonstrations with the Scampi robot (Fig. 1) displaying a range of preprogrammed animal behaviours, after which they were divided into two sub-groups where they could control Scampi or play with some additional multi-function robots that could play tunes, follow lines or avoid objects.

Activity #3 – Teaching Kaspar
This activity focused on teaching the children about how robots are designed and manufactured. In this session the children had a 30 min lesson where they learned how to use a piece of Computer Aided Design (CAD) software called SketchUp [4] and as part of this they would design a house or a castle to learn the basic concepts of CAD. At the end of this lesson the children were broken into 3 groups where they rotated though three different activities, spending 10 min on each. These activities were: (a) interacting with the Kaspar robot in a game where they could teach the robot, after which children filled out the post-interaction questionnaire (items of which were used as dependent measures in this study); (b) thinking about how a number of robotic toys worked; (c) learning about conductivity and which objects were conductive.

Since the study we are reporting in this paper is focusing on the results of the post-interaction questionnaire children filled out after interacting with Kaspar in the teaching scenario, we are going to provide a few more details on this interaction below.

The interaction involved small groups of 2–3 children at a time and Kaspar. During the interaction children had to teach Kaspar how to recognize different animal toys. Before the sessions Kaspar was programmed to know that there were six potential toys in the room with different names. However, it was the task of the children to teach Kaspar which name was associated with which animal toy. The children took turns to teach this to Kaspar. Teaching was realised by Kaspar autonomously pointing at each of the toys and saying one of the animal names to find out if that is the right one. The children answered by using a key fob and pressing either the green or the red button depending on Kaspar's actions (green = correct or red = incorrect). Kaspar continued to guess the names of the animal toys until it could name each one of them correctly. Details of technical realisation of this experiment were reported in the paper of Zaraki et al. [15]. Once the interaction was over, children were asked to fill out the post-interaction questionnaire (Table 1) in the presence of a researcher who made sure that all questions were clear to the children. Items 1–4 and Item 6 were measured on a 5-point Likert scale, depicted with happy/sad faces to make the choice easier for the children. Item 5 was a dichotomous question.

Table 1. Questionnaire items used as dependent measures

Questionnaire item
1. Did you think Kaspar was capable of showing emotions?
2. Did you find Kaspar being capable of caring?
3. Do you think Kaspar can have real emotions and feelings?
4. Do you think Kaspar could be a real playmate to you? (Like one of your friends)
5. Do you think Kaspar is more like a toy or a friend? (Tick one of the boxes)
6. Playing with Kaspar was? (Rate from very boring to very fun)

3.3 Experimental Conditions

Experimental groups were created based on the children's order of exposure to the different activities. Accordingly, participants of Group 1 took part in Activity #3 first, having had no previous exposure to either Scampi or programming Kaspar before interacting with Kaspar in Activity #3 and filling out the post-interaction questionnaire on their perception of Kaspar. Group 2 started with Activity #2 followed by Activity #3, and so filled out the questionnaire before taking part in Activity #1, programming Kaspar. Group 3 took part in both Activity #1 (programming Kaspar) and Activity #2 (observing Scampi) before interacting with Kaspar in Activity #3 and filling out our post-interaction questionnaire.

4 Results

4.1 Statistical Analysis

IBM SPSS Statistics 21 was used for the statistical analysis. Since we collected ordinal and nominal questionnaire data, non-parametric procedures were used for the data analysis. Kruskal-Wallis test was used to examine the effects of previous exposure to robots and the effects of year groups. Post-hoc tests with Bonferroni corrections were used to identify specific differences among the three groups. Effects of gender were examined by Mann-Whitney U-test. Effects of exposure and year groups on the binomial nominal data of the Item 5 were tested by χ^2 test, while effects of gender on the same item were tested by Fisher's exact test.

4.2 Effect of Previous Exposure

Significant effects of previous exposure were found on children's subjective perception of the Kaspar robot on Items 1, 5 and 6. Kruskal-Wallis test revealed significant differences in participants' rating of the robot on the items "Did you think Kaspar was capable of showing emotions?" ($\chi^2(2) = 11.11$; $p = 0.004$) (Fig. 2) and "Playing with Kaspar was ..... - Rate from Very Boring to Very Fun" ($\chi^2(2) = 8.08$; $p = 0.018$) (Fig. 3). Post-hoc tests with Bonferroni corrections showed significant difference between Group 1 (starting with Activity #3 with no previous exposure to other robots) and Group 3 (taking part in both Activities #1 and #2 before interacting with Kaspar in

Activity #3) in case of both of the above items (p = 0.03 and p = 0.014 respectively). No significant differences were found between Group 1 and Group 2 (taking part in Activity #2 first followed by Activity #3) suggesting that having had the experience of programming Kaspar made the children rate Kaspar higher on these items, while their exposure to Scampi only had no effect on their ratings.

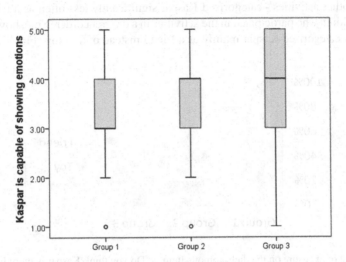

Fig. 2. Effect of exposure on Item 1 "Did you think Kaspar was capable of showing emotions?", ranging from 1 = definitely no to 5 = definitely yes.

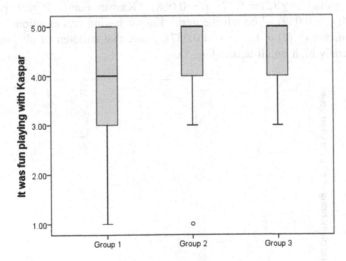

Fig. 3. Effect of exposure on Item 6 "Playing with Kaspar was? (Rate from very boring to very fun)?", ranging from 1 = boring to 5 = fun.

We found further significant effect of exposure on the item "Did you think Kaspar is more like a toy or a friend?" ($\chi^2(2) = 7.69$; p = 0.021). Adjusted residuals and p values after Bonferroni corrections revealed that the difference was explained by Group 1 (Group 1: Adjusted residual Z = 2.72; $\chi^2(2) = 7.39$; p = 0.007; Group 2: Z = −0.73; $\chi^2(2) = 0.53$; p = 0.465; Group 3: Z = −2.00; $\chi^2(2) = 4.00$; p = 0.046; Bonferroni adjusted significance level: p = 0.016). Children in Group 1 – interacting with Kaspar before the other activities - categorised Kaspar significantly less often as a friend compared to children who participated in the activities in a different order. Note, however, that all 3 groups categorised Kaspar mainly as a friend instead of as a toy (Fig. 4).

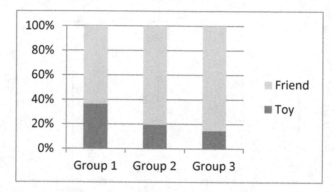

Fig. 4. Effect of exposure on the dichotomous Item 5 "Do you think Kaspar is more like a toy or a friend?".

No significant difference was found in case of any other items ("Kaspar being capable of caring": $\chi^2(2) = 5.37$; p = 0.068; "Kaspar being a real playmate": $\chi^2(2) = 4.84$; p = 0.089), although the item "Kaspar having real emotions" was marginally significant ($\chi^2(2) = 11.11$; p = 0.057). Note, that children of all groups rated Kaspar generally high on all items (Fig. 5).

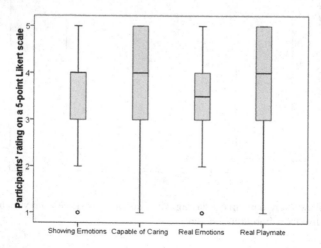

Fig. 5. Children's rating of Kaspar on Items 1, 2, 3, and Item 4. Since there was no significant effect of exposure on these items, this figure shows the medians for all participants (N = 166).

4.3   Effect of Age and Gender

Year groups had no significant effect on any of the items ("Kaspar being capable of showing emotions": $\chi^2(2) = 0.28$; $p = 0.86$; "Kaspar being capable of caring": $\chi^2(2) = 1.98$; $p = 0.37$; "Kaspar having real emotions": $\chi^2(2) = 0.66$; $p = 0.71$; "Kaspar being a real playmate": $\chi^2(2) = 0.45$; $p = 0.79$; "Kaspar is more like a toy or a friend" ($\chi^2(2) = 3.09$; $p = 0.21$; "fun playing with Kaspar": $\chi^2(2) = 0.78$; $p = 0.67$).

Girls categorised Kaspar significantly more often as a friend (vs being a toy) than boys (Fisher's exact test $p = 0.033$). In addition, there was a marginally significant effect on the item "Did you find Kaspar being capable of caring?", girls rating this item marginally significantly higher than boys ($U = 2446.5$, $p = 0.051$). No further gender effect was found ("Kaspar being capable of showing emotions": $U = 2928.5$, $p = 0.78$; "Kaspar having real emotions: $U = 2827.0$, $p = 0.93$"; "Kaspar being a real playmate": $U = 2602.5$, $p = 0.27$; "fun playing with Kaspar": $U = 2449.0$, $p = 0.07$.)

5   Discussion

Findings showed significant effect of exposure on children's perception of Kaspar. Children who have been exposed to the Scampi robot and have had the opportunity to program Kaspar to express simple emotions before interacting with it in the teaching scenario, rated Kaspar higher on several items and categorised it significantly more often as a friend than children who have not been previously exposed to the other activities. We have to note, however, that this change in perception could be related to several factors other than children's experience of programming Kaspar, such as the time spent on each activity. In Activity #1children had more time to interact with Kaspar than in Activity #3. Additionally, in Activity #1 children worked in pairs, which allowed them to acquire more hands-on experience with Kaspar, which could further explain why participating in Activity #1altered their perception. It is also important to note, that children's perception of Kaspar was generally very positive after the interaction with Kaspar in the teaching scenario even without any previous exposure, with 63.4% of children categorising Kaspar as a friend instead of a toy. This positive perception of Kaspar may seem to contradict earlier findings of Peca et al. [11], who found that Kaspar was among the least preferred robots by TD children (although our results are not directly comparable to theirs). These seemingly contradictory results may provide further evidence for the effect of exposure and emphasize the importance of measuring perception of robots based on real human-robot interactions as opposed to using images only, especially with children. A robot's appearance only does not convey enough information on its movements or expressive behavior.

No significant effect of Year groups was observed, which is in line with earlier findings of Tung et al. [16] who found that the effect of children's age on their attitude towards robots with various degrees of anthropomorphic appearance was less significant than the effect of gender. We have to note however, that using Year groups is not the best way to measure age effect and using the actual chronological age of the children might have shown a different result. In addition, our Year groups were not perfectly balanced in numbers, which we could not control. Regarding the gender effects on children's perception of Kaspar, we found that girls categorised Kaspar significantly more often (55.8%) as a friend than boys (44.2%) and rated Kaspar slightly more capable of caring (51.3%) than boys did (48.7%). These results further strengthen Tung et al.'s [16] findings that girls are more accepting of human-like robots, than boys. Interestingly, Peca et al. [11] did not find any significant gender effect among TD children, they did find however significant gender effects among children with ASD. With regards to Kaspar it appears that among children with ASD boys mainly categorised Kaspar as a human while girls categorised it mainly as a toy.

Although this study offered a real human-robot interaction scenario for gauging perception of children against the Kaspar robot, it still has several limitations. These limitations involve the lack of objective behaviour analysis that could provide more reliable results than subjective ratings of questionnaire items. A further limitation is the lack of behaviour manipulation of the robot, which could give us a much clearer picture of how robotic behaviour affects the perception of robots. Additionally, our three activities took place on the same day, and thus our study did not assess impact of novelty versus repeated exposure, which also leaves room for further exploration.

6 Conclusion

Our results emphasize the importance of using actual robots when measuring perception of robots as it is a complex question - dependent on several factors - that cannot be solely based on robot appearance only. In addition, the findings have important implications to all HRI studies, informing the HRI community that caution has to be taken when recruiting participants for a human-robot interaction study, considering participants' previous exposure to robots as it can influence the results greatly.

The positive perception and attitude towards Kaspar that TD children showed in this study supports the potential usability of Kaspar in several different scenarios in the future. Kaspar could work as an educational tool for TD children as well as for children with ASD, or as previous studies suggested, it could potentially even provide advantages in robot-mediated interviews with children in challenging situations [7, 8].

Acknowledgments. The authors wish to thank the institution that was involved in the study, the children who took part in the event and their parents. The authors also thank Luke Hickton and Silvia Moros for their assistance in the sessions. This work as part of the UK Robotics week was supported by the UK-RAS Network.

References

1. Wood, L.J., Zaraki, A., Walters, M.L., Novanda, O., Robins, B., Dautenhahn, K.: The iterative development of the humanoid robot Kaspar: an assistive robot for children with autism. In: Kheddar, A., et al. (eds.) ICSR 2017. LNCS, pp. 53–63. Springer, Cham (2017). https://doi.org/10.1007/978-3-319-70022-9_6
2. Dautenhahn, K., et al.: KASPAR: a minimally expressive humanoid robot for human–robot interaction research. Appl. Bionics Biomech. **6**, 369–397 (2009)

3. Moreno-León, J., Robles, G.: Code to learn with scratch? A systematic literature review. In: 2016 IEEE Global Engineering Education Conference (EDUCON). IEEE, pp. 150–156 (2016)
4. Chopra, A.: Google SketchUp for Dummies. Wiley, Hoboken (2007)
5. Robins, B., Dautenhahn, K., Dickerson, P.: Embodiment and cognitive learning – can a humanoid robot help children with autism to learn about tactile social behaviour? In: Ge, S. S., Khatib, O., Cabibihan, J.-J., Simmons, R., Williams, M.-A. (eds.) ICSR 2012. LNCS (LNAI), vol. 7621, pp. 66–75. Springer, Heidelberg (2012). https://doi.org/10.1007/978-3-642-34103-8_7
6. Wood, L.J., Robins, B., Lakatos, G., Syrdal, D.S., Zaraki, A., Dautenhahn, K.: Developing a protocol and experimental setup for using a humanoid robot to assist children with autism develop visual perspective taking skills. Paladyn J. Behav. Robot. **10**(1), 167–179 (2019)
7. Wood, L.J., Dautenhahn, K., Rainer, A., Robins, B., Lehmann, H., Syrdal, D.S.: Robot-mediated interviews-how effective is a humanoid robot as a tool for interviewing young children? PLoS ONE **8**(3), e59448 (2013)
8. Wood, L.J., Lehmann, H., Dautenhahn, K., Robins, B., Rainer, A., Syrdal, D.S.: Robot-mediated interviews with children: what do potential users think? Interact. Stud. **17**(3), 439–461 (2016)
9. Cerqui, D., Arras, K.O.: Human beings and robots: towards a symbiosis? A 2000 people survey. In: International Conference on Socio Political Informatics and Cybernetics (PISTA 2003) (2003)
10. Woods, S., Dautenhahn, K., Schulz, J.: The design space of robots: investigating children's views. In: RO-MAN 2004, 13th IEEE International Workshop on Robot and Human Interactive Communication (IEEE Catalog No. 04TH8759), pp. 47–52. IEEE (2004)
11. Peca, A., Simut, R., Pintea, S., Costescu, C., Vanderborght, B.: How do typically developing children and children with autism perceive different social robots? Comput. Hum. Behav. **41**, 268–277 (2014)
12. Toh, L.P.E., Causo, A., Tzuo, P.-W., Chen, I.-M., Yeo, S.H.: A review on the use of robots in education and young children. J. Educ. Technol. Soc. **19**(2), 148–163 (2016)
13. Mori, M., MacDorman, K.F., Kageki, N.: The uncanny valley [from the field]. IEEE Robot. Autom. Mag. **19**(2), 98–100 (2012)
14. Moros, S., Wood, L., Robins, B., Dautenhahn, K., Castro-González, Á.: Programming a humanoid robot with the scratch language. In: Merdan, M., Lepuschitz, W., Koppensteiner, G., Balogh, R., Obdržálek, D. (eds.) RiE 2019. AISC, vol. 1023, pp. 222–233. Springer, Cham (2020). https://doi.org/10.1007/978-3-030-26945-6_20
15. Zaraki, A., et al.: A novel paradigm for typically developing and autistic children as teachers to the Kaspar robot learner. In: BAILAR-2018 in Conjunction with RO-MAN 2018 (2018)
16. Tung, F.-W.: Influence of gender and age on the attitudes of children towards humanoid robots. In: Jacko, J.A. (ed.) HCI 2011. LNCS, vol. 6764, pp. 637–646. Springer, Heidelberg (2011). https://doi.org/10.1007/978-3-642-21619-0_76

The Attitude of Elderly and Young Adults Towards a Humanoid Robot as a Facilitator for Social Interaction

Lizzy Sinnema[(✉)] and Maryam Alimardani

Department of Cognitive Science and AI, Tilburg University,
Tilburg, The Netherlands
lizzysinnema95@gmail.com

Abstract. The main objective of this research was to gain insight in the attitude that groups of elderly and young students have towards social robots. A total of 52 participants (24 elderly vs. 28 students) took part in a short-term interaction with a humanoid social robot. In small groups of two to four people, they engaged in a conversation with a Nao robot. Their attitude was measured before and after the interaction using the Unified Theory of Acceptance and Use of Technology (UTAUT) questionnaire. Furthermore, the role of the robot as a facilitator for conversation was assessed by observing the interaction between individuals after the robot was removed. This research explored the use of social robots as a means to improve socialization between individuals rather than aiming to replace the human contact. Results from the questionnaire and an additional observational analysis showed a positive attitude towards the robot and the interaction from both age groups. After the interaction, elderly perceived the robot as significantly more useful than students, which could be assigned to a difference in needs and expectations they had from it. Furthermore, anxiety towards the robot for both groups decreased after the interaction. Future research can investigate the effect of long-term interaction with a similar robot. In the long-term, social robots could possibly be deployed to decrease loneliness, a common issue among elderly.

Keywords: Socially assistive robots · Elderly · Young adults · Acceptance of technology · Attitude towards robots · Social interaction

1 Introduction

There is a worldwide increase in elderly population, a large part of which resides in care homes. Especially in Western countries life expectancy has improved, resulting from increased health care knowledge and access to it [1]. This ageing of the population has led to a shortage of caregivers and places available in care homes [2]. A serious problem among elderly in general and in care homes is loneliness; they often lack valuable social contacts and support in the social relationships they have [3].

Feeling lonely has some severe effects in the long term. People that persistently feel lonely are more prone to depression and generally have a lower quality of life and mental health [4]. Social interaction is one of the factors that plays an important role in

© Springer Nature Switzerland AG 2019
M. A. Salichs et al. (Eds.): ICSR 2019, LNAI 11876, pp. 24–33, 2019.
https://doi.org/10.1007/978-3-030-35888-4_3

keeping elderly from being lonely [5]. Meaningful interactions with friends reduce feelings of loneliness, however, improving social interaction for residents in care homes seems a complicated task [4, 6].

Therefore, many new technologies are deployed to improve health and mental well-being of the user that focus on increasing social participation of elderly. Examples are the use of robot animals as a therapy aid to improve a person's social and emotional well-being [6, 7]. Robot Paro has extensively been studied in the context of Robot-Assisted Therapy (RAT), mainly in experiments with elderly. Wada et al. [7] showed for example that interaction with the robotic seal reduced the stress levels of the elderly, their moods improved and they were more energetic than before the interaction.

Usually, interaction with animal-like robots consists of stroking, hugging or touching, while more extensive social interaction in the form of real conversations could be a valuable extension to combat loneliness and improve socialization among elderly [5]. However, introduction of language to Human-Robot Interaction (HRI) requires advanced computational models for natural language processing, dialogue management and speech synthesis. Moreover, as soon as the robot becomes humanlike and its social abilities increase, the attitude towards it might differ from the attitude users have towards animal-like robots. Naturally, the attitude of users towards a robot depends not only on the type of robot, but also on the target group. In general, elderly have significantly less experience with novel technologies in comparison to younger adults. Prior experience with technological devices could influence the attitude or thoughts about the robot itself and the perceived usefulness of it [8]. So far, not many studies have been carried out that compare the attitude of different target groups towards a social humanoid robot. Stafford et al. [9] studied the attitude change over time towards a mobile robot and compared a group of residents of a care home to a group of staff members. They found that attitude can be influenced by experiences with the robot, however, the robot in this study was not a humanoid one. Other studies that did use humanoid robots, focus on a limited number of aspects of the attitude. An example is [10], in which the influence of age on the experience of the interaction is measured.

Our study will measure a broader range of aspects that together form the complete attitude of two different age groups towards Nao robot as a social companion. The attitude of a group of elderly volunteers at a care home is compared to a group of students before and after a short interaction with the robot. The interaction took place in small groups to encourage social interaction between the participants. Furthermore, this research will focus on the role of the robot as a facilitator for conversations between the target groups. We hypothesized that the participants, especially the group with less experience with similar technologies, would be interested in the robot and robot-related topics, and start talking about it together.

2 Method

2.1 Participants

A total of 65 participants took part in the experiment, from which 8 students and 5 seniors had to be removed due to technical issues. They were all Dutch natives.

24 participants were seniors (16 female) and 28 were students (17 female). The elderly ranged in age from 59 to 91 years (Mean = 69, SD = 7). Their experiments were carried out at care home 'De Wever' in Tilburg, the Netherlands, spread out over three consecutive days in January 2019. Inclusion criteria were no cognitive impairment and the ability to appropriately hear, speak and fill out questionnaires. The students were aged between 18 and 27 (Mean = 22, SD = 3). Their experiments were performed at Tilburg University in February 2019, in a room with a similar set-up as for the elderly. They were recruited through the university with the inclusion criteria being a student at Tilburg University. All participants received explanation about the study and signed an informed consent form prior to the experiment. The study was approved by the Research Ethics Committee of Tilburg School of Humanities and Digital Sciences.

2.2   Questionnaire

A pre- and post-interaction questionnaire using a 5-point Likert scale were used in this study. The pre-questionnaire consisted of two parts: Prior experience with technology and Unified Theory of Acceptance and Use of Technology (UTAUT) [11]. The post-questionnaire repeated UTAUT (with modifications specific to this study) and contained additional questions to verify whether the robot provided a topic for discussion.

In the first part, participants were asked how they would rate their own prior experience with phones/computers and robots and could choose 'no experience', 'beginner', 'intermediate', 'experienced' or 'expert'.

The UTAUT questionnaire measures the general attitude towards technology and can be adapted to the technology it evaluates, which in this case was a social robot. It consists of several constructs; Anxiety, Attitude Towards Technology, Perceived Enjoyment, Perceived Sociability, Perceived Usefulness, Social Influence, and Trust. Each construct consists of several sub questions. The questionnaire was adapted to this study and gave a full picture of the general attitude towards robots. Also, the wording of the questions were adjusted to the moment of collection; the questions from the pre-questionnaire were put in a speculative form and the ones in the post-questionnaire targeted subject's experience in the experiment (*e.g.*, for the construct Perceived Sociability, 'I think the robot might understand me' versus 'I think Charlie understood me'). In the pre-questionnaire, the name of the robot, Charlie, was avoided, since it had not officially introduced itself to the participants yet. The construct Perceived Enjoyment was only included in the post-questionnaire, because it could not be measured without the experience with the robot. Since participants were Dutch natives, the questions had been translated to Dutch in the official questionnaire. For each question, participants could choose from 'Strongly agree', 'Agree', 'Neutral', 'Disagree' or 'Strongly disagree'. Responses were then transformed into numerical scores ranging from 1 (Strongly disagree) to 5 (Strongly agree).

In the post-questionnaire, eight additional questions measured the level of social interaction between the participants during the experiment. These questions were the following; Q24: 'Charlie gave me a topic of discussion with the other participants', Q25: 'I thought the discussion with the other participants, when Charlie was removed, was positive', Q26: 'I felt uncomfortable sitting together after the experiment was finished', Q27: 'After the experiment I wanted to leave as soon as possible', Q28: 'I felt a connection with the other participants', Q29: 'After the experiment, I felt like discussing Charlie with the other participants', Q30: 'I would have preferred one-on-one interaction with Charlie' and Q31: 'If there was the possibility, I would have liked to continue talking to Charlie more'. Again, a 5-point Likert scale was used, with responses ranging from 1 (Strongly disagree) to 5 (Strongly agree).

2.3   Procedure

The participants were split up into groups of two to four people, to stimulate social interaction. In total, 9 groups of elderly and 8 groups of students participated. The participants did not know each other beforehand.

The experiments for the students and elderly took place at different locations, but the set-up of the rooms was similar. After signing the consent form and filling in the pre-questionnaire, the participants were placed in a room with no other distractions and faced the robot with three cameras placed in front of them (Fig. 1).

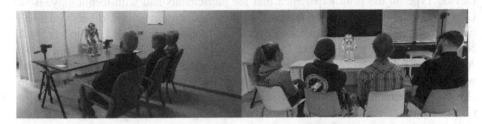

Fig. 1. Images of interaction setup with robot Charlie from elderly (left) and students (right) groups

The robot used for this experiment was Nao, a humanoid robot developed by Aldebran Robotics [12]. For the purpose of this experiment, the robot was named Charlie. Charlie's behavior and movements were programed in advance, but there were occasional input that were given to the robot by an experimenter hidden behind a partition and thus not visible to the participants during the whole experiment (Wizard of Oz).

At the beginning of the interaction, Charlie introduced itself and said it had been looking forward to the visit. It asked some questions from the participants (*e.g.* 'Did you know I was coming today?') and suggested to perform a dance. This was an icebreaker for the participants and allowed them to see the complex movements the robot was capable of. After the dance was finished, the robot asked the participants for feedback and proposed to solve riddles together. Since an important aspect of this experiment was to encourage participants to interact with each other, the robot stimulated the participants to actively discuss the possible answers together. The participants could ask for a hint if they were lost or ask the robot to repeat the riddle if they did not hear it properly. They could also give an answer to the riddle and the robot would give feedback.

Once the specified interaction time was over, one of the experimenters stepped forward and took away the robot. The experimenters left the room carrying the robot and the participants remained alone for approximately 2.5 min. The cameras were there to record the conversation between individuals and later evaluate whether they talked about the robot, talked about other topics, or just waited quietly. In total, each interaction lasted around 10 min.

Then, the experimenters returned without Charlie and distributed the post-questionnaire. As soon as all participants handed in their questionnaire, it was announced that the experiment had ended. Charlie was brought out again, cameras were turned off, the Wizard was introduced and participants were debriefed and had the opportunity to ask questions about the experiment.

3 Results

3.1 Prior Experience with Technology

A two-way ordinal ANOVA was conducted to compare the main effects of Group and Device Type on the prior experience that the participants had with technology. Both Group (elderly, students) and Device Type (phones/computers and robots) included two levels. A significant main effect was found for both Group (χ^2 (1, N = 52) = 52.66, p < .001), and Device Type (χ^2 (1, N = 52) = 89.53, p < .001). A post-hoc Tukey showed that the students had significantly more prior experience with phones/computers (p < .001), as well as with robots (p < .001) compared to elderly. Furthermore, the prior experience between device types showed a p-value of p < .001 for both students and elderly, indicating a significantly higher usage of phones and computers in comparison to robots for all individuals.

3.2 Attitude Towards Robots

A boxplot of the constructs and the corresponding scores can be found in Fig. 2. A two-way ordinal ANOVA was conducted for each construct of the UTAUT questionnaire to compare the main effects of Group and Time on the collected scores. Both Group (elderly, students) and Time (pre, post) included two levels. The construct Perceived Enjoyment was only included in the post-questionnaire and since the scores were not normally distributed, the comparison between the two groups was conducted using a Mann-Whitney U test. This section will discuss the constructs that were found significant either between groups or over time.

Anxiety. A significant main effect was found in Anxiety levels for both Group (χ^2 (1, N = 52) = 19.45, p < .001), and Time (χ^2 (1, N = 52) = 43.73, p < .001). This indicates a significant difference between both elderly vs. students and pre- vs. post-questionnaires for Anxiety. A post-hoc Tukey showed a significant difference between pre- and post-questionnaire scores for both groups (p < .001). This indicates that anxiety towards the robot decreased in both elderly and students after the interaction. However, the post-interaction anxiety differed significantly between the students and elderly groups (p < .01), indicating that students rated their anxiety towards the robot significantly lower than the elderly after the interaction. This is while elderly were generally more anxious than students even at the beginning.

Perceived Sociability. A significant main effect was found in Perceived Sociability for both Group (χ^2 (1, N = 52) = 6.25, p < .05), and Time (χ^2 (1, N = 52) = 11.14, p < .001). A post-hoc Tukey showed significantly different scores for the students between the pre- and post-questionnaires (p < .05), indicating an increase in Perceived Sociability of the robot (how social the robot was) after the interaction had taken place.

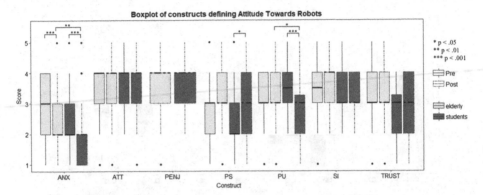

Fig. 2. Boxplot of the constructs defining Attitude Towards Robots (UTAUT questionnaire); Anxiety (ANX), Attitude Towards Technology (ATT), Perceived Enjoyment (PENJ), Perceived Sociability (PS), Perceived Usefulness (PU), Social Influence (SI) and Trust

Perceived Usefulness. A significant main effect for Time was found (χ^2 (1, N = 52) = 13.96, p < .001) as well as a significant interaction effect (χ^2 (1, N = 52) = 7.11, p < .05). A post-hoc Tukey showed a significant decrease in students' responses after the interaction (p < .001), indicating that for students the Perceived Usefulness of the robot decreased over time. Also, there was a significant difference between post scores of groups (p < .05), indicating that students generally rated the robot as less useful in comparison to elderly.

3.3 Topic of Discussion

The boxplot in Fig. 3 displays the results of the eight questions about whether or not the robot gave the participants a topic of discussion. The scores were not normally distributed and hence a Mann-Whitney test indicated that question 26 "I felt uncomfortable sitting together after the experiment was finished" was rated higher by the elderly (W = 475.5, p < .01). Question 30 "I would have preferred one-on-one interaction with Charlie" was also rated higher by the elderly (W = 541.5, p < .001), and so was question 31 "If there was the possibility, I would have liked to continue talking to Charlie more" (W = 441.5, p < .05).

3.4 Observational Video Analysis

An additional observational analysis was performed to verify how much time the participants actually talked about the robot together. The first author analyzed video recordings of the participants when they were left alone after the interaction with the robot. A stopwatch was used to verify how long the robot or related topics were discussed over the total time. A Mann-Whitney U test showed no significant differences, indicating that elderly did not significantly discuss the robot more than the students did.

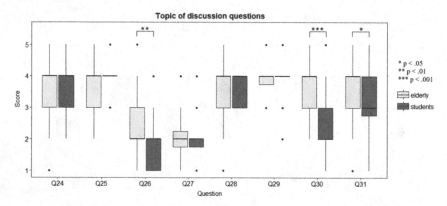

Fig. 3. Boxplot of the questions defining topic of discussion

4 Discussion

In this study, we compared two groups of elderly and young students in their attitude toward a social robot before and after interacting with it. The fact that a group of older adults were compared to a group of young adults, and such comparison was done in the Dutch population makes this study unique. Furthermore, a broad range of aspects was taken into account including prior experience with technology, attitude towards robots, and socialization between individuals.

4.1 Attitude Towards Robots

We found that for both groups, the construct of Anxiety decreased significantly after interaction with the robot and the anxiety level of the students after interaction was significantly lower than that of the elderly. This indicates that the experience with the robot helped decrease uncomfortable feelings in both groups, particularly the elderly, who might have experienced more anxiety due to little prior experience with robots. As Louie et al. [13] suggest in their research with a socially assistive robot, prior experiences with a robot decreases anxiety of the user towards it and increases the perception of ease of use. Our results from a single interaction support this statement.

Results from the construct Perceived Usefulness showed that students perceived the robot significantly less useful after the interaction whereas elderly did not. This is while students reported a significantly higher Perceived Sociability after they participated in the interaction. This could be explained by a difference in needs that both groups have. Nomura et al. [14] explain that elderly expect a robot to perform communicative tasks like serving in public settings or providing health care. Young adults seem to have other needs; they prefer an assistive robot that does repetitive tasks for them, as helping with household chores. Since the robot in our experiment performed a social task, elderly possibly perceived it as more useful than students.

No construct of the UTAUT questionnaire differed significantly between elderly and students before the interaction had taken place, even though previous studies show discrepancy in attitude towards technology between age groups [8]. An explanation for this could be that the number of participants recruited by this study was too small. The study can be expanded in the future to see if significant differences can be seen. Another limitation is the influence of a potential novelty effect, which could have had a distinct effect on the attitude of both groups due to a different prior experience with similar technologies. At last, it should be taken into consideration that the tasks of the robot were pre-defined, and at times were controlled by the Wizard. Future studies could make the conversation more adaptive to the user, by giving the robot the ability to generate sentences itself.

Among the non-significant results, Trust towards robots is more thoroughly discussed in previous literature and is an important aspect for the maintainance of relationships between the user and robot [15, 16]. A meta-analysis by Hancock et al. [15] set out factors that influence trust towards robots and concluded that factors related to the performance of the robot were associated with the level of trust towards it. Other studies state that appearance of the robot is an important factor to influence trust [16]. Future research can give deeper insight into these concepts by changing aspects of the interaction, such as the appearance of the robot, duration of the interaction, and the role of the robot, in order to evaluate changes in Trust and other constructs such as Perceived Usefulness and Enjoyment.

4.2 Topic of Discussion

So far, little research has been done on the improvement of social interaction between individuals with the usage of humanoid robots, where the social robot is used as a facilitator for conversations between individuals. Usually, animal-like robots are used for such experiments, e.g. in [6] and [7].

In our study, elderly generally were positive about the discussion they had, indicated by relatively high scores for Q24 ("Charlie gave me a topic of discussion with the other participants"), Q25 ("I thought the discussion with the other participants, when Charlie was removed, was positive") and Q29 ("After the experiment, I felt like discussing Charlie with the other participants"). An additional observational analysis showed no significance between both groups in time the robot was discussed. A trend was visible; elderly discussed the robot slightly more than the students did (63% and 53% of the total time respectively). Either the small number of groups that was compared, or the differences in group size, could explain the non-significant results. In future research, a similar analysis could be done with a larger number of equally sized groups, to verify whether or not the amount of time that both groups talk about the robot will differ.

Other results from the questionnaire show that most participants felt comfortable with each other, indicated by a low score for Q26 ("I felt uncomfortable sitting together after the experiment was finished") and Q27 ("After the experiment I wanted to leave as soon as possible") and a higher score for Q28 ("I felt a connection with the other participants"). Q26 was significantly different for elderly and students, indicating that elderly felt less comfortable than the students. This could be due to the fact that the students were more used to an experimental setting, given that they participate in experiments on campus regularly. Furthermore, elderly preferred one-on-one interaction more often, as scores for Q30 ("I would have preferred one-on-one interaction with Charlie") were significantly different between the groups. They felt like having insufficient opportunity to talk to the robot, either because they did not always hear what Charlie said properly, or because other participants were responding before they could. This could be linked to Q31 ("If there was the possibility, I would have liked to continue talking to Charlie more"), which was rated significantly higher by elderly than by students. This might be influenced by a different motivation between the groups as well; students mainly participated for credits while elderly were more intrinsically motivated to participate and therefore might have been more positive about continuing the conversation.

As Sharkey and Sharkey [17] explain in their paper, there are numerous ethical concerns for robots in elderly care. One has to make sure a robot does not replace human contact, and in care home settings there will always have to be a care giver present to keep an eye on the situation. However, if carefully introduced, robots have the potential to increase the quality of life of elderly in several ways. This research is the first step in improving social interaction between individuals using a humanoid social robot, and a first attempt to evaluate the attitude of different target groups towards such robot.

5 Conclusion

This study measured the attitude of 9 groups of elderly and 8 groups of students towards a social humanoid robot, before and after they engaged in a conversation with it. Results showed that the attitude of the groups were comparable before the interaction, but that it did change over time and between groups after the interaction. Anxiety towards the robot decreased for both groups, and elderly perceived it as more useful than young adults did. These differences could be assigned to a distinct prior experience with technology, age, or different prior expectations from the robot. In general, both elderly and young adults were positive towards usage of and interaction with the robot.

Promising results were found when it came to using a social humanoid robot as facilitator for social conversations between individuals. The participants generally started discussing the robot or related topics when they were left alone, and indicated that they enjoyed the conversation. This study shows the possibility of a social robot as a tool to increase socialization between individuals, thereby it should not be a replacement for human beings. Future work should consider long-term interactions and other social tasks performed by the robot in order to assess influencing parameters in attitude change of target groups.

References

1. Wright, J.D.: The graying of America: implications for health professionals. Care Manag. J. **6**, 178 (2006)
2. Broekens, J., Heerink, M., Rosendal, H.: Assistive social robots in elderly care: a review. Gerontechnology **8**, 94–103 (2009)
3. De Jong Gierveld, J.: A review of loneliness: concept and definitions, determinants and consequences. Rev. Clin. Gerontol. **8**, 73–80 (1998)
4. Victor, C.R., Scambler, S.J., Bowling, A., Bond, J.: The prevalence of, and risk factors for, loneliness in later life: a survey of older people in Great Britain. Ageing Soc. **25**, 357–375 (2005)
5. Singh, A., Misra, N.: Loneliness, depression and sociability in old age. Ind. Psychiatry J. **18**, 51 (2009)
6. Banks, M.R., Willoughby, L.M., Banks, W.A.: Animal-assisted therapy and loneliness in nursing homes: use of robotic versus living dogs. J. Am. Med. Dir. Assoc. **9**, 173–177 (2008)
7. Wada, K., Shibata, T., Saito, T., Sakamoto, K., Tanie, K.: Psychological and social effects of one year robot assisted activity on elderly people at a health service facility for the aged. In: Proceedings - IEEE International Conference on Robotics and Automation (2005)
8. Baack, S.A., Brown, T.S., Brown, J.T.: Attitudes toward computers: views of older adults compared with those of young adults. J. Res. Comput. Educ. **23**, 422–433 (1991)
9. Stafford, R.Q., et al.: Improved robot attitudes and emotions at a retirement home after meeting a robot. In: Proceedings - IEEE International Workshop on Robot and Human Interactive Communication (2010)
10. Feingold-Polak, R., Elishay, A., Shahar, Y., Stein, M., Edan, Y., Levy-Tzedek, S.: Differences between young and old users when interacting with a humanoid robot: a qualitative usability study. Paladyn. J. Behav. Robot. **9**(1), 183–192 (2018)
11. Venkatesh, V., Morris, M.G., Davis, G.B., Davis, F.D.: User acceptance of information technology: toward a unified view. MIS Q. **27**, 424–478 (2003)
12. Hugel, V., et al.: Mechatronic design of NAO humanoid (2009)
13. Louie, W.Y.G., McColl, D., Nejat, G.: Acceptance and attitudes toward a human-like socially assistive robot by older adults. Assist. Technol. **26**, 140–150 (2014)
14. Nomura, T., Kanda, T., Suzuki, T., Kato, K.: Age differences and images of robots: Social survey in Japan. Interact. Stud. Stud. Soc. Behav. Commun. Biol. Artif. Syst. **10**, 374–391 (2009)
15. Hancock, P.A., Billings, D.R., Schaefer, K.E., Chen, J.Y.C., De Visser, E.J., Parasuraman, R.: A meta-analysis of factors affecting trust in human-robot interaction. Hum. Factors **53**, 517–527 (2011)
16. Haring, K.S., Matsumoto, Y., Watanabe, K.: How do people perceive and trust a lifelike robot. In: Proceedings of the World Congress on Engineering and Computer Science 2013 (2013)
17. Sharkey, A., Sharkey, N.: Granny and the robots: ethical issues in robot care for the elderly. Ethics Inf. Technol. **14**, 27–40 (2012)

Spatiotemporal Coordination Supports a Sense of Commitment in Human-Robot Interaction

Alessia Vignolo[1,2(✉)], Alessandra Sciutti[3], Francesco Rea[2], and John Michael[1]

[1] Department of Philosophy, Social Sciences Building, University of Warwick,
Coventry CV4 7AL, UK
[2] Robotics Brain and Cognitive Sciences Unit, Istituto Italiano di Tecnologia,
Via Enrico Melen 83, 16152 Genoa, Italy
alessia.vignolo@iit.it
[3] CONTACT Unit, Istituto Italiano di Tecnologia,
Via Enrico Melen 83, 16152 Genoa, Italy

Abstract. In the current study, we presented participants with videos in which a humanoid robot (iCub) and a human agent were tidying up by moving toys from a table into a container. In the High Coordination condition, the two agents worked together in a coordinated manner, with the human picking up the toys and passing them to the robot. In the Low Coordination condition, they worked in parallel without coordinating. Participants were asked to imagine themselves in the position of the human agent and to respond to a battery of questions to probe the extent to which they felt committed to the joint action. While we did not observe a main effect of our coordination manipulation, the results do reveal that participants who perceived a higher degree of coordination also indicated a greater sense of commitment to the joint action. Moreover, the results show that participants' sensitivity to the coordination manipulation was contingent on their prior attitudes towards the robot: participants in the High Coordination condition reported a greater sense of commitment than participants in the Low Coordination condition, except among those participants who were a priori least inclined to experience a close sense of relationship with the robot.

Keywords: Cognitive human-robot interaction · Sense of commitment · iCub

1 Introduction

As robots become increasingly prevalent throughout everyday life and in domains ranging from health care to education and manufacturing [2,4,6,8,15], researchers are devoting ever more attention to developing new ways of optimizing human-robot-interaction. In the industrial context, for example, there has already been a shift from the use of robots as fully pre-programmed devices performing single predefined tasks towards the adoption of co-bots, able to adapt

M. A. Salichs et al. (Eds.): ICSR 2019, LNAI 11876, pp. 34–43, 2019.
https://doi.org/10.1007/978-3-030-35888-4_4

to new tasks and new human partners. One challenge in this regard is to boost human interactants' willingness to invest time and effort when interacting with a robot partner and in persisting in an interaction as the robot adapts to a new context and a new human partner. While there is a risk of human interactants becoming frustrated or impatient when a robot is slow to adapt, the potential benefits of adaptation are high insofar as they can maximize a robot's ability to contribute to new tasks with new partners.

To address this challenge, Powell and Michael [10] (cf. also [11]) have recently proposed that a potentially effective and low-cost strategy could be to develop design features that serve to maintain a human's sense of commitment to an interaction with a robot. By boosting a human agent's sense of commitment, it may be possible to increase her or his willingness to remain patient and persistent when the robot makes errors or is slow to perform a task. To achieve this, they recommend the implementation of features that have been shown to promote a sense of commitment in human-human interaction.

For example, recent research on human-human interaction provides evidence that spatiotemporal coordination may boost a sense of commitment [12] (cf. also [13]), leading people to persist longer and to invest greater effort in joint actions. This is because, when two agents coordinate their contributions to a joint action, they form and implement interdependent, i.e. mutually contingent, action plans. The agents thus form interdependent action plans. Each agent must therefore have – and rely upon – expectations about what the other agent is going to do. This may generate social pressure on the other agent to perform the expected actions. It is not yet known, however, to what extent spatiotemporal coordination may have similar effects in the context of human-robot interaction.

1.1   Aim of the Study

In the current study, we extend the research on spatiotemporal coordination and commitment to the context of human-robot interaction. To this end, we adapted a paradigm used in research on human-human joint action [8]. Specifically, we designed and implemented an online study in which we presented participants with videos in which a humanoid robot (iCub [9]) and a human agent were tidying up by moving toys from a table into a container. In the High Coordination condition, the two agents formed a chain, with the human picking up the toys and passing them to the robot. In the Low Coordination condition, they worked in parallel without forming a chain. Participants were asked to imagine themselves in the position of the human agent and to respond to a battery of questions to probe the extent to which they felt committed to the joint action. We predicted that they would indicate a higher degree of commitment in the High Coordination condition than in the Low Coordination condition.

2   Methods

We used SurveyMonkey to administer a web-based observational paradigm. Participants were recruited via prolific academic. Since each participant gave only one judgment per condition, and since online experiments produce greater variability than lab-based experiments, we aimed for a large sample size: 100 per condition in a between-subjects design. Anticipating that about 25% of our participants may need to be excluded, we solicited 250 participants and also included an additional nine participants who completed the survey before prolific had registered that the target number had been reached. Each of the 259 participants received a payment of 1 Pound. We excluded 19 participants who either did not complete the experiment or did not correctly answer the question "What items were John and the robot clearing away?". The final dataset was thus composed by 240 participants (129 males, 107 females, 1 other and 2 preferred not to say) between the ages of 16 and 74 ($M = 28.95$ years, $SD = 10.52$ years). The experiment was conducted in accordance with the Declaration of Helsinki, and was approved by the Humanities & Social Sciences Research Ethics Sub-committee (HSSREC) at the University.

2.1 Stimuli

iCub's movements of all the body parts (arms, torso, neck and eyes) were controlled entirely with the Constant Time Position Service (CTP Service) that takes as input the desired position in joint space and the timing, and conforms to biological motion (minimum jerk model). In both conditions, the robot and the human partner do not perform mutual gaze during the interaction. In both conditions, the robot's gaze anticipates the right hand movement (e.g. in the Low Coordination condition, the robot's gaze anticipates the reaching and the grasping of the object), to conform to biologically-inspired behaviour.

2.2 Procedure

After providing their informed consent and answering basic demographic questions, participants are asked to respond to a preliminary question ("Have you ever interacted with a robot?"). Then, participants are shown a brief video (the introductory video) in which the humanoid robot iCub is tidying up by moving toys from a table into a container. In the video, a human agent who is passing by stops and begins to help the robot.

Participants are then asked to imagine being in the position of the human agent, to assess how close they feel to the robot, and to report this using the 7-point Inclusion of Other in the Self (IOS) Scale [19]. (before seeing the video of the joint action and after). Next, a brief text explaining the scenario is shown:

· The robot in the picture has the task of cleaning up a bunch of small items from the morning activity. As you will see in a very brief video, John is walking by to get his laptop when he notices the robot cleaning up. Since he is going to need to use this table later on, he stops to help for a bit to ensure that the cleaning up is going well.

Participants then watch a video composed of the introductory video and the video of the joint action (repeated twice) in one of the two conditions: in the Low Coordination condition, the human agent and the robot act independently of each other, with each of them grasping toys individually and putting them into the container (Fig. 1, left). In the High Coordination condition, they form a chain in which the human grasps toys and passes them to the robot, whereupon the robot drops them into the container (Fig. 1, right). In the High Coordination condition, the video lasts about 40 s; in the Low Coordination condition, the video lasts 37 s. In both conditions, the overall number of toys placed in the box is 4 (in the Low Coordination condition each agent puts two toys into the container; in the High Coordination condition all four toys are passed from the human to the robot).

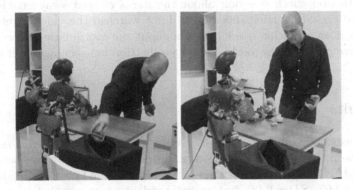

Fig. 1. Screenshots of the video stimuli: low coordination (left) and high coordination condition (right).

After the video, participants are asked the following questions:

- The "persistence question": How long would you keep helping if you were in John's place? (1, Not at all - 5, Until all objects are cleared away)
- The "resistance to distraction question": If you were in John's place and your phone were to start ringing...how likely is that you would take the call? (1, Highly likely - 4, Highly unlikely)
- The "patience question": Sometimes the robot has to stop to recalibrate its sensors. This requires that the entire activity be stopped and can take anywhere from a few seconds to 10 min. If you were in John's place and the robot had to pause to recalibrate, how long do you think you would wait for him before giving up and leaving? (1, Not at all - 6, As long as it takes)
- The "coordination question": To what extent did John and the robot seem to be coordinating with each other? (1, Not at all - 5, Completely)
- The "human coordination question": To what extent did John seem to be coordinating with the robot? (1, Not at all - 5, Completely)
- The "robot coordination question": To what extent did the robot seem to be coordinating with John? (1, Not at all - 5, Completely)
- The "attention check question": What items were John and the robot clearing away?

The persistence question, the resistance to distraction question and the patience question all operationalize commitment. They enable us to assess whether participants that were exposed to the High Coordination condition would continue longer, would be less likely to be distracted by an external stimulus, and would wait longer if the robot had to stop.

The three coordination questions enable us validate the stimuli and to demonstrate that participants in the High Coordination condition indeed perceived a higher degree of coordination. Moreover, they also enable us to probe whether participants perceived the coordination to be driven more by the robot or by the human.

The attention check question about the items cleared away enables us to identify and exclude participants who had not watched the video carefully. We did not insert an attention check question about the coordination as we did not want to force participants to observe a coordination between agents if they did not notice it.

3   Results

For the persistence question, we observed a quantitative difference such that participants in the High Coordination condition indicated that they would help for longer ($M = 3.36$, $SD = 1.53$) than participants in the Low Coordination condition ($M = 3.07$, $SD = 1.43$), but an independent t-test revealed no significant difference, t (238) $= 1.477$, $p = 0.141$. For the resistance to distraction question, we did not observe a significant difference between participants in the High Coordination condition ($M = 1.47$, $SD = 0.64$) and participants in the Low Coordination condition (M$= 1.45$, $SD = 0.71$), independent t-test t (238) $= 0.176$, $p = 0.860$. For the patience question, participants in the High Coordination condition indicated that they would help longer ($M = 3.31$, $SD = 1.49$) than participants in the Low Coordination condition ($M = 3.01$, $SD = 1.35$), and an independent t-test revealed a marginal effect, t (238) $= 1.661$, $p = 0.098$.

As a manipulation check, we analysed the data from the coordination question and the robot coordination question. Regarding the coordination question, participants who observed the High Coordination condition video perceived a higher degree of coordination between the human and the robot ($M = 4.09$, $SD = 0.88$) than participants who observed the Low Coordination condition video ($M = 3.29$, $SD = 1.12$), and an independent t-test revealed a significant effect, $t(238) = 6.207$, $p = 2.382 \cdot 10^{-9}$.

Regarding the robot coordination question, participants who observed the High Coordination condition video perceived a higher degree of coordination on the part of the robot ($M = 3.96$, $SD = 1.05$) than participants who observed the Low Coordination condition video ($M = 2.68$, $SD = 1.27$), and an independent t-test revealed a significant effect, t (238) $= 8.488$, $p = 2.284 \cdot 10^{-15}$.

We then conducted a series of one-way ANCOVAs with the perceived coordination (coordination question) as covariate (Fig. 2). For the persistence question, it revealed a significant effect of the covariate on perceived commitment,

$F(1, 237) = 13.62$, $p = 0.0003$, but no significant effect of the condition, $F(1, 237) = 0.02$, $p = 0.884$, or of the interaction, $F(1, 237) = 2.72$, $p = 0.100$. For the resistance to distraction question, it revealed no significant effect of the covariate, $F(1, 237) = 1.11$, $p = 0.293$, of the condition, $F(1, 237) = 0.06$, $p = 0.815$ or of the interaction, $F(1, 237) = 1.78$, $p = 0.183$. For the patience question, it revealed a significant effect of the covariate on the perceived commitment, $F(1, 237) = 15.27$, $p = 0.0001$, but no significant effect of the condition, $F(1, 237) = 0.07$, $p = 0.796$, or of the interaction, $F(1, 237) = 0.34$, $p = 0.562$.

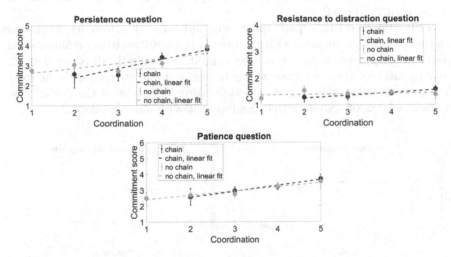

Fig. 2. Effect of condition (high coordination vs. low coordination), with perceived coordination (i.e. response to the coordination question) as covariate, on perceived commitment (i.e. responses to the persistence question, the resistance to distraction question, and the patience question).

We also conducted a series of one-way ANCOVAs with the perceived coordination of the robot (i.e. responses to the robot coordination question) as covariate. For the persistence question, it revealed a significant effect of the covariate on perceived commitment, $F(1, 237) = 6.21$, $p = 0.013$, but no significant effect of the condition, $F(1, 237) = 0.11$, $p = 0.747$, or of the interaction, $F(1, 237) = 0.65$, $p = 0.423$. For the resistance to distraction question, it revealed no significant effect of the covariate, $F(1, 237) = 2.35$, $p = 0.127$, of the condition, $F(1, 237) = 0.41$, $p = 0.522$, or of the interaction, $F(1, 237) = 0.55$, $p = 0.457$. For the patience question, it revealed a significant effect of the covariate on the perceived commitment, $F(1, 237) = 24.27$, $p = 1.58 \cdot 10^{-6}$, but no significant effect of the condition, $F(1, 237) = 0.54$, $p = 0.462$, or of the interaction, $F(1, 237) = 0.004$, $p = 0.947$.

Next, we probed whether participants' responses to the three commitment questions varied according to the closeness which they reported to the robot prior to the experiment. To do so, we conducted a series of one-way ANCOVAs with closeness as covariate. For the persistence question, it revealed a significant effect of the interaction between the condition and the covariate on perceived commitment, $F(1, 237) = 6.43$, $p = 0.012$, but no significant effect of the covariate, $F(1, 237) = 1.30$, $p = 0.255$, or of the condition, $F(1, 237) = 2.26$, $p = 0.134$. For the resistance to distraction question, it revealed a marginal effect of the covariate, $F(1, 237) = 3.68$, $p = 0.056$, no significant effect of the condition, $F(1, 237) = 0.04$, $p = 0.847$, or of the interaction, $F(1, 237) = 0.03$, $p = 0.857$. For the patience question, it revealed a marginal effect of the covariate, $F(1, 237) = 2.75$, $p = 0.099$, of the condition, $F(1, 237) = 2.86$, $p = 0.092$, and of the interaction, $F(1, 237) = 3.29$, $p = 0.071$,

As illustrated in Fig. 3, participants who indicated that they felt least close with the robot (i.e. responded with a '1') were least sensitive to our manipulation. In fact, for the persistence question, they exhibit a trend in the direction opposite to our hypothesis: they are more willing to persist in interacting with the robot when there is not a high degree of coordination. The rest of the participants exhibit a pattern of responses that is consistent with our hypothesis.

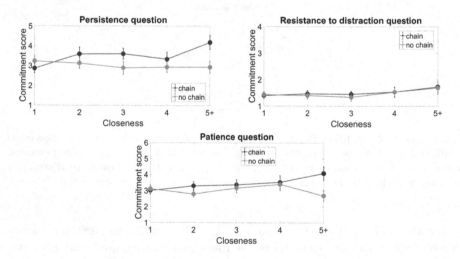

Fig. 3. Effect of the closeness which they reported to the robot prior to the experiment on perceived commitment (i.e. responses to the persistence question, the resistance to distraction question, and the patience question).

A linear regression was calculated to predict perceived commitment (i.e. responses to the persistence question, the resistance to distraction question, and the patience question) based on perceived coordination (i.e. responses to the coordination question). For the persistence question, a significant regression equation was found ($F(1, 238) = 13.57$, $p = 0.0003$), with an R^2 of 0.054. Participants' perception of commitment was equal to $2.039 + 0.318$ (perceived coordination score). Commitment increased 0.318 for each point of perceived coordination. For the resistance to distraction question, no significant regression equation was found ($F_{(1, 238)} = 1.112$, $p = 0.293$), with an R^2 of 0.005. Participants predicted commitment is equal to $1.3026 + 0.042$ (perceived coordination score). Commitment increased 0.042 for each point of perceived coordination score. For the patience question, a significant regression equation was found ($F_{(1, 238)} = 15.37$, $p = 0.0001$), with an R^2 of 0.061. Participants' perception of commitment was equal to $1.961 + 0.325$ (perceived coordination score). Commitment increased 0.325 for each point of perceived coordination.

A linear regression was calculated to predict perceived commitment (i.e. responses to the persistence question, the resistance to distraction question, and the patience question) based on perceived robot's coordination (i.e. responses to the robot coordination question). For the persistence question, a significant regression equation was found ($F_{(1, 238)} = 6.245$, $p = 0.013$), with an R^2 of 0.026. Participants predicted commitment is equal to $2.621 + 0.179$ (perceived coordination score). Commitment increased 0.179 for each point of perceived coordination score. For the resistance to distraction question, no significant regression equation was found ($F_{(1, 238)} = 2.358$, $p = 0.126$), with an R^2 of 0.010. Participants predicted commitment is equal to $1.293 + 0.050$ (perceived coordination score). Commitment increased 0.050 for each point of perceived coordination score. For the patience question, a significant regression equation was found ($F_{(1, 238)} = 24.41$, $p = 1.465 \cdot 10^{-6}$), with an R^2 of 0.093. Participants predicted commitment is equal to $2.072 + 0.328$ (perceived coordination score). Commitment increased 0.328 for each point of perceived coordination score.

4   Discussion

Current research in HRI is more and more devoted to trying to obtain seamless and pleasant interactions and transfer of skills between humans and robots [1,16]. However, extended interaction also requires patience from human partners in face of errors or simply to slow robot behaviours. Previous work in robotics has investigated how to deal with errors or lack of knowledge, suggesting different strategies for robots to ask the right questions [3] or to be transparent about its errors in order to mitigate negative human reactions - and to reduce the risk of humans abandoning the interaction [5]. In this work we explored a different approach, testing the hypothesis that a high degree of spatiotemporal coordination promotes a sense of commitment in the context of human robot interaction. To this end, participants were instructed to imagine themselves in the role of a human agent interacting with a humanoid robot either with a high degree of spatiotemporal coordination (High Coordination condition) or with a low degree of spatiotemporal coordination (Low Coordination condition), and asked to respond to a battery of questions to probe the extent to which they felt committed to the joint action. We predicted that they would indicate a greater sense of commitment in the High Coordination condition than in the Low Coordination condition. Though we did not observe a main effect of our coordination manipulation, the exploratory analyses did reveal that those participants who perceived a higher degree of coordination – and particularly those participants who perceived that the robot was actively coordinating with the human agent – also indicated a greater sense of commitment to the joint action. This is consistent with our hypothesis, though it suggests that our stimuli may not have been optimally designed to present contrasting degrees of coordination. The results also show that participants' sensitivity to the coordination manipulation was contingent on their prior attitudes towards the robot: participants in the High Coordination condition reported a greater sense of commitment than participants in the Low Coordination condition, except among those participants who were a priori least inclined to experience a close sense of relationship with the robot.

Our findings contribute to a growing body of research investigating how simple design features may be used to elicit a human agent's sense of commitment to a joint action with a robot, thereby increasing the human's willingness to remain patient and invest effort in the joint action. In particular, Székely et al. (forthcoming; cf. also Vignolo, under review) have shown that noticing a robot's investment of effort in a joint action, beyond improving subjects' performance [17], can boost a human agent's sense of commitment, thereby enhancing their persistence and patience. The current findings extend this research by providing preliminary evidence that a second factor, namely spatiotemporal coordination, may have similar effects. This provides roboticists with a further tool to use in designing robots that can elicit a sense of commitment on the part of human agents. These results also suggest that developing new approaches to enable robots to detect sensorimotor regularities in human partners' behaviours [18] and adapt to them [7,14] could bring in advantages beyond simple efficiency, potentially also leading to higher degrees of commitment toward robotic partners. It would be valuable for further research to explore the effects of spatiotemporal coordination in other contexts and with other tasks. Moreover, an important next step would be to investigate the effects that spatiotemporal coordination with a robot has upon the sense of commitment when people are directly involved in the interaction rather than watching a video and imagining themselves in the interaction.

Acknowledgment. This research was supported by a Starting Grant from the European Research Council (nr. 679092, SENSE OF COMMITMENT).

References

1. Argall, B.D., Chernova, S., Veloso, M., Browning, B.: A survey of robot learning from demonstration. Robot. Auton. Syst. **57**(5), 469–483 (2009)
2. Breazeal, C., Brooks, A., Gray, J., Hoffman, G., Kidd, C., Lee, H.: Humanoid robots as cooperative partners for people. J. Hum. Robot. **1**, 34 (2004)
3. Cakmak, M., Thomaz, A.L.: Designing robot learners that ask good questions. In: Proceedings of the Seventh Annual ACM/IEEE International Conference on Human-Robot Interaction, HRI 2012, pp. 17–24. ACM, New York (2012). https://doi.org/10.1145/2157689.2157693

4. Clodic, A., Cao, H., Alili, S., Montreuil, V., Alami, R., Chatila, R.: SHARY: a supervision system adapted to human-robot interaction. In: Khatib, O., Kumar, V., Pappas, G.J. (eds.) Experimental Robotics, vol. 54, pp. 229–38. Springer, Heidelberg (2009). https://doi.org/10.1007/978-3-642-00196-3_27
5. Fischer, K., Weigelin, H., Bodenhagen, L.: Increasing trust in human-robot medical interactions: effects of transparency and adaptability. Paladyn J. Behav. Robot. 9(1), 95–109 (2018)
6. Grigore, E., Eder, K., Pipe, A., Melhuish, C., Leonards, U.: Joint action understanding improves robot-to-human object handover. IEEE/RSJ International Conference on Intelligent Robots and Systems,pp. 4622–9 (2013)
7. Iqbal, T., Rack, S., Riek, L.D.: Movement coordination in human - robot teams: a dynamical system approach. IEEE Trans. Robot. 34, 909–919 (2016)
8. Lenz, C., Nair, S., Rickert, M., Knoll, A., Rosel, W., Gast, J.: Joint-action for humans and industrial robots for assembly tasks, pp. 130–135. IEEE (2008)
9. Metta, G., et al.: The iCub humanoid robot: an open-systems platform for research in cognitive development. Neural Netw. 23(8–9), 1125–1134 (2010)
10. Michael, J., Powell, H.: Feeling committed to a robot: why, what, when, and how? Philos. Trans. R. Soc. B: Biol. Sci. 374(1771), 20180039 (2019)
11. Michael, J., Salice, A.: The sense of commitment in human-robot interaction. Int. J. Soc. Robot. 9(5), 755–63 (2017)
12. Michael, J., Sebanz, N., Knoblich, G.: Observing joint action: coordination creates commitment. Cognition 157, 106–113 (2016)
13. Michael, J., Sebanz, N., Knoblich, G.: The sense of commitment: a minimal approach. Front. Psychol. 6, 1968 (2016)
14. Rea, F., Vignolo, A., Sciutti, A., Noceti, N.: Human motion understanding for selecting action timing in collaborative human-robot interaction. Front. Robot. AI 6, 58 (2019)
15. Sciutti, A., Bisio, A., Nori, F., Metta, G., Fadiga, L., Pozzo, T.: Measuring human-robot interaction through motor resonance. Int. J. Soc. Robot. 4(3), 223–34 (2012)
16. Sciutti, A., Mara, M., Tagliasco, V., Sandini, G.: Humanizing human-robot interaction: on the importance of mutual understanding. IEEE Technol. Soc. Mag. 37(1), 22–29 (2018)
17. Vignolo, A., Powell, H., McEllin, L., Rea, F., Sciutti, A., Michael, J.: An adaptive robot teacher boosts a human partner's learning performance in joint action. In: The 28th IEEE International Conference on Robot & Human Interactive Communication (RO-MAN 2019), New Delhi, India (2019)
18. Vignolo, A., Noceti, N., Rea, F., Sciutti, A., Odone, F., Sandini, G.: Detecting biological motion for human-robot interaction: a link between perception and action. Front. Robot. AI 4, 14 (2017)
19. Woosnam, K.M.: The inclusion of other in the self (IOS) scale. Ann. Tour. Res. 37, 857–60 (2010)

Subject Selection Bias in Intervention Experiments with Socially Assistive Robots and the Impact on the Representativeness of the Population

Toshiharu Igarashi[1], Misato Nihei[1,2(✉)], Jumpei Mizuno[3],
Takenobu Inoue[3], and Minoru Kamata[1,2]

[1] Department of Human and Engineered Environmental Studies,
The University of Tokyo, 5-1-5 Kashiwanoha, Kashiwa, Chiba, Japan
mnihei@edu.k.u-tokyo.ac.jp
[2] Institute of Gerontology, The University of Tokyo,
Faculty of Engineering Bldg.8., 7F, 7-3-1 Hongo, Bunkyo-ku, Tokyo, Japan
[3] Research Institute of National Rehabilitation Center for Persons
with Disabilities, 1 Namiki 4-chome, Tokorozawa,
Saitama Prefecture 359-8555, Japan

Abstract. The subjects of all studies have their own personalities and characteristics. For example, the characteristics of elderly individuals being assisted by Socially Assistive Robots (SARs) needs to be investigated. However, the attributes of subjects' personalities that affect the outcome of intervention experiments involving SARs have been analyzed mainly by gender so far. The purpose of this study is to clarify the selection criteria of the subjects in intervention experiments with SARs and their influence on subjects' attributes. Semi-structured interviews were conducted to clarify the criteria by which subjects were selected and the relationship between the subjects and the facility personnel. We interviewed 13 staff members who were involved in the selection of subjects for SAR intervention experiments in six facilities. According to the subject selection criteria discovered in these interviews, we did follow-up research to clarify the influence on the attributes of the selected subjects. In conclusion, the subject selection criteria reported by the staff were analyzed according to four categories based on the interview surveys. It was verified that the selection criteria affected the selection attributes of subjects' degree of involvement, relationship, and character. Going forward, it is necessary to link this research to not only the personality of the elderly person being assisted but also to their family structure and hobbies, friendship characteristics, and the function of the SARs.

Keywords: Socially assistive robots · Selection Bias · Representativeness of the population

1 Introduction

The lifestyle of the elderly in Japan is currently changing. While two or three families living together was commonplace in the past, in recent years, there has been an increase in households consisting of single adults and elderly married couples [1]. Therefore,

© Springer Nature Switzerland AG 2019
M. A. Salichs et al. (Eds.): ICSR 2019, LNAI 11876, pp. 44–53, 2019.
https://doi.org/10.1007/978-3-030-35888-4_5

elderly care has become a significant issue in Japan: to secure the 2.45 million care workers in demand, it is necessary to secure 60,000 new care workers each year by fiscal year 2025 [2]. Because of this, the elderly care staff shortage in Japan is considered to be serious and prolonged. In this context, intervention with socially assistive robots (SARs) for the elderly was recently proposed as a solution [3]. Previous studies have shown that appropriate intervention can help prevent the progression of cognitive decline and decrease depression among the elderly [4, 5]. However, there are large individual differences in usage and retention rates and inappropriate use has been reported despite proper introduction [6].

What are the issues that influence the use of SARs? Based on the opinions of older adults, four issues related to the use of SARs have emerged: (1) the roles of an SAR; (2) the appearance of an SAR; (3) the normative/ethical issues regarding the use of SARs in elderly care; and (4) the interaction between an older adult and an SAR. The last point can be further subdivided into (a) the technical aspects of this interaction and (b) the human aspects of this interaction [7].

All these issues have been investigated intensively with the exception of theme 4b; the human aspect of the interaction between SARs and older adults. SARs are defined as "the intersection of AR and SIR" [8]. SARs share with assistive robotics the goal of providing assistance to human users but specifically, this assistance is through social interaction. As important as interpersonal relationships are for people, understanding the characteristics of the elderly using SARs is also a very important research subject. However, the personality attributes of subjects that affect the outcome of SAR intervention experiments have been analyzed mainly by gender [9]. The purpose of this study is to clarify the selection criteria of the subjects in the intervention experiments with SARs and their influence on subject attributes.

2 Related Works

2.1 Research Design and Bias

Intervention studies with SARs can be divided into three types: randomized controlled trials (RCTs), crossover trials, and studies without control. Most previous research on SARs corresponded to studies without control, while a few of them comprised of RCTs and crossover-controlled trials.

Biases affecting these intervention studies include (a) selection, (b) information, and (c) confounding. Therefore, researchers must control the attributes of subjects in line with the research design [10]. In fact, in 2010, Martinson reported that research programs for the elderly may have limited reach and substantial volunteer bias [11]. Since it is unrealistic to conduct an exhaustive survey, researchers need to carefully consider the representativeness of the population of the sampled subjects.

2.2 Bias Entered by Facility Staff

So far, we have developed a robot called "PaPeRo" (Partner-type-Personal-Robot) in a 10-year project started in 2010 [12]. The robot is equipped with speech recognition, speech synthesis, facial image recognition, autonomous mobility, head motion, light indication functions, and tactile sensors. Intervention experiments were conducted in nursing homes and serviced apartments for the elderly (Fig. 1). While the approach to residents in these facilities has been through the facility staff, this "staff" factor can also be a bias. In addition to our research, other experiments were also conducted to introduce SARs to users in such facilities. However, there has been no in-depth discussion on the criteria for subject selection and the relationship between the subjects and facility staff has not yet been clarified.

Size	20 cm(width) × 30 cm(length) × 23 cm(height)
Weight	2000 g
Main function	Text-to-speech, voice recognition, emotion expression by the LED lamp, face recognition.
Sensor	Infrared sensor (for human detection), acceleration sensor, illuminance sensor temperature and humidity sensor,

Fig. 1. The size, weight, main function and equipped sensor of "PaPeRo".

2.3   Relationship Between Subject Personality and Bias

Among the recent theories on personality characteristics, the Big-Five Inventory (Goldberg, 1990, 1992) and the Five-Factor Model of Personality (McCrae & Costa, 1987) have accumulated the most solid knowledge [13]. As a common point, both models capture personality in five large frameworks, namely Extraversion, Agreeableness, Conscientiousness, Neuroticism, and Openness. Regarding the relationship between personality and bias, Dollinger points out the influence of an individual's agreeableness and openness traits on volunteer bias [14]. However, there are hardly any research involving intervention studies with SARs that conduct experiments while paying attention to the influence of such individual personality characteristics. Therefore, studies were conducted to clarify the bias related to subject selection by facility staff and the relationship between subject personality and representativeness of the population among the elderly in Japan.

3   Semi-structured Interview with Facility Staff Involved in Subject Selection

3.1   Method

In this study, semi-structured interviews were conducted to clarify the criteria by which subjects were selected and the relationship between the subjects and the facility staff.

Target Audience. Our ten-year project was supported by 30 facilities in Japan, including serviced apartments for the elderly. We interviewed 13 staff members (five men and eight women) who were involved in the selection of subjects for intervention experiments with SARs in six facilities. All six facilities were serviced apartments for the elderly belonging to the same company but administered by different managers as separate facilities. We conducted interviews with all staff who participated in the selection of subjects in the demonstration experiments at the six facilities.

Interview Guide. An interview guide for semi-structured interviews was created with the help of care experts associated with intervention experiments. The interview guide included five hearing items: (1) basic information on the interviewee, (2) basic information on the selected subjects, (3) subject selection criteria, (4) relationship with selected subjects, and 5) emotional burden scale of work. As for basic information on the interviewee (1), we asked for age, years of work experience in the company, job title, and the user correspondence ratio in their work. Regarding information on the selected subjects (2), we asked for age, gender, and information about physical function, cognitive function, and mental condition. Considering the subject selection criteria (3), we asked about the selection of subjects in intervention experiments. The criteria were sufficient for each subject selection after all hearing items were completed. In the case of the interviewee's relationship with selected subjects (4), we asked about the opportunities of involvement with subjects and the degree of relationship (five-point scale evaluation). In the scale, "5" comprises the top 20% in involvement opportunities, while "1" refers to the bottom 20%. For emotional burden scale of work (5), Fig. 2 showed the five personal questions of the Japanese version of the Zarit Burden Interview (ZBI) [15]. The survey was conducted with all the facilities' users and the selected subjects while the order of the questions was changed.

Q1. Do you have any problems with users' behavior?
Q2. Do you feel strained when you are around users?
Q3. Are there situations in which you do not know how to respond to users?
Q4. Do you wish you could leave the care of users to someone else?
Q5. Do you feel angry when you are around users?

Fig. 2. Five personal questions of the Japanese version of the Zarit Burden Interview

3.2 Results

Basic Information on the Interviewee (1). The average age of the 13 staff members was 48.7 years (±12.7 years) and the average service time in the group company was 11.2 years (±4.2 years). Regarding job title, seven persons were facility managers, five were life support coordinators, and one person was a part-time employee. The ratio of user correspondence to work was 50.9% overall; however, the average was 37.1% for facility managers and 61.2% for the other staff.

Basic Information on Selected Subjects (2). A total of 18 subjects (2 men and 16 women) were selected in six facilities. The average age was 85.33 years (±6.06 years, mean of 84.0 years for men, and mean of 85.5 years for women). In terms of physical function, there were people who were able to live independently despite anxiety about walking and age-related hearing loss. Regarding cognitive function, none had a previous diagnosis of dementia, although a few subjects presented with forgetfulness due to aging. Regarding mental status, only one subject had been diagnosed with schizophrenia and depression; none of the other subjects had been specifically diagnosed.

Subject Selection Criteria (3). Based on the raw data recorded, we summarized the concepts that were investigated based on similar intentions for the staff and the subjects, although the wording was different. Concerning the selection of the elderly subjects for SAR experiments, eight of the staff reported selection of subjects based on an interest in new things/no resistance (smartphones, tablets, etc.), five reported selection based on an interest in robots/no resistance, five presented a cooperative character, and four reported selection due to a need for life support today or in the near future. Additionally, four staff reported ease of understanding of the subjects and their families, three reported the presence of forgetfulness and mild cognitive impairment, three reported usually staying in the room, two reported considerable involvement with facility staff, two reported symptoms of forgetfulness, two reported owning a robot such as Aibo, one reported being a former employee of an affiliated company of the robots, and one reported a strong desire for approval. Items leading to exclusion comprised of severe hearing loss and dementia, an inability to speak frequently due to cerebrovascular disease, and not liking staff intervention.

Relationship with Selected Subjects. Regarding frequency of involvement, the interviewees expressed 4.33 (SD = 0.88) in a five-point Likert scale as an average of 13 staff. As for opportunities for involvement, they mentioned meals (16 people), interaction on the floor, in-facility events, and paid services.

Emotional Burden Scale of Work (5). Concerning the personal questions of the Zarit Burden Interview on staff work, there were differences in all items when comparing the answers concerning all apartment users with the answers on the study subjects. In "Q1. Do you have any problems with users' behavior?" the all-residents group factored 3.83, while the only-subjects group factored 2.5. For "Q2. Do you feel strained when you are around users?" the all-residents group factored 2.33, while only-subjects group factored 2.0. In "Q3. Are there situations in which you do not know how to respond to users?" the all-residents group factored 3.58, while the only-subjects group factored 2.0. For "Q4. Do you wish you could leave the care of users to someone else?" the all-residents group factored 2.33, while only-subjects group factored 1.75. Finally, in "Q5. Do you feel angry when you are around users?" the all-residents group factored 2.75, while the only-subjects group factored 1.83.

3.3   Analysis

Concerning the frequency and opportunity of involvement, it was found that most of the subjects were selected from among the top 40% regarding degree of involvement, while there were tenants who were completely unrelated among the facilities. Moreover, with the emotional burden scale, the burden awareness for all residents and for the study subject group differ (Table 1). A Mann–Whitney U test on the same sample confirmed a significant difference between all five items ($p < 0.05$). Regarding the subject selection criteria, we divided criteria concepts into four categories based on the Modified Grounded Theory Approach (M-GTA) by Kinoshita et al. [16].

Table 1. Results of the emotional burden scale

	Whole user	Subject only	
Q1. Do you have any problems with users' behavior?	3.83	2.5	**
Q2. Do you feel strained when you are around users?	2.33	2.0	*
Q3. Are there situations in which you do not know how to respond to users?	3.58	2.0	**
Q4. Do you wish you could leave the care of users to someone else?	2.33	1.75	*
Q5. Do you feel angry when you are around users?	2.75	1.83	*

* = $P < 0.05$; ** = $P < 0.01$.

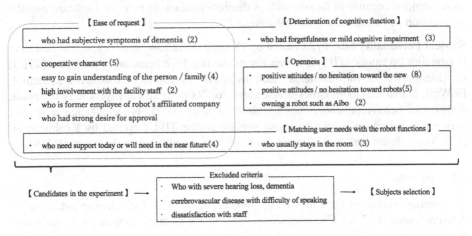

Fig. 3. Selection criteria categories and their inclusive concepts (n = 13)

Figure 3 shows the 12 concepts divided into four categories and plotted for visualization.

The first category is "openness," which includes three concepts related to positive attitudes toward new concepts. This includes the case of owning a robot such as Aibo. The second Category is "deterioration of cognitive function" and includes people who had forgetfulness or mild cognitive impairment and who presented with symptoms of forgetfulness. The third category is "matching users' needs with the robot functions" and includes those who need support at present or will need it in the near future and those who usually stay in their rooms. The fourth category is "ease of request" and includes the concepts of "cooperative character" and "high involvement with the facility staff." Additionally, although subjective symptoms of forgetfulness and need for support at present or in the near future are included in other categories, we consider them to overlap because it was also reported that those who were aware of their forgetfulness found it easy to ask. The candidates who participated in the experiment were organized based on these four categories. Subjects with severe hearing loss, dementia, cerebrovascular disease with difficulty of speaking, and dissatisfaction with staff were excluded.

4   Follow-up Subject's Research

4.1   Method

According to the subject selection criteria examined in Sect. 3, we followed up research to clarify what kind of influence on the attributes of the selected subject. A personality survey to measure openness and Agreeableness was conducted.

Target Audience. Participants were nine women from the original survey who were able to follow up from April 1 to June 15, 2019. Their average age was 87.56 years (± 3.88 years). A follow-up investigation could not be conducted with the other previous subjects because of factors such as death, relocation to external facilities, and the progression of dementia or other illnesses.

Subject Personality Survey. Created by Gosling, Rentfrow, and Swann, the Ten Item Personality Inventory (TIPI) is a measure of the Big-Five personality attributes [17]. It is widely used in various fields, such as social psychology (Baumeister, Gailliot, DeWall, & Oat-en, 2006; Crocker & Canevello, 2008), political psychology (Caprara, 2008), and behavioral economics (Amir & Ariely, 2007). We conducted a subject personality survey using the Japanese version of the TIPI prepared by Koshio et al. [18]. The validity and credibility of the scale were confirmed by Iwasa et al. [19].

4.2   Results

The average scores of the followed-up subjects were: 4.78 for extroversion, 5.78 for Agreeableness, 4.72 for Conscientiousness, 3.56 for Neuroticism, and 4.33 for openness 4.33.

4.3   Analysis

Relationship Between Personality and Selection Criteria, Frequency of Involvement. In a previous study by Iwasa et al. [19], the national average mean scores for Japanese women aged 80 to 84 years (n = 49) were 3.95 for extroversion, 5.63 for

Agreeableness, 4.37 for Conscientiousness, 4.13 for Neuroticism, and 3.46 for openness. When compared with the data of this study, the follow-up subjects above showed increases of 0.83 for extroversion, 0.15 for Agreeableness, 0.35 for Conscientiousness, and 0.87 for openness, which were all higher than average (Table 2 and Fig. 4). Those with neuropathy tendencies showed a decrease of 0.57 from the average.

Table 2. Score comparison between the subjects' personality and the national average

	Subjects average	Japanese average	Difference (a–b)
Extroversion	4.78	3.95	0.83
Agreeableness	5.78	5.63	0.15
Conscientiousness	4.72	4.37	0.35
Neuroticism	3.56	4.13	−0.57
Openness	4.33	3.46	0.87

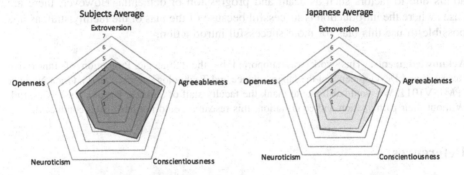

Fig. 4. Score visual comparison between the subjects' personality and the national average

5 Discussion

5.1 Sufficiency of the Sample Size of Facility Staff

Interviews were conducted with 13 staff members related to subject selection. In qualitative interviews with subjects with homogeneous attributes, a number of 13 is considered sufficient because saturation often occurs between 12 and 15. Homogeneous attributes refer to a particular type of employee (e.g., customer service representatives). For example, Guest, Bunce, and Johnson proposed that saturation often occurs around 12 participants in homogeneous groups [20]. This is consistent with a study by Latham, in which saturation occurred at around 11 participants [21].

However, the sample size of follow-up subjects is not sufficient, as only nine people could be surveyed due to factors such as death, relocation to external facilities, and progression of dementia and other illnesses. Moreover, since all the subjects in this survey were women, it is necessary to conduct further surveys including male subjects to increase the validity.

6   Conclusion

In this study, subject selection criteria according to staff were analyzed based on four categories in interview surveys with facility staff. It was verified that the selection criteria affected the selected attributes of subjects' degree of involvement, relationship, and character. As a result, subject selection is made by "Matching user needs with the robot functions", "Deterioration of cognitive function", "Openness" and "Ease of request" in the elderly facilities. However, character refers to "a feature of a person that explains a consistent pattern of emotion, thinking, and behavior" [22]. Depending on the character of the individual, the relationship with the facility staff and the degree of involvement may change, which may cause the subject group to lose their representativeness within a population. The results of this study suggest that it is necessary to carefully examine the generalizability of the selected subjects when designing a study. It is strongly recommended that the subjects' attributes be investigated along with the intervention experiment, otherwise it is necessary to consider a robust study design such as RCT with a large number of subjects since it was difficult to follow up on older adults due to factors such as death and progression of dementia. However, there are cases where the introduction is successful because of the bias of the facility staff, as it is possible to use this bias for more successful introduction.

Acknowledgments. This work was supported by the "Strategic Promotion of Innovative Research and Development" of the Japan Science and Technology Agency (JST), Grant Number JPMJSV1011. We would also like to thank the faculty staff of Seikatsu Kagaku Un-Ei Co., Ltd. Without their participation and contribution, this research could not have been conducted.

References

1. Ministry of Health, Labor and Welfare. Annual report for aging society (2018)
2. Ministry of Health, Labor and Welfare. Required number of care personnel based on the 7th care insurance plan (2018)
3. Nihei, M., et al.: Relaxed watching system for elderly by using communication robot. JSMBE 53(Suppl.) S143_03–S143_03 (2015)
4. Góngora Alonso, S., Hamrioui, S., de la Torre Díez, I., Motta Cruz, E., López-Coronado, M., Franco, M.: Social robots for people with aging and dementia: a systematic review of literature. Telemed J. E Health. (2018). https://doi.org/10.1089/tmj.2018.0051
5. Chen, S.C., Jones, C., Moyle, W.: Social robots for depression in older adults: a systematic review. Nurs. Sch. 50(6), 612–622 (2018). https://doi.org/10.1111/jnu.12423
6. Igarashi, T., Nihei, M., Nakamura, M., Obayashi, K., Masuyama, S., Kamata, M.: Socially assistive robots influence for elderly with cognitive impairment living in nursing facilities: micro observation and analysis. AAATE (2019)
7. Vandemeulebroucke, T., de Casterlé, B.D., Gastmans, C.: How do older adults experience and perceive socially assistive robots in aged care: a systematic review of qualitative evidence. Aging Ment Health. 22(2), 149–167 (2018). https://doi.org/10.1080/13607863.2017.1286455
8. Feil-Seifer, D., Mataric, M.J.: Defining socially assistive robotics. In: IEEE 9th ICRR (2005)

9. Sakuma, M.: Current status and issues of interaction to communication robots: focusing on negative feeling. Bull. Shiraume Gakuen Univ. Jr. Coll. **54**, 119–134 (2018)
10. Tsushima, E.: Fundamentals of research design and statistical analysis. Physiotherapy **44**(6), 463–469 (2017)
11. Martinson, B.C.: Population reach and recruitment bias in a maintenance RCT in physically active older adults. J. Phys. Act Health. Author manuscript; available in PMC, 2010 July 2010
12. Inoue, T., et al.: Field-based development of an information support robot for persons with dementia. Technol. Disabil. **24**, 263–271 (2012). https://doi.org/10.3233/tad-120357
13. Briggs, S.R.: Assessing the five–factor model of personality description. J. Pers. **60**, 253–293 (1992)
14. Dollinger, S.J., Leong, F.T.L.: Volunteer bias and the five-factor model. J. Psychol. Interdiscip. Appl. **127**(1), 29–36 (1993)
15. Kumamoto, K., Arai, Y.: Validation of 'personal strain' and 'role strain': subscales of the short version of the Japanese version of the Zarit Burden Interview (J-ZBI_8). Psychiatry Clin. Neurosci. **58**(6), 606–610 (2004)
16. Kinoshita, Y.: Analysis method of modified grounded theory approach (M-GTA). J. Nurs. Toyama Univ. **6**(2), 1–10 (2007)
17. Gosling, S.D., Rentfrow, P.J., Swann Jr., W.B.: A very brief measure of the Big-Five personality domains. J. Res. Pers. **37**(504–528), 2003 (2003)
18. Shinji, K., Satoshi, A., Cutrone, P.: Attempt to create Japanese version of ten item personality inventory (TIPI-J). Pers. Res. **21**(1), 40–52 (2012)
19. Iwasa, H., Yoshida, Y.: Examination of standard value and sex difference and age difference of "Japanese version Ten-Item Personality Inventory" (TIPI-J) in middle-aged and older adults. Jpn. Public Health J. **65**(7), 356–363 (2018)
20. Guest, G., Bunce, A., Johnson, L.: How many interviews are enough? An experiment with data saturation and variability. Res. Artic. **18**(1), 59–82 (2006)
21. Latham, J.R.: A framework for leading the transformation to performance excellence part I: CEO perspectives on forces, facilitators, and strategic leadership systems. Qual. Manag. J. **20**, 12–33 (2013)
22. Cervone, D., Pervin, L.A.: Personality Psychology, 12th edn. Wiley, Singapore (2013)

Investigating the Effects of Gaze Behavior on the Perceived Delay of a Robot's Response

Vivienne Jia Zhong[✉] [iD], Theresa Schmiedel, and Rolf Dornberger

Institute for Information Systems, FHNW University of Applied Sciences
and Arts Northwestern Switzerland, Basel, Switzerland
{viviennejia.zhong, theresa.schmiedel,
rolf.dornberger}@fhnw.ch

Abstract. Slow responses of social robots cause user frustration in human-robot communication. This paper investigates how far the gaze behavior of a robot, meaning the way the robot looks at its conversation partner, influences the perceived delay of a robot's response in human-robot conversations. To enhance a natural conversation pattern, a gaze behavior was designed and implemented into a humanoid robot. A within-subject experiment involving 31 test subjects was designed with two conditions (with and without gaze behavior). The results generally show a positive correlation between the gaze behavior that the robot exhibits and the perceived responsiveness of the robot (in the condition with gaze behavior). However, the perceived responsiveness is the same in both conditions. One reason for this finding may be that the response time of the robot might have been generally too short to identify an effect in the experimental setting. Future research can directly build on our research to assess the relation between gaze behavior and perceived responsiveness in further detail and draw upon the finding that gaze behavior generally plays an important role with regard to the perceived responsiveness of a robot. Robot designers can also build on our research and consider both gaze behavior and additional factors to address a perceived delay in a robot's response.

Keywords: Human-robot interaction · Gaze behavior · Robot response time

1 Introduction

The ability to conduct natural language dialogues is considered one of the crucial characteristics of social robots [1]. Although silent pauses frequently occur in human natural conversation [2, 3], silence in human-robot communication is often seen as a technical delay respectively defect that may be caused, for example, by failure of speech recognition [4]. Research has suggested that slow responsiveness of a conversational system causes user stress [5] and long waiting times also lead to dissatisfaction at the customer side. Furthermore, prior research suggests avoiding awkward silence in the behavioral design of communication robots as it causes embarrassing social situations [6]. In addition, delayed robot responses can also confuse conversation partners because it might not be clear whether the robot actually intends to take the turn in a conversation or not.

© Springer Nature Switzerland AG 2019
M. A. Salichs et al. (Eds.): ICSR 2019, LNAI 11876, pp. 54–63, 2019.
https://doi.org/10.1007/978-3-030-35888-4_6

To address the perceived delay in human-robot communication, most research proposes the use of filled pauses (e.g. "urmm") to buy time (e.g. [7, 8]). The underlying strategy is to keep the robot talking until it finishes the generation of the response to the asked question. This approach is similar to the one used for conversational systems like chatbots (e.g. [9]). Another approach to address conversational breaks makes use of the way the robot looks at its conversation partner, that is, its gaze behavior. Specifically, previous research demonstrates that gaze behavior can smoothen turn transition in conversations and increase the willingness to wait for robots' responses [10].

While the improvement of robot's responsiveness has been studied in different contexts, small talk has remained an untouched domain. Small talk fulfils a variety of social functions [11]. Therefore, silence in small talk needs to be addressed particularly properly.

The aim of this paper is to investigate the effect of gaze behavior on the perceived delay of a robot's responses in small talk dialogues. To do so, we implemented gaze behavior into a social robot and conducted a within-subject experiment with two conditions (with and without gaze behavior).

2 Related Works

2.1 Time-Buying in Human-Robot Communication Using Filled Pauses

Existing research has studied the effects of filled pauses, so-called fillers, in situations that require time-buying. [12] investigated the upper and lower boundary of a robot's response time in a Wizard of Oz manner: The authors demonstrated that the use of verbal fillers alleviated negative user impressions towards the robot. In their case, the robot simply repeated "etto..." (i.e. "uhm") until the robot is technically able to give the desired response.

[8] proposed two mechanisms for the wait time management, when the tele-operator needs to control multiple robots for social interactions. When a conflict arose in requiring the operator's attention, the robot that did not receive the attention executed the first mechanism "proactive timing control", i.e. uttering a set of predefined phrases until it was stopped by the operator. During the conversation, filled pauses (e.g. "let me think...", "uh") were then used to give the operator time to process the request.

An approach more tailored to the conversation partner's utterance is proposed by [7] for a task-oriented dialogue. The authors created a handful of verbal fillers. Some of these fillers had a placeholder, which was filled with the information collected from the user at runtime. This approach allowed personalized fillers and was more favored than not employing fillers at all.

The only study that used means other than verbal filled pauses was reported by [13]. The authors examined how filled pauses and self-adaptive behaviors recover the awkward silence occurring in a discussion. The filler and the self-adaptive behavior used in their study was "ummm" respectively touching the robot's own chin. Their results showed that these fillers help mitigate awkwardness and express a cooperative attitude.

In conclusion, verbal fillers are effective means to bridge the gap before a robot is able to utter a response in different scenarios. However, means other than verbal fillers and time-buying strategies in the context of small talk conversations have not received much attention in research, yet.

2.2 Gaze Behavior

[14] identified four types of gaze: mutual gaze, referential gaze, gaze related to joint attention and gaze aversion. The research findings show that the robot can perform all types of gaze, and humans are capable to respond to a robot's gaze. However, the robot's gaze capabilities depend on the mechanical possibilities of the robot's face and software technical implementation of the eye movement [14].

As a particularly important nonverbal behavior, gaze plays an important role in conversations. People usually look at the person, to whom their speech is targeted and to whom they are listening [15]. Moreover, gaze has been proven effective in the regulation of conversational turn transitions, which follow a typical pattern: The speaker shows the intention of turn yielding by looking at the listener. The agreement of turn accepting of the listener is then achieved by mutual gaze. This mutual gaze is broken by the listener who looks away once the planning of the utterance starts [10, 16, 17].

Mutual gaze can ease the start of a conversation [18] and increase the engagement in social interaction [19]. Researchers found that by using appropriate gaze aversion behaviors, conversation partners interpreted a robot's behavior as intentional and engaged in a thinking process and were more likely to wait for the robot's response [10]. Interestingly, when gaze aversion is used for turn-yielding by the robot, the conversation partner took significantly more time to response [20].

3 Design of the Robot Gaze Behavior

Following the gaze pattern as described above, we designed a gaze behavior consisting of three steps to investigate the effects of the gaze behavior on the perceived delay of a robot's response.

3.1 Step One: Mutual Gaze and Gaze Aversion

The robot first establishes mutual gaze with the conversation partner after he/she finishes his/her utterance. Studies found that mutual gaze increasingly occurs towards the end of the previous speaker's speech [16] and lasts approx. 2.4 s before the turn transition takes place [21]. Keeping the estimated lower boundary of the response time in mind [12], we designed that the robot keeps looking at its conversation partner for one second before performing the gaze aversion.

When changing speaker, gaze aversion is usually directed down and to the side [10]. Therefore, five gaze aversion behaviors were designed: left, right, down, left down, right down. A random selector picks one of these five behaviors to perform gaze aversion.

3.2   Step Two: Robot's Response Generation

A speech generator is responsible for producing the robot's response. The goal of the speech generator is, on the one hand, to utter the response as soon as possible once it is available. On the other hand, the speech generator needs to bridge the time, when the response is still not finally processed and available after step one.

Inspired by [22] and [23], who step-wise produced scripted utterances to tackle the delayed responses of a task-oriented conversational system, two kinds of time-buying strategies are designed: fillers (e.g. "urrmm") and wait requests (e.g. "Wait a moment. I am trying to understand what you said."). These two time-buying categories are inserted on-demand. Fillers are used when the response has not arrived within two seconds after the mutual gaze (i.e. three seconds after the conversation partner finishes his/her turn). Furthermore, an event-based mechanism enables the robot to decide autonomously what and when to utter in such a way that the current utterance is not interrupted, and thus not overlaid with a second utterance at once.

3.3   Step Three: Interlocutor-Directed Gaze

The last step is the interlocutor-directed gaze during responding. The robot's head rotates to the previously recorded conversation partner's location. This step helps the conversation partner to recognize the robot's turn yielding signal and, therefore, smoothens the subsequent conversational turn transition.

4   Research Design

4.1   Study Design

The gaze behavior was implemented in a 58 cm tall humanoid robot called NAO (version V5), produced by Softbank Robotics[1]. We designed a within-subject experiment with two conditions (see Fig. 1): In the baseline condition, NAO performed no gaze behavior (i.e. no head movement). During the entire conversation, NAO remained stiff, looked at the conversation partner and uttered the response as soon as it was available. In the evaluation condition, NAO performed the designed gaze behavior. Two videos were recorded for the study where NAO conduced the same small talk with a conversation partner: once with and once without gaze behavior. The length of the videos was around 100 s each. NAO held nine conversational turns.

To study how far the gaze behavior and the perceived responsiveness of the robot relate, we designed a questionnaire that captured ratings on the robot's responsiveness (see Table 1, left), on the perception of the designed gaze behavior (see Table 1, right), and demographical data of the participants. The statements measuring the responsiveness of the robot were derived and adjusted from [22]. Further, statements measuring gaze behavior were developed in an iterative item development process [24], as

---

[1] https://www.softbankrobotics.com/.

we could not identify similar items in prior research. The rating used a five-point Likert scale (1 = strongly disagreed; 3 = neutral; 5 = strongly agree).

Fig. 1. Robot without the designed gaze behavior in the baseline condition (left), always fixed eye contact with human, and robot with the designed gaze behavior in the evaluation condition (right), designed mutual gaze and gaze aversion

Table 1. Items measuring the responsiveness and the gaze behavior of the social robot

Statements on responsiveness	Statements on gaze behavior
1. The robot responded in a timely manner	1. I felt the robot tried to establish eye contact with the conversation partner
2. I would prefer a faster response from the robot	2. The way the robot looked around seemed random to me
3. I felt the robot responded as soon as possible	3. I felt the robot gazed strictly at the conversation partner without any movement
4. At some point, I felt the robot was not going to answer the question	4. The head movements of the robot seemed human-like

4.2 Participants

The study involved 31 participants working in various industries. All of them were associated with the host university through their studies or work relation. We invited all participants personally to support our study. Regarding demographics, a light majority of the participants were male ($n = 18$; 58%). The age of the participants ranged between 20 and 40 ($M = 30.13$, $SD = 4.67$). While 13 participants had no experience with a humanoid robot at all, the remaining 18 participants have seen others interacting with a humanoid robot. Three participants even have programmed a humanoid robot.

4.3 Procedure of the Study

The participants were randomly assigned into two groups. Then, they filled in the questionnaire collecting their demographical data such as gender, age etc. Afterwards, the two groups started watching the two videos, but in different order: In Group 1, the participants first watched the video displaying the baseline condition, while in Group 2, the participant first watched the video displaying the evaluation condition. The participants then filled in the questionnaire regarding the robot's responsiveness and the perception of the designed gaze behavior. After finishing the questionnaire, the participants watched the remaining video and filled in the same questionnaire (with a different order of items) again.

5   Results

Our analyses comprised three steps: (1) We first did a manipulation check to assess how far the study participants actually perceived the implemented gaze behavior in the evaluation condition. (2) We assessed how far the responsiveness of the robot differed between the baseline and the evaluation condition. This analysis included an examination of potential differences based on gender and robot experience. And (3), we examined the correlation of the gaze behavior and the responsiveness variables.

5.1   Manipulation Check of the Implemented Gaze Behavior

We first compared the ratings of the gaze behavior items between the baseline and the evaluation condition using the two-side Wilcoxon signed rank test, since our analysis builds on ordinal scales and non-normally distributed data. The results show that the designed gaze behavior of the robot is apparent to the study participants (see Table 2). We can observe a difference in median rating for almost all items. Even though the robot did not stare at the conversation partner, but alternated the gaze in the evaluation condition (as confirmed in Statement 3), the participants still recognized the mutual gaze the robot established (see Statement 1) and that the behavior was perceived more humanlike (see Statement 4). Statements 3 and 4 showed particularly small p-values between the two conditions.

Table 2. Results regarding gaze behavior

Statement	Baseline		Evaluation		Wilcoxon
	Mdn	Range	Mdn	Range	
1	4	1–5	4	1–5	$z = -0.35, p = 0.72$
2	2	1–4	3	1–5	$z = -2.27, p = 0.023$
3	3	1–5	2	1–4	$z = -3.30, p = 0.001^{**}$
4	2	1–4	3	1–4	$z = -2.71, p = 0.007^{*}$

Bonferroni-adjusted $\alpha = 0.0125^{*}$, $\alpha = 0.0025^{**}$, $\alpha = 0.00025^{***}$

5.2   Assessment of the Perceived Responsiveness

We compared the differences in the perceived responsiveness of the social robot between the baseline and the evaluation condition. We again applied the two-side Wilcoxon signed rank test and found no difference in the median ratings between both conditions. The results show that overall, most participants neither agree nor disagree with the statements. Only Statement 2 indicates that most participants would prefer an even faster response (see Table 3). When it comes to whether the robot answered timely, females ($Mdn = 4$) seemed to be more patient than males ($Mdn = 3$), $U = 69.5$, $p = 0.047$. Further, experienced participants were more likely to prefer a faster response ($Mdn = 4$) than those with no robot experience ($Mdn = 3$), $U = 68.5$, $p = 0.04$.

Table 3. Results regarding perceived responsiveness

Statement	Baseline		Evaluation		Wilcoxon
	Mdn	Range	Mdn	Range	
1	3	1–5	3	1–5	$z = -0.67, p = 0.5$
2	4	2–5	4	1–5	$z = -0.67, p = 0.5$
3	3	1–4	3	1–5	$z = -0.16, p = 0.87$
4	3	1–5	3	1–5	$z = -0.45, p = 0.66$

5.3 Examination of the Association Between Gaze Behavior and Responsiveness

We consolidated the results of the perceived responsiveness and the gaze in each condition by calculating a responsiveness score and an gaze score (as in [25]) for each participant: We summed up the rating considering whether the statement favors the responsiveness respectively the gaze behavior, and vice versa. The higher the score the more responsive the participant rated the robot respectively the stronger the designed gaze behavior is perceptible to the participants. We assessed the internal consistency reliability with the composite reliability score [26], which has the advantages not to assume equal outer loading of construct indicators and to be sensitive to the number of indicators of a construct. The scores for the perceived responsiveness and the gaze behavior were 0.91 and 0.71 respectively, which exceed the satisfactory threshold of 0.7 [26].

As we expect that the gaze behavior of a robot positively affects its perceived responsiveness, we investigated their association with the Pearson correlation coefficient between the perceived responsiveness and the perceived gaze behavior for each condition. The results indicate a clear positive correlation between the perceived gaze behavior and the perceived responsiveness of the robots in the evaluation condition. The coefficient of determination between the perceived gaze behavior and responsiveness in the evaluation condition is $R^2 = 41\%$. Finally, we investigated how much the difference of the responsiveness score between both conditions correlates with the one of gaze score. We observe a moderate positive correlation between the differences (see Table 4).

Table 4. Correlation of the perceived responsiveness and the robot's gaze behavior

	Baseline	Evaluation	Difference between the two conditions
r	0.05	0.64[***]	0.33

$\alpha = 0.05^{*}, \alpha = 0.01^{**}, \alpha = 0.001^{***}$

6   Discussion

This paper quantitatively examines the effects of gaze behavior on the perceived delay of a robot's response. The results show a significant, positive correlation between the perceived responsiveness and a robot's gaze behavior in the evaluation condition. This means that participants who recognized the gaze behavior that we implemented into the robot tended to rate the responsiveness higher and vice versa. This finding emphasizes the importance of studying gaze behavior as a variable influencing the responsiveness of a robot.

Derived from the correlation, the coefficient of determination between gaze and responsiveness in the evaluation condition is $R^2 = 41\%$, which suggests that a large proportion of the variance from the responsiveness construct might be explained through factors in addition to gaze behavior.

As to the response time of the robot, fillers, which were automatically triggered after a two-second time out, occurred only twice in the evaluation setting. In other words, the robot managed to utter a response within two seconds in most cases after the mutual gaze. This period might be too short to reveal a strong effect of the gaze behavior on the perceived responsiveness of a robot since the effects of gaze aversion could not unfold properly and the robot directed its gaze too soon to the conversation partner again. Potentially, the short response times of the robots were due to nature of the conversation (small talk). Thus, future research should investigate the effect of gaze behavior on a larger delay of response and in alternative conversation contexts.

Our study also provides important implications for robot designers. The results show that the gaze of a robot conveys an impression of a better responsiveness to the conversation partner even in the case of delayed responses. To address the perceived delay of a robot's response, the gaze behavior of a social robot should be properly designed and implemented in combination with other means (e.g. blinking).

Finally, our study contains limitations. First, we assessed the perceived responsiveness of a social robot through videos without a direct interaction between participants and robots. We decided to choose this setting to avoid technical difficulties through language barriers in small talk conversations. While speech recognition is already advanced, we still experience related technical challenges. Once the technical difficulties can be minimized, we recommend conducting the experiment in a condition of actual human-robot interactions. Second, the robot in the videos did not face the study participants in a frontal way. This might have alleviated the effects of the gaze behavior. Since small talk conversations often involve several people, a non-frontal angle is often given. Thus, we chose this approach. Finally, the results of this paper apply mainly to those robots that use head turn to perform gaze behavior. Robots that can perform a more behaviorally realistic gaze might yield different results under the same settings.

7 Conclusions

Slow responses of robots represent a key challenge in human-robot communication. This paper investigates the effects of gaze behavior on the perceived delay of a robot's response in small talk scenarios by using the humanoid robot NAO. For this purpose, we have designed a gaze behavior setting consisting of mutual gaze, gaze aversion and interlocutor-directed gaze. The results of an experiment with 31 test persons show a positive correlation between the designed gaze behavior and the robot's responsiveness. However, comparing the perceived responsiveness in both conditions, we could not observe any differences. A possible explanation might be that the response time of the robot might have been generally too short to reveal a strong effect of gaze behavior on the responsiveness of a social robot. Our findings show that gaze behavior generally plays an important role with regard to the perceived responsiveness of a robot. Researchers and practitioners can build on these findings and further examine and shape gaze behavior as a factor relevant to address a perceived delay in a robot's response.

References

1. Fong, T., Nourbakhsh, I., Dautenhahn, K.: A survey of socially interactive robots. Robot. Auton. Syst. **42**, 143–166 (2003)
2. Kurzon, D.: Discourse of Silence. John Benjamins Publishing (1998)
3. Bruneau, T.J.: Communicative silences: forms and functions. J. Commun. **23**, 17–46 (1973)
4. Oto, K., Feng, J., Imai, M.: Investigating how people deal with silence in a human-robot conversation. In: 2017 26th IEEE International Symposium on Robot and Human Interactive Communication (RO-MAN), pp. 195–200 (2017)
5. Ward, N.G., Rivera, A.G., Ward, K., Novick, D.G.: Root causes of lost time and user stress in a simple dialog system. Presented at the INTERSPEECH-2005 (2005)
6. Mukawa, N., Sasaki, H., Kimura, A.: How do verbal/bodily fillers ease embarrassing situations during silences in conversations? In: The 23rd IEEE International Symposium on Robot and Human Interactive Communication, pp. 30–35 (2014)
7. Galle, M., Kynev, E., Monet, N., Legras, C.: Context-aware selection of multi-modal conversational fillers in human-robot dialogues. In: 2017 26th IEEE International Symposium on Robot and Human Interactive Communication (RO-MAN), pp. 317–322. IEEE, Lisbon (2017)
8. Zheng, K., Glas, D.F., Kanda, T., Ishiguro, H., Hagita, N.: Designing and implementing a human-robot team for social interactions. IEEE Trans. Syst. Man Cybern.: Syst. **43**, 843–859 (2013)
9. Skantze, G., Hjalmarsson, A.: Towards incremental speech generation in conversational systems. Comput. Speech Lang. **27**, 243–262 (2013)
10. Andrist, S., Tan, X.Z., Gleicher, M., Mutlu, B.: Conversational gaze aversion for humanlike robots. In: Proceedings of the 2014 ACM/IEEE International Conference on Human-robot Interaction, pp. 25–32. ACM, New York (2014)
11. Coupland, J.: Small talk: social functions. Res. Lang. Soc. Interact. **36**, 1–6 (2003). https://doi.org/10.1207/S15327973RLSI3601_1

12. Shiwa, T., Kanda, T., Imai, M., Ishiguro, H., Hagita, N.: How quickly should a communication robot respond? Delaying strategies and habituation effects. Int. J. Soc. Robot. **1**, 141–155 (2009)
13. Ohshima, N., Kimijima, K., Yamato, J., Mukawa, N.: A conversational robot with vocal and bodily fillers for recovering from awkward silence at turn-takings. In: 2015 24th IEEE International Symposium on Robot and Human Interactive Communication (RO-MAN), pp. 325–330 (2015)
14. Admoni, H., Scassellati, B.: Social eye gaze in human-robot interaction: a review. J. Hum.-Robot Interact. **6**, 25–63 (2017)
15. Vertegaal, R., Slagter, R., van der Veer, G., van der Veer, G., Nijholt, A.: Eye gaze patterns in conversations: there is more to conversational agents than meets the eyes. In: Proceedings of the SIGCHI Conference on Human Factors in Computing Systems, pp. 301–308. ACM, New York (2001)
16. Oertel, C., Włodarczak, M., Edlund, J., Wagner, P., Gustafson, J.: Gaze patterns in turn-taking. In: 13th Annual Conference of the International Speech Communication Association 2012 (INTERSPEECH 2012), Portland, OR, pp. 2243–2246 (2012)
17. Heylen, D.: Head gestures, gaze and the principles of conversational structure. Int. J. Human. Robot. **03**, 241–267 (2006)
18. Satake, S., Kanda, T., Glas, D.F., Imai, M., Ishiguro, H., Hagita, N.: How to approach humans?: Strategies for social robots to initiate interaction. In: Proceedings of the 4th ACM/IEEE International Conference on Human Robot Interaction, pp. 109–116. ACM, New York (2009)
19. Bruce, A., Nourbakhsh, I., Simmons, R.: The role of expressiveness and attention in human-robot interaction. In: Proceedings 2002 IEEE International Conference on Robotics and Automation (Cat. No.02CH37292), vol. 4, pp. 4138–4142 (2002)
20. van Schendel, J.A., Cuijpers, R.H.: Turn-yielding cues in robot-human conversation. Presented at the AISB Convention 2015, Society for the Study of Artificial Intelligence and Simulation of Behaviour, Canterbury, April 20 (2015)
21. Andrist, S., Mutlu, B., Gleicher, M.: Conversational gaze aversion for virtual agents. In: Aylett, R., Krenn, B., Pelachaud, C., Shimodaira, H. (eds.) Intelligent Virtual Agents, pp. 249–262. Springer, Berlin Heidelberg (2013). https://doi.org/10.1007/978-3-642-40415-3_22
22. Gambino, S.L., Zarrieß, S., Schlangen, D.: Testing strategies for bridging time-to-content in spoken dialogue Systems. In: Proceedings of the Ninth International Workshop on Spoken Dialogue Systems Technology (IWSDS 2018), p. 7, Singapore (2018)
23. Gambino, S.L., Zarrieß, S., Schlangen, D.: Beyond on-hold messages: conversational time-buying in task-oriented dialogue. In: SIGDIAL Conference (2017)
24. Schmiedel, T., vom Brocke, J., Recker, J.: Development and validation of an instrument to measure organizational cultures' support of Business Process Management. Inf. Manag. **51**, 43–56 (2014)
25. Zhang, Y., Beskow, J., Kjellström, H.: Look but don't stare: mutual gaze interaction in social robots. In: Kheddar, A., et al. (eds.) Social Robotics, pp. 556–566. Springer, Cham (2017). https://doi.org/10.1007/978-3-319-70022-9_55
26. Hair, J., Hult, G.T.M., Ringle, C.M., Sarstedt, M.: A Primer on Partial Least Squares Structural Equation Modeling. SAGE Publications Inc., Los Angeles (2016)

Individual Differences in Attitude Toward Robots Predict Behavior in Human-Robot Interaction

Nina-Alisa Hinz[1] , Francesca Ciardo[2](✉) ,
and Agnieszka Wykowska[2]

[1] General and Experimental Psychology, Ludwig-Maximilians-University,
Geschwister-Scholl-Platz 1, 80539 Munich, Germany
[2] Social Cognition in Human-Robot Interaction, Italian Institute of Technology,
Via Enrico Melen, 83, 16152 Genoa, Italy
francesca.ciardo@iit.it

Abstract. Humans are influenced by the presence of other social agents, sometimes performing better, sometimes performing worse than alone. Humans are also affected by how they perceive the social agent. The present study investigated whether individual differences in the attitude toward robots can predict human behavior in human-robot interaction. Therefore, adult participants played a game with the Cozmo robot (Anki Inc., San Francisco), in which their task was to stop a balloon from exploding. In individual trials, only the participants could stop the balloon inflating, while in joint trials also Cozmo could stop it. Results showed that in joint trials, the balloon exploded less often than in individual trials. However participants stopped the balloon earlier in joint than in individual trials, although this was less beneficial for them. This effect of Cozmo joining the game, nevertheless, was influenced by the negative attitude of the participants toward robots. The more negative they were, the less their behavior was influenced by the presence of the robot. This suggests that robots can influence human behavior, although this influence is modulated by the attitude toward the robot.

Keywords: Individual differences · Attitude toward robots · Human-robot interaction

1 Introduction

Robotic agents are already present in many aspects of our everyday-life, whether they greet us at the airport [1], assist in elderly care [2] or work side-by-side with human employers in manufacturing [3]; and wider applications are probably going to emerge. Therefore, humans face the need to act more and more often in the presence of robots or to interact with them. In situations with social or work-related responsibility, it appears important to know how people behave in the presence of robots and how this eventually diverges from individual situations.

Although evidence showed that the presence of social agents in the environment may improve performance, it may also create difficulties [4, 5]. For instance, in human-

© Springer Nature Switzerland AG 2019
M. A. Salichs et al. (Eds.): ICSR 2019, LNAI 11876, pp. 64–73, 2019.
https://doi.org/10.1007/978-3-030-35888-4_7

human interaction, a well-known phenomenon is social facilitation, i.e. the fact that the presence of another human can enhance performance [4]. However, this effect is dependent on the nature of the task [6]. For complex and difficult tasks, for example, the presence of a co-agent can lead to social inhibition, i.e. deteriorated performance [5]. Similar effects have been demonstrated with artificial agents [7, 8]. As has been demonstrated before in other aspects of social cognition [9], embodiment seems to affect the social presence effect, as presence induced by images of social agents did not affect performance [10]. These studies, however, have used fairly simple tasks, such as arithmetic operations, that do not accurately resemble the complexity that characterizes practical applications of robots. Indeed, most of the applications in which a human has to interact with a robot rather deal with uncertainty and risky contexts.

Another crucial aspect to examine in human-robot interaction is how individual differences in robot perception translate to differences in behavior [11, 12]. Indeed, individual differences, such as personality traits or attitudes, have been found to affect the perception and acceptance of robots in social situations [13–16]. For example, higher levels of neuroticism seem to predict the preference of more machine-like robots [13]. Similarly, differences in assigning human-like characteristics to non-human agents lead to differences in the trustworthiness assigned to a robot [14]. A full range of individual differences, like anxiety, perfectionism or religious fundamentalism, have been proposed to explain feelings of eeriness towards the robot [15]. Differences in trustworthiness perception of a robot have been demonstrated to predict behavior in a human-robot team [16, 17].

1.1 Aim of the Study

Our study aimed at investigating whether human behavior is influenced by the presence of a robotic agent in a task necessitating risk-taking, and how this influence is moderated by individual differences in the attitude towards robots. Therefore, we asked participants to perform a game in which they had to stop a balloon from exploding alone or playing with the Cozmo robot (Anki Inc., San Francisco).We used a non-anthropomorphic robot in order to avoid that differences in assigning human-likeness might affect trustworthiness toward the robot [14]. We expected Cozmo to improve the performance of participants in the task due to social facilitation effects as a function of individual differences.

2 Methods

2.1 Participants

Thirty-two healthy adults participated in this study. Data of one participant were not analyzed because the robot crashed during the experimental session. The remaining sample consisted of thirty-one participants (12 male, 1 left-handed, age range: 19–44 years, $M = 23.85$, $SD = 4.81$). All had normal or corrected- to-normal vision. Participants provided informed written consent before participation, received financial reimbursement and were debriefed after the experiment. The study was approved by the local ethical committee (Comitato Etico Regione Liguria).

2.2 Apparatus and Materials

Participants were seated in front of a desk on which lay a computer screen (22 inches diagonal, 1366 × 768 pixels resolution, 59 Hz refresh rate). The Cozmo robot was placed directly in front of them (see Fig. 1). For both the participant and the Cozmo robot, the response device was one of the Cozmo cubes on top of which an in-house-built one-key-keyboard was mounted.

Fig. 1. Experimental setup.

The Cozmo Robot

The Cozmo robot (Anki Inc., San Francisco) is a commercial robot designed for educational purposes. It consists of a horizontally moveable head with an LED screen on which eyes are displayed, four wheels, three LEDs on the back and a horizontally moveable lift. Cozmo is controlled by an application compatible with iOS and Android. A Python 3.6-based Software development kit (SDK) can be used to program Cozmo.

During the experiment a mobile Android device with the Cozmo application in "SDK mode" was used to control Cozmo, connected to a laptop through the Android Debug Bridge (adb) as described in [18]. Commands were sent to the Cozmo application by using OpenSesame Version 3.1.9 [19], running on Python 3.6.

Questionnaires

To assess the participant's attitude towards robots, before the experiment we administered three different questionnaires. All of the questionnaires were presented on a computer screen, using OpenSesame Version 3.1.9 [19] and responded to with a standard computer mouse. The questionnaires were:

- the *Frankenstein Syndrome Questionnaire* (FSQ; [20]), composed of thirty items, measuring the "Frankenstein Syndrome", the fear of creating new entities. Four different subscales are evident in the questionnaire: "General Anxiety toward Humanoid Robots", "Apprehension toward Social Risks of Humanoid Robots", "Trustworthiness for Developers of Humanoid Robots" and "Expectation for Humanoid Robots in Daily Life". The subscales have medium to good internal consistency, the questionnaire in general, however, demonstrated good reliability [21]. Higher scores stand for a more severe Frankenstein Syndrome, i.e. more negative attitude towards robots.

- the *Negative Attitude Towards Robots Scale* (NARS; [13]) consisting of fourteen items, organized in three different subscales: "Negative Attitudes toward Situations and Interactions with Robots", "Negative Attitudes toward Social Influence of Robots" and "Negative Attitudes toward Emotions in Interaction with Robots". The questionnaire demonstrated high internal consistency and validity. Higher scores stand for more negative attitude towards robots.

- the *Robotic Social Attributes Scale* (RoSAS; [22]) consisting of eighteen items in which participants are presented with an adjective (e.g. social) and have to express on a 9-point Likert scale how much they believe that the adjective can be used to describe a robot. Items are classified into three psychometrically validated subscales: "Warmth", "Competence" and "Discomfort". While higher scores on the subscales "Warmth" and "Competence" are related to a more positive attitude towards robots, higher scores on the "Discomfort" subscale signify a more negative attitude.

2.3 Task and Trial Procedure

The task was based on the Balloon Analogous Risk Task [23]. Participants played a game, in which they had to stop an inflating balloon before it exploded when reaching a pin on the top of the display. In every trial the participants would lose points from an initial amount of 4000 points, with the amount of lost points depending on when the balloon was stopped. The later the balloon was stopped, the less points were lost. The exact number of lost points per trial was randomly chosen from a range of points, depending on four different clusters of sizes at which the balloon was stopped (see Table 1). The maximal amount of points was lost when the balloon exploded. The goal of the game was to save the maximal amount of points; therefore the best strategy would have been to wait as long as possible before stopping the balloon. In 50% of trials, participants played alone (individual trials), while in the remaining trials also Cozmo was in charge to stop the balloon inflation (joint trials). Cozmo was programmed to act only in the 60% of joint trials. When Cozmo stopped the balloon, it would lose the respective amount of points, whereas the participant would lose no points. In case of an explosion both agents would lose the points. Cozmo always acted when approximately 90% of the inflation time was reached. In joint trials, the best strategy for the participant would have been to wait for an action of Cozmo and only react in trials, in which it did not, to prevent an explosion of the balloon. However, participants could not predict a priori when Cozmo would act.

At the beginning of each trial participants were told whether they were playing alone (individual trial) or with Cozmo (joint trial) with a text presented on the screen for 1000 ms (see Fig. 2). During the first trial of each block Cozmo either went to sleep (transition from joint to individual trial) or woke up and approached the cube (transition from individual to joint trial). After the initial instruction about the type of trial, a sketchpad displaying "The trial is starting" was presented on the screen, so participants could prepare for the beginning of each trial. Then, a fixation point was presented for a random duration of 800–1000 ms (note that the fixation point duration was randomly set at the beginning of each trial and kept constant for all fixation points presented in the respective trials). After that, the images of a pin and of the balloon at its starting size were presented for 500 ms. Following, the balloon started inflating. The inflation speed was variable across and within trials, in order to make the explosion time not predictable. In each block ten different inflation speeds were used. Additionally, during the inflation sequence, two grey circles were presented on the bottom right and top left corner. When a response was given one of the circles turned blue, indicating whose reaction was counted (with top left corner representing Cozmo and bottom right corner representing the participant). After a response was executed, the balloon was displayed in its final size for 1000 ms. If the balloon exploded, an image representing the bursting event was presented. Then a fixation point was followed by a sketchpad (2000 ms) showing the amount of lost points.

Participants were explicitly instructed that their goal was to save as many points as possible to defeat previous participants and they would not be able to defeat Cozmo since it was playing in only half of trials. This was done to try to avoid that they would perceive the task as a competition between themselves and Cozmo.

The task consisted of 180 trials presented in 18 blocks of 10 trials each. The type of trials (individual or joint) was manipulated across blocks. The order of the blocks was randomly selected. A practice session of six trials (three individual trials, three joint trials) was administered before the experiment. During the practice participants experienced one trial in which Cozmo was not reacting.

Table 1. Lost points depending on the balloon size at reaction. Balloon sizes were separated into four clusters. Depending on in which cluster the reaction was, a random number was drawn from the corresponding range.

Time of reaction (percentage of inflation time)	Range of points lost
$\geq 50\%$	1–15
33–49%	16–29
17–33%	31–45
$\leq 17\%$	46–60
(explosion) 100%	80–100

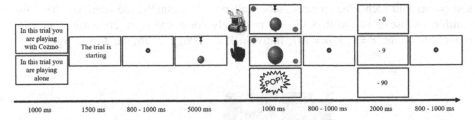

Fig. 2. Trial procedure. In joint trials Cozmo and the participant could stop the balloon from exploding. If Cozmo stopped the balloon the participant was not losing points. In individual trials only the participant could stop the balloon from exploding. (Color figure online)

2.4 Statistical Analysis

Each trial was classified as a "Human" trial if the participant stopped the balloon and as a "Cozmo" trial if Cozmo stopped the balloon. If no one stopped the balloon and it exploded, the trial was classified as "No reaction". Performance was assessed by the amount of reactions in each trial type, reaction time (i.e. the amount of time in ms from the starting of the inflation until the balloon was stopped) and the points lost after the reaction. This behavioral data was analyzed using paired-sample t-tests. Ratings from the questionnaire subscales were summed up to a total score. Pearson correlations were conducted to examine the relationship between questionnaire (subscale and total) scores and the behavioral data. All analyses were performed using R Version 3.5.1 [24]. Plots were created using the ggplot2 package Version 3.0.0 [25].

3   Results

Participants successfully stopped the balloon in 85.4% ($SD = 7.7\%$; see Fig. 3) of individual trials and 47.3% ($SD = 9.5\%$) of joint trials. In 42.1% ($SD = 6.7\%$) of joint trials they let Cozmo react. The balloon exploded in 14.6% ($SD = 7.7\%$) of individual trials, but only 10.6% ($SD = 4.4\%$) of joint trials. The number of explosions differed significantly between the two types of trials ($t_{29} = -3.55, p < .001$).

Given that Cozmo's actions were influencing the information contained in outcome and balloon size, only trials in which the participant successfully stopped the balloon (Human trials) were further analyzed. No difference was found between the points lost in each trial type (Joint: $M = 9.05$, $SD = 0.85$; Individual: $M = 8.79$, $SD = 0.74$; $t_{29} = 1.32, p = .19$; see Fig. 4 left). However, reaction times were different between the trial types ($t_{29} = -3.42, p < .001$), showing faster performance in joint ($M = 4078$ ms, $SD = 93$ ms) compared to individual trials ($M = 4130$ ms, $SD = 66$ ms; see Fig. 5 left).

The analysis of correlations between questionnaires and performance (i.e. lost points and reaction times) showed that the FSQ total score correlated negatively with the amount of lost points in the joint trials only (Joint: $r = -.45, p < .01$; Individual: $r = .09, p = .62$; see Fig. 4 right). The "General Anxiety toward Humanoid Robots" subscale of the FSQ showed a similar pattern (Joint: $r = -.38, p < .05$; Individual: $r = -.07, p = .70$). No other significant correlations were found between the amount of lost points and each FSQ-subscale score (all $p > .23$). Finally, the score on the "Discomfort" subscale of the RoSAS was positively correlated to reaction times in joint trials only (Joint: $r = .33$, $p = .07$; Individual: $r = .06$, $p = .76$; see Fig. 5 right).

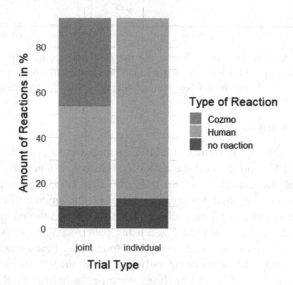

Fig. 3. Proportions of reactions in the two trial types. Cozmo was only acting in joint trials.

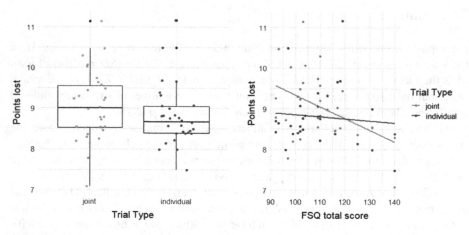

Fig. 4. Left panel: Average amount of lost points when participants successfully stopped the balloon as a function of trial type (individual vs. joint). Right panel: Correlations between the amount of lost points in Human trials and the FSQ total score.

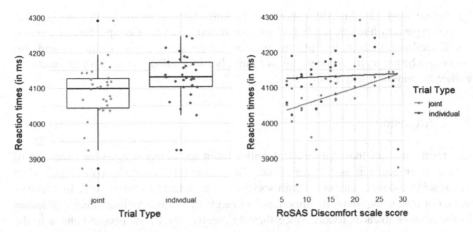

Fig. 5. Left panel: Average reaction times of trials in which the participants successfully stopped the balloon across trial type (individual vs. joint). Right panel: Correlations between reaction times in Human trials and the RoSAS Discomfort scale score.

4 Discussion

In the present study, we investigated how someone's behavior is influenced by the presence of a robotic agent and especially how this influence is moderated by individual differences in the attitude towards robots. Our results showed that when playing with Cozmo, participants overall performance in the game improved as indicated by a smaller number of explosions for joint than individual trials. This effect was clearly driven by Cozmo's actions. When only analyzing trials in which participants successfully stopped the balloon themselves (Human trials), results showed that participants stopped the balloon slightly earlier, as evident from faster reaction times, in the joint compared to the individual trials. Such a difference in the performance suggests that the presence of Cozmo triggered the action in joint trials, leading to a social facilitation effect exerted by the robot. Interestingly, the social facilitation effect occurred despite that the optimal strategy to lose as few points as possible was to react as late as possible (i.e. withholding the action). It should be noted that social facilitation was not observed in the number of lost points because the relation between stopping the balloon and actual feedback was not fully linear (see Table 1).

Our results showed that the effect exerted by the social presence of Cozmo varied as function of individual attitude towards robots, with higher scores on the FSQ questionnaire being associated with better performance (i.e. fewer points lost) in joint trials, and higher scores on the Discomfort subscale of the RoSAS leading to later balloon stops (i.e. slower reaction times) in joint trials. Together the correlation patterns suggest that the more negative someone is regarding robots, the less s/he is influenced by the presence of the robot and the less s/he shows social facilitation effect. Such a result is in line with the hypothesis of Schellen and Wykowska [11], that negative attitudes towards robots might be a moderating factor for social presence effects.

Future work should look at how the present effects translate to the use of other robots, especially humanoid robot. Humanoid robots could for example further increase social facilitation effects by inducing more social presence. Future studies should also account whether trustworthiness toward the robot may affect the decision to intervene earlier to prevent losing points.

5   Conclusion

Our results indicate that sharing a task with a robot apparently triggers the execution of action, even when it is not beneficial. This should be carefully considered when introducing robots in situations with social or work-related responsibility. In a similar vein, our results highlight the importance of carefully examining individual differences in the attitude towards robots, since they differently affect how people behave in the presence of a robotic agent.

Acknowledgements. This project has received funding from the European Research Council (ERC) under the European Union's Horizon 2020 research and innovation program (grant awarded to AW, titled "InStance: Intentional Stance for Social Attunement." G.A. No: ERC-2016-StG-715058).

References

1. Flughafen München GmbH: Hi! I'm Josie Pepper. https://www.munich-airport.com/hi-i-m-josie-pepper-3613413
2. Kachouie, R., Sedighadeli, S., Khosla, R., Chu, M.-T.: Socially assistive robots in elderly care. A mixed-method systematic literature review. Int. J. Hum.-Comput. Interact. **30**, 369–393 (2014)
3. Innovative human-robot cooperation in BMW Group Production, Munich, Germany (2013)
4. Zajonc, R.B.: Social facilitation. Science **149**, 269–274 (1965)
5. Myers, D.G., DeWall, C.N.: Psychology (2018)
6. Ciardo, F., Wykowska, A.: Response coordination emerges in cooperative but not competitive joint task. Front. Psychol. **9**, 1919 (2018)
7. Park, S., Catrambone, R.: Social facilitation effects of virtual humans. Hum. Factors **49**, 1054–1060 (2007)
8. Riether, N., Hegel, F., Wrede, B., Horstmann, G.: Social facilitation with social robots? In: Proceedings of the Seventh Annual ACM/IEE International Conference on Human-Robot-Interaction, pp. 41–48 (2012)
9. Kompatsiari, K., Ciardo, F., Tikhanoff, V., Metta, G., Wykowska, A.: On the role of eye contact in gaze cueing. Sci. Rep. **8**, 17842 (2018)
10. Hertz, N., Wiese, E.: Social facilitation with non-human agents. Possible or not? In: Proceedings of the Human Factors and Ergonomics Society Annual Meeting, vol. 61, pp. 222–225 (2017)
11. Schellen, E., Wykowska, A.: Intentional mindset toward robots—open questions and methodological challenges. Front. Robot. AI **5**, 71 (2019)
12. Marchesi, S., Ghiglino, D., Ciardo, F., Perez-Osorio, J., Baykara, E., Wykowska, A.: Do we adopt the intentional stance toward humanoid robots? Front. Psychol. **10**, 450 (2019)

13. Syrdal, D.S., Dautenhahn, K., Kony, K.L., Walters, M.L.: The negative attitudes towards robots scale and reactions to robot behaviour in a live human-robot interaction study. In: Adaptive and Emergent Behaviour and Complex Systems (2009)
14. Waytz, A., Cacioppo, J., Epley, N.: Who sees human? The stability and importance of individual differences in anthropomorphism. Perspect. Psychol. Sci. **5**, 219–232 (2010)
15. MacDorman, K.F., Entezari, S.O.: Individual differences predict sensitivity to the uncanny valley. IS **16**, 141–172 (2015)
16. Rossi, S., Staffa, M., Bove, L., Capasso, R., Ercolano, G.: User's personality and activity influence on HRI comfortable distances. In: Kheddar, A., et al. (eds.) ICSR 2017. LNCS, vol. 10652, pp. 167–177. Springer, Cham (2017). https://doi.org/10.1007/978-3-319-70022-9_17
17. Rossi, S., Santangelo, G., Staffa, M., Varrasi, S., Conti, D., Di Nuovo, A.: Psychometric evaluation supported by a social robot. Personality factors and technology acceptance. In: 2018 27th IEEE International Symposium on Robot and Human Interactive Communication (RO-MAN), pp. 802–807. IEEE (2018)
18. Anki Inc.: Android Debug Bridge (2016)
19. Mathôt, S., Schreij, D., Theeuwes, J.: OpenSesame. An open-source, graphical experiment builder for the social sciences. Behav. Res. **44**, 314–324 (2012)
20. Nomura, T., Sugimoto, K., Syrdal, D.S., Dautenhahn, K.: Social acceptance of humanoid robots in Japan. A survey for development of the frankenstein syndrome questionnaire. In: 12th IEEE-RAS International Conference on Humanoid Robots (Humanoids 2012), pp. 242–247 (2012)
21. Syrdal, D.S., Nomura, T., Dautenhahn, K.: The frankenstein syndrome questionnaire – results from a quantitative cross-cultural survey. In: Herrmann, G., Pearson, M.J., Lenz, A., Bremner, P., Spiers, A., Leonards, U. (eds.) ICSR 2013. LNCS (LNAI), vol. 8239, pp. 270–279. Springer, Cham (2013). https://doi.org/10.1007/978-3-319-02675-6_27
22. Carpinella, C.M., Wyman, A.B., Perez, M.A., Stroessner, S.J.: The robotic social attributes scale (RoSAS). In: Proceedings of the ACM/IEEE International Conference on Human-Robot Interaction, pp. 254–262 (2017)
23. Lejuez, C.W., et al.: Evaluation of a behavioral measure of risk taking. The balloon analogue risk task (BART). J. Exp. Psychol.: Appl. **8**, 75–84 (2002)
24. R Core Team: R: A language and environment for statistical computing, Vienna (2018)
25. Wickham, H.: ggplot2: Elegant Graphics for Data Analysis. Springer, New York (2016). https://doi.org/10.1007/978-3-319-24277-4

Cognition and Social Values
for Social Robots

Transferring Adaptive Theory of Mind to Social Robots: Insights from Developmental Psychology to Robotics

Francesca Bianco[✉] and Dimitri Ognibene

University of Essex, Colchester CO4 3SQ, UK
fb18599@essex.ac.uk

Abstract. Despite the recent advancement in the social robotic field, important limitations restrain its progress and delay the application of robots in everyday scenarios. In the present paper, we propose to develop computational models inspired by our knowledge of human infants' social adaptive abilities. We believe this may provide solutions at an architectural level to overcome the limits of current systems. Specifically, we present the functional advantages that adaptive Theory of Mind (ToM) systems would support in robotics (i.e., mentalizing for belief understanding, proactivity and preparation, active perception and learning) and contextualize them in practical applications. We review current computational models mainly based on the simulation and teleological theories, and robotic implementations to identify the limitations of ToM functions in current robotic architectures and suggest a possible future developmental pathway. Finally, we propose future studies to create innovative computational models integrating the properties of the simulation and teleological approaches for an improved adaptive ToM ability in robots with the aim of enhancing human-robot interactions and permitting the application of robots in unexplored environments, such as disasters and construction sites. To achieve this goal, we suggest directing future research towards the modern cross-talk between the fields of robotics and developmental psychology.

Keywords: Mental states · Computational modelling · Theory of Mind

1 Introduction

The robotic field has greatly advanced in the last decades and the complexity and sophistication of robots have highly improved. However, the application of robotics in everyday scenarios still faces some challenges. For example, humans' positive attitude towards non-human agents has increased with the humanoid aspect of robots, however, this drops when a mismatch of agent features is noticed [1] due to the robots' still limited (non-human-like) social capabilities (uncanny valley effect). Currently, robots' architectures generally rely on association and simulation principles to learn about the social world, which enable them to recognize and predict actions from observing other agents performing such actions [2, 3]. However, robots' recognition of complex mental states is still limited, as is their understanding of the humans they interact with. For example, although robots can recognize the action of digging through rubble, they do

© Springer Nature Switzerland AG 2019
M. A. Salichs et al. (Eds.): ICSR 2019, LNAI 11876, pp. 77–87, 2019.
https://doi.org/10.1007/978-3-030-35888-4_8

not necessarily understand the deeper mental state of the observed agent, such as the desire to search for survivors.

In robotics, the perception of social contexts mostly relies on the passive view of stimuli (with few exceptions [4]) and highly prewired knowledge. This means that missing elements and features are not actively searched by robots and that their adaptability to new contexts/tasks/agents' behaviors is limited. Similarly, multiple-agent interactions may be too computationally and sensorially expensive given the inability to exploit context-specific information to optimize the computations underlying robots' social interactions. Therefore, one of the main challenges in robotics is to create robots that can act as social (human-like) agents to increase robots' acceptance as social companions and ameliorate human-robot interactions, also in challenging situations [5].

Substantial advancements in robotics resulted from the introduction of Deep Neural Networks (DNNs). However, online action perception, online learning and generalization to new contexts with a sufficient level of spatial and temporal detail to support human-robot interaction is still difficult [6]. One of the main issues related to the application of DNNs for social interaction is their reliance on suitable datasets. Current DNNs algorithms require huge datasets which are mostly recorded by humans, who however select points of view which may completely differ from those adopted by robots. While the performance of these bottom-up recognition methods is continuously improved through new architectures [7] and datasets [8], the high dependency of human activities on multiple contextual factors and actors' mental states suggests that the size of the datasets necessary to achieve a high enough precision for predictive physical interaction would be prohibitive. Furthermore, this approach requires substantial training time and reconfiguration or retraining when new tasks are added.

An initial solution to these issues was provided by simulation-based methods for the extension of datasets through the generation of virtual training data [9] and digital manipulation of the training data [10]. However, these methods are particularly difficult to scale to social interaction tasks because both the virtual training data and the robot's response are strongly affected by contexts of high dimensionality (e.g., other agent's previous actions, current posture, relative position of other objects). The DNNs approach is also limited given that learning is based on short frames and does not allow for an interpretation of the situation or the agent's mental state. Therefore, this only enables the understanding of short and stereotyped interactions. This is in contrast to humans' ability to comprehend the world by adding sequences together, putting them into context and relating them to other similar events or their own experiences, feelings, mental states. Ultimately, the lack of data in uncertain, previously unexperienced environments (e.g., natural disasters) prevents the utilization of standard machine learning methods to provide robots with the correct behaviors.

A way to deal with the strong limits of DNNs and endow robots with social skills would be to integrate them in a principled manner with a model-based reasoning system [11]. Indeed, we propose to develop future computational models inspired by our knowledge of human infants' mentalizing abilities, as they may provide solutions at an architectural level to ameliorate the limits of existing robotic systems. In this paper, we present the functional advantages that adaptive mentalizing systems would support in robotics and contextualize them in practical applications. Specifically, we review current models and robotic implementations to identify the current limitations and suggest a possible future developmental pathway.

2 Adaptive Theory of Mind for Robots

Theory of Mind (ToM), or mentalizing, refers to the cognitive capacity to attribute and represent others' mental states [12–14]. Although a definite age at which mentalizing develops in humans is yet to be determined, possessing a ToM from an early age [15] is an evident demonstration of its importance for human social navigation. In fact, "externally observable actions are just observable consequences of unobservable, internal causal structures" [16], i.e., mental states. In other words, if a person is running down a mountain, his immediate goal is to displace himself from a location to another, whereas his underlying intention (e.g., to run away from an avalanche) is not clear until the context is analyzed. To a certain extent, humans are able to predict and understand others' actions by observing their behavior, however, having the capability to infer the underlying reasons provides an invaluable advantage during social interactions. Given that mental states are characterized differently in the literature (see Table 1 for further details), a clear definition of ToM is yet to be identified. However, compared to the association, simulation and teleological paradigms underlying social perception, the highlight of ToM relies on the quantities it extracts (i.e., mental states) rather than the computational processes that realize the inferences. A better understanding of how these methodologies can support ToM is provided in Sect. 3.

Table 1. Different characterization of mental states in the literature.

Types of mental states:
Intentions, desires, beliefs [15]
Desires, beliefs and percepts [32]
Desires, values, beliefs and expectations [29]
Perceptions, bodily feelings, emotional states and propositional attitudes [12]
Long-term dispositions, short-term emotional states, desires and their associated goal-directed intentions and beliefs about the world [13]

2.1 Functional Advantages for Robotics

Equipping robots with a ToM would allow them to also access human's hidden mental states, such as intentions, desires and beliefs, and to reason about and react to them much like humans do. More specifically, it would facilitate the adaptive attribution of mental states to agents, meaning for example that beliefs would be acquired and intentions would be inferred by the robot itself. By equipping robots with an adaptive ToM, their application to situations in which specific data are not currently available, due to high variability or uncertainty of environments/agents, will be possible (e.g., searching and rescuing during disasters or helping in construction sites). In fact, internal beliefs/mental states are generally shared by humans and provide important context for higher detail and perceptually-demanding behavior understanding. Finally, providing robots with mentalizing abilities would enable them to "express their internal states through social interaction" [17], which will answer to the issue expressed by the uncanny valley effect. The functional advantages of an adaptive ToM for robotics (see paper [18] for further details) will now be described (Table 2).

Table 2. Functional advantages of equipping robots with a Theory of Mind.

Functional advantages of ToM for robotics	Current systems	ToM contribution
Mentalizing for coordinating and managing false beliefs	- Spatial perspective taking - Robot has access to states and actions of all agents ($\neq$ real-life)	- Mental perspective taking
Mentalizing for proactivity and preparation	- Reliance on bottom-up inputs	- Top-down control: proactivity - Improved preparation for interaction with other agents
Mentalizing for active perception	- Passive exploration/understandding of environments/agents	- Active search of cues: better explain current situation and enable more precise predictions
Mentalizing for learning	- Deep neural network limits - Same learning process for passive object dynamics and human behavior	- Time- and cost-efficient learning - Different learning processes: object dynamics VS human behavior - Improved multi-agent interactions

Mentalizing for Coordinating and Managing False Beliefs. Until now, ToM has mainly been implemented in robotics to allow for the understanding and ability to track beliefs in humans [19, 20]. In fact, determining whether a human partner holds true beliefs about a situation is an essential requirement for successful human-robot inter-actions [20], especially during collaborative tasks. Previous studies introduced in robots the ability to assume the spatial perspective of the agent they were interacting with [19, 21], which is a fundamental characteristic of human mentalizing. By enabling robots to put themselves in the agents' shoes and infer their sensorial access, they showed a better recognition of mental states and increased performances in belief recognition tasks. Interestingly, false-belief tasks (standard experimental paradigm to test ToM in humans [22]) were implemented in robots [20] and were passed with the aid of spatial perspective taking. Future studies should create adaptive ToM architectures which aim at also equipping robots with mental perspective taking. This would mean systems in which robots are able to autonomously attribute a wider set of mental states, reason about them and appropriately react to them. Another approach was recently presented by Rabinowitz et al. [8], who proposed a NN able to predict the behavior of multiple agents in a false-belief situation given their past and current trajectories. However, as the authors mention in their paper, they assume the observer to have access to states and actions of all agents, which is not always the case for an embodied agent. Therefore, fully understanding and reasoning about agents' beliefs still represents a challenge for robotics.

Mentalizing for Proactivity and Preparation. Characterizing other agents through their beliefs, desires and intentions may allow the anticipation of their behavior before they perform any concrete action. Proactivity implies a lower reliance on bottom-up inputs in favor of additional top-down control influencing the response of the robot to the situation. This is important for the successful application of robots in everyday social settings and collaborative tasks, as social contexts are highly dynamic and robots are required to prepare and act prior to an event rather than just to react to it. An interesting study by Milliez et al. [20] provided an example of a proactive robot which was able to reason about the beliefs of a human partner and to communicate important information that the human had missed for the successful completion of a collaborative task. Although the architecture of this robot was based on the ToM principle of perspective taking to interact with an agent, the robot was readily provided with several hard-coded position hypotheses to make when an object was not visible (contrary to the automaticity seen in human behavior). Ultimately, equipping robots with an adaptive ToM would allow more efficient and fluid human-robot interactions (e.g., by independently positioning themselves in a position easy to spot).

Mentalizing for (Active) Perception. Associating intentions and mental states to agents' behavior may encourage observers to search for cues that better explain the current situation and enable more precise predictions [23]. Active perception may be necessary to eliminate the passive nature of robots' exploration and understanding of environments/agents. For example, in Görür et al. [19] the robot was fed with 100 different observation sequences from which states were estimated with a hidden Markov model. This suggests that the important information/features of the scene were readily provided to the robot, which was not left to explore and act in the environment to increase the information content derived from its sensorial data. In contrast with the ecological behavior seen in humans, this limits the quality of human-robot interactions.

Mentalizing for Learning. An adaptive ToM for robots would also tackle many of the challenges identified in the robotics field by Lake et al. [24]. Integrating ToM development principles in the blueprint of an adapting neural architecture for social interaction may result in a more time- and cost-efficient learning process compared to DNNs [6]. Furthermore, it would decrease the need to select and feed appropriate content to robots through expensive datasets, also reducing human errors involved in their preparation and permitting increased accuracy. In addition, mentalizing for learning would imply a different way of learning about the world. More specifically, most DNN-based action recognition systems do not currently distinguish the learning of passive objects dynamics (e.g., the movement of clouds) from that of agents' behavior (e.g., opening several boxes to find lost glasses while searching) and do not take into consideration the intentionality that marks humans' behaviors. In contrast, we propose that equipping robots with mental states understanding and contextualization would provide a means to distinguish between passive object dynamics and agents behaviors. Finally, predicting interactions and perceiving the mental states of multiple agents simultaneously may be particularly demanding both for the sensory and the general cognitive load of the agent. However, humans swiftly deal with these conditions by adaptively allocating their attention to the most significant users based on contextualized knowledge (e.g., while playing football, only the intentions of the player with the most relevant location and role will be considered) [25]. Therefore, providing robots with similar capabilities would alleviate the current issues associated with multi-agent interactions.

3 Computational Modelling of ToM

In the literature, several theories describing human ToM exist [12, 26], however, developing a computational model inspired by the brain processes underlying human mentalizing is particularly challenging. Here, we attempt to better delineate the possible brain processes responsible for the development of the mentalizing ability in humans with the aim of transferring such features to social robots and stimulating future research in the direction proposed. Specifically, we will describe the limitations and advantages of two principal accounts which have been contrasted and implicated in the development of a ToM in humans, i.e., the teleological and simulation theories.

3.1 Teleological Theory for ToM

The teleological theory is one of the principal accounts utilized to describe the intention recognition ability based on observable actions in both adults and infants [27]. Specifically, infants were suggested to attribute a causal intention to an agent according to the rationality principle [28]. However, whether this teleological account is a suitable candidate mechanism underlying ToM remains questioned. Firstly, the concepts represented in the mentalistic account can be considered more complex compared to those of the teleological account. In fact, although the teleological account is able to process actions to derive the goal of an agent in various situations, it is unlikely that the rationality principle may provide access to the unobservable, abstract mental states [29, 30]. Indeed, a recent review noted that there are kinds of mindreading contexts that have nothing to do with rationality or efficiency [12]. Similarly, rationality, thus the teleological account, is not very effective when trying to infer mental states which are subjective, as efficiency may not be the prerogative of the agent observed. In addition, while the teleological account suggests that infants should not be able to distinguish their representation of a scene from that of an agent (thus, reality should be as construed by the infants), the mentalistic account presupposes the attribution of a perspective to another agent, which may be similar or differ from their own [31].

Nonetheless, Gergely and Csibra [28] proposed a continuum between the teleological constructs (i.e., action, goal-state and situational constraints) and the mentalistic ones, with the latter presupposing the same computations and constructs of the former but representing more sophisticated, abstract constructs (i.e., intentions, desires and beliefs). Furthermore, Baker et al. [32] developed a Bayesian computational model for

ToM based on the teleological principle that was tested on both adults and infants [33], who were suggested to follow this model to infer the mental states behind an agent's behavior using priors. However, this model is computationally demanding and could not be directly used to support online interactions.

3.2 Simulation Theory for ToM

The simulation theory is the other principal account utilized to describe the intention recognition ability based on observable actions in both adults and infants [34, 35]. Specifically, activation of infants' motor system was shown both during the observation of a grasping action and prior to the visual input once the action could be predicted [35]. However, similarly to the teleological account, whether the simulation account is a suitable candidate mechanism underlying ToM remains questioned. The simulation theory "proposes that we can understand the mental states of others on the basis of our own mental states" [12, 13, 34, 36]. Therefore, in contrast to the teleological account, the simulation theory permits the representation of the same abstract mental states, given that we experience our own mental states. However, having the same desire as another person does not necessarily permit the inference of their intentions. Hence the simulation theory can be considered only a first step for mentalizing [13]. Furthermore, the simulation account can account for the subject-specific nature of the mental states only when the observer and the subject observed are very similar [13]. This has also consequences on the metarepresentational ability of mentalizing. In fact, while similarity is essential to permit the transfer of mental perspectives, it may also be a disadvantage and lead to the quarantine failure [12]. That is the failure to both exclude own mental states (which are lacking in the agent observed) and include those possessed by the target (as lacking in the observer). Against the simulation theory as a base for mentalizing is also some evidence of its inability to support action understanding in novel situations [36], which does not support the context-specific nature of mental states.

Nonetheless, Keysers and Gazzola [37] proposed a model integrating the simulation and mentalistic accounts based on neural evidence. More specifically, the authors suggested that the brain areas associated with both accounts reflect simulation, even though at different levels, rather than radically different processes.

3.3 Integrating the Models for a Better ToM

Although the teleological and simulation models in some respects rely on different representations and computations, they may be important in different situations or when dealing with specific mental states. For example, while the teleological model might be useful to predict mental states early in development given its more innate nature (due to the central rationality principle) compared to the simulation model, the latter may become valuable when humans start learning from experience and relating to other people. Similarly, while the simulation approach may be more suitable to infer mental states triggered by bottom-up stimuli, the teleological model may be important when an increasing top-down control is necessitated. In turn, the top-down control enabled by the mentalistic and teleological models may enable different preparation strategies for interaction, such as adopting a convenient posture (e.g., looking for a possible target of a predator before it approaches it [4]).

In this paragraph we suggest an innovative view which is not usually taken in robotics, that is the integration of the simulation and teleological models for ToM as a means to improve robots' social skills. We thus propose a complementary view of the models described up to date, rather than a contrasting one. In fact, although mirroring does not necessarily imply inference and prediction of the final intentions and beliefs of an agent, it may help with the action sequences necessary to reach that goal state (i.e., the trajectory to reach the final state). This may favor the teleological reasoning which may provide further information to infer and predict the mental states of the agent observed. The same might be true also in the opposite direction. While the teleological model might provide information on possible trajectories of observed actions to infer the agent's mental states, simulation may allow the correct inference of intentions, desires or beliefs by choosing between such options through internal simulation.

4   Questions and Future Directions

A great debate currently exists on whether the abstract mental states can be accessed through learning or if they can be innately understood. Based on what mentioned above, it would be reasonable to assume that they can be inferred after learning about an agent through repeated observations, in different contexts, with the aid of language and communication [13, 14, 38]. However, the assumption that this capacity may be innate (i.e., derived from the supposition that conspecifics share general mental states) or driven by innate stimulus cues (e.g., direction of gaze or movement) also seems valid [28, 39]. It is possible that a combination of the two inference mechanisms occurs in humans [40].

Another debate concerns whether such mental states can be inferred directly from automatic, bottom-up effects, such as the automatic tendency to share another person's experiences, or whether mostly top-down control is involved [30]. Again, these recognition mechanisms may act in concert to achieve optimal mental states understanding.

Shedding light on these processes for ToM would also mean assessing which current models are better describing the mentalizing ability and whether they cooperate or compete with each other. Nevertheless, assigning an innate component to and a top-down control over the mental states inference process would support the teleological account as a precursor of ToM. In contrast, if a learning component and a bottom-up control are assumed, the simulation account could be identified as the precursor of ToM. Finally, if all these properties are present during ToM at different instances or when attributing different mental states, both the teleological and simulation models might be precursors of the mentalizing ability. They may however be important for specific parts of ToM.

We would like to urge future studies to focus on the modern cross-talk between developmental studies and robotics to answer these questions. In fact, on the one hand, developing architectures for robots inspired by developmental mechanisms resulted in more sophisticated robots with increasingly complex abilities and behavior [41]. On the other hand, robots have been useful in the modelling of human developmental processes within an embodied agent and the prediction of developmental phenomena which were successively validated by infants studies [2]. Therefore, developing robot architectures based on ToM can result in increasingly complex adaptive social robots as well as in a new tool for investigating models from developmental psychology and provide insights into human capabilities which are yet to be fully understood, including the mentalizing ability itself.

References

1. Abubshait, A., Wiese, E.: You look human, but act like a machine: agent appearance and behavior modulate different aspects of human-robot interaction. Front. Psychol. **8**, 1393 (2017)
2. Cangelosi, A., Schlesinger, M.: From babies to robots: the contribution of developmental robotics to developmental psychology. Child. Dev. Perspect. **12**, 183–188 (2018)
3. Demiris, Y., Dearden, A.: From motor babbling to hierarchical learning by imitation: a robot developmental pathway. In: Proceedings of the 5th International Workshop on Epigenetic Robotics, pp. 31–37 (2005)
4. Ognibene, D., Demiris, Y.: Towards active event recognition. In: Proceedings of IJCAI AAAI, pp. 2495–2501 (2013)
5. Wiese, E., Metta, G., Wykowska, A.: Robots as intentional agents: using neuroscientific methods to make robots appear more social. Front. Psychol. **8**, 1663 (2017)
6. Pierson, H., Gashler, M.: Deep learning in robotics: a review of recent research. Adv. Robot. **31**, 821–835 (2017)
7. Singh, G., Saha, S., Sapienza, M., Torr, P., Cuzzolin, F.: Online real time multiple spatiotemporal action localisation and prediction on a single platform. arXiv preprint arXiv: 1611.08563 (2017)
8. Rabinowitz, N.C., Perbet, F., Song, H.F., Zhang, C., Eslami, S.M.A., Botvinick, M.: Machine Theory of Mind. arXiv preprint arXiv:1802.07740 (2018)
9. Mariolis, I., Peleka, G., Kargakos, A., Malassiotis, S.: Pose and category recognition of highly deformable objects using deep learning. In: International Conference on Advanced Robotics (ICAR), pp. 655–662 (2015)
10. Polydoros, A.S., Nalpantidis, L., Kruger, V.: Real-time deep learning of robotic manipulator inverse dynamics. In: IEEE/RSJ International Conference on Intelligent Robots and Systems (IROS), pp. 3442–3448 (2015)
11. Silver, D., Schrittwieser, J., Simonyan, K., Antonoglou, I., Huang, A., Guez, A., et al.: Mastering the game of Go without human knowledge. Nature **550**, 354–359 (2017)
12. Goldman, A.I.: Theory of mind. In: The Oxford Handbook of Philosophy of Cognitive Science. Oxford University Press, Oxford (2012)
13. Frith, C.D., Frith, U.: The neural basis of mentalizing. Neuron **50**, 531–534 (2006)
14. Devaine, M., Hollard, G., Daunizeau, J.: The social Bayesian brain: does mentalizing make a difference when we learn? PLoS Comput. Biol. **10**, e1003992 (2014)
15. Yott, J., Poulin-Dubois, D.: Are infants' theory-of-mind abilities well integrated? Implicit understanding of intentions, desires, and beliefs. J. Cogn. Dev. **17**, 683–698 (2016)
16. Kosakowski, H.L., Saxe, R.: "Affective theory of mind" and the function of the ventral medial prefrontal cortex. Cogn. Behav. Neurol. **31**, 36–50 (2018)
17. Scassellati, B.: Theory of mind for a humanoid robot. Auton. Robots **12**, 13–24 (2002)

18. Bianco, F., Ognibene, D.: Functional advantages of an adaptive theory of mind for robotics: a review of current architectures. In: The 11th Computer Science and Electronic Engineering Conference. IEEE Xplore, University of Essex (2019)
19. Görür, O.C., Rosman, B., Hoffman, G., Albayrak, A.: Toward integrating theory of mind into adaptive decision-making of social robots to understand human intention. In: Workshop on Intentions in HRI at ACM/IEEE International Conference on Human-Robot Interaction (2017)
20. Milliez, G., Warnier, M., Clodic, A., Alami, R.: A framework for endowing an interactive robot with reasoning capabilities about perspective-taking and belief management. In: The 23rd IEEE International Symposium on Robot and Human Interactive Communication, pp. 1103–1109 (2014)
21. Devin, S., Alami, R.: An implemented theory of mind to improve human-robot shared plans execution. In: The Eleventh ACM/IEEE International Conference on Human Robot Interation, pp. 319–326 (2016)
22. Grosse, W.C., Friederici, A.D., Singer, T., Steinbeis, N.: Implicit and explicit false belief development in preschool children. Dev. Sci. **20**, e12445 (2017)
23. Ognibene, D., Chinellato, E., Sarabia, M., Demiris, Y.: Contextual action recognition and target localization with an active allocation of attention on a humanoid robot. Bioinspiration Biomimetics **8**, 035002 (2013)
24. Lake, B.M., Ullman, T.D., Tenenbaum, J.B., Gershman, S.J.: Building machines that learn and think like people. Behav. Brain Sci. **40**, 1–101 (2016)
25. Lee, K., Ognibene, D., Chang, H.J., Kim, T.-K., Demiris, Y.: STARE: spatio-temporal attention relocation for multiple structured activities detection. IEEE Trans. Image Process. **24**, 5916–5927 (2015)
26. Schaafsma, S.M., Pfaff, D.W., Spunt, R.P., Adolphs, R.: Deconstructing and reconstructing theory of mind. Trends Cogn. Sci. **19**, 65–72 (2015)
27. Southgate, V., Johnson, M.H., Csibra, G.: Infants attribute goals even to biomechanically impossible actions. Cognition **107**, 1059–1069 (2008)
28. Gergely, G., Csibra, G.: Teleological reasoning in infancy: the naive theory of rational action. Trends Cogn. Sci. **7**, 287–292 (2003)
29. Koster-Hale, J., Richardson, H., Velez, N., Asaba, M., Young, L., Saxe, R.: Mentalizing regions represent distributed, continuous, and abstract dimensions of others' beliefs. NeuroImage **161**, 9–18 (2017)
30. Frith, C.D., Frith, U.: How we predict what other people are going to do. Brain Res. **1079**, 36–46 (2006)
31. Luo, Y., Baillargeon, R.: Toward a mentalistic account of early psychological reasoning. Curr. Dir. Psychol. Sci. **19**, 301–307 (2010)
32. Baker, C.L., Jara-Ettinger, J., Saxe, R., Tenenbaum, J.B.: Rational quantitative attribution of beliefs, desires and percepts in human mentalizing. Nat. Hum. Behav. **1**, 0064 (2017)
33. Hamlin, J.K., Ullman, T., Tenenbaum, J., Goodman, N., Baker, C.: The mentalistic basis of core social cognition: experiments in preverbal infants and a computational model. Dev. Sci. **16**, 209–226 (2013)
34. Gallese, V., Goldman, A.: Mirror neurons and the simulation theory of mind-reading. Trends Cogn. Sci. **2**, 493–501 (1998)
35. Southgate, V., Johnson, M.H., Osborne, T., Csibra, G.: Predictive motor activation during action observation in human infants. Biol. Let. **5**, 769–772 (2009)
36. Brass, M., Schmitt, R.M., Spengler, S., Gergely, G.: Investigating action understanding: inferential processes versus action simulation. Curr. Biol. **17**, 2117–2121 (2007)
37. Keysers, C., Gazzola, V.: Integrating simulation and theory of mind: from self to social cognition. Trends Cogn. Sci. **11**, 194–196 (2007)

38. Frith, C.D., Frith, U.: Social cognition in humans. Curr. Biol. **17**, 724–732 (2007)
39. Kovacs, A.M., Teglas, E., Endress, A.D.: The social sense: susceptibility to others' beliefs in human infants and adults. Science **330**, 1830–1834 (2010)
40. Baron-Cohen, S.: Mindreading: evidence for both innate and acquired factors. J. Anthropol. Psychol. **17**, 26–27 (2006)
41. Bhat, A.A., Mohan, V., Sandini, G., Morasso, P.: Humanoid infers Archimedes' principle: understanding physical relations and object affordances through cumulative learning experiences. J. Roy. Soc. Interface **13** (2016)

Robots Improve Judgments on Self-generated Actions: An Intentional Binding Study

Cecilia Roselli[1,2(✉)], Francesca Ciardo[1], and Agnieszka Wykowska[1]

[1] Social Cognition in Human Robot Interaction,
Fondazione Istituto Italiano di Tecnologia, Center for Human Technologies,
Via Enrico Melen 83, 16040 Genoa, Italy
cecilia.roselli@iit.it

[2] DIBRIS, Dipartimento di Informatica, Bioingegneria, Robotica e Ingegneria
dei Sistemi, Via all'Opera Pia 13, 16145 Genoa, Italy

Abstract. In near future, robots will become a fundamental part of our daily life; therefore, it appears crucial to investigate how they can successfully interact with humans. Since several studies already pointed out that a robotic agent can influence human's cognitive mechanisms such as decision-making and joint attention, we focus on Sense of Agency (SoA). To this aim, we employed the Intentional Binding (IB) task to implicitly assess SoA in human-robot interaction (HRI). Participants were asked to perform an IB task alone (Individual condition) or with the Cozmo robot (Social condition). In the Social condition, participants were free to decide whether they wanted to let Cozmo press. Results showed that participants performed the action significantly more often than Cozmo. Moreover, participants were more precise in reporting the occurrence of a self-made action when Cozmo was also in charge of performing the task. However, this improvement in evaluating self-performance corresponded to a reduction in SoA. In conclusion, the present study highlights the double effect of robots as social companions. Indeed, the social presence of the robot leads to a better evaluation of self-generated actions and, at the same time, to a reduction of SoA.

Keywords: Human robot interaction · Sense of Agency · Intentional Binding

1 Introduction

In recent years, artificial agents (e.g. Siri, Alexa, Google Assistant) have started appearing more commonly in our houses. They are able to perform a huge number of autonomous activities: playing our favorite music, reminding us to take a pill or helping us to reach a friend's place. However, since these artificial agents are not embodied, they are not able to manipulate the physical world. In the near future, also robots will take part in our everyday life, as useful supportive assistants at home or at work [1]. Thanks to their embodiment, robots not only will comply with our requests, but also will act directly on our environment and manipulate it [2]. Therefore, it appears crucial to understand whether robots as social companions can affect basic cognitive mechanisms in humans.

© Springer Nature Switzerland AG 2019
M. A. Salichs et al. (Eds.): ICSR 2019, LNAI 11876, pp. 88–97, 2019.
https://doi.org/10.1007/978-3-030-35888-4_9

Some evidences showed that the mere presence of a robot influenced the behavior of a human partner, leading her/him to follow robot's recommendation in a decision-making task [3], or even to afford a greater peri-personal space [4]. Beyond the mere presence, the actions of a robotic agent actually have an impact on human's behavior. For example, when performing a target discrimination task with the iCub robot, participants' attentional orienting was biased by robot's gaze direction similarly to when human eyes are presented [5, 6]. Similar findings have been shown also for joint actions. For instance, when performing a joint Simon task [7, 8], participants coordinated their actions with a non-humanoid robot, however this was true only when they believed that the robot was controlled by a human being [9].

Together, these findings demonstrated that robots are able to modify humans' cognitive mechanisms, such as decision-making and joint attention, in a similar fashion as they occur in human-human interaction. However, other mechanisms of human cognition are still poorly investigated in HRI; one of this is Sense of Agency (SoA). SoA has been defined as the feeling of control that we experience over our own actions and their outcomes [10]. Given its pivotal role in the embodied nature of the Self, disruption of SoA may lead to unpleasant consequences, like the misrecognition of ourselves as the authors of our thoughts, feelings and actions. For instance, disruption of SoA has been reported in schizophrenia patients, who find difficult to distinguish between self- and externally-generated events [11, 12].

In the context of HRI, Ciardo and colleagues demonstrated that SoA over self-generated actions is reduced when performing a task with a robotic agent [13]. Specifically, when participants performed costly actions (i.e. losing a various amount of points) together with a robot, they rated their SoA lower compared to when they performed the same task alone. However, although interesting, these results have been obtained with explicit measures only, thus it remains unclear whether the social presence of a robot can affect SoA in humans also at an implicit level.

One of the most common implicit measure to investigate SoA is based on recording variations in time perception related to action effects (see [14] for a review). The typical result is to perceive the time interval between a self-voluntary action and its sensory consequence (e.g. a tone) as shorter in time than its actual duration. This effect is known as *Intentional Binding* (IB) [15], and it occurs only when people perform self-voluntary actions. Indeed, if the same action-effect chain is produced either by other people or by involuntary movements, then the IB effect is not reported [16, 17]. In terms of SoA in a social context, Sahaï and colleagues [18] showed that IB for self-generated actions does not differ if people perform the task alone or interact with another human, but it decreases when they interact with a computer.

1.1 Aim

In the present study, we aimed to investigate whether the social presence of the robot can affect SoA in humans by using an implicit measure. To this end, participants were asked to perform an IB task [19, 20] alone (Individual Condition) or with the Cozmo robot (Anki Robotics) (Social Condition). Notably, both participants and Cozmo performed the task by executing the action, i.e. the keypress, at the time of their own choice. We hypothesized that, if the social presence of the robot can actually influence participants' SoA, inducing a reduction of SoA as in Ciardo et al. [13], then participants' performance is expected to differ across conditions. Specifically, in Social blocks participants would be better in judging the position of the clock-hand compared to the Individual blocks. As a consequence, smaller or null IB was expected in the Social compared to the Individual Condition.

2 Materials and Methods

2.1 Participants

Seventeen right-handed young adults (mean age = 22.47, sd = 3.14, 5 males) have been recruited to take part in the study. Sample size has been estimated according to previous experiments [19, 20] and to *a priori* power analysis indicating that a sample size of N = 12 was needed in order to detect a medium effect size [Cohen's d for repeated measures (Dz) = 0.63, alpha (one-tailed) = .05 and power = 0.80] for within-subjects comparisons. The study has been conducted in accordance with the ethical standards laid down in the 2013 Declaration of Helsinki and has been approved by the local ethical committee (Comitato Etico Regione Liguria). All participants gave written informed consent prior to the experiment. They received an honorarium of 10€ per hour for their participation. The experimental session lasted around 60 min. At the end of the experiment, participants were debriefed about the purpose of the study.

2.2 Apparatus and Stimuli

The experimental setup consisted of a mobile Android device with the standard Cozmo application running in 'SDK enabled option' [21]; one computer connected with Cozmo through the Android Debug Bridge (cosmosdk.anki.com/docs/adb.html) [22]; one 21' inches screen (1920 × 1080 pixels) to display the task; two keyboards to collect responses during the experiment.

Participants and Cozmo were seated side by side at approximately 60 cm away from the computer screen. A keyboard was placed in front of the participants and in front of Cozmo (see Fig. 1). Stimuli presentation, response collection, and the Cozmo robot were controlled with OpenSesame (see [13] for the procedure of how to integrate Cozmo).

2.3 Procedure

Participants were asked to perform the Intentional Binding task alone (Individual Condition) or with Cozmo (Social Condition). They were presented with an image of the clock (10.6° visual angle) with a red rotating clock-hand. Each trial started with a black fixation dot on a white background for 1000 ms, followed by the image of a clock with a static clock-hand for 500 ms. Then, the clock-hand started to rotate randomly from one of the 12 five-minutes positions of the clock, in order to complete a unique full rotation in 2560 ms. At the end of each trial, participants were asked to report the position of the clock-hand at the time of the event of interest (either keypress or tone play). The task comprised four different type of blocks: two types of Baseline blocks (*tone* or *action*), and two types of Operant blocks (*tone* or *action*) (see Table 1). For both the Individual and the Social Condition, each block was repeated twice; following the procedure of [23], only the *Baseline-Tone* block was performed once, since no action was required.

Table 1. The Baseline and the Operant blocks.

Block type	Task
Baseline-tone (BT)	A tone (440 Hz, 700 ms) is played at a random time while the clock-hand (length = 170 pixels) is rotating. Participants have to judge at which time on the clock the sound event occurs. No action is required.
Baseline-action (BA)	Participants have to press the spacebar at any moment while the clock-hand is rotating. They have to report the position of the clock-hand when they act. No auditory feedback occurs.
Operant-tone (OT)	Participants have to press the spacebar at the time of their own choice while the clock-hand is rotating. 250 ms after the keypress, the tone (440 Hz, 700 ms) is presented while the clock-hand is still rotating. Participants have to judge at which time on the clock the sound event occurs.
Operant-action (OA)	Participants have to press the spacebar at any moment during the clock-hand rotation. 250 ms after the keypress, the tone (440 Hz, 700 ms) is presented while the clock-hand is still rotating. Participants have to report the position of the clock-hand when they act.

At the beginning of each block, participants were informed whether they were performing the task alone (Individual Condition) or with Cozmo (Social Condition). If the block belonged to the Individual condition, Cozmo moved away from its keyboard and entered into the sleep mode. When a block of the Social Condition started, Cozmo was programmed to wake up and reach the keyboard. In those blocks belonging to the Social Condition, participants were instructed that if they wanted they could let Cozmo do the task alone in their place. Cozmo was programmed to tap the bar during the clock-hand rotation at a random time. The task comprised 14 blocks of 24 trials each, for a total number of 336 trials. Blocks were randomly assigned to either Individual (7 blocks) or Social Condition (7 blocks). Therefore, once in the Individual and once in the Social Condition each participant performed 1 BT, 2 BA, 2 OT and 2 OA blocks. In order to prevent any habituation effect, both Individual and Social blocks were presented in a random order within participants. A practice session of the entire task (i.e. 14 trials, one per condition) was administered.

Fig. 1. Experimental setup.

2.4   Data Analysis

Our dependent measures were the percentages of human's and Cozmo's responses in the Social blocks and the *judgment error* (JE) in reporting the critical event across the Individual and the Social Blocks. To this aim, only Social blocks were considered and the percentages of responses for each agent were estimated for those trials in which an action occurred and compared with a chi-square test.

JEs were estimated as the difference between the position of the clock-hand reported by participants and the actual onset of the critical event (i.e. action or tone play). For Social blocks, JE was estimated only for those trials in which participants acted. Then, for each block, we calculated the average JE and its standard deviation; trials in which the JE deviated more than ±2.5. SD from the participants' mean were excluded from the analysis. After the outliers' removal, participants with a total number of valid trials lower than 24 were excluded from the subsequent analysis. According to this criterion, for action blocks four participants were excluded, whereas, for tone blocks, data of seven participants were not analyzed. Therefore, for 14 participants in action blocks, and for 10 participants in tone blocks, IB effect was estimated as the difference between the mean JE for the Baseline (Individual condition) and the mean JE for the corresponding Operant block (Social condition).

Given that JEs were not normally distributed, Wilcoxon signed- rank tests were used to compare JEs and IB across conditions (Individual, Social) and Block Types (Baseline, Operant). The threshold for level of significance was set at $p < .05$, rank-biserial correlation coefficient (r_b) is reported as an index of the effect size. 95% confidence intervals of the means are reported.

3 Results

In Social Blocks, participants acted in the 75.3% of trials (95% CI [73.5%, 77%]), letting Cozmo to perform the task in their place the remaining 24.7% of trials (95% CI [23%, 26.5%]). This difference was statistically significant from chance ($\chi^2 = 4.468$, p < .001). Interestingly, Human/Cozmo action ratio was constant across all the Social blocks in which an action was required (see Fig. 2).

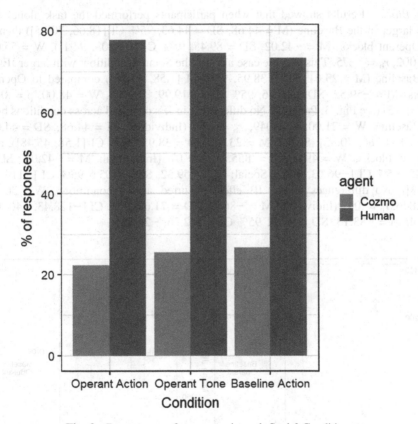

Fig. 2. Percentages of responses in each Social Condition.

Action Blocks. Results showed that when participants performed the task alone, JEs were smaller in the Baseline (M = −28.250, SD = 33.39, 95% CI [−43.94, −12.43]) than in the Operant blocks (M = 26.829, SD = 112.61, 95% CI [−30.16, 83.67]), W = 13.00, p = .011, r_b = −.75. However, this was not true for the Social Condition, as no differences occurred in JEs between the Baseline (M = −15.257, SD = 38.08,

95% CI [−35.58, 4.19]) and the Operant blocks (M = 5.082, SD = 68.73, 95% CI [−30.775, 41.468]), W = 25.00, p = .091, r_b = − .524 (see Fig. 3, Panel A). Moreover, results showed that JEs marginally differed across conditions for Baseline blocks only, W = 21.00, p = .049, r_b = −.60 (Individual: M = −28.250, SD = 33.39, 95% CI [−43.94, −12.43]; Social: M = −15.257, SD = 38.08, 95% CI [−35.58, 4.19]). No differences in JEs across conditions occurred for Operant blocks, W = 49.00, p = .855, r_b = −.07 (Individual: M = 26.829, SD = 112.61, 95% CI [−30.16, 83.67]; Social: M = 5.082, SD = 68.73, 95% CI [−30.775, 41.468]). Finally, the comparison between IB effects across conditions showed a larger IB in the Individual (M = 55.080, SD = 106.30, 95% CI [2.10, 107.29]) compared to the Social Condition (M = 20.339, SD = 39.45, 95% CI [0.44, 39.52]), W = 85.00, p = .042, r_b = .619.

Tone Blocks. Results showed that when participants performed the task alone, JEs were larger in the Baseline (M = 44.68, SD = 44.63, 95% CI [18.66, 70.85]) then in the Operant blocks (M = −42.02, SD = 89.45, 95% CI [−96.03, 9.91]), W = 55.00, p = .002, r_b = − .75. This was the case also for the Social Condition, with larger JEs in the Baseline (M = 23.61, SD = 38.95, 95% CI [1.58, 45.48]) compared to Operant blocks (M = −59.52, SD = 105.6, 95% CI [−119.99, −0.04]), W = 48.00, p = .037, r_b = − .75) (see Fig. 3, Panel B). No differences in JEs occurred across conditions both for Baseline, W = 21.00, p = .049, r_b = −.60 (Individual: M = 44.68, SD = 44.63, 95% CI [18.66, 70.85]; Social: M = 23.61, SD = 38.95, 95% CI [1.58, 45.48]), and Operant blocks, W = 49.00, p = .855, r_b = −.07 (Individual: M = −42.02, SD = 89.45, 95% CI [−96.03, 9.91]; Social: M = −59.52, SD = 105.6 95% CI [−119.99, −0.04]). No differences in the IB effect occurred across conditions, W = 30.00, p = .846, r_b = .091 (Individual: M = −86.70, SD = 71.69, 95% CI [−128.43, −46.03]; Social: M = −83.13, SD = 99.11 95% CI [−142.26, −24.25]).

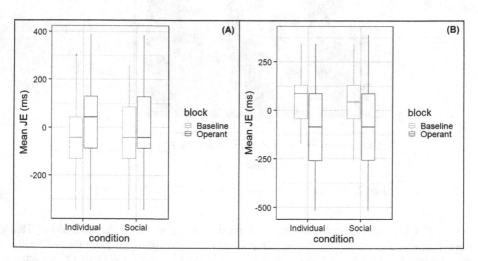

Fig. 3. Panel (A): Mean JEs for Baseline and Operant block as a function of condition (Individual, Social) when the critical event was the action (action blocks). Panel (B): Mean JE for Baseline and Operant block as a function of condition (Individual, Social) when the critical event was the tone (tone blocks).

4 Discussion

In this experiment, we sought to determine whether the social presence of the robot might influence SoA for self-generated actions. To this end, we employed an Intentional Binding experiment as an implicit measure to investigate SoA. As in the standard version of the IB task where participants knew they always were the initiator of the action [23], we let participants choose whether they wanted to press the spacebar, of let Cozmo press in their place. We predicted that, if the social presence of the robot can actually have an impact on human's SoA, participants' performance would be different across conditions, i.e. they would judge better the occurrence of self-voluntary actions when doing the task with the robot compared to when they perform the task alone. Otherwise, if the robot does not influence humans' SoA, participants' performance in Social Condition would have mirrored the one in Individual Condition.

Overall participants let Cozmo responding only in the 30% of the Social trials. This trend in responses was constant across different block types, suggesting a general attitude toward a robot. It may be possible that they perceived the Social Condition as a competition between themselves and the robot. If this has been the case, then participants may have been triggered to act faster than Cozmo, resulting into a lower percentage of Cozmo's trials. Another possible explanation is that given the nature of the robot we used, i.e. Cozmo, participants might have perceived the robot as not competent enough to perform the task, thus they took the responsibility of the task and acted above the level of chance. Future studies should investigate these possibilities by addressing how individual differences in attitude towards the robot and perceived competence may affect the possibility to let it act. In line with previous studies [16, 23], when participants performed the task alone (Individual Condition) JEs for action events were smaller for the Baseline than for the Operant blocks, whereas, when the critical event was a tone, JEs were smaller for the Operant than for the Baseline blocks. The reversed pattern can be explained by the fact that the direction of the IB effect depends on when the critical event occurred on the temporal line in the Operant blocks.

When the critical event was the action (i.e. the keypress), since it preceded the sensory effect (i.e. the sound) on the temporal line, the actual occurrence of the action was bounded to the occurrence of the tone, leading to perceive the temporal interval between the action and the sensory outcome as longer. Thus, participants reported the action as delayed compared to a condition in which it did not produce any sensory outcome. In operant blocks, in which participants had to judge when the sound occurred, given that the tone followed the keypress on the temporal line, its occurrence was bounded to the preceding event (i.e. the action). Therefore, participants perceived the temporal interval between the action and the sensory outcome as shorter. Thus, in operant blocks participants reported the tone earlier compared to when the sound is passively presented. Our results showed that the presence of the robot affected JEs only when the critical event is an action, as indicated by the lack of IB in the Social condition only. The robot did not affect JEs when the critical event was a tone. Interestingly, previous studies showed that a lack of IB is typically reported for unintentional self-generated actions [15, 24]. In our Social condition for action blocks, the lack of IB was driven by a reduction in JEs both in the Baseline and in the Operant blocks, suggesting that when the robot was also in charge to perform the task, participants were better in reporting when their own action occurred. These latter results can be due to a well-known phenomenon in psychology named social facilitation, i.e. the fact that in the presence of a social companion, humans' performance is enhanced [25].

Our results suggest that the social presence of Cozmo had a double effect. Indeed, on one hand the presence of the robot led to an improvement in the evaluation of self-generated actions. On the other hand, it might bring to a reduction of self-agency, similarly to what occurred in human-human cooperative contexts [26].

5 Conclusions

In the present study, we raised the question of whether a robot, as a social companion, can have an influence on human's SoA. According to our results, participants were better in judging the occurrence of their own actions when Cozmo was also in charge to perform the task, confirming that the social presence of the robot actually influences human's agency. On the other side, in action blocks a lack of IB in Social Condition compared to Individual Condition correspond to a reduction of SoA. Future studies should provide further evidences about the influence of robots on human's SoA, in order to build new robotic agents well-tailored on human's cognition.

Acknowledgments. This project has received funding from the European Research Council (ERC) under the European Union's Horizon 2020 research and innovation program (grant awarded to AW, titled "InStance: Intentional Stance for Social Attunement." G.A. No: ERC-2016-StG-715058).

References

1. Glasauer, S., Huber, M., Basili, P., Knoll, A., Brandt, T.: Interacting in time and space: investigating human-human and human-robot joint action. In: 19th International Symposium on Robot and Human Interactive Communication, pp. 252–257 (2010)
2. Wykowska, A., Chaminade, T., Cheng, G.: Embodied artificial agents for understanding human social cognition. Philos. Trans. B **371**, 20150375 (2016)
3. Shinozawa, K., Naya, F., Yamato, J., Kogure, K.: Differences in effect of robot and screen-agent recommendations on human decision-making. Int. J. Hum Comput Stud. **62**(2), 267–279 (2005)
4. Bainbridge, W.A., Hart, J., Kim, E.S., Scassellati, B.: The Effect of presence on human-robot interaction. In: Proceedings of the 17th IEEE International Symposium on Robot and Human Interactive Communication, Technische Universität München, Munich, Germany, 1–3 August 2008
5. Kompatsiari, K., Pèrez-Osorio, J., De Tommaso, D., Metta, G., Wykowska, A.: Neuroscientifically-grounded research for improved human-robot interaction. In Proceedings of 2018 IEEE/RSJ International Conference on Intelligent Robots and Systems (IROS), Madrid, Spain, 1–5 October 2018, pp. 3403–3408. IEEE (2018)
6. Kompatsiari, K., Ciardo, F., Tikhanoff, V., Metta, G., Wykowska, A.: On the role of eye contact in gaze-cueing. Sci. rep. 14, 8(1), 17842 (2018)

7. Sebanz, N., Knoblich, G., Prinz, W.: Representing others' actions: Just like one's own? Cognition **88**, B11–B21 (2003)
8. Ciardo, F., Wykowska, A.: Response coordination emerges in cooperative but not competitive joint task. Front. Psychol. **9**, 1919 (2018)
9. Stenzel, A., Chinellato, E., Tirado Bou, M.A., Del Pobil, A.P., Lappe, M., Liepelt, R.: When humanoid robots become human-like interaction partners: corepresentation of robotic actions. J. Exp. Psychol. Hum. Percept. Perform. **38**(5), 1073–1077 (2012)
10. Gallagher, S.: Philosophical conception of the self: implication for cognitive science. Trends Cogn. Sci. **4**(1), 14–21 (2000)
11. Daprati, E., Franck, N., Georgieff, N., Proust, J., Pacherie, E., Dalery, J., et al.: Looking for the agent: an investigation into consciousness of action and self-consciousness in schizophrenic patients. Cognition **65**, 7186 (1997)
12. Gallagher, S.: Multiple aspects in the sense of agency. New Ideas in Psychology **30**, 15–31 (2012)
13. Ciardo, F., De Tommaso, D., Beyer, F., Wykowska, A.: Attribution of intentional agency toward robots reduces one's own sense of agency. Cognition **194**, 104109 (2020)
14. Haggard, P.: Sense of agency in the human brain. Nat. Rev. Neurosci. **18**(4), 196–207 (2017)
15. Haggard, P., Clark, S.: Kalogeras, J: Voluntary action and conscious awareness. Nat. Neurosci. **5**, 382–385 (2002)
16. Haggard, P., Clark, S.: Intentional action: conscious experience and neural prediction. Conscious. Cogn. **12**, 695–707 (2003)
17. Tsakiris, M., Haggard, P.: Awareness of somatic events associated with a voluntary action. Exp. Brain Res. **149**, 439–446 (2003)
18. Sahaï, A., Desantis, A., Grynszpan, O., Pacherie, E., Berberian, B.: Action co-representation and the sense of agency during a joint Simon task: comparing human and machine co-agents. Conscious. Cogn. **67**, 44–55 (2019)
19. Obhi, S.S., Hall, P.: Sense of agency in joint actions: influence of human and computer co-actors. Exp. Brain Res. **211**, 663–670 (2011)
20. Strother, L., House, K.A., Obhi, S.S.: Subjective agency and awareness of shared actions. Conscious. Cogn. **19**, 12–20 (2010)
21. Cozmo SDK Installation for Windows. https://cozmosdk.anki.com/docs/install-win-dows.html. Accessed 22 May 2019
22. Android Debug Bridge. cozmosdk.anki.com/docs/adb.html, Accessed 22 May 2019
23. Obhi, S.S., Hall, P.: Sense of agency and intentional binding in joint actions. Exp. Brain Res. **22**, 655–662 (2011)
24. Chambon, V., Moore, J.W., Haggard, P.: TMS stimulation over the inferior parietal cortex disrupts prospective sense of agency. Brain Struct. Funct. **220**(6), 3627–3639 (2015)
25. Zajonc, R.B.: Social facilitation. Science **149**(3681), 269–274 (1965)
26. Beyer, F., Sidarus, N., Bonicalzi, S., Haggard, P.: Beyond self-serving bias: diffusion of responsibility reduces sense of agency and outcome monitoring. Soc. Cogn. Affect. Neurosci. **12**(1), 138–145 (2017)

Perception of Creative Responses to Moral Dilemmas by a Conversational Robot

Felix Lindner[✉], Barbara Kuhnert, Laura Wächter, and Katrin Möllney

Albert-Ludwigs-University, Freiburg, Germany
{lindner,kuhnertb,waechtel,moellnek}@informatik.uni-freiburg.de

Abstract. Moral HRI is investigating humans' perception and reasoning regarding robots' responses to moral dilemmas. Understanding moral dilemmas as cases of tragedy, we identify creative responses as an alternative to responses based on ethical principles such as deontology or utilitarianism. We propose a computational procedure based on AI planning that can generate such responses. We report results from an exploratory study to obtain a preliminary understanding of how the character of creative ethical reasoning robots is perceived compared to the more commonly discussed utilitarian and deontological robots.

Keywords: Moral HRI · Moral dilemmas · Creativity

1 Introduction

Moral human-robot interaction (HRI) is a discipline devoted to the investigation of social robots that reason and act in ethical domains. Moral HRI can be subdivided into *normative* questions addressing how a robot *should* reason and act in ethical domains, and *descriptive* questions regarding how robots that reason and act in ethical domains are actually *perceived* by humans. Both, normative and descriptive research in moral HRI so far has mainly investigated dilemmatic situations by asking people which choice a robot should make between two outcomes [2], or by asking participants to attribute blame to robots that act in one way or the other, e.g., [10,13].

The common depiction of moral dilemmas in moral HRI studies thus renders ethical dilemmas as problems that have to be solved by some individual facing the choice between several bad outcomes. Then, it is up to the human participants of these studies to judge the robot's action right or wrong. This depiction does not take the tragedy of a moral dilemma into account [12,14]. The tragedy of a moral dilemma points to the fact that the protagonist will feel negatively affected no matter how they decides. Being unsolvable, a moral dilemma can thus be better understood as a burden the failure of society or other circumstances put on individuals rather than a puzzle an individual is supposed to solve [15]. One example is the well-known dilemma of Heinz stealing medicine for his wife,

© Springer Nature Switzerland AG 2019
M. A. Salichs et al. (Eds.): ICSR 2019, LNAI 11876, pp. 98–107, 2019.
https://doi.org/10.1007/978-3-030-35888-4_10

who is seriously ill [5]. The very fact that Heinz is confronted with the dilemma to either steal or to let his wife die points to the immorality of societal circumstances and is calling for action by society rather than him as an individual. This way of reasoning about moral dilemmas requires going beyond the original framing of the dilemma, i.e., creativity. Creativity is often defined as a novel and appropriate solution to a problem or situation [11]. In context of our study, we understand creativity as a type of reasoning which involves originality. Recognizing a moral dilemma as a tragedy constitutes an invitation to exercise creative out-of-the-box reasoning with the goal to avoid such tragedies in future. For example, in the Heinz dilemma creativity may result in formulating the need for health insurance for everyone.

In our earlier studies [9,13], we employed a conversational robot to discuss ethical dilemmas with people in a more open face-to-face dialogue setting. Participants had the opportunity for explicating their uncertainty about what is the right thing to do. Some of them argued neither of the options is morally superior, because it actually does not matter how the protagonist decides. Other participants imagined action possibilities available to the protagonist the original framing of story did not explicitly suggest: For instance, faced with the task to make a judgment about the Coal Dilemma (similar to the classical Trolley Problem), one participant said they still had hope there is another way out, for instance that the protagonist could tell someone about the danger, who then can warn the person about the approaching train. These two kinds of responses show how people are not just either utilitarians or deontologists, but that they can also be fatalistic or creative moral reasoners.

The research questions we investigate in this paper are motivated by the above observations: The first research question asks how a conversational robot can be equipped with the capability to also generate creative responses to moral dilemmas. To this end, we describe an implemented computational method for generating creative responses based on AI planning. The second research question asks how a conversational robot that gives creative responses to moral dilemmas is perceived by people. To this end, we report results from a study with our conversational robot Immanuel [7] which indicate that the robot giving creative responses to three ethical dilemmas is perceived as more appealing compared to the robot giving principle-based (i.e., utilitarian, deontological) or fatalistic responses. As we refer to the three dilemmas throughout the paper, we provide them here:

Coal Dilemma [10]. *The robot currently works in a coal mine, where it is responsible for checking the rail control system. While checking the switching system, the robot noticed that four miners are caught in a train that has lost control. The robot immediately realized if the train continues on its path, it will crash into a massive wall and kill the four miners. If redirected onto the side rail it will slow down and the four miners would be saved; but, on that side rail, the train would kill a single miner who was working there.*

Lying Dilemma [9]. *The robot currently works in the household of a sick elderly man called Mr. Smith. The robot's task is to motivate him to do more exer-*

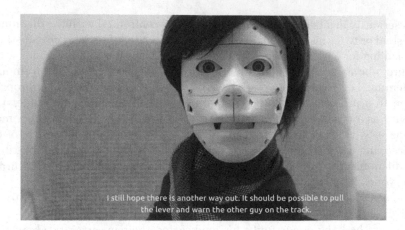

Fig. 1. From the video material used in the study: Immanuel presenting the creative solution to the Coal Dilemma (see below).

> *cises. However Mr. Smith is very hard to motivate. In order to increase his health the robot thought about telling Mr. Smith the lie that its employer will fire the robot, if it cannot succeed in motivating him.*

Child Dilemma [13]. *The robot currently works as child-sitter for a lone-raising parent with a ten year-old child. Recently, the child wanted to watch a movie which is rated as inappropriate for children under twelve years, and which all of the other children have already seen. But it had been forbidden by the parent.*

2   Ethical Dilemmas: Representation and Reasoning

Our argument departs from a classical machine-ethics point of view according to which the basic problem is to judge a given plan (i.e., a possible course of action to respond to the dilemma) for a given planning task (i.e., the description of the dilemma) as morally permissible or not. More specifically, we imagine that the dilemma is modeled as a triple consisting of a planning task Π, a utility function u, and a possible solution π to that planning task. We call this triple a *moral situation* (Definition 1).

Definition 1 (Moral Situation). *A moral situation* S *is a triple* (Π, u, π)*, such that*

- $\Pi = \langle \mathcal{V}, A, s_0, s_\star \rangle$ *is a planning task consisting of*
  - *a set of Boolean variables* $\mathcal{V}$
  - *a set* $A = A_{\mathrm{endo}} \cup A_{\mathrm{exo}} \cup \{\epsilon\}$ *of endogenous actions* A_{endo}, *exogenous events* A_{exo} *and the empty action* ϵ; *All actions and events in* A *are described in terms of preconditions and effects on the values of the variables in* $\mathcal{V}$; *Events have a set of time points associated to them denoting the times at which the events happen;*

- *an initial state s_0, and*
- *a specification of a goal state s_**
- *u is a evaluation of actions and facts, and*
- *π is a plan that solves Π*

As an example, consider the following model of the moral situation $(\langle \mathcal{V}, A_{\text{endo}} \cup A_{\text{exo}}, s_0, s_* \rangle, u, \pi)$ representing the Lying Dilemma that was outlined in the introduction:

$$\mathcal{V} = \{motivated, healthy\}, A_{\text{endo}} = \{lie\}, A_{\text{exo}} = \{improve\}$$
$$lie = \langle \top, motivated:=\top \rangle, improve = \langle motivated=\top, healthy:=\top \rangle$$
$$t(improve) = \{1\}, s_0 = motivated=\bot \wedge healthy=\bot, s_* = healthy=\top$$
$$u = \{lie \mapsto -1, motivated=\top \mapsto 0, motivated=\bot \mapsto 0,$$
$$healthy=\top \mapsto 3, healthy=\bot \mapsto -3\}$$
$$\pi = [lie]$$

Two aspects are relevant here: The motivation of Mr. Smith and his health. Each aspect is modeled as a Boolean variable. There is one endogenous action *lie*, which can always be executed (precondition $\top$) and sets the motivation Mr. Smith to true ($\top$). Moreover, there is an event *improve*, which models the health improvement: If at time point 1 Mr. Smith is motivated (precondition $motivated=\top$), then Mr. Smith will be healthy (as a result of his non-modeled exercises).

A dilemma can be represented as a set of moral situations each describing an alternative way of achieving a (possibly different) goal by executing a plan as a means to accomplish that goal.

Definition 2 (Moral Dilemma). *A moral dilemma is a set of moral situations $\{(\Pi, u, \pi)_i\}$ (Definition 1), such that each situation represents an alternative way of resolving the dilemma.*

We usually assume that $\mathcal{V}$, A, s_0, and u are the same for each moral situation in a moral dilemma, but π and s_* may differ. For example, in the Lying Dilemma, one moral situation is composed of the plan $\pi = [lie]$ with goal $s_* = healthy=\top$, and the alternative is given by $\pi = [\epsilon]$ with goal $s_* = \top$.

Given a moral dilemma, each of the moral situations can be analysed using ethical principles (cf. [8]). Definitions 3, 4, and 5 introduce three of them: Deontology, Utilitarianism, and a principle inspired by Isaac Asimov [1].

Definition 3 (Deontology). *Given a moral situation $S = (\Pi, u, \pi)$, the plan $\pi = \langle a_0, \dots, a_{n-1} \rangle$ is morally permissible according to the deontological principle if and only if $u(a_i) \geq 0$ for all $i = 0, \dots, n-1$.*

Definition 4 (Utilitarian Principle). *Given a moral situation $S = (\Pi, u, \pi)$, the plan $\pi = \langle a_0, \dots, a_{n-1} \rangle$ is morally permissible according to the utilitarian principle if and only if $u(s_n) \geq u(s')$ for all reachable states s', where s_n is the final state reached by π.*

Definition 5 (Asimovian Principle). *Given a moral situation* $S = (\Pi, u, \pi)$, *the plan* $\pi = \langle a_0, \ldots, a_{n-1} \rangle$ *is morally permissible according the Asimovian principle if and only if for all facts* $v=d$, *if* $s_n \models v=d$ *and* $u(v=d) < 0$, *then there is no alternative plan* π', *such that* $s'_{n'} \not\models v=d$, *where* s_n *and* $s'_{n'}$ *are the final states reached by* π *and* π', *respectively.*

Applied to the Lying Dilemma, Child Dilemma, and Coal Dilemma from the introduction, these three principles yield different judgments: Both the Asimovian principle and the utilitarian principle permit lying in the Lying Dilemma (as long as no long-term bad consequences such as possible loss of trust are assumed) and forbid refraining from it, deontology forbids lying and permits not lying. For the Child Dilemma, deontology permits only not showing the movie (given the action is modeled as an instance of rule breaking), utilitarianism and the Asimovian principle permit only showing the movie (given the model does not assume any long-term bad consequences). Deontology permits both pulling the lever (given it is not modeled as an instance of murder) and refraining from it, utilitarianism only permits pulling the lever, and the Asimovian principle forbids either possibility. Hence, the Asimovian principle, which forbids causing any harm, may trigger a case for fatalistic or creative responses.

As a first step towards simulating various moral responses, we calculate a moral response of an agent embracing some ethical principle p by considering the following distinctions:

1. The moral dilemma $\{(\Pi, u, \pi)_i\}$ consists of some moral situation $(\Pi, u, \pi)_j$, such that π is judged permissible by ethical principle p. In this case, the agent can explain it will perform plan π, because the plan is morally permissible.
2. If none of the plans in the alternative moral situations is permissible according to p, two different responses are possible: The *fatalistic response* argues that any of the plans in $\{(\Pi, u, \pi)_i\}$ can be performed, because none of them is permissible. Conversely, the *creative response* first constructs an alternative moral situation (Π^*, u^*, π^*) which was not already part of the moral dilemma and which is permissible according to p. The manipulations done to (Π, u, π) to obtain (Π^*, u^*, π^*) may consist of postponing events (e.g., to let the trolley in the trolley problem move slower to have time for a rescue attempt), adding variables (e.g., introducing health insurance for everyone in the Heinz dilemma), changing moral utility (e.g., explaining that some bad consequence is actually not as bad), or adding endogenous actions such as reminding Mr. Smith how great life is with his grandchildren:

$$\mathcal{V}^* = \{motivated, healthy\}, A^*_{endo} = \{lie, remind\}, A^*_{exo} = \{improve\}$$
$$lie = \langle \top, motivated := \top \rangle, remind = \langle \top, motivated := \top \rangle$$
$$improve = \langle motivated = \top, healthy := \top \rangle, t(next\_activity) = \{1\}$$
$$s^*_0 = motivated = \bot \wedge healthy = \bot, s^*_\star = healthy = \top$$
$$u^* = \{lie \mapsto -1, motivated = \top \mapsto 0, motivated = \bot \mapsto 0,$$
$$healthy = \top \mapsto 3, healthy = \bot \mapsto -3, remind \mapsto 0\}$$
$$\pi^* = [remind]$$

Due to space constraints, we refer to our project website http://www.hera-project.com for more detailed explanations of the computational implementation of the creative-response generation.

3   Perception of a Robot's Creative Responses

One objection against creative responses may be that people avoid to solve the original problem by making up their own one, i.e., they change the rules. It is far from clear, whether such kind of behavior is appealing, especially if it is shown by a robot who was asked for its ethical judgment to a given dilemma. To investigate this question, we set up an online study where four responses (fatalistic, utilitarian, deontological, and creative) were given by our robot. We predict that the four configurations implemented in the conversational robot are perceived as different personalities (**Hypothesis 1**), and that the conversational robot offering creative responses and solutions is perceived as creative (**Hypothesis 2**). From our earlier study we know that people strongly prefer the deontological solution to the Child Dilemma (i.e., obey the parent), but that they are very uncertain regarding the other two dilemmas. In these cases of uncertainty, creativity may be a welcomed alternative, and we predict that a creative robot is something new and appealing. Thus, our further hypotheses were: The creative problem solution is the most preferred one in the Coal Dilemma group (G_{CD}) and the Lying Dilemma group (G_{LD}) (**Hypothesis 3a**), the deontological problem solution is the most preferred one in the Child Dilemma group (G_{ChD}) (**Hypothesis 3b**), and the creative personality is the most appealing one (**Hypothesis 4**).

3.1   Methods

Participants. Participants were recruited by self-selection on the online research platform Prolific. They received a monetary compensation of $1.30 £$ for participation. A total of 200 participants (f = 119, m = 78, other = 3) completed the online questionnaire ($M_{age} = 29.6$, $SD_{age} = 10.21$, $min_{age} = 18$, $max_{age} = 66$).

Procedure, Design, and Materials. We conducted an experiment, designed as between-participant study, consisting of four parts. Initially the participants had to read about a moral dilemma a conversational robot is faced with. Depending on which group the participants were randomly assigned to, they either faced the Coal Dilemma (G_{CD}), the Lying Dilemma (G_{LD}), or the Child Dilemma (G_{ChD}). Afterwards, the participants watched four short video sequences showing our conversational robot presenting one different problem solution each. Then the participants had to rate which of the four configurations is best described by 19 different attributes from the RoSAS-Scale [3], as well as the two terms *Companion* and *Advisor*. Three further questions asked for the most preferred problem solution, the most appealing configuration, and if the four different robot configurations represent different personalities. As last part of the experiment the participants were asked to self-assess their own creativity on the Creative Personality Scale (CPS) [4].

3.2   Results

As predicted in H_1, 175 (87,5%) participants experienced the four configurations as different personalities (exact binomial test, two-sided, $p < .001$, $n = 200$). There are further hypothesis-confirming results for H_2: 51 (79,7%) of the participants in the Coal Dilemma group, 52 (71,2%) in the Lying Dilemma group, and 49 (77,8%) in the Child Dilemma group perceived the conversational robot offering creative responses and solutions as creative. For each dilemma, the χ^2 goodness-of-fit test reveals highly significant differences in creativity perception between the four robot types (G_{CD}: $\chi^2(3, N = 64) = 102.45, p < .001$; $G_{LD} : \chi^2(3, N = 73) = 86.29, p < .001$; $G_{ChD} : \chi^2(3, N = 63) = 93.76, p < .001$). The slight differences between the three dilemmas were not significant ($\chi^2(6, N = 200) = 10.87, n.s.$). In accordance with H_{3a} and H_{3b}, the creative problem solution is most preferred in the Coal Dilemma group and the Lying Dilemma group, while the deontological problem solution is the most preferred solution in the Child Dilemma group. 39 (60,9%) of the participants in the Coal Dilemma group ($\chi^2(3, N = 64) = 46.13, p < .001$) and 57 (78,1%) in the Lying Dilemma group ($\chi^2(3, N = 73) = 110.84, p < .001$) stated the creative solution to be their preferred one. 31 (49,2%) of the participants in the Child Dilemma group ($\chi^2(3, N = 64) = 28.87, p < .001$) stated the deontological solution to be their preferred one. Across the three groups, the creative personality is the most appealing one (H_4): 39 (60,9%) of the participants in the Coal Dilemma ($\chi^2(3, N = 64) = 45.38, p < .001$), 54 (74,0%) in the Lying Dilemma ($\chi^2(3, N = 73) = 94.73, p < .001$) and 27 (42,9%) in the Child Dilemma ($\chi^2(3, N = 64) = 13.13, p < .01$) expressed this attitude. See absolute frequencies in Table 1.

Table 1. Most preferred solution and most appealing personality (absolute frequencies per group).

Group	Personality	Preferred	Appealing
G_{CD}	Fatalistic	9	6
	Utilitarian	12	12
	Deontological	4	7
	Creative	**39**	**39**
G_{LD}	Fatalistic	3	3
	Utilitarian	4	6
	Deontological	9	10
	Creative	**57**	**54**
G_{ChD}	Fatalistic	2	10
	Utilitarian	11	9
	Deontological	**31**	17
	Creative	19	**27**

Further Results. Concerning the evaluation of the four robot characters by means of different attributes the results are as follows: 29 (45,3%) of the Coal Dilemma participants, 37 (50,7%) in the Lying Dilemma, and 27 (42,9%) in the Child Dilemma assigned the creative personality to the attribute *Organic*. For each dilemma, the χ^2 goodness-of-fit test reveals highly significant differences between the four robot types ($G_{CD} : \chi^2(3, N = 64) = 15.63$, $p < .01$; $G_{LD} : \chi^2(3, N = 73) = 25.8, p < .001$; $G_{ChD} : \chi^2(3, N = 63) = 11.6$, $p < .01$). The slight differences between the three dilemmas were not significant ($\chi^2(6, N = 200) = 4.31$, *n.s.*). A different outcome shows up for the attribute *Principled*: 22 (34,4%) of the participants in the Coal Dilemma group, 37 (50,7%) in the Lying Dilemma group, and 48 (76,2%) in the Child Dilemma group assigned the utilitarian personality to the attribute *Principled*. For each dilemma, the χ^2 goodness-of-fit test reveals highly significant differences between the four robot types ($G_{CD} : \chi^2(3, N = 64) = 8.38, p < .05$; $G_{LD} : 2(3, N = 73) = 30.4, p < .001$; $G_{ChD} : \chi^2(3, N = 63) = 90.71, p < .001$). Except for the attributes *Just, Honest, Knowledgeable,* and *Fair* in the Coal Dilemma we overall find highly significant differences in the distribution of the absolute frequencies for all other attributes of the RoSAS-Scale. Participants in the Coal and in the Lying Dilemma most frequently rated the creative personality as a companion ($G_{CD} : \chi^2(3, N = 64) = 27.88, p < .001$; $G_{LD} : \chi^2(3, N = 73) = 42.23, p < .001$), whereas in the Child Dilemma the utilitarian personality was most frequently rated as a companion ($G_{ChD} : \chi^2(3, N = 63) = 47.79, p < .001$). Similar results can be observed for the attribute *Advisor*: the Child Dilemma group most frequently rated the deontological personality as an advisor ($G_{ChD} : \chi^2(3, N = 63) = 15.92, p < .01$), whereas the other two groups again chose the creative personality ($G_{CD} : \chi^2(3, N = 64) = 12.88, p < .01$; $G_{LD} : \chi^2(3, N = 73) = 24.04, p < .001$). For absolute frequencies see Table 2. Calculations concerning correlations between the values of the Creative Personality Scale (CPS) and the preferred problem solution respectively the most appealing configuration led to no significant results.

3.3 Discussion

In the present study we examined humans' perception of a robot reasoning differently about various ethical dilemmas. As intended, the participants experienced the four configurations as different personalities, and across the three groups participants perceived the robot offering creative responses as the creative one. The creative personality is the most appealing one across all three groups and is clearly assigned to the attribute *Organic*, i.e., this personality seems to most closely approximate the human being. Conversely, the utilitarian personality is distinctively perceived as *Principled*. Participants in the Coal Dilemma and the Lying Dilemma group favour a creative problem solution. This is not the case in the Child Dilemma. In [13], it has been found that people are very uncertain in the Coal Dilemma and the Lying Dilemma, but not in the Child Dilemma. This suggest that creative responses are particularly appealing if there are no clear preferences. Future studies should investigate in more detail the relationship between moral uncertainty and the appeal of creative responses. In our study,

Table 2. Rating concerning the attributes *Companion* and *Advisor* (absolute frequencies per group).

Group	Personality	Companion	Advisor
G_{CD}	Fatalistic	11	18
	Utilitarian	7	16
	Deontological	12	5
	Creative	**34**	**25**
G_{LD}	Fatalistic	7	9
	Utilitarian	13	13
	Deontological	11	15
	Creative	**42**	**36**
G_{ChD}	Fatalistic	8	11
	Utilitarian	**39**	7
	Deontological	4	**28**
	Creative	12	17

we were not able to detect whether the solution preference or the personality preference depends on the extend of the participant's creativity. The selection of an appropriate instrument to measure creativity will be subject of further research.

Further research is aimed to increase transferability of our work beyond the three dilemmas and beyond the robot we have used. We plan to replicate the study using a more expressive robot. Moreover, in line with [13] the choice of dilemma is critical, and future work will have to take this factor more seriously into account. Research on a systematic analysis of dilemmas is necessary to be able to generalize from responses to particular dilemmas to classes of dilemmas. One way could be to classify dilemmas based on their causal structure as proposed by Kuhnert and colleagues [6]. A limitation of the current computational model of moral dilemmas and the generation of creative responses consists in the need to manually model both the original moral situations and the creative ones. An interesting challenge is how creative moral situations can be generated automatically by systematic variations of the original dilemma.

4 Conclusions

We have presented an argument in favor of considering creative responses to moral dilemmas based on the observation that people sometimes conceptualize a moral dilemma more as a tragedy with no definite solution rather than as a puzzle. We have described an implemented procedure for computing moral responses in the framework of AI planning. In case no action plan is morally permissible, the agent can exercise creativity to derive a new moral situation by alter the original ones, such that the plan in the new moral situation is morally permissible. In an online study we found that creative responses were rated as most appealing across three different moral dilemmas. This result paves the way for exploring creative responses for ethical reasoning robots further.

References

1. Asimov, I.: Runaround. Gnome Press, New York (1950)
2. Awad, E., et al.: The moral machine experiment. Nature **563**, 59–64 (2018)
3. Carpinella, C.M., Wyman, A.B., Perez, M.A., Stroessner, S.J.: The robotic social attributes scale (RoSAS): development and validation. In: HRI 2017 Proceedings of the 2017 ACM/IEEE International Conference on Human-Robot Interaction, pp. 254–262 (2017)
4. Kaufman, J.C., Baer, J.: Sure, i'm creative – but not in mathematics!: self-reported creativity in diverse domains. Empirical. Stud. Arts. **22**(2), 143–155 (2004)
5. Kohlberg, L.: The Philosophy of Moral Development Moral Stages and the Idea of Justice. Harper & Row, San Francisco (1981)
6. Kuhnert, B., Lindner, F., Bentzen, M.M., Ragni, M.: Perceived difficulty of moral dilemmas depends on their causal structure: a formal model and preliminary results. In: Proceedings of the COGSCI 2017 (2017)
7. Lindner, F., Bentzen, M.M.: The hybrid ethical reasoning agent IMMANUEL. In: Proceedings of the Companion of the 2017 ACM/IEEE International Conference on Human-Robot Interaction, pp. 187–188. ACM (2017)
8. Lindner, F., Mattmüller, R., Nebel, B.: Moral permissibility of action plans. In: Proceedings of AAAI, vol. 2019, no. 33, pp. 7635–7642 (2019). https://doi.org/10.1609/aaai.v33i01.33017635
9. Lindner, F., Wächter, L., Bentzen, M.M.: Discussions about lying with an ethical reasoning robot. In: Proceedings of the 26th IEEE International Symposium on Robot and Human Interactive Communication (RO-MAN), pp. 1445–1450. IEEE, New York (2017)
10. Malle, B.F., Scheutz, M., Arnold, T., Voiklis, J., Cusimano, C.: Sacrifice one for the good of many?: people apply different moral norms to human and robot agents. In: HRI 2015 Proceedings of the 2015 ACM/IEEE International Conference on Human-Robot Interaction, pp. 117–124. ACM, New York (2015)
11. Runco, M.A.: Everyone has creative potential. In: Sternberg, R.J., Grigorenko, E.L., Singer, J.L. (eds.) Everyone Has Creative Potential, pp. 21–30. American Psychological Association, Washington (2004)
12. Sommaggio, P., Marchiori, S.: Break the chains: a new way to consider machine's moral problems. BioLaw J. Rivista di BioDiritto **3**, 241–257 (2018)
13. Wächter, L., Lindner, F.: An explorative comparison of blame attributions to companion robots across various moral dilemmas. In: Proceedings of the 6th International Conference on Human-Agent Interaction (HAI 2018), pp. 269–276. ACM, New York (2018)
14. Weber, T.B.: Tragic dilemmas and the priority of the moral. J. Ethics. 4(3), 191–209 (2000). https://doi.org/10.1023/A:1009864421398
15. Weston, A.: Creative Problem-Solving in Ethics. Oxford University Press, New York (2006)

Detection of Generic Human-Object Interactions in Video Streams

Lilli Bruckschen[1]([✉]), Sabrina Amft[3], Julian Tanke[2], Jürgen Gall[2], and Maren Bennewitz[1]

[1] Humanoid Robots Lab, University of Bonn, Bonn, Germany
`brucksch@cs.uni-bonn.de`
[2] Institute of Computer Science III, University of Bonn, Bonn, Germany
[3] Human-Centered Security, Leibniz University Hannover, Hanover, Germany

Abstract. The detection of human-object interactions is a key component in many applications, examples include activity recognition, human intention understanding or the prediction of human movements. In this paper, we propose a novel framework to detect such interactions in RGB-D video streams based on spatio-temporal and pose information. Our system first detects possible human-object interactions using position and pose data of humans and objects. To counter false positive and false negative detections, we calculate the likelihood that such an interaction really occurs by tracking it over subsequent frames. Previous work mainly focused on the detection of specific activities with interacted objects in short prerecorded video clips. In contrast to that, our framework is able to find arbitrary interactions with 510 different objects exploiting the detection capabilities of R-CNNs as well as the *Open Image* dataset and can be used on online video streams. Our experimental evaluation demonstrates the robustness of the approach on various published videos recorded in indoor environments. The system achieves precision and recall rates of 0.82 on this dataset. Furthermore, we also show that our system can be used for online human motion prediction in robotic applications.

Keywords: Intention understanding · Video understanding · Domestic robots

1 Introduction

The ability to detect interactions of humans with objects is of great use for a variety of applications, especially for service robots. Examples include the identification of customer browsing patterns in retail scenarios [8], activity recognition based on used objects and monitoring of daily activities [14,15], and, as we

This work has been supported by the DFG Research Unit FOR 2535 Anticipating Human Behavior.

showed in our previous paper, the prediction of human movements based on subsequent object interactions [1]. We now present a system that extracts such interactions from RGB-D streams. Most work regarding interaction detection focuses on well-constrained scenarios often with the goal to identify a small set of potential activities in prerecorded videos [10,12]. In this paper, we present a novel approach to detect and extract arbitrary human-object interactions from video streams, which is based on spatio-temporal and pose information. To achieve robustness, our framework verifies interactions found in one frame using subsequent observations. In contrast to existing detection approaches, we do not assume specific activities but allow for the detection of arbitrary human-object interactions with 510 different objects from the *Open Image* dataset [7]. Our framework focuses on video streams, but can also be applied to static images or pre-recorded videos. We define a human-object interaction as an action in which a human places at least one hand on an object while facing it, see Fig. 1 for a demonstration. Our method detects relevant objects inside each frame using regional convolutional neural networks (R-CNNs) [3] and estimates humans and their body pose using the *OpenPose* system [2]. We then detect possible interactions based on the pose of the human and spatial information about humans and objects. To deal with uncertainty in the observations, our system computes for each found interaction the likelihood that it really occurs by tracking it over subsequent frames. The output of our framework is the set of all detected human-object interactions with a sufficiently high likelihood. Figure 1 illustrates the methodology of our approach.

As our approach is constrained by the types of recognizable objects our framework is able to utilize a vast amount of available training data [7]. This allows us to recognize any interaction with objects known by an interchangeable R-CNN.

(a) (b)

Fig. 1. Our system detects human-object interactions based on object positions (purple) as well as pose and orientation information of the human (green) (a). To deal with uncertainty in the observations, we then compute for each found human-object interaction the likelihood that this interaction really occurs using previous observations (b). In this example, the human interacts with the coffee machine over several frames, resulting in a high likelihood for this interaction. (Color figure online)

At the time of publication, our system is able to detect interactions with 510 different objects. We will publish the source code of our framework.

As we show in the experimental evaluation our system achieves recall and precision rates of 0.82 with respect to the detection of human-object-interactions. We additionally show the application of our system to predict human motions online and improve existing motion prediction systems [1].

2   Related Work

The detection of interactions between humans and objects is closely intertwined with activity recognition, as the type of the used object is typically associated with an activity.

An interesting work in this context is presented by Prest *et al.* [10]. The goal of the authors is to detect smoking and drinking activities in realistic videos. To accomplish this, Prest *et al.* trained an action classifier on example interactions and use this classifier in combination with a generic, part-based human detector [11] to spot the previously learned interactions in a prerecorded video. The system tracks objects and persons in space and time and uses the action classifier on the tracked data. In contrast to our approach the application domain of this system is limited, as it is only able to detect interactions with cigarettes and glasses. Similarly Yang *et al.* [14] proposed to use object and interaction information to assign a predefined role, in their example *kidnapper* and *hostage*, to a human. To detect human-object interactions, the authors apply depth information and R-CNNs [3] and assume that an object is in use when it is very close to a human in terms of position and depth. As interaction detection is primarily done using position information obtained from an R-CNN, detection errors can easily lead to wrong results. While our framework also uses an R-CNN, we additionally make use of pose and spatio-temporal information to increase the robustness of the detection.

Several other related systems use static images rather than videos for example the work by Yao *et al.* [15]. The authors use the assumption that objects are associated with activities with the goal to increase object detection rates in static scenes by utilizing information about pose and activities of humans. The work of Gupta *et al.* [5] follows a similar idea. The authors propose a Bayesian model that incorporates functional and spatial context for object and action recognition. Another approach that focuses on action detection in static images was presented by Gkioxari *et al.* [4]. The authors detect humans and objects with an R-CNN and estimate action-type specific densities to localize the used object. In most cases, this corresponds to the position of a hand of the human.

In our work we use pose information [5,15], especially about the hands of the human [4], alongside R-CNNs [3] to detect possible interactions in individual frames. We then apply a verification step in the video stream to deal with false positive detections. We extend the state of the art by allowing arbitrary interactions with known objects, thereby shifting the focus from action recognition to the detection of human-object interactions, allowing the use of a large amount of freely available training data [7]. Several applications can utilize the information provided by our framework ranging from motion prediction, as we show in this work, to intention or activity recognition at a larger scale.

3 Detection of Human-Object Interactions

Our goal is to detect all human-object interactions that occur in a video stream. We define a human-object interaction as an action in which a human places at least one hand on the object while facing it, see Fig. 1 for an illustration.

A video stream is a sequence of frames $V = [f_0, ..., f_t]$ with f_0 as the first observed frame and f_t as the currently observed frame at time t. Our approach uses the current frame f_t and all previously found interactions on $[f_0, ..., f_{t-1}]$ as input and returns all human-object interactions in V.

In summary, our approach to find all human-object interactions inside V works as follows:

1. Apply an R-CNN to detect objects and the *OpenPose* system [2] to detect humans and their poses from RGB data.
2. Use position and depth data to find overlaps between object bounding boxes and human hand positions. Use pose information of the human to check whether they are facing an object that overlaps with their hand, if so, record a possible interaction.
3. Update the likelihood of interactions based on the new observations. This step is necessary to verify that a detected interaction really occurs.

The output of our system are all human-object interactions with a likelihood over a threshold min_L, which is determined using a training data set. A learning process for min_L is shown in our evaluation. An example video demonstrating our approach is shown on our website[1].

3.1 Detection of Objects and Humans and Estimation of the Human Pose

To efficiently detect objects in the current frame we use an R-CNN from Google's object detection API [6], which was trained on the Open Images dataset [7]. Note that the R-CNN is interchangeable and its object detection capabilities can be extended using transfer learning techniques [9] in case new objects need to be detected. For the detection of humans and their poses we apply the *OpenPose* framework [2]. The estimated pose directly contains information about the position of ears, eyes, nose, shoulders, hands, and legs of the human. We further trained an estimator to classify the general direction in which the human is oriented. We use as orientations with respect to the point of view of the camera: *right*, *left*, *back*, and *frontal*. The estimation is based on information about the visibility of the ears, eyes, nose and shoulders. During this step, we used pre-existing systems. In the following, novel approaches are presented.

---

[1] https://www.hrl.uni-bonn.de/icsr_interaction_demo.mp4.

3.2 Detection of Possible Human-Object Interactions

Depending on the results of the orientation estimation we can infer which objects the human is facing based on their x coordinates in the frame and depth levels with respect to the human. In particular, our approach processes each detected object in the current frame and checks whether the following conditions are satisfied for f_t:

- The position of a human hand is inside the bounding box of the object.
- The human is facing the object.
- The depth level of the hand and the object are similar.

If an object fulfills all these conditions, a possible interaction of the human with this object is recorded for f_t.

3.3 Dealing with False Positive and False Negative Detections of Human-Object Interactions

A common problem of human-object interaction systems are false positive object detections [10], e.g., when image regions are wrongly classified as objects. Furthermore, we observed in early tests of our framework a drop in the recall rates due to occlusions while the human interacted with an object, e.g., while drinking from a cup. To deal with such effects, we explicitly consider uncertain observations and compute the likelihood of possible human-object interactions to estimate the probability that the interaction really occurs based on their detection in subsequent frames.

To define the likelihood function, we evaluated the typical minimal length of human interaction with an object on a training data set collected in an university setting. Most interactions were shorter than 12 s. Longer interactions often last for several minutes, e.g., working with a laptop. This results in a distribution with a significant amount of data points during the first 12 s and very scattered data points for longer durations. Using fitting techniques with common probability functions we found that the *gamma probability density function*

$$G(x) = \frac{1}{\Gamma(k)\theta^k} x^{k-1} \exp(-\frac{x}{\theta}) \tag{1}$$

with $k = 5$ and $\theta = 0.9$ and $\Gamma(a)$ as the *gamma function* [13], is a close approximation to the data. The resulting distribution for the first 12 s is visualized in Fig. 2a. As can be seen its fits the data points closely.

Given this distribution we compute the cumulative distribution function $G_C(x)$ of $G(x)$, which models the probability that an interaction has a duration of x or less seconds

$$G_C(x) = \frac{1}{\Gamma(k)} \gamma(k, \frac{x}{\theta}) \tag{2}$$

with $\gamma(a, b)$ as the *incomplete gamma function* [13], see Fig. 2b for a visualization of this cumulative distribution function.

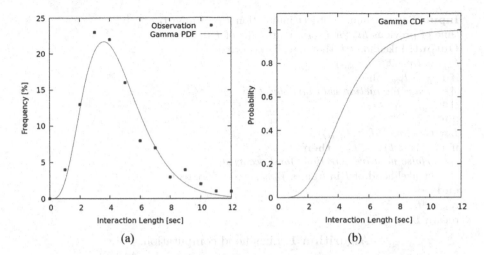

Fig. 2. Gamma probability density function (green) approximating the observed interaction durations (purple) in our real-world data set (a). Cumulative form of the *gamma probability density function* (b) that indicates the probability that an interaction lasts for at most x seconds. Both functions were modeled with $k = 5$ and $\theta = 0.9$. (Color figure online)

Using $G_C(x)$, we determine the likelihoods of the detected possible human-object interactions (see Sect. 3.2) using their estimated duration. In more detail, for an interaction with a given object we say that a frame is a *hit* if an interaction with this object was detected and a *miss* otherwise. To get the length of an interaction over several frames we mark a *hit* as the start point of a new interaction if the elapsed time since the last *hit* for this interaction is greater than a threshold $t_{max} = 5\,s$. We determined this value from $G_C(x)$ as 50% of the interactions are within a duration of 5 s. Not detecting a single *hit* for a specific human-object interaction during this time is a strong indication that no interaction with the object took place. First, each likelihood is initialized with 0 for all objects in each frame. Then, we compute the likelihoods of all detected interactions and possibly update the likelihoods of object interactions on previous frames where the interaction was not detected. Algorithm 1 lists our complete approach to compute the likelihood of an observed human-object interaction, with *timeDiff*(a, b) as the time difference between a and b.

Input: Possible human-object interaction I on frame f_t,
time of previous *hit* for I t_{phit}, start time of I t_{start}.
Output: Likelihood L that I really occurred.
$t_{diff} = timeDiff(t, t_{phit})$
if $t_{diff} > t_{max}$ **then**
    | *//new interaction with this object*
    | $t_{start} = t$
end
$L = G_C(timeDiff(t, t_{start}))$
if $(t - 1) < t_{diff} < t_{max}$ **then**
    | *//false negative detections for I occurred*
    | set likelihood of I in frames $f_{tphit+1}, \cdots, f_{t-1}$ to L
end
$t_{phit} = t$
return L

Algorithm 1. Likelihood computation.

4 Experimental Evaluation

We performed extensive experiments to demonstrate the robustness of our approach with respect to precision and recall. Furthermore, we show the improvement that can be achieved by computing the likelihood that an interaction is really happening by considering subsequent observations. In particular, we collected a dataset containing 195 human-object interactions of 10 different people with objects from the *Open Image* dataset [7], over 27 min of video data. All videos were recorded with 12 frames per second in indoor environments[2]. Figure 3 shows 6 example interactions from our dataset in different environments.

We manually created the ground truth for each frame, i.e., the information which human-object interactions are taking place.

4.1 Precision and Recall

We compare the output of our approach on each frame with the ground truth to compute the recall and precision rates. We hereby perform the evaluation with respect to the likelihood value min_L from which on we assume our framework to be certain enough to return a found interaction with an object. Figure 4 shows the evolution of the precision and recall for 100 different values of min_L equally distributed in the range from 0 to 1. The results were fitted with a function using least squares.

Using a min_L value of 0.21 our framework is able to achieve recall and precision rates of 0.82. Accordingly, in practice we use this as threshold for the likelihood as both the recall and precision are relatively high. As can be seen

---

[2] Videos from our dataset are availably under https://www.hrl.uni-bonn.de/icsr2019.

Fig. 3. Six example interactions from our evaluation dataset in different environments.

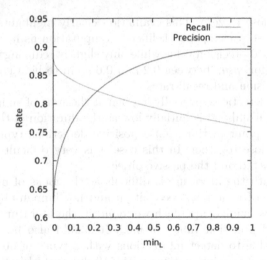

Fig. 4. Evolution of precision and recall rates of our approach with respect to different values of min_L. The precision rate strongly increases with higher min_L values while the recall rate only slowly decreases.

in Fig. 2b this corresponds to a minimal interaction length of approximately 2 s. Shorter minimal interaction lengths are possible but would result in a high precision loss.

Increasing min_L to a value close to 1 results in higher precision values up to 0.88 and lower recall values of 0.75. Decreasing min_L on the other hand has the opposite effect resulting in a precision rate of 0.62 and recall rate of 0.82 for

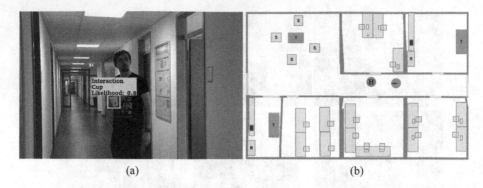

(a)   (b)

Fig. 5. Example application of our approach to predict human movement goals. The robot (red) detects a human-object interaction with a cup using our framework (a). Based on a pre-learned probability distribution about interaction transitions, the likelihood of possible next interaction objects is computed (b). The darker the green the higher the likelihood. Object names are abbreviated: table (T), sofa (S), refrigerator (R), coffee machine (C). (Color figure online)

a value of min_L close to zero. This evaluation clearly highlights the usefulness of the verification step using the likelihood computation as it can significantly improve the returned precision value while only slightly reducing the recall value. In general, values for min_L between 0.2 and 0.6 seem to be a good compromise between high precision and recall rates.

False negative detections naturally happen at the start of an interaction since the corresponding likelihood is initially low as the duration of the interaction is very short at this point in time. False positive detections typically happen if objects are very close together. In this case it is very difficult to differentiate between the interacted and the passive object.

Comparison with the literature is difficult as the focus of most approaches that we are aware of is activity recognition and not human-object interaction detection. The most similar approach we found in the literature [10] lists recall values of 0.90 and precision values of 0.62. It should also be noted that this system was only able to detect interactions with 2 types of objects, while our approach is able to detect interactions with 510 different objects.

4.2   Application to Human Motion Prediction

As demonstrated, our framework is able to robustly detect human-object interactions in video streams. By applying the system online to the video stream recorded with the camera of a real robot, the robot is able to predict human motions. To do so, we first learn a distribution from collected data to represent the probability that after an interaction with an object A the human will next interact with an object B. The robot can then use this knowledge to predict future movement goals of the human based on the known locations of objects in the environment when it detects human-object interactions.

Figure 5 shows an application example. In this scenario, the robot detects a human-object interaction with a cup and computes based on an interaction model transition probabilities to other known objects. The most likely next objects in this example are sofas, tables, refrigerators, and coffee machines.

In our previous work[3], we showed that such knowledge about subsequent object interactions can improve the prediction of human motions compared to approaches which rely on learned trajectories [1].

5   Conclusion

In this paper, we present a novel approach to automatically extract human-object interactions from video streams. In comparison to existing frameworks, our system focuses on the detection of general interactions with objects rather than specific activities. Furthermore, we use spatio-temporal information to verify found interactions. We use an R-CNN to detect objects and the *OpenPose* pose estimator [2] to detect humans and their poses. Based on this information, we find human-object interactions on the current frame and compute for each interaction the likelihood that it is really happening based on subsequent observations.

As the experimental evaluation demonstrates, our approach is able to robustly detect human-object interactions with recall and precision rates of 0.82 on our test dataset.

Acknowledgments. We would like to thank Nils Dengler, Sandra Höltervennhoff, Sophie Jenke, Saskia Rabich, Jenny Mack, Marco Pinno, Mosadeq Saljoki and Dominik Wührer for their help during our experiments.

References

1. Bruckschen, L., Dengler, N., Bennewitz, M.: Human motion prediction based on object interactions. In: Proceedings of the European Conference on Mobile Robots (ECMR) (2019)
2. Cao, Z., Simon, T., Wei, S.E., Sheikh, Y.: Realtime multi-person 2d pose estimation using part affinity fields. In: Proceedings of the IEEE Conference Computer Vision Pattern Recognition (CVPR) (2017)
3. Girshick, R., Donahue, J., Darrell, T., Malik, J.: Rich feature hierarchies for accurate object detection and semantic segmentation. In: Proceedings of the IEEE Conference Computer Vision Pattern Recognition (CVPR) (2014)
4. Gkioxari, G., Girshick, R., Dollár, P., He, K.: Detecting and recognizing human-object interactions. In: Proceedings of the IEEE Conference Computer Vision Pattern Recognition (CVPR) (2018)
5. Gupta, A., Kembhavi, A., Davis, L.S.: Observing human-object interactions: using spatial and functional compatibility for recognition. IEEE Trans. Pattern Anal. Mach. Intell. **31**(10), 1775–1789 (2009)

---

[3] A video showing the capabilities of this approach can be found under https://www.hrl.uni-bonn.de/icsr_application_demo.mp4.

6. Huang, J., et al.: Speed/accuracy trade-offs for modern convolutional object detectors. In: Proceedings of the IEEE Conference Computer Vision Pattern Recognition (CVPR) (2017)
7. Krasin, I., et al.: Openimages: a public dataset for large-scale multi-label and multi-class image classification (2017)
8. Li, H., Ye, C., Sample, A.P.: IDSense: a human object interaction detection system based on passive UHF RFID. In: Proceeding of the ACM Conference on Human Factors in Computing Systems. ACM (2015)
9. Li, Z., Hoiem, D.: Learning without forgetting. IEEE Trans. Pattern Anal. Mach. Intell. (TPAMI) **40**(12), 2935–2947 (2018)
10. Prest, A., Ferrari, V., Schmid, C.: Explicit modeling of human-object interactions in realistic videos. IEEE Trans. Pattern Anal. Mach. Intell. (TPAMI) **35**(4), 835–848 (2013)
11. Prest, A., Schmid, C., Ferrari, V.: Weakly supervised learning of interactions between humans and objects. IEEE Trans. Pattern Anal. Mach. Intell. (TPAMI) **34**(3), 601–614 (2012)
12. Rohrbach, A., et al.: Coherent multi-sentence video description with variable level of detail. In: Jiang, X., Hornegger, J., Koch, R. (eds.) GCPR 2014. LNCS, vol. 8753, pp. 184–195. Springer, Cham (2014). https://doi.org/10.1007/978-3-319-11752-2_15
13. Weisstein: Gamma function. http://mathworld.wolfram.com/GammaFunction.html. Accessed 24 Feb 2019
14. Yang, C., et al.: Knowledge-based role recognition by using human-object interaction and spatio-temporal analysis. In: Proceedings of IEEE International Conference on Robotics and Biomimetics (ROBIO) (2017)
15. Yao, B., Fei-Fei, L.: Modeling mutual context of object and human pose in human-object interaction activities. In: Proceedings of Computer Vision and Pattern Recognition (CVPR) (2010)

More Than You Expect: Priors Influence on the Adoption of Intentional Stance Toward Humanoid Robots

Jairo Perez-Osorio[1(✉)], Serena Marchesi[1], Davide Ghiglino[1],
Melis Ince[2], and Agnieszka Wykowska[1]

[1] Instituto Italiano di Tecnología, 16152 Genoa, Italy
jairo.perez-osorio@iit.it
[2] Universitá di Trento, 38068 Rovereto, Italy

Abstract. Humans predict others' behavior based on mental state inferences and expectations created on previous interactions. On the brink of the introduction of artificial agents in our social environment, the question of whether humans would use similar cognitive mechanisms to interact with these agents gains relevance. Recent research showed that people could indeed explain the behavior of a robot in mentalistic terms. However, there is scarce evidence regarding how expectations modulate the adoption of these mentalistic explanations. The present study aims at creating a questionnaire that measures expectations regarding the capabilities of the robot and testing whether these priors modulate the adoption of the intentional stance toward artificial agents. We found that individual expectations might influence the adoption of mentalistic explanations. After a show period of observation, participants with higher expectations tended to explain iCub's behavior in mentalistic terms; meanwhile, participants with lower expectations maintained their mechanistic explanations of behavior. Our findings suggest that expectations about capabilities and purpose of the robot might modulate the adoption of intentional stance toward artificial agents.

Keywords: Expectations · Adoption of intentional stance · iCub robot · Priors · Human-robot interaction

1 Introduction

Social interaction strongly depends on predictions. The rich social environment requires to anticipate the next step, predict and understand others' behavior by inferring their mental states [2–4]. When we predict others' behavior using mental states, we adopt the intentional stance. Humans adopt the intentional stance or use mentalistic explanations to understand the behavior of complex systems like other animals, computers, and groups of people. This predictive strategy is crucial for social interaction. However, nowadays, the type of agents with whom humans interact has diversified. From the hated chatbots to humanoid robots, passing through virtual agents, we face a wide variety of social interaction counterparts. In this context, it is plausible to ask whether humans would use the intentional stance to interact and predict

---

The original version of this chapter was revised: the acknowledgement section was added. The correction to this chapter is available at https://doi.org/10.1007/978-3-030-35888-4_70

M. A. Salichs et al. (Eds.): ICSR 2019, LNAI 11876, pp. 119–129, 2019.
https://doi.org/10.1007/978-3-030-35888-4_12

the behavior of artificial agents [5]. Moreover, if that is the case, it is still unknown which factors would modulate the adoption of this strategy.

Research in HRI has turned toward understanding whether adopting the intentional stance plays a role in social interaction with artificial agents. However, there is mixed evidence. For instance, Krach et al. [6] and Chaminade et al. [7] suggested that robots do not naturally evoke the adoption of the intentional stance. Both studies found that interactions with artificial agents failed to elicit neural correlates of the intentional stance. On the contrary, a couple of studies [8, 9] revealed that observing a robot performing goal-directed actions elicit similar mirror neuron system activity compared to observing other humans; suggesting that artificial agents indeed evoke the intentional stance. In the same line, Wykowska et al. [10] found that observing a robotic agent performing grasping and pointing actions can bias perceptual processing in a similar way as observing a human agent does. In other words, participants judged robots and humans as goal-driven agents.

More recently, particular interest has been driven toward how and when humanoid robots evoke mentalistic explanations of behavior [10–13]. In particular, [14] asked participants to observe images of robots and people performing comparable actions and asked to explain their behavior. Participants tended to adopt the intentional stance toward the robot (use mentalistic explanations of its behavior). Furthermore, Marchesi et al. [1] found that, in specific contexts, participants tended to adopt the intentional stance towards humanoid robots. These authors developed the Instance Questionnaire (ISQ), which systematically explores the spontaneous adoption of intentional stance toward the humanoid robot iCub [15, 16]. The aim was to evaluate whether people explained the behavior of iCub using mentalistic or mechanistic terms. Each item of the questionnaire depicted the robot in a sequence of three photographs. Participants were asked to rate whether the behavior of the robot was motivated by a mechanical cause or by a mentalistic reason. Results showed that participants had a preference for mechanistic explanations, in line with previous findings [6, 12, 17]. However, two interesting findings were reported: some scenarios evoked more mentalistic explanations (relative to the mean scores), and some participants were more likely to choose mentalistic explanations; meanwhile, others preferred mechanistic explanations. Authors concluded that (a) human-like appearance of the robot, the kind of action context and the goal-oriented behavior are crucial for attribution of mentalistic explanations; and (b) individual differences play a role in the explaining robot's behavior. Thus, it seems that expectations regarding artificial agents' capabilities modulate the likelihood of adoption of the intentional stance. However, results did not allow to determine how these expectations influenced participants' responses.

1.1 Expectations About Robot Behavior

Robots are all over the media. Every day news and social media mention how robots are smarter and more capable. Although, we are far from achieving all that the media promises, such exposure to technology has created high expectations regarding what robots capable of. In this context, researchers have focused on developing tools that measure general preferences and expectations toward robots and assessing how preferences might impact HRI [18]. Users preferred robots that look like machines, that are predictable, smart but controllable, polite, and with human-like speech (for review see [19] and [20]). People also expect robot behavior to be coherent and sensitive to the (social) context [21]. The expectations seem to be tightly connected to the purpose/task of the robot. In general, people expect robots to be reliable [22], simple, predictable, precise (without errors), autonomous but not independent, without a human-like personality [19], and in general to be taking care of repetitive tasks instead to be involved in social tasks [20]. These general expectations have been measured using open questions, interviews or with standardized questionnaires. For example, scales like the Negative Attitudes towards Robots Scale (NARS) [23] (that evaluates reactions and expectations about the behavior of robots) and the Frankenstein Syndrome Questionnaire (FSQ) [24] (that measures people's acceptance of humanoid robots) have been widely used.

In summary, findings reveal that humans tend to create personal impressions of robots in general based on their previous knowledge and expectations. Such stereotype-like ideas might cascade down and adjust regarding a specific robot and its desired functions (i.e., schools, counters or homes). Ultimately, these priors and expectations might play a crucial role in the social interactions with robots, and, therefore, might modulate the adoption of intentional stance towards artificial agents.

1.2   Aim of the Study

Previous studies have suggested that individual expectations (regarding a determined robot and its role/task/purpose) might influence the adoption of intentional stance toward humanoid robots. However, scarce evidence supports this idea. Hence, the present study aims at identifying whether participants' expectations have an impact on the adoption of intentional stance to explain robot behavior. For this purpose, we first designed and tested a questionnaire to evaluate the expectations of participants about robots. In a subsequent step, we devised an experiment to measure whether individual expectations influence the scoring of Instance questionnaire after observing an iCub performing a task. We aimed at designing a questionnaire sensitive to the inter-individual variations in expectations and measuring whether such variations play a role in the adoption of intentional stance.

2   RobEx Questionnaire Design

We designed a questionnaire, RobEx, to measure the expectations toward a specific robot. Identify this information might facilitate the interpretation of the subjective and objective data collected in HRI experiments. The items evaluate expectations about the capabilities, usefulness, behavioral repertoire, pleasantness, and safety during the interaction with iCub. The items were inspired by previous questionnaires and by our own observations during previous experiments. Note that the questionnaire was developed and tested using the humanoid robot iCub, but it was designed for any robot platform. Participants were asked to observe a picture of iCub (Fig. 1, panel A) before answering the questions. The picture depicted iCub in a neutral position to avoid creating any positive or negative bias. Table 1 shows the items of the questionnaire in the first column. The items were designed in English and then translated to Italian. Participants responded to each question of the sub-scales using a 6-point Likert scale (6 - "Completely agree" to 1 - "Completely disagree"). The questionnaire includes 18 items with positive and reverse-formulated items. For its administration, the items were divided into two sections into different pages, each one containing either the positive or the reverse item. The order of the items was randomized before data collection, and each participant solved the questions in the same order.

2.1 Participants

The questionnaire was administered online to 101 Italian people (66 men) using the platform SoSci (https://www.soscisurvey.de). Eighty-two participants were between 18–35, nine between 35–49 and nine between 50–65 years old. Responders were recruited via email or through social media. Before responding to the questionnaire, participants signed an informed consent digital form, followed by a demographic survey including age, gender, marital status, education level, and work field.

Table 1. Items from the RobEx questionnaire, component identified, and saturation.

Item (I think this robot…)	Component and saturation	Item (I think this robot…)	Component and saturation
1. Can protect personal privacy	1 (.494)	10. Would not be able to hurt anyone	3 (.700)
2. Would not be a good home assistant	1 (.724)	11. Can violate personal privacy	3 (.814)
3. Is capable of easing daily tasks for people	1 (.775)	12. Could harm people	3 (.825)
4. Would do a great job as a home assistant	1 (.819)	13. Has limited mechanistic movements	4 (.461)
5. Is unable to help people on daily task	1 (.821)	14. Has human-like movements	4 (.660)
6. Would be a boring interaction partner	2 (.600)	15. Can do only a few tasks	4 (.720)
7. Is capable of being an enjoyable interaction partner	2 (.765)	16. Is constantly controlled by someone	5 (.884)
8. Is not able to hold a conversation	2 (.783)	17. Can adapt to the environment	6 (.626)
9. Can hold a conversation with people	2 (.834)	18. Can operate itself without human intervention	6 (.767)

2.2 Analysis

Descriptives of each item and inter-item correlations with reliability were examined. Additional analysis of the principal component analysis (PCA) was performed to identify the effect of the different component on the total variance. Further analyses included calculation Cronbach's alpha. Besides, to investigate the effects of the education level, and field of work within two groups as Humanities (i.e., psychology) vs. Non-humanities (i.e., engineer) occupations. All the analysis were performed using SPSS.

2.3 Results

Reliability. The Principal Component Analysis (PCA) showed six main components. Initial eigenvalues indicated that the first two factors explained 35% and 14% of the variance, respectively. The third, fourth, and fifth factors had eigenvalues just over one, and each explained 6%, 5% and 5% of the variance, respectively. Reliability test revealed that Cronbach's alpha for the questionnaire was .837. We also checked for the checked the similarities between the items based on their factor loadings (Table 1).

Regarding the expectations, participants seemed to be predominately optimistic (M = 71.60, SD = 13.80) independent of gender and education. Male participants had higher expectations from iCub (M = 73.80, SD = 14.33) compared to female participants (M = 67.45, SD = 11.86). Male participants expected iCub to have the capability to speak, move, operate itself and be less dependent on human control compared to female participants. All participants expected that iCub would be capable of holding a conversation with a human, operate itself, and have human-like movements rather than mechanical movements. They also expected iCub to be a good home assistant and to protect the privacy of the users. However, only some participants think the robot could help with daily tasks. Finally, participants do not associate iCub with the possibility of physically harm people. Altogether, statistical results showed that questionnaire evaluates the diverse priors regarding any robot, and in this case also about iCub.

3 Implementation of RobEx

After testing the questionnaire, we were interested in measuring whether initial expectations regarding robots (as measured by our RobEx questionnaire) would have an effect on the attribution of mental states to the robot before and after the observation. We assumed that being exposed to an embodied robot might make a difference in the adoption of mental states to explain iCub's behavior. However, we hypothesize that possible differences would depend on the initial expectations of each participant.

3.1 Methods

A total of 44 participants took part in the experiment (M = 24.75 y/o, SD = 3.49, 20 men, 4 left-handed), all had normal or corrected to normal vision, and no one reported a clinical history of psychiatric or neurological diseases. All the volunteers were naïve regarding the purpose of the experiment and provided written informed consent.

Procedure. The whole experiment lasted for about an hour. After completing the informed consent, and before seeing the robot, participants filled in the pre-test questionnaires that included: half of the ISQ, the RobEx questionnaire, the FSQ,

NARS, and RoSAS [25]. Subsequently, they were moved inside a room where they sat down in front of iCub and were asked to attend to the behavior of the robot. The robot was standing in front of a screen. Participants were told that the robot was performing a cognitive task. This was done in order to expose participants to the physical presence of the robot.

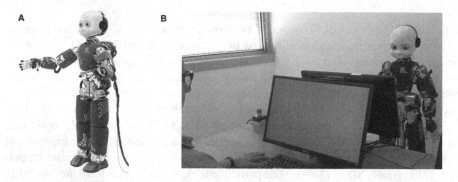

Fig. 1. Panel A shows the picture presented at the beginning of the RobEx questionnaire. Panel B depicts the exposure phase.

During the "exposure" phase, the robot was looking at the screen carefully and fixating a location to simulate that it was making a choice. Participants were not able to see what was on the screen in front of the robot. From the perspective of the participants, the robot always scanned the screen from left to right. From the robot perspective, the robot always gazed first at the right and then to the center of the screen for 5–7 s, alternating these positions. Subsequently, it looked at the left, the center and right of the screen for another 7–10 s, also alternating between them. In some trials, iCub took longer time gazing at the screen, changed facial expressions, and moved the torso back and forth simulating that the task required a more significant effort. Such behavior was presented randomly to all the participants. The objective of this change in behavior was to keep the participants engaged with the observation of the robot. Each participant had a total of 40 trials. Each trial lasted about 20 s. On every trial participants were asked about "what do you think is iCub doing?" to be sure that they were attending to the robot. Participants reported that the behavior was different across trials. The responses to this question are not within the scope of this paper. Right after observing the robot, the participants responded the second part of the ISQ, the God-Speed questionnaire [26], and the Big Five inventory [27]. Finally, participants were debriefed regarding the purpose of the experiment.

Apparatus and Stimuli. The experiment was performed in a noise-attenuating room. Participants were seated in front of a desk. Two screens were used (21 inches), one positioned in front of the robot, and the other in front of the participant, parallel to each other (See Fig. 1, panel B). Participants wrote with a keyboard the response to the question about iCub's behavior at the end of the trial. The screens were tilted back at an angle of 12° from the vertical position. During the experiment iCub was looking at three different locations on the screen relative to the point of view of the robot: (1) right, (2) center and (3) left of the screen.

iCub moved eyes and neck to indicate the position on the screen. The eyes and the neck were controlled by the YARP Gaze Interface, iKinGazeCtrl [28]. The vergence of the eyes was set to 3° and maintained constant. iCub's movements, the screen presentation of the images, and the collection of the responses of the participants were controlled in OpenSesame (an open-source, graphical experiment builder for social sciences [29]) in combination with the iCub middleware YARP (Yet Another Robot Platform [30]), using the Ubuntu 12.04 LTS operating system.

Analysis. Data analysis was conducted on a sample of 44 participants. Similar to Marchesi et al. [1] we calculated the InStance Score (ISS) for each participant converting the bipolar scale into a 0–100 scale. The value 0 corresponded to completely mechanistic and 100 to an utterly mentalistic explanation. The ISS score was computed as the average score of all questions. The ISS was calculated PRE and POST the interaction with the robot. The items were randomly selected to create two groups of 17 items and presented in counterbalanced order to the participants. The aim was to evaluate whether observing the robot performing a task would have any impact on the adoption of mentalistic or humanistic explanations.

Importantly, to measure whether participants expectations' regarding iCub affected the perception of the mentalistic or mechanistic scores, we divided the sample into two groups based on the RobEx scores (median score cutoff = 74, range between 49 and 100). This resulted in two groups of 22 participants each: low expectations (M = 66.27; SD = 6.42) and high expectations (M = 83.45; SD = 6.74). These groups have significantly different scores [$t(42) = -8.657$, $p < .0000$]. We conducted analyses to compare the ISS-PRE and -POST intra and intergroup.

Furthermore, before the interaction, we assessed the general expectations regarding robots using the FSQ, NARS, and ROSAS. That would help us to determine whether these scales that measure the general expectation regarding robots are predictive of the ISS-PRE and -POST. We also analyzed the responses to the Godspeed questionnaire and the BFI. Correlations among all the questionnaires were performed accordingly. All statistical analyses were performed used SPSS.

3.2 Results

In general, participants tended to explain the behavior of the robot in mechanistic terms, similar to the findings reported by [1]. Interestingly, independent sample t-test revealed that PRE scores were not different between groups, $t(42) = 1.414$, p = .165. However, POST scores were significantly different, $t(42) = -2.139$, $p = .038$. These findings suggest that participants' expectations modulated the attribution of mentalistic explanations of iCub's behavior. Planned post hoc comparisons within-group (paired sample t-test) showed that there was no difference between PRE and POST in the low expectations group, $t(21) = 1.069$, $p = .297$; but a significant difference in the High expectations group $t(21) = -2.38$, $p = .027$. Findings suggest that participants that have higher expectations tend to explain the behavior of the robot in mentalistic terms after observation (Table 2).

Table 2. Mean ISS pre- and post-observation for both groups (SD inside the parenthesis).

Group	ISS-PRE	ISS-POST
Low expectations	37.91(9.81)	33.99(15.77)
High expectations	32.31(15.5)	43.27(13.22)

Further analysis of the subscales of the questionnaires applied before the observation of the robot (FSQ, NARS, and ROSAS) did not show any significant differences between groups. Regarding the questionnaires applied after observing the robot, the subscale of animacy from the GodSpeed showed only a trend to significance between the scores of both groups, $t(42) = -1.74$, $p = .089$, slightly higher for the high expectations group (M = 19.00, SD = 4.63) compared to the low expectations group (M = 16.77, SD = 3.80). Similarly, subscales of the Big Five inventory showed no differences between the groups.

Correlations Between Questionnaires

Low Expectations Group: The was a significant inverse correlation between RobEx score and the Situations and Interactions subscale of the NARS, $r(22) = -.472$, $p = .026$. Lower scores on the Situations subscale are linked with higher expectations. RobEx scores were also inversely correlated with the neuroticism score in the BFI, $r(22) = -.544$, p = .009. We also found a significant positive correlation between ISS-POST with both the Expectations subscale of FSQ, $r(22) = .543$, $p = .009$, and the warmth judgement subscale of the RoSAS, $r(22) = .585, p = .004$. Similarly, we found a positive correlation between ISS-POST and the Anthropomorphism subscale, $r(22) = .667, p = .001$.

High Expectations: No significant correlations were found between RobEx scores and any questionnaires. There was only a significant inverse correlation between ISS-POST with the RoSAS Discomfort subscale, $r(22) = -.423$, $p = .049$; and a positive correlation between ISS-POST and the Openness score in the BFI, $r(22) = .485, p = .022$.

4   Discussion

The present study aimed at designing and testing a questionnaire that evaluates participants' expectations regarding a particular humanoid robot and measures whether individual expectations influenced the adoption of mental state based explanations of the behavior of an artificial agent. Our questionnaire proved to be sensitive to the inter-individual variations in expectations across 101 participants on the validation phase. Furthermore, in the experimental phase, we found that expectations play a crucial role in the attribution on mentalistic/mechanistic explanations of the behavior iCub when participants were exposed to the same type of robot behavior. Participants with higher expectations judged the robot more mentalistic after observation, as reflected in the difference between PRE and POST ISQ scores. On the contrary, participants with lower expectations judged the robot as more mechanistic after observation. These suggest that participants approach the robot with a certain level of expectations and tend to confirm their predictions during the observation phase. Interestingly, we found that lower expectations were associated with anxiety during interaction with robots and neuroticism. Meanwhile, high expectations were linked to feeling less discomfort during interaction and a higher degree of openness. Altogether, our findings suggest that individual expectations regarding the capabilities and purpose of a robot might need to be included in the design of experiments and interpretation of data in HRI research. Although some of the components of the standardized scales were related to the Intentional Stance scores, expectations about the robot seemed to have a stronger influence on the explanations that participants gave regarding the behavior of the robot.

In line with the findings of experimental and social psychology (for review see [31]), our findings support the notion that predictions about the behavior of other agents might modulate the adoption of intentional stance. The extensive expertise people have using intentional explanations of behavior might be used to interpret the behavior of artificial agents. However, similar to social interactions with humans, expectations regarding the counterpart capabilities might have an impact on HRI. In this context, our RobEx questionnaire has proven to be a useful and easy tool to measure such expectations. It provides an additional perspective regarding the priors of participants related to the functionality, capabilities, and behavior of a humanoid robot. Future studies should further increment the understanding of the influence of individual priors and ideas and how these are connected with education, occupation, personal interests and the effect of pop culture. Similarly, our findings need to be extended to other humanoid robots and include more interactive scenarios.

In conclusion, we suggest that beyond the general ideas and attitudes about robots, expectations related to the functionality and capabilities of robots might play an essential role in the adoption of intentional stance toward artificial agents and HRI in general.

Acknowledgement. This work received support from the European Research Council (ERC) under the European Union's Horizon 2020 research and innovation program (grant awarded to AW, titled "InStance: Intentional Stance for Social Attunement." G.A. No: ERC-2016-StG-715058).

References

1. Marchesi, S., Ghiglino, D., Ciardo, F., Perez-Osorio, J., Baykara, E., Wykowska, A.: Do we adopt the intentional stance toward humanoid robots? Front. Psychol. **10**, 450 (2019)
2. Dennett, D.C.: Intentional systems. J. Philos. **68**(4), 87–106 (1971)
3. Searle, J.R.: Construction of Social Reality (1995)
4. Malle, B.F.: Attribution theories: how people make sense of behavior. Theor. Soc. Psychol. **23**, 72–95 (2011)
5. Waytz, A., Epley, N., Cacioppo, J.T.: Social cognition unbound: insights into anthropomorphism and dehumanization. Curr. Dir. Psychol. Sci. **19**(1), 58–62 (2010)
6. Krach, S., Hegel, F., Wrede, B., Sagerer, G., Binkofski, F., Kircher, T., et al.: Can machines think? Interaction and perspective taking with robots investigated via fMRI. PLoS One **3**(7), e2597 (2008)

7. Chaminade, T., et al.: How do we think machines think? An fMRI study of alleged competition with an artificial intelligence. Front. Hum. Neurosci. **6**, 103 (2012)
8. Gazzola, V., Rizzolatti, G., Wicker, B., Keysers, C.: The anthropomorphic brain: the mirror neuron system responds to human and robotic actions. Neuroimage **35**(4), 1674–1684 (2007)
9. Oberman, L.M., McCleery, J.P., Ramachandran, V.S., Pineda, J.A.: EEG evidence for mirror neuron activity during the observation of human and robot actions: toward an analysis of the human qualities of interactive robots. Neurocomputing **70**, 2194–2203 (2007)
10. Wykowska, A., Chellali, R., Al-Amin, M.M., Müller, H.J.: Implications of robot actions for human perception. How do we represent actions of the observed robots? Int. J. Soc. Robot. **6**(3), 357–366 (2014)
11. Wykowska, A., Kajopoulos, J., Obando-Leitón, M., Chauhan, S.S., Cabibihan, J.J., Cheng, G.: Humans are well tuned to detecting agents among non-agents: examining the sensitivity of human perception to behavioral characteristics of intentional systems. Int. J. Soc. Robot. **7**(5), 767–781 (2015)
12. Wiese, E., Metta, G., Wykowska, A.: Robots as intentional agents: using neuroscientific methods to make robots appear more social. Front. Psychol. **8**, 1663 (2017)
13. Admoni, H., Srinivasa, S.: Predicting user intent through eye gaze for shared autonomy (2016)
14. Thellman, S., Silvervarg, A., Ziemke, T.: Folk-psychological interpretation of human vs. humanoid robot behavior: exploring the intentional stance toward robots. Front. Psychol. **8**(Nov), 1–14 (2017)
15. Metta, G., et al.: The iCub humanoid robot: an open-systems platform for research in cognitive development. Neural Netw. **23**(8–9), 1125–1134 (2010)
16. Natale, L., Bartolozzi, C., Pucci, D., Wykowska, A., Metta, G.: iCub: the not-yet-finished story of building a robot child. Sci. Robot. **2**(13), eaaq1026 (2017)
17. Chaminade, T., et al.: Brain response to a humanoid robot in areas implicated in the perception of human emotional gestures. PLoS ONE **5**(7), e11577 (2010)
18. Horstmann, A.C., Krämer, N.C.: Great expectations? Relation of previous experiences with social robots in real life or in the media and expectancies based on qualitative and quantitative assessment. Front. Psychol. **10**, 939 (2019)
19. Dautenhahn, K., Woods, S., Kaouri, C., Walters, M.L., Koay, K.L., Werry, I.: What is a robot companion - friend, assistant or butler? In: 2005 IEEE/RSJ International Conference on Intelligent Robots and Systems, IROS (2005)
20. Ray, C., Mondada, F., Siegwart, R.: What do people expect from robots? In: 2008 IEEE/RSJ International Conference on Intelligent Robots and Systems, IROS (2008)
21. Goetz, J., Kiesler, S., Powers, A.: Matching robot appearance and behavior to tasks to improve human-robot cooperation. In: Proceedings - IEEE International Workshop on Robot and Human Interactive Communication (2003)
22. Arras, K.O., Cerqui, D.: Do we want to share our lives and bodies with robots? A 2000-people survey (2005)
23. Syrdal, D.S., Dautenhahn, K., Koay, K.L., Walters, M.L.: The negative attitudes towards robots scale and reactions to robot behaviour in a live human-robot interaction study. Adapt. Emergent Behav. Complex Syst. (2009)
24. Nomura, T.T., Syrdal, D.S., Dautenhahn, K.: Differences on social acceptance of humanoid robots between Japan and the UK. In: Salem, M., Weiss, A., Baxter, P., Dautenhahn, K. (eds.) Proceedings 4th International Symposium on New Frontiers in Human-Robot Interaction, pp. 115–120. The Society for the Study of Artificial Intelligence and the Simulation of Behaviour (AISB) (2015)

25. Carpinella, C.M., Wyman, A.B., Perez, M.A., Stroessner, S.J.: The robotic social attributes scale (RoSAS). In: Proceedings of the 2017 ACM/IEEE International Conference on Human-Robot Interaction - HRI 2017 (2017)
26. Bartneck, C., Kulić, D., Croft, E., Zoghbi, S.: Measurement instruments for the anthropomorphism, animacy, likeability, perceived intelligence, and perceived safety of robots. Int. J. Soc. Robot. 1(1), 71–81 (2009)
27. John, O.P., Srivastava, S.: Big five inventory (BFI). In: Handbook of Personality Second Edition: Theory and Research (1999)
28. Roncone, A., Pattacini, U., Metta, G., Natale, L.: A cartesian 6-DoF gaze controller for humanoid robots. In: Proceedings of Robotics: Science and Systems (2016)
29. Mathôt, S., Schreij, D., Theeuwes, J.: OpenSesame: an open-source, graphical experiment builder for the social sciences. Behav. Res. Methods 44(2), 314–324 (2012)
30. Metta, G., Fitzpatrick, P., Natale, L.: YARP: yet another robot platform. Int. J. Adv. Robot. Syst. 3(1), 8 (2006)
31. Frith, C.D., Frith, U.: How we predict what other people are going to do. Brain Res. 1079(1), 36–46 (2006)

Verbal Interaction with Social Robots

Optimal Use of Verbal Instructions for Multi-robot Human Navigation Guidance

Harel Yedidsion[✉], Jacqueline Deans, Connor Sheehan, Mahathi Chillara, Justin Hart, Peter Stone, and Raymond J. Mooney

Department of Computer Science, The University of Texas at Austin, Austin, USA
harel@cs.utexas.edu

Abstract. Efficiently guiding humans in indoor environments is a challenging open problem. Due to recent advances in mobile robotics and natural language processing, it has recently become possible to consider doing so with the help of mobile, verbally communicating robots. In the past, stationary verbal robots have been used for this purpose at Microsoft Research, and mobile non-verbal robots have been used at UT Austin in their multi-robot human guidance system. This paper extends that mobile multi-robot human guidance research by adding the element of natural language instructions, which are dynamically generated based on the robots' path planner, and by implementing and testing the system on real robots.

Generating natural language instructions from the robots' plan opens up a variety of optimization opportunities such as deciding where to place the robots, where to lead humans, and where to verbally instruct them. We present experimental results of the full multi-robot human guidance system and show that it is more effective than two baseline systems: one which only provides humans with verbal instructions, and another which only uses a single robot to lead users to their destinations.

Keywords: Multi robot coordination · Natural language · Human robot interaction · Indoor navigation

1 Introduction

Finding one's way in an unfamiliar office building, university, or hospital can be a daunting task. Even when provided with navigational instructions, the lack of an indoor localization system, and the lack of reliable pedestrian odometry makes it difficult for humans to successfully follow them. Following instructions is efficient for short sequences, but memorizing a long sequence of instructions is difficult, and the tendency to make mistakes increases with the length of the instruction sequence and the complexity of the environment.

Electronic supplementary material The online version of this chapter (https://doi.org/10.1007/978-3-030-35888-4_13) contains supplementary material, which is available to authorized users.

© Springer Nature Switzerland AG 2019
M. A. Salichs et al. (Eds.): ICSR 2019, LNAI 11876, pp. 133–143, 2019.
https://doi.org/10.1007/978-3-030-35888-4_13

As service robots become increasingly abundant in large buildings [4,12], and steadily more capable of autonomous navigation, there has been growing interest in using them to guide humans in buildings. However, for safety reasons, even state-of-the-art service robots still travel much slower than the average human; therefore, following them is reliable but tedious. Additionally, robots have difficulties changing floors and opening doors.

To mitigate these problems, we developed a system of mobile robots that provides guidance to newcomers to the GDC building at UT Austin. Once a visitor approaches one of the robots and requests to reach a goal location, the system calculates the shortest path to the desired destination, and then, based on the characteristics of each region of the path, decides where a robot will lead the person and where verbal instructions will be provided. The characteristics that are considered for each region are: (i) the length of the path through that region, (ii) the region's traversability by a robot, and (iii) the probability of a human going wrong there.

The use of multiple robots allows for separate intervals of leading and instructing within a single navigational path. The robots that are used in this research are the BWIBots (See Fig. 1), a custom-built fleet of robots that are part of the Building Wide Intelligence (BWI) project [8]. The generation of natural language navigational instructions is based on the robot's planned path and a map annotated with landmarks.

Fig. 1. Three BWIBots used in this study.

We empirically tested the system on human participants who were not familiar with the GDC building, and measured the time it took them to reach a given goal location. Empirical results show that compared to baselines of instructions only and leading only, the combination of leading and instructing provides the best results in terms of minimizing the time to destination and maximizing the success rate.

The remainder of the paper is structured as follows. Section 2 reviews related work. Section 3 formally defines the problem, and Sect. 4 outlines our approach to optimally solving it. Section 5 describes the technical details of implementing of the system on the BWIBots. Section 6 presents the natural language instruction generation module. Section 7 details the experimental evaluation and discusses the results, and Sect. 8 concludes.

2   Related Work

Previous studies of the multi-robot human guidance problem developed a central system whose goal is to guide a person to the destination efficiently, while limiting the robots' time away from their background tasks [6], and later extended it to multiple concurrent guidance tasks [7]. Both of these systems did not make use of natural language instructions, but rather used arrows on the screen to indicate the position of the next robot the human should go to. We extend this research by adding natural language instructions, and by applying and testing the system on real robots.

Another relevant project used a single stationary robot to give verbal instructions inside a building [1]. The paper provides some valuable insights and directions for future work regarding the effectiveness of the robot's generated instructions. The authors discuss the challenge of communicating long paths, which result in directions that are difficult for the listener to understand and retain. We propose to mitigate this challenge by using multiple mobile robots which enable breaking up long instruction sequences to shorter, and more user-friendly ones. This paper [1], and others [5], highlight the use of landmarks as navigational waypoints – a technique we leverage in our work.

Generating natural language navigational instructions has been attempted using a Seq-to-Seq network that was trained on a dataset of human generated instructions for navigating a grid-world domain [2]. Other approaches such as the top performing one in the GIVE 2.5 challenge [10], a competition for natural language generation systems that guide human users through solving a task in a virtual environment, use a template-based method [3]. We use a similar template-based method for generating natural language instructions.

3   Problem Definition

Our problem formulation is similar to that of the Multi-Robot Human Guidance (MRHG) problem [6]. A MRHG problem begins when a human approaches a robot and requests assistance to reach a destination in the building, and ends when the destination is reached. At our disposal we have a team of mobile robots that can autonomously navigate the building. The problem we are studying is how to efficiently utilize them to guide humans to their desired destination in the building as quickly as possible.

Unlike Khandelwal et al. [6], where the set of available guidance actions were either *Direct* (Display a directional arrow on the display interface of a robot) or

Lead (Have the human follow a robot as it navigates to a required location), in our system the robots are augmented with the ability to generate and vocalize natural language instructions and therefore use the action *Instruct* instead of *Direct*.

Our primary objective is to minimize the time it takes the human to reach the destination. Khandelwal et al. [6] also considered minimizing the robots' time away from their background tasks as a secondary objective, which we do not actively try to optimize for. However by simply supplementing the robots with the *Instruct* action, the system is able to reduce the robots' leading time and consequently improve this secondary objective as well.

The notations we use and assumptions we make are as follows. The environment, E, in which guidance assistance is required is a fully connected space which is divided into a set of non overlapping domains D such that $E = \bigcup_{i=1}^{|D|} d_i$. Each domain, $d_i \in D$ has one robot $r_i \in R$ assigned to perform a background task in that domain.

A guidance task, $T(o, g)$ is a request by a human to get from origin location o to goal location g. We assume that at the time a guidance task is created, the human and one robot are co-located at origin o.

The robots can communicate with each other and announce that a new guidance task needs to be performed. We assume that the environment is divided into domains which are small enough to enable the robots to get into the required position in their domain in time to support a high priority guidance task, once it is communicated. The robots can navigate the environment autonomously with an average speed of v_r. We assume that humans travel at an average speed of v_h, and that $v_h > v_r$.

We assume that robots have a map of the environment and can use it to plan the shortest path, p, from origin to goal. The map is divided into a set of regions, L, which correspond to rooms, corridors, elevators, and open spaces, each with attributes of: physical dimensions, neighboring regions, how traversable this region is to a robot, and what is the probability of a human going wrong there while following navigational instructions. Each domain contains several regions. We denote the subset of regions of L that contain path p as L^p.

The robots can reach any given location reliably, i.e., do not make any wrong turns. However, for the robots, some regions are more traversable than others, e.g, the elevator, or the very busy regions are difficult to navigate through. We denote the traversability of region l_j for a robot as trv_j. The harder a region is to traverse, the lower its trv value will be.

Regarding humans, we assume and validate the following assumption empirically: given a set of navigational instructions, humans have some probability of going wrong in every region, and that probability increases as the length of the instruction sequence increases. We denote the inherent navigational complexity of region l_j for a human as cmp_j. The dynamic parameter that represents the number of previously consecutive instructed regions before l_j is denoted as cir_j. The actions that a robot can take to guide a human are:

- *Lead* - The robot asks the human to follow it as it navigates to a desired destination.
- *Instruct* - The robot generates and vocalizes natural language instruction from its current location to a desired destination.

The robots chose one action per region.

We assume that action durations are not fixed and are dependent on the state i.e, the complexity of the region and the number of consecutive previously instructed regions. We also assume that when navigating to a location in a building, humans will eventually reach their destination even if they take a wrong turn, at the expense of longer travel time. This assumption allows us to trade off state transition probabilities with action durations, i.e., if a human is given navigational instructions from origin to goal, and the regions in the path have some probability of going wrong, the human will reach the goal successfully but the time it takes to traverse these regions will be directly affected by the respective probabilities of going wrong. We assume that the time required to say the instructions for a single region is constant and equals t_c.

Thus, the MRHG can be formulated as a stochastic planning algorithm where the goal is to find the plan that results in the shortest time in expectation.

Formally, the MRHG problem is: Given a guidance task $T(o, g)$ in environment E, populated by a set R of robots, each located in its respective domain, find an optimal sequence of actions that will minimize the human's expected time to reach the destination goal g. Denoting t_j as the time estimation per region l_j in the shortest path p from o to g:

$$min \sum_{l_j \in L^p} t_j \quad S.T.$$

- Only one consecutive *lead* sequence per robot.
- The robot can use the *lead* action only at the start of its guidance sequence.
- A robot can only lead in its domain, but can instruct through other domains.
- When a robot instructs to a region in another robot's domain, a transition occurs and requires the robot in that domain to navigate to that region and wait for the human there to start its portion of the guidance task.
- The number of transitions is limited to the number of domains (and robots) in the path.

4   Optimal MRHG Problem Solver

In this section we outline our approach to optimally solve a guidance task $T(o, g)$ for the MRHG problem. First, by using the robot's planner we calculate the shortest path p from o to g. Second, we calculate for each region in the path, $l_j \in L^p$, the length of the path through that region $length(p, l_j)$. Third, the solver calculates a time estimation for each possible combination of *Lead/Instruct* for each robot. In order to calculate the time estimate for a path, we dynamically calculate the additional time per region that is a result of it being in a long chain of consecutive instructed regions. The parameter that represents the number of previously consecutive instructed regions for region l_j is denoted as cir_j. Since a robot is located in transition regions, the probability of going wrong there is reduced by a factor denoted as the robot observably factor, rof. The time estimation per region, t_j, is calculated as follows:

$$
t_j = \begin{cases} (length(p,l_j)/v_r)/trv_j & \text{if } action = Lead \\ (length(p,l_j)/v_h) \cdot cmp_j \cdot (cir_j + 1) + t_c & \text{if } action = Instruct \\ (length(p,l_j)/v_h) \cdot cmp_j \cdot (cir_j + 1)/rof + t_c & \text{if } Transition \text{ at } l_j \end{cases}
$$

For a region where a *Transition* occurs, the probability of going wrong is reduced since we place a robot at the intersection of the two regions and it is harder to miss it as opposed to other less noticeable landmarks.

Finally, the solver chooses the action combination that results in the shortest time. It runs a branch-and-bound search on the tree of possible combinations saving the current minimal combination time and abandoning combinations that result in longer times. This approach speeds up computation compared to brute force search and allows for real-time optimization of paths with up to 10 regions, i.e., without creating an awkward pause in the dialog.

5   Robot Implementation

In this section, we briefly describe the hardware design of the BWIBots [8] used in this study. The robotic platform is built on top of the Segway RMP mobile base. The robots are equipped with a Hokuyo lidar (for navigation and obstacle avoidance), a Blue Snowball microphone, and a speaker (for conducting the dialog). One of the robots is equipped with a Kinova MICO arm (useful for gesturing the initial orientation of the very first sequence).

On the non-armed robots, a Dell Inspiration computer executes all necessary computation and doubles as a user interface. For the arm robot, an Alienware computer is used. The robots' mobile Segway base is reinforced with additional 12V Li-Ion batteries to power the base, arm, computer, and sensors for up to 6 h of continuous operation. The software architecture used on the BWIBots is built on top of the Robot Operating System (ROS) framework [9]. It includes a custom built layered architecture that spans high level planning to low level motion control and allows autonomous navigation in our department building.

Multi-robot communication is achieved using the *rosbridge_suite* and *Node.js* packages running on a central server, and passing ROS messages between the different ROS masters that manage each individual robot. Robot-spoken instructions are delivered using Google's WaveNet text-to-speech [11].[1]

---

[1] The BWI code is open source and can be found here: https://github.com/utexas-bwi.

6   Generating Natural Language Instructions

In this section we present the system for generating natural language instructions for indoor navigation. Given a starting point, ending point, and an annotated map, our system produces landmark-based instructions to a goal location. These instructions are generated by translating the robot's planned path into an intermediate abstract syntax, and then into natural language, using a template-based method [3]. In order to validate the quality of the generated instructions, we conducted a preliminary human study comparing our system's generated instructions to human-generated ones. For human directions, we asked a student who was very familiar with the building, but not with our system, to generate instructions as if someone had asked him how to get there.

Twenty five participants each traveled to four different locations on the GDC third floor after receiving random combinations of human/robot-generated instructions. After each trial, participants answered six questions, each on a 6-point semantic differential scale, each measuring one metric of the quality of the instructions. The metrics were: understandability ("How easy was it to understand the instructions?"), memorability ("How easy was it to remember the instructions?"), informativeness ("How much information did the instructions provide?"), efficacy ("How easily did you arrive at the destination?"), usefulness of landmarks ("How helpful were the landmarks provided in the instructions?"), and naturalness ("How natural did the instructions sound?").

Our system was ranked within 0.75 points of the human generated instructions for each metric, with no statistically significant differences found for understandability ($p = 0.089$) memorability ($p = 0.367$) and informativeness ($p = 0.289$). Most importantly, we timed all participants through each trial and found no statistically significant differences between human- versus robot-generated instructions, according to two-sample t-tests. Thus, following the results of this preliminary system validation, we concluded that our instruction generating module provides sufficiently effective instructions to be used in the full MRHG system.

7   Experiments

Setup - To study the performance of this system, we chose a typical navigation task facing a newcomer to the building. The path starts from the GDC entrance hall and ends in front of an office on the third floor. We recruited 30 participants with no prior knowledge of the building, (12 male, 18 female, ages 12–58), from the UT Austin campus by fliers, email, and word of mouth. We conducted a two-condition inter-participant study contrasting the MRHG condition to the *Instructions* condition, defined as follows. The participants were divided into two groups. The first 15 were only given instructions by the robot and had to follow those instructions to the best of their abilities. The results from this group were used both as a benchmark for the full multi-robot system, and as a means of tuning the parameters for the probability of people going, based on the frequency

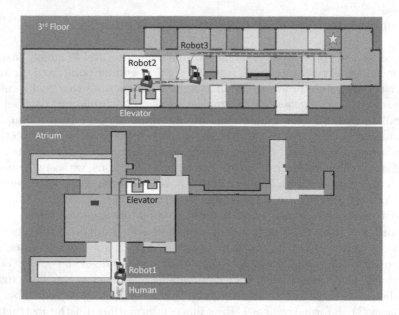

Fig. 2. In this example, a human approaches a robot in the atrium and asks for guidance to an office on the 3rd floor, marked with a star. The robot calculates a plan to optimally guide the human using two other robots through 10 regions. Solid lines represent *Lead* and dashed lines represent *Instruct* regions. Regions are colored uniquely. (Color figure online)

of that occurrence in each region. These parameters were later used by the MRHG optimization module to determine where to lead and where to instruct. The other 15 participants interacted with the full *MRHG* system which utilized 3 robots to lead and instruct the humans to the goal. As another benchmark, we timed a single robot as it navigated from the origin to the destination, averaged over 15 runs. This was done to simulate a *Leading* only guidance solution. A visualization of the path can be seen in Fig. 2 and a demo video of the BWIBots performing a MRHG task with verbal instructions can be viewed here https://youtu.be/5MSdMwfw6QI.

Results - We collected data on the time it took participants to complete each section of the path, if and where they went wrong, and had them fill out a short survey on their impression of the interaction. The time it took to wait and go up the elevator was deducted from all the trials.

Five participants in the instructions-only case got lost and never made it to the destination, whereas all of the MRHG participants made it to the goal, a large difference in success rate of 66% vs. 100%. The participants who went wrong could not remember the entire sequence of instructions, and at some point they got lost and took a wrong turn.

In terms of timing, the *Leading* condition was the slowest with an average of 206 s. Next was the *Instructions* condition with 164 s on average. The fastest was

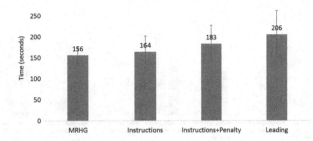

Fig. 3. Comparison of the average time for each guidance method. Error bars represent one standard deviation above and below the average.

the MRHG condition with 156 s on average. The difference in timing between the *Instructions* (164 s) and the MRHG (156 s) condition was not statistically significant (p = 0.254). However, this does not account for the fact that 5 *Instructions* participants failed to reach the destination: we stopped timing their runs once they gave up. Note that this does not contrast our assumption that humans eventually reach the destination since we did not allow participants to ask for additional instructions.

To account for this effect, we add a penalty by assigning them the average time for the participants who got lost but kept looking and eventually reached the destination. For the adjusted *Instructions + Penalty* case we get an average of 183 s which is statistically significantly different from the MRHG condition *(p = 0.026) for a two sample t-test. The *Leading* condition took 206 s on average and is statistically significantly difference from MRHG **(p = 0.003).[2] A bar chart of the results is shown in Fig. 3.

Participants responded to a post-interaction survey of their reactions to the interaction. The questions on the survey were chosen specifically to measure the utility of the robots in this task as well as users' enjoyment of the interaction. Questions were posed on a 5-point scale. The survey results were somewhat inconclusive. On the one hand, the MRHG participants ranked the robots as more friendly (p = 0.064), useful (p = 0.329), helpful **(p = 0.003) and intelligent (p = 0.085). They also ranked the interaction to feel more natural (p = 0.06) than the *Instructions* participants ranked their interaction. On the other hand, they ranked the interaction to feel longer (p = 0.054), and the instructions harder to remember **(p = 0.000), follow **(p = 0.000), and understand **(p = 0.004) compared to the ranking provided by the *Instructions* participants. This result is surprising considering that 100% of the *Instructions* participants requested that the robot repeat the instructions and a third of them didn't make it to the destination. We emphasize that no participant witnessed both the cases, and conclude that more testing should be conducted to establish the perceived ease-of-use of the system. The survey results can be seen in Fig. 4.

---

[2] We mark by * the paired measures for which there is significance at $p \leq 0.05$ and ** for measures at $p \leq 0.01$.

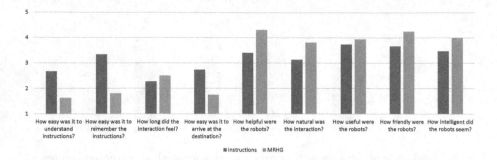

Fig. 4. Survey results of *MRHG* and *Instructions* participants.

8   Conclusions

In this study we developed a system for guiding humans in indoor environments that integrates multi-robot coordination with natural-language instruction generation, which, to the best of our knowledge, is the first system to do so. The system optimizes the guidance process by choosing the robots' locations, the regions through which they lead and the regions through which they instruct, in order to minimize the human's travel time. The instruction-generation module uses the robots' navigational path planner coupled with a landmark annotated map to generate natural language instructions.

The full MRHG system was tested on human participants and performed better than the *Instructions* benchmark in terms of both success rate and time to destination. It also outperformed the *Leading* benchmark in terms of time to destination.

This project showed, for the first time, that using natural language generation is beneficial in multi-robot human guidance systems. In this study we focused on generating natural language instructions based on the robots' planned path which is the shortest path in terms of distance, but might not be the shortest path to guide a human through as there might be a longer path that is easier to guide through. Future work might consider extending this study by optimizing over all possible paths.

Acknowledgment. This work has taken place in the Learning Agents Research Group (LARG) at UT Austin. LARG research is supported in part by NSF (IIS-1637736, CPS-1739964, IIS-1724157), ONR (N00014-18-2243), FLI (RFP2-000), ARL, DARPA, and Lockheed Martin. Peter Stone serves on the Board of Directors of Cogitai, Inc. The terms of this arrangement have been reviewed and approved by the University of Texas at Austin in accordance with its policy on objectivity in research.

References

1. Bohus, D., Saw, C.W., Horvitz, E.: Directions robot: in-the-wild experiences and lessons learned. In: AAMAS, pp. 637–644 (2014)
2. Daniele, A.F., Bansal, M., Walter, M.R.: Navigational instruction generation as inverse reinforcement learning with neural machine translation. In: HRI, pp. 109–118 (2017)
3. Denis, A.: The loria instruction generation system l in give 2.5. In: The European Workshop on Natural Language Generation, pp. 302–306. Association for Computational Linguistics (2011)
4. Eaton, E., Mucchiani, C., Mohan, M., Isele, D., Luna, J.M., Clingerman, C.: Design of a low-cost platform for autonomous mobile service robots. In: The IJCAI Workshop on Autonomous Mobile Service Robots (2016)
5. Hile, H., Grzeszczuk, R., Liu, A., Vedantham, R., Košecka, J., Borriello, G.: Landmark-based pedestrian navigation with enhanced spatial reasoning. In: Tokuda, H., Beigl, M., Friday, A., Brush, A.J.B., Tobe, Y. (eds.) Pervasive 2009. LNCS, vol. 5538, pp. 59–76. Springer, Heidelberg (2009). https://doi.org/10.1007/978-3-642-01516-8_6
6. Khandelwal, P., Barrett, S., Stone, P.: Leading the way: an efficient multi-robot guidance system. In: AAMAS, pp. 1625–1633 (2015)
7. Khandelwal, P., Stone, P.: Multi-robot human guidance: human experiments and multiple concurrent requests. In: AAMAS, pp. 1369–1377 (2017)
8. Khandelwal, P., et al.: Bwibots: a platform for bridging the gap between ai and human-robot interaction research. Int. J. Robot. Res. 36(5–7), 635–659 (2017)
9. Quigley, M., et al.: ROS: an open-source robot operating system. In: ICRA Workshop on Open Source Software, vol. 3, p. 5 (2009)
10. Striegnitz, K., Denis, A., Gargett, A., Garoufi, K., Koller, A., Theune, M.: Report on the second second challenge on generating instructions in virtual environments (GIVE-2.5). In: The European Workshop on Natural Language Generation, pp. 270–279 (2011)
11. Van Den Oord, A., et al.: WaveNet: a generative model for raw audio. In: SSW, p. 125 (2016)
12. Veloso, M.M., Biswas, J., Coltin, B., Rosenthal, S.: CoBots: robust symbiotic autonomous mobile service robots. In: IJCAI, p. 4423. Citeseer (2015)

What Makes a Good Robotic Advisor? The Role of Assertiveness in Human-Robot Interaction

Raul Paradeda[1,2]([✉]), Maria José Ferreira[1,2], Raquel Oliveira[2,3], Carlos Martinho[1,2], and Ana Paiva[1,2]

[1] Instituto Superior Técnico-University of Lisbon, Lisbon, Portugal
{raul.paradeda,maria.jose.ferreira,carlos.martinho}@tecnico.ulisboa.pt
[2] INESC-ID (GAIPS), Lisbon, Portugal
ana.paiva@inesc-id.pt
[3] Instituto Universitário de Lisboa (ISCTE-IUL), CIS-IUL, Lisbon, Portugal
rsaoa@iscte-iul.pt

Abstract. The display of different levels of assertiveness by a robot can be an essential factor in determining the way it is perceived and the extent to which it can influence its users. To explore the persuasive abilities of social robots, we devised an interactive storytelling scenario, in which users had to make several decisions while being persuaded by two autonomous robots (each one displaying low, high or neutral levels of assertiveness). To evaluate how different levels of assertiveness affected the decision-making process, we conducted a user study ($n = 61$) in which we measured participants' perceptions of the robots, the valence of their emotional state and level of assertiveness. Our findings revealed that (a) the user's perception of assertive robots differed from their initial expectations about robots in general and (b) that robots displaying personality were more effective at influencing participants to change their decisions than robots displaying a neutral arrangement of traits.

Keywords: Human-robot interaction · Interactive storytelling · Personality · Persuasion · Autonomous robots

1 Personalization, Assertiveness and Decision-Making in Human-Robot Interaction

The personality of the user is an important factor to take into consideration when designing interactive technological artefacts. Rosenthal-von der Pütten and colleagues [23] demonstrated that the user's personality influenced their feelings

We would like to thank the National Council for Scientific and Technological Development (CNPq) program Science without Border: 201833/2014-0 - Brazil and Agência Regional para o Desenvolvimento e Tecnologia (ARDITI) - M1420-09-5369-000001, for PhD grants to first and second authors respectively. This work was also supported by Fundação para a Ciência e a Tecnologia: (FCT) - UID/CEC/50021/2019 and the project AMIGOS:PTDC/EEISII/7174/2014.

© Springer Nature Switzerland AG 2019
M. A. Salichs et al. (Eds.): ICSR 2019, LNAI 11876, pp. 144–154, 2019.
https://doi.org/10.1007/978-3-030-35888-4_14

towards robots, their evaluation of these agents and actual behaviour towards them. Moreover, Callejas and colleagues [7] observed that the similarity between the user's and the agent's personalities had a moderating effect on the user's satisfaction with the interaction. This is also demonstrated by the work of Nass and Lee [17], in which participants felt more attracted and evaluated more positively robotic voices that showed a similar personality to their own. Furthermore, a study conducted by Aly and Tapus [2] also suggested that interaction with a robot is perceived as more engaging and natural when the robot adjusts to the interaction style of the participant, thus lending further credence to the idea that personalised Human-Robot Interaction (HRI) has the potential to offer a number of benefits not present in traditional HRI.

Although previous work has extensively acknowledged the importance of certain personality traits, it left others mostly in the shadows in regards to their effects in HRI, such as assertiveness [14]. Assertiveness is a valuable trait that people develop throughout their lifetime and that facilitates the achievement of one's goals while considering the rights, needs and desires of others [1]. The currently existing work concerning the role of assertiveness in HRI has presented mixed results. For instance, a pilot study conducted by Xin and Sharlin [26] found that users assigned more trust to a robot displaying a high level of assertiveness than to a robot displaying a low level of this trait, however a further investigation by the same authors returned inconclusive results [27]. Congruently, Chidambaram and colleagues [8] found no significant association between the level of assertiveness displayed by the robot and the participants' willingness to comply with its suggestions. However, the level of assertiveness seems to affect participants' evaluations of robots. For instance, Woods and colleagues observed that there was an association between the assertiveness level of the female participants and those participants' evaluation of the assertiveness level of the robot [25]. This is in line with the results reported by other authors who have also observed that the level of assertiveness displayed by participants is a good predictor of their evaluations of the assertiveness displayed by the robot [8]. But, it remains unclear what the direction of this effect is. In the first study, the authors observed a positive relationship between the individual's and the robot's reported levels of assertiveness. In the second study, this association seemed to go in the opposite direction, with subjects who scored higher on assertiveness, rating the robot lower on this trait [8,25].

These mixed results can be partly explained by the complexity of persuasive communications. Indeed, communication among humans is a complex phenomenon that involves both verbal and non-verbal cues. Within the realm of non-verbal communication, the display of negative emotions coupled with assertive behaviour can increase the effectiveness of a persuasion attempt [14]. Besides, several studies have shown that despite personality being an instrumental factor in predicting decision-making (e.g. [6]), especially in group scenarios [22], individuals are more likely to be persuaded when the persuasive situation presents determined characteristics (see [12,14]).

From an HRI perspective, studies on persuasion have focused mostly in explorations of the effectiveness of persuasive approaches using both verbal [3] and
non-verbal cues [8] and in the role of the robot embodiment [15]; thus, paying
little attention to contextual, task and user-related attributes. In this paper, we
seek to fill that gap by taking into consideration a personality trait of the user
(i.e., the level of assertiveness) and the role of the robots' emotional expression
(in terms of its valence: positive or negative) in determining the effectiveness of
the persuasion attempts.

2   Goals and Hypothesis

Our goal is to analyse how the display of different levels of assertiveness can
affect people's responses to two robotic agents in the context of an interactive
storytelling game. More specifically, we will analyse how the display of different
levels of assertiveness (high, low or neutral) by a robot can influence (a) peoples'
perception of the robot; (b) peoples' emotional state during the interaction and
(c) participants' decision-making process.

To achieve this goal, we devised a mixed design study in which the level
of assertiveness displayed by the robots was manipulated. As such, we had two
conditions: (1) both robots presented a neutral level of assertiveness (henceforth,
neutral or control condition) and (2) each robot presented different levels of
assertiveness (high or low; henceforth, test or personality condition).

In this study, sought to test the following hypotheses:

- **H1:** Participants will change their decisions more often when being persuaded
  by a robot displaying a negative facial emotion than by one displaying a
  positive facial emotion.
- **H2:** Participants who report a high level of assertiveness will evaluate the
  robots as being more assertive than participants who score low on this trait.
  As an exploratory hypothesis, we will also analyse possible gender differences
  in this attribution effect.
- **H3:** We also expect to observe differences in the perception of robots displaying different levels of assertiveness both between robots displaying different
  levels of assertiveness and between each robot and the participants' general
  perception of robots prior to the interaction.

3   Research Methods

3.1   Participants

A sample of 61 participants (40 male) was recruited on the campus of a technological institute. Participants were on average 24 years old $(SD = 7.1)$.

3.2   Materials

We conducted a quantitative study using two autonomous EMYS robots programmed to display different levels of assertiveness and act as advisers in an interactive storytelling scenario. A speaker was placed next to each robot to communicate its verbal utterances. A touchscreen was used to display the elements of the interactive story and to enable the user to chose her/his path in the story.

3.3   Manipulations

Four physical aspects of the robots' behaviour were manipulated to display different levels of assertiveness in accordance with a previous validation reported in [20]: (a) pitch (with values x-low, default and x-high), (b) rate of speech (values set as medium and +20%), (c) posture, and (d) eye gaze behaviour[1]. To ease the distinction between the two robots, they were given different names: *Emys* (high assertiveness) and *Glin* (low assertiveness). In the neutral condition, the names were assigned randomly (Fig. 1).

Fig. 1. EMYS robot with postures pride at left and shame at right.

3.4   Procedures and Measures

Pre-interaction. After signing the informed consent, participants were asked to answer to the Myers-Briggs Type Indicator (MBTI) [5] to assess their personality. Secondly, to determine their own level of assertiveness, they answered a personality scale from [9]. Thirdly, to measure participants perceptions and feelings towards robots, they responded to the Godspeed Questionnaire [4] and PANAS (Positive and Negative Affect Schedule) [11]. Because participants had not interacted with the robots yet, the items of these questionnaires were framed to refer to participant's perceptions of robots in general. Finally, they were asked to respond to a brief sociodemographic questionnaire.

---

[1] More details regarding the configurations of the robots for the display of assertiveness can be consulted in [20].

Interaction. Participants were told that they would be playing a game in which they would take on the role of the leader of a country that receives an invasion threat from an enemy country. Participants were also told that to defend their country, they would have to make some important decisions and that to do so, they would receive help from two robotic advisors. Participants were told that they would have to state their intention of a decision at each *Decision Point* (DP) and then, after hearing the advice of the robot, indicate their final choice. The narrative is a short story set in the medieval period, with approximately 30 min of duration.

Post-interaction. In this stage, participants were asked to assess their emotional state subsequent to the interaction and the assertiveness level that they displayed during the game. Afterwards, they evaluated their perceptions and feelings towards each one of the robots and the extent to which their decisions were affected by them. Participants received a cinema ticket as compensation for their participation.

3.5 The Platform

The platform was developed using the language $C\#$, which allows the integration with the framework described in [24] and supports the communication with the robots. The flow of the system with the user intervention has: the Scene Generator, the Persuasion Module, the Robot Selection Function, the Personality Module, and the System Settings. For a visual representation of the system architecture, consult [18].

Scene Generator (SG). Determines the next scene of the story flow by taking into consideration the user's final decision. The story follows a parallel interactive storytelling structure where the user can go to different parts of the story and face different decisions depending on the choices made. In total, the story has 30 distinct DPs, and to reach the end, the user must pass through a minimum of 20. This way, the SG is responsible for: (a) showing the selected scene for each DP, (b) call the text-to-speech to process the corresponding utterance for the narrator and (c) present two decisions after the narration finishes. After this last point, the user must inform his/her intention of decision for the DP. In [18] it is presented a persuasion flow that depicts a small part of the scheme that represents the full story with the DPs and the MBTI dimensions that it measures (details in Subsect. 3.5 PEM).

System Settings (SS). It is responsible for storing the information related to the user's personality (collected in the pre-interaction stage) and the robots' characteristics (personality and congruence with the user personality). The robots features are updated every time the Sect. 3.5 RSF is called.

Persuasion Module (PM). It has in consideration information from the Sect. 3.5 SS and combines these settings and the user's intention to produce the corresponding persuasive gestures. As a result, the PM determines the type of persuasion (verbal and non-verbal) that the robot will make. The Non-Verbal Cues are associated with facial expressions and head movements (nodding yes or shaking the head for no); while the Verbal Cues are the utterances said by the robots after the user intention has been indicated.

After the players' final decision, this module is reactivated by the Personality Module (see Sect. 3.5 PEM), by sending information about the decision and the personality classification. This data will then define the final response of the robot based on whether the participants' decision was congruent (joy) or incongruent (anger) with his/her personality.

Robot Selection Function (RSF). During the story, each user will interact with the system and one of the two robots in each DP through a specific order. The process has into consideration that: (a) the story has DPs associated with the MBTI dichotomies pairs **EI** (Extroverted-Introverted), **SN** (Sensing-iNtuition), **TF** (Thinking-Feeling) and **JP** (Judging-Perceiving); (b) for each pair exists a maximum number of DPs (**K**) in the story and (c) the robot can act in **favour** or **against** the player's personality. For example, having into consideration the first DP (DP1), that measures the pair **EI**, and in all story, there are 5 DPs for this pair, **K** maximum is 5. This way, following the process in Fig. 2, the random robot selected was the less-assertive one; $K = 1$, so $K\%2 \neq 0$ (remainder of 1 per 2) which means the robot will be performing the advice against the user personality; finally, K is incremented. This process will be repeated until each dichotomy pair has reached their limit ($K = max$) or the user has finished the game. The flow for the selection of traits and the scheme of the story flow can be consulted in [18].

Personality Module (PEM). It does a real-time classification of the user personality based on the dichotomy associated with the DP received. This classification was generated through a parallel mechanism based on the findings presented in [19], which shows that each DP in this game is "connected" to one of the dimensions of the MBTI questionnaire. In this sense, we devised a story that considers all MBTI dimensions and follows the same principles of [19]. After the user final decision in each DP, the PEM will activate the PM again by sending the user's personality classification for the DP and the final decision that was selected. With the features described above, at the end of the interaction, the system presents information about both (a) the game outcome (victory or defeat) and (b) the MBTI dimensions score for each user.

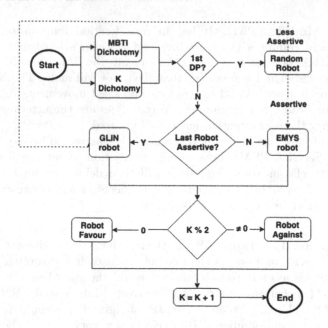

Fig. 2. Flow for the selection of traits for the assertive and/or less-assertive robot acting in favour or against the user's personality.

4   Results

H1. In order to examine the relationship between the valence of the facial emotion displayed by the robot (positive or negative) and the participants' final decision (congruent or incongruent with their initial intention), we conducted a χ^2 test. This test yielded that the relation between these two variables was significant (χ^2 (1, $N = 1220$) $= 547.06$; $p < .01$). Although most participants did not alter their decisions ($n = 756$), they were more likely to make a choice that differed from their initial intentions when the robot displayed a negative emotion (*i.e. anger*; $n = 290$) than when the robot displayed a positive emotion (*i.e. joy*; $n = 174$). On the other hand, participants were more likely to maintain their decisions in the game, when the robot displayed joy ($n = 737$), than when it displayed anger ($n = 19$).

H2. We computed the average score of participants' self-reported level of assertiveness (pre-interaction) and the average score given to each robot and then categorised them as being high or low assertive depending on weather their scores were above or below the middle point of the scale. We then performed a χ^2 test, which revealed no significant difference in the distribution of these two variables, neither for the high assertiveness robot (χ^2 (1, $N = 60$) $= .43$; $p = .51$) nor for the low assertiveness robot (χ^2 (1, $N = 60$) $= .90$; $p = .34$). Moreover, we also analysed the relation between the evaluation of the level of assertiveness displayed by the robots by participants and the participants' gender. In this regard, we observed a significant difference in the evaluation of the high assertiveness robot (χ^2 (2, $N = 60$) = 19.45; $p < .01$), suggesting that male participants rated this robot higher in assertiveness ($N = 37$) than female participants ($N = 20$). However, no differences were found in the evaluation of the low assertiveness robot according to the gender of the participant (χ^2 (3, $N = 60$) = 4.03; $p = .26$). Furthermore, we also did not observe any differences in the level of self-reported assertiveness between female and male users (χ^2 (2, $N = 60$) = 1.09; $p = .58$).

H3. To test this hypothesis, we analysed the answers of the Godspeed Questionnaire given by the participants in the pre and post stages of the study. Because our data did not present a normal distribution, we opted for a nonparametric test (Wilcoxon). Results suggest that participants had a different perception of the high assertiveness robot (Emys) after interacting with it than they had about robots in general (pre-interaction) in terms of appearance ($Z = -2.612; p = .009$), consciousness ($Z = -3.03; p = .002$) and friendliness ($Z = -3.28; p = .001$). Furthermore, the low assertiveness robot was also found to differ in terms of appearance ($Z = -2.44; p = .015$), consciousness ($Z = -2.98; p = .003$), friendliness ($Z = -2.68; p = .007$) and its ability to display emotions ($Z = -2.06; p = .039$) (see Fig. 3), in comparison to the perception of participants about robots in general before the interaction. Regarding the robots that did not present an assertive trait (neutral robots), participants also perceived them differently after interacting with them when compared with their general perceptions of robots. Our results revealed that both neutral robots presented sig. differences in impression (Emys ($Z = -1.96; p = .050$), Glin ($Z = -2.57; p = .01$)) and, only Glin was sig. difference in competence ($Z = -2.31; p = .021$). Concerning the statistical dif-

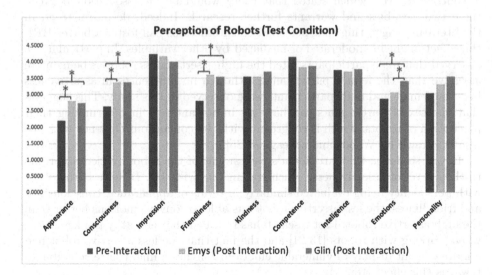

Fig. 3. The x-axis is the mean of the answers and Y-axis is the features measured for the Assertive and less-assertive robots (test condition).

ferences between both robots after the interaction, only the capacity of expressing emotions was perceived differently by the participants for the test condition
($Z = -2.500; p = .012$). Regarding the control condition, no statistical differences were found among the two robots.

5   Discussion

5.1   The Role of Emotions (H1)

Our results suggest that robot's persuasion attempts were more effective when
the robot displayed a negative facial emotion, than when it displayed a positive
facial emotion. In this instance, the negative emotion displayed by the robot
might have emphasised the importance of the decision requested of the participant (and the potential negative consequences that would result of a wrong
decision). This is congruent with previous literature that suggests that the perceived importance of a decision to the individual's self construct and attitudes
presents a negative relation to the likelihood that the same individual has to be
persuaded to take a course of action that is incongruent with his self-concept
[10]. Moreover, in the specific context of HRI, some authors have speculated that
negative emotions (in particular anger), can facilitate persuasion by easing the
individual to make a concession [28].

5.2   The Role of Assertiveness (H2-H3)

Congruently with the results presented by Chidambaram et al. [8], we observed
no relationship between the level of assertiveness of the participant (high or
low) and the evaluation that participants made of the robots for this trait. This
is contrary to H2, which stated that there would be an association between
these two variables and warrants further research. Indeed, despite a trend in
the literature suggesting that personalised interactions can foster a better HRI,
this effect might be moderated or mediated by other variables. In particular, we
observed that male participants rated the high assertiveness robot as being more
assertive than the female participants, although no differences in assertiveness
between female and male participants were observed in this study. This suggests
that the sex of participants can have an important role in determining their
perception of robots, which is congruent with the conclusions (but not with the
results) drawn by Woods and colleagues [25].

In our scenario, the participant's assessment of the robots varied according
to their level of assertiveness, which was in line with H3. Despite both robots
with personality being evaluated similarly in terms of appearance, consciousness
and friendliness, the less assertive robot was able to convey emotions better than
the high assertive robot. Past research has revealed that empathy is a key factor
when working with robots [13,21] and the fact that the less assertive robot had
a more evident display of vulnerable emotions (shyness) might have contributed
towards this effect [16].

Overall, our results offer valuable insights regarding the role of assertiveness
in the context of persuasive HRI.

References

1. Alberti, R., Emmons, M.: Your Perfect Right: Assertiveness and Equality in Your Life and Relationships. New Harbinger Publications, Oakland (2017)
2. Aly, A., Tapus, A.: A model for synthesizing a combined verbal and nonverbal behavior based on personality traits in human-robot interaction. In: Proceedings of the 8th ACM/IEEE International Conference on Human-Robot Interaction, pp. 325–332. IEEE Press (2013)
3. Andrist, S., Spannan, E., Mutlu, B.: Rhetorical robots: making robots more effective speakers using linguistic cues of expertise. In: Proceedings of the 8th ACM/IEEE International Conference on Human-Robot Interaction, pp. 341–348. IEEE Press (2013)
4. Bartneck, C., Kulić, D., Croft, E., Zoghbi, S.: Measurement instruments for the anthropomorphism, animacy, likeability, perceived intelligence, and perceived safety of robots. Int. J. Soc. Robot. $1(1)$, 71–81 (2009)
5. Briggs, K.C.: Myers-Briggs Type Indicator. Consulting Psychologists Press, Palo Alto (1976)
6. Byrne, K.A., Silasi-Mansat, C.D., Worthy, D.A.: Who chokes under pressure? The big five personality traits and decision-making under pressure. Pers. Individ. Differ. 74, 22–28 (2015)
7. Callejas, Z., Griol, D., López-Cózar, R.: A framework for the assessment of synthetic personalities according to user perception. Int. J. Hum. Comput. Stud. $72(7)$, 567–583 (2014)
8. Chidambaram, V., Chiang, Y., Mutlu, B.: Designing persuasive robots: how robots might persuade people using vocal and nonverbal cues. In: Proceedings of the Seventh Annual ACM/IEEE International Conference on Human-Robot Interaction, pp. 293–300. ACM (2012)
9. Costa, P., McCrae, R.: Revised NEO personality inventory (NEO PI-R) and NEP five-factor inventory (NEO-FFI): professional manual. Psychological Assessment Resources, Lutz (1992)
10. Crano, W.D., Prislin, R.: Attitudes and persuasion. Annu. Rev. Psychol. 57, 345–374 (2006)
11. Crawford, J., Henry, J.: The positive and negative affect schedule (panas): construct validity, measurement properties and normative data in a large non-clinical sample. Br. J. Clin. Psychol. $43(3)$, 245–265 (2004)
12. Dillard, J.P., Shen, L.: The Sage Handbook of Persuasion. Sage, Thousand Oaks (2013)
13. Duhaut, D.: A way to put empathy in a robot. In: International Conference on Artificial Intelligence ICAI 2010, Las Vegas, Nevada, United States (2010). https://hal.archives-ouvertes.fr/hal-00504748
14. Greene, J.C.: Handbook of Communication and Social Interaction Skills. Psychology Press, London (2003)
15. Herse, S., et al.: Bon appetit! robot persuasion for food recommendation. In: Companion of the 2018 ACM/IEEE International Conference on Human-Robot Interaction, pp. 125–126. ACM (2018)
16. Kalliopuska, M.: Personality variables related to shyness. Psychol. Rep. $102(1)$, 40–42 (2008)
17. Nass, C., Lee, K.: Does computer-generated speech manifest personality? An experimental test of similarity-attraction. In: Proceedings of the SIGCHI Conference on Human Factors in Computing Systems, pp. 329–336. ACM (2000)

18. Oliveira, R.A., Paradeda, R.B., Ferreira, M.J.: System information, July 2019. osf.io/puh9d
19. Paradeda, R., Ferreira, M.J., Martinho, C., Paiva, A.: Using interactive storytelling to identify personality traits. In: Nunes, N., Oakley, I., Nisi, V. (eds.) ICIDS 2017. LNCS, vol. 10690, pp. 181–192. Springer, Cham (2017). https://doi.org/10.1007/978-3-319-71027-3_15
20. Paradeda, R., Ferreira, M.J., Martinho, C., Paiva, A.: Communicating assertiveness in robotic storytellers. In: Rouse, R., Koenitz, H., Haahr, M. (eds.) ICIDS 2018. LNCS, vol. 11318, pp. 442–452. Springer, Cham (2018). https://doi.org/10.1007/978-3-030-04028-4_51
21. Pereira, A., Leite, I., Mascarenhas, S., Martinho, C., Paiva, A.: Using empathy to improve human-robot relationships. In: Lamers, M.H., Verbeek, F.J. (eds.) HRPR 2010. LNICST, vol. 59, pp. 130–138. Springer, Heidelberg (2011). https://doi.org/10.1007/978-3-642-19385-9_17
22. Planas-Sitja, I., Deneubourg, J.L., Gibon, C., Sempo, G.: Group personality during collective decision-making: a multi-level approach. Proc. Roy. Soc. B: Biol. Sci. **282**(1802), 20142515 (2015)
23. von der Pütten, A.M., Krämer, N.C., Gratch, J.: How our personality shapes our interactions with virtual characters - implications for research and development. In: Allbeck, J., Badler, N., Bickmore, T., Pelachaud, C., Safonova, A. (eds.) IVA 2010. LNCS (LNAI), vol. 6356, pp. 208–221. Springer, Heidelberg (2010). https://doi.org/10.1007/978-3-642-15892-6_23
24. Ribeiro, T., Pereira, A., Di Tullio, E., Paiva, A.: The sera ecosystem: socially expressive robotics architecture for autonomous human-robot interaction. In: Enabling Computing Research in Socially Intelligent Human-Robot Interaction: A Community Driven Modular Research Platform (2016)
25. Woods, S., Dautenhahn, K., Kaouri, C., te Boekhorst, R., Koay, K.L., Walters, M.L.: Are robots like people?: relationships between participant and robot personality traits in human-robot interaction studies. Interact. Stud. **8**(2), 281–305 (2007)
26. Xin, M., Sharlin, E.: Exploring human-robot interaction through telepresence board games. In: Pan, Z., Cheok, A., Haller, M., Lau, R.W.H., Saito, H., Liang, R. (eds.) ICAT 2006. LNCS, vol. 4282, pp. 249–261. Springer, Heidelberg (2006). https://doi.org/10.1007/11941354_26
27. Xin, M., Sharlin, E.: Playing games with robots-a method for evaluating human-robot interaction. In: Human Robot Interaction. IntechOpen (2007)
28. Yoshino, K., Ishikawa, Y., Mizukami, M., Suzuki, Y., Sakti, S., Nakamura, S.: Dialogue scenario collection of persuasive dialogue with emotional expressions via crowdsourcing. In: Proceedings of the Eleventh International Conference on Language Resources and Evaluation (LREC-2018) (2018)

Online Evaluation of Text to Speech Systems for Three Social Robots

Fernando Alonso-Martín[✉], María Malfaz, Álvaro Castro-González,
José Carlos Castillo, and Miguel A. Salichs

Department of Systems Engineering and Automation,
Universidad Carlos III de Madrid, Leganés, Spain
famartin@ing.uc3m.es

Abstract. The success of social robots is mainly based on their capacity
for interaction with people. In this regard, verbal and non-verbal communication skills are essential for social robots to get a natural human-robot
interaction. This paper focuses on the first of them since the majority
of social robots implement a Text to Speech system. We present a comparative study of 8 off-the-shelf systems used in social robots where 125
participants evaluated the performance of the systems. The results show
that, in general, the participants detect differences between the Text to
Speech systems, being able to determine which are the more intelligible,
expressive, and artificial ones. Besides, the participants also conclude
that there are some systems more suitable than others depending on the
physical appearance of the robots.

1 Introduction

Humans tend to prioritize speech over other modes to receive information from
their peers. Therefore, systems that allow robots to generate an artificial voice
are key elements for Human-Robot Interaction (HRI) systems. Since most of
these systems convert written text into voice, they are known as Text to Speech
(TTS) These systems have been an important research topic for years. For example, several authors have analysed the technological foundations of text to voice
conversion using a computer in the early '90s [10]. Additionally, Klatt presented
one of the first analyses of the TTS systems available in the late 1980s [8].

Currently, there are many TTS systems available with different features and
performance. According to the reviewed literature, there are no recent comparative studies about the performance of the currently available TTS systems, in
particular, those used in social robots. Therefore, in this paper, we study the
following TTS systems: *Ivona, Nuance, Google, Microsoft, AT&T, Espeak, Pico,*
and *Loquendo.*

To carry on the tests, each system has been deployed in three social robots
of the Social Robotics group of the Carlos III University: *Mini* [14], *Maggie* [14],
and *Mbot* [5]. This comparative study focuses on the evaluation of three features:

© Springer Nature Switzerland AG 2019
M. A. Salichs et al. (Eds.): ICSR 2019, LNAI 11876, pp. 155–164, 2019.
https://doi.org/10.1007/978-3-030-35888-4_15

(i) *intelligibility* of the generated speech, to evaluate if the robot communicates with clarity and if the utterances are well understood; (ii) *Expressiveness* of the generated voice, to assess if the voice sounds monotonous or not; and (iii) The *artificiality* of the voice, that is, if it is perceived as more or less robotic (in the sense of less human-like).

This paper is structured as follows: Sect. 2 reviews the TTS systems that are currently available, and which ones are used in social robots and other electronic devices. Section 3 describes the experimental procedure followed in this study. Section 4 presents the results obtained for each evaluated feature. Finally, in Sect. 5, the main outcomes of the study are discussed.

2   Related Work

Social robots usually integrate verbal communication skills for interaction together with other means for expressiveness. For example, the robot *Nao* [15] is able to interact with people naturally by voice and gestures. This robot uses the TTS web service of *Nuance*[1]. The social robot Pepper [9] has been also designed to interact with people in a natural way using voice, gestures, sounds, etc. Besides, it adds another interaction channel: a tactile screen situated in its chest. This robot uses the same TTS system as *Nao*. Another social robot with verbal communication skills is *iCub* [19]. This robot is conceived as a research platform to test learning algorithms, cognitive skills, and artificial intelligence algorithms. In this case, the TTS system used is *Acapela*. The *Yamaha Vocaloid Humanoid Robot* [17] integrates a different TTS approach that is able to sing and talk, Vocaloid [7], that creates realistic artificial voices.

Android-based devices have another assistant, called *Google Now*, *Google Assistant* and *Google Duplex*, which uses the *Google TTS*, especially the device *Google Home*[2]. Furthermore, the *Amazon* devices, such as the Amazon Echo, use *Alexa-Ivona*. Finally, there are other electronic devices, developed by *Microsoft*, which are equipped with the voice assistant that uses *Microsoft TTS*.

Regarding the analysis of TTS systems, there are few comparative studies of the performance of these systems.

In 2006, Roehling et al. presented a comparative study of 12 TTS systems for robotic platforms [12]. In this analysis, the authors studied the different features of the TTS systems needed for synthesizing expressive speech: pitch, duration, loudness, and voice quality. A more recent study was presented by Handley in 2009 [6]. This was focused on setting the requirements of a TTS system to be used in Computer-Assisted Language Learning PC applications. According to this author, the TTS system should have control over the characteristics of the generated speech (in French): the different styles (familiar or formal styles), the different communicative rhythms (speech rate), and the different tones of voice (timbre). The study analysed four TTS systems: *AT&T*, *Nuance Vocalizer* (the predecessor software of Nuance NaturalSpeak), *eLite*, and

---

[1] https://developer.nuance.com/public/index.php?task=mix.
[2] https://store.google.com/es/product/google_home.

Acapela BrightSpeech[3]. There are other comparative studies of TTS systems for non-Latin languages [3,16] but the tools analysed are still in early stages and mainly focused on accessibility for visually impaired people.

There are many TTS systems that are currently available in the market, but in this section, we are going to describe some of them. There are several references where the most relevant TTS systems are listed [1,11]. Some of them are the following:

- *Mbrola*: This is an open-source system which allows the user to have a great degree of control over the synthesized speech. In this sense, the user can set up a set of parameters to get precise prosodic control [4].
- *Loquendo*: This speech synthesis software synthesizes a human-like voice in multiple languages.
- *Pico*: This is the TTS system, developed by SVOX, installed by default in Android devices (at least until the 4.2 version).
- *Nuance Real Speak*: This is the speech synthesis system of the Nuance company. It allows generating voices in several languages. It is the voice of the virtual assistant of Apple, Siri.
- *Festival*: This is an open-source framework used to generate artificial voices in several languages.
- *Ivona*: This is the TTS system developed by the Amazon company. It is widely used in Amazon devices, such as the Kindle electronic reader.
- *Google*: This is the voice system developed by Google and is used in its applications, web services, and in its virtual assistant 'Google Now'. The generated voice is different in each language (supports over 80 languages and dialects).
- *Microsoft*: This is the voice system of the Microsoft company, and it is used in its services, applications, operative systems, and in its virtual assistant 'Cortana'.
- *AT&T*: This is the system developed by the AT&T company. It generates speech in 8 different languages and it is used in its call centres.
- *Verbio*: This is the system developed by the Spanish company Verbio. It is mainly used by call-centre services of companies and public institutions.

3 Analysis and Experimentation with the Selected TTS Systems

This section describes the experimental procedure to assess the TTS systems tested in this work, giving some insights about the systems evaluated as well as the robotic platform used in the experiments.

The social robots used in this study have been developed in the RoboticsLab, a research group of the Carlos III University of Madrid (Spain). These robots have been designed as research platforms in HRI. They incorporate natural dialogue skills, so the selection of the most appropriate TTS is crucial to enhance

---

[3] https://www.acapela-group.com.

Fig. 1. The social robots employed in this work: Maggie, Mini, and Mbot, respectively

the HRi experience with users. Also, the robots are equipped with broadcast-quality loudspeakers, microphones, and sound cards, among other interaction means. The robot *Maggie* (see Fig. 1, left) [14], 1.40 m tall, moves through the environment using a mobile base. This robot was designed to improve the HRI users' experience. The interaction is based on verbal communication, sound, gestures, and it also uses a touch-screen situated in its belly. The robot *Mini* (see Fig. 1, centre) [13] is a desktop robot designed to be used mainly by the elderly. This robot is about 55 cm tall, and its external shell is covered by a plush fabric. The interaction capabilities are also based on verbal communication, sound, gestures, and it also incorporates an external touch-screen. Finally, the robot *Mbot* (see Fig. 1, right) is 1.05 m tall and its shell is made of carbon fibre. This is also a mobile robot, developed as part of a European Project, MOnarCH[4], which focus is on social interaction with h children, staff, and visitors engaging in edutainment activities in the paediatric ward at an oncological hospital.

These robots integrate an interaction system known as Robotic Dialog System (RDS) [2] that allows interacting with humans through speech dialogues. In this study we have improved the TTS module of the RDS, incorporating the eight off-the-shelf TTS systems analyzed in this study, namely: Wizzard AT&T TTS[5], Espeak[6], Google TTS[7], Microsoft TTS[8], Ivonna (now knows as by Amazon as Amazon Polly[9], Loquendo TTS[10], Nuance RealSpeak Vocalizer[11], and Pico[12].

---

[4] http://monarch-fp7.eu.
[5] http://www.wizzardsoftware.com/text-to-speech-sdk.php.
[6] http://espeak.sourceforge.net.
[7] https://cloud.google.com/text-to-speech.
[8] https://azure.microsoft.com/es-es/services/cognitive-services/text-to-speech.
[9] https://www.ivona.com.
[10] https://www.nuance.com/es-es/omni-channel-customer-engagement/support/loquendo.html.
[11] https://www.nuance.com/es-es/omni-channel-customer-engagement/voice-and-ivr/text-to-speech/vocalizer.html.
[12] https://github.com/naggety/picotts.

The first five systems require an internet connection (they use web services), while the last three run in the robot.

The selection of these eight TTS systems is based on three requirements. The first one is that the TTS system must be commonly used, mainly, by the robotic research community. The second requisite is that the TTS system should be cost-free or, at least, it must offer a trial version. Finally, The TTS system must have a Spanish version with acceptable technical support. Considering these requisites, other systems such as *Festival* [18] was discarded since it does not offer robust Spanish support, and *Verbio*[13] was also rejected since it did not offer a trial version.

3.1 Methodology and Set-Up

The experiments required defining a set of characteristics to be measured. In this regard, we can find different works in the literature proposing sets of characteristics that could be evaluated to determine the performance of a TTS system under certain contexts. In this study, we consider the outcomes from the works of Handley [6] and Viswanathan [20] extracting three characteristics to evaluate: *Intelligibility*, that has to do with how easily can individual phonemes/sounds and words be discriminated one from another; *Expressiveness*, that establishes how monotonous a voice is; and *Artificiality*, which measures how "robotic" a voice sounds. Each of these questions has been rated using a 5-point Likert scale.

We created three types of online questionnaires, one for each robot[14]. In all cases, the first page of the questionnaire includes some instructions and personal questions about the user (age, gender, and educational level). The rest of the questionnaire is formed of 8 pages, each page related to a different TTS system. These questionnaires were used to obtain a ranking of the TTS systems for each of the evaluated features.

The number of participants filling each questionnaire was balanced and we obtained 125 participants in total: 44 participants for the questionnaire for Maggie, 42 for Mini, and 39 for MBot. Most of these participants were male (94 of the total). Concerning the age of the participants, the distribution is the following: 33 participants 17–30 years old; 86 participants 31–40 years old; and just 6 participants more than 41 years old. Finally, regarding the educational level, 24 participants indicated that they had just primary or secondary studies, 101 reported having university-level education (a bachelor's degree, masters, or PhD).

---

[13] https://www.verbio.com.

[14] Online questionnaires (in Spanish): Mini: http://bit.ly/2K3a4I6; Mbot: http://bit.ly/2XwlAyC; and Maggie: http://bit.ly/2WoUIUS.

Table 1. Results of the evaluation of the eight TTS systems under the three features compared

	Intelligibility		Expressiveness		Artificialness	
	M	SD	M	SD	M	SD
AT& T	2.22	1.06	2.09	0.98	3.94	1.16
Espeak	2.20	1.02	1.84	0.99	4.51	1.04
Google	4.70	0.64	3.79	0.93	2.81	1.13
Ivona	4.56	0.69	3.20	1.02	2.92	1.13
Loquendo	4.06	1.04	3.21	1.11	3.62	1.17
Microsoft	3.65	1.13	2.99	0.99	3.25	1.21
Nuance	3.83	0.98	2.97	1.16	3.00	1.16
Pico	3.29	1.19	2.40	0.97	3.46	1.21

4   Results

This section presents the results obtained for each feature evaluated. The scores obtained for each TTS system (the independent variable) for these features (the dependent measures) were analysed considering the mean and the standard deviation. Moreover, to confirm the RQs proposed, it was necessary to verify that there was a significant difference between the mean values of the scores obtained for each TTS system with each dependent measure, using a one-way repeated measures ANOVA.

4.1   Analysis of the Three Features Studied

The first feature we analyzed was **intelligibility**. As already said, a one-way repeated measures ANOVA was conducted to compare the scores obtained for each TTS system. The means and standard deviations are presented in Table 1. According to this ranking, *Google* is the best TTS system in terms of the intelligibility of its synthesized voice, followed closely by *Ivona* (there is not a significant difference between these two TTS systems: $p = 0.228$). After this second TTS system, there is a group formed by *Loquendo, Nuance, Microsoft*, and *Pico*, in that order. All of them are significantly different from the best-rated systems, $p < 0.05$, and even between themselves. Finally, *AT&T* and *Espeak* are noticeably worse understood (both are significantly different from *Pico*, $p < 0.05$, and there is no significant difference between them, $p = 1$).

Next, we evaluated the feature corresponding to the **expressiveness** of a TTS system refers to whether the voice is perceived as monotonous, or, on the contrary, as very expressive. As in the previous section, first, we must observe the results obtained by the multivariate test. The means and standard deviations are presented in Table 1. Presenting the means and the standard deviations in order, we also obtain a ranking of the TTS systems in terms of their expressiveness: from the most expressive one to the most monotonous one.

There is one TTS system, *Google*, that has a very different evaluation result in comparison with all the other TTS systems ($p < 0.05$). This system is also the best rated one, which means that it is perceived as the most expressive system. *Google* is followed by *Loquendo, Ivona, Microsoft*, and *Nuance*. These TTS systems have a similar evaluation in terms of their expressiveness (they do not have significant differences between them, $p = 1$). Finally, at the end of the ranking, there is another group of three TTS systems which are perceived as the least expressive (or most monotonous) ones: *Pico, AT&T*, and *Espeak* (in that order). In fact, *AT&T* has similarities with *Pico* ($p = 0.26$) and *Espeak* ($p = 1$).

The third feature, **artificiality**, tries to determine if the voice of the TTS system is perceived as 'robotic' (in the sense of a metallic, or not a human-like voice). Again, Table 1 presents the descriptive statistics for this feature. The TTS system that has been perceived as the most artificial is *Espeak*, which is also significantly different from the rest of the TTS systems. The ranking of the TTS systems in terms of the perceived artificiality starts with *Espeak*. After that, the rest of the TTS systems are presented in the following order: *AT&T, Loquendo, Pico, Microsoft, Nuance, Ivona* and *Google*.

In this case, there are no clearly differentiated sets of similar TTS systems, as it was for *intelligibility* and *expressiveness*. This means that most of the TTS systems have similarities ($p > 0.05$) with the ones situated at their sides in the ranking. It can be noticed that the TTS system perceived as the least artificial one, *Google*, is also considered the most clearly understood and expressive one. In contrast, *Espeak* is considered as the most 'robotic', and at the same time as the least intelligible and the most monotonous. Therefore, it seems that there is some correlation between the considered features.

4.2   Correlations Between the Three Features Analysed

The relations between the evaluated features have been analysed using the Pearson product-moment correlation coefficient. A preliminary analysis was performed to ensure there was no violation of the assumptions of normality, linearity, and homoscedasticity.

The results showed that there is a strong positive correlation between *intelligibility, expressiveness*, and *suitability* ($r > 0.476, p < 0.01$), and a negative correlation between these three features and *artificiality* ($r < -0.225, p < 0.01$).

We summarize the obtained Pearson correlation scores in Table 2:

The results of the Pearson test show that the questions related to *intelligibility, expressiveness*, and *suitability* are directly correlated. This relation could be because most intelligible TTS systems are usually also the most expressive ones. This causes these systems to also be the most preferred for use in social robots.

As also observed, *artificiality* has an inverse correlation with *intelligibility* and *expressiveness*. This fact can be observed in the previous sections where the results show that the TTS systems that are better understood and more expressive are also perceived as the less robotic, probably because the tone and timbre of those voices are very similar to the human ones.

Table 2. Pearson product-moment correlations between the three features analysed.

Measures	Intelligibility	Artificiality	Expressiveness
Intelligibility			
Artificiality	−0.301		
Expressiveness	0.548	−0.358	

5   Conclusions and Discussion

We conducted a comparative study of eight TTS systems, implemented in three different social robots. In order to evaluate the performance of these systems, three features have been considered in this study: *intelligibility, expressiveness*, and *artificiality*. The first two are the most commonly analysed features of a TTS system, that is, they are the 'desired' features to be optimized.

The participants in this study were asked to rate these features for each TTS system for just one robot. These results have been analysed, using a one-way repeated measures ANOVA, to determine if there were significant differences between the scores obtained by the TTS systems about each feature.

Analysing the results obtained, we can draw the following conclusions: (i) There are significant statistical differences between the TTS systems evaluated concerning Intelligibility, expressiveness, and artificiality. This means that the RQs are confirmed, and so we can present a ranking of the TTS systems, indicating the most and the least intelligible, expressive and artificial ones; (ii) These results show that there is a correlation between intelligibility and expressiveness, and an inverse correlation between these two and artificiality. Google was the best evaluated TTS system in terms of intelligibility and expressiveness and, at the same time, it was evaluated as having the lowest degree of artificiality; and (iii) Espeak is the most 'robotic' one and the least intelligible and the most monotonous TTS system.

5.1   Limitations of This Study and Lessons Learned

The research presented in this paper has some limitations. First, The language used is Spanish. This is not a limitation per se, but the problem is that we decided to make this comparative study using TTS systems that offered this language option.

It is important to indicate that the questionnaires used to evaluate each feature were administered after watching a video, not after having a real HRI experience. This allowed reaching a higher number of participants although we acknowledge that using videos for the evaluation could have introduced some bias due to the lack of direct interactions with the robot and the system chosen for reproducing the sounds. The quality of the voice perceived by participants could be affected by some aspects as the microphone used to collect and record the audio, the audio codec used in the video, the distance and position regarding the robot, and the sound equipment used by the participants. These first aspects have been treated carefully to avoid discrepancies between the use of different robots and TTS systems, trying to preserve the fidelity and quality of the sound, however, the sound system used by the volunteers could not be controlled.

Acknowledgement. The research leading to these results has received funding from the projects: Development of social robots to help seniors with cognitive impairment (ROBSEN), funded by the Ministerio de Economia y Competitividad; and RoboCity2030-DIH-CM, funded by Comunidad de Madrid and co-funded by Structural Funds of the EU.

References

1. Comparison of speech synthesizers (2017). https://en.wikipedia.org/wiki/Comparison_of_speech_synthesizers
2. Alonso-Martín, F., Castro-González, A., Luengo, F., Salichs, M.: Augmented robotics dialog system for enhancing human-robot interaction. Sensors **15**(7), 15799–15829 (2015)
3. Bakhsh, N.K., Alshomrani, S., Khan, I.: A comparative study of arabic text-to-speech synthesis systems. Int. J. Inf. Eng. Electron. Bus. **6**(4), 27 (2014)
4. Dutoit, T., Pagel, V., Pierret, N., Bataille, F., Van der Vrecken, O.: The mbrola project: towards a set of high quality speech synthesizers free of use for non commercial purposes. In: Proceeding of Fourth International Conference on Spoken Language Processing, ICSLP 1996, vol. 3, pp. 1393–1396. IEEE (1996)
5. González-Pacheco, V., Castro-González, Á., Malfaz, M., Salichs, M.A.: Human-robot interaction in the MOnarCH project. In: Robocity2030 13th Workshop, pp. 1–8 (2015)
6. Handley, Z.: Is text-to-speech synthesis ready for use in computer-assisted language learning? Speech Commun. **51**(10), 906–919 (2009)
7. Kenmochi, H., Ohshita, H.: VOCALOID-commercial singing synthesizer based on sample concatenation. In: INTERSPEECH 2007, 8th Annual Conference of the International Speech Communication Association, Antwerp, Belgium, pp. 4009–4010 (2007)
8. Klatt, D.H.: Review of text-to-speech conversion for English. J. Acoust. Soc. Am. **82**(3), 737 (1987)
9. Lafaye, J., Gouaillier, D., Wieber, P.B.: Linear model predictive control of the locomotion of Pepper, a humanoid robot with omnidirectional wheels. In: 2014 IEEE-RAS International Conference on Humanoid Robots, pp. 336–341. IEEE (2014)
10. O'Malley, M.: Text-to-speech conversion technology. Computer **23**(8), 17–23 (1990)
11. Pappas, C.: Top 10 text to speech (TTS) software for elearning (2015). https://elearningindustry.com/top-10-text-to-speech-tts-software-elearning
12. Roehling, S., MacDonald, B., Watson, C.: Towards expressive speech synthesis in English on a robotic platform. In: Proceedings of the Australasian International Conference on Speech Science and Technology, pp. 130–135 (2006)
13. Salichs, E., Fernández-Rodicio, E., Castillo, J.C., Castro-González, Á., Malfaz, M., Salichs, M.Á.: A social robot assisting in cognitive stimulation therapy. In: Demazeau, Y., An, B., Bajo, J., Fernández-Caballero, A. (eds.) PAAMS 2018. LNCS (LNAI), vol. 10978, pp. 344–347. Springer, Cham (2018). https://doi.org/10.1007/978-3-319-94580-4_35

14. Salichs, M., et al.: Maggie: a robotic platform for human-robot social interaction. In: 2006 IEEE Conference on Robotics, Automation and Mechatronics, Bangkok, pp. 1–7. IEEE (2006)
15. Shamsuddin, S., et al.: Humanoid robot NAO: review of control and motion exploration. In: 2011 IEEE International Conference on Control System, Computing and Engineering, Penang, Malaysia, pp. 511–516 (2011)
16. Shruthi, G., et al.: Comparative study of text to speech system for Indian language. Int. J. Adv. Comput. Inf. Technol. **1**, 199–209 (2012)
17. Tachibana, M., Nakaoka, S., Kenmochi, H.: A singing robot realized by a collaboration of VOCALOID and cybernetic human HRP-4C. In: Interdisciplinary Workshop on Singing Voice (InterSinging 2010), Tokyo, Japan (2010)
18. Taylor, P., Black, A.W., Caley, R.: The architecture of the festival speech synthesis system. In: The Third ESCA Workshop in Speech Synthesis, pp. 147–151 (1998). 10.1.1.52.2650
19. Tsagarakis, N., Metta, G., Sandini, G.: iCub: the design and realization of an open humanoid platform for cognitive and neuroscience research. Adv. Robot. **21**(10), 1151–1175 (2007)
20. Viswanathan, M., Viswanathan, M.: Measuring speech quality for text-to-speech systems: development and assessment of a modified mean opinion score (MOS) scale. Comput. Speech Lang. **19**(1), 55–83 (2005)

Lexical Entrainment in Multi-party Human–Robot Interaction

Mitsuhiko Kimoto[1,2,3](✉), Takamasa Iio[3,4,5], Michita Imai[1],
and Masahiro Shiomi[3]

[1] Keio University, Kanagawa, Japan
{kimoto,michita}@ailab.ics.keio.jp
[2] JSPS Research Fellow, Tokyo, Japan
[3] ATR-IRC, Kyoto, Japan
{kimoto,iio,m-shiomi}@atr.jp
[4] University of Tsukuba, Ibaraki, Japan
iio@sce.iit.tsukuba.ac.jp
[5] JST PRESTO, Saitama, Japan

Abstract. This paper reports lexical entrainment in a multi-party human–robot interaction, wherein one robot and two humans serve as participants. Humans tend to use the same terms as their interlocutors while making conversation. This phenomenon is called lexical entrainment. In the field of human–robot interaction, lexical entrainment has been investigated as a one-to-one interaction, and it is still unknown how humans entrain to a robot and/or another human interlocutor in a multi-party interaction. In this study, we investigate which participant, a robot or a human, strongly entrains to the other human's lexical choices in a multi-party group interaction. Moreover, we investigate whether witnessing interaction about whether a human is entrained to a robot affects the entrainment frequency of the other human participant. We conducted a map navigation task wherein a robot and two humans guide each other by describing icon images on the map. Our results showed that the human participants were lexically entrained to a greater extent to the robot than the human participant in the multi-party interaction. We found no significant effect proving that a human participant witnessing an interaction between a human and a robot would become more entrained to the robot or the other human participant.

Keywords: Human–robot interaction · Lexical entrainment · Multi-party

1 Introduction

Social robots provide services to one or more persons (e.g., guiding visitors in a museum [1] and providing information to people [2]). To achieve successful communication with people, social robotics researchers have incorporated a wide range of communication elements in a robot's conversation model, including emotion [3], gaze [4], and attention [5]. In human–human communication, it is known that humans unconsciously tend to imitate terms that their conversation partners use. This phenomenon is called lexical entrainment [6, 7]. According to Pickering and Garrod, entrainment is a critical element for successful communication [8]. Nenkova et al. [9] found that high frequency of

© Springer Nature Switzerland AG 2019
M. A. Salichs et al. (Eds.): ICSR 2019, LNAI 11876, pp. 165–175, 2019.
https://doi.org/10.1007/978-3-030-35888-4_16

lexical entrainment was correlated with task success and turn-taking in dialogues. Brennan and Clark [10] explained lexical entrainment as a consequence of conceptualizations of a "common pact," namely finding common ground [11].

Lexical entrainment is observed not only in conversation with a human, but also with a robot [12, 13]. However, past research in the field of human–robot interaction investigated lexical entrainment only in terms of one-to-one interaction (e.g., between one person and one robot, and between one person and one computer agent); it is unknown how humans are entrained to other participants in multi-party conversations in which a human and a robot participate. Thus, we investigate how humans are entrained to a robot and/or a human leads a robot to create common ground and successful communication in multi-party conversations.

We also investigate what kind of interaction unconsciously encourages a human to be entrained to a robot to a greater extent than to human participants. In multi-party conversations, participants try to establish a shared conceptualization among the group, and a participant's attempt would affect other participants' entrainment tendency. If a robot can align the tendency of lexical entrainment in multi-party conversations, it would help the robot create common ground with humans and develop successful communication. For this reason, we investigate the effect of witnessing the interaction of a participant entrained to a robot as the first step to identify the interaction-encouraging entrainment.

Therefore, in this study, we analyze how a human is entrained to a robot and/or a human participant in a multi-party group interaction. In addition, we test whether witnessing the interaction of a human being entrained to a robot affects the entrainment frequency of another human participant. Accordingly, we design a multi-party human–robot interaction and test the following two questions:

1. Does a robot or a human strongly entrain another human's lexical choices in a multi-party human–robot interaction?
2. Does witnessing the interaction of a human entrained to a robot affect the entrainment frequency of another human participant in that interaction?

2   Task Design

2.1   Overview

To investigate how a human is entrained to a robot and a human participant, we expanded the map navigation task proposed by Brandstetter et al. [13] to a multi-party human–robot interaction. Their map navigation task was designed to investigate how often humans switch their own term choices when conversing with their human or robot partner in a one-to-one interaction. Our task had three participants: a robot and two humans. One human participant was instructed by the experimenter to control the terms he/she used; we called this participant a confederate, and the other was known as the target participant. The participants see a map displayed on a computer screen, with their avatar icon representing each participant's position. The map comprises cells with an icon image that can be expressed using multiple terms. Each participant could see the correct path of the partner but could not see his/her own path (Fig. 1a shows an example of such a map). Each participant said out loud the partner's next cell on the correct path and guided the partner to not turn off the correct path in turns. We investigated the entrainment tendency by controlling the robot's and confederate's terms during map navigation. The task was divided into three parts: pre-task, main-task, and post-task. The pre-task was designed to gather how a target participant described the icons before map navigation took place. In the main task, the conversation partners, a robot and a confederate, described some icons on the correct path using terms other than those uttered by the target participant for that particular icon in the pre-task. In the post-task, the target participant described the icons on the correct path again, as in the pre-task. The aim here was to investigate how the target participant changed his/her term choices through the main task (i.e., how the target participant was entrained to the conversation partners, who were a robot and a confederate).

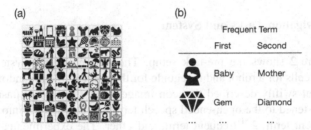

Fig. 1. (a) Example of a map displayed to the participant allotted the yellow icon (henceforth "Participant Y," and so on) to guide the robot. The correct path of the robot is highlighted by the yellow line, whereas Participant Y's correct path is not highlighted; hence he/she needs to be guided by another participant. In this case, Participant Y guides the robot, the robot guides Participant R, who guides Participant Y in turn. (b) Example of frequently used terms (all the terms are translated from Japanese to English). We collected the top two frequent terms for each icon.

2.2   Icon Images and Preparation of Terms

During map navigation, participants guided their partners on the correct path by saying the icons out loud using open-ended terms. If an icon is difficult to describe using such terms and/or if only one term exists for many people to describe it, identifying changes in lexical choices through interactions can be complicated. In addition, it is important that the icon be described as an interesting term during the main task because the extent of the commonality of the term used to describe an icon affects whether the participant becomes entrained to the term. For these reasons, we collected icons and possible terms beforehand using the following steps.

First, we chose 101 terms that were ranked the highest in terms of imageability rating in the MRC Psycholinguistic Database [14], and we collected images corresponding to these terms as icons from an online icon database[1]. Next, we gathered

---

[1] We used the database at https://www.flaticon.com/. All the chosen icons are licensed under the Flaticon Basic License and created by Freepik.

terms people use to express these icons. For this purpose, we asked 12 volunteers (6 females and 6 males, averaging 22.7 years in age, $SD = 1.30$) to describe each icon using as many terms as possible in Japanese. After gathering the data, we analyzed it and selected the top two terms used by the volunteers for each icon (we call these terms "frequent terms," as seen in Fig. 1b). Next, we selected icons that are described by a robot and a confederate based on the difference between the number of times each frequent term, first and second frequent term, was used. We did so because we aimed to investigate how a target participant changes his/her lexical expressions for the icons, and the difference in the number may influence whether the participant is easily entrained or not. For example, in Fig. 1b the term "Baby" was used more than "Mother" by the volunteers, and a human might be easily entrained to the term "Baby". We allocated icons to the routes that a robot and a confederate navigated, in order, from the smallest number of differences, at an equivalent rate.

2.3   Map Navigation Tasks and System

Pre-task. Figure 2 shows the pre-task setup. The term-collecting system displayed icon images on cells for a robot and in a guide for the confederate in random order. The target participant swiftly described the icon image, as in the case of flash cards. The experimenter listened to the open-ended speech term and classified it into one of three types: 1st frequent term, 2nd frequent term, and other. The experimenter inputted the classification into the system, and it was stored as the pre-term list. After all the images were displayed and the classifications were inputted, the system decided which terms a robot and a confederate would use when guiding a partner. To investigate whether a target entrains to a robot and a confederate, both parties need to use terms different from those used in the pre-task by the target participant. In the main task, a robot and a confederate described the icon images using terms different from those used by the target participant in the pre-task for the same icon images, but they used the same terms for some words. This is because if the robot and the confederate were to always use different terms when guiding a partner, the target participant would probably notice the obvious attempt to control the use of the terms. To hide this aspect, the following procedure was used to decide which icon image will be expressed using a term different from the one used in the pre-task.

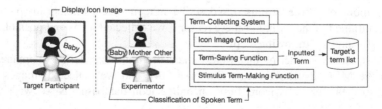

Fig. 2. Pre-task setup and architecture of the term-collecting system.

First, the experimenter divided the icon images along the routes navigated by the robot and the confederate into two types: *change* and *match* icon images. The change icon images denote the icon images for which the robot and the confederate will use different terms compared to the target participants' pre-task term. By contrast, the match icon images denote the images for which the robot and the confederate will not use different terms. We set the ratio of the change and match icon images to 50:50 based on Brandstetter et al. [13]. Next, the stimulus term-making function of the system decided what term the robot and the confederate should use in the main task based on the target participant's choice of the term in the pre-task. Figure 3 shows the procedure followed for this purpose. Finally, the number of change and match icon images differed for the robot and the confederate because different icon images were assigned to the routes used by the robot and the confederate to guide the partner. The change terms were used to assess how a target participant was entrained to a robot and a confederate.

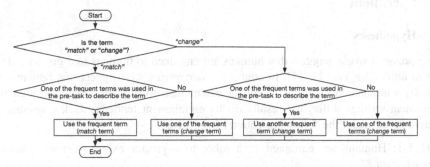

Fig. 3. Procedure to create the stimulus terms. Based on the terms used in the pre-task by the target participant, some *match* icon images were finally assigned to the *change* icon images. The robot and the confederate used these terms in the main task.

Main task. In the main task, the three participants alternately described an icon image and guided a partner to his/her goal along the correct displayed route. The rotation used was robot-confederate-target or robot-target-confederate. When they were told to move, they moved their respective display agent to the indicated cell by clicking the cell on the monitor. The roles of the three participants (target, confederate, and robot) during the main task were as follows. The target participant freely guided a partner, who was either a confederate or a robot. A confederate guided a partner using the requested terms to direct the partner about which cell to move to next. The terms were displayed for his/her map based on the pre-task results (Fig. 4 shows an example of the displayed terms that were used). The robot also guided the partner in the same manner as the other participants. In our task, we employed the Wizard-of-Oz design and the robot was operated by the experimenter. The experimenter listened to the other participants' speech and controlled the speech timing of the robot. The robot's motions were thus predetermined and run automatically (e.g., idling and facing motions during speech). When all the participants had moved to the end of their respective routes, the robot was notified that the main task had ended.

Fig. 4. Example of the displayed terms to use in the confederate map. If the confederate moused over the icon image on the route, the term used to describe the icon was displayed.

Post-task. In the post-task, the target participant again described the icon image in the manner of flash cards for the terms displayed in the pre-task. The experimenter listened to the speech terms and stored the classifications as the 1st frequent term, 2nd frequent term, and other, as the post-term list.

3   Experiment

3.1   Hypotheses

Some previous works suggest that humans are entrained to humans to a greater extent than to artificial agents [7, 15]. In contrast, other researchers suggest that humans are lexically entrained to robots to a greater extent than to humans [13]. Although the experiment settings differ, the results of the entrainment tendency lack consistency. Therefore, we make the following counter hypotheses:

H 1-1: Humans are entrained to a robot to a greater extent than to a human participant.
H 1-2: Humans are entrained to a human participant to a greater extent than to a robot.

Lexical entrainment occurs as a consequence of establishing shared conceptualization [10, 11]. If a human witnessed the entrainment interaction of another participant to a robot, the human may be also become entrained to the robot so as to establish a shared conceptualization with his/her group. Therefore, we make the following hypothesis:

H 2: If a participant is entrained to a robot, another participant in the same group is more likely to be entrained to the robot.

3.2   Conditions

Our experiment used a mixed factorial design, where we combined within- and between-participant designs. The within-participant factor concerned the partner to which the target participant showed more entrainment (partner factor). The between-participant factor determined whether the confederate was entrained to the robot during the main task (witnessing entrainment factor).

Partner Factor: This factor involved two conditions: confederate and robot. We analyzed which conversation partners (the confederate or the robot) entrained the target participant to a greater extent.

Witnessing Entrainment Factor: We controlled whether the confederate was entrained to the terms of the robot; that is, we controlled whether the target participant witnessed the interaction of the other (human) participant being entrained to the robot. We used the following two conditions: with- and without-entrainment condition. We assigned two participants to one of the conditions. In the with-entrainment condition, the two icon images on the cells the robot and the confederate described at the beginning of the route were designed the same. The confederate used the same term as the robot for the same icon image. In the without-entrainment condition, the top two icon images of the robot's and the confederate's route differed. Figure 5 shows the example maps of the with- and without-entrainment conditions.

(a) with-entrainment condition   (b) without-entrainment condition

Map for the robot Map for the confederate   Map for the robot   Map for the confederate

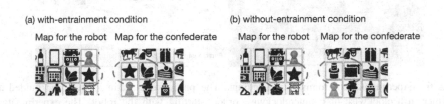

Fig. 5. Maps for the robot and the confederate for the with- and without-entrainment conditions

3.3 Procedure

Before the map navigation task was implemented, the two human participants were given brief descriptions of the experiment procedure and the rules of the map navigation tasks. Thereafter, the confederate and the target participant were given detailed explanations about how to use the system and were allowed to practice the system operation individually. The participants were given these explanations in private (the other participant would be waiting outside the room). After the practice was complete, the experimenter asked the target participant to conduct the pre-task using the following instructions: "Next, please practice describing the icon images in the cells. Please describe the displayed image intuitively, as in the manner of a flash card." After the practice was complete, the confederate was informed that he/she was assigned the confederate role and needed to follow the terms displayed on his/her map when describing the icons in the cells to a partner. The task thus had three participants: the robot, the confederate, and the target participant. There were two rotation directions. If the target participant were guided only by the robot or the confederate, the guiding partner would influence the entrainment tendency. Therefore, the participants implemented the main task twice to change the rotation directions (clockwise and counter-clockwise). After the main task was complete, the target participant conducted the post-task.

3.4 Participants and Experimental Environment

Thirty-eight participants (19 females and 19 males, averaging 33.0 years of age, $SD = 9.53$) participated in our experiment. They did not meet beforehand. All trials included a participant of each gender. In all trials, a male participant was assigned as the confederate and a female participant was assigned as the target participant. This is because gender differences in lexical entrainment tendency have been reported [16], and we intended to align these effects. During the experiment, the roles of the participants were not changed.

Figure 6 shows the experimental environment and settings. The tables were arranged circularly, and each participant could not see the other participants' monitors. The experimenter was seated behind the participants, checking the robot's monitor and controlling it.

Fig. 6. Experimental environment and settings. The participants sat in a circle and guided a partner in a clockwise or counterclockwise order, starting with the robot. The experimenter controlled the robot from the partitioned area situated behind the participants' desks.

3.5 Measurement

We measured how often the target participant was entrained (namely, the percentage of entrainment) to the robot and the confederate. We measured this value based on the percentage of *change* icon images for which the target participant changed her lexical terms between the pre-task and the post-task. Here, the *change* icon images denote the icon images for which the robot and the confederate used expression terms different from those used by the target participant in the pre-task, respectively, as described in Sect. 3.3. The two icon images at the beginning of the routes were not included to the *change* icon images because those were used to control the witnessing entrainment factor.

4   Results: Verification of Hypotheses

Figure 7 shows the percentage of entrainment (i.e., to what extent the participants changed terms to express the icon images as a result of the effects of the robot and the confederate during the main task). We conducted a two-factor mixed analysis of variance and identified significant main effects in the partner factor ($F(1,17) = 6.405$, $p = 0.022$, $\eta_p^2 = 0.274$). We did not find significant main effects in the witnessing entrainment factor ($F(1,17) = 0.147$, $p = 0.706$, $\eta_p^2 = 0.009$) and the simple interaction effects between the two factors ($F(1,17) = 2.64$, $p = 0.122$, $\eta_p^2 = 0.135$). This result indicates that the target participant was entrained to a greater extent to the robot than to the other human participant in the multi-party conversations. Thus, H 1-1 was supported while H 2 was not.

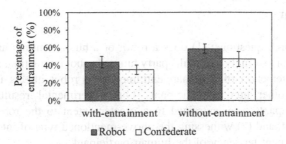

Fig. 7. Results of the percentage of entrainment with *SE*. The results of the statistical test suggest that the target participant was entrained to a greater extent to the robot than to another human participant.

5   Discussion and Limitations

Our experimental results revealed that the human in the experiment was entrained to the robot to a greater extent than to the other human participant in the multi-party conversation. Regarding one-to-one communication, it has been reported that humans are entrained to humans to a greater extent than to artificial agents [7, 15]. Our results are in line with these findings. However, our results do not agree with those of Brandstetter et al. [13], who reported that humans are entrained to a greater extent to a human than to a robot. These results provide interesting implications regarding the presence of the robot changing the tendency of lexical entrainment in groups. We found no significant difference with regard to the entrainment tendency caused by witnessing an interaction of another participant entrained to the robot. This may be because the stimuli in our experiment were not strong enough to change the entrainment tendency. In our settings, the confederate used the same terms as the robot only twice, but additional and repeated stimuli may cause changes in entrainment tendency. Moreover, it has been suggested that people do not increase lexical entrainment to robots when they witness an interaction of another person entrained to a robot.

This study also suffers from some limitations. Our work involved investigation of changes in terms by female participants. It has been reported that gender affects lexical entrainment in human–robot interactions [16]. Thus, we need to conduct additional experiments to investigate this effect. Further, we conducted the experiments with a pair of male and female participants and ignored same-gender settings. In addition, social relationships among friends, family, colleagues as participants would be important factors in entrainment in multi-party conversations. We used an existing robot, whose appearance was limited. Past studies have suggested that entrainment is related to a person's belief in an agent [17]. For example, Pearson et al. [17] showed that participants became entrained to a greater extent to a system when they believed that they interacted with an unsophisticated one compared to a sophisticated system. The appearance of the robot would project such beliefs; therefore, we need to investigate whether robots with different appearances may be able to entrain a human participant to a greater extent than other human participants.

6 Conclusion

We set two research questions: (1) does a robot or a human entrain another human's lexical choices more strongly in a multi-party human–robot interaction, and (2) whether witnessing an interaction of a human entrained to a robot affects the entrainment frequency of another human participant? Our experimental results showed that (1) human participants were entrained to a greater extent to the robot than another human participant, and (2) witnessing the above-mentioned type of interaction did not affect the entrainment tendency of the human participant.

Acknowledgements. This research work was supported in part by JSPS KAKENHI Grant Numbers JP19J01290 and JP18H03311, and JST PRESTO Grant Number JPMJPR1851, Japan.

References

1. Shiomi, M., Kanda, T., Ishiguro, H., Hagita, N.: Interactive humanoid robots for a science museum. In: Proceedings of the 1st ACM SIGCHI/SIGART Conference on Human-Robot Interaction, pp. 305–312. ACM, 1121293 (2006)
2. Satake, S., Hayashi, K., Nakatani, K., Kanda, T.: Field trial of an information-providing robot in a shopping mall. In: 2015 IEEE/RSJ International Conference on Intelligent Robots and Systems (IROS), pp. 1832–1839 (2015)
3. Shibata, H., Kanoh, M., Kato, S., Itoh, H.: A system for converting robot 'emotion' into facial expressions. In: Proceedings 2006 IEEE International Conference on Robotics and Automation, ICRA 2006, pp. 3660–3665 (2006)
4. Admoni, H., Scassellati, B.: Social eye gaze in human-robot interaction: a review. J. Hum.-Robot Interact. **6**(1), 25–63 (2017)
5. Imai, M., Ono, T., Ishiguro, H.: Physical relation and expression: joint attention for human-robot interaction. IEEE Trans. Industr. Electron. **50**(4), 636–643 (2003)
6. Brennan, S.E.: Lexical entrainment in spontaneous dialog. In: 1996 International Symposium on Spoken Dialogue, pp. 41–44 (1996)
7. Branigan, H.P., Pickering, M.J., Pearson, J., McLean, J.F.: Linguistic alignment between people and computers. J. Pragmat. **42**(9), 2355–2368 (2010)
8. Pickering, M.J., Garrod, S.: Toward a mechanistic psychology of dialogue. Behav. Brain Sci. **27**(02), 169–190 (2004)
9. Nenkova, A., Gravano, A., Hirschberg, J.: High frequency word entrainment in spoken dialogue. In: The 46th Annual Meeting of the Association for Computational Linguistics on Human Language Technologies: Short Papers, pp. 169–172. Association for Computational Linguistics, 1557737 (2008)
10. Brennan, S.E., Clark, H.H.: Conceptual pacts and lexical choice in conversation. J. Exp. Psychol. Learn. Mem. Cogn. **22**(6), 1482–1493 (1996)
11. Clark, H.H., Brennan, S.E.: Grounding in communication. Perspect. Soc. Shared Cogn. **13**, 127–149 (1991)
12. Iio, T., Shiomi, M., Shinozawa, K., Shimohara, K., Miki, M., Hagita, N.: Lexical entrainment in human robot interaction. Int. J. Soc. Robot. **7**(2), 253–263 (2015)
13. Brandstetter, J., Beckner, C., Bartneck, C., Benitez, E.: Persistent lexical entrainment in HRI. In: The 2017 ACM/IEEE International Conference on Human-Robot Interaction, pp. 63–72 (2017)

14. Coltheart, M.: The MRC psycholinguistic database. Q. J. Exp. Psychol. Sect. A **33**(4), 497–505 (1981)
15. Branigan, H.P., Pickering, M.J., Pearson, J., McLean, J.F., Nass, C.: Syntactic alignment between computers and people: the role of belief about mental states. In: 25th Annual Conference of the Cognitive Science Society, pp. 186–191 (2003)
16. Kimoto, M., Iio, T., Shiomi, M., Tanev, I., Shimohara, K., Hagita, N.: Gender effects on lexical alignment in human-robot interaction. IEEJ Trans. Electron. Inf. Syst. **137**(12), 1625–1632 (2017)
17. Pearson, J., Hu, J., Branigan, H.P., Pickering, M.J., Nass, C.I.: Adaptive language behavior in HCI: how expectations and beliefs about a system affect users' word choice. In: Proceedings of the SIGCHI Conference on Human Factors in Computing Systems, pp. 1177–1180. ACM, 1124948 (2006)

No Need to Scream: Robust Sound-Based Speaker Localisation in Challenging Scenarios

Tze Ho Elden Tse[1], Daniele De Martini[2] (ID), and Letizia Marchegiani[3(✉)] (ID)

[1] Electronic Systems, BAE Systems, Farnborough, UK
eldentseb@gmail.com
[2] Oxford Robotics Institute, University of Oxford, Oxford, UK
daniele@robots.ox.ac.uk
[3] Department of Electronic Systems, Aalborg University, Aalborg, Denmark
lm@es.aau.dk

Abstract. This paper is about speaker verification and horizontal localisation in the presence of conspicuous noise. Specifically, we are interested in enabling a mobile robot to robustly and accurately spot the presence of a target speaker and estimate his/her position in challenging acoustic scenarios. While several solutions to both tasks have been proposed in the literature, little attention has been devoted to the development of systems able to function in harsh noisy conditions. To address these shortcomings, in this work we follow a purely data-driven approach based on deep learning architectures which, by not requiring any knowledge either on the nature of the masking noise or on the structure and acoustics of the operation environment, it is able to reliably act in previously unexplored acoustic scenes. Our experimental evaluation, relying on data collected in real environments with a robotic platform, demonstrates that our framework is able to achieve high performance both in the verification and localisation tasks, despite the presence of copious noise.

Keywords: Speaker localisation · Speaker verification · Speech in noise

1 Introduction

Human-robot social interaction greatly relies on accurate detection and localisation of the various interlocutors [28]. In many instances, this interaction requires voiced communication (*e.g.* a robot personal assistant executing commands uttered by a specific user). Such social contexts, however, can be characterised by a high levels of noise of a various nature, including the noise emitted by the robot while moving. For instance, elderly people trying to communicate with a robot might struggle to be perceived, because they might be simultaneously watching TV at a high volume, there might be other people talking, or they

© Springer Nature Switzerland AG 2019
M. A. Salichs et al. (Eds.): ICSR 2019, LNAI 11876, pp. 176–185, 2019.
https://doi.org/10.1007/978-3-030-35888-4_17

might have developed, through the years, non-coordination or weakness of the speech mechanism, resulting in the production of very feeble sounds. This paper explores the possibility of spotting and localising a specific speaker in challenging scenarios, characterised by a significantly low Signal-to-Noise Ratio (SNR) level, relying on the use of Convolutional Neural Networks (CNNs). Specifically, we are interested in enabling a mobile robot assistant to spot the presence of its intended user in the acoustic scene (known in the literature as *speaker verification*), and estimate his/her position on the horizontal plane (*i.e.* *speaker localisation*).

Literature in robotics has provided us with several speaker detection and recognition frameworks, most of which rely on face and voice characteristics (see [19,26] among others). Despite the accuracy of such frameworks, situations where noise might play a crucial role and heavily compromise the quality of the sound perceived by the robot have not been yet investigated. This paper aims to move a step in this direction by exploring the performance of an audio-only perceptual system when challenged by extreme environmental conditions, which are not known *a priori*. As the conditions of the application scenarios are not necessarily either predictable or available, verification and localisation cannot take into account and leverage the structure of the operation environment, or the nature and characteristics of the overlapping noise. To address such constraints, we build a dataset containing several kinds of potential maskers, combined in a different fashion, and we opt for a pure data-driven approach, in the attempt of developing a framework able to generalise to unexplored acoustic scenes. We focus on binaural perception (*i.e.* stereo signals), and thus, on horizontal localisation (*i.e.* estimation of the direction of arrival of the sound on the horizontal plane), as a *proof-of-concept*. Yet, additional audio channels as well as sensing modalities could be considered to extend the analysis to 3D localisation. Despite the use of deep learning frameworks which, traditionally, require a large amount of training data, in our scenario we are able to obtain remarkable performance relying only on 30 min of *target speech*, allowing the use of such technology also in scenarios where data collection might be particularly challenging (*e.g.* nursing homes). Our experimental evaluation proves that our system is able to accurately spot the presence of a specific speaker in the acoustic scene with an average verification rate of 94%, and a median localisation error lower than $6°$.

2 Related Works

Speaker Verification. While traditionally this task has been addressed relying on Gaussian Mixture Models (*e.g.* [19,21]), recent advances in machine learning, particularly in the form of deep learning architectures (*e.g.* [8,9]) have dictated and driven the development of new methods able to achieve great precision, and to overcome the need of defining hand-crafted features. Several speaker verification systems, for instance, both text-dependent and text-independent have been introduced (*cf.* [2,25] among others). While those frameworks show particularly high accuracy in the classification process, not much can be said on how well they operate in harsh noisy conditions. Our work, which aims to verify the presence of a target speaker in the acoustic scene without relying on the use of specific text (*i.e.* text-independent), shares the aspirations of [25] and [2], and, as [2] explores the possibility of treating the acoustic signals as images to which directly apply CNNs. With respect to [2], however, in this paper we further challenge the verification procedure, by considering scenarios characterised by the presence of heavy noise, of a different nature and coming from different sources. The goal is to investigate the robustness of similar systems when acting in the real-world, when the presence of maskers of variegate types can, indeed, be plenteous.

Speaker Localisation. Speaker or, more generally, sound source localisation, has followed a similar pattern, and more traditional geometrical methods [19,22] have been now superseded by deep learning approaches, such as [7,14]. Both those studies rely on cross-correlation information to train CNN-based models to perform localisation. We are close in spirit to both those instances; but, as in the case of the speaker verification task, we wish to explore the behaviour of our system when coping with remarkably noisy scenes (*e.g.* while in [14], $SNR \geq 0\,$dB, in this work we consider scenarios with $-5\,$dB $\leq SNR \leq -20\,$dB), where the competitive maskers can be of a different nature and not only represented by other speakers in known indoor scenes, to evaluate its performance beyond laboratory and restrained environments. Furthermore, rather than utilising cross-correlation information, we propose the use of a stereo spectral representation of the signals, based on the Gammatone filterbanks (*cf.* Sect. 3.1).

In summary, the use of deep learning for speaker verification and localisation has been already investigated in the literature. Yet, with respect to those studies, this paper offers three main contributions:

- we consider challenging scenarios where $-5\,$dB $\leq SNR \leq -20\,$dB, while previous works only operate on positive levels of SNR;
- we consider both indoor and outdoor scenarios, and propose solutions able to operate robustly in both situations, overcoming any dependence on the structure of the operation environment and on the noise's characteristics;
- we propose the use of spectral stereo features, rather than ones based on cross-correlation, generally used for speaker localisation, to better cope with the presence of massive noise.

3   Technical Approach

Similarly to previous works in the area [19], our framework relies on a two-stage approach: firstly the incoming audio signal is fed to a CNN to verify the presence of the target speaker; secondly, in case the target speaker is present, further analysis is performed to estimate the Direction of Arrival (DoA) of the sound (*i.e.* horizontal localisation). A description of the feature representation of the various signals is given in Sect. 3.1, while the deep learning architectures employed are illustrated in Sect. 3.2.

3.1 Feature Representation

Traditionally, speaker recognition and verification tasks have been performed employing Mel-Frequency Cepstrum Coefficients (MFCCs) as feature representations of the audio signals; yet, recent works (*e.g.* [3,18]) demonstrated that the discriminative power of MFCCs greatly decreases when dealing with more realistic, dynamic and complex noisy scenarios. In this work, we adopt gammatonegrams, which are a visual representation of the energy of a signal based on short-time Fourier transform (STFT) and the application of Gammatone filterbanks [13], which have been firstly introduced in [11]. It has been proved, indeed, that such filtering, is able to guarantee robustness to noise for speech analysis tasks [15,24]. The gammatonegrams are generated following the specification illustrated in [29] and [17], employing a bank of 64 filters. Examples of gammatonegrams from our dataset representing, respectively, target speech, noise and their combination at −20 dB are reported in Fig. 1.

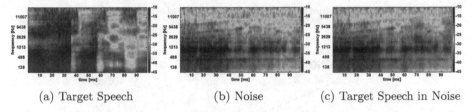

(a) Target Speech   (b) Noise   (c) Target Speech in Noise

Fig. 1. Example of the gammatonegram representation of sound frames of 1 s. From left to right: target speech, noise, and their combination at −20 dB. The energy of the time-frequency bins is expressed in decibel (dB).

3.2 Architecture

We approach both tasks using CNN-based models. We refer to the CNN used for verification as *VER-MONO*, and to the one used for localisation as *LOC-STEREO*. The two architectures differ in the input size and, consequently, in the size of the fully-connected layer, and in the structure of the output layer. Indeed, while the former takes the gammatonegram of a single channel as input, the latter considers a stereo gammatonegram, where the gammatonegrams corresponding the audio channels are disposed *side by side*. Further details are provided in Fig. 2. Furthermore, different loss functions are utilised in the training phase: while in the case of *VER-MONO*, we optimise a soft-max combined with a cross-entropy loss function to implement classification (*i.e.* target speaker vs anything/anyone else), in the case of the *LOC-STEREO* network, we minimise the Euclidean loss between the estimated DOA of the sound and the ground truth value.

4 Experimental Evaluation

We performed four kinds of experiments to validate our framework.

- Experiment 1: we train the *VER-MONO* network and evaluate its performance at verifying the presence of the target speaker against other random speakers, robot's, and environmental noise.
- Experiment 2: we compare the behaviour of the *VER-MONO* network with a different one, having the same architecture, but where verification is performed on a stereo gammatonegram (organised side by side, as in *LOC-STEREO*), and which we name *VER-STEREO*. The goal is to investigate whether having a stereo combination of the audio signals might help the network in the verification process.
- Experiment 3: we train the *LOC-STEREO* network, and evaluate its performance in the DoA estimation of the speaker's voice.
- Experiment 4: we compare the behaviour of the *LOC-STEREO* network with a different one, having the same architecture, but where localisation is performed on the cross-correlation between the gammatonegrams corresponding to the audio signals in the two channels, named *LOC-CROSS* and used as a benchmark. We also compare the behaviour of *LOC-STEREO* and *LOC-CROSS* with a more traditional geometrical method [19], indicated as *BASELINE*.

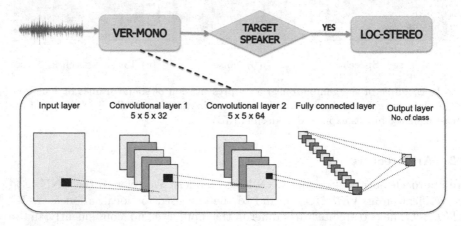

Fig. 2. The figure reports the two-stage approach operating in the framework: firstly the incoming audio signal is fed to a CNNs to verify the presence of the target speaker (*VER-MONO*) through a binary classification paradigm; secondly, in case the target speaker is present, further analysis is performed to estimate the DoA of the sound through a regression model (*LOC-STEREO*). The figure reports details on the architecture used for verification, which consists of two 5×5 convolutional layers, followed by a 2×2 max pooling, and one fully connected layer. All layers are equipped with a Rectified Linear Unit (ReLU). The regression employs the same architecture, but while *VER-MONO* operates on the gammatonagram of only one of the two channels available, *LOC-STEREO* acts on the gammatonegrams of both channels, disposed side by side. The fully-connected layer will have, thus, a different size as well. Lastly, the regression network counts only one unit in its output layer.

4.1   The Dataset

To evaluate our framework, we built a dataset where the voices of three speakers are combined with several kinds of noise, at different level of SNRs. Specifically, we consider particularly challenging scenarios characterised by significantly low SNRs: $SNR \in \{-5\,\mathrm{dB}, -15\,\mathrm{dB}, -20\,\mathrm{dB}\}$. As our goal is enabling mobile robots to spot the presence of a speaker of reference in the acoustic scene, and localise him/her on the horizontal plane, the speech utterances were recorded with the speaker standing at different angles with respect to the front of the robot, and the sound emitted by the motors of the robot was also considered as one of the potential sources of noise (*i.e.* the robot might move to follow the speaker, or being already moving while it encounters the voice of the speaker). The data was recorded by using two Knowles omnidirectional boom microphones, mounted in proximity of each of the two front wheels of a *Clearpath Husky A200* platform (shown in Fig. 3), and an ALESIS IO4 audio interface, at a sampling frequency of 44.1 kHz and a resolution of 16 bits. The speakers' voices were recorded in a silent, but realistic environment (*i.e.* perturbations due to reflections etc are present), accounting for a total of around 90 min minutes of speech data (*i.e.* 30 min minutes per speaker used as a reference). In addition to the robot's noise, we also considered other sources of stereo environmental noise from the *Urban Sound Dataset* [23], and from other publicly available databases, such as www.freesound.org, as well as random speech from [6]. Care was taken so that the environmental noise selected is characterised by moving sound sources, and covering both outdoor and indoor scenarios. Following previous works (*e.g.* [4,16,20]), we opted for collecting the data corresponding to the target speech and the masking noise separately, because this would allow us to directly control the level of SNR, and to isolate and accurately quantify the impact of the noise on the verification and localisation tasks.

4.2   Implementation Details

We trained the networks using mini-batch gradient descent based on back-propagation, employing the Adam optimisation algorithm [12]. Dropout [10] was applied to each layer for both architectures with a keeping probability of 0.75. The models were implemented using the Tensorflow [1] libraries. Similarly to previous works on deep learning in the auditory domain (cf. [5,27]), we randomly split our dataset into training set (70%) and testing set (30%).

4.3   Experiment 1 and 2: Speaker Verification

We perform speaker verification at different SNR levels ($SNR \in \{-5\,\mathrm{dB}, -15\,\mathrm{dB}, -20\,\mathrm{dB}\}$), comparing the behaviour of the *VER-MONO* and *VER-STEREO* networks, when operating on frames of $1s$. In both cases, the verification is implemented as a binary classification problem, where one class refers to a combination of the target speaker and different kinds of noise (as described in Sect. 4.1), and the other class is obtained as random combinations of urban noise, robots' noise and voices from one or more speakers different from the target one. Table 1 reports the results of those experiments. We observe that both networks are characterised by high accuracy, with the *VER-MONO* providing slightly greater performance. This suggests that the verification process does not benefit from the use of stereo information.

Fig. 3. Clearpath Husky A200 used in the experiments.

Table 1. Verification accuracy (mean and variance), when employing the *VER-MONO* and the *VER-STEREO* networks in scenarios characterised by different SNRs. Accuracy is expressed as the percentage of correct verifications.

SNR	Verification accuracy	
	VER-MONO	*VER-STEREO*
$-5\,$dB	**99.1 ± 0.80**	99.88 ± 0.56
$-15\,$dB	**98.65 ± 0.46**	95.20 ± 0.82
$-20\,$dB	**86.02 ± 2.42**	82.26 ± 2.21
Average	**94.85**	92.19

4.4 Experiment 3 and 4: Speaker Localisation

We perform speaker horizontal localisation at different SNR levels ($SNR \in \{-5\,dB, -15\,dB, -20\,dB\}$), comparing the behaviour of the *LOC-STEREO* and *LOC-CROSS* networks, when operating on frames of either 1 s or 500 ms. We also compare the results obtained by both deep learning approaches with a more traditional geometric method based on Interaural Time Difference [19], indicated as *BASELINE*. In all cases, localisation of the target speaker is carried out against different noise combinations, as described in Sect. 4.1. Table 2 reports the results of those experiments. We observe that by employing either the *LOC-STEREO* or the *LOC-CROSS* networks, localisation accuracy degrades when dealing with shorter frames. This might be due to the fact that, since we do not apply any voice activity detection algorithm neither in training or testing, we might get more 500 ms-frames with not enough speech information for the network to train a reliable model. Indeed, the performance of the *BASELINE* approach, which doesn't rely on a specific learned model, greatly drop at lower SNRs, but shows consistent results independently on the frame size. We also see that using a stereo gammatonegram (*i.e.* gammatonegrams from both channels put side by side) remarkably help the localisation process, with respect to using the representation based on cross-correlation. We believe this is due to the presence of heavy noise, which might mask cues useful for speaker localisation when computing the cross-correlation. The difference between the behaviour of the two networks is reported in Figs. 4 and 5. The greatest performance is obtained when using the *LOC-STEREO* on frames of 1 s, which provides a median error lower than 6° even when $SNR = -20\,SNRdB$. Considering that the frames are

Table 2. The table reports the median of the absolute error (expressed in degrees) in the DoA prediction obtained by using the *LOC-STEREO*, the *LOC-CROSS* networks, and the *BASELINE* approach. *FL* refers to the frame length.

	Localisation accuracy											
	LOC-STEREO				LOC-CROSS				BASELINE			
FL	−5 dB	−15 dB	−20 dB	All	−5 dB	−15 dB	−20 dB	All	−5 dB	−15 dB	−20 dB	All
500 ms	16.47	21.01	21.90	18.45	21.02	22.7	21.75	22.10	6.6	17.8	26.5	15.9
1 s	**5.09**	**5.32**	**5.43**	**5.24**	19.93	22.38	23.4	21.57	5.5	16.7	27.1	15.3

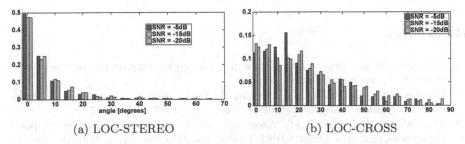

(a) LOC-STEREO   (b) LOC-CROSS

Fig. 4. From left to right: histogram of the absolute error in the localisation, when using the *LOC-STEREO* and the *LOC-CROSS* networks, operating on frames of 1 s.

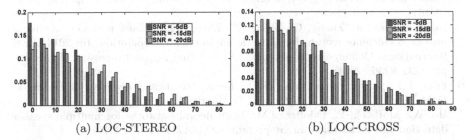

(a) LOC-STEREO   (b) LOC-CROSS

Fig. 5. From left to right: histogram of the absolute error in the localisation, when using the *LOC-STEREO* and the *LOC-CROSS* networks, operating on frames of 500 ms.

randomly selected, and that, in reality, those will come as a consecutive audio stream, the error could be further decreased through outlier removal (*i.e.* by applying a median filter).

5   Conclusions

In this work, we explored speaker verification and horizontal localisation in challenging indoor and outdoor acoustic scenarios characterised by the presence of copious and unpredictable noise. We addressed both tasks employing a fully data-driven approach, based on CNN architectures. Our experimental evaluation, implemented on a robotic platform, demonstrated that the framework presented is able to perform both tasks (*i.e.* verification and localisation) robustly and with a high level of accuracy. Future work will investigate the possibility of developing multi-modal systems (*e.g.* audio-visual) to enable more robust and accurate in-noise human-robot interaction. Furthermore, domain adaptation techniques could be used to reduce the amount of data necessary to train the models to extend the use of this framework to situations where only few speech data from the target speaker is available (*e.g.* a guide robot interacting with people in museums, airports or malls.)

References

1. Abadi, M., et al.: TensorFlow: large-scale machine learning on heterogeneous systems (2015). http://tensorflow.org/
2. Bhattacharya, G., Alam, M.J., Kenny, P.: Deep speaker embeddings for short-duration speaker verification. In: Interspeech, pp. 1517–1521 (2017)
3. Chakrabarty, D., Elhilali, M.: Abnormal sound event detection using temporal trajectories mixtures. In: 2016 IEEE International Conference on Acoustics, Speech and Signal Processing (ICASSP), pp. 216–220 (2016)
4. Chan, W., Jaitly, N., Le, Q., Vinyals, O.: Listen, attend and spell: a neural network for large vocabulary conversational speech recognition. In: 2016 IEEE International Conference on Acoustics, Speech and Signal Processing (ICASSP), pp. 4960–4964 (2016)
5. Deng, S., Han, J., Zhang, C., Zheng, T., Zheng, G.: Robust minimum statistics project coefficients feature for acoustic environment recognition. In: 2014 IEEE International Conference on Acoustics, Speech and Signal Processing (ICASSP), pp. 8232–8236 (2014)
6. Feng, L.: Speaker recognition. Ph.D. thesis, Technical University of Denmark, IMM-THESIS, DK-280, Kgs. Lyngby, Denmark (2004)
7. He, W., Motlicek, P., Odobez, J.M.: Deep neural networks for multiple speaker detection and localization. arXiv preprint arXiv:1711.11565 (2017)
8. Heigold, G., Moreno, I., Bengio, S., Shazeer, N.: End-to-end text-dependent speaker verification. In: 2016 IEEE International Conference on Acoustics, Speech and Signal Processing (ICASSP), pp. 5115–5119 (2016)
9. Hinton, G., et al.: Deep neural networks for acoustic modeling in speech recognition: the shared views of four research groups. IEEE Signal Process. Mag. **29**(6), 82–97 (2012)
10. Hinton, G.E., Srivastava, N., Krizhevsky, A., Sutskever, I., Salakhutdinov, R.R.: Improving neural networks by preventing co-adaptation of feature detectors. arXiv preprint arXiv:1207.0580 (2012)
11. Holdsworth, J., Nimmo-Smith, I., Patterson, R., Rice, P.: Implementing a gammatone filter bank. Annex C of the SVOS Final Report: Part A: The Auditory Filterbank, vol. 1, pp. 1–5 (1988)
12. Kingma, D., Ba, J.: Adam: a method for stochastic optimization. arXiv preprint arXiv:1412.6980 (2014)
13. Lyon, R.F., Katsiamis, A.G., Drakakis, E.M.: History and future of auditory filter models. In: Proceedings of 2010 IEEE International Symposium on Circuits and Systems, pp. 3809–3812 (2010)

14. Ma, N., May, T., Brown, G.J.: Exploiting deep neural networks and head movements for robust binaural localization of multiple sources in reverberant environments. IEEE/ACM Trans. Audio Speech Lang. Process. (TASLP) **25**(12), 2444–2453 (2017)
15. Maganti, H.K., Matassoni, M.: Auditory processing inspired robust feature enhancement for speech recognition. In: Fred, A., Filipe, J., Gamboa, H. (eds.) BIOSTEC 2011. CCIS, vol. 273, pp. 205–218. Springer, Heidelberg (2013). https://doi.org/10.1007/978-3-642-29752-6_15
16. Marchegiani, L., Fafoutis, X.: On cross-language consonant identification in second language noise. J. Acoust. Soc. Am. **138**(4), 2206–2209 (2015)
17. Marchegiani, L., Newman, P.: Learning to listen to your ego-(motion): metric motion estimation from auditory signals. In: Giuliani, M., Assaf, T., Giannaccini, M.E. (eds.) TAROS 2018. LNCS (LNAI), vol. 10965, pp. 247–259. Springer, Cham (2018). https://doi.org/10.1007/978-3-319-96728-8_21
18. Marchegiani, L., Posner, I.: Leveraging the urban soundscape: auditory perception for smart vehicles. In: 2017 IEEE International Conference on Robotics and Automation (ICRA), pp. 6547–6554 (2017)
19. Marchegiani, M.L., Pirri, F., Pizzoli, M.: Multimodal speaker recognition in a conversation scenario. In: Fritz, M., Schiele, B., Piater, J.H. (eds.) ICVS 2009. LNCS, vol. 5815, pp. 11–20. Springer, Heidelberg (2009). https://doi.org/10.1007/978-3-642-04667-4_2
20. Noda, K., Hashimoto, N., Nakadai, K., Ogata, T.: Sound source separation for robot audition using deep learning. In: 2015 IEEE-RAS 15th International Conference on Humanoid Robots (Humanoids), pp. 389–394 (2015)
21. Reynolds, D.A.: An overview of automatic speaker recognition technology. In: 2002 IEEE International Conference on Acoustics, Speech, and Signal Processing, vol. 4, pp. IV–4072 (2002)
22. Rudzyn, B., Kadous, W., Sammut, C.: Real time robot audition system incorporating both 3D sound source localisation and voice characterisation. In: 2007 IEEE International Conference on Robotics and Automation, pp. 4733–4738 (2007)
23. Salamon, J., Jacoby, C., Bello, J.P.: A dataset and taxonomy for urban sound research. In: 22nd ACM International Conference on Multimedia (ACM-MM 2014), Orlando, FL, USA, November 2014
24. Schluter, R., Bezrukov, I., Wagner, H., Ney, H.: Gammatone features and feature combination for large vocabulary speech recognition. In: 2007 IEEE International Conference on Acoustics, Speech and Signal Processing-ICASSP 2007, vol. 4, pp. IV–649 (2007)
25. Snyder, D., Garcia-Romero, D., Povey, D., Khudanpur, S.: Deep neural network embeddings for text-independent speaker verification. In: Interspeech, pp. 999–1003 (2017)
26. Stefanov, K., Sugimoto, A., Beskow, J.: Look who's talking: visual identification of the active speaker in multi-party human-robot interaction. In: Proceedings of the 2nd Workshop on Advancements in Social Signal Processing for Multimodal Interaction, pp. 22–27. ACM (2016)
27. Takahashi, N., Gygli, M., Van Gool, L.: Aenet: Learning deep audio features for video analysis. arXiv preprint arXiv:1701.00599 (2017)
28. Tapus, A., Bandera, A., Vazquez-Martin, R., Calderita, L.V.: Perceiving the person and their interactions with the others for social robotics-a review. Pattern Recogn. Lett. **118**, 3–13 (2019)
29. Toshio, I.: An optimal auditory filter. In: IEEE ASSP Workshop on Applications of Signal Processing to Audio and Acoustics, pp. 198–201 (1995)

Social Cues and Design of Social Robots

Static and Temporal Differences in Social Signals Between Error-Free and Erroneous Situations in Human-Robot Collaboration

Dito Eka Cahya[1,2(✉)], Rahul Ramakrishnan[1(✉)], and Manuel Giuliani[1(✉)]

[1] Bristol Robotics Laboratory,
University of the West of England, and University of Bristol, Bristol, UK
dito.cahya@bristol.ac.uk, rahul2.ramachandran@live.uwe.ac.uk,
manuel.giuliani@brl.ac.uk
[2] Agency for the Assessment and Application of Technology (BPPT),
Jakarta, Indonesia

Abstract. The capability of differentiating error situations from error-free situations in human-robot collaboration is a mandatory skill for collaborative robots. One of the variables that robots can analyse to differentiate both situations are the social signals from the human interaction partner. We performed an extensive human-robot collaboration user study involving 50 participants in which the robot purposefully executed erroneous behaviours. We annotated the occurrences and the duration of multimodal social signals from the participants during both error-free situations and error situations using an automatic video annotation method based on OpenFace. An analysis of the annotation shows that the participants express more facial expressions, head gestures, and gaze shifts during erroneous situations than in error-free situations. The duration of the facial expressions and gaze shifts is also longer during error situations. Our results additionally show that people look at the robot and the table with a longer duration and look at the objects with a shorter duration in error situations compared to error-free situations. The results of this research are essential for the development of automatic error recognition and error handling in human-robot collaboration.

Keywords: Human-robot collaboration · Faulty robots · Social signal processing

1 Introduction

Collaborative robots must be managed by a cognitive architecture which has various social and physical skills [2] such as the ability to detect error situations accurately and to react appropriately to resolve error situations in order to achieve fluent and natural human-robot collaboration (HRC). Error situations which are either created by the robot or by the human usually recur during HRC.

© Springer Nature Switzerland AG 2019
M. A. Salichs et al. (Eds.): ICSR 2019, LNAI 11876, pp. 189–199, 2019.
https://doi.org/10.1007/978-3-030-35888-4_18

Most error situations in HRC are induced by the robot due to hardware or programming flaws. These error situations often lead to disturbances, distractions, or even a full stop of the collaboration [4]. Therefore, robot system architectures need to be extended by the ability to handle error situations in HRC. To detect error situations in HRC, we adopt the concept of Humanistic Intelligence, which is defined as "intelligence that arises because of a human being in the feedback loop of a computational process" [7]. Based on this view, the collaborative robot can observe social signals from its human partner to detect if error situations happen during HRC.

This paper is a part of our research into stable detection of error situations in HRC using human's social signals. We conducted a wizard-of-oz (WoZ) user study involving 50 participants and collected a dataset of HRCs between a human and an erroneous robot in a within-subject design setup. We intentionally introduced three types of faulty behaviours which includes *social norms violations*, *planning errors* and *execution errors* during the collaboration session and recorded the participants' social signals with a microphone and an RGB-D camera. In this paper, we analysed our dataset to produce the three following contributions: (1) Annotation and analysis of multimodal human social signals in error situations and error-free situations during HRC. (2) Comparison of differences in occurrence (static aspect) and duration (temporal aspect) of social signals that people show in error situations and error-free situations. (3) Identification of informative social signals which should be used to train a statistical model for automatic recognition of error situations in HRC.

2   Background and Related Work

Error situations during HRC is a new topic in the HRC research field. Salem et al. [11] reported that people considered faulty robots as less reliable than flawless ones. Hamacher et al. [6] implemented expressive communication strategies on robots and found that erroneous but expressive robots are preferable than error-free robots. Giuliani et al. [4] and Mirnig et al. [8] analysed 201 videos which contain error situations from four human-robot interaction (HRI) user studies. Mirnig et al. [8] discovered that people frequently perform a leaning forward body movement followed by verbal utterances in reaction to error situations. Giuliani et al. [4] found that humans show noticeable facial expressions and head gestures during error situations. Mirnig et al. [9] experimented with deliberate faulty robot behaviour. The results of their study show that interpreting a human's social signals, especially gaze shifts and smile/laughter, can help robots to determine when error situations happen. Trung et al. [12] used Mirnig et al.'s [9] dataset to train the first automatic error recognition in HRC based on human's head and shoulder movements using k-nearest neighbour learning algorithms.

Giuliani et al. [4] noticed two distinguishable types of error situations in HRI, *social norms violations* (SNV) and *technical failures* (TF). A social norm violation happens when a robot acts differently from the social script which are normally executed in a certain social situation. A technical failure occurs when a human perceives the robot as having a technical problem. In this paper, we introduce two new sub-types of technical failures. Inspired by Rasmussen [10], we divide TF into two additional error types, *planning errors* (PE) and *execution errors* (EE). *Planning errors* occur when a robot executes an action correctly although it is the wrong action. *Execution errors* happen when a robot initiates the correct action but unsuccessfully executes the action. The error situation taxonomy that we present in this research is based on how humans perceive error events; hence, we analysed humans' multimodal feedback.

3   User Study

User Study Design. We conducted a wizard-of-oz (WoZ) HRC user study to analyse humans' social signals during error situations and error-free situations. We used a dual-arm ABB Yumi[1] collaborative robot for the study. The robot was equipped with a pan/tilt unit holding a tablet PC attached on top of the robot showing an animated face from the *homer robot face* library[2]. The tablet screen showed seven types of facial expressions and subtitles for the robot's speech. The user study consisted of three parts, one interview session and two assembly sessions, with a total of 20 episodes. In the interview session, the robot asked five questions to the participant. In the second session, which we call the robot plan assembly (RPA) session, the robot gave step by step instructions to the participants to build seven simple shapes using wooden blocks in the participant's area. In the third session, the human plan assembly (HPA) session, the participant had eight assembly plans but did not have some of the wooden parts to build them. The participant needed to ask the robot to handover the missing wooden blocks which were placed in the robot area.

(a) The human-robot collaboration session

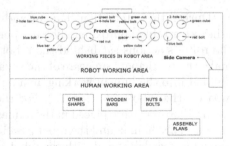

(b) User study table layout

Fig. 1. User study setup

[1] https://new.abb.com/products/robotics/industrial-robots/irb-14000-yumi.
[2] https://gitlab.uni-koblenz.de/robbie/homer_robot_face-release.

Table 1. Collaboration sessions details

Session	#	Question/Task	Error type	Error event
Interview	1	Have you interacted with a robot before?	-	None
	2	Name three words related to robots!	-	None
	3	What do you think is a robot?	SNV	The robot starts speaking after 2.5 s, cutting off the participant
	4	In which areas robots are implemented?	SNV	The robot talks to the participant but looking at a different direction
	5	Tasks would you never trust a robot with?	-	None
RPA	6	Build a windmill	-	None
	7	Build a T shape	SNV	The robot stops talking for 15 s before moving to the next instruction
	8	Build an H shape	SNV	Unusual request to throw the shape on the floor instead of showing it to the robot
	9	Build an L shape	EE	The robot stops talking in the middle of the instruction for 15 s before starts talking again
	10	Build an F shape	EE	The robot repeats a word seven times as if it stucks in a loop
	11	Build a cross	EE	The robot repeats the instruction four times
	12	Build an arrow	-	None
HPA	13	Build a U shape	-	None
	14	Build a V shape	EE	The robot opens its hand too early during handover process
	15	Build a biped robot	PE	The robot picks the wrong object with the right colour
	16	Build an anchor	PE	The robot picks a right object with the wrong size
	17	Build a Z shape	PE	The robot picks the right object with the wrong colour
	18	Build a hammer	PE	The robot picks the wrong object with the wrong colour
	19	Build a rook	-	None
	20	Build an E shape	-	None

During the interaction, human and robot were both sitting opposite each other at a table approximately 1 m apart (Fig. 1a). A researcher who wizarded the robot's actions sat behind the robot and was covered by a portable wall to make the participant unaware of the wizarding process. The user study table was divided into the human working area on the human side and the robot working area on the robot side (Fig. 1b). For the RPA session, the build plans and all required objects were placed in the human area. In the HPA session, objects were placed in the human and the robot area in order to elicit interaction. Every study participant collaborated with the robot in 12 erroneous episodes and 8 error-free episodes within the span of three consecutive collaboration sessions. The interview session included two SNV, the RPA session contained two SNV and three EE, while the HPA session involved three PE and one EE. We decided to split the user study into three sessions to maintain the participants' attention on the interaction and to balance the error situation types across different interaction modes. The setup also allowed us to elicit more error situations while minimising *saturation effects*, because the error situations only made up 7.5% of the

Table 2. Annotated social signals' thresholds (angles given in radians)

Head	
Tilting	|head roll| > 0.25 and |head pitch| < 0.5 and |head yaw| < 0.5
Move forward	head z position < 0.87 m (absolute distance to the robot)
Move backward	head z position > 1.15 m (absolute distance to the robot)
Gaze shifts	
Look at robot	−0.1 < gaze yaw <= 0.2 and |gaze pitch| <= 0.6 and head yaw > −0.2 and |head_pitch| <= 0.6
Look at objects	gaze yaw >= 0.2 and |gaze pitch| <= 0.18 and head yaw <= −0.2 and |head pitch| <= 0.18
Look at table	gaze yaw > 0.25 and |gaze pitch| >= 0.25 and head yaw <= −0.25 and |head pitch| >= 0.25
Wandering	gaze yaw < 0 and head yaw >= −0.15
Action units	AU value > 1.6 and AU duration > 300 ms

whole interaction. We also randomised the order of the collaboration episodes in each session to reduce *ordering effects*. Table 1 describe the details of collaboration episodes and error situations that occurred during the interview, RPA, and HPA session. We conclude the study with a semi-structured interview in which the experimenter asked four questions related to the participants' interaction experience with the robot.

The error situations that we introduced in the study were mostly adopted from a previous study by Mirnig et al. [9]. However, we extended the error taxonomy by dividing technical errors into EE and PE. We also added the erroneous behaviours 'giving the wrong object' and 'dropping object' to the list of PE and EE, respectively. Finally, we added the 'talking while looking away' behaviour into the list of SNV, because Giuliani et al. [4] noted this unusual robot behaviour in their research. Generally, our aim in this study was to introduce error situations that might happen in real 'in the wild' human-robot interactions.

Data Collection and Annotation. We recorded depth and colour videos of the participants during the user study with a RealSense D415 RGB-D camera which was placed in front of the robot's body to record the participants' facial expressions and body posture (Fig. 1a). The collaboration sessions were also recorded from the side using a wide angle GoPro camera. A head-mountable microphone was used to capture the participants' speech. We adopted an automatic annotation method on our audio-video dataset to extract more detailed social signals than in manual annotation and also to speed up the process of annotation. For the automatic social signal annotation, we used OpenFace [1], the facial behaviour analysis toolkit. OpenFace is able to extract 17 types of facial action units (AU) following the Facial Action Coding System (FACS) [3], head orientation, head position, and gaze direction. All extracted social signals from OpenFace were saved in rosbag[3] files along with the audio-video recording.

OpenFace gave us the head orientation and gaze direction estimates in the form of roll-pitch-yaw angles, where tilting movements were represented by roll

---

[3] https://wiki.ros.org/rosbag.

angle, right and left turn were indicated by pitch angle, and the up and down movement were given by yaw angle. Meanwhile, the facial AU results were represented in a scale between 0 to 5, which indicates the intensity of each AU's facial muscle movements. Since we were interested in extracting the frequency and duration of social signals from the participants, we wrote a python script to convert the continuous values from OpenFace into discrete and meaningful social signals. For the discretisation, we applied heuristically defined thresholds based on manual examination of the dataset, and then extracted the AU's occurrences timestamps to calculate their duration. Table 2 indicates the automatically annotated social signals and their definition in terms of OpenFace outputs.

4   Results

Dataset. We collected audio-video data of 1200 HRCs from 50 participants (23 male, 27 female). From the data set, we extracted 600 error situations (200 SNV, 200 EE, and 200 PE) and 600 error-free situations. Each error-free situation corresponds to one of the error situations. For example, when we extracted the part where the robot performed the unusual request to throw the shape on the floor as an SNV error situation, we also extracted the part where the robot asked the participant to show the finished object to the robot as a corresponding error-free situation. Both, the erroneous and the corresponding error-free situation are similar in terms of the modalities used by the robot. We obtained the frequency and duration of participants' social signals during both situation types using our automatic annotation method and ran a statistical test to compare them. Because of the large sample size ($N = 50$), we skipped the normality test and chose a parametric test. We used a paired student's t-test on the data to check the difference in the static and temporal aspects of the social signals between erroneous and error-free situations, and between different error situation types and their error-free counterparts.

Frequency of Social Signals. Table 3 shows a summary of the average frequency (static aspect) of participants' social signals and the statistical analysis results. The statistically different social signals ($p < 0.05$) are printed in bold. Column 2 and 3 of Table 3 show the frequency of social signals in all error situations and error-free situations. A t-test revealed that people show more facial expressions ($t(49) = 6.95, p < .001$), head gestures ($t(49) = 3.74, p < .001$) and gaze shifts ($t(49) = 6.39, p < .001$) during error situations compared to error-free situations. In the *gaze shifts* category, we found that people shift their gaze to the robot and the study table more frequently during error situations. In the *head gestures* modality, we noticed that people tilt and move their head forward more often during error situations. Meanwhile in the *facial expression* category, people show more AU01 (Inner Brow Raiser), AU02 (Outer Brow Raiser), AU04 (Brow Lowerer), AU05 (Upper Lid Raiser), AU15 (Lip Corner Depres), AU17 (Chin Raiser), AU20 (Lip Stretcher), AU25 (Lips Part), AU26 (Jaw Drop), and AU28 (Lip Suck) in error situations than error-free situations. The frequency

Table 3. Social signals frequency in error vs. Error-free situations

Signals	All Errors Mean/SD	All Normals Mean/SD	t-test t/Sig.	SNV Mean/SD	Normal Mean/SD	t-test t/Sig.	EE Mean/SD	Normal Mean/SD	t-test t/Sig.	PE Mean/SD	Normal Mean/SD	t-test t/Sig.
AU	10.8/4.98	8.00/4.44	**6.95/.000**	5.40/3.12	4.50/3.05	**2.08/.043**	7.32/5.07	6.81/3.95	0.68/.502	19.6/11.2	12.7/8.57	**7.11/.000**
AU01	0.56/0.43	0.31/0.36	**4.95/.000**	0.33/0.46	0.13/0.21	**3.35/.002**	0.45/0.60	0.31/0.51	1.27/.212	0.91/0.78	0.49/0.70	**4.01/.000**
AU02	0.23/0.27	0.15/0.17	**2.05/.046**	0.12/0.26	0.07/0.16	1.59/.118	0.25/0.54	0.13/0.22	1.37/.178	0.34/0.43	0.26/0.38	1.32/.194
AU04	0.24/0.66	0.14/0.49	**3.26/.002**	0.20/0.57	0.09/0.39	**2.56/.014**	0.23/0.56	0.16/0.51	**2.60/.012**	0.31/1.03	0.19/0.61	1.45/.153
AU05	0.11/0.20	0.04/0.07	**2.33/.024**	0.04/0.14	0.04/0.15	0.17/.868	0.13/0.39	0.05/0.12	1.47/.149	0.16/0.27	0.06/0.10	**2.77/.008**
AU06	0.43/0.73	0.42/0.71	0.15/.883	0.28/0.41	0.38/0.59	-1.51/.138	0.25/0.55	0.29/0.59	-0.53/.598	0.76/1.52	0.60/1.22	1.50/.141
AU07	0.74/1.19	0.73/1.24	0.19/.854	0.63/1.08	0.45/0.98	1.67/.101	0.60/1.04	0.62/1.13	-0.25/.806	0.99/1.90	1.12/2.11	-1.29/.202
AU09	0.01/0.03	0.02/0.05	-0.88/.382	0.02/0.06	0.00/0.00	1.77/.083	0.01/0.04	0.04/0.11	-1.77/.083	0.02/0.07	0.03/0.08	-0.63/.533
AU10	0.95/1.18	0.87/1.06	1.14/.259	0.44/0.60	0.37/0.69	0.79/.432	0.42/0.80	0.60/0.83	-2.18/.034	1.98/2.61	1.65/2.15	**2.14/.037**
AU12	0.47/0.55	0.47/0.59	0.02/.988	0.34/0.44	0.37/0.49	-0.34/.737	0.27/0.42	0.38/0.57	-1.52/.134	0.81/1.25	0.67/1.10	1.04/.303
AU14	0.91/1.32	0.87/1.12	0.53/.600	0.47/0.68	0.33/0.56	**2.02/.048**	0.57/1.01	0.57/0.88	0.00/.999	1.70/2.55	1.72/2.33	-0.12/.902
AU15	0.42/0.39	0.32/0.35	**2.12/.039**	0.16/0.43	0.13/0.18	0.53/.595	0.34/0.39	0.35/0.41	-0.13/.894	0.76/0.85	0.49/0.67	**3.36/.002**
AU17	1.07/0.63	0.73/0.51	**4.17/.000**	0.55/0.59	0.53/0.53	0.20/.846	0.84/0.91	0.57/0.64	1.93/.059	1.82/1.52	1.12/0.89	**3.68/.001**
AU20	0.20/0.23	0.12/0.17	**2.07/.044**	0.07/0.20	0.06/0.10	0.31/.755	0.21/0.35	0.18/0.46	0.39/.699	0.32/0.47	0.14/0.25	**2.83/.007**
AU23	0.33/0.25	0.27/0.20	1.61/.113	0.08/0.16	0.12/0.17	-1.31/.197	0.27/0.28	0.24/0.32	0.49/.629	0.66/0.68	0.46/0.44	**2.09/.042**
AU25	2.04/1.19	1.27/0.74	**6.61/.000**	0.92/0.77	0.85/0.63	0.71/.480	1.05/0.87	1.17/0.99	-0.73/.468	4.14/3.03	1.78/1.46	**7.79/.000**
AU26	1.56/0.65	0.90/0.54	**8.51/.000**	0.66/0.58	0.58/0.55	0.86/.392	1.12/0.84	0.84/0.66	1.90/.064	2.91/1.47	1.27/1.15	**8.53/.000**
AU28	0.51/0.48	0.37/0.33	**2.86/.006**	0.13/0.32	0.05/0.10	1.83/.073	0.36/0.57	0.36/0.47	0.00/.999	1.04/1.06	0.70/0.78	**2.76/.008**
Head	1.63/0.98	1.33/0.83	**3.74/.000**	0.65/0.68	0.62/0.69	0.34/.737	1.49/1.27	1.09/0.91	**2.45/.018**	2.77/1.85	2.30/1.54	**2.20/.032**
Tilt	0.48/0.30	0.39/0.28	**2.18/.034**	0.18/0.26	0.16/0.26	0.40/.693	0.35/0.38	0.27/0.33	1.09/.280	0.91/0.73	0.74/0.70	1.55/.127
Forward	0.63/0.89	0.46/0.70	**3.54/.001**	0.27/0.57	0.25/0.59	0.34/.733	0.62/1.01	0.50/0.71	1.02/.314	1.01/1.42	0.64/1.02	**3.29/.002**
Backward	0.53/0.51	0.48/0.64	0.89/.380	0.20/0.42	0.21/0.41	-0.23/.819	0.53/0.70	0.32/0.65	**2.42/.019**	0.85/0.95	0.92/1.24	-0.57/.570
Gaze	7.72/1.41	6.51/1.20	**6.39/.000**	4.65/1.46	3.51/1.16	**5.41/.000**	5.07/1.45	5.62/1.63	-1.92/.060	13.5/3.13	10.4/2.45	**7.10/.000**
At robot	2.83/1.23	1.85/1.16	**9.14/.000**	2.56/1.28	2.08/1.18	**3.38/.001**	2.33/1.12	1.37/1.17	**6.62/.000**	3.60/2.32	2.12/1.90	**6.80/.000**
At objects	2.54/1.27	2.66/1.02	-1.12/.266	1.71/1.45	1.04/0.84	**4.40/.000**	1.94/1.32	2.74/1.38	**-4.93/.000**	3.98/1.93	4.20/1.52	-1.05/.298
At table	2.11/1.05	1.82/1.10	**3.43/.001**	0.15/0.38	0.09/0.21	1.34/.188	0.63/0.55	1.41/1.16	**-4.67/.000**	5.57/2.92	3.96/2.38	**6.68/.000**
Wander	0.24/0.52	0.18/0.40	1.76/.084	0.24/0.69	0.32/0.75	-1.66/.104	0.17/0.51	0.10/0.28	1.44/.155	0.32/0.54	0.14/0.30	**2.84/.006**

of social signals between SNV error situations and their error-free situations counterparts are represented in column 5 and 6 of Table 3. A t-test also showed that people display more facial expressions ($t(49) = 2.08, p = .043$) and gaze shifts ($t(49) = 5.41, p < .001$) during SNV situations compared to the corresponding error-free situations. We found that during SNV situations, people look at the robot ($t(49) = 3.38, p = .001$) and at the working objects more ($t(49) = 4.40, p < .001$) compared to their error-free situations pairs.

Column 8 and 9 of Table 3 collate the frequency of social signals in EE situations and their error-free situations equivalent. Results showed that people exhibit more head gestures ($t(49) = 2.45, p = .018$) during EE situations compared to the corresponding error-free situations. It is also interesting to note that people show more gaze shifts to the robot ($t(49) = 6.62, p < .001$) and less gaze shits at the objects ($t(49) = -4.93, p < .001$) and the table ($t(49) = -4.67, p < .001$) during EE situations although the overall occurrences of gaze shifts during the error situations ($t(49) = -1.92, p < .060$) is not significantly different from error free situations. In the *facial expression* category, people show more AU04 (Brow Lowerer) ($t(49) = 2.60, p = .012$) and AU10 (Upper lip raiser) ($t(49) = -2.18, p = 0.034$) during EE situations. The occurrences of social signals of PE situations and their error-free situations are indicated in column 11 and 12 of Table 3. People show more facial expressions ($t(49) = 7.11, p < .001$) and gaze shifts ($t(49) = 7.10, p < .001$) during PE situations when compared to its equivalent error-free situations. We also observed that people move their head forward ($t(49) = 3.29, p = .002$,), shift their gaze towards the robot ($t(49) = 6.80, p < .001$) and at the table ($t(49) = 6.68, p < .001$) more in PE situations.

Table 4. Social signals duration (seconds) in error vs. Error-free situations

Signals	All Errors Mean/SD	All Normals Mean/SD	t-test t/Sig.	SNV Mean/SD	Normal Mean/SD	t-test t/Sig.	EE Mean/SD	Normal Mean/SD	t-test t/Sig.	PE Mean/SD	Normal Mean/SD	t-test t/Sig.
AU	11.9/8.42	9.57/7.64	**4.27/.000**	5.80/4.26	4.26/3.97	**2.46/.017**	7.44/6.73	8.19/7.93	-0.65/.520	22.5/18.4	16.3/14.7	**4.95/.000**
AU01	0.59/0.63	0.31/0.43	**3.91/.000**	0.36/0.66	0.12/0.23	**2.73/.009**	0.56/0.99	0.25/0.48	**2.01/.050**	0.87/1.00	0.55/0.93	**2.20/.032**
AU02	0.18/0.25	0.10/0.11	**2.31/.025**	0.07/0.16	0.04/0.08	1.83/.073	0.24/0.55	0.08/0.19	1.84/.073	0.23/0.32	0.17/0.27	1.26/.213
AU04	0.28/0.95	0.17/0.68	**2.44/.018**	0.28/0.96	0.10/0.54	**2.27/.028**	0.26/0.95	0.16/0.57	1.59/.119	0.28/1.15	0.25/0.99	0.51/.609
AU05	0.08/0.14	0.03/0.06	**2.33/.024**	0.03/0.14	0.02/0.09	0.58/.568	0.09/0.28	0.02/0.06	1.77/.082	0.11/0.22	0.05/0.14	1.78/.081
AU06	0.60/1.19	0.62/1.27	-0.21/.835	0.37/0.62	0.49/0.98	-0.95/.346	0.30/0.88	0.44/1.32	-0.74/.463	1.12/2.56	0.93/2.32	0.85/.399
AU07	0.86/1.81	0.76/1.59	1.10/.275	0.71/1.36	0.52/1.33	1.17/.249	0.76/1.68	0.60/1.22	1.41/.166	1.10/2.81	1.17/2.87	-0.85/.398
AU09	0.01/0.03	0.02/0.08	-1.24/.219	0.01/0.04	0.00/0.00	1.68/.099	0.00/0.01	0.05/0.21	-1.74/.089	0.02/0.07	0.02/0.06	-0.10/.920
AU10	1.33/2.15	1.27/2.13	0.44/.663	0.50/0.77	0.41/0.81	0.84/.406	0.55/1.21	0.91/2.02	**-2.05/.046**	2.93/4.96	2.50/4.15	1.48/.144
AU12	0.83/1.52	0.90/1.58	-0.73/.471	0.48/0.71	0.47/0.81	0.13/.895	0.42/0.99	0.76/1.81	-1.54/.131	1.59/3.58	1.47/2.99	0.46/.648
AU14	1.07/1.93	1.18/1.99	-1.14/.259	0.47/0.78	0.24/0.45	**2.93/.005**	0.56/1.27	0.92/1.98	-1.66/.103	2.19/4.16	2.40/4.17	-0.78/.441
AU15	0.35/0.41	0.30/0.37	0.86/.392	0.14/0.45	0.09/0.17	0.77/.444	0.25/0.37	0.36/0.58	-1.11/.271	0.65/0.93	0.44/0.75	1.78/.081
AU17	1.00/0.64	0.65/0.56	**3.68/.001**	0.53/0.70	0.39/0.43	1.16/.254	0.72/0.76	0.44/0.63	**2.19/.033**	1.76/1.64	1.13/1.19	**2.94/.005**
AU20	0.15/0.22	0.12/0.25	1.00/.323	0.03/0.11	0.04/0.10	-0.26/.794	0.15/0.25	0.23/0.65	-0.84/.407	0.27/0.56	0.11/0.25	**2.29/.026**
AU23	0.30/0.28	0.24/0.23	1.69/.096	0.07/0.21	0.07/0.11	-0.05/.962	0.25/0.33	0.22/0.37	0.49/.624	0.58/0.74	0.43/0.50	1.55/.128
AU25	2.23/1.97	1.58/1.38	**3.26/.002**	1.03/1.21	0.79/0.82	1.40/.168	0.98/1.21	1.51/1.61	-1.89/.064	4.69/4.83	2.45/2.93	**4.42/.000**
AU26	1.55/1.01	0.91/1.02	**5.72/.000**	0.61/0.85	0.44/0.49	1.37/.177	1.01/1.02	0.89/1.13	0.73/.470	3.03/2.34	1.40/2.08	**6.13/.000**
AU28	0.53/0.60	0.40/0.45	**2.09/.042**	0.10/0.33	0.04/0.09	1.40/.168	0.36/0.68	0.36/0.59	0.02/.987	1.12/1.37	0.80/1.09	1.94/.059
Head	2.24/1.79	2.16/2.04	0.81/.423	1.73/2.19	1.54/2.21	1.12/.269	1.93/2.01	1.78/2.22	0.66/.510	3.05/2.67	3.15/2.78	-0.35/.730
Tilt	0.51/0.44	0.44/0.37	1.28/.208	0.26/0.47	0.14/0.27	1.44/.157	0.36/0.52	0.40/0.67	-0.39/.701	0.91/0.98	0.78/0.88	0.85/.399
Forward	0.89/1.58	0.90/1.88	-0.18/.861	0.85/1.96	0.78/1.96	0.51/.609	0.76/1.46	0.90/2.00	-0.79/.433	1.08/1.94	1.04/2.19	0.26/.794
Backward	0.84/1.29	0.81/1.32	0.40/.692	0.63/1.38	0.61/1.28	0.20/.845	0.82/1.61	0.49/1.20	**2.82/.007**	1.07/1.71	1.34/2.18	-1.54/.130
Gaze	12.2/3.63	10.3/2.05	**4.74/.000**	8.94/2.89	6.60/3.07	**7.20/.000**	8.69/4.25	8.99/2.66	-0.46/.648	19.1/8.84	15.4/3.99	**3.19/.003**
At robot	5.11/4.14	3.04/2.44	**6.01/.000**	5.91/3.49	4.48/2.91	**4.00/.000**	3.91/3.05	1.98/2.47	**7.80/.000**	5.51/8.24	2.65/3.25	**3.05/.004**
At objects	3.75/2.41	4.64/1.74	**-3.93/.000**	2.62/2.21	1.73/1.32	**3.60/.001**	3.98/4.02	5.28/2.42	**-2.63/.011**	4.64/3.29	6.92/2.85	**-5.36/.000**
At table	3.13/2.03	2.49/1.86	**3.77/.000**	0.13/0.34	0.05/0.15	**2.08/.043**	0.64/0.70	1.67/1.64	**-4.29/.000**	8.64/5.82	5.75/4.31	**5.60/.000**
Wander	0.24/0.71	0.17/0.42	1.48/.147	0.28/1.10	0.34/0.97	-0.93/.357	0.16/0.54	0.07/0.23	1.81/.077	0.28/0.63	0.08/0.21	**2.27/.028**

Duration of Social Signals. Table 4 shows a summary of the duration (temporal aspect) of participants' social signals in seconds and the statistical analysis results. Column 2 and 3 of Table 4 show the duration of social signals in all error situations and all error-free situations. A t-test revealed that the duration of people's facial expressions ($t(49) = 4.27, p < .001$) and gaze shifts ($t(49) = 4.74, p < .001$) is longer during error situations compared to error-free situations. In the *gaze shifts* category, the duration of people's gaze at the robot and the table is longer during error situations. In the *facial expression* category, the duration of the following peoples' expression is longer in error situations than in error-free situations: AU01 (Inner Brow Raiser), AU02 (Outer Brow Raiser), AU04 (Brow Lowerer), AU05 (Upper Lid Raiser), AU17 (Chin Raiser), AU25 (Lips Part), AU26 (Jaw Drop), and AU28 (Lip Suck). Column 5 and 6 of Table 4 represents the duration of social signals between SNV error situations and their error-free situations counterparts. The facial expressions ($t(49) = 2.46, p = .017$) and gaze shifts ($t(49) = 7.20, p < .001$) duration is longer during SNV situations compared to the corresponding error-free situations. We also found that in the facial expressions category, the duration of AU01 (Inner Brow Raiser), AU04 (Brow Lowerer), and AU14 (Dimpler) in SNV situations is longer. In the *gaze shifts* category, the duration of gaze shifts by the people to the robot, the objects, and the table is significantly longer during SNV situations.

The duration of social signals in EE situations and their error-free situations equivalent are collated in column 8 and 9 of Table 4. We discovered that the backward movement of head gestures ($t(49) = 2.82, p = .007$) and gaze shifts at robot ($t(49) = 7.802, p < .001$) duration is longer during EE situations compared to the corresponding error-free situations. In the *facial expression* category, people express longer AU01 (Inner Brow Raiser) ($t(49) = 2.01, p = .050$) and AU17

(Chin Raiser) $(t(49) = 2.19, p = .033)$ during EE situations. In column 11 and 12 of Table 4, the duration of social signals in PE situations and their error-free situations are presented. We found that people prolonged facial expressions $(t(49) = 4.95, p < .001)$ and gaze shifts $(t(49) = 3.19, p = .003)$ during PE situations when compared to the equivalent error-free situations.

5 Discussion

The outcomes of the statistical analysis of our dataset agree with results of previous studies [4,9] that people exhibit specific social signals during error situations in HRI. Previous studies [4,9] only analysed the frequency (static aspect) of people's social signals in different types of error situations in HRI. We enrich the current understanding on error situations in human-robot interaction by analysing the frequency (static aspect) and the duration (dynamic aspect) of people's social signals during both error situations and error-free situations in HRI. In general, we found that people show more head movements, gaze shifts, and facial expressions during error situations than in error-free situations. We also discovered that the duration of facial expressions and gaze shifts are statistically longer during erroneous situations. The agreement of the previous research results and our results further indicates the importance of observing people's head movements, gaze shifts, and facial expression upon detecting error situations in HRC.

From the statistical analysis results, we learned that people tilt their head more often during error situations, we assume to express their confusion. We also noticed that people move their head forward more often during error situations to read the instruction on the robot's screen because they want to verify the robot's speech. We believed that people shift their gaze more frequently between the robot and the table in erroneous situations to find a solution to that situation. In terms of facial expressions, we found that people show more AU01, AU02, AU04, AU05, AU20, and AU27 during error situations which are usually associated with surprise and fear [3]. This finding is aligned with the post-study interview results in which most participants admitted that they were surprised, confused, or even scared when the robot made errors.

Statistical analysis further showed that during EE situations, people look at the robot more often and with a longer duration, while rarely look at the objects and the table. We hypothesised that people were frustrated during EE situations which made them stare at the robot and 'freeze', a phenomenon that people show in reaction to anxiety or stress [5]. Results showed that during PE situations, people look at the robot and the table longer while they look at objects with a shorter duration compared to the error-free equivalents. We believe that during PE situations, people look at the robot and the table to resolve the problem, while in error-free situations counterparts, they tend to keep working and look at objects longer as a result. Finally, we noticed that people show more facial expressions during PE situations compared to EE and SNV situations. Based on that result, we theorise that people give more reactions to the errors that strongly influence the continuity of the interaction.

6   Conclusion, Limitations and Future Work

This paper reports the differences between social signals' frequency and duration that people show in error situations and error-free situations in a human-robot collaboration scenario. These results are essential toward achieving our final aim of detecting and managing error situations in human-robot collaboration. The findings were extracted from a dataset of 600 error situations and 600 error-free situations that we collected in an extensive user study with 50 participants. The results show that during error situations, people express significantly more head movements, gaze shifts, and facial expression than in error-free situations. We also found that people show more extended facial expressions and gaze shifts during error situations. Further statistical analysis showed that there are also significant distinctions in the frequency and duration of people's social signals between social norm violations, execution errors, planning errors, and their respective error-free situation pairs. Based on these results, we are confident to choose humans' facial expressions, gaze shifts, and head gestures as input features of an automatic error situation detection module that we will develop in the future research.

The accuracy of our automatic annotation method is bound by our subjectivity upon determining the discretisation limits and the accuracy of the facial analysis pipeline which supports it. Another limitation of our work is that we do not have an absolute ground truth whether the study participants actually experienced each induced error situation as such. To solve these limitations, we plan to enrich the automatic annotation tool further by implementing dynamic thresholds and add the ability to annotate more social signal types such as speech and hand gestures. We will also assign human raters to label the dataset based on the participant's perspective to get the real ground truth of our dataset. We plan to pursue this research further by analysing the differences in people's social signals between error situation types. We also plan to publish our dataset together with automated and manual annotations. It will be the first publicly available dataset that contains erroneous and error-free situations in human-robot interaction. Finally, we will use our dataset to train a machine-learned model for automatic recognition of error situations in human-robot collaboration.

Acknowledgments. The first author acknowledges the scholarship support from the Ministry of Research and Higher Education (KEMENRISTEKDIKTI) of Republic of Indonesia through the Research and Innovation in Science and Technology (RISET-Pro) Program (World Bank Loan No. 8245-ID).

References

1. Baltrusaitis, T., Zadeh, A., Lim, Y.C., Morency, L.P.: OpenFace 2.0: facial behavior analysis toolkit. In: Proceedings - 13th IEEE International Conference on Automatic Face and Gesture Recognition, FG 2018, pp. 59–66. Institute of Electrical and Electronics Engineers Inc. (2018)
2. Cahya, D., Giuliani, M.: Towards a cognitive architecture incorporating human feedback for interactive collaborative robots. Lecture Notes in Computer Science (including subseries Lecture Notes in Artificial Intelligence and Lecture Notes in Bioinformatics), LNAI, vol. 10965, pp. 486–488 (2018)
3. Ekman, P., Friesen, W.V.: Facial Action Coding System - The Manual, vol. 160. Research Nexus division of Network Information Research Corporation (2002)
4. Giuliani, M., Mirnig, N., Stollnberger, G., Stadler, S., Buchner, R., Tscheligi, M.: Systematic analysis of video data from different human-robot interaction studies: a categorization of social signals during error situations. Front. Psychol. 6(July), 931 (2015)
5. Hagenaars, M.A., Oitzl, M., Roelofs, K.: Updating freeze: aligning animal and human research (2014). https://doi.org/10.1016/j.neubiorev.2014.07.021
6. Hamacher, A., Bianchi-Berthouze, N., Pipe, A.G., Eder, K.: Believing in BERT: using expressive communication to enhance trust and counteract operational error in physical Human-robot interaction. In: 25th IEEE International Symposium on Robot and Human Interactive Communication, RO-MAN 2016, pp. 493–500. Institute of Electrical and Electronics Engineers Inc. (2016)
7. Mann, S.: Humanistic computing: "WearComp" as a new framework and application for intelligent signal processing. Proc. IEEE 86(11), 2123–2151 (1998). https://doi.org/10.1109/5.726784
8. Mirnig, N., Giuliani, M., Stollnberger, G., Stadler, S., Buchner, R., Tscheligi, M.: Impact of robot actions on social signals and reaction times in HRI error situations. In: Tapus, A., André, E., Martin, J.C., Ferland, F., Ammi, M. (eds.) Social Robotics. LNCS (LNAI), vol. 9388, pp. 461–471. Springer, Cham (2015). https://doi.org/10.1007/978-3-319-25554-5_46
9. Mirnig, N., Stollnberger, G., Miksch, M., Stadler, S., Giuliani, M., Tscheligi, M.: To err is robot: how humans assess and act toward an erroneous social robot. Front. Robot. AI 4(May), 1–15 (2017)
10. Rasmussen, J.: Human errors. A taxonomy for describing human malfunction in industrial installations. J. Occup. Accid. 4(2–4), 311–333 (1982)
11. Salem, M., Lakatos, M., Amirabdollahian, F., Dautenhahn, K.: Would you trust a (faulty) robot?: effects of error, task type and personality on human-robot cooperation and trust. In: Proceedings of the Tenth Annual ACM/IEEE International Conference on Human-Robot Interaction, pp. 141–148 (2015)
12. Trung, P., et al.: Head and shoulders: automatic error detection in human-robot interaction. In: Proceedings of the 19th ACM International Conference on Multimodal Interaction - ICMI 2017, pp. 181–188 (2017)

Using Human Eye Gaze Patterns as Indicators of Need for Assistance from a Socially Assistive Robot

Ulyana Kurylo(✉) and Jason R. Wilson

Northwestern University, Evanston, IL 60208, USA
uk@u.northwestern.edu, jrw@northestern.edu

Abstract. With current growth in social robotics comes a need for well developed and fine tuned agents which respond to the user in a seamless and intuitive manner. Socially assistive robots in particular have become popular for their uses in care for older adults for medication adherence and socializing. Since eye gaze cues are important mediators in human-human interactions, we hypothesize that gaze patterns can be applied to human-robot interactions to identify when the user may need assistance. We reviewed videos ($N = 16$) of robot supported collaborative work to explore how recognition of gaze patterns for an assistive robot in the context of a medication management task can help predict when a user needs assistance. We found that *mutual gaze* is a better predictor than *confirmatory request*, *gaze away*, and *goal reference*. While eye gaze serves as an important indicator for need for assistance, it should be combined with other indicators, such as verbal cues or facial expressions to sufficiently represent assistance needed in the interaction and provide timely assistance.

Keywords: Gaze detection · Gaze patterns · Assistive agents

1 Introduction

As assistive robots become more prevalent, there is an increasing need to design robots that know how and when they should provide assistance, as not all users want constant assistance. Instead users may prefer to have the autonomy to make their own decisions, especially in regards to their care [10]. In the growing world of user-centered design constant assistance is often not preferable and the robot needs to know when is the proper time to give assistance. In human-human interactions, we use a variety of social cues to guide our interaction so we can predict the appropriate times to engage. Similarly, robots may use these social cues to create a more natural and seamless interaction. In particular, gaze cues are important indicators that assist in conversation management and mutual understanding; most people inherently give off and interpret such cues in social interactions. Given their importance in human interactions, it is natural

© Springer Nature Switzerland AG 2019
M. A. Salichs et al. (Eds.): ICSR 2019, LNAI 11876, pp. 200–210, 2019.
https://doi.org/10.1007/978-3-030-35888-4_19

to extend their utility to assistive robots, where understanding the users' needs can help in assisting them in accomplishing their goals.

A growing area of assistive robotics is socially assistive robots [7], which provide assistance in a social manner rather than a physical one where a robot is completing a task for the subject. Applications of socially assistive robots include physical therapy and rehabilitation [5,14], companionship for an older adult living in a care facility [20], helping children with autism [16], and medication management for older adults [21]. The use of robots in assistance with medication adherence in older adults is a relatively new application of assistive robots. Here, the robot is used to facilitate medication management while ensuring the user is still in control of the task [21]. Researchers used a Nao robot to provide assistance in a medication sorting task, where users were given a grid and two medications to sort in the grid. The intent of this task was for the user to feel they have control of the task while ensuring the correct medication sorting. In such a task, it is crucial for the robot to provide assistance at the correct time to increase the fluidity of the interaction and provide a more positive user experience.

Since gaze cues have already been shown to have important roles within social interactions between people, the analysis of gaze cues in the context of the collaborative human-robot medication sorting task can provide similar patterns of gaze, which can then be used to predict the user's need for assistance. Our data consists of videos taken from a previous study [21] that depicted interaction between a subject and a Nao robot during a robot-assisted task. The subject is engaged in a medication sorting task, relying on the robot to indicate when they make a mistake. Our goal is to identify a pattern, or patterns, of gaze which indicate this need for assistance before the subject makes an error or becomes disengaged. While gaze alone does not fully encapsulate the collaborative interaction, we postulate it is an important element in the development of a model of need. We hypothesize that there exists a simple model of gaze where just looking up at the robot indicates a need for assistance, unless the robot is speaking. In this paper, we evaluate four simple gaze models using annotated video data to determine which model best predicts when the user needs assistance.

2   Background

The importance of gaze, gesture, and facial expressions in social interaction have been well studied and documented in psychology literature. Gaze is a type of non-verbal feedback that is used to moderate conversations and other social interactions. Mutual gaze (or eye contact) is an important social tool used for helping gauge attentiveness, interest, competence, credibility and social skills within interactions [13]. Additionally, gaze provides feedback for turn taking in conversation to indicate when one is finished speaking, or expects to start their turn [11,12]. Gaze patterns are thus important indicators and mediators in human social interaction.

Mutual gaze is specifically important because of the role it plays in collaborative interactions. Perception of mutual gaze in collaborative tasks increased task completion [18]. Specific gaze patterns, including mutual gaze, have been identified and corroborated [1]. These include *joint attention, confirmatory requests, goal reference,* and *gaze aversion* [9]. Joint attention is defined as the initiation of gaze towards an object with another subject. This is a gaze at the subject, the object, and back to the subject. Confirmatory requests also involve another subject, but with the intention to confirm mutual gaze at an object rather than initiate it. This means a glance at the object, at the subject, then back to the object. Goal referencing is a gaze towards the goal state of the task. Gaze aversion is looking away, signaling disengagement or thoughtfulness [9].

With a clear understanding of how gaze mediates human-human social interactions, it is logical to extend these observations to human-robot interactions. The incorporation of eye gaze into the field of robotics and virtual agents spans two broad categories: agents producing gaze cues and agents interpreting human gaze cues. First, we will discuss the work being done in virtual agents producing gaze cues. Because gaze cues are used for communication, the use of such cues by robots increases subject engagement and fluidity of interaction [4,17]. Human-like robots which demonstrate timely gaze version appeared more thoughtful and were more successful in conversational turn taking [3]. Work has been done on task collaboration with gaze-producing agents, which showed that subjects made fewer mistakes on the task when the agent would produce human-like gaze cues in addition to responding to the subject's gaze cues [2].

As for robots interpreting gaze cues, there are a several works which explore this interaction. For example, human gaze feedback has been used as indicator for object identification tasks between a human subject and a Nao robot [6]. In human robot collaboration tasks, object handover is most successful when the robot waits for a gaze cue before releasing the object [8]. The initiation of joint attention is important in collaborative tasks with an assistive agent to establish common ground. Previous work has shown that agents which make use of these gaze cues as well as produce them demonstrate higher levels of understanding and fluidity of interaction [15]. In assistive environments with service robots, it has been suggested that the use of gaze patterns which naturally occur between a caretaker and a patient can aid in the development of service robots which display availability, recipiency, and acknowledgement [23].

3   Data Collection

We analyzed 19 audio-video recordings of humans completing a medication sorting task while being assisted by a social robot that were recorded for [21]. Of the 19 videos, the robot had technical difficulties in three of the videos. With the malfunction resulting in a lack of human-robot interaction; we removed these three videos from our analysis.

For the study in the videos, subjects were either graduate students (N = 10) or undergraduates (N = 10). Half of the subjects were male, half were female and all subjects were randomly assigned to either a virtual or physical robot. One participant was not recorded, resulting in 19 videos. Videos consisted of a Nao robot situated in front of a subject. The subject had in front of them two pill bottles and a grid representing the week. The goal of the task was to follow the labels on the medication containers to sort the medication into the weekly grid. The robot would provide a verbal introduction to the task, as well as other constraints for the task (for example, dance class or appointments that needed to be considered). When the subject made a mistake, the robot would offer varying levels of verbal assistance. The task was the same for all subjects, while the robot was either physically embodied or a virtual representation on a screen. The subject collaborated with the robot to complete the task by following the robots instructions and hints. The task is completed when the medication is correctly placed and the robot verbalizes successful completion of the task to the subject.

To analyze the videos, we annotated each video using the ChronoViz[1] annotation tool (see Fig. 1). Annotations consisted of gaze events in addition to vocal and gesture cues. Gaze events are continuous, as the subject is always looking somewhere within the environment. All annotated events show the start and end times of the event.

Fig. 1. The Chronoviz video annotation tool with a frame from one video, which shows the setup of the robot with the medication grid on the table between the robot and the person. The bottom portion of the image shows the annotation bar, with the different rows representing various annotation categories (i.e. gaze at robot, gaze away, etc.)

There are four types of eye gaze events that we capture:

- **Gaze at robot:** Subject is gazing at the robot, including the face or body.
- **Gaze at the task:** Subject is gazing at the sorting grid or the pills in their hand.
- **Gaze at goal reference:** Gaze at the pill containers, or reading the container labels.
- **Gaze away:** Any gaze that is not one of the three above is a gaze away, such as a gaze at the ceiling or other elements of the environment not included above.

---

[1] http://chronoviz.com.

Table 1. Frequency of gaze annotations, percentages of instances and annotation time.

	Robot	Task	Away	Goal	Total
No. of instances	328	429	14	185	956
% of total instances	34	45	2	19	100
% of total annotated time	14	61	1	24	100

In addition to the gaze events, we capture vocal cues and gestures, as defined here:

- **Vocal cue:** An utterance by the subject or the robot.
- **Gesture:** A movement of the hands or arms, either by the subject or the robot.

Gaze events occurred continuously, while vocal and gesture cues were either continuous or discreet. All of the annotations were made by the first author, resulting in the numbers of annotations reported in Table 1.

In addition to the objective annotations for the eye gaze, vocal, and gesture events, we had subjective ratings for when a person needs assistance. We define needing assistance as confused glances, periods of inactivity, verbalization of need, or appearing frustrated. Since this is a subjective rating, three annotators labeled each video with the start and end times at which the person in the video (the person being assisted by the robot) appears to need assistance. Final ratings are all times at which at least 2 annotators judged the person to be in need of assistance. There are 872 help events representing 1010.9 s of help needed out of 3837.7 s of total video times. These annotations are used for the validation of our models.

4   Eye Gaze Model to Predict Need for Assistance

Our ultimate goal is develop a model that can predict when a person needs assistance so that a socially assistive robot can respond at the appropriate time. A successful model could be integrated into a system that determines the timing and level of assistance based on the needs of the person, such as proposed in [22]. The assistive robot may use a variety of modalities to infer when a person needs assistance, but the models we consider here focus primarily on the direction of eye gaze of the person.

4.1   Atomic Model Design

We hypothesize that a simple glance from the task at the robot while the robot is not speaking is a powerful predictor of the person's need for assistance. To validate our hypothesis, we compare four models, with each model considering different features from the data. Models are made to include the relevant gaze cues from prior research. They are not learned for the purpose of assessing which features are most relevant. There are four atomic models used to compare the effectiveness of each gaze pattern to predict need, each representing a single eye gaze pattern, described below.

Mutual Gaze (MG). The *mutual gaze* model represents the subject initiating mutual gaze with the robot by directing its gaze at the robot. When this gaze is initiated, the model will predict the subject needs assistance from the robot, with a couple of exceptions. The model does not include instances where the robot was speaking and the person was looking at the robot because it is natural to react to the robot speaking by looking up at it.

Confirmatory Gaze (C). The *confirmatory gaze* model attempts to recognize when a person is looking back and forth between the task and the robot with the intention of getting feedback on the task. This is when a person places a pill but is unsure as to whether it is correct, and the person glances at the robot and back at the placement to indicate that they are unsure about the action. To recognize this, the model categorizes one of two situations as need for assistance: (1) the person briefly looks at the task and then briefly looks at the robot, or (2) the person briefly looks at the robot followed by briefly looking at the task. A brief glance is considered to be less than 2.5 s (time defined through experimentation).

Goal Referencing (G). The *goal referencing* model attempts to capture the case where a person is visually referencing a "goal" state and needs assistance. We consider the goal to be the instructions on the medication bottles. In addition to the person looking at the goal, we constrain the model to include only the instances where the subject does not exhibit any hand gesture motions. The subject only needs assistance when they are looking at the goal but are not completing the task, as this signals some sort of confusion or delay in understanding.

Gaze Away (A). The *gaze away* model uses a gaze aversion longer than a second as a predictor of need. Gaze aversion for longer periods of time is often a signal of disengagement or boredom. We defined gaze away to be any gaze that is not the other 3 gaze categories. This is done because gaze is continuous; if the person is not looking at the task, robot, or pill bottles, they could be looking at the ceiling or floor, and this is considered a gaze away.

All models included a 10 s "orienting" period at the beginning of each video, during which the subject gets accustomed to the environment and robot. The subject may look around, at the robot, at the pill bottles, etc., but none of these events will be classified as the person needing assistance during this time period.

4.2 Atomic Model Evaluation

We evaluated each model by comparing the results of the model to the ratings of the annotators. To process the annotations of each video, we created a sequence of events, each characterized by a new annotation representing change in the environment. For example, if the person is looking down at the task and then begins and finishes speaking while still looking at the task, there will be four events for the beginning of looking down at the task, the beginning of speaking (while still looking down), the end of speaking, and finally the end of looking down (which coincides with the beginning of looking elsewhere). Over all videos there were 2145 events with a mean of 134 events per video (SD = 121.8).

For each event, the model classified the event as either a time in which the person needs assistance or not. Each model classification was compared with the subjective annotation at that time. Inter-rater agreement was used to confirm subjective measures. Of the 2145 events, 834 of them (38.9% of the events) correspond with a time in which an annotator has indicated the person needs assistance.

4.3   Atomic Model Results

We analyzed how each model performs on the annotations from each video, and our results show that mutual gaze as well as confirmatory gaze are both good predictors of need for assistance (see Fig. 2). The Mutual Gaze model performs best and the Confirmatory Gaze model is better than both the Gaze Away and Goal Reference models (see Fig. 2).

The Mutual Gaze model produces accuracy significantly above chance (.637, p < .001) the highest precision score of the atomic models (.703), and the second highest recall score (.116). The next best is the Confirmatory Gaze model, which results in .629 accuracy, .611 precision, and .207 recall.

The Gaze Away and Goal Reference models do not perform as well. The Gaze Away model results in an accuracy of .610, precision of .4, and recall of .005. The Goal Reference model is still better than the Goal Away model, yielding an accuracy of .508, precision of .209, and recall of .094.

We also compare the precision and recall of each of the models. As for the precision of the models, the Mutual Gaze model is significantly better than that of the Gaze Away (paired t-test, p = .026) and Goal Reference (p = .029) models, and the precision of the Confirmatory Gaze model approaches is better than the Gaze Away model (p = .023) and possibly better than Goal Reference (p = .085). There are statistical differences between the other pairs of models.

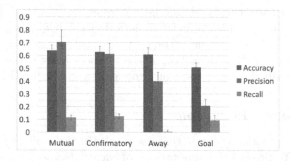

Fig. 2. The accuracy, precision, and recall for each of the atomic models shows that the precision of the Mutual Gaze and Confirmatory Gaze models are clearly better than the other two models.

As for the recall of the models, the Mutual Gaze model is significantly better than that of the Gaze Away (paired t-test, $p = .002$) and approaches being significantly better than Goal Reference ($p = .07$) and approaching significance for the Goal Reference model ($p = .073$). Similarly, the recall of the Confirmatory Gaze model is better than the Gaze Away model ($p = .003$) and possibly better than Goal Reference ($p = .089$). The recall of the Gaze Away model is also statistically better than the Goal Reference model ($p = .009$). There are statistical differences between the other pairs of models.

5   Discussion

Our development of gaze models was based on patterns and cues found in human-human interactions. Mutual gaze, including joint attention and confirmatory gaze, were major cues in human-human collaborative tasks [2]. We extended these cues to a human-robot task to identify a pattern of gaze that indicate a subject needs assistance in a collaboration task. Our results show that gaze cues, particularly mutual gaze, are good indicators for help needed in robot supported collaborative work. These results align with previous work on the use of gaze cues to understand and embody interactions with assistive agents [1,2,8,15].

In support of our hypothesis, mutual and confirmatory gaze models were the best predictors of need in a collaborative task. This is because a simple look at the robot is enough to indicate that the subject needs assistance, without the need for other gaze cues. Our Gaze Away and Goal Reference models had the lowest precision scores across all models. This supports the idea that a gaze at the robot is sufficient for identifying need. There may be instances where the subject is gazing away as a sign of thoughtfulness rather than disengagement. The data has relatively low amounts of gaze away instances, the importance of away gaze in predicting need for assistance is thus inconclusive. Frequent goal referencing gazes may be for clarification of the medication label rather than an explicit signal of confusion.

While our most successful gaze models had relatively high precision scores, the recall score for each of the models was lower. This is because gaze patterns do not encapsulate the full breadth of interactions with assistive agents. The range of human communication spans more than just gaze (e.g., also speech, body posture, facial expressions). As such, the need for assistance is displayed through more than just gaze cues, and it is expected that a model focusing on gaze would not be able to identify all the occurrences of when a person needs assistance. The analysis of gaze cues must be combined with other modalities to provide a holistic model of need for assistance in a collaborative task.

This work provides a starting point for the development of a holistic model for assistive agents in the context of HRI. While previous work has identified benefits for gaze producing agents, development of a holistic model which includes gaze can improve interaction and facilitate decision making on the part of the assistive agent. This work has implications for the improvement and development of future assistive systems, and offers a strong argument for the use of gaze cues in such systems.

6   Limitations

This work built upon a previous study [21] from which the videos were annotated and used for model testing and validation. While the models focused on gaze cues, gaze alone does not represent a holistic view of a collaborative interaction, which is seen through the relatively low recall scores. Gaze should be an element of a much larger representation which can include indicators such as vocalizations, types of gestures, facial expressions, emotions, or more. This idea is supported by previous work done on assistive agents, which shows a range of considerations for assistive agents; these interactions cannot be reduced down to a single gaze pattern or behavior [19]. The assistive agent in our work did not produce gaze cues, this limits our analysis of gaze patterns as we hypothesized them based on human-human interactions where both subjects produce gaze cues. While it did produce vocal corrections and some gestures, these were not based on the gaze cues of the subject.

7   Future Work

While this work focused entirely on the use of gaze cues as predictors of assistance, future work should expand the model of need to include other empirically decided indicators, and develop a holistic model of need. Thus, further work with assistive agents in this context should seek to develop such a model of need with the goal of optimally supporting the subject in the task. Future work should also explore the production of communication cues, such as human-like gaze or gestures, in assistive agents to aid in task completion and robot usability. While work has been done for gaze producing agents [3,4,17], the integration of gaze production with a robust model of need should be explored. A holistic model would better represent the collaborative interaction and likely improve the low recall scores observed with gaze-only models.

To improve the validity and application to real world situations, our model should be generalized across other environments, agents, and tasks. Such future work can explore the use of assistive agents with other physical and cognitive tasks. To further generalize, we must validate that these models apply to other agents, both virtual agents and physical robots, as there could be differences in gaze patterns with different agent embodiment. To provide real-time data, eye tracking software and hardware should be explored to validate the model of gaze and provide more precise integration with an assistive agent.

8   Conclusion

The simple model of mutual gaze performed best as a predictor for need of assistance in a medication sorting task. However, for improved results, mutual gaze should be incorporated with other cues in the development of a robust assistance model for use in socially assistive agents. The model of gaze draws from cues found in human-human collaboration, and provides a framework for continued development of a holistic assistance model. The development of such a model has implications for robots in health care, particularly for physical therapy, companionship, and medication adherence. With an increasing need for elderly and disability care in care facilities and at home, assistive agents can be used to support human autonomy within an activity or assist with daily tasks to ease the reliance on nurses [23]. While there remains a considerable amount of work to develop assistive agents, our work here is an important step toward enabling socially assistive robots to better recognize when a person needs assistance and thereby better support the person's goals and autonomy.

References

1. Admoni, H., Scassellati, B.: Social eye gaze in human-robot interaction: a review. J. Hum.-Robot Interact. **6**(1), 25–63 (2017)
2. Andrist, S., Gleicher, M., Mutlu, B.: Looking coordinated: bidirectional gaze mechanisms for collaborative interaction with virtual characters. In: Proceedings of the 2017 CHI Conference on Human Factors in Computing Systems, pp. 2571–2582. ACM (2017)
3. Andrist, S., Tan, X.Z., Gleicher, M., Mutlu, B.: Conversational gaze aversion for humanlike robots. In: Proceedings of the 2014 ACM/IEEE International Conference on Human-Robot Interaction, pp. 25–32. ACM (2014)
4. Bruce, A., Nourbakhsh, I., Simmons, R.: The role of expressiveness and attention in human-robot interaction. In: Proceedings 2002 IEEE International Conference on Robotics and Automation (Cat. No. 02CH37292), vol. 4, pp. 4138–4142. IEEE (2002)
5. Casas, J., et al.: Architecture for a social assistive robot in cardiac rehabilitation. In: 2018 IEEE 2nd Colombian Conference on Robotics and Automation (CCRA), pp. 1–6. IEEE (2018)
6. Fang, R., Doering, M., Chai, J.Y.: Embodied collaborative referring expression generation in situated human-robot interaction. In: 2015 10th ACM/IEEE International Conference on Human-Robot Interaction (HRI), pp. 271–278. IEEE (2015)
7. Feil-Seifer, D., Matarić, M.J.: Defining socially assistive robotics. In: 9th International Conference on Rehabilitation Robotics, ICORR 2005, pp. 465–468 (2005)
8. Grigore, E.C., Eder, K., Pipe, A.G., Melhuish, C., Leonards, U.: Joint action understanding improves robot-to-human object handover. In: 2013 IEEE/RSJ International Conference on Intelligent Robots and Systems, pp. 4622–4629. IEEE (2013)
9. Huang, C.M., Andrist, S., Sauppé, A., Mutlu, B.: Using gaze patterns to predict task intent in collaboration. Front. Psychol. **6**, 1049 (2015)
10. Jeste, D.V., Depp, C.A.: Positive mental aging. Am. J. Geriatr. Psychiatry **18**(1), 1–3 (2010)
11. Jokinen, K.: Gaze and gesture activity in communication. In: Stephanidis, C. (ed.) UAHCI 2009. LNCS, vol. 5615, pp. 537–546. Springer, Heidelberg (2009). https://doi.org/10.1007/978-3-642-02710-9_60
12. Kendon, A., Cook, M.: The consistency of gaze patterns in social interaction. Br. J. Psychol. **60**(4), 481–494 (1969)

13. Kleinke, C.L.: Gaze and eye contact: a research review. Psychol. Bull. **100**(1), 78 (1986)
14. Matarić, M.J., Eriksson, J., Feil-Seifer, D.J., Winstein, C.J.: Socially assistive robotics for post-stroke rehabilitation. J. NeuroEng. Rehabil. **4**(5), 1–9 (2007)
15. Mehlmann, G., Häring, M., Janowski, K., Baur, T., Gebhard, P., André, E.: Exploring a model of gaze for grounding in multimodal HRI. In: Proceedings of the 16th International Conference on Multimodal Interaction, pp. 247–254. ACM (2014)
16. Pennisi, P., et al.: Autism and social robotics: a systematic review. Autism Res. **9**(2), 165–183 (2016)
17. Satake, S., Kanda, T., Glas, D.F., Imai, M., Ishiguro, H., Hagita, N.: How to approach humans?: strategies for social robots to initiate interaction. In: Proceedings of the 4th ACM/IEEE International Conference on Human Robot Interaction, HRI 2009, pp. 109–116. ACM, New York (2009)
18. Schneider, B., Pea, R.: Real-time mutual gaze perception enhances collaborative learning and collaboration quality. Int. J. Comput.-Supported Collab. Learn. **8**(4), 375–397 (2013)
19. Tapus, A., Maja, M., Scassellatti, B.: The grand challenges in socially assistive robotics. IEEE Robot. Autom. Mag. **14**(1), 35–42 (2007)
20. Wada, K., Shibata, T.: Robot therapy in a care house - change of relationship among the residents and seal robot during a 2-month long study. IEEE Trans. Robot. **23**(5), 972–980 (2007)
21. Wilson, J.R., Lee, N.Y., Saechao, A., Tickle-Degnen, L., Scheutz, M.: Supporting human autonomy in a robot-assisted medication sorting task. Int. J. Soc. Robot. **10**(5), 621–641 (2018)
22. Wilson, J.R., Wransky, M., Tierno, J.: General approach to automatically generating need-based assistance. In: Proceeding of Advances in Cognitive Systems (2018))
23. Yamazaki, K., et al.: Prior-to-request and request behaviors within elderly day care: implications for developing service robots for use in multiparty settings. In: Bannon, L.J., Wagner, I., Gutwin, C., Harper, R.H.R., Schmidt, K. (eds.) ECSCW 2007, pp. 61–78. Springer, London (2007). https://doi.org/10.1007/978-1-84800-031-5_4

Knock on Wood: The Effects of Material Choice on the Perception of Social Robots

Sanne van Waveren$^{(\boxtimes)}$, Linnéa Björklund, Elizabeth J. Carter,
and Iolanda Leite

KTH Royal Institute of Technology, Stockholm, Sweden
{sannevw,iolanda}@kth.se

Abstract. Many people who interact with robots in the near future will not have prior experience, and they are likely to intuitively form their first impressions of the robot based on its appearance. This paper explores the effects of component material on people's perception of the robots in terms of social attributes and willingness to interact. Participants watched videos of three robots with different outer materials: wood, synthetic fur, and plastic. The results showed that people rated the perceived warmth of a plastic robot lower than a wooden or furry robot. Ratings of perceived competence and discomfort did not differ between the three robots.

Keywords: Social robotics · Robot material design · Social perception

1 Introduction

In science fiction, robots are often depicted as human-like or as metallic, machine-like creatures. Now, social robots are going beyond their roles in science fiction and taking a place in our daily lives. Currently, these commercially available robots for personal use do not look like realistic humans, and their component materials are often metal or plastic. However, it is possible to incorporate other materials into robot design, including wood, fabric, and fur, that could make robots more pleasing and comfortable to use in different contexts.

As many people interacting with robots will not have prior experience, they are likely to intuitively form their impressions of a robot based on its outer appearance during the first milliseconds of interaction, as is typical among humans [31]. In fact, people ascribe social attributes, such as warmth and competence, to social robots based on their physical characteristics [21].

While studies have been done on robot embodiment (e.g., physical vs. virtual [11,15,30]), robot body shape (e.g., size [19], waist-to-hip ratio and shoulder width [1]) and facial features (e.g., eyebrows, eyes [6,14,26]), less attention has been given to component materials. Some works have investigated how robot skin can convey emotions through skin textures [13] and skin temperature [24]. One research team developed a robot with customizable skin [29]. However, the

© Springer Nature Switzerland AG 2019
M. A. Salichs et al. (Eds.): ICSR 2019, LNAI 11876, pp. 211–221, 2019.
https://doi.org/10.1007/978-3-030-35888-4_20

question of how the choice of component material affects people's perception of robots remains open.

Human-robot interaction (HRI) may benefit if people's perceptions of a robot can be shaped through choice of component material. In this work, we examine if the choice of outer material affects people's perception of a social robot; we study the effects of using wood, plastic, and synthetic fur on people's impressions of warmth, competence, and discomfort. We expect that a robot made of plastic (an inorganic material) will be rated less positively than a wooden or a furry robot. We expect fur to score similarly to wood, as both materials resemble organic materials. Specifically, we hypothesize that:

- H1: A robot constructed of wood will be rated as more positive than a robot constructed of plastic.
- H2: A robot constructed of fur will be rated as more positive than a robot constructed of plastic.
- H3: A robot constructed of wood will be rated equally positive as a robot constructed of fur.

2 Related Work

The design of a robot should match its intended function [6,17]; prior work has focused on different aspects of robot appearance, such as the body's shape and the design of the face. Social robots that are intended for human interaction should have a degree of humanness that evokes positive reactions from the people with whom they interact, without being too similar to humans, as this may elicit feelings of uncanniness [22].

To date, many works have investigated what level of the human-likeness is appropriate to increase the effectiveness of HRIs [7,9]. An fMRI study by Krach et al. [17] showed that a robot's degree of human-likeness influences people's cortical activity in regions associated with Theory of Mind [27]; perceived human-likeness was positively correlated with the tendency to attribute mental states to the robot. However, Phillips et al. [25] argued that there is little systematic understanding of what constitutes a robot's human-likeness and identified four different dimensions (body-manipulators, facial features, mechanical locomotion, and surface look) that contribute to the perceived human-likeness of a robot. We discuss prior work on the facial features and surface appearance of social robots.

The face plays a crucial role in human interactions: it conveys information about what a person is thinking or feeling, their age and physical condition, and sometimes even their personalities. Early work focused on the mechanical design of expressive humanoid robot faces. For example, Hegel et al. [10] designed the social robot 'Flobi', which appears cartoon-like and can express both primary emotions (e.g., happy, sad) and even some secondary emotions with moderate success (e.g., shame). The design used baby-face cues (e.g., relatively large eyes, small chin, small lips and nose, and round head shape) to make the robot appear warmer, more naive, less dominant and less competent. DiSalvo et al. [6] conducted a study on the design and perception of a humanoid robot head and found that a humanoid robot head and face with a small forehead, small chin, and a head that is wider than that it is long, create a positive experience in HRI.

Luria et al. [20] studied the effects of a social robot's eye designs on how it was perceived. The authors created sixteen eye options for paper prototypes of a tabletop robot, ranging from lifelike eyes to abstract eyes, and no eyes as a control. The results showed that robots with more lifelike eyes were perceived as more personable and as a better fit for entertainment roles and domestic environments relative to robots with more abstract eyes or no eyes.

While robots typically have mechanical faces, rendering robot faces on a screen has endowed robots with more facial expressivity. Carpinella et al. [4] manipulated the masculinity vs. femininity and machine-likness vs. human-likeness of rendered robot faces and found that robots with a higher degree of human-likeness and femininity were perceived as warmer, and machine-like or masculine robots were seen as more discomforting. Similarly, Kalegina et al. [14] studied people's preferences in realism and detail of rendered robot faces; the authors manipulated one face feature at a time and found that less realistic and less detailed robots are preferred in domestic settings and highly detailed, whereas not too realistic, robots are preferred for service tasks. Lehmann et al. [18] used a user-centered design approach to design the face display of a humanoid robot companion. An online survey showed that people rejected abstract designs for the robot face, and preferred an iconic face without too much details. In summary, the design of a robot face needs to consider the social role and function of the robot, as well as its human-likeness, gender facets, and realism.

Prior work focused mostly on the body shape and facial features of robots, and an open question is what material should be used for the surface of robots' bodies. Some research has looked into how robot skin can convey emotions using skin textures and form [2,13] and skin temperature [24]. One work addressed the need for customizable robots with SPRITE, a socially assistive robot with a modifiable skin to tailor the robot to a target population or specific domain [29]. The authors stated that robot's small size and colorful outer appearance made people perceive it as non-threatening.

This work draws inspiration from other domains, such as industrial design, that have studied material choice in the process of product design. One study examined the link between the outer material of a bowl and what emotions it evoked within the participants [5]. It was found that wood scored high on all positive attributes measured, including joy and satisfaction, and low on negative attributes, such as disgust and fear. Contrarily, plastic generally scored high on negative and low on positive attributes. In this work, we investigate to what extent these effects translate to robots. Our work extends existing literature by investigating how surface material of a robot affects people's perception of its social attributes.

3   Robot Design

The robots were constructed from three different materials: birch plywood, birch plywood covered in synthetic fur, and acrylic plastic; see Fig. 1. Besides that prior interior design research showed that wood scored higher on eliciting positive emotions and lower on negative emotions than plastic [5], these materials are easy to work with, being both cheap and workable with a laser cutter. The robots possessed three degrees of freedom with MG90s micro servos in the shoulder joints and the neck, using Arduino Uno for motion control.

Fig. 1. The three versions of the robot: wood, plastic, and fur.

4   Method

4.1   Participants and Design

120 participants were recruited from Amazon's Mechanical Turk (MTurk), they were compensated for their participation. As control questions, participants were asked to report the color of the square shown at the end of each video (*"What color was the square at the end of the video?"*), and we added the following item to the questionnaire: *"To make sure you are still paying attention, we have added this question. Please choose 9 'definitely associated' for the next item 'check question'."* Three workers were excluded from the analysis because they failed to answer two or more of the control questions correctly, resulting in a total of 117 participants (43 female and 74 male). Participants' mean age was 32.82 (SD = 8.63), and they described themselves as White/Caucasian (53.8%), Black or African American (5.1%), Asian or Pacific Islander (26.5%), Hispanic, Latino, or Spanish origin (7.7%), Native American, American Indian, or Alaska Native (2.6%), Native Hawaiian (0.9%), mixed (0.9%), unknown (2.7%). A total of 56 (47.9%) participants reported to have completed a bachelor's degree, 23 (19.7%) participants a master's degree, 16 (13.7%) participants some college credit but no degree, 14 (12%) participants had a high school graduate, diploma or equivalent, four (3.4%) completed trade/technical/vocational training, three

(2.6%) participants completed an associate degree, and one (0.9%) reported to have completed a doctorate degree. Overall, participants reported that they were somewhat familiar with robots, with a mean of 2.4 (SD = 1.1) on a scale from zero (not at all) to four (extremely). Specifically, 25 (21.4%) participants reported to work with robots, 27 (23.1%) participants study or have studied robots, nine (7.7%) reported to own a robot, 73 (62.4%) participants said to watch or read media that includes robots, and one participant reported to have no experience with robots. We manipulated within-subjects the independent variable of robot material (wood vs. fur vs. plastic). To account for order effects, the order in which the robots were presented was counterbalanced.

4.2 Materials and Procedure

Participants viewed a video of each robot in which the robot was angled 45 degrees away from the viewer, then turned its head 45 degrees to face the viewer, raised the arm closest to the viewer and waved up and down three times[1]. After each video, participants were asked to rate the robot they just watched on warmth, competence, and discomfort dimensions on a scale from 1 (definitely not associated) to 9 (definitely associated) adapted from Carpinella et al. [4]. We included the following items as they were most relevant to the current study: *reliable, competent, knowledgeable,* and *capable* (resulting in four items on the competence dimension); *organic, sociable, emotional, happy,* and *feeling* (resulting in five items on the warmth dimension); and *awkward, scary, strange, awful,* and *aggressive* (resulting in five items on the discomfort dimension). All three dimensions for all three robots were found to have adequate internal consistency, with Cronbach's α levels all above 0.9. Therefore, we averaged the individual items of each dimension to obtain the final score for that dimension. Additionally, we asked how much they liked the robot (1 = dislike, 7 = like) and their willingness to interact/spend time with the robot (1 = not at all willing, 7 = very willing). Finally, participants were asked to give each robot a name, to report which robot they preferred and why (*"Please explain in a minimum of 20 words why you prefer this robot. This helps us understand your responses better."*), and to provide demographic information.

5 Results

We analyzed the ratings on perceived warmth, competence, discomfort, likability, people's willingness to interact with each of the three robots, and which robot the participants preferred. To gain additional insight into why people preferred a specific robot, we performed qualitative analysis on the free-text answers.

---

[1] Videos are available at bit.ly/2IsnMSW, bit.ly/2Iph28i, bit.ly/2L1vBAz.

5.1   Social Attribute Judgments

A repeated-measures ANOVA with skin type (wood vs. fur vs. plastic) as the within-subjects factor showed that warmth differed statistically significantly across materials ($F(2,232) = 11.15$, $p < 0.0005$, $\eta^2 = 0.09$) (See Fig. 2). Post hoc tests using the Bonferroni correction revealed that the plastic robot scored statistically significantly lower (M = 4.72, SD = 2.35) than the wooden (M = 5.10, SD = 2.25, $p < 0.005$) and the furry robot (M = 5.19, SD = 2.15, p < 0.0005). Wood and fur did not differ significantly from each other ($p = 1.0$). In line with the low ratings of warmth for the plastic robot, examples of names that the participants gave the plastic robot include "Snowman robot", "ice cold robot", and "pale robot". Both ratings for competence and discomfort did not differ statistically significantly. A repeated-measures ANOVA for skin type showed no significant difference in perceived competence ($F(2, 232) = 1.28$, $p = 0.28$; wood: M = 5.57, SD = 1.94, fur: M = 5.45, SD = 2.09 and plastic: M = 5.44, SD = 2.10). A repeated-measures ANOVA for skin type showed no significant difference in discomfort ($F(2, 232) = 0.77$, $p = 0.46$; wood M = 4.55, SD = 2.41, fur: M = 4.58, SD = 2.44 and plastic: M = 4.44, SD = 2.46).

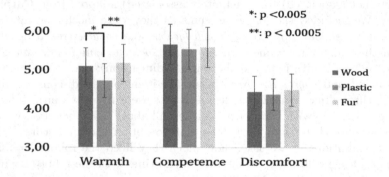

Fig. 2. Mean warmth, competence, and discomfort ratings. Error bars indicate standard errors.

5.2   Likability

The participants rated the three robots moderately on likability. The wooden (M = 5.14, SD = 1.6, Mdn = 5.0) and furry (M = 5.21, SD = 1.66, Mdn = 6.0) robots were rated slightly higher than the plastic robot (M = 4.97, SD = 1.6, Mdn = 5.0), but a repeated-measures ANOVA showed that the scores did not differ significantly ($p = 0.096$).

5.3   Willingness to Interact

The participants rated their willingness to interact with the thee robots as moderately high (furry robot M = 5.26, SD = 1.54, Mdn = 6.0; wooden robot

M = 5.16, SD = 1.60, Mdn = 6.0; plastic robot M = 5.09, SD = 1.63, Mdn = 5.0). A repeated-measures ANOVA found no statistically significant difference in the mean scores of the three robots ($p = 0.37$).

5.4 Robot Preference

45 (38.5%) participants reported preferring the plastic robot, 40 (34.2%) preferred the furry robot, and 32 (27.4%) preferred the wooden robot; statistically, the three robots were not unequally preferred; $\chi^2(2) = 2.205$, $p = 0.33$. This suggests that despite the difference in ratings on the warmth dimension, participants prefer the three types of robots equally. To gain insight into participants' robot preferences, two independent coders coded the open-ended question in which participants were asked to explain their choice and we report the main findings. 101 out of 117 answers were coded with substantial inter-rater agreement (fuzzy κ [16] = 0.76), the other 16 answers were either unrelated or incomprehensible.

People's reason to prefer the furry and wooden robots seems to often relate to their material, which reminds people of pets or wooden objects they have seen before (kid's toy or cartoon), and their social character traits, such as kindness and friendliness, e.g., *"I prefer this robot because it us furry, which makes it look more animal like and friendly. It's almost like a pet. I think it's cute."* (Fur robot) and *"Something about the design makes it feel more like a kids toy or a cartoon. The dashes that run around the edges kind of remind me of animated characters. (...) it reminds me of Awesom-O (from the TV show South Park)."* (Wooden robot). The people who preferred the plastic robot seem to comment positively on its appearance and usefulness, e.g., *"I like this white color robot and i think this one is very knowledgeable, responsive, capable robot [more] than the other robots"*.

6 Discussion and Conclusion

Robot design is a crucial aspect of HRI research and in this study, we shed some light on the role of robot component material and pave the way for further research on the effects of robot materials on people's perceptions of social robots. We hypothesized that a robot constructed of wood would be rated more positively than a robot constructed of plastic (*H1*), that a robot constructed of fur would be rated more positively than a robot constructed of plastic (*H2*), and that a robot constructed of wood would be rated equally positively as a robot made of fur (*H3*).

The results showed that people rated the plastic robot significantly lower on perceived warmth as compared to the wooden and furry robots. The warmth ratings for the wooden and furry robots did not differ significantly, which confirms all three hypotheses for the warmth dimension. Interestingly, people did not rate the three robots differently in terms of competence or discomfort. Open answers revealed that the robot's resemblance with for example, a pet or a toy, and its positive social traits may be a reason to prefer the wooden or furry robot, whereas the plastic robot may be preferred because of its perceived usefulness.

As people have shown the same tendency to form impressions for robots as they do for humans [21], our findings may be explained by what we know about human impression formation. From social psychology, it is known that warmth and competence are the primary focus in impression formation among people. Specifically, wood as a furnishing material has been shown to be perceived as a warmer, more natural, and more inviting material, compared to glass or plastic [28]. Fur may remind people of (stuffed) animals, making the robot appear more organic and causing people to imbue it with emotion, as has been seen in animal-like robots [23], even when the robot is minimalistic in design [3].

The robots in this study were small, not highly detailed, table-top robots, which may explain why participants did not rate them differently on the discomfort dimension, as they were not uncanny [22]. In contrast to warmth, which reflects characteristics that benefit others, for example, whether someone is friendly, competence reflects characteristics that benefit the self, for example, being intelligent or skilled [12]. Competence is related to people's expectations of the robot's function, e.g., which task or what behavior they expect the robot to perform, but the robots did not have a specific task or function, which may explain why the robots were note rated differently in terms of competence.

Another interpretation for why we found an effect for warmth but not competence is that morality judgments may be more important in a first evaluation of someone. Fiske et al. [8, p. 77] argued that "*[f]rom an evolutionary perspective, the primacy of warmth is fitting because another person's intent for good or ill is more important to survival than whether the other person can act on those intentions.*" Similarly, people's ratings of warmth may carry more weight than competence ratings when forming their first impressions of robots based on their outer appearance, where the weighting may have been further impacted by unspecified function of the three robots.

However, effects in video have been shown to differ between live results [2], and to develop real-world human-robot interactions, we need to validate our findings with live results. Also, the robots in this study did not have a function, which may have made it difficult to rate their perceived competence. Prior work showed that robot appearance affects which roles people see the robot fit [20]. As robots will take on specific roles in our daily lives, it is important to further investigate the effects of robot appearance on ratings of competence and discomfort when the robots are assigned specific tasks. Finally, the sample of participants included both a large portion of people who worked with or studied robots and a large portion of people who did not interact with robots before. Hence, future work needs to determine whether there is a difference between the first impressions of people with different levels of experience with robots.

To summarize, we studied how component material (wood, synthetic fur, and plastic) affects people's first impressions of social robots. We found that people rated the plastic robot lower on warmth than the wooden and fur robot. Open answers revealed that people felt familiar with the wooden and fur robot, as they reminded them of pets and toys. We did not find differences in ratings of competence, discomfort, which may be explained by the fact that the robots lacked a specific function and by their benign appearance. Although the robots were equally preferred, the reasons behind this seem to be influenced by their component material, which needs to be further studied in future research.

Acknowledgments. This work was partially funded by a grant from the Swedish Research Council (reg. number 2017-05189).

References

1. Bernotat, J., Eyssel, F., Sachse, J.: Shape it – the influence of robot body shape on gender perception in robots. In: Kheddar, A., et al. (eds.) ICSR 2017. LNCS, vol. 10652, pp. 75–84. Springer, Cham (2017). https://doi.org/10.1007/978-3-319-70022-9_8
2. Bucci, P., et al.: Sketching cuddlebits: coupled prototyping of body and behaviour for an affective robot pet. In: Proceedings of the 2017 CHI Conference on Human Factors in Computing Systems, pp. 3681–3692. ACM (2017)
3. Bucci, P., Zhang, L., Cang, X.L., MacLean, K.E.: Is it happy? Behavioural and narrative frame complexity impact perceptions of a simple furry robot's emotions. In: Proceedings of the 2018 CHI Conference on Human Factors in Computing Systems, p. 509. ACM (2018)
4. Carpinella, C.M., Wyman, A.B., Perez, M.A., Stroessner, S.J.: The robotic social attributes scale (RoSAS): development and validation. In: Proceedings of the 2017 ACM/IEEE International Conference on Human-Robot Interaction, pp. 254–262. ACM (2017)
5. Crippa, G., Rognoli, V., Levi, M.: Materials and emotions, a study on the relations between materials and emotions in industrial products. In: 8 International Conference on Design & Emotion: Out of Control, pp. 1–9. Central Saint Martins College of Arts & Design, London(2012)
6. DiSalvo, C.F., Gemperle, F., Forlizzi, J., Kiesler, S.: All robots are not created equal: the design and perception of humanoid robot heads. In: Proceedings of the 4th Conference on Designing Interactive Systems: Processes, Practices, Methods, and Techniques, pp. 321–326. ACM (2002)
7. Eyssel, F., De Ruiter, L., Kuchenbrandt, D., Bobinger, S., Hegel, F.: 'If you sound like me, you must be more human': on the interplay of robot and user features on human-robot acceptance and anthropomorphism. In: 2012 7th ACM/IEEE International Conference on Human-Robot Interaction (HRI), pp. 125–126. IEEE (2012)
8. Fiske, S.T., Cuddy, A.J., Glick, P.: Universal dimensions of social cognition: warmth and competence. Trends Cogn. Sci. **11**(2), 77–83 (2007)
9. Green, R.D., MacDorman, K.F., Ho, C.C., Vasudevan, S.: Sensitivity to the proportions of faces that vary in human likeness. Comput. Hum. Behav. **24**(5), 2456–2474 (2008)
10. Hegel, F., Eyssel, F., Wrede, B.: The social robot 'Flobi': key concepts of industrial design. In: 19th International Symposium in Robot and Human Interactive Communication, pp. 107–112. IEEE (2010)
11. Hoffmann, L., Krämer, N.C.: Investigating the effects of physical and virtual embodiment in task-oriented and conversational contexts. Int. J. Hum Comput Stud. **71**(7–8), 763–774 (2013)

12. Holoien, D.S., Fiske, S.T.: Downplaying positive impressions: compensation between warmth and competence in impression management. J. Exp. Soc. Psychol. **49**(1), 33–41 (2013)
13. Hu, Y., Hoffman, G.: Using skin texture change to design emotion expression in social robots. In: 2019 14th ACM/IEEE International Conference on Human-Robot Interaction (HRI), pp. 2–10. IEEE (2019)
14. Kalegina, A., Schroeder, G., Allchin, A., Berlin, K., Cakmak, M.: Characterizing the design space of rendered robot faces. In: Proceedings of the 2018 ACM/IEEE International Conference on Human-Robot Interaction, pp. 96–104. ACM (2018)
15. Kennedy, J., Baxter, P., Belpaeme, T.: Comparing robot embodiments in a guided discovery learning interaction with children. Int. J. Soc. Robot. **7**(2), 293–308 (2015)
16. Kirilenko, A.P., Stepchenkova, S.: Inter-coder agreement in one-to-many classification: fuzzy kappa. PLoS ONE **11**(3), e0149787 (2016)
17. Krach, S., Hegel, F., Wrede, B., Sagerer, G., Binkofski, F., Kircher, T.: Can machines think? Interaction and perspective taking with robots investigated via fMRI. PLoS ONE **3**(7), e2597 (2008)
18. Lehmann, H., Sureshbabu, A.V., Parmiggiani, A., Metta, G.: Head and face design for a new humanoid service robot. In: Agah, A., Cabibihan, J.-J., Howard, A.M., Salichs, M.A., He, H. (eds.) ICSR 2016. LNCS (LNAI), vol. 9979, pp. 382–391. Springer, Cham (2016). https://doi.org/10.1007/978-3-319-47437-3_37
19. Lucas, H., Poston, J., Yocum, N., Carlson, Z., Feil-Seifer, D.: Too big to be mistreated? Examining the role of robot size on perceptions of mistreatment. In: 2016 25th IEEE International Symposium on Robot and Human Interactive Communication (RO-MAN), pp. 1071–1076. IEEE (2016)
20. Luria, M., Forlizzi, J., Hodgins, J.: The effects of eye design on the perception of social robots. In: 2018 27th IEEE International Symposium on Robot and Human Interactive Communication (RO-MAN), pp. 1032–1037. IEEE (2018)
21. Mieczkowski, H., Liu, S.X., Hancock, J., Reeves, B.: Helping not hurting: applying the stereotype content model and bias map to social robotics. In: 2019 14th ACM/IEEE International Conference on Human-Robot Interaction (HRI), pp. 222–229. IEEE (2019)
22. Mori, M., MacDorman, K.F., Kageki, N.: The uncanny valley [from the field]. IEEE Robot. Autom. Mag. **19**(2), 98–100 (2012)
23. Nakata, T., Sato, T., Mori, T., Mizoguchi, H.: Expression of emotion and intention by robot body movement. In: Proceedings of the 5th International Conference on Autonomous Systems (1998)
24. Peña, D., Tanaka, F.: Validation of the design of a robot to study the thermo-emotional expression. In: Ge, S.S., et al. (eds.) ICSR 2018. LNCS (LNAI), vol. 11357, pp. 75–85. Springer, Cham (2018). https://doi.org/10.1007/978-3-030-05204-1_8
25. Phillips, E., Zhao, X., Ullman, D., Malle, B.F.: What is human-like? Decomposing robots' human-like appearance using the Anthropomorphic RoBOT (ABOT) database. In: Proceedings of the 2018 ACM/IEEE International Conference on Human-Robot Interaction, pp. 105–113. ACM (2018)
26. Powers, A., Kiesler, S.: The advisor robot: tracing people's mental model from a robot's physical attributes. In: Proceedings of the 1st ACM SIGCHI/SIGART Conference on Human-Robot Interaction, pp. 218–225. ACM (2006)
27. Premack, D., Woodruff, G.: Does the chimpanzee have a theory of mind? Behav. Brain Sci. **1**(4), 515–526 (1978)

28. Rice, J., Kozak, R.A., Meitner, M.J., Cohen, D.H.: Appearance wood products and psychological well-being. Wood Fiber Sci. **38**(4), 644–659 (2007)
29. Short, Y.F.E., Short, D., Mataric, M.J.: SPRITE: stewart platform robot for interactive tabletop engagement. Technical report, Department of Computer Science, University of Southern California (2017)
30. Wainer, J., Feil-Seifer, D.J., Shell, D.A., Mataric, M.J.: The role of physical embodiment in human-robot interaction. In: ROMAN 2006-The 15th IEEE International Symposium on Robot and Human Interactive Communication, pp. 117–122. IEEE (2006)
31. Willis, J., Todorov, A.: First impressions: making up your mind after a 100-ms exposure to a face. Psychol. Sci. **17**(7), 592–598 (2006)

Personality Synthesis Using Non-humanoid Cues

Sam Lee[1], Kotaro Funakoshi[2(✉)], Ritsuko Iwai[2], and Takatsune Kumada[2]

[1] University of British Columbia, Kelowna, BC V1V 1V7, Canada
sam.lee@alumni.ubc.ca
[2] Kyoto University, Sakyo-ku, Kyoto 606-8501, Japan
funakoshi.k@i.kyoto-u.ac.jp

Abstract. Currently there exists literature and research done on the role of personality in robots. However the existing research involves exhibiting personality on some platform which contains human cues. On the other hand, there exists little research on attempts to synthesize and exhibit personality without the use of any humanoid cues. In our research, we explore this challenge. In concrete, we define four parameters that modulate the migration behavior (motion path and schedule) of an information-seeking agent in a virtual 2D environment where only moving triangles and static rectangles reside. The presented model will be applicable to any mobile social robots. We setup five different agent behaviors as video stimuli and asked subjects to evaluate the agent's personality based on the Big Five personality traits model. The results suggest that people perceive different personalities from different parameter settings. We will discuss the future direction and issues based on the results.

Keywords: Mobile robots · Motion · Animacy · Personality types · Big Five

1 Introduction

Personality science is not a new domain, however, its application to the fields of human-robot interaction and social robotics has been gaining more attention as the role of robots in human society continue to increase [3,16]. Currently there exists literature and research done on the role of personality in robots (*e.g.*, [7,11,13]). However the existing research involves exhibiting personality on some platform which contains human cues. These human cues include humanoid robots, human faces, voices and other such cues that suggest an attempt to "humanize" the platform by which the personality is exhibited.

There exists little research on attempts to synthesize and exhibit personality without the use of any humanoid cues. To our best knowledge, this paper is the first attempt to explore this challenge in the robot's interaction with the

This work is supported by Honda Research Institute Japan Co., Ltd.

M. A. Salichs et al. (Eds.): ICSR 2019, LNAI 11876, pp. 222–234, 2019.
https://doi.org/10.1007/978-3-030-35888-4_21

environment. Research in this specific branch may help us understand the nature of personality, and the effectiveness or ineffectiveness of using humanoid cues to exhibit it.

This paper presents a model consisting of a virtual 2D simulation environment inspired by Heider and Simmel's experiment [6] and a formal framework to manipulate the behavior of an information-seeking agent in the simulation where only moving triangles and static rectangles reside. The framework defines four parameters that modulate the behavior (motion path and schedule) of the agent to exhibit different personalities.

We setup five different agent behaviors as video stimuli and asked subjects to evaluate the agent's personality based on the Big Five personality traits model in a crowd-sourcing based experiment, from which we obtained promising results.

In what follows, we first explore related work in the past literature. Then we present our personality synthesis model and experimental design. Finally we show and discuss the results.

2 Related Work

The currently existing field of personality science is broad in both scope and reach. The three main domains within this field applied to engineering are automatic personality recognition (self-assessment of one's personality from its behavior), automatic personality perception (attribution of personalities to others based on observable behavior), and automatic personality synthesis (synthesis of artificial personalities) [18].

Another seminal topic in the field is the five-factor or Big Five personality model [8]. The model describes personality using five traits: openness-to-experience (op), conscientiousness (co), extraversion (ex), agreeableness (ag) and neuroticism (ne). This model is generally accepted as the standard model by which research in the field is conducted. Our research is in the domain of automatic personality synthesis and is based on the five-factor personality model.

While most previous approaches to automatic personality synthesis rely on humanoid cues such as synthetic voice [1,17], artificial face [7] or head [13], and gestures [12], Koppensteiner [9] examined personality perception over synthesized motion cues exhibited by a moving ball in a computer animation. However, the examined motion was limited to the locomotion on a sine curve, which were modulated through primitive parameters such as frequency and amplitude. Thus, it is not easy to directly apply his personality synthesis method to actual robots in general.

Heider and Simmel [6] explored how subjects anthropomorphize a simple animation made up of rudimentary shapes and lines, without the use of any humanoid cues. Our research is inspired by this work but focuses on personality synthesis. People perceive different personalities in dogs and cats [5], and they attribute emotions to non-humanoid but dog-like robots based on motion-based cues [10]. This work examines whether or not people perceive different personalities in different migration behaviors of an agent with a rudimentary shape.

3   Personality Synthesis Model

This section describes the personality synthesis model we designed to attempt to exhibit personality without the use of humanoid cues. The model is made up of two main components: the framework, which represents the theory and computations; and the simulation, which is the platform on which the framework is implemented. First we describe the simulation and then the framework.

3.1   Simulation

The main purpose of the simulation is to act as the visual platform on which the personality synthesis model is implemented. The personality is exhibited by the target agent, through its interaction with its environment. In simplest terms, the simulation consists of the target agent and the environment. Figure 1 shows a screen-shot of the simulation.

The target agent (highlighted red) is the main vehicle by which personality is exhibited. The target agent is unlike all other entities in the simulation in that its behavior is variable and can change based on four behavior parameters (to be explained in detail in Sect. 3.2). This target agent's interaction with the environment is governed by its behavior parameters. It is through this interaction with the environment that the target agent displays personality.

The environment consists of the other agents and objects with which the target agent interacts. They are constrained to the area of the simulation. These other agents and objects are called peripheral entities. There are five peripheral agents and five peripheral objects present at all times in the environment. The target agent is defined as an information-seeking agent, whose motive is to know about (or get familiar with) other peripheral entities by moving around the environment.

All the agent are isosceles triangular shaped so that they have a natural orientation. When the target agent and a peripheral agent interact they face to each other as shown in Fig. 1. Peripheral agents are all agents that are not the target agent. They have some localized motion and wander around the simulation area at random. Peripheral objects are square shaped objects of the environment. They are static and do not move.

All the peripheral entities are gray colored. The brightness of each entity represents the target agent's familiarity with the entity. The longer the target agent interacts a peripheral entity, the more the agent gets familiar with the entity, and the brighter the entity is. That is, a view of the simulation reflects the mental state of the target agent at the moment in terms of the familiarity with the environment.

3.2   Framework

The framework contains all the mathematical formulation and algorithms to synthesize the behavior and personality of the target agent. The most important components of the framework are the four behavior parameters. The actual

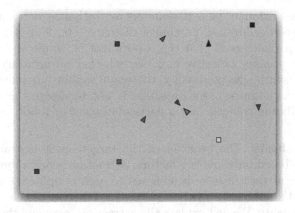

Fig. 1. A screen-shot of the simulation. (Color figure online)

behavior of the target agent is synthesized by a fixed algorithm based on the four behavior parameters.

Behavior Parameters. The behavior of our target agent is governed by these behavior parameters: curiosity, sociality, thoroughness, and impulsivity (described below). These parameters are variable and as they are changed, the behavior changes accordingly. The four behavior parameters are curiosity, sociality, thoroughness and impulsivity. These parameters are properties of the target agent only, not the environment.

Curiosity: Curiosity is the tendency of the target agent to prefer either familiar or unfamiliar entities. If the target agent has a high curiosity level, it prefers unfamiliar entities. If it has a low curiosity, it prefers familiar ones. Curiosity is represented as a weight W_c.

Sociality: Sociality is the tendency of the target agent to prefer either agents or objects. If the target agent has a high sociality level, it prefers other agents over objects. If is has a low sociality, it prefers objects over other agents. Sociality is represented as a weight W_s.

Thoroughness: The thoroughness parameter determines the length of each of the target agent's interactions with peripheral entities. A high thoroughness level stochastically results in longer interactions. A low thoroughness level results in shorter interactions. The value of thoroughness T ranges from 0 to 1.

Impulsivity: The impulsivity parameter affects the likelihood or probability of the target agent switching goals while pursuing a peripheral entity. The value of impulsivity I ranges from 0 to 1. The probability of goal-switching is determined by a sigmoid function of I so that a high impulsivity level results in a higher probability.

We hypothetically chose these four parameters to exhibit personality in a Heider-Simmel-like environment in consideration of the Big Five personality traits [8].

Of course, we can introduce more parameters to synthesize more complex behaviors, such as speed, vibration, proximity distance, etc. Nevertheless we limit the number of parameters so that the experiment is simple and as general as possible, as our primary objective is to see whether an arbitrary social agent can potentially synthesize personality thorough vanilla but universal interactions with the environment. Our objective is not to design the most optimal personality-exhibiting behaviors for a particular agent or robot.

Behavior Synthesis. The behavior of the target agent is synthesized by a fixed algorithm based on three key factors: attraction score, thoroughness and impulsivity. The attraction score is assigned to each peripheral entity based on the target agent's familiarity to the entity as a function of the target agent's curiosity and sociality. We first explain the attraction score and then present the specific algorithm to synthesize the target agent's migration behavior.

Attraction Score: The attraction score represents the attractiveness of each peripheral entity to the target agent at the moment. The target agent stochastically chooses the next entity to interact with according to the attraction scores of the entities.

Curiosity weight W_c and sociality weight W_s are predefined properties of the target agent as described above. The values of these weights determine the behavior of the target agent (*i.e.*, how "curious" or how "social" it behaves). The variables f (familiarity) and a (agency) are properties of the peripheral entities. Given the properties of the target agent and properties of the peripheral entities, two scores are computed as:

$$C_{score} = -W_c \cdot f$$

$$S_{score} = W_s \cdot a$$

Both of these scores combine to form the overall attraction score A in $[0, 1]$:

$$A = \frac{C_{score} + S_{score} + 2}{4}$$

Here we describe W_c, W_s, f, and a in detail:

Curiosity weight W_c: The curiosity weight is a property of the target agent. A high (positive) W_c represents a preference for unfamiliar entities. A low (negative) W_c represents a preference for familiar entities. Zero W_c represents neither preference for either. Values range from -1 to 1.

Sociality weight W_s: The sociality weight is a property of the target agent. A high (positive) W_s represents a preference for other agents. A low (negative) W_s represents a preference for objects. Zero W_s represents neither preference for either. Values range from -1 to 1.

Familiarity property f: Familiarity is a property of a peripheral entity in relation to the target agent. A low familiarity represents an unfamiliar peripheral entity. A high familiarity represents a familiar peripheral entity. Values range from -1 to 1.

Algorithm 1. Behavior synthesis procedure in the simulation

Require: Target agent a_t's properties: curiosity W_c, sociality W_s, thoroughness T, impulsivity I.
Require: Set of 10 randomly positioned peripheral entities E.
Require: Migration parameters (in pixels): interaction distance d, step length l, proximity range r.
  // 0. Initializing familiarity values.
  for each entity $e \in E$ **do**
    familiarity(e) $\sim$ Uniform($-1, 0$)
  end for
  while $\exists e \in E$, familiarity(e) < 1 **do**
    // 1. The target agent a_t chooses a target entity e_t.
    for each entity $e \in E$ **do**
      attraction score of e: $A_e \leftarrow$ attractionScore(W_c, W_s, familiarity(e), agency(e))
    end for
    $e_t \sim$ Attractiveness(E)
    // 2. Target agent a_t migrates to target peripheral entity e_t.
    while distance(a_t, e_t) $> d$ **do**
      Move a_t toward e_t by l.
      // 2-1. Impulsive goal-switching
      if a_t finds $\exists e' \in E$ ($e_t \neq e'$) in front of a_t with range r **then**
        $G \sim$ Bernoulli(p) where $p =$ goalSwitchingProbability(I)
        if $G = 1$ **then**
          $e_t \leftarrow e'$
        end if
      end if
    end while
    // 3. Agent a_t interacts with entity e_t for t_i seconds.
    $t_i \leftarrow D + 10T$ where $D \sim \mathcal{N}(0, 1)$
    Change direction of e_t toward a_t if e_t is a peripheral agent.
    while elapsed time $t < t_i$ and familiarity(e_t) < 1 **do**
      Increase familiarity(e_t) slightly.
      Sleep for a short time.
    end while
  end while

Agency property a: Agency is an innate property of a peripheral entity independent of the target agent. A negative agency represents an object. A positive agency represents an agent. This property is a binary state so far, meaning a peripheral entity has either an agency of -1 or 1. There are no values in between at the moment.

Synthesis Algorithms: Algorithm 1 describes the overall procedure to synthesize the behavior of the target agent and the behavior of a peripheral agent that interacts with the target agent. The procedure consists of the three steps: (1) choosing the target entity to which the target agent chases, (2) moving the target agent to the target entity, and (3) making the target agent interacts with the target entity. All peripheral entities are initially generated with a familiarity level below 0. In the first step, the target entity is determined according to a probabilistic distribution Attractiveness(E) that is based on the attraction scores of the entities. In the second step, the target agent stochastically changes its target entity to another entity when the target agent passes by it. This goal-switching behavior is controlled by impulsivity I. In the third step, when the target agent reaches the target entity, the target agent interacts with the entity for a while. That increases the target agent's familiarity with the entity in proportion to the interaction length. This interaction length is controlled by thoroughness T.

The attractiveness distribution was determined *ad hoc* by the authors to synthesize a naturally-looking target selection behavior according to the ranks in the order of the attraction scores of the ten entities. In this distribution, the first and second ranks take 95% of a chance and the rest take 5%. Then the 95% chance is allocated to the first and the second rank as 85% and 15%, respectively. The 5% chance of the rest is allocated to the remaining eight ranks as 40%, 15%, 15%, 7.5%, 7.5%, 5%, 5%, 5%, respectively. With this distribution, the first ranked entity is chosen in most cases with a chance of 80.75%. The other entities are chosen infrequently.

We introduced this stochastic target entity selection mechanism to enhance the life-likeness of the target agent, which is expected to be perceived from some sort of weak randomness/unpredictability or complexity. When we use either a simple distribution proportional to score values (*i.e.*, Attractiveness(E) = $A_e / \sum_{e' \in E} A_{e'}$) or a modified distribution as a soft-max function (*i.e.*, Attractiveness(E) = $\exp(A_e) / \sum_{e' \in E} \exp(A_{e'})$), however, the selection looks almost completely random. Therefore, we devised the above rank-based distribution.

4   Experiment Design

4.1   Personality Profiles and Video Stimuli

Using the four parameters outlined in the previous section (curiosity, sociality, thoroughness and impulsivity), we manually generated five different one-dimensional personality profiles based on the Big Five Factor model as shown in Table 1.

Table 1. Parameter value combinations for the five personality profiles

Profile	Curiosity	Sociality	Thoroughness	Impulsivity
Open-profile (OP)	High	Neutral	Low	Neutral
Conscientious-profile (CP)	Neutral	Neutral	High	Low
Extrovert-profile (EP)	High	High	Low	High
Agreeable-profile (AP)	Neutral	High	High	High
Neurotic-profile (NP)	High	Low	Low	High

Each personality profile was generated using a "high", "low" or "neutral" value for each of the four parameters. In general, for the parameters with values from -1 to 1 (curiosity and sociality) a "high" value refers to 1, a "low" value refers to -1 and a "neutral" value refers to 0. For the parameters with values from 0 to 1 (thoroughness and impulsiveness) a "high" value refers to 1, a "low" value refers to 0 and a "neutral" value refers to 0.5.

The Big Five personality traits are not the categories but the dimensions of human personality. That is, the personality of each person is not classified into the five but explained as a point in the five-dimensional space. Nevertheless, for the sake of simplicity, we dared prepare five prototypical profiles inspired by the five traits of the Big Five model. Each combination of the parameter values presented in Table 1 was, according to our introspection, set to be in line with a typical (but imaginary) person who would be regarded as open, conscientious, extrovert, agreeable, or neurotic commonly. Thus, we name these profiles based on the name of the Big Five traits, *i.e.*, OP, CP, EP, AP, and NP as shown in Table 1. We will refer to the five experimental conditions or levels with these five profile names.

These five personality profiles were implemented onto the framework, and the simulation was run. Short videos up to 1.5 min as experimental stimuli were captured of the simulation running each of the five personality profiles. Additionally, a "neutral" state video as a reference was also captured of the simulation running with all four parameters set at "neutral" values.[1]

4.2 Participants

We conducted our subjective evaluation experiment using a crowd-sourcing web service *Yahoo! Crowd Sourcing*[2]. This web service is operated in Japanese and its users are mostly native Japanese who speak Japanese only. Therefore, we conducted our experiment in Japanese.

Our experiment was designed as an inter-subject experiment of the five conditions, each of which corresponds to one of the five video stimuli. We recruited 45 subjects for each condition, 225 subjects in total. We did not set any personal constraints (*i.e.*, sex, age, and residence regions). The subjects were anonymous. Any demographic information is not available as we did not collect any personal profile information this time.

We designated on the service the identity numbers of the crowd-sourcing workers who participated in our previous test tasks as the banned workers for this experiment. Therefore, these workers were not included in the subject set, and all the subjects were new to our experiment. Moreover, we provided the web service with several check questions that confirm whether a worker correctly understands and obeys instructions. These check questions were systematically presented to the workers while they were working on our experiment task, and those who wrongly answered a check question were rejected by the service automatically. The workers were required to finish the task within 20 min while the expected task completion time was about 10 min. The successful workers were paid by 50 points on the service (almost equivalent to 50 JPY).

---

[1] The six videos are accessible with the following URL: https://drive.google.com/open?id=1eLNT7Bv7k1ETtRDlo3LqTaZDHRLxRhqW.

[2] https://crowdsourcing.yahoo.co.jp.

4.3   Procedure

As a subject, each crowd sourcing worker engaged in the task that was implemented on the web service according to the following five-step procedure.

1. **General instruction:** The overall description of the task is presented, that is, (1) the worker observes two short videos in order and answer a questionnaire on the second video (one can observe the videos as many times as he/she wants); (2) both of the videos show moving triangles and static rectangles; (3) the worker pays attention to the sole red triangle whose purpose is to know the environment; (4) the color of an entity (triangle or rectangle) changes according to whether the red triangle knows the entity well; and (5) the more the red triangle knows the entity, the brighter the entity's color becomes.
2. **Observing the reference video:** The worker is instructed to observe the behavior of the red triangle in the first video as the reference to the next video.
3. **Observing a stimulus video:** The worker is instructed to observe the behavior of the red triangle in the second video and is noticed that he/she will be asked to answer ten questions on the red triangle in the second video in comparison to that in the first video in a seven-point scale. The exact video is assigned randomly by the service.
4. **Answering the questionnaire on agent:** The worker is instructed to answer the ten items of TIPI-J [14], a Japanese version of the TIPI questionnaire [4] designed based on the Big Five personality model with respect to the red triangle in the second video.
5. **Answering the questionnaire on self:** The worker is instructed to answer the same ten items of TIPI-J, this time, with respect to the worker oneself.

Apart from the aforementioned systematic check questions, each worker answered additional questions that check the worker's understanding of the task at appropriate timings.[3] At the end of the task, each worker was asked whether they could watch the videos without problems. They were allowed to use PCs to engage in the task only. Smart phones were not allowed.

5   Analysis and Results

We dispatched the same crowd-sourcing task twice. The first round was conducted in a Tuesday evening with 75 participants, 15 for each condition. The second one was conducted in a Wednesday evening one week after the first with 150 participants, 30 for each condition. From among the collected responses, we excluded the responses of the participants who gave unexpected answers to any

---

[3] These questions were (A) whether the worker is confident in the understanding of the instruction; (B) the direction of the red triangle's final movement in the first video; (C) the color of an entity that the red triangle knows very well; and (D) the target of the second questionnaire (self or other).

of the additional questions. We also excluded apparently malicious or cheating participants such as those who chose all 4 in the 7-point Likert scales. The numbers of the remaining valid responses for the conditions were OP: 33, CP: 40, EP: 38, AP: 37, NP: 37. Due to space limitation, we show only the aggregated results of the two crowd-sourcing rounds. Note that, however, the characteristics of the two subject groups were seemingly different. We will revisit this point in Sect. 6.

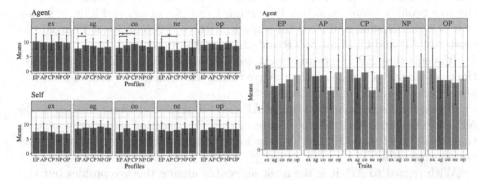

Fig. 2. The calculated TIPI mean scores with standard deviations. Left: the agent and self evaluations grouped by the Big-Five traits (see Sect. 2 for abbreviations), right: the agent evaluation grouped by the profiles. (The two agent evaluation graphs show the same data in different views.)

Each trait of the Big Five model has two corresponding items in TIPI and one of the two is in an inverse scale, *i.e.*, 1 is the most positive and 7 is the most negative. Therefore, the score for each trait is calculated as the inter-subject average of the sums of the response values of the normal-scale item and the inverted response value of the inverse-scale item. Then, the neutral score becomes 8. Figure 2 shows the calculated TIPI mean scores.

As subjects were randomly assigned to conditions (*i.e.*, profiles), the self evaluation was expected to show no significant difference among profiles. Indeed, self-evaluated trait scores were subjected to a three-way analysis of variance (ANOVA) with the profile and the round as between-subject factors and with the trait as a within subject factor, and the result showed no significant main effect of the profile and the round, and their interaction with the trait. On the other hand, the same ANOVA performed for the agent evaluation detected the main effect of the trait and the profile x trait interaction as significant ($p < .0001$, $p = .018$, respectively). Simple main effect analyses revealed that the main effects of the profile were significant in "ag", "co", and "ne" ($p < .033$). The result of the multiple comparisons is shown in Fig. 2 (left. $*$ $p < .05$, $+$ $p < .10$).

This indicates that the subjects give more divergent or biased evaluations to the agent than themselves among the conditions. Therefore, we think that the results suggest that our primary question is positively confirmed: People perceive different personalities even from non-human-like simple migrating behaviors that are modulated by only a few parameters.

6 Discussion

While we are positive with the conclusion that our proposed model makes people perceive different personalities in non-humanoid agents or robot just by motion cues, it is questionable whether we could exhibit five distinct personalities by the five profiles as we expected. Observing the right graph in Fig. 2, it seems that the participants evaluated the stimuli in three different ways. That is, the cluster of AP and CP, that of NP and OP, and EP alone.

It seems that EP successfully exhibited an intended personality with a distinctively high "ex" score among the five traits. The other four profiles, however, also received similar high "ex" scores.

The score distribution patterns of AP and CP seem to be very similar. So do NP and OP. Moreover, the "ne" score of the NP condition is not only smaller than those of EP and OP, but also the lowest within NP. It seems that NP was not so successful.

With regard to AP, it is the most agreeable among the five profiles but the advantage from CP is quite small. Therefore, AP might be partially successful case. The "co" score is, however, higher than the "ag" score in AP. In the same way, CP has the highest "co" score, but the difference with AP is not large. This suggests that we could exhibit agreeable and conscientious personalities by both AP and CP, but they were not distinctive from each other. In short, there is much room for further investigation to exhibit an intended personality with the presented model in a clear distinctive manner. On the other hand, the clinical literature suggests that there are three replicable distinct personality types [2,15]. The three personality profile clusters identified in this work may link to these three types.

When we compare our scores of the self evaluation to the literature, we find that the observed scores were not so much different from the past observations, except for extraversion. For the first round, the mean "ex" score of 6.6 is seemingly much lower than past studies based on more public surveys such as [14] (7.8). In the preliminary tests with crowd-sourcing, we repeatedly observed such low "ex" scores. This would be partially explained by the use of a computer-based crowd-sourcing service for recruiting. However, for the second round, the mean "ex" score is 7.3. This indicates the two subject groups have different characteristics as mentioned above. Thus, there would be some limitations using crowd-sourcing for such research because of the nature of the available subject groups, even subject to date and time.

7 Conclusion

This paper presented a personality synthesis model that uses only migrating behaviors as non-humanoid motion-based cues to exhibit personalities. The model consists of a simulation environment inspired by Heider and Simmel's experiment [6] and a formal framework to manipulate the behavior of the agent to exhibit a personality in the simulation based on just four parameters. The presented model is designed to be universal and it will be applicable to any mobile social robots. We conducted an inter-subject crowd-sourcing experiment with 225 Japanese subjects and obtained promising results. At the same time, however, the results suggested the need of further studies to express intended distinctive personalities. Investigations with different subject groups are also necessary, especially with non-Japanese subjects.

References

1. Aylett, M.P., Vinciarelli, A., Wester, M.: Speech synthesis for the generation of artificial personality. IEEE Trans. Affect. Comput. (2017). (early access)
2. Bohane, L., Maguire, N., Richardson, T.: Resilients, overcontrollers and under-controllers: a systematic review of the utility of a personality typology method in understanding adult mental health problems. Clin. Psychol. Rev. **57**, 75–92 (2017)
3. Dautenhahn, K.: Roles and functions of robots in human society: implications from research in autism therapy. Robotica **21**, 443–452 (2003)
4. Gosling, S.D., Rentfrow, P.J., Swann Jr., W.B.: A very brief measure of the big five personality domains. J. Res. Pers. **37**, 504–528 (2003)
5. Gosling, S.D., Sandy, C.J., Potter, J.: Personalities of self-identified "dog people" and "cat people". Anthrozoös **23**(3), 213–222 (2010)
6. Heider, F., Simmel, M.: An experimental study of apparent behavior. Am. J. Psychol. **57**, 243–259 (1944)
7. Hu, X., Xie, L., Liu, X., Wang, Z.: Emotion expression of robot with personality. Math. Prob. Eng. **2013**(132735), 1–10 (2013)
8. John, O.P., Srivastava, S.: The Big Five trait taxonomy: history, measurement, and theoretical perspectives. In: Pervin, L.A., John, O.P. (eds.) Handbook of Personality: Theory and Research, pp. 102–138. Guilford Press, New York (1999)
9. Koppensteiner, M.: Perceiving personality in simple motion cues. J. Res. Pers. **45**, 358–363 (2011)
10. Lakatos, G., Gácsi, M., Konok, V., Brúder, I., Bereczky, B., Korondi, P.: Emotion attribution to a non-humanoid robot in different social situations. PLoS ONE **9**(12), e0121929 (2014)
11. Lee, K.M., Peng, W., Jin, S.A., Yan, C.: Can robots manifest personality? An empirical test of personality recognition, social responses, and social presence in human–robot interaction. J. Commun. **56**(4), 754–772 (2006)
12. McRorie, M., Sneddon, I., McKeown, G., Bevacqua, E., de Sevin, E., Pelachaud, C.: Evaluation of four designed virtual agent personalities. IEEE Trans. Affect. Comput. **3**(3), 311–322 (2012)
13. Miwa, H., Takanishi, A., Takanobu, H.: Experimental study on robot personality for humanoid head robot. In: International Conference on Intelligent Robots and Systems, pp. 1183–1188 (2001)
14. Oshio, A., Abe, S., Cutrone, P.: Development, reliability, and validity of the Japanese version of ten item personality inventory (TIPI-J). Jpn. J. Pers. **21**(1), 40–52 (2012)

15. Robins, R.W., John, O.P., Caspi, A., Moffitt, T.E., Stouthamer-Loeber, M.: Resilient, overcontrolled, and undercontrolled boys: three replicable personality types. J. Pers. Soc. Psychol. **70**(1), 157–171 (1996)
16. Sequeira, J.S.: Can social robots make societies more human? Information **9**, 295 (2018)
17. Tapus, A., Tapus, C., Mataric, M.: User-robot personality matching and robot behavior adaptation for post-stroke rehabilitation therapy. Intell. Serv. Robot. **1**(2), 169–183 (2008)
18. Vinciarelli, A.: A survey of personality computing. IEEE Trans. Affect. Comput. **5**(3), 273–291 (2014)

Exploring the Causal Modeling
of Human-Robot Touch Interaction

Soheil Keshmiri[1]([⊠]), Hidenobu Sumioka[1], Takashi Minato[1], Masahiro Shiomi[1],
and Hiroshi Ishiguro[1,2]

[1] Advanced Telecommunications Research Institute International (ATR),
Kyoto, Japan
{soheil,sumioka,minato,m-shiomi}@atr.jp
[2] Osaka University, Osaka, Japan
ishiguro@sys.es.osaka-u.ac.jp

Abstract. The growing emergence of socially assistive robots in our
daily lives inevitably entails such interactions as touch and hug between
robots and humans. Therefore, derivation of robust models for such physical interactions to enable robots to perform them in naturalistic fashion
is highly desirable. In this study, we investigated whether it was possible to realize distinct patterns of different touch interactions that were
general representations of their respective types. For this purpose, we
adapted three touch interaction paradigms and asked human subjects
to perform them on a mannequin that was equipped with a touch sensor on its torso. We then applied Wiener-Granger causality on the time
series of activated channels of this touch sensor that were common (per
touch paradigm) among all participants. The analyses of these touch time
series suggested that different types of touch can be quantified in terms
of causal association between sequential steps that form the variation
information among their patterns. These results hinted at the potential
utility of such generalized touch patterns for devising social robots with
robust causal models of naturalistic touch behaviour for their human-
robot touch interactions.

1 Introduction

Interpersonal touch plays a pivotal role in formation and growth of the individuals' emotional bonds and physical well-being [1]. This observation is evident in compelling results that identify the therapeutic effects of interpersonal
touch on alleviating the individuals' physical and mental stress [2]. These findings on psychological power of such physical interactions as touch and hug have
direct implications for the field of socially-assistive robotics [3], considering their
demonstrated effectiveness in health-related services [4]. In fact, the growing

M. Shiomi—This research work was supported by JST CREST Grant Number
JPMJCR18A1, Japan, and JSPS KAKENHI Grant Numbers JP19K20746 and
JP17K00293.

emergence of interactive social robots [5] in our daily lives points at an evolving scenario which inevitably entails more physically engaged interactions (e.g.,
handshakes, hug, touch) between humans and their synthetic companions.

However and despite limited number of studies in which robots exhibited
some degree of reciprocal physical interaction with humans [6], most previous
studies treated these agents as "objects of interest" in which it was almost always
the humans who performed part of physical interactions on the robots and not
vice a versa. Apart from such issues as safety for humans during a physical
interaction with robots, the limited capabilities of these agents to comprehend
and reciprocate such interactions as hug and touch are among the core issues
that resulted in such one-directional interaction paradigms. Although imitation
learning approaches [7] that rely on a human demonstrator to teach a robot about
human behaviour may present themselves as solutions, these techniques can be
time-consuming as they require every type of action along with its variations to
be demonstrated to the robots.

However, these issues can be (at least partly) alleviated if we can realize
distinct patterns of touch interactions. For instance, such realizations can allow
for generalized representations of different touch interactions that capture their
subtle differences in their varieties. These representations, in turn, can enable
the social robots to not only differentiate between their types based on their
distinct patterns but also to exhibit naturalistic touch behaviour during their
human-robot touch interactions that are generated based on such generalized
representations.

In this study, we investigated the possibility of realizing such generalized
representations through the application of Granger causality (G-causality) [8].
In the language of G-causality, a variable X is said to G-cause a variable Y if the
past of X contains information that helps predict the future of Y over and above
information already in the past of Y. In the context of touch interaction then,
this translates to whether time series that are associated with different touch
interactions can potentially result in differential causal patterns that distinctively
define their respective type of touch interactions.

To verify the utility of Granger causality in the context of touch interaction, we asked human subjects to perform three types of touch interactions on
a mannequin that was equipped with a touch-sensor on its torso. We then used
touch-sensor's time series associated with these touch interactions and applied
the G-causality on them to determine whether different touches resulted in differing causal networks that underlined the activation patterns of touch-sensor's
input channels.

Our results suggested that different touch interactions can be quantified in
terms of causal association between sequential steps that form the variation
information among their patterns. These results hinted at the potential use of
such distinct patterns of embodied actions to devise social robots to more con-
veniently recognize and replicate naturalistic interactions with humans through
causal reasoning of the perceived patterns of their human companions' touch
interactions.

2 Methodology

In this study, we utilized the Wiener-Granger causality (G-causality) analysis [8,9] to determine the potential distinct patterns that may underlie different types of touch interaction. The Granger causality (G-causality) is based on predictability and precedence among two or more events that occur at the same time. Specifically, it examines whether the past information of a subset of these events can help predict the future of the remaining events that are not members of this subset better than the past of those non-member events themselves do. In other words, G-causality is a measure of directed functional connectivity that provides a statistical description of the observed events. G-causality has been used in such broad areas of research as economics and statistics [8,9] and neuroscience [10]. The full treatment of the theory behind G-causality is described in [8,11].

Let $X_{N \times T}$ represent a touch sensor (i.e., in a matrix form) in which every row entry i is a real-valued column-vector touch time series that is collected over a period $\tau = 1, \ldots, T$ through the channel i of the touch sensor X. In this setting, the Granger causal analysis of X is analogous to identifying a subset of channels $x_i \in X$, $i = 1, \ldots, N$ in such a way that the past information of x_i's can help predict the future of the remaining channels $x_j \in X, j = 1, \ldots, N$, $j \neq i$ beyond the predictions that are based solely on x_j's own past information. This subset $x_i \in X$, $i = 1, \ldots N$ of the touch sensor X, if existed, can then be interpreted as the backbone of touch event that all of the time series sequences $x \in X$ of length T were collectively associated with.

3 Experimental Setup

Twenty-two younger adults (eleven females and eleven males, age M = 32.95, SD = 6.41) participated in our study. Data from four participants (three males and one female) were not recorded properly and therefore they were excluded from our analysis.

In our experiment, participants performed three types of touch-based interactions on a mannequin that was wearing a touch-sensor on its torso (Fig. 1(A)). This vest consisted of two Tactilus^{TM} touch sensor mats manufactured by SENSOR PRODUCTS INC. Each sensor mat has 16×16 sensor cells (i.e., input channels). We put the sensor mats on the front and the back of the mannequin (Fig. 1(A)). The size of sensor mat was 17.9×17.9 in. The size of a single sensor cell on each mat was 1.12×1.12 in. The sampling rate of the touch-sensor in this study was 50.0 Hz.

The three touch-based interactions in our study included (1) patting the mannequin's chest gently (*chest-pat*) (Fig. 1(B)), (2) rubbing the mannequin's chest (*chest-rub*) (Fig. 1(C)), and (3) hitting the mannequin's chest (*chest-hit*) (Fig. 1(D)). We chose *chest-rub* to determine the utility of causal analysis of touch-based interaction in which the touched surface allowed for a continuous action (i.e., rubbing the mannequin's chest). On the other hand, we used

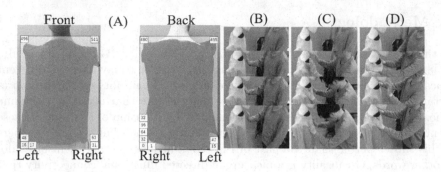

Fig. 1. (A) Touch-sensor vest along with the arrangement of sensor's channels through which touch interaction data was collected. In the right subplots, an experimenter demonstrates the three experimental setups: (B) patting the mannequin's chest gently (*chest-pat*) (C) rubbing the mannequin's chest strongly (*chest-rub*) (D) hitting the mannequin's chest (*chest-hit*).

chest-pat and *chest-hit* to validate the use of causal analysis when the embodied interaction was discontinuous (i.e., patting/hitting the mannequin's chest) while keeping the spatial information intact. The latter two experiment also allowed us to determine the effect of touch-intensity on our analysis results. On average, *chest-pat*, *chest-rub*, and *chest-hit*, lasted for 12.99, 12.31, and 11.80 s (M = 12.36, SD = .60).

3.1 Data Processing

For every experiment, we first eliminated, per participant, the row entries of the touch-sensor that had all its cells (i.e., data acquisition channels) zero (i.e., not activated). Among the remaining channels, we then found the channels that were common among participants and averaged those channels (e.g., 10th channel of all participants in the second experiment), thereby generating the averaged representative touch interaction pattern for a given experiment. On these averaged representative patterns, we then performed Augmented Dickey Fuller (ADF) [11], followed by Kwiatkowski-Phillips-Schmidt-Shin (KPSS) [12] tests to ensure that the selected channels were covariance stationary and subsequently discarded those channels that did not pass these tests. This was a crucial step since for the result of Granger causality to be meaningful, it is necessary to ensure that every time series that is included in the analysis is covariance stationary (trend-stationary) i.e., its mean and variance does not change over time.

After this step, we utilized Akaike and Bayesian information criteria (AIC and BIC) to determine the best model order and time lag for modeling the touch interactions' time series. Both AIC and BIC indicated 2 and 22 as best model order and suitable time lag for our touch interactions' data. Therefore, we used these values in our analysis. We also ensured that our data passed the model consistency and the residual independence checks (empirical thresholds: >.80 and >.30, respectively) [13] and found all channels satisfied these two conditions.

In essence, these tests ensure that the model accounts for a sufficient amount of the variance in the data therefore the model can be trusted [13].

Last, we used the channels, per experiment, that passed all these tests and computed the overall time-domain causal density of the averaged representative touch interaction along with unit causal density of each of the channels that were included in their corresponding causal network. The unit causal density quantifies the predictive power of a given element of causal touch network (i.e., specific activated channels of the touch-sensor in response to a touch interaction) in determining the future values of the entire touch time series that is associated with this causal network. On the other hand, the causal density of the network reflects the network predictive power (i.e., as an aggregate of all its elements) for such predictions. More specifically, causal density is a measure of the total amount of causal interactivity among the elements of a causal network. A significant causal density indicates that these elements are both globally (i.e., with respect to the entire network that they form) coordinated (and therefore useful for its predictions) and dynamically distinct (i.e., each contributes differentially for such predictions). To determine the significance of calculated causal densities, we performed permutation tests (bonferroni corrected) on these values to assess whether they significantly differed from zero. We used the multivariate Matlab-based Granger causality toolbox [13] in our analyses. We used the measured pressures on sensors' channels during the touch interactions as inputs to our G-causal model analysis.

4   Results

In our experimental settings, we used *chest-rub* to determine the utility of causal analysis of touch interaction in which the touched surface allowed for a continuous action (i.e., rubbing the mannequin's chest). On the other hand, we used *chest-pat* and *chest-hit* to validate the use of causal analysis when the touch interaction entailed a different intensity (i.e., patting versus hitting the mannequin's chest) while keeping the spatial information intact.

4.1   Patting the Mannequin's Chest Gently (*chest-pat*)

Figure 2(A) shows the *chest-pat*'s causal network. We observed a significant overall casual effect in *chest-pat* (causal density (cd) $= .071$, corrected $p < .001$), implying that one or more channels (i.e., their measured touch pressures) had more predictive information about the current states of their neighbouring channels than those channels' own past observations. Further scrutiny of this results indicated that channel 432 (unit causal density (ucd) $= .38$, $M_{pressure} = .25$, $SD_{pressure} = .01$) was significantly (corrected $p < .001$) predictive of channels 464 (ucd $= .25$, $M_{pressure} = .34$, $SD_{pressure} = .01$) and 465 (ucd $= .25$, $M_{pressure} = .26$, $SD_{pressure} = .01$). Similarly, we observed that channel 464 was significantly (corrected $p < .001$) more predictive of channel 496 (ucd $= .13$, $M_{pressure} = .17$,

$SD_{pressure} = .002$) than 496's own past information and that channel 465 was significantly (corrected $p < .001$) predictive of channel 464. Last, the z-score of these ucd values (Fig. 2(B)) identified that difference between channel 432's ucd and the other channels was above one standard deviation ($z_{432} = 1.6733$, $z_{463} = -.84$, $z_{432} = .84$, $z_{465} = .84$, $z_{469} = -.84$, $z_{470} = -.84$, $z_{486} = -.84$, $z_{496} = 0.0$), thereby implying its significantly above average predictability of other channels in *chest-pat*'s causal network.

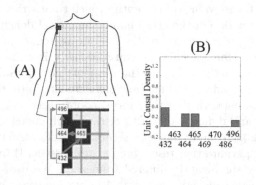

Fig. 2. *chest-pat* (patting the mannequin's chest gently): (A) Causal network (corrected $p < .001$). (B) Channels' unit causal density.

4.2   Rubbing the Mannequin's Chest Strongly (*chest-rub*)

Figure 3(A) depicts the *chest-rub*'s causal network which showed a significant overall casual effect (cd = .023, corrected $p < .001$). However, there were only two causally associated channels present in the case of *chest-rub*'s causal network

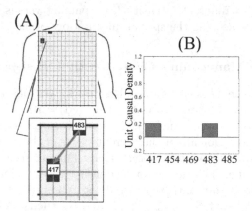

Fig. 3. *chest-rub* (rubbing the mannequin's chest strongly): (A) Causal network (corrected $p < .001$). (B) Channels' unit causal density.

in which channel 485 (ucd $= .14$, $M_{pressure} = .03$, $SD_{pressure} = .002$) was significantly predictive of channel 454 (ucd $= .14$, $M_{pressure} = .04$, $SD_{pressure} = .002$). The z-scores of *chest-rub*'s channels also indicated that the difference between the ucd values corresponding to channels 485 and 454 and the other channels in *chest-rub* was above one standard deviation ($z_{417} = 1.46$, $z_{454} = -.59$, $z_{469} = -.59$, $z_{483} = 1.46$, $z_{485} = -.59$). Figure 3(B) shows these results.

4.3 Hitting the Mannequin's Chest (*chest-hit*)

We observed a significant overall casual effect in the case of *chest-hit*'s casual network (Fig. 4(A)) (cd $= .05$, corrected p $< .001$). We also observed that channel 470 (ucd $= .25$, $M_{pressure} = .37$, $SD_{pressure} = .02$) was significantly (corrected p $< .001$) predictive of both channels 451 (ucd $= .13$, $M_{pressure} = .11$, $SD_{pressure} = .01$) and 483 (ucd $= .12$, $M_{pressure} = .16$, $SD_{pressure} = .01$). In addition, the channel 470's ucd showed (Fig. 4(B)) above one standard deviation difference from the average ucd values of *chest-hit*'s network while those of the channels 451 and 483 remained within one standard deviation from the average ucd values of this network ($z_{438} = -.66$, $z_{454} = .66$, $z_{464} = -.66$, $z_{469} = -.66$, $z_{485} = 1.98$, $z_{489} = .66$, $z_{496} = -0.66$, $z_{505} = -0.66$).

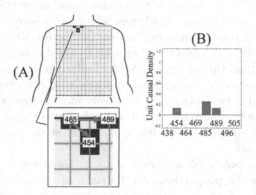

Fig. 4. *chest-hit* (hitting the mannequin's chest): (A) Causal network (corrected p $< .001$). (B) Channels' unit causal density.

5 Discussion

In this study, we utilized the Wiener-Granger causality (G-causality) [8,9] to investigate whether different types of touch interaction can be differentiated based on their potential underlying distinct patterns that were general representations of their types. For this purpose, we designed three touch interaction paradigms that our participants executed on a mannequin's chest. The first paradigm, *chest-rub*, was to determine the utility of causal analysis of touch interaction in which the touched surface allowed for a continuous action. On the other hand, the second and the third paradigms (i.e., *chest-pat* and *chest-hit*) were designed to validate the use of causal analysis when the touch interaction entailed a different intensity (i.e., measured touch pressure) on the same spatial touch surface.

Our results suggested that the touch interactions that were adapted in our study resulted in distinct activation patterns of touch-sensor's channels with differential causal association. For instance, we observed that the intensity of a touch interaction was identified by the presence of hubs i.e., channels with high causal densities (i.e., based on their measured touch pressures). In this regard, whereas we observed higher unit causal densities in the case of *chest-pat* (i.e., the channel 432) and *chest-hit* (i.e., channel 485), the unit causal densities were rather uniform in the case of *chest-rub* setting (i.e., channels 417 and 483). More importantly, the interconnectivity among the elements of these causal networks appeared to reflect the interplay between temporal and intensity information of these touch interactions. Specifically, we observed that *chest-rub* was associated with least interconnected causal network. On the other hand, such interconnections consistently increased from *chest-hit* (i.e., shorter in duration but more intense than rubbing) to *chest-pat* (i.e., moderately intense but longer in duration than *chest-hit*).

Such an interplay between temporal information and the intensity of the touch showed a direct correspondence with the causal networks' density of these touch interactions. In this regard, whereas *chest-pat* whose type of interaction entailed both a moderately longer interaction than *chest-hit* and a more intense interaction than *chest-rub* was associated with a causal network that exhibited a higher complexity than that of the *chest-hit*. Similarly, the higher intensity of the interaction in the case of *chest-hit* in comparison with the *chest-rub* interaction resulted in a causal network that was relatively more complex than that of the *chest-rub*. On the other hand, the causal network that corresponded to *chest-rub* comprised of two elements: the activated channels at the start and the end of this touch interaction.

Considering the potential activated areas in these touch interactions that should, in principle, be proportional to the palm of the individuals, the resulting causal networks of adapted touch interactions in our study also suggested that not all the channels that were potentially activated during a particular touch interaction were fundamental part of its distinct formational pattern. This observation suggested the potential presence of redundancy in data acquired through such interactions, thereby implying the possibility of distinguishing between different types of touch by identifying the minimal sets of most relevant and informative channels.

In this respect, our results made a clear distinction between essential constituents of a touch interaction and the physical manifestation of such an interaction (i.e., the aggregate of activated channels by a touch). Specifically, the principle of causal analysis requires the given time series to not only be occurring in parallel (i.e., at the same time) but also these time series must be stationary. In the context of touch interaction in our study, we observed that the individuals' execution of designated touch interactions resulted (i.e., on average) in activation of 18 touch-sensor channels (M = 17.75, SD = .50) out of which 8 channels (M = 7.00, SD = 1.41) constituted to the causal analysis of these touch interactions and the remaining 10 channels (M = 11.00, SD = 1.41) were discarded due to exhibiting non-stationarity in their patterns of activation during these touch interactions. As a result, those channels that were included in the analysis corresponded to the activation patterns that were necessary to compute the causal network of their corresponding touch interaction in which an average of 3 of these channels (M = 3.00, SD = 1.00) contributed to the formation of causal networks of these touch interactions. In fact, we observed that there were 4, 2, and 3 channels that had significant unit casual densities and that formed the causal networks associated with *chest-pat*, *chest-rub*, and *chest-hit*, respectively. On the other hand, those channels that were discarded by the analysis contributed to the manifestation (e.g., aggregate of the activated channels due to the touch area covered by the palm of a toucher on the mannequin's chest). In the context of social robots, such information and clear distinction between essential and complementary patterns of activation that were reliably distinguished through causal analysis of the touch interactions in our study can enable the robots to not only robustly differentiate between the type of touch (i.e., differential causal networks that are formed on the basis of minimalist most informative activated patterns) but also to reciprocate such touch interactions through the combination of essential activation patterns and their complementary activated channels that describe the manifestation of a touch interaction.

In this context, our results suggested the potentials that such analyses can offer to the solution concept of more robust approach to human-robot interaction that can meet the requirement for naturalistic and real-world interactions. For instance, such causal networks can be adapted for defining probabilistic graphs whose nodes are the observed activated channels in a given embodied action. Such graphs that are the backbones of probabilistic reasoning in intelligent systems [14] can not only be utilized to enable robots to distinguish between different types of embodied actions based on their causal reasoning of observed patterns in their companions' touch interaction but also to allow them to replicate such interactions through following the causal connectivity among the nodes of their probabilistic graphs that are associated with their identified type of touch interaction.

The most apparent limitation of our study is the absence of robots. One reason for not using a robot was due to the touch-sensor that was more suitable for fitting on a mannequin than a robot. In addition and considering the exploratory nature of the present study, the use of a mannequin allowed for a more controlled setting. We were also concerned with the safety of our participants to perform such touch interactions as hitting on a hard object such as a robot. Another limitation of our study was the small sample of touch interactions which made the implication of the observed causal networks to be limited in their interpretation. It is also crucial to examine the results of these analyses on different parts of the body (i.e., other than the chest) to verify that the observed results whose extents were indicative of the level of complexity of the performed touch interactions will preserve. The effect of gender on formation of such causal networks is another interesting issue that requires further consideration. Last, the number of participants in our study was small and limited to young adults. Therefore, future studies that will address these shortcomings while including larger number of participants that cover broader age groups are necessary to draw an informed conclusion on these results.

6   Conclusions

In this article, we presented our preliminary results toward causal modeling of touch interaction. Our results based on three different types of touch interactions suggested that different types of touch can be quantified in terms of causal association between sequential steps that form the variation information among their patterns. These results hinted at the potential utility of such generalized touch patterns for devising social robots with robust causal models of naturalistic touch behaviour for their human-robot touch interactions.

References

1. Gallace, A., Spence, C.: The science of interpersonal touch: an overview. Neurosci. Biobehav. Rev. **34**, 246–259 (2010)
2. Field, T.: Touch for socioemotional and physical well-being: a review. Dev. Rev. **30**, 367–383 (2010)
3. Matarić, M.J.: Socially assistive robotics: Human augmentation versus automation. Sci. Robot. **2**, eaam5410 (2018)
4. Mann, J.A., MacDonald, B.A., Kuo, I., Li, X., Broadbent, E.: People respond better to robots than computer tablets delivering healthcare instructions. Comput. Hum. Behav. **43**, 112–117 (2015)
5. Broadbent, E.: Interactions with robots: the truths we reveal about ourselves. Ann. Rev. Psychol. **68**, 627–652 (2017)
6. Nakagawa, K., Shiomi, M., Shinozawa, K., Matsumura, R., Ishiguro, H., Hagita, N.: Does a robot's touch encourage human effort? Int. J. Soc. Robot. **9**, 5–15 (2017)
7. Schaal, S.: Is imitation learning the route to humanoid robots? Trends Cogn. Sci. **3**, 233–242 (1999)
8. Granger, C.W.J.: Investigating causal relations by econometric models and cross-spectral methods. Econometrica **37**, 424–438 (1969)
9. Geweke, J.: Measures of conditional linear dependence and feedback between time series. J. Am. Stat. Assoc. **79**, 907–915 (1984)
10. Pereda, E., Quiroga, R.W., Bhattacharya, J.: Nonlinear multivariate analysis of neurophysiological signals. Prog. Neurobiol. **77**, 1–37 (2005)
11. Hamilton, J.D.: Time Series Analysis. Princeton University Press, Printceton (1994)
12. Kwiatkowski, D., Phillips, P.C., Schmidt, P., Shin, Y.: Testing the null hypothesis of stationarity against the alternative of a unit root. J. Econ. **54**, 159–178 (1992)
13. Barnett, L., Seth, A.K.: The MVGC multivariate Granger causality toolbox: a new approach to Granger-causal inference. J. Neurosci. Methods **223**, 50–68 (2014)
14. Pearl, J.: Probabilistic Reasoning in Intelligent Systems: Networks of Plausible Inference. Elsevier, San Fransisco (1988)

Emotional and Expressive Interaction with Social Robots

Hug Behavior Request Model
with Approaching Human
for Hug Robots

Mitsuru Jindai(✉), Shunsuke Ota, Toshiyuki Yasuda, and Tohru Sasaki

University of Toyama, 3190, Gofuku, Toyama, Toyama 930-8555, Japan
{jindai,ota,yasuda,tsasaki}@eng.u-toyama.ac.jp
http://enghp.eng.u-toyama.ac.jp/labs/me07/

Abstract. Hug behavior can promote synchronization of embodied rhythms effectively as it is one of the types of embodied interactions wherein humans contact whole-body with each other. In the case of a human and a robot, it is likely that a robot effectively synchronizes an embodied rhythm with a human using hug behavior. Therefore, in this paper, a hug behavior request model with an approaching human is proposed for hug robots. Furthermore, a hug robot system that employs the proposed model is developed. In this model, the robot requests hug behavior when a human approaches it, and generates hug behavior with humans. Using the developed robot system, a preferred timing which begins with the hand motion of the robot is determined to request hug behavior by sensory evaluations.

Keywords: Human-robot system · Embodied interaction · Hug behavior

1 Introduction

In human face-to-face communication, embodied sharing using a synchrony of embodied rhythms is promoted by embodied interactions. Therefore, embodied interactions are critical for smoothly initiating coexistence and communication. In particular, hug behavior can promote synchronization of embodied rhythms effectively as it is one of the types of embodied interactions wherein humans contact whole-body with each other. In the case of a human and a robot, it is likely that a robot effectively synchronizes an embodied rhythm with a human using hug behavior. A robot that can generate such an interaction is emotionally acceptable to humans because it produces feelings of security [1]. Furthermore, by applying hug behavior, robots can hold humans without feeling uncomfortable.

Embodied interactions between humans and robots that involve direct contact have been discussed [2,3]. In particular, hug behavior between humans and

Supported by KAKENHI Grant Number JP18K11393 of the Japan Society for the Promotion of Science (JSPS), Japan.

robots has been discussed in previous studies [4–6]. These studies examined remote hug communications between partners and shapes of hugging robots. However, these studies did not discuss to generate hug behavior with humans for embodied interactions. Thus, we have proposed a hug behavior response model with humans based on an analysis of hug behavior between humans [7]. Furthermore, we demonstrated the effectiveness of the proposed hug behavior response model by the sensory evaluation using a hug robot system. In the proposed model, a robot generates hug behavior when a human requests the robot for it. Thus, this model generates passive hug behavior. Robots should generate active hug behavior in order to promote its embodied interaction with humans. Therefore, the robots also request humans to hug.

Therefore, in this paper, a hug behavior request model with an approaching human is proposed for hug robots. In this model, the robot requests hug behavior when a human approaches it. The robot generates a hug behavior with the human. Furthermore, a hug robot system that employs the proposed model is developed. In the hug behavior, the timing of when the robot begins its hand motion influences human emotions. Thus, a preferred timing which begins with its hand motion is determined to request hug behavior by sensory evaluations using the developed hug robot system.

2 Analysis of Hug Behavior Between Humans

2.1 Hugging Experiment

Hug behavior between humans was measured to provide the basis for hug behavior between humans and robots. A three-dimensional motion capture system was used in the experiment, and the requester and responder were determined beforehand. The experimental scene is shown in Fig. 1. They initially stand face-to-face at a distance of 3 m with their right arms stretching downward. For the hug behavior, the responder approaches the stationary requester, and the requester starts to move his or her hand at an arbitrary time to request hug behavior. Then, the responder moves his or her hand according to this motion. In the experiment, research participants hug each other accompanied by voice greetings. The research participants were 30 healthy right-handed students (15 pairs) aged between 20 and 24, and each pair hugged 10 times.

2.2 Results of Analysis

In our previous study on handshakes between humans and robots, a time at which the requester begins the hand motion is influenced by the walking rhythm of the responder [8]. Furthermore, a robot can generate a preferred handshake motion by timings based on steps. Therefore, relationships between the beginning of the requester's hand motion and steps of the responder's walking were analyzed. Figure 2 shows a histogram of the relationships. The horizontal axis shows the time at the beginning of hand motion based on the steps of the walking:

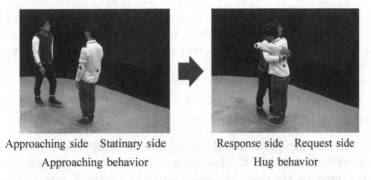

Approaching side   Statinary side   Response side   Request side

Approaching behavior   Hug behavior

Fig. 1. Experimental scene of hug behavior between humans

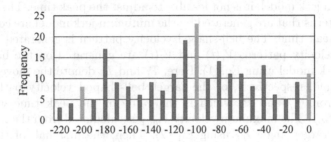

Fig. 2. Relationship between requester's hand motion and responder's steps

0 indicates that the requester begins the hand motion simultaneously with the stop of the responder. −100 indicates that the requester begins the hand motion at the one step before the responder stops. −200 indicates that the requester begins the hand motion at the two steps before the responder stops. It can be observed from Fig. 2 that the time distribution has one peak at −100. Therefore, most humans of the request side begin their hand motions at the one step before the stop of the responder. From this result, it can be inferred that the time humans begin the request motion is influenced by the walking rhythm of the others.

In addition, a time gap between the beginning of the requester's hand motion and the utterance of his or her voice greeting was recorded. As a result, many humans utter the voice greeting around 0.3 s after the beginning of their hand motions.

3   Generation of Hand Motion

In this study, right and left hand motions for hug behavior are generated by bell-shaped and wave-shaped velocity patterns. The generation method of hand motions using these velocity patterns has already been proposed in our previous study [7]. In this method, rotations of shoulder, elbow, forearm, and wrist joints are generated using the bell-shaped velocity pattern, and the external and internal rotations of upper arms are generated using the wave-shaped velocity pattern. To produce hand motions similar to those of a human, the movement time, maximum velocity, peak time, and initial and target angles are matched to those of humans.

The bell-shaped and wave-shaped velocity patterns are generated as follows:

3.1   Bell-Shaped Velocity Pattern

A bell-shaped velocity pattern with an adjustable peak time is generated with the minimum jerk model as the foundation [9]. The minimum jerk model can accurately reproduce the point-to-point motion of human hands. In this model, the acceleration and velocity patterns exhibit smooth transitions. However, in the minimum jerk model, it is not feasible to adjust the peak time. Therefore, two velocity patterns that are generated by the minimum jerk model are combined to adjust the peak time. The bell-shaped velocity pattern is generated as follows: First, two velocity patterns $V_1(t)$ and $V_2(t)$ are generated on the basis of the minimum jerk model using Eq. (1). Here, T_f and T_p denote the movement time and peak time, respectively, of the target bell-shaped velocity pattern. T_p is calculated from T_f and P, which is the value of the peak time when T_f is normalized to 1. The maximum velocity V_{max} is calculated from the initial angle R_0 and the target angle R_f using Eq. (2). Then, the first half of the velocity pattern $V_1(t)$ and the latter half of the velocity pattern $V_2(t)$ are combined as illustrated in Fig. 3. As a result, the target bell-shaped velocity pattern is generated. In this pattern, the position and velocity vary smoothly, and it is feasible to adjust the peak time.

$$V_i(t) = V_{max}\frac{16}{T_i^4}(t^4 - 2T_it^3 + T_i^2t^2) \qquad (i = 1, 2) \qquad (1)$$

Here, $T_1 = 2PT_f$, $\quad T_2 = 2(1-P)T_f$, $\quad T_p = PT_f$

$$V_{max} = \frac{15}{8T_f}(R_f - R_0) \qquad (2)$$

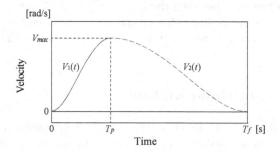

Fig. 3. Bell-shaped velocity pattern

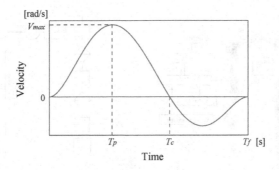

Fig. 4. Wave-shaped velocity pattern

3.2 Wave-Shaped Velocity Pattern

The wave-shaped velocity pattern is generated using a fifth-order curve. The wave-shaped velocity pattern is illustrated in Fig. 4. In the wave-shaped velocity pattern, its shape is determined by the movement time, maximum velocity, and initial and target angles. The fifth-order curve is expressed by Eq. (3). The movement time and peak time are denoted by T_f and T_p, respectively. The time T_c is the time at which the velocity becomes zero. The value of the constant K is calculated from the initial angle R_0 and target angle R_f using Eq. (4). The peak time T_p is calculated using Eq. (5). Then, the time T_c is determined as the velocity at time T_p attains the maximum velocity V_{max}.

$$V(t) = K(T_f - t)^2 (T_c - t)t^2 \tag{3}$$

$$K = \frac{60(R_f - R_0)}{2T_f{}^5 T_c - T_f{}^6} \tag{4}$$

$$T_p = \frac{(4T_c + 3T_f) - \sqrt{16T_c{}^2 - 16T_f T_c + 9T_f{}^2}}{10} \tag{5}$$

4 Hug Robot System

A hug robot system that employs the proposed hug behavior request model was developed. The hug robot system is illustrated in Fig. 5. The robot system incorporates two arms, each of which has seven degrees-of-freedom (three at the shoulder and one each at the upper arm, elbow, forearm, and wrist), as illustrated in Fig. 6. The robot arms were fabricated based on the average size of a human arm [10]. The required joint angles of the robot were calculated using the proposed model.

Accelerometers and a laser range finder were used to measure human steps and the distance between a human and the robot, respectively. A speaker was used for utterance of a voice greeting. The sampling time of the system was 5 ms. The robot was capable of achieving the desired position accurately.

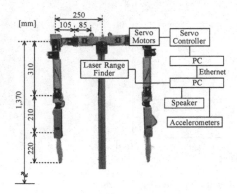

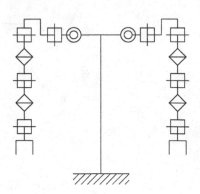

Fig. 5. Hug robot system   **Fig. 6.** Mechanism diagram

5   Experiment with Hug Behavior Request Model

In the hug behavior request model, the hand of the robot began moving before that of humans. Therefore, it is considered that a timing which begins with its hand motion, influences human emotions. Thus, an experiment was performed to determine the preferred timing of the beginning to request hug behavior.

5.1   Experimental Method

In the experiment, a research participant and the robot initially stand face-to-face at a distance of 3 m. Next, the research participant approaches the robot. Then, the robot moves its hand to request hug behavior, and the research participant starts to move his or her hand at an arbitrary time according to it. The research participant and the robot hug accompanied by voice greetings. Figure 7 shows the experimental scene.

In the analysis of hug behavior between humans, the time at which the requester begins the hand motion is influenced by the walking rhythm of the responder. Therefore, three modes were used in a sensory evaluation. In mode (a), the robot begins its hug behavior at the two steps before the stop of the human during approach. In mode (b), the robot begins its hug behavior at the one step before the stop of the human during approach. Most humans begin the hand motion at the one step before the stop of the other person in hug behavior between humans. In mode (c), the robot begins its hug behavior simultaneously with the stop of the approaching human. In the experiment, the robot uttered of the voice greeting 0.3 s after the beginning of its hand motions.

A paired comparison was performed for all six pairs of mode combinations, and then a seven-point bipolar rating on a scale from −3 (not at all) to 3 (extremely) was determined for the following four items: "Easiness of hug," "Comfortable velocity," "Security," "Politeness," and "Vitality." The research participants were 30 healthy students aged between 20 and 24 years. They used the modes randomly.

Fig. 7. Experimental scene using hug robot system

5.2   Experimental Results

Result of Paired Comparison. The result of the paired comparison is shown in Table 1. It shows the number of research participants that preferred the row mode to the column mode. From the table, it is indicated that mode (b) was preferred by the largest number of research participants. Furthermore, the Bradley-Terry model [11] was fitted to the result to analyze the result quantitatively by using Eq. (6).

$$P_{ij} = \frac{\pi_i}{\pi_i + \pi_j} \tag{6}$$

$$\sum_i \pi_i = Const. \ (= Total : 100)$$

π_i is the intensity of the preference for model i. P_{ij} is the probability of the judgment that i is better than j.

Table 1. Result of paired comparison

	(a)	(b)	(c)	Total
(a)		18	32	50
(b)	42		50	92
(c)	28	10		38

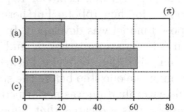

Fig. 8. Result of Bradley-Terry model

Using this model, the results of the paired comparison were expressed by the intensity of preference π, as shown in Fig. 8. The suitability of the model was validated by the goodness-of-fit and likelihood ratio tests. It indicates that mode (b) was rated as the best mode.

254   M. Jindai et al.

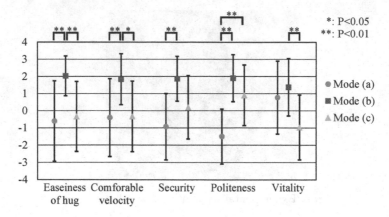

Fig. 9. Result of seven-point bipolar rating

Result of Seven-Point Bipolar Rating. The results of the seven-point bipolar rating are shown in Fig. 9. Mode (b) was evaluated as better than modes (a) and (c) with a significant difference of 1% or 5% in the "Easiness of hug" and "Comfortable velocity" items. This result agrees with the result of the Bradley-Terry model. Therefore, it can be concluded that the hug behavior of mode (b) is most preferred by humans. This result indicates that humans prefer the timing of the beginning that the robot begins its hug behavior at the one step before the stop of the human during approach. Furthermore, in the seven-point bipolar rating, all items of mode (b) were evaluated as positive. Therefore, the result shows that the proposed model is useful to request hug behavior from a human, when the human approaches a robot.

6   Conclusion

In this paper, a hug behavior request model with an approaching human was proposed for hug robots. Furthermore, a hug robot system that employs the proposed model was developed. In this model, the robot requests hug behavior when a human approaches it, and generates hug behavior with humans. From the analysis of hug behavior between humans, most humans began the request motion at the one step before the stop of the other. Then, based on this analysis, a sensory evaluation was performed using the developed robot system. From the results, it was indicated that humans prefer the timing of the beginning that the robot begins its hug behavior at the one step before the stop of the human during approach. Furthermore, the results showed that the proposed model is useful to request hug behavior from a human, when the human approaches a robot.

References

1. Rani, P., Sarkar, N., Smith, C.A.: Affect-sensitive human-robot cooperation-theory and experiments. In: Proceedings of the 2003 IEEE International Conference on Robotica & Automation, pp. 2382–2387 (2003)
2. Watanabe, T., Miwa, Y.: Duality of embodiment and support for co-creation in hand contact improvisation. J. Adv. Mech. Des. Syst. Manuf. **6**(7), 1307–1318 (2012)
3. Nakanishi, J., Kuwamura, K., Minato, T., Nishio, S., Ishiguro, H.: Evoking affection for a communication partner by a robotic communication medium. In: Proceedings of the 1st International Conference on Human-Agent Interaction, vol. 3, pp. 1–4 (2013)
4. Tsetserukou, D.: HaptiHug: a novel haptic display for communication of hug over a distance. In: Kappers, A.M.L., van Erp, J.B.F., Bergmann Tiest, W.M., van der Helm, F.C.T. (eds.) EuroHaptics 2010. LNCS, vol. 6191, pp. 340–347. Springer, Heidelberg (2010). https://doi.org/10.1007/978-3-642-14064-8_49
5. Teh, J.K.S., Cheok, A.D., Peiris, R.L., Choi, Y., Thuong, V., Lai, S.: Huggy Pajama: a mobile parent and child hugging communication system. In: Proceedings of the 7th International Conference on Interaction Design and Children, pp. 250–257 (2008)
6. DiSalvo, C., Gemperle, F., Forlizzi, J., Montgomery, E.: The hug: an exploration of robotic form for intimate communication. In: Proceedings of 12th IEEE Workshop on Robot and Human Interactive Communication, pp. 403–408 (2003)
7. Jindai, M., Ota, S., Yasuda, T., Sasaki, T.: Hug behavior response model for generation of hug behavior with humans. J. Adv. Mech. Des. Syst. Manuf. **12**(2), 1–11 (2018)
8. Jindai, M., Watanabe, T.: Development of a handshake request motion model based on analysis of handshake motion between humans. In: Proceedings of the 2011 IEEE/ASME International Conference on Advanced Intelligent Mechatronics, pp. 560–565 (2011)
9. Flash, T., Hogan, N.: The coordination of arm movements: an experimentally confirmed mathematical model. J. Neurosci. **5**(7), 1688–1703 (1985)
10. Kouchi, M., Mochimaru, M., Iwasawa, H., Mitani, S.: Anthropometric database for Japanese population. Japanese Industrial Standards Center 1997–98 (AIST, MITI) (2000)
11. Bradley, R.A., Terry, M.E.: Rank analysis of incomplete block designs. Biometrika **39**, 324–345 (1952)

Influence of Variable Environments and Character-Specific Design on Perception of Virtual Robots with Affective Labels

Wali Rizvi[✉], Ishaan Pakrasi, and Amy LaViers

Mechanical Science and Engineering Department,
University of Illinois Urbana-Champaign, Urbana, IL 61801, USA
{smrizvi2,pakrasi2,alaviers}@illinois.edu

Abstract. As robotic systems move out of the factory, it is essential that they adapt to changing environments. Distinct contextual settings may cause users to have a different perception of these systems. This paper explores the relationship between context and expression by looking at various combinations of robot characters and environments in a virtual setting. The robots are designed after characters from pop-culture. Physical traits such as color, eye shape, and motion profiles are abstractly analyzed and infused onto the robot. Six different robot characters and six different environments are used to see if individuals perceive each robot differently in varying environments. Additionally, the effect of character-specific priming as a context generator is also surveyed. It is found that the character with an affect label with positive valence was rated more favorably than characters with negative valence affect labels in positive valence environments and vice versa is true for environments with negative valence associated. Qualitative feedback from participants provides a meaningful description for each rating choice. This study shows the importance of contextual realizations while designing robotic systems that can be considered in future work looking at user perception.

Keywords: Context · Robot characters · Robotics design methodology

1 Introduction

Mobile robots navigating physical spaces need to take dimensions and parameters of the environment, such as the size of an obstacle or the friction of the ground, into account. These functional parameters of the environment guide the successful navigation of aerial and ground robots. When navigating in human environments, perceptions by human counterparts become part of the task definition for the successful operation of these devices. Mobile robots in social and human-facing settings need to be able to generate features of their motion that

© Springer Nature Switzerland AG 2019
M. A. Salichs et al. (Eds.): ICSR 2019, LNAI 11876, pp. 256–266, 2019.
https://doi.org/10.1007/978-3-030-35888-4_24

integrate seamlessly in their environment; to do this, they need to be able to measure aspects of their environment that impact the perception of this motion.

One lens through which human perception can be measured is the Circumplex Model of Affect [15]. This two-dimensional model uses *valence* and *arousal* to characterize human affect perception (alternatively, pleasure, arousal, and, a third dimension, dominance, has been proposed [12]). Prior work, which built from animator-derived stylized motion [4], has shown how context modifies the interpretation of motion by human viewers and that the Circumplex Model is an effective way to improve our prediction of affective labeling by humans [7].

Other work has looked at bodily generation by experts of stylized motion [2,6,18], including for mobile robots on ground [8] and in air [16]. Many of these prior studies use labels derived from affect studies, such as happy and sad. Parallel work has examined the role of narrative in changing user perception and behavior; robots given meaningful backstories were less likely to be destroyed by human subjects [3].

The tendency of humans to extract information and intentionality in robot motion has been discussed through the lens of "body language" as well [9], even for distinctly non-anthropomorphic bodies [1]. Often the narratives human viewers draw are unintentional: people have described the iRobot Roomba robot as both "cute" and "pathetic" [5]. Thus, it is reasonable to conclude that social acceptance is an important factor in the adoption of robots [11].

Thus, this paper will use existing Disney characters as in our prior work where characters from Winnie the Pooh were utilized [13], to design distinct robot characters with different affective labels. We will then test these characters in variable environments to see the effect these environments have on human perception of the intended characters. We will use established instruments for testing the perception of human viewers, utilizing agreement with the intended label by human subjects. Subjects watch robot motion in virtual reality, a platform that allows for quick iteration on the design of scenario features. Our results show that characters of negative valence in environments similar to those with negative valence (a Negative Scenario) perform differently than characters with positive valence in environments similar to those with positive valence (a Positive Scenario). Moreover, priming participants with the Disney animations seems to dampen this response, suggesting that the robot characters do not live up to the richness of the Disney animations.

Section 2, we will describe the six distinct robot characters created (including a "neutral" design) along with the virtual environment design. The user study design is presented in Sect. 3, and results and analysis of the experiment are presented in Sect. 4. Concluding remarks with future directions of work are outlined in Sect. 5.

2   Character-Based Robot and Environment Design

The plot of *Inside Out* revolves around creatures, shown in Fig. 1, that portray the five emotions inside the head of a human named Riley. We study the

258   W. Rizvi et al.

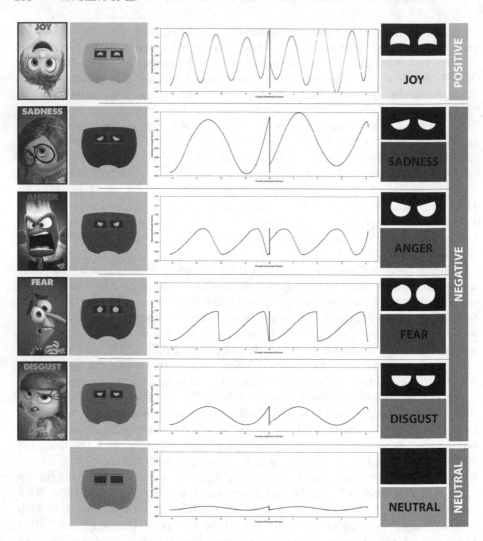

Fig. 1. The robot design of each 'emotion' (*Inside Out* character) and an additional neutral design. The first column shows the original *Inside Out* characters from Disney-Pixar© and the second column shows the final renditions of each robot. The third column shows the motion profile used by the aerial robots. The y-axis is the vertical movement of the robot while the x-axis shows the forward movement. The progression of time is from left to right. The vertical line in each motion profile is the point where the robot stops and until after a while it starts proceeding forward again. The fourth column shows the eye shapes and the color used. The fifth column presents broader classification.

physical characteristics of each emotion representation from publicly available descriptions [17]. Features of these characters that could be applied to our virtual aerial robot were distilled. We looked at body-color, eye-shape, and movement style. This resulted in the creation of five virtual robot designs. An additional neutral design was created to act as a control and a baseline for comparisons. The six design of the virtual robots has been described in our prior work [14]. A summary is shown in Fig. 1. Designs are also grouped based on the valence of emotions that they represent [15]. Joy is labeled positive while Sadness, Anger, Fear, and Disgust are labeled negative.

Fig. 2. First row: nature, urban, rural and destruction environments from the OASIS database with their ratings on the Circumplex Model of Affect [10]. These environments are similar to the ones developed and used in the user study. Bottom pictures: Panoramic views of the six environments with corresponding labels (clockwise from top-left): urban, nature, room, control, destruction, rural.

In order to test how the perception of these characters changed in distinct environments, five contextual settings were selected as environments for the characters. An effort was made to have these environments be as different as possible and be common enough that the audience is easily able to identify them.

As a result, *Urban, Rural, Nature, Destruction* and *Room* were chosen. Four of these have rather positive connotations while *Destruction* has a negative feel. This is supported by similar environments pulled from the OASIS database [10], where environments have been characterized according to the Circumplex Model of Affect [15]. These environments are shown in Fig. 2; the relatively high values for valence of the Urban, Rural, and Nature scene versus the Destruction scene support this classification.

The Room environment does not have a correlate in this database and was determined to be relatively positive, given its familiar, comfortable scene. This environment was selected due to an interest in studying the designs in a human-facing environment. An additional control environment containing an almost white room was also created, which was assigned to be 'Neutral' in valence. Future work will validate the assumed valences for each of these environments.

The environments were created in Unity3D, a publicly available game development engine. Objects in each environment were either created using built-in Unity3D tools or obtained online through the Unity asset store or open-source platforms. Figure 2 shows the panoramic scene of each environment. Environments were devoid of dynamic objects except few minor background details.

3   User Study Design

The efficacy in changing user perception through varying contexts is tested through user studies with three treatment groups, each having unique participants. All three groups require the participant to watch videos of our virtual aerial robot in an environment and then rate the robot's corresponding affective label from a scale of 1 to 10. An additional question asks them to explain their choice. The participants then proceed to the demographic questions where they are asked about their age, gender, education, location, and language.

Videos of each robot environment pair were created using Unity3D. Each video is choreographed similarly and the camera is programmed to follow the virtual aerial robot from a fixed position. The robot motion can be seen in Fig. 3. Six environments and six robot characters result in 36 videos.

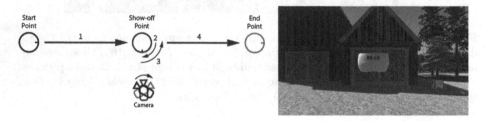

Fig. 3. Left: (1) The robot moves to the show-off position (2) The robot rotates 90° clockwise to face the camera. (3) After 10 s, the robot rotates 90° counterclockwise. (4) The robot proceeds to the end point. Right: Example scene of virtual robot in an environment.

Participants were recruited on Amazon Mechanical Turk and reimbursed according to a typical rate for that platform under a university-approved human subjects protocol. In all the participant groups, we randomized the presentation of the videos to reduce order bias. Participants were mostly English-speaking people aged 25–34 with Bachelor's degrees located in either the US or India.

The first group (unprimed) was used to validate the character based robots. Each participant watched, successively, videos of each robot design in the control environment. A total of 93 people (59 males and 34 females) were part of this user group. The second group was used to survey the role of priming as a context generator. It followed the same format of the first participant group. However, only this group was required to watch a short clip introducing the *Inside Out* character before watching the respective robot character video. The results from this group can be compared with the first group to understand the role of priming. 155 participants (92 males, 62 females and 1 non-binary) completed this user study. Lastly, the third group tested how varying backgrounds impacts our movement design profiles. The 36 videos were divided into six blocks of six videos each. Each design and environment combination occured once in each block. This was done to have the participants complete the survey in an acceptable amount of time. This treatment was completed by 89 participants (48 males and 41 females) and each participant only saw one of the blocks to keep the task from becoming overwhelming and repetitive.

4 Results and Analysis

The purpose of this study was to explore the influence, if any, of variable contexts on the perception of our virtual aerial robots. This paper achieves changing contexts in two ways. The first way was to prime the participants with character introduction videos before they rated the robot design. The second way was to place the robot in distinct virtually created environments. The quantitative results from all treatments grouped by character is shown in Fig. 4.

4.1 Quantitative Results

The results from the first group can be seen as validation for our robot designs. Since we only use the control environment, we assume that the participants largely rate the affective label of each robot based on the design. All robot designs receive, on average, a rating of more than 5. The Disgust and Fear based designs scored low comparatively, achieving an average rating less than 6. Ratings at this range were expected. Not only certain physical characteristics of the *Inside Out* characters were observed in the robots but also translating them from such fluid characters into rigid robots is not possible.

In the second group, priming the participants before they watched the robot videos with videos of the characters did not have the effect we originally intended. We expected the average affective label ratings to be higher when compared to ratings from Group 1. The difference was either the opposite or negligible enough to ignore. Joy, Sadness and Fear scored lower while Anger and Disgust were almost the same. This suggests that the participants did not find the robot characters as vivid when compared to the animations that they watched. It is also possible that some participants did not watch the animations closely and absorb their meaning deeply.

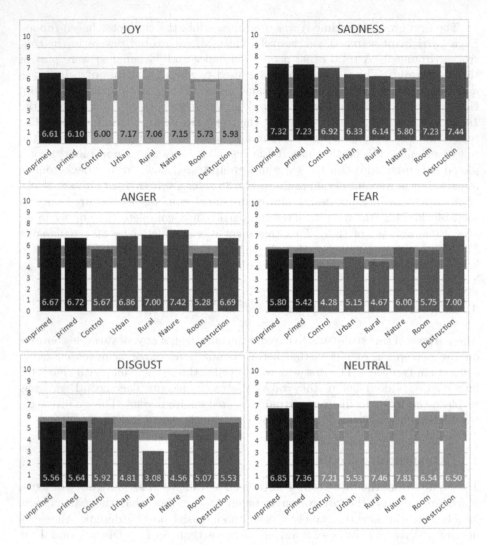

Fig. 4. All six virtual robots in the unprimed (N = 93), primed (N = 155), and each environmental condition (N = 89). These plots show how environments with a similar valence boosted the perception of robot characters (of that valence) and how priming dampened the perception of the intended characters.

Varying environments had mixed results. In the control environment, Anger and Fear had lower average ratings compared to Group 1 ratings for the same videos. Disgust scored poorly in all environments except Control, and Fear scored poorly in the Control and Rural environments. Fear and Disgust are perhaps more complex or lesser seen emotions. Other robot characters scored fairly well in all environments especially the positive character in positive environments and the negative characters in the negative environment. This can visually be seen in Fig. 5. Negative characters scored the highest in the negative environment of Destruction. Positively labeled character that only includes Joy scored highest in the Urban, Rural and Nature environment that are labeled positive. Positive labeled Room did not have as high a rating compared to its counterparts. Thus, the Room environment is perhaps a better choice for a neutral environment than the overly bleak Control environment as it was still a realistic environment.

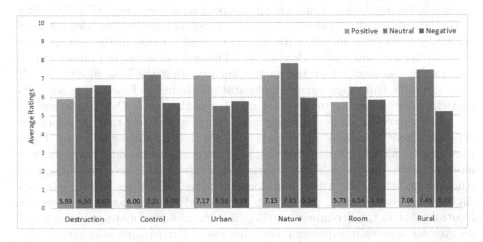

Fig. 5. Grouping the characters into positive (blue), neutral (grey), or negative (orange) valence highlights how environments of a similar valence boost this perception compared to a neutral character. (Color figure online)

4.2 Qualitative Feedback

In all studies, we asked participants in a free response box to explain their choice after each affective label rating. It was essential in learning each participant's motivation of their rating choice. Though many of the responses were mere 1–3 words, some were detailed enough to provide valuable insights. Every participant thinks differently and this was evident from the subjective qualitative comments.

Robot character Joy was received very positively by the participants. We saw comments like "The object seems to be skipping happily. Furthermore, its eyes seem upbeat a clear sign of joy" and "The jumping, bright color, and upbeatness are the tell-tale signs here." Some participants did not agree with Joy's motion profile observing that "the movements are too slow."

Many participants clearly identified the features we implemented for the Sadness robot. One participant commented "The face looks sad and the color blue feels sad to me. This one seems to bob listlessly around and I think that conveys a sense of sadness." One participant who saw the video of Sadness in the Destruction environment wrote that "The video shows a great deal of sadness because of the abandoned land and buildings" suggesting an important role of context in their decision. The eyes and color of Anger were widely noted in comments like "The color red is often associated with anger. Its movements are somewhat restless and its eyes look menacing." and "The color red signifies anger to me. It's eyes look angry. The background is not hospitable." Some participants wanted the movement to be faster saying "The movement though is too slow."

Participants were divided on Fear's movement. Some agreed with it saying "slow doubtful move makes me to say it express some fear" while others said "moves too slowly for real fear". One participant who gave a high affective rating to the Fear robot said "The coloring and eyes again matched the idea (at least according to societal norms), with the addition of a pause in the movement it gives further credence to the idea of fear." The opposite effect of priming can be seen in this comment where the participant says that the Fear robot "doesn't have the same thin appearance or physical attributes as Fear." This suggests participants were hoping to see exact matches of the *Inside Out* characters.

Disgust received many comments where participants said that the character expressed more "Annoyed" or "Bored" behavior than disgusting behavior. There were some qualities that depicted disgust. One participant said "There was one moment when the robot slightly turned and that could have been disgust". Another said that "Bot's slow and doubtful move, immediate leaving suggests slightly disgust." Finally, participants mentioned the absence of eyes on the Neutral robot in their comments saying "moving in a very unassuming way and its eyes are not really expressing anything else." Participants also agreed with the coloring of that robot saying "This video was about as neutral as it gets. The beige colors are exactly what I think of when I think of the word neutral."

5 Conclusions

This paper has presented the use of physical design, movement profile, environment features, and the role that narrative elements can play in the perception of robots by humans. We found that changing environment heightened the effectiveness of the perception of designed robot characters when the environment matched the valence of the robot. We also found that priming with more expressive animations created by professional animators [17] reduced the perceived efficacy of the robot characters. In future work, we will characterize robot characters and environments on the Circumplex Model separately as in [7]. This approach will reduce our reliance on 'similar' environments previously studied and avoid mistakes like our assumption here about the room environment having inherently positive associations. Moreover, we would like to work with animators directly to create unique narratives and character-types in order to see if these designs can better enhance the perceived characters of limited robotic platforms. This work is an important part of developing a robust understanding of how people perceive a given robotic device across multiple contexts, needed to prevent misunderstandings and, thus, system failures in social settings.

Acknowledgement. This work was conducted under IRB #17427 and funded by NSF grant #1528036.

References

1. Bianchini, S., Levillain, F., Menicacci, A., Quinz, E., Zibetti, E.: Towards behavioral objects: a twofold approach for a system of notation to design and implement behaviors in non-anthropomorphic robotic artifacts. In: Laumond, J.-P., Abe, N. (eds.) Dance Notations and Robot Motion. STAR, vol. 111, pp. 1–24. Springer, Cham (2016). https://doi.org/10.1007/978-3-319-25739-6_1

2. Burton, S.J., Samadani, A.-A., Gorbet, R., Kulić, D.: Laban movement analysis and affective movement generation for robots and other near-living creatures. In: Laumond, J.-P., Abe, N. (eds.) Dance Notations and Robot Motion. STAR, vol. 111, pp. 25–48. Springer, Cham (2016). https://doi.org/10.1007/978-3-319-25739-6_2

3. Darling, K., Nandy, P., Breazeal, C.: Empathic concern and the effect of stories in human-robot interaction. In: 2015 24th IEEE International Symposium on Robot and Human Interactive Communication (RO-MAN), pp. 770–775. IEEE (2015)

4. Etemad, S.A., Arya, A.: Expert-driven perceptual features for modeling style and affect in human motion. IEEE Trans. Hum.-Mach. Syst. 46(4), 534–545 (2016)

5. Forlizzi, J., DiSalvo, C.: Service robots in the domestic environment: a study of the roomba vacuum in the home. In: Proceedings of the 1st ACM SIGCHI/SIGART Conference on Human-Robot Interaction, pp. 258–265. ACM (2006)

6. Gemeinboeck, P., Saunders, R.: Towards socializing non-anthropomorphic robots by harnessing dancers' kinesthetic awareness. In: Koh, J.T.K.V., Dunstan, B.J., Silvera-Tawil, D., Velonaki, M. (eds.) CR 2015. LNCS (LNAI), vol. 9549, pp. 85–97. Springer, Cham (2016). https://doi.org/10.1007/978-3-319-42945-8_8

7. Heimerdinger, M., LaViers, A.: Modeling the interactions of context and style on affect in motion perception: stylized gaits across multiple environmental contexts. Int. J. Soc. Robot. (SORO) 11(3), 495–513 (2019)

8. Knight, H., Simmons, R.: Expressive motion with x, y and theta: laban effort features for mobile robots. In: The 23rd IEEE International Symposium on Robot and Human Interactive Communication, pp. 267–273. IEEE (2014)

9. Knight, H., Simmons, R.: Laban head-motions convey robot state: a call for robot body language. In: 2016 IEEE International Conference on Robotics and Automation (ICRA), pp. 2881–2888. IEEE (2016)

10. Kurdi, B., Lozano, S., Banaji, M.R.: Introducing the open affective standardized image set (OASIS). Behav. Res. Methods 49(2), 457–470 (2017)

11. Manyika, J., et al.: A future that works: automation, employment and productivity. McKinsey Global Institute, January 2017

12. Mehrabian, A.: Pleasure-arousal-dominance: a general framework for describing and measuring individual differences in temperament. Curr. Psychol. 14(4), 261–292 (1996)

13. Pakrasi, I., Chakraborty, N., LaViers, A.: A design methodology for abstracting character archetypes onto robotic systems. In: Proceedings of the 5th International Conference on Movement and Computing, p. 24. ACM (2018)

14. Rizvi, W., Pakrasi, I., LaViers, A.: Movement design of virtual aerial robots with distinct affective labels. In: 6th International Conference on Movement and Computing (Extended Abstract). ACM (2019, to appear)

15. Russell, J.A.: A circumplex model of affect. J. Pers. Soc. Psychol. 39(6), 1161–1178 (1980)

16. Sharma, M., Hildebrandt, D., Newman, G., Young, J.E., Eskicioglu, R.: Communicating affect via flight path: exploring use of the laban effort system for designing affective locomotion paths. In: Proceedings of the 8th ACM/IEEE International Conference on Human-Robot Interaction, pp. 293–300. IEEE Press (2013)
17. Pixar Animation Studios: Inside out. Technical report, Disney (2015). https://www.pixar.com/feature-films/inside-out
18. Zhou, A., Dragan, A.D.: Cost functions for robot motion style. In: 2018 IEEE/RSJ International Conference on Intelligent Robots and Systems (IROS), pp. 3632–3639. IEEE (2018)

Social Emotions for Social Robots - Studies on Affective Impressions in Human-Human and Human-Robot Interactions

Kristiina Jokinen[✉]

AI Research Center, AIST Tokyo Waterfront, Tokyo, Japan
kristiina.jokinen@aist.go.jp

Abstract. In this paper, social emotions and expressive interaction are discussed in the context of human-robot interaction. The focus is on understanding natural human behaviour and how human socio-emotional stance manifests itself in various interactive settings. The paper compares two different types of agents, human partners and humanoid robot agents, and studies how the subjects' behaviour and their impressions of the interaction differ depending on the agent type. The paper concludes that there is no statistically significant difference between the two conditions, but that the subjects are more certain and unanimous about their views when interacting with humans, but less sure and also less unanimous about their socio-emotional stance concerning a robot partner.

Keywords: Social robots · Human-robot interaction · Affect

1 Introduction

Social robots are expected to make important contributions in society in the coming years. The use of robots for assistive robotics, elder-care, and everyday life is expected to increase: the robots can act as companions [8, 11, 15, 17, 18], instruct novice care-givers about daily routines and how to perform particular care-giving tasks [11, 13], read news or weather forecasts or Wikipedia articles [24, 25], or provide support for those who have age-related challenges [19, 22]. Consequently, spoken interactions with robot agents are expected to increase, and it is important to design interfaces that support natural, affordable interactions, based on natural interaction models that the human partners can understand. The design of social robots which are intended for everyday situations and various educational, health and care services should be based on a human-centred approach which focusses on natural multimodal communication and social aspects of interaction. The perceived social emotions convey the agent's intentions, thoughts and feelings, and can equip the robot with a capability to interact with the human in a more socially competent manner that also addresses the user's emotional needs [11]. Moreover, the robot should provide truthful and reliable information, and deal with sensitive information, e.g. a patient's physical state, in a way that is socially tactful and can be regarded as trustworthy. In smart environments with interconnected devices, safe and ethical data management becomes crucial [6, 14].

© Springer Nature Switzerland AG 2019
M. A. Salichs et al. (Eds.): ICSR 2019, LNAI 11876, pp. 267–277, 2019.
https://doi.org/10.1007/978-3-030-35888-4_25

Social robots pose challenges for interaction modelling due to their dual characteristics as agents and as sophisticated computer tools [11]. This paper discusses the robot as an agent in the context of a case study where the robot interacts with human interlocutors and provides task-based information and entertaining facts. Technical details of the dialogue model can be found elsewhere [11, 13], and this paper focuses on the enablements of interaction, the user's socio-emotional stance, and perception of the robot's interaction capability. The main questions are:

- How to model socio-emotional interaction using various multimodal signals?
- What is the users' socio-emotional stance and their self-reported impressions of a humanoid robot in natural interactions?
- How do these compare with human-human interactions in similar situations?

The paper first discusses the CDM-based affective agent model used in our robot application (Sect. 2), then presents an empirical study of user interaction with the robot (Sect. 3) and the results of the questionnaire concerning the user's impressions of the human-human and human-robot interactions (Sect. 4). The paper concludes with future views and a brief discussion of the implications of the findings for the design of robots enhancing social interaction between users and robot agents (Sect. 5).

2 Affective Agent Model

According to the Constructive Dialogue Model [10], communicative situations are interactions where the interlocutors construct shared understanding of the intentions and beliefs of their partners. Interactions take place through a cycle of interpretation and generation processes based on four central enablements for communication: Contact, Perception, Understanding, and Reaction. The agent must first detect the partner's signals, such as vocalization and gesturing (Contact), then recognize that the signals have communicative intention (Perception), and analyse potential interpretations in the context as the intended communicative act (Understanding). The agent then needs to generate behaviour that acknowledges the partner's communicative act and conveys their own intention as a suitable response (Reaction). The interlocutors are thus engaged in a dynamic building of the dialogue through monitoring of the enablements and grounding of information in the shared dialogue context. This also creates affective bonds between the partners which are stored in the memory and can influence their future behaviour. If the enablements are not met, the agents attempt to specify the problem and initiate clarification with respect to the failing enablement: the partner may not be contactable, does not perceive communicative intention, has difficulties to understand it, or produces irrelevant reaction. If the enablement is broken beyond reasonable expectations of clarification, communication simply fails as it is not possible to build mutual understanding and engage the partner in interaction.

The CDM-based human-robot interaction is depicted in Fig. 1. The framework distinguishes the *speaker's perspective* from the *partner's perspective*, the former referring to the speaker's intentions and expressions to convey a certain meaning, the latter to the partner's interpretation of the speaker's behaviour. The agents maintain two views of the interaction depending on whether the focus is on planning own behaviour or interpreting and evaluating the partner's behaviour.

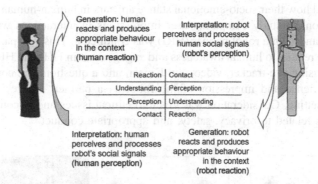

Fig. 1. Human-robot interaction and the cycle of interpretation and generation, with communicative enablements in the middle grid.

The model defines *social emotions* as the agent's basic attitudes towards partners and the environment in general. They represent the agent's emotions in a wider sense than the six basic emotions [2, 5], and are linked to the agent's personality traits [21]. Social emotions manifest themselves through multimodal behaviour patterns (micro gestures, facial expressions, head nods, laughter types, etc.) learnt in interactive situations via dynamic categorisation of observed behaviours into a set of social emotions. The set of behaviour patterns constitutes a *repertoire for expressive behaviour* and it can change as a result of the agent's exposure to feedback that rewards different types of manifestations. At a given time, the agent's behaviour patterns form a particular *socio-emotional stance* which can have a label describing the closest underlaying social emotion. In our questionnaire, *enjoyable, awkward, impressive, ordinary*, etc. are used as higher-level abbreviations for the subject's socio-emotional stance.

Interpretation of social emotions need not be what the agent intended or assumed to have conveyed. If the mismatch between the intended and perceived intentions is small it can be clarified, but if the difference is too big, communication becomes difficult because there is no basis for shared understanding. Non-verbal communication is especially prone to misunderstandings due to cultural differences that lead to differences in how people think, feel and act [4, 5]. Different cultures have been found to exhibit different non-verbal "accents" [18], and non-verbal behaviour can vary significantly even in closely related cultures [20]. Comparisons are often conducted against Western and Eastern cultural backgrounds, especially in interactions with virtual characters [1, 4], but considerations on empathic concern and perspective taking are also relevant, e.g. in sharing of personal information in care-giving situations [14].

3 Experiment

In order to explore how human users perceive social emotions in natural interactions with robots and how their socio-emotional stance appears in human-human and human-robot interactions, a study comparing user impressions in interactions with a human partner (HHI) and with a robot partner (HRI) was conducted. This was part of a bigger data collection related to human awareness and engagement in HHI and HRI [12]. Data was recorded using eye-tracker, video, and Kinect, and a questionnaire concerning the subjects' experience and impression of the robot as a partner. Figure 2 depicts the experimental setting. Consideration was given to ethical issues and to complying with the regulations related to privacy, safety, and appropriate conduct.

Fig. 2. Experimental setting.

A humanoid robot was installed with software that allowed the user to conduct natural language dialogues with the robot on care-giving tasks, and other software that enabled chat-type conversations on music and movies, complete with a short quiz game. The dialogue design took into consideration dialogue activity (task-based instructions vs. chatty conversations on music and movies) known to have impact on social interaction and affect. Instructions for the subjects were similar in both HRI and HHI conditions. After the instructions, the subjects interacted with their partner (a human or a robot) alone, but the experimenters monitored the session in the next room and could intervene if needed. The subjects interacted with the robot in Japanese or English depending on their preference. The languages provide an implicit cultural conditioning on the interaction, dividing subjects into native Japanese speakers and English speakers with backgrounds in Europe, US, and South-East Asia.

The questionnaire contains questions about the subjects' background and the topics of the interaction, and an extensive set of questions about the user's perception of the robot and its interaction capabilities. There are also free questions about the subject's expectations of the robot interaction, influence of their background on the scores, and suggestions for improvements. The subjects' socio-emotional stance was measured by asking them to self-evaluate the interaction in terms of six descriptive adjectives (*enjoyable, impressive, relaxed, natural, interesting, friendly*), based on our earlier work on HRI evaluation. Each adjective was paired with a corresponding negative one (*awkward, ordinary, tense, unnatural, boring, anxious*), for which the score was expected to be the opposite of the positive one (see Fig. 3). The negative adjectives were used as control questions to check consistency and reliability of the subjects' self-evaluation. The rationale is that, if consistent, the participant would give higher rates for positive and lower rates for negative stance. All answers were recorded on a 7-point Likert scale.

There were 30 subjects (20 Japanese, 10 English speakers, 10 females), each having one dialogue with a human experimenter and one with a robot either on instruction giving or free chatting domain. The subjects were students and researchers, age 20-60, with some experience in IT but no experience of robots. 14 subjects had instructional and 16 had chat dialogues.

This paper focuses on the participants' socio-emotional stance as evidenced in the questionnaire. Analyses of eye-gaze in interaction are presented in other papers [9, 16].

4 Results

4.1 Expectations and Background on Social Interaction

We first checked subjects' answers to free questions concerning their expectations of the robot's social and technical capabilities. A majority (60%) commented on social aspects like *If I am bored or excited by the conversation, recognize my emotions a little* or *Look at my eyes. Behaviors should be natural according to what we are talking about at the time.* Many (40%) also commented on the technical issues related to speech and repetitive questions like *To interrupt the talk and ask simple questions while the robot speaks* or *At least a bit more options for navigating the conversation tree.* However, when checking the distribution of self-initiated comments over gender and language varieties, the results seem to refute the stereotypical views.

4.1.1 Gender Differences

There were no gender differences in the comments on the robot's social and technical capabilities: 60% of the male as well as of female subjects focused on social capabilities and 40% on technical aspects. The data thus does not support gender-based views of the "soft" vs "hard" aspects of interaction: both male and female subjects have similar experience on IT technology, and both commented on the social rather than technical aspects.

4.1.2 Cultural Differences

If the self-initiated comments are clustered with respect to language, it is interesting that English-speaking subjects commented more on the robot's social capabilities (70%) whereas Japanese subjects were more balanced between technical and social capabilities (55% vs 45%, respectively). As the dataset is small, definite conclusions about cultural differences cannot be drawn, especially as the English speaking group had varied cultural backgrounds, but it is interesting that the data seems to refute stereotypical views of Japanese emphasis on social interaction design, and instead indicates that social aspects are paid more attention among the English speaking subjects, whereas the Japanese subjects focus on both social and technical aspects. The difference may be related to the subjects' prior experience and views of robots in general, which play a tacit role in their answers. This was recognized by the subjects themselves: 75% of Japanese speakers and 80% of English speakers considered that their background in robots and agents biased their expectation and comprehension of the system. Indeed, the Japanese subjects have a long and wide exposure to various types of robots and robot interactions aiming to help humans, while in the Western world robots are more associated with industrial robots or hostile robot agents which need emotional and social modelling. We thus assume that in our corpus, expectations of the "standard" robot features among the Japanese subjects include both social and technical aspects, i.e. social aspects are not singled out, whereas the comments by the other subjects emphasise socio-emotional aspects as a response to their expectations about the technical aspects being more developed. A larger subject population may of course even out the differences.

4.2   Socio-Emotional Stance

To study how the subjects experienced their interaction with the robot agent, we used the part of the questionnaire where the subjects were asked to map their experience with the robot in regard to a set of social emotions and compared this with the ranking of their experience with a human partner. Consistency of the subjects' ratings was checked by the control questions, which paired the selected positive socio-emotional types with negative socio-emotional ones (see Fig. 3, where the negative control adjective is below the corresponding positive one).

The hypothesis was that there is a difference in subject's impressions of their interaction with human or robot partners. We thus analyse the data statistically across the HHI and HRI categories. The ratings were analysed using Student's two-tailed t-test and the results presented with $\alpha = 0.05$. Pearson's correlation coefficient was used to measure linear correlations among the variables. Figure 3 visualises the average scores for each socio-emotional stance, and Table 1 summarizes the findings.

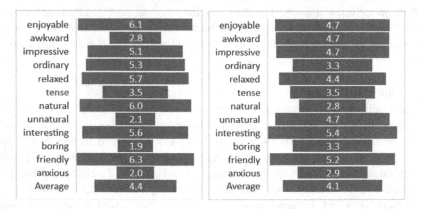

Fig. 3. Visualisations of the subjects' average scores concerning their socio-emotional stance in interaction with the human (left) and with the robot (right).

The average score on a 7-point Likert scale is 4.4 for HHI and 4.1 for HRI. The mean values are not significantly different (Student's two-tailed t-test, p = 0.63, α = 0.05), so the original hypothesis that there is a difference in the subject's impressions concerning their interaction with a human or a robot partner is not supported. However, the scores show a slight correlation (Pearson r = 0.32), i.e. the subjects' socio-emotional stance seems to have a similar tendency in HHI and HRI and differ only in the strength of the subjects' confidence ratings.

Looking deeper into the data, we compare the questions related to positive and negative socio-emotional stance separately across HHI and HRI. The mean average score for positive questions is μ = 5.8 for HHI and μ = 4.5 for HHR, and these appear significantly different (two-tailed t-test, p = 0.03, α = 0.05). However, the mean score differences between the corresponding negative control questions (μ = 2.9 in HHI and μ = 3.7 in HRI) are not significantly different (two-tailed t-test, p = 0.28, α = 0.05). The standard deviation shows that the subjects are rather unanimous on their high positive impressions in HHI (μ = 5.8, σ = 0.4), but less certain about their interaction with the robot partner in HRI, and there was also more variability among the subjects' scores (μ = 4.5, σ = 0.9). As for the negative control questions, the ratings are lower, but variation in HHI is large (μ = 2.9, σ = 1.3), while in HRI variation is of similar magnitude as in the other cases (μ = 3.7, σ = 0.8), indicating consistency and similarity in the subjects' impression of the interaction with the robot partner. Furthermore, if we compare the corresponding positive and negative responses across HHI and HRI, t-test with α = 0.05 indicates significant difference (p = 0.03) between the positive question scores, but not between the negative question scores across HHI and HRI (p = 0.28). This is supported by Pearson correlation: there is no correlation between positive HHI and HRI scores (r = −0.07) and only a weak correlation between negative HHI and HRI scores (r = −0.18).

Table 1. Average ratings with standard deviation, Student t-test (α = 0.05), and Pearson correlations between all, positive, and negative ratings on the subjects' socio-emotional stance across human-human (HHI) and human-robot (HRI) interactions.

	Ave HHI	Ave HRI	t-test (p) HHI vs HRI	Pearson (r) HHI vs HRI
All	4.4 ± 1.8	4.1 ± 0.9	0.63	0.32
Positive	5.8 ± 0.4	4.5 ± 0.9	**0.03**	−0.07
Negative	2.9 ± 1.3	3.7 ± 0.8	0.28	−0.18

Table 2 summarizes the comparison between positive and negative ratings within the HHI and HRI conditions, i.e. with respect to the interaction partner. Pearson correlation shows that there is a strong negative correlation between the positive and negative scores within both HHI (r = −0.79) and HRI (r = −0.69), indicating that the subjects provided their positive and negative ratings with strong internal consistency (high positive score was accompanied by low negative score and vice versa).

Table 2. Student's t-test ($\alpha = 0.05$) and Pearson correlation concerning the subjects' positive and negative socio-emotional stance ratings within HHI and within HRI.

Interaction type	Positive	Negative	t-test p	Pearson r
HHI	5.8 ± 0.4	2.9 ± 1.3	**0.01**	−0.79
HRI	4.5 ± 0.9	3.7 ± 0.8	0.28	−0.69

A similar tendency seems to occur concerning positive and negative scores as in the previous across-category comparison: the difference between the positive and negative scores is significant in HHI (t-test p = 0.01, α = 0.05), but not in HRI (t-test p = 0.28, α = 0.05). In other words, the subjects expressed clearer and more confident views in rating human interactions than human-robot interactions. This may indicate their familiarity with human partners, and uncertainty to consider a robot as an interactive partner. It is also interesting that in HHI, the subjects seem more uniform in evaluating their positive emotional stance than the corresponding negative one (σ = 0.4 and σ = 1.3, respectively), whereas in HRI, variation is similar for both positive and negative ratings (σ = 0.9 and σ = 0.8, respectively). This observation can also support the view that HRI is not a typical form of interaction and that the subjects have not yet "fixed" their views on a robot as an interactive partner.

Table 3 shows differences in rating between HHI and HRI. The biggest differences are found in the ratings for *natural* and *ordinary* (3.2 and 2.0 points, respectively), and the smallest for *tense* (no difference) and for *interesting* and *impressive* (0.29 and 0.41 points, respectively). On the negative control questions, the biggest differences are in the ratings for *unnatural* and *awkward* (−2.6 and −1.9, respectively).

Table 3. Average scores of the subjects' impressions and their absolute difference.

Type	Enjoyable	Awkward	Impressive	Ordinary	Relaxed	Tense	Natural	Unnatural	Interesting	Boring	Friendly	Anxious	Ave
HHI	6.1	2.8	5.1	5.3	5.7	3.5	6.0	2.1	5.6	1.9	6.3	2.0	4.37
HHR	4.7	4.7	4.7	3.3	4.4	3.5	2.8	4.7	5.4	3.3	5.2	2.9	4.13
Δ	1.38	−1.94	0.41	2.00	1.29	0.00	3.21	−2.59	0.29	−1.38	1.12	−0.88	0.24

The pair *impressive-ordinary* may seem counterintuitive: we expected HHI be more impressive and less ordinary based on the richness and variation of the interaction, and HRI be less impressive and more ordinary due to the limited interaction capability. However, in HHI *ordinary* was rated higher (5.3) than *impressive* (5.1). The reason for this is probably an ill-selected adjective "ordinary" which associates with "normal", "common", "usual" rather than the opposite of "impressive".

Figure 4 summarizes the mean scores of the subjects' impressions together with the corresponding Δ-ratings between HHI and HRI. Although the general trend seems to rate HRI worse than HHI, the difference, as mentioned, is not statistically significant. Rather, the tendency to evaluate one's socio-emotional stance in HHI and HRI seems to be the same, and the biggest differences concern ratings for the *natural* and *ordinary*, i.e. how intuitive and "normal" the interaction was perceived by the user.

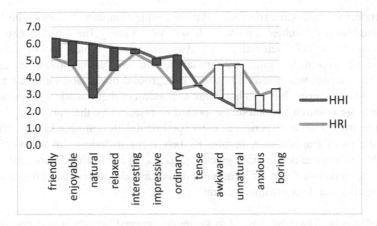

Fig. 4. Comparison of HHI and HRI along the positive and negative ratings. The black bars show difference in positive questions, the white bars show the difference in the corresponding negative questions. (See the text for the scores on *ordinary*).

5 Discussion and Conclusions

The paper discussed human subjects' socio-emotional impressions concerning their interactions with a human and with a robot partner. It presented a dialogue model based on the CDM framework which emphasises the enablements of communication and the cyclic and dynamic construction of dialogue, and discussed how this model takes into account various modalities to build an affective model of the interaction, by distinguishing the speaker's and the partner's perspectives and defining the agent's socio-emotional stance as the set of behaviour patterns at a given time.

Users' self-reported socio-emotional behaviour was analysed using questionnaires where subjects ranked their interactions with human (HHI) and robot (HRI) partners. Statistical analysis showed there is no statistically significant difference between the two conditions: users rate their socio-emotional stance along the same lines in HHI and HRI. However, the subjects' confidence varies across the cases: they are certain and unanimous in their impressions and socio-emotional stance when interacting with humans, but less sure and less unanimous in their views of a robot partner. Although the human and robot interactions clearly have differences in terms of versatility and richness of expressions, it is interesting that subjects exhibited similar patterns in both interactive conditions. We assume that this is due to the robot's dual characteristics as a computer and as an agent, and it paves way towards the robot acting as a boundary-crossing agent, i.e. an entity that extends the borders of typical autonomous agents to include inanimate robots with their human-like capabilities [11].

The subjects were also more uniform in evaluating their positive emotional stance than the corresponding negative ones. This may be due to the selected adjectives, but the phenomenon has been observed in other studies, and may be related to human cognition and differences in recognizing positive and negative emotions (concerning facial expressions, see [3]). Due to lack of data here, this is left for future research.

An important methodological point typical in questionnaire studies is the level of background bias in the subjects' answers. In the current study, the subjects' exposure to robot interactions affects their ratings, e.g. expectations of "typical" robot features, or evaluation of natural vs. unnatural human-human and human-robot interactions. A larger sample size will alleviate possible background biases and eliminate noise in the observed differences. It is also important to remember that statistical differences and correlations are research hypotheses supported or rejected by the data.

To maximize human experience, the experimental design should also take into account the robot's appearance, besides its behaviour including the socio-emotional stance and multimodal actions in a given situation. An interesting future study would replicate experiments using a different robot design and different capabilities to take the communicative enablements into account.

Acknowledgments. The paper is based on the results obtained from the project commissioned by the New Energy and Industrial Technology Development Organization (NEDO).

References

1. Aylett, R., Paiva, A., Vannini, N., Enz, S., Andre, E., Hall, L.: But that was in another country: agents and intercultural empathy. In: The 8th International Conference on Autonomous Agents and Multiagent Systems (2009)
2. Barrett, L.F.: Solving the emotion paradox: categorization and the experience of emotion. Pers. Soc. Psychol. Rev. **10**(1), 20–46 (2006)
3. Cowie, R., et al.: Emotion recognition in human computer interaction. IEEE Sig. Process. Mag. **18**(1), 32–80 (2001)
4. Endrass, B., Andre, E., Rehm, M., Nakano, Y.: Investigating culture-related aspects of behavior for virtual characters. In: The 12th International Conference on Autonomous Agents and Multiagent Systems, AAMAS (2013)
5. Ekman, P., Friesen, W.V., O'Sullivan, M., Chan, A., et al.: Universals and cultural differences in the judgments of facial expressions of emotion. J. Pers. Soc. Psychol. **53**(4), 712 (1987)
6. Grieco, L.A., et al.: IoT-aided robotics applications: technological implications, target domains and open issues. Comput. Commun. **54**, 32–47 (2014)
7. Heberlein, A.S., Saxe, R.: Dissociation between emotion and personality judgments: convergent evidence from functional neuroimaging. Neuroimage **28**, 770–777 (2005)
8. Heylen, D., Krenn, B., Payr, S.: Companions, virtual butlers, assistive robots: empirical and theoretical insights for building long-term social relationships. In: Trappl, R. (ed.) Cybernetics and Systems 2010, pp. 539–570. Austrian Society for Cybernetic Studies, Vienna (2010)
9. Ijuin, K., Jokinen, K., Kato, T., Yamamoto, S.: Eye-gaze in social robot interactions. In: Grounding of Information and Eye-Gaze Patterns. JSAI 2019 (2019)
10. Jokinen, K.: Constructive Dialogue Modelling: Speech Interaction with Rational Agents. Wiley, Chichester (2009)
11. Jokinen, K.: Dialogue models for social robots. In: Proceedings of ICSR 2018, Qingdao, China (2018)
12. Jokinen, K.: The AICO corpus. Technical report, AI Research Center, AIST (2019)

13. Jokinen, K., Nishimura, S., Watanabe, K., Nishimura, T.: Human-robot dialogues for explaining activities. In: D'Haro, L.F., Banchs, R.E., Li, H. (eds.) 9th International Workshop on Spoken Dialogue System Technology. LNEE, vol. 579, pp. 239–251. Springer, Singapore (2019). https://doi.org/10.1007/978-981-13-9443-0_20
14. Jokinen, K., et al.: Privacy and sensor information in the interactive service applications for elder people. In: Proceedings of 7th National Conference of Servicology, Tokyo (2019)
15. Kanda, T., Hirano, T., Eaton, D., Ishiguro, H.: Interactive robots as social partners and peer tutors for children: a field trial. Hum.-Comput. Interact. **19**(1–2), 61–84 (2004)
16. Laohagangvalvit, T., Jokinen, K.: Eye-gaze behaviours in natural human-human and human-robot interactions. In: ECEM Conference, Alicante (2019)
17. Leite, I., Martinho, C., Paiva, A.: Social robots for long-term interaction: a survey. Int. J. Soc. Robot. **5**(2), 291–308 (2013)
18. Montemayor, J., et al.: From pets to storykit: creating new technology with and intergenerational design team. In: Proceedings of the Workshop on Interactive Robots and Entertainment (WIRE), Pittsburgh (2000)
19. Montemerlo, M., Pineau, J., Roy, N., Thrun, S., Verma, V.: Experiences with a mobile robotic guide for the elderly. In: Proceedings of AAAI National Conference on Artificial Intelligence (2002)
20. Navarretta, C., Ahlsen, E., Allwood, J., Jokinen, K., Paggio, P.: Feedback in Nordic first encounters: a comparative study. In: The 8th International Conference on Language Resources and Evaluation (LREC) (2012)
21. Okada, S., Nguyen, L.S., Aran, O., Gatica-Perez, D.: Modeling dyadic and group impressions with intermodal and interpersonal features. ACM Trans. Multimed. Comput. Commun. Appl. **15**, 13 (2019)
22. Petrica, R., Moscovitch, M., Grady, C.: Proficiency in positive vs. negative emotion identification and subjective well-being among long-term married elderly couples. Front. Psychol. **5**, 338 (2014)
23. Pollack, M.E.: Intelligent technology for an aging population: the use of AI to assist elders with cognitive impairment. AI Mag. **26**(2), 9–24 (2005)
24. Sidner, C., Rich, C., Shayganfar, M., Bickmore, T., Ring, L., Zhang, Z.: A robotic companion for social support of isolated older adults. In: The 10th Annual ACM/IEEE International Conference on Human-Robot Interaction Extended Abstracts, pp. 289–289 (2015)
25. Wilcock, G., Jokinen, K.: Advances in Wikipedia-based interaction with robots. In: Proceedings of ICMI Workshop on Multi-Modal, Multi-Party, Real-World Human-Robot Interaction, pp. 13–18 (2014)

The Contribution of Art and Design to Robotics

Ioana Ocnarescu[(✉)] and Isabelle Cossin

Strate School of Design, Sèvres, France
{i.ocnarescu, i.cossin}@strate.design

Abstract. Today the industrial interests for technological objects, the increasing number of robotic solutions that appear on the market and the powerful imaginative stories on robotics demand a deep exploration on what living with robots means. This article shows how art and design could contribute to the field of social robotics by proposition a new paradigm shift based on aesthetic and ethical challenges intimately linked to the quality of living. It shows different explorations coming from artists and designers whose goals are finally very similar to those of roboticists. These experiments allow not only to create technical and artistic objects but also propose new ways to better understand the human-robot interaction on notions like the design of the robotic body, the different types of relationships with robots and the narrative context.

Keywords: Robotic art · Human-Robot Interaction · Experience · Movement · Human-robot relationship · Fiction

1 Introduction

Today the increasing number of robotic solutions that appear on the market, the industrial interests for this sector, and the powerful imagination around robotics, demand that we explore what living with robots means. Just like in the 1990s, the robotic industry will need designers and other creators of imaginative worlds to change the vision on this discipline. While the studies in Human-Robot Interaction have long integrated cognitive sciences, engineering, computer science and recently also designers, psychologists, sociologists, anthropologists [1], this scientific multi-disciplinary approach undoubtedly lacks in addressing more imaginative field oriented questions. These considerations bring together aesthetic and ethical challenges intimately linked to the quality and the experience of living with robots. For these notions, we need to conduct more than quantitative studies that intend to break the human experience into small tasks. Often, a slight paradigm shift, an overview of the imaginative field or a field research insight can redirect an exploration focused solely on the technical feasibility. This is why a vision based on experiences coming from art and design could bring a complementary approach to that of roboticists.

Artists showed an interest in robotics for a long time, but the term "robotic art" was defined only in 1997 by Edouardo Kac, a Brazilian-American artist in his paper entitled "Foundation and development of robotic art" [2]. For him, the experience with robotic artefacts, as opposed to the object (the artefact), is unstable, open and ephemeral, but

M. A. Salichs et al. (Eds.): ICSR 2019, LNAI 11876, pp. 278–287, 2019.
https://doi.org/10.1007/978-3-030-35888-4_26

yet closely linked to the body. His definition is part of a very broad artistic landscape that includes the media arts, interaction, digital art and robotic or automated technologies [2]. Studying artistic installations and performances related to robotic art could bring valuable insights in the field of social robotics and the human-robot interaction. Therefore our goal is to show through experimentations led in the field of art, that artists address notions and questions on experience, meaning and interaction with robotic artefacts. Further on we present these contributions on three dimensions: the body (how to design a robotic body that is perceived having a self, how to create an effect of presence etc.), the different types of relationships with robots, and the fiction (how a story contributes to the human-robot relationship).

2 The "Body" and Its Role in the Human-Robot Interaction

2.1 A Figure that Plays with Its Ambiguity

In 1965, artist Nam June Paik became interested in robotics and created K456, a human sized remotely-operated robot designed to become, according to the artist, "the first non-human action of the history" to wander around the streets in order to startle passers-by – see Fig. 1a. A kind of aluminium skeleton with fake breasts, K456 was presented as a caricature of the human being that was to replace the body of a performer. It was built in reaction to the idea that robots in the industry would suppress men's jobs by rationalizing the production [3]. With Nam June Paik, comes the question of the ambiguity of robotic representations: the artist builds a humanoid from scratch, recognizable as an artificial figure and that needs humans to move (5 persons in this case). This representation is here to denounce a societal situation: K456 is a technical object incapable of operating without human intervention; it takes a stance as an effigy and as the representation of a given situation that operates in an environment halfway between art (the Whitney museum) and life (the street). Therefore Nam June Paik's staging questions even today our relationship to technological objects and provoke the viewers to rethink their interaction with robotics in their daily life.

2.2 A "Statue" that Questions or Engages the Viewer

Since the Renaissance, artists have intended to create a presence through their works and make the viewer experience strong emotions through their different ways of representing the human body. In some artworks one could find figures that are static yet in action, like sculptures that show characters absorbed in their activities or in contemplation. In others more interactive works, forms and features are in action to make the viewer react in a more complex way: gazes converging towards the viewer such as in Velasquez's painting Las Meninas [4]. One can say that in the first instance, the spectator remains a simple viewer whereas in the second instance, the spectator is engaged almost physically with the artwork. Moreover, in the classical conception of sculpture, the shape is decisive because it gives the meaning of sculpture. Rodin is the first artist to invent new representation showing the body dynamics. For him "the sculpture does not consist in carving a shape out of stone, but in carving the effect" [5].

This effect lies in the link between form and movement. Furthermore, while Rodin still focuses on static representations, with Alexandre Calder's mobiles, sculpture evolves from a represented movement to a real movement.

At this point, one can say that the robot is close to a new form of statue. Robots are not only objects that move but they also play on the two modes of representation mentioned above. These two modes of representation can be found in the work of the French artist and roboticist France Cadet. During the exhibition "Robot pour être vrai" (translated from French in "Robot for real"), one could observe robotic statues in a determined position to question the notion of desire (for example: can a robot be desirable and can one be desired in return by a robot?) – see Fig. 1b. In another work of art, the artist uses an Aibo and plays with its first mode of representation by creating a robotic "ready-made": the dog behaves like a cat looking at a goldfish in a bowl – see Fig. 1b. Moreover, the artist offers the viewer the opportunity to interact with the works by touching it. These types of installation force viewers to have a direct relationship with the work. It is even more interesting because in general it is forbidden to touch works of art. Looking at robots as dynamic sculptures and working with sculptors in order to strongly engage the user could definitely improve the field of social robotics. On the other hand studying people's reaction to this type of artworks could also be useful for robot design.

2.3   The Humanoid or Anthropomorphic Form and the "Presence Effects"

One of the questions that can be found among both artists and designers as well as in social robotics is that of the humanoid form of robots. Do we need the machine to take the spitting image of a human in order to become a social robot? Would the humanoid form be the ideal support to make the individual feel empathy? As anthropologist Denis Vidal shows, this feeling of immediate empathy is what Mori describes as the reaction in front of a Buddha [6]. For him, it is the result of a balance that must be found between the effect of a person and a formal abstraction. Mori was already referring to sculpture and to the way of representing gods in eastern sculpture when he wrote his article in 1970. According to Mori a human-machine relationship works due to the "fluctuation" between the individual, the machine, the gods and the fact of never knowing really at which moment the human recognizes it as one of these entities [7].

Researchers in robotics have understood this well and they also use anthropomorphism to create this ambiguous relationship; although we know for a fact that is a machine, an artefact. Some experimentations show that the more anthropomorphic reactions a machine creates, the greater the implicit expectation of the users to see it as a human will be and the more disappointed they will be if the machine does not hold its promises [7]. This is precisely an implicit anthropomorphic pact between the man and the machine. Other results show that as humanoid robots become more social in their interaction, we are led to grow more and more intimate and trusting relationships with them [8]. Yet, even if it is not enough, an individual's engagement towards a robot's sociality (i.e. the belief in the possibility of a robot's social behaviour) is a necessary condition to develop a trusting relationship with it. This is actually what researcher

Véronique Aubergé means when she explains that it is about "revealing a self in a thing that is only a thing" [9].

The artist and robotician Zaven Paré became interested in robotics after working in mise-en-scène industry and after inventing his first electronic puppets in 1996. In 2009, he joined the Intelligent Robotics Laboratory led by professor Hirosho Ishiguro in Japan. For him, our relations with robots are based on representations. The interaction can only take place if the person develops empathy towards the robot s/he faces and if s/he is able to project free will onto this machine. Yet, to create a genuine relationship between the person and the robot, it is necessary to simulate a robot's "intelligence" that will allow the human to identify him/herself to the machine or to recognize it as one of his peers. As Emmanuel Grimaud shows in [10], a robot immediately incites to action or interaction in a game mode. But if one gets attached to machines, it is also because they are confused with other living beings. For Zaven Paré this is about making the spectator "feel" some "embodiment effect" through the movement by suggesting unconscious gestures. This is what he calls "the presence effects" [11]. He explains that a character can be recreated in the form of "tics" with 6 or 7 movements. The goal is to play on some micro-movements that will allow for a few moments to create an ambiguity in the perception of these machines. These presence effects will allow the viewer to feel physically the robot as one of his/her kinds. This principle can be found in animation film as this technique allows to create ex-nihilo characters through movement [12]. Moreover, Zaven Paré creates boards on which he details these movements as animators creating an animated character – see Fig. 1c.

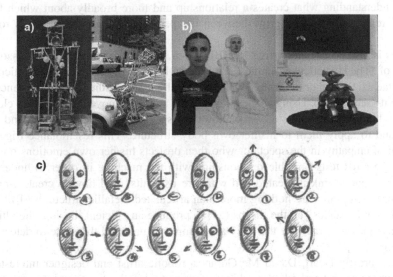

Fig. 1. (a) Robot K-456 by Nam June Paik and Shuya Abe. Japan, 1964. On the right, the performance organised in New York: a car driven by William "Bill" Anastasi has an accident with K-456, (b) France Cadet – on the left robotic figure; on the right the Aibo dog that interacts with the image of a goldfish on a screen in the exhibition "Robot pour être vrai" at the Cube in 2015, (c) Zaven Paré's animated character preliminary drawing. Courtesy of Galerie Charlot, Paris.

The animated body and the robotic body have the same goal: to create the illusion that they are alive and preserve viewers with an open space to project themselves. This is possible as long as the relationship between the form and the movement was carefully designed. As design researchers, Guy Hoffman and Wendy Ju, underline a focus on movement design could create interactive robots "able to communicate intentions, display internal states, and evoke emotions through the way they move". This perspective "has the potential to usher in a new era in human-robot relationships" [13]. Further on working on simple and recognisable artefacts like robjects - a robotic entity embedded in an everyday object [14], and focusing on movement and presence effects might be more easily accepted into people's day-to-day lives.

3   Relationship(s)

The artistic experimentations dealing with robotic forms lead us to ask the question of the spectator. Which relationship can s/he maintain with a creature that s/he knows to be artificial? Some other artists attempted to stage this human-robot relationship. This is what interested for instance choreographer Emmanuelle Grangier when she created in 2015 the performance "LINK Human/Robot". The goal of this performance is to stage an interaction between a Nao robot and a female dancer – see Fig. 2a. This multi-disciplinary project was born thanks to the collaboration between an artist and a researcher in developmental robotics, Arnaud Revel. In the choreography, Nao does not imitate the dancer but it reacts to her movements. This performance is therefore about understanding what creates a relationship and more broadly about which forms of new relationships could grow between the person and these autonomous robotic forms.

This is also what other artists like Bill Vorn, a Canadian artist and professor and creator of "The Hysterical Machines" try to do in his works. Composed of 8 articulated arms attached to a spherical body, Hysterical Machines detect the visitors' presence and react to it– see Fig. 2b. Using shapes (arms, legs) and their movements that are close to those of human beings, this artwork allows the spectator to quickly understand these forms and to apply them to his/her own body structure. This resemblance triggers a reaction of empathy in the spectator who then projects his/her own emotions onto the robot. The artist tests possible relationships with the machine in order to understand how the empathic link is created and what are its limits. And how to create empathy when these sculptures are nothing more than articulated metallic structures? Bill Vorn explains that he stages "all the means (…) to produce an efficient illusion, the ultimate goal was to make us believe that they are living creatures and therefore to detect their autonomy" [15].

In the project Heart, David Mc Goran, a robotic artist and designer interested in primal emotions and embodied machines, designed a small robot to test the attachment effect – see Fig. 2c. The term attachment is defined here according to Emmanuel Grimaud's definition: "a term that is sufficiently vague to allow for all degrees of intensity: utility relations, friendship, love, dependences" [10]. Designed as an interface, this robot that looks like a small child blinks and simulates breathing. A small red light flickers on its chest more or less quickly according to a simulated internal state.

It is in the movement and the breathing simulation that the artistic performance and therefore the relationship will take place.

As we have previously seen with the last two examples, the artistic experimentations allow to stage the human-robot relationship in order to better understand, as Zaven Paré says, how the robot can move from the status of object to that of a subject. Yet, as Cynthia Breazeal shows it is important to consider the specific ways in which we understand and interact with the social world. If done well, humans will be able to engage with the robot by utilizing their natural social machinery instead of having to overly and artificially adapt their way of interaction [16]. That is why it is important for robot designers to consider the way the robot's physical actions are interpreted by people around them [13]. For example Cynthia Breazeal explains that if a robot "looks and behaves as a very young creature, people will be more likely to treat it as such and naturally exaggerate their prosody when addressing the robot. This manner of robot-directed speech would be spontaneous and seems quite appropriate" [17]. Understanding the human emotions and their adaptability helps this relationship. Thus, the emergence of robotics for personal use in society raises questions like: what will be our relationships with these assistants that present themselves as life companions? As anthropologist Denis Vidal argues, the point is to wonder if we are not going to be led to gradually modify the scope that has been traditionally associated to the notion of a person [18].

Fig. 2. (a) LINK Human/Robot by Emmanuelle Grangier is a choreographic performance for a dancer and a Nao robot (b) Bill Vorn's Hysterical machines exhibited at the Gallery Crawl USA, (c) David McGoran, with his robot Heart Robot, during the opening of the exhibition Emotibots, at the Science Museum in 2008, (d) Reborn by Justine Emard. The artist uses Alter (robot developed by the associated laboratories of Hiroshi Ishiguro and Takashi Ikegami) to create a meeting point between two forms of life.

This is indeed what some artists are experimenting in their performances in which people could interact with evolving systems. Such artistic installations using artificial intelligence algorithms could show new ways to think and to design robots behaviours and their interactions with the real world. The robot Alter (created by Takashi Ikegami, professor at the Department of General Systems Sciences at Tokyo University and developed in collaboration with Hiroshi Ishiguro) was actually used in a performance of the French artist Justine Emard – see Fig. 2d. With the video installation Reborn, the artist offers a change of perspective by creating a meeting point between two forms of life that dialogue through interposed screens. In this staging, the robot Alter is equipped with an artificial intelligence that allows to deploy its own space through a specific body language and a voice. It analyses its environment and reacts to it in an autonomous way. In parallel, the dancer Mirai Moriyamase lets himself be impregnated by "the life" of this artificial creature. As Pascal Beausse (art critic and exhibition curator) "[the dancer's] body relearns the movement through the new vitality of the robot. Together, they invent the possibility of a world" [19].

4   Fiction

When we talk about a complex machine like a social robot and its predisposition to enter into a relationship with a person, it is necessarily to understand the impact of fiction. Indeed, if we want to make the viewer or user react by arousing empathy, artists and designers need to build a situation (even very simple) that will guide the viewer in this direction. It is about building life scenarios and stories with these machines intended to become companions. The viewpoint is subjective, because it is imagined and thought according to the use, even the commercialization of something that does not exist yet.

Thus, after more than one month in immersion with professor Ishiguro's famous geminoids in order to understand what would be a relationship with these machines, Zaven Paré concluded that it is necessary to decentre the action. This means to create forms of trivial interaction, like for instance "eating an apple" [20], in which the robot is no longer the centre of attention but the social interaction still takes place. This experience allowed the artist to work on the implementation of a platform dedicated to research and theatrical experimentation for robotics, "the Robot Actors Project", based on playwright Oriza Hirata's repertoire with humanoids and androids. This is also the case showed by Bill Vorn. In Hysterical Machines, the affect of the viewer is not the result of the robot observation but of its integration in the staging (the fiction). This mechanism triggers the viewer's empathy. And the experience is complete only if it managed to provoke this empathy.

In design research one could find the use of fiction in Speculative Design, a movement created by Anthony Dunne & Fiona Raby. This design movement finds its meaning in a "shift from thinking about applications to implications" [21]. The implications go beyond the resolution of a local problem or offering solutions that can be consumed and used today; they address broader societal questions and sometimes present uncomfortable scenarios, narratives that integrate the repercussions of a technological development [22]. This design approach is brought to a vast audience through design exhibitions but also through publications [23]. The goal to exhibit speculative design objects and situations is to challenge the ethos of new technological artefacts and to open a discussion on the place of technology in people's lives.

For instance the project "Uninvited Guests", by the Superflux laboratory, questions through speculative design the concept of remote healthcare for the elderly. In this project – see Fig. 3 – a senior struggles with rules and orders imposed by some smart objects: a smart fork tells him what and how to eat, a smart cane calculates his number of steps per day and encourages him to walk, a smart bed monitors his sleeping program. These objects were designed to help the person for a better health: to count the vegetables, number of steps, sleeping hours etc. However, a video presents the psychological pain that these objects can bring in one's life. The person feels controlled by these objects, as he is no longer able to make his own decisions and ends up losing his freedom and daily habits. Finally, the video shows how the person invents solutions to disobey these smart objects.

Fig. 3. Uninvited Guests project by Superflux Laboratory: Thomas, aged 70, lives alone after the death of his wife. His children send him smart objects to follow and to monitor remotely his eating habits, his health and his sleep.

Even if the video remains hypothetical and offers no solution on how to design assistance devices, it shows thanks to fiction the complexity of human behaviour and incites the HRI researchers to think more thoroughly on the consequences of their proposals. Indeed, the value of design and of artistic devices is to create objectifications of lived experiences and embodiments of a culture [24]. If the robots are meant to leave the laboratory to become social objects, it is necessary to understand the very nature of what a robot is, to question the relationships that we will have with them and what they will be able to do, and especially the way we stage them. As Heudin argues we realize the importance of the environment in which the robot is going to evolve and that it will be able to "manipulate" [22]. The robotic form will become one of the elements of the robotic system that will include the artefact, the environment where it operates, and the spectator (or the user). It becomes, as Anne Marie Duguet shows, a "generative system that structures the sensitive experience" [25]. This approach, that we believe is complementary to the more "scientific" approach represented in the community of Human-Robot Interaction, could only be brought by artists and designers; they will confront the audience to these artefacts in new scenarios and forms and thus question our own relationship to technology on a societal dimension.

5 Conclusion

The artistic experimentations permit a deep understanding of our relationship to technological devices and the way this relationship could evolve in time. When artists and designers approach the technological object and more particularly social robots, their goal is to question us about the promising (or not) relationships with these objects. In which conditions could an object be considered a subject? These experiments allow not only to create technical and artistic objects but also to work on the way to give them meaning. Therefore the point is to create frameworks that crystallize life situations and new forms in order to understand the relationships that we have with these artefacts. Without wishing to offer answers, the projects mentioned before explore how we as people position ourselves in front of these technical objects. Thus, we can clearly imagine that these experiences (that for most of them took place in determined contexts of museums or stages) can become testifying experiences and shift towards an everyday life context, as the spectator becomes the user. As Joffrey Becker underlines when speaking about robotics in art, "the fiction forms a space dedicated to experimentation". Finally this space becomes a "way to study the interactions between humans" [26].

References

1. Dautenhahn, K.: Human-robot interaction. In: The Encyclopedia of Human-Computer Interaction, 2nd edn. The Interaction Design Foundation, Aarhus (2004)
2. Kac, E.: The origin and development of robotic art. Convergence **7**(1), 76–86 (2001)
3. Becker, J.: Humanoïdes. Expérimentations croisées entre arts et sciences. Presses universitaires de Paris Ouest, Nanterre, coll. Frontières de l'humain, pp. 238–240 (2015)
4. Dufrêne, T.: Au jeu de la présence-absence dans l'art, catalogue de l'exposition Persona, étrangement humain, dir. T. Dufrêne, E. Grimaud, D. Vidal, A.C. Taylor, Hors collection, Actes Sud, coedition Musée du quai Branly, pp. 23–24 (2016)
5. Ruskin, J.: Les sept lampes de l'architecture , V. 31, translation G. Elwall, 1900, in Jarassé, D. Rodin: la passion du mouvement, Paris, Terrail (1993)
6. Mori, M., MacDorman, K., Kageki, N.: The uncanny valley [from the field]. IEEE Robot. Autom. Mag. **19**, 98–100 (2012)
7. Vidal, D.: Vers un nouveau pacte anthropomorphique! Les enjeux anthropologiques de la nouvelle robotique. Gradhiva Revue d'anthropologie et d'histoire des arts (15) (2012)
8. Kahn Jr, P.H., et al.: Will people keep the secret of a humanoid robot? Psychological intimacy in HRI. In: HRI 2015 Proceedings, pp. 173–180 (2015)
9. Auberjé, V.: L'art est-il une partie de go? Les relations entre artistes et intelligence artificielles. Experimenta, Salon arts, sciences, technologies, (2016)

10. Grimaud, E.: Androïde cherche humain pour contact électrique. Gradhiva Revue d'anthropologie et d'histoire des arts (15) (2012)
11. Paré, Z.: Effets de présence: relations hommes-androïdes, Cultures-Kairós [Enligne], Métamorphoses digitales: Expérimentations esthétiques et construction du sensible dans l'interaction humain-machine (2014)
12. Cossin, I.: Le robot – Une post-sculpture? In: La Sculpture et le vivant. Issue n°4, T. Dufrêne (dir.). Presses universitaires de Rouen et du Havre (2017)
13. Hoffman, G., Ju, W.: Designing robots with movement in mind. J. Hum.-Robot Interact. 3 (1), 89–122 (2014)
14. Mondada, F., Fink, J., Lemaignan, S., Mansolino, D., Wille, F., Franinović, K.: Ranger, an example of integration of robotics into the home ecosystem. In: Bleuler, H., Bouri, M., Mondada, F., Pisla, D., Rodić, A., Helmer, P. (eds.) New Trends in Medical and Service Robots. MMS, vol. 38, pp. 181–189. Springer, Cham (2016). https://doi.org/10.1007/978-3-319-23832-6_15
15. https://www.poptronics.fr/Bill-Vorn-Jouer-de-la%20psychosedes. Accessed 20 Aug 2019
16. Breazeal, C.: Designing Sociable Robots. Intelligent Robotics and Autonomous Agents Series. MIT Press, Cambridge (2002). https://doi.org/10.1016/s0898-1221(03)80129-3
17. Breazeal, C., Aryananda, L.: Recognition of affective communicative intent in robot-directed speech. Auton. Robots 12, 83–104 (2002)
18. Vidal, V., Gaussier, P.: Ressemblances de famille et robotique humanoïde, catalogue de l'exposition Persona, étrangement humain, dir. Dufrêne, T. Grimaud, E. Vidal, D. Taylor, A. C. Hors collection, Actes Sud (2016)
19. http://justineemard.com/coaixistence-2/. Accessed 20 Aug 2019
20. Grimaud, E., Paré, Z.: Le jour où les robots mangeront des pommes: conversations avec un Geminoïd, éditions Petra, coll. Anthropologiques, Paris (2011)
21. Dunne, A., Raby, F.: Design for debate (2007). http://www.dunneandraby.co.uk/content/bydandr/36/0
22. Heudin, J.C.: Robots & avatars, éditions Odile Jacob (2009)
23. Auger, B.: Living with robots: a speculative design approach. J. Hum.-Robot Interact. 3(1), 20–42 (2014)
24. Cupchik, G.C., Hilscher, M.C.: Holistic perspective on the design of experience. In: Elsevier, S., Hekkert, P., Schifferstein, H.N.J. (eds.) Product Experience (2008)
25. Sermon, J.: Marionnettes contemporaines: de la manipulation à l'installation. In: La marionnette: objet d'histoire, œuvre d'art, objet de civilisation, dir. Dufrêne, T. et Huthwol, J. Editions l'Entretemps (2014)
26. Becker, J.: Le corps humain et ses doubles. Sur les usages de la fiction dans les arts et la robotique. Gradhiva, op. cit., p. 108 (2006). Robot Hum. Interact. Commun., p. 51–5

Creating Context Through Performance: Perception of the 'Dancing Droid' Robotic Platform in Variable Valence Interactions in Distinct Office Environments

Erin Berl[✉], Ishaan Pakrasi, and Amy LaViers

Mechanical Science and Engineering Department, University of Illinois
Urbana-Champaign, Urbana, IL 61801, USA
{berl1,pakrasi2,alaviers}@illinois.edu

Abstract. Operating robots in multiple contexts and environments is currently a challenge, both in functional aspects of design as well as expressive aspects. This paper presents a pilot study using performance and environment to create distinct contexts around the same robotic system. Three distinct environments and three distinct performative interactions with the robot were used to test whether or not individuals experienced the same robotic system differently based on which condition they were exposed to and whether they noticed differences between the distinct scenarios when viewing in series. This study used three observation scenarios (Positive, Negative, and Neutral), combining choreographic design (a human performer's movement and behavior, especially in relation to robots) and interior design (the elements of the physical observation space). This study found that the Positive Scenario robot was most successful as a companion robot, and that the Negative Scenario robot made participants the least comfortable, aligning with the predicted effect. Qualitative feedback provides further insight into why participants rated the robots this way. This work gives an example of how moving the same robot in between new contexts may result in unanticipated expressive characteristics or interpretation by human viewers.

Keywords: Performance · Context · Choreography · HRI

1 Introduction

Bringing robots out of the factory into human-facing scenarios creates an increased opportunity for humans to create complex impressions of these moving mechanical devices. When humans see moving objects in an environment, we tend to construct narratives for why movement is occurring, leading to a need to predict narratives people may create for robotic devices. Directors and choreographers face similar challenges in the successful staging of a play or a dance,

© Springer Nature Switzerland AG 2019
M. A. Salichs et al. (Eds.): ICSR 2019, LNAI 11876, pp. 288–298, 2019.
https://doi.org/10.1007/978-3-030-35888-4_27

respectively. This observation provides an opportunity to leverage techniques from theater and performance to modulate perceptions of robotic devices.

Classic experiments have shown that even moving shapes in a two-dimensional fields can produce complex narratives that are robustly recreated in human viewers [11]. Further work in artificial motion has shown how context modifies the interpretation of *the same movement pattern* [12]. Thus, we cannot simply create a robot that "works", but must consider – and even manipulate – the context and priming of human users for successful integration of these systems. Socially assistive robots have been proposed as a potentially positive method to prolong elderly populations' independence, but researchers acknowledging the socio-demographic factors preventing elderly populations from adopting socially assistive robotic systems call for a higher level of adaptability and customization [8]. Because of the human tendency to interpret behavior as intentional [11,18], there is also a strongly suggested link between user perception of a robotic system and this future user behavior towards the system [13]. Attributing a greater sense of intentionality to robot behavior can be linked to a more anthropomorphic viewing of the robot, which in turn can lead to a greater social acceptance [7]. Examples of people naming their Roomba robot point to how giving anthropomorphic qualities to a robot can indicate higher adoption of the technology into homes and lives [9]. Humans also try to apply similar logic to robotic actions, extracting information towards intentionality in robots as well, even for non-humanoid robots [3].

Many prior efforts have leveraged the use of artists to construct variable robotic behavior that imparts different impressions on human viewers, including work with dancers [10], Certified Movement Analysts [4], animators, and actors. A seminal demonstration of using factors outside the "intelligence" or design of a robotic system showed that providing a back story to robots led human participants to resist destroying the devices [6]. Thus, this paper will explore the use of performance to modulate some of these factors and impact human perception of a robotic system. The same robotic system (hardware and software) will be used in three distinct office-like environments with a human performer using three distinct choreographed interactions with the device. The environments in this study will be open enough to allow for movement, will be perhaps most similar to office hallways, lobbies, and entryways, but future work will consider more complex, chaired, and even people-filled office environments. Participants then record their responses via a survey including Godspeed scales [2] and with qualitative feedback. We find overall that participants' perceptions of the robot were somewhat influenced by which environment and interaction they viewed. Next, in Sect. 2, we will describe how three scenarios were developed, comprised of both interior and choreographic designs. Section 3 describes the study design. Results and analysis are presented in Sect. 4, and concluding remarks with future directions of work are outlined in Sect. 5.

2   Performance, Context, and Environment

In this section we present the design of three scenarios used to present the same robotic system to human viewers. Each scenario is constructed from the combination of choreographed interactions with either positive, neutral, or negative valence and a physical environment that has positive, neutral, or negative associated valence as well. Thus, the Positive Scenario combines the positive valence human performer behavior and the positive valence physical environment. The determination of the physical environments' valences were based on previous research in the field relating to interior design and the power of environment. This research acknowledges the lens of the Circumplex Model of Affect, as especially the Likeability and Engagement scales of the Godspeed questionnaire include words indicative of highly positive or negative valence. Backgrounds in the arts of the authors (one of whom was the human performer in the experiments) also influenced the design of these scenarios. Performance alongside robots has been explored in several venues. Challenges with putting machines onstage, including analysis of gender and other anthropomorphic features, have been discussed inside the opportunity this theatrical element allows to address themes. Interestingly, this medium is inherently embodied and ethereal, making quantified measures of experience difficult to obtain. However, the practicality of these methods has been exploited in many scenarios, including human-robot interaction [5] and even retail sales for consumers [1].

Interior designers have considered how to design supportive work environments to facilitate collaboration, but more decorative factors like windows and accessibility to natural light have also been found to be important [16]. The power of environment was identified by patients in rooms with a beautiful natural window view having shorter postoperative hospital stays than patients in rooms with windows facing a brick wall [19]. Broadly, this body of work supports the thesis that environment affects human perception, mood, and productivity.

2.1   Selection of Office Environments

Offices are an important area where robots may assist or monitor human workers; however, every office space is not the same. Thus, three distinct environments, pictured in Fig. 1, were selected in a campus building. Specifically, this study focused on environments representing office areas with movement potential, such as hallways, entryways, or lobbies, but future work may expand to a wider variety of office spaces, including areas such as cubicles or corner offices. The following details on Interior and Choreographic Design are summarized in Fig. 1.

The Positive Scenario was observed in a small, carpeted room with large windows allowing for natural light with a beautiful view of nature outside. The Negative Scenario was observed in a similarly small room that instead had a rough, neutrally colored tile floor, with no windows and only fluorescent lights. The Neutral Scenario was observed in a small portion of the main room where the surveys were conducted, using tables to create a barrier, blocking off a space around the same size as the two other scenarios' rooms for the robot and human performer to be separated from the observer. This scenario had a window behind with some natural light but not with a particularly beautiful view as the blinds were partially drawn, using this as a middle ground between the Positive Scenario's light/view and the Negative Scenario's absence of any windows.

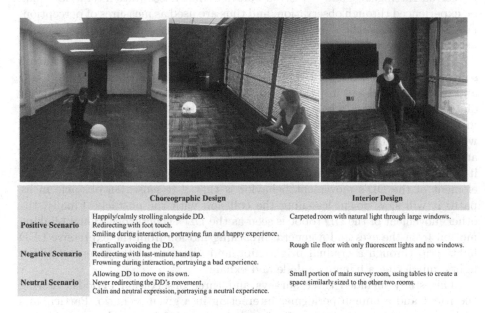

	Choreographic Design	Interior Design
Positive Scenario	Happily/calmly strolling alongside DD. Redirecting with foot touch. Smiling during interaction, portraying fun and happy experience.	Carpeted room with natural light through large windows.
Negative Scenario	Frantically avoiding the DD. Redirecting with last-minute hand tap. Frowning during interaction, portraying a bad experience.	Rough tile floor with only fluorescent lights and no windows.
Neutral Scenario	Allowing DD to move on its own. Never redirecting the DD's movement. Calm and neutral expression, portraying a neutral experience.	Small portion of main survey room, using tables to create a space similarly sized to the other two rooms.

Fig. 1. The three observation scenarios (pictured left to right).

2.2   Variable Interaction Design

The human performer's interaction with the Dancing Droid (DD) robot was specifically designed for each scenario. In the Positive Scenario, the human performer strolled calmly alongside the DD, redirecting with a playful foot touch, seeming to play with it. The performer often smiled at the DD, indicating she was having a fun and happy interaction. In the Negative Scenario, the human performer frantically avoided the robot, moved on a low level by sitting or crawling, and redirected it at the last second with sharp taps. The performer openly frowned or appeared scared, indicating a bad experience with the DD. In the Neutral Scenario, the human performer let the robot move on its own, never redirected its movement, and simply existed in the same scenario space as the robot by standing or sitting. The performer maintained a calm, neutral expression, overall indicating an experience that was not strongly positive or negative.

3   Methodology

This section outlines the robot, study, and survey designs used in this work. An existing robotic system was used for each of three scenarios (described in the previous section). Participants were randomly assigned a first scenario and filled out Godspeed questionnaires with a few additional qualitative questions after their viewing of the device and performer in context. The metrics measured in the Godspeed questionnaire, especially Anthropomorphism, Animacy, Likeability, Perceived Intelligence, and Perceived Safety do not necessitate interaction, may be experienced through observation, and thus are used as measures of perception. For example, researchers examining how ambient light affects user perception used the Godspeed questionnaire as one of the bases of their evaluation [17].

This study used a previously developed hardware prototype with supporting software called the Dancing Droid (DD), which is pictured three times in Fig. 1 and described in detail in prior work [14, 15]. The primary movement behavior of the DD robot as a whole unit is that of its base. Once turned on and set in motion, the DD will move smoothly in straight lines around the room, but when it hits an obstacle in its path, the robot will stop and rotate before again attempting a straight-line trajectory forward. If it again encounters an obstacle, it will repeat the rotating process until it finds an unobstructed path. The other element of the DD's movement behavior is that if it senses an obstacle in its path, it will slow down, lessening the collision with the obstacle. Finally, the other movement of the DD robot is seen as the DD's generic occasional blinking motion from the eyes and a general breathing motion from the expressive LED light strip through a gradual brightening and dimming of the intensity of the lights, mimicking a human's inhale and exhale.

This study included three surveys and three observation periods, viewing the robot and a human performer interacting in a given scenario. Participants were assigned a randomized order for their observation periods. Questions in all surveys were phrased about perception of the robot, rather than about perception of the human performer or the scenario overall. The human performer was a white female in her early 20's who performed movement according to the choreography description in Fig. 1. The DD robot's behavior was the same for all three scenarios, thus making the human performer's interaction with the robot and the physical environment the main differing factors for the participant to observe. The differences in the rooms of the scenarios themselves were chosen to heighten the effect of the human performer's interaction in each scenario.

The pre-survey included demographic questions, such as age, native language as culture may affect prior movement experiences, gender, highest level of education. It also gauged participants' relationship to robots, asking about past robotic experience, whether they had an in-home robot, and how likely they were to have an in-home robot in the future. While the study is looking specifically at robots in an office-like environment, the research used the in-home robot questions as an imperfect indication of acceptance and even of trust of robots in the participants' personal lives (although these responses are likely to be correlated with other factors like socioeconomic status). Having an in-home robot is a choice they have more control over, while an in-office robot may not be their decision or may not be as applicable, depending on their job-status.

The next survey, completed after their first observation (of only one randomly selected scenario), leveraged the established Godspeed questionnaire, which asks participants to rate the robot on four main scales: Engagement, Anthropomorphism, Animacy, and Likeability [2]. Participants were also asked to rate the robot on how successful it was at fulfilling its intended function as well as at providing companionship, and participants were asked again how likely or unlikely they were to want an in-home robot in the future based on their observation of the robot. Participants provided feedback on what seemed to be motivating the robots' movements, as well as characteristics of the robot that made them feel comfortable and uncomfortable. Finally, they provided a name for the robot in this scenario and described if the robot reminded them of any character.

The final survey, completed after viewing all three scenarios, asked which robot was most successful/least successful at fulfilling its function, which robot participants most/least wanted to take home, which made them most/least comfortable, as well as similar questions to the first main survey on the first robot they viewed but answering them for the second and third robots they viewed. They were asked a final time about the likelihood that they would want an in-home robot in the future, based on their observations of all three scenarios. Qualitative feedback was also gathered, using open-ended questions with space to write a free response, such as if the second or third robots reminded them of any characters. They also provided a name for the second and third robots, thus providing three total names, one for each robot scenario observed). These surveys together helped to paint a comprehensive picture of participants' initial robot experience, how they were affected by the scenarios they viewed, and what they thought of the design of the DD robot.

This study used twelve participants with an average age of 21.7, (0.9 standard deviation). There were nine males and three females, including eight native English speakers. Four participants reported their highest education level as high school, five Bachelor's degrees, and three Associates degrees. The participants reported an average level of familiarity with robots of 46.3 out of 100.

4   Results and Analysis

This study aimed to explore how manipulating the context around the same robotic system could change people's preferences of that system. The results show some support for our hypothesis that the same platform viewed in different environments and contexts would produce different impressions on human viewers; moreover, these results support our predicted outcomes as designed through selection of interior and choreographic design to create Positive, Negative, and Neutral Scenarios. Though quantitative conclusions are limited by our small participant pool size, these results give us initial support, and qualitative feedback gives an important initial view into how the device was perceived.

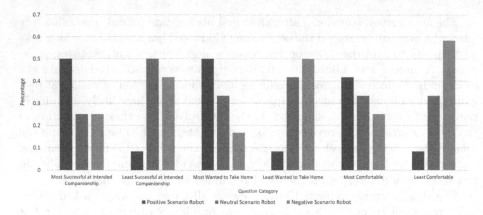

Fig. 2. Participant responses regarding robot/scenario pairs (left to right): most/least successful as a companion, wanted to take home, and comfortable. The highest percentage of participants rated the Positive Scenario as most successful as a companion robot, as shown by the first bar on the left (which was also the preferred robot to take home). The highest percentage rated the Negative Scenario as making them feel least comfortable.

4.1   Quantitative Feedback

After seeing all scenarios, participants selected which scenario (answering "first room", "second room", or "third room", which was coded by researchers to the corresponding scenario) displayed a robot that would be most desirable as a companion robot. Overall, participants saw the Positive Scenario robot as the most successful as a companion robot, as can be seen in Fig. 2. All participants who observed the Negative Scenario first identified the Positive Scenario robot as most successful as a companion robot. Another finding showed that the Negative Scenario made participants overall the least comfortable When asked which robot made them least comfortable, 58.3% of participants answered the Negative Scenario robot, while only 8.3% of participants answered the Positive Scenario robot. When asked which robot they least wanted to take home, 50% of participants answered the Negative Scenario robot, in comparison to 8.3% of participants answered the Positive Scenario robot, all as shown in Fig. 2.

After viewing only one of the scenarios, participants rated the robotic system on the Godspeed questionnaire. We were interested in how this detailed measure of robot perception might correlate with scenario and participant background, which can be seen in the upper left plot in Fig. 3. Averaged across all scenarios, Anthropomorphism received the lowest ranking (which was low for all three cases as might be expected of robots without articulated limbs), then Animacy, Engagement, and Likeability, which displayed greater differences across scenarios. The Neutral Scenario had a lower Engagement rating (43.8) than Positive and Negative (57.2 and 54.3, respectively), which both received fairly high scores for this measure. On the other hand, this Neutral Scenario was seen as the most Likeable robot when viewed first, with an average score of 72.6; while Positive

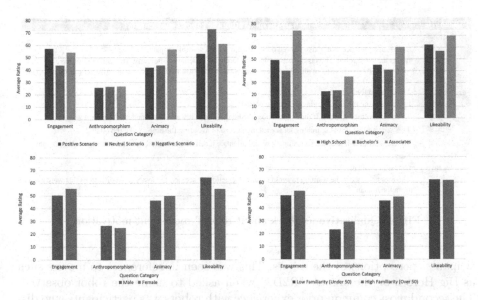

Fig. 3. DD Godspeed ratings indexed by initial scenario viewed, educational level, gender, and previous level of familiarity with robots (N = 12). Those who viewed the Neutral Scenario first provided the lowest Engagement rating but highest Likeability rating. Those who viewed the Negative Scenario first provided the highest Animacy rating.

and Negative had relatively low scores on this scale (52.8 and 60.8, respectively). Finally, the Negative Scenario received the highest Animacy rating (56.4).

Participant demographic data did not have a major effect on the Godspeed questionnaire ratings, which can be seen in the upper right and lower two plots in Fig. 3. However, slight differences in gender are seen where female participants displayed higher Engagement ratings while male participants found the robot more likeable, over all scenarios (with male average Likeability score of 64.2, compared to female average Likeability score of 55.4). Those with Associates degrees provided generally higher ratings for all four categories, but especially for Engagement (those with Associates degrees provided an average Engagement score of 74.1, High School 49.3, and Bachelors 40.3).

4.2 Qualitative Feedback

Participant answers to the qualitative questions of the surveys gave further insight into their impressions of the scenarios, summarized in Fig. 4. Because of each person's unique background with robots prior to the study, it was helpful to understand more about why participants provided their answers. The results indicate that previous robotic experience was a key influence on participants' ratings as well as the priming effect of which scenario they viewed first.

While many participants claimed little to no experience with robots, society has exposure to robots through popular media sources, which may impact par-

Scenario	What was motivating the robot's movements?
Positive	Love
Positive	Collision avoidance, but it also slowed down when it sensed possible impact.
Positive	It was the same robot... It was the person that was forcing it to behave differently. The same things were motivating its movements in all cases; the obstacles and terrain it actively experiences (whether that be a wall or a human foot)
Positive	The kicks to the sensor
Positive	I think that the robot was trying to find the person
Neutral	The robot seemed lifeless. It didn't care about the human and just wanted to wander wherever it wanted to.
Neutral	This seemed like it was searching for something instead of avoiding the objects like the other 2
Neutral	Touch, whenever it touched something it would orientate it self in a new direction and continue going straight
Negative	Fear
Negative	Collision avoidance
Negative	The robot seemed to be wanting to avoid human interaction. It seemed to mostly go in directions that were away from the human.

Fig. 4. Qualitative feedback about robots' movement motivation.

ticipants' perceptions of the robots. This was seen in references to movies such as Big Hero 6 or the answer "R2D2" when asked to name the robot observed. The second most common prior experience with robots was participants who discussed a Roomba vacuum. Thus, while some perceived the robot to be following the human performer, one participant said the DD's movement motivation was cleaning, and many participants identified correctly that the DD robot changed directions when its sensor was touched.

Almost all participants reported how responsive and interactive the DD was, as well as saying the eyes and lights made it seem friendlier. The friendliness of the eyes was reported even by participants who observed the Negative Scenario first, mentioning "the lights on the front" made them feel comfortable. One reported that "it reminded me of Big Hero 6 with the white surrounding parts and the happy eyes without a mouth." Reporting on if the robot made them uncomfortable, participants noted the noise and moments when it failed by getting stuck in a corner it had been to already. Participants generated names for the robot, including "Floorinator", "iHelp", and "R2D2". When asked what was controlling the robot's behavior, 8 of the 12 participants noted the robot's redirection if it encountered an obstacle, whether that was the human performer or the wall. Also, 4 of the 12 participants noted the robot's tendency to slow down if it sensed a potential obstacle, saying the DD's goal was collision avoidance.

5   Conclusions

This paper has presented the use of interior and choreographic design in human-robot interaction and the role these contextual elements can play in the perception of robots by humans. Although in each scenario the robot (and its behavior) was exactly the same, people perceived differences between scenarios and rated the robot differently based on which scenario they had seen. Overall, the positive interactions in the sunnier, newer office space produced a more desirable product and the impression of better companionship. Previous interaction with robots may have influenced participants' functional and expressive perceptions of the robots. Future work may recruit a larger, more balanced participant pool to separate effects of participant background from interior and choreographic design, including a more heightened strength of narrative. Because the robot was reactive to the performer's choices and environment features, its exhibited behavior was distinct in each room, for each participant. Future work needs to examine these influences more. Because of humans' natural tendency to connect narrative and intentionality to movement they observe, perhaps using techniques from performance to influence perceptions of new robotic systems will be a useful tool. Particularly with elderly populations who are wary of new technologies, creating scenarios such as in this study may assist in the acceptance of robotic systems that could truly improve quality of life and prolong future independence.

Acknowledgement. This work was conducted under IRB #17427 and funded by National Science Foundation (NSF) grant #1528036. Thanks to the Illinois Program for Research in the Humanities (IPRH) and Wali Rizvi for providing space and staff support.

References

1. Baron, S., Harris, K., Harris, R.: Retail theater: the "intended effect" of the performance. J. Serv. Res. 4(2), 102–117 (2001)
2. Bartneck, C., Kulić, D., Croft, E., Zoghbi, S.: Measurement instruments for the anthropomorphism, animacy, likeability, perceived intelligence, and perceived safety of robots. Int. J. Soc. Robot. 1(1), 71–81 (2009)
3. Bianchini, S., Levillain, F., Menicacci, A., Quinz, E., Zibetti, E.: Towards behavioral objects: a twofold approach for a system of notation to design and implement behaviors in non-anthropomorphic robotic artifacts. In: Laumond, J.-P., Abe, N. (eds.) Dance Notations and Robot Motion. STAR, vol. 111, pp. 1–24. Springer, Cham (2016). https://doi.org/10.1007/978-3-319-25739-6_1
4. Burton, S.J., Samadani, A.-A., Gorbet, R., Kulić, D.: Laban movement analysis and affective movement generation for robots and other near-living creatures. In: Laumond, J.-P., Abe, N. (eds.) Dance Notations and Robot Motion. STAR, vol. 111, pp. 25–48. Springer, Cham (2016). https://doi.org/10.1007/978-3-319-25739-6_2
5. Cuan, C., Pakrasi, I., Berl, E., LaViers, A.: Curtain and time to compile: a demonstration of an experimental testbed for human-robot interaction. In: 2018 27th IEEE International Symposium on Robot and Human Interactive Communication (RO-MAN), pp. 255–261. IEEE (2018)
6. Darling, K., Nandy, P., Breazeal, C.: Empathic concern and the effect of stories in human-robot interaction. In: 2015 24th IEEE International Symposium on Robot and Human Interactive Communication (RO-MAN), pp. 770–775. IEEE (2015)
7. Eyssel, F., Kuchenbrandt, D.: Social categorization of social robots: anthropomorphism as a function of robot group membership. Br. J. Soc. Psychol. 51(4), 724–731 (2012)
8. Flandorfer, P.: Population ageing and socially assistive robots for elderly persons: the importance of sociodemographic factors for user acceptance. Int. J. Population Res. 2012, 13 (2012)

9. Forlizzi, J., DiSalvo, C.: Service robots in the domestic environment: a study of the roomba vacuum in the home. In: Proceedings of the 1st ACM SIGCHI/SIGART Conference on Human-Robot Interaction, pp. 258–265. ACM (2006)
10. Gemeinboeck, P., Saunders, R.: Towards socializing non-anthropomorphic robots by harnessing dancers' kinesthetic awareness. In: Koh, J.T.K.V., Dunstan, B.J., Silvera-Tawil, D., Velonaki, M. (eds.) CR 2015. LNCS (LNAI), vol. 9549, pp. 85–97. Springer, Cham (2016). https://doi.org/10.1007/978-3-319-42945-8_8
11. Heider, F., Simmel, M.: An experimental study of apparent behavior. Am. J. Psychol. **57**(2), 243–259 (1944)
12. Heimerdinger, M., LaViers, A.: Modeling the interactions of context and style on affect in motion perception: stylized gaits across multiple environmental contexts. Int. J. Soc. Robot. **11**(3), 1–19 (2018)
13. Hendriks, B., Meerbeek, B., Boess, S., Pauws, S., Sonneveld, M.: Robot vacuum cleaner personality and behavior. Int. J. Soc. Robot. **3**(2), 187–195 (2011)
14. Pakrasi, I., Chakraborty, N., Cuan, C., Berl, E., Rizvi, W., LaViers, A.: Dancing droids: an expressive layer for mobile robots developed within choreographic practice. In: Ge, S.S., et al. (eds.) ICSR 2018. LNCS (LNAI), vol. 11357, pp. 410–420. Springer, Cham (2018). https://doi.org/10.1007/978-3-030-05204-1_40
15. Pakrasi, I., Chakraborty, N., LaViers, A.: A design methodology for abstracting character archetypes onto robotic systems. In: Proceedings of the 5th International Conference on Movement and Computing, p. 24. ACM (2018)
16. Reinhart, C.F.: Effects of interior design on the daylight availability in open plan offices. In: 2002 ACEEE Summer Study on Energy Efficiency in Buildings, pp. 309–322 (2002)
17. Song, S., Yamada, S.: Ambient lights influence perception and decision-making. Front. Psychol. **9**, 2685 (2018)
18. Terada, K., Shamoto, T., Ito, A., Mei, H.: Reactive movements of non-humanoid robots cause intention attribution in humans. In: 2007 IEEE/RSJ International Conference on Intelligent Robots and Systems, pp. 3715–3720. IEEE (2007)
19. Ulrich, R.S.: View through a window may influence recovery from surgery. Science **224**(4647), 420–421 (1984)

Collaborative SR and SR
at the Workplace

Collaborative Human-Robot Hierarchical Task Execution with an Activation Spreading Architecture

Bashira Akter Anima[✉], Janelle Blankenburg, Mariya Zagainova,
S. Pourya Hoseini A., Muhammed Tawfiq Chowdhury, David Feil-Seifer,
Monica Nicolescu, and Mircea Nicolescu

Department of Computer Science and Engineering, University Nevada,
Reno, NV 89557, USA
banima@nevada.unr.edu

Abstract. This paper addresses the problem of human-robot collaborative task execution for hierarchical task plans. The main contributions are the ability for dynamic allocation of tasks in human-robot teams and opportunistic task execution given different environmental conditions. The human-robot collaborative task is represented in a tree structure which consists of sequential, non-ordering, and alternative paths of execution. The general approach to enable human-robot collaborative task execution is to have the robot maintain an updated, simulated version of the human's task representation, which is similar to the robot's own controller for the same task. Continuous peer node message passing between the agents' task representations enables both to coordinate their task execution, so that they perform the task given its required execution constraints and they do not both work on the same task component. A tea-table task scenario was designed for validation with overlapping and non-overlapping sub-tasks between a human and a Baxter robot.

1 Introduction

The fast pace of advancements in the development of autonomous robotic systems opens new possibilities for the use of robots in daily tasks, holding a significant potential for improving the quality of our lives. While autonomy and the ability of robots to perform complex tasks have significantly improved, the challenges of operating in collaborative domains prevent current robotic systems from working effectively alongside with people as collaborators and assistants. The focus of the proposed work is to develop a control architecture that enables robots and humans to work collaboratively on a joint task that has a complex hierarchical structure and multiple types of execution constraints.

The underlying assumption is that both the robot and the human have knowledge of the requirements of the task. However, there is no pre-defined allocation

© Springer Nature Switzerland AG 2019
M. A. Salichs et al. (Eds.): ICSR 2019, LNAI 11876, pp. 301–310, 2019.
https://doi.org/10.1007/978-3-030-35888-4_28

that indicates what the human or the robot should do, and both teammates are allowed to work on any aspect of the task, as long as they obey the execution constraints imposed for the task (e.g., ordering of steps). As a result, the robot's decision making process (i.e., deciding what part of the task to work on) is tightly interconnected with its ability to understand the human teammate's goals and intentions. For this, each robot needs to take into account what are the overall (sub-)goals of the task, and also which (sub-)goals are already being worked on by the human. In a team comprising only of robots, such information may be transmitted through direct communication; when interacting with human users, a robot would need to rely on direct observations (e.g., using cameras) in order to track the humans' actions.

In this paper, we propose a solution where the robot uses its own task representation (e.g., controller) both to plan its own future actions, and to keep track of its human teammate's current and future goals. The general solution is as follows: the robot maintains a duplicate representation of the task controller for the human teammate, representing the human's mental model of the task. This second representation "runs" in parallel with the robot's own representation, and the status of various nodes in the human's task (e.g., *working*, or *done*) is updated by the robot using its camera. Peer nodes on both the robot's and the human's controllers continuously exchange messages that communicate their status information, enabling the robot to infer what part of the task the human is working on. The robot decides its next action based both on the constraints of the defined task and the behavior of the human partner.

2   Related Work

Collaboration between robots and humans is crucial to the effective utilization of modern robots in the real world. Our experiments focus on the capability of a robot's identification of human intention while working collaboratively with a human. Much prior work has been done in this area. Intent recognition encompasses many domains, including: entertainment [1]; museum documents [2]; personal assistants [3]; health care [4]; space exploration [5]; police SWAT teams [6]; military robotics [6]; and rescue robotics [7]. The proposed work demonstrates the ability for dynamic allocation of tasks in human-robot teams based on intent recognition, while also observing hierarchical constraints.

Approaches exist for recognizing human intent. A recognition task was categorized into two categories: explicit intention communication and implicit intention communication, and using weighted probabilistic state machines were utilized [8]. Recurrent Convolutional Neural Networks (RCNNs) [9] and Neural networks [10] were used to detect human intention, and an online estimation method was developed to deal with the nonlinear and time-varying property of a limb model. Human-aware motion planning was examined in [11,12]. The ability of a robot to work with a human in close proximity [13] without colliding with the human was demonstrated. A Gaussian Mixture Model (GMM) representation [14] of a human's motion was used. In our work, collision avoidance after collision detection has been emphasized unlike other works that focused on avoiding collision based on predefined mechanisms.

Given detected intent, it is an open question whether and when a robot should take initiative during joint human-robot task execution [15]. In this work, robot-initiated reactive assistance triggers the robot's help when it senses that the user needs help and robot-initiated proactive assistance makes the robot help whenever it can. In our architecture, we combined the processes of the robot's recognition of human actions and it's decision making to determine when it should take initiative during a human-robot joint task.

A collaborative robot should be able to execute complex tasks, be aware of its teammates' goals and intentions, as well as be able to make decisions for its actions based on this information. Recent work addresses these challenges using a probabilistic approach for predicting human actions and a cost based planner for the robot's response [16]. Tasks are represented as Bayes networks and prediction of human actions is performed using a forward-backward message passing algorithm in the network. This inference process is however dependent on knowledge of the full conditional probability table for the task, which increases computational complexity for large tasks and limits adaptability to changes in the task at run-time. This approach has been extended in [17], with a new task representation that can encode tasks with multiple paths of execution. The initial representation for the task is a compact AND-OR tree structure, but for action prediction and planning, it has to be converted into an equivalent Bayes network, which has to explicitly enumerate all possible alternative paths.

Our task tree representation includes a THEN-AND-OR tree structure which further allows for sequential, alternative paths of execution, and non-ordering constraints. Additionally, our approach is able to choose actions based on a human's intent without having to enumerate all possible alternative paths.

3   Human-Robot Collaborative Architecture

3.1   Hierarchical Task Representation

In this work, we augmented our robot control architecture that enables the system to encode tasks involving various types of constraints such as sequential (THEN), non-ordering (AND), and alternative paths of execution (OR) [18]. Tasks are represented in a tree structure where leaf nodes represent tasks to be completed and behavior nodes represent the hierarchical relationships between those tasks. An example task for arranging a tea table scenario is shown in Fig. 1.

In order to execute a controller represented by such a hierarchical task, each node in the architecture maintains a state consisting of several components: (1) **Activation Level:** a number provided by the node's parent and represents the priority placed on executing and finalizing a given node, (2) **Activation Potential:** a number representing the node's perceived efficiency, which is sent to the parent of the node, (3) **Active:** a boolean variable that is set to true when the node's activation level exceeds a predefined threshold, indicating that the behavior is currently executing, and (4) **Done:** a boolean variable that is set to

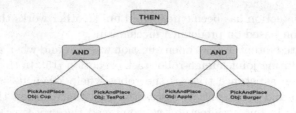

Fig. 1. Hierarchical task representation

true when the node has completed its required work. The above state information is continuously maintained for each node and is used to perform top-down and bottom-up activation spreading that ensures the proper execution of the task given the constraints.

To execute a task, *activation spreading messages* are sent from the root node of a task toward its children to spread the *activation level* throughout the task tree. At the same time, each node sends its current state to its parent node as *status messages* to spread the *activation potential* throughout the tree in a bottom-up fashion. An update loop is run at each cycle which helps to maintain the state of each node in the task structure. This loop performs a series of checks of the node's state and updates the various components of the state accordingly.

The controller architecture scales to multiple robots by maintaining a copy of the task tree for each robot noting when that robot is currently working on a behavior, when a robot has completed one, and the activation potential and level for each robot and each behavior. Message passing between peer nodes (equivalent nodes across all robots' copies of the task tree) allow each robot to represent the complete task status, not just its own view. The full details of this approach are presented in [18].

3.2   Human-In-The-Loop Hierarchical Architecture

In order to extend the previously developed architecture described in Sect. 3.1 from the multi-robot domain to the human-robot domain, several adjustments must be made. The robot can perform a task with a human instead of another robot by maintaining an updated, simulated version of the human's task representation. The person completes the task with the same constraints as the robot. Message passing between peer nodes of the human's and robot's task representation enables the task execution to perform as in the robot-robot scenario.

If the human's sub-task can be inferred, the corresponding node's activation potential in the human's architecture will be increased making the node *active*. As a result, the robot will be able to know what the human is working on. For task execution we distinguish between the following two cases:

1. The human and the robot choose to work on *non-overlapping tasks* in Fig. 1. If the human and the robot decide to work on the cup and the teapot respectively, the robot will infer that its sub-task is safe to continue by checking the status of the peer node of the teapot on the human's controller.

2. The human and robot decide to work on *the same sub-task* in Fig. 1. If both agents decide to work on the cup, the node status will indicate to the robot that the human is also working on this sub-task. The robot will initiate a dialogue in order to negotiate the conflict. A *dialogue* topic and *issue* topic to each corresponding node are added to the architecture to initiate the dialogue.

The likelihood that the person is intending to pick up each object based on the updated hand position for each frame is published as an object status message. The behavior node of an object in the human architecture will be updated based on the value of the object status message for each object.

3.3 Human Intention Recognition

During execution of the task, the robot continuously updates the hand position of the human as shown in Fig. 2. By finding the largest skin contour in the image frame, we are able to detect the position of the human hand because the only skin in the robot's view is the hand.

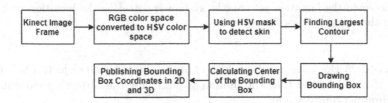

Fig. 2. A step-by-step description of the continuous hand detection system from the Kinect image frame to infer the human intention

From the motion of the hand, we calculate similarity score (*SimScore*), chance score (*Chance*), started value (*Started*) and done value (*Done*) for each object.

- **Similarity Score:** The similarity score (*SimScore*) for each object is calculated for the updated hand position $(h_{x,y,z})$ in the frame. The initial normalized vector between the initial hand position $(h_{X,Y,Z})$ and an object's position $(obj(i)_{x,y,z})$ are calculated for each object $i \in 1, ..., n$. For each new hand position, the cosine similarity between the initial normalized vector and the updated normalized vector are calculated and stored in the *SimScore* list as shown in Eq. 1.

$$SimScore_i = Cosine\_Similarity(V_{\hat{X_i,Y_i,Z_i}}, V_{\hat{x_i,y_i,z_i}}) \tag{1}$$

where $V_{\hat{X_i,Y_i,Z_i}}$ and $V_{\hat{x_i,y_i,z_i}}$ are the initial normalized vector and updated normalized vector for object $i \in 1, ..., n$.

- **Chance:** The *Chance* value for the object that has the highest *SimScore* is incremented for every new hand position. If multiple objects have the same maximum score, the *Chance* value will be incremented for all of them. In this situation, the *Chance* value of the object which had the highest similarity score in the previous iteration will instead be incremented twice.

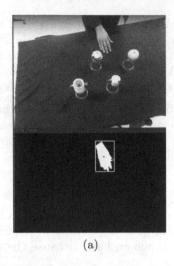

(a)   (b)

Fig. 3. Human intention system with the contour of the hand detection (a) The system hasn't detected the intention yet (b) The system is detecting the intention with a red circle on the object. (Color figure online)

- **Started:** A Boolean variable which is initially 0 for each object; it will be set to 1 if it is inferred that the human is going for the object by checking the maximum *Chance* value.
- **Done:** A Boolean variable that will be initially 0 for each object; it will be set to 1 if the task for the object is completed by the human.

The above information (*Chance*, *Started*, and *Done*) is contained in the object status messages which are published to each object's dedicated status topic using ROS [19]. The messages allow the human architecture to activate an object node when the *Started* value is 1.

3.4   Collision Detection and Handling

In most human-robot collaborative tasks, there can be *collisions* where both the human and the robot can go for the same object at the same time. Collisions must be handled for smooth collaboration between human and robot. As mentioned before, each node of each agent's task tree is updated continuously with the status of its corresponding node of the other agent. If both the human and robot are going to the same object simultaneously, then the status of both nodes will be *active*, which will trigger a collision.

Figure 3 shows the human hand going for the cup during the task. The system hasn't detected the intention yet in Fig. 3a. However, in Fig. 3b the human's intention can now be inferred and is being shown with a red circle on the object.

If a collision is detected, a ROS message will be published to the corresponding node's *issue* topic which will enable the callback function to publish a ROS message to the *dialogue* topic. This initiates the negotiation between the robot and the human. The robot will ask, "It appears that you are going to grab the (Object Name). Should I grab the (Object Name)?" If the human replies "Yes" then the robot will answer "Alright I will place the (Object Name)". The robot will then continue on its path to pick and place the object, while the human will instead go for the next available object in the task tree. If the human replies "No", then the robot will answer "Okay, then please place the (Object Name). Thank you". It will then let the human finish the pick and place task and instead go for the next object according to the task tree.

4 Experiment Design

To demonstrate the capabilities of this augmentation of the architecture, a distributive task between a human and a robot was designed. The task was performed in a lab environment with a human and a Baxter humanoid robot standing on opposite sides of a table containing the objects as shown in Fig. 4. The 3D location of each object is provided by the vision system [20]. A Kinect v1 camera, next to the Baxter was used to observe human intent, and a Kinect v2 camera on top of the Baxter's head was used for the robot end of the architecture.

A joint tea-making task was designed based on the task tree which encodes the constraints of both THEN and AND nodes (Fig. 1). The scenario contained both overlapping and non-overlapping sub-tasks between human and robot.

The robot and the human both went for the cup to pick and place, which resulted in a collision. The robot started to negotiate; the human told the robot to finish the current task. While the robot was performing the task, the human moved to the next object, which was picking and placing the teapot. A collision was again detected as the human and the robot were both going for the apple which started the dialogue between the robot and the human again. The human wanted to perform the current task and informed the robot. The robot stopped going for the apple and moved to the next task to pick and place the burger.

Fig. 4. A sample view of the experimental setup to perform a human-robot distributive collaborative tea table task

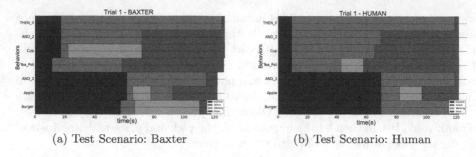

(a) Test Scenario: Baxter   (b) Test Scenario: Human

Fig. 5. The timing diagrams of the tea-table task scenario on the human and the Baxter. These show the times at which the state of a node in a given task tree changed. Each row corresponds to a behavior node named as its corresponding object. The horizontal axis is increasing time. Brown → *inactive*, Orange → *active*, Green → *working*, and Blue → *done*. (Color figure online)

5   Results

The timing diagrams (Fig. 5) illustrate the state for each node during scenario execution using the task structures of the human and robot shown in Fig. 1. There are four state types in the diagram: *inactive*, *active*, *working*, and *done*. Each state is shown with different color bars in the diagram for each node.

When the task starts, both the cup and teapot are eligible for both agents to grasp (due to the task tree constraints), thus becoming *active*. At first, both agents choose to go for the cup which caused a collision and began a dialogue. As in the task design, the human let the robot finish the task for this collision resulting in the cup status of the robot being changed to *working* (Fig. 5a). While the robot was finishing the task, the human moved on to pick and place the teapot, which changed the teapot node status for the human to *working* in Fig. 5b, due to the human's action. After placing the cup and the teapot, the status of both objects became *done* in both agents.

After the teapot and cup were completed, the apple and burger became eligible for grasping by both agents (due to the task tree constraints), and so their status became *active*. The second collision occurred on the apple task. After the Baxter began working on the apple task, the human started the same task, which triggered a collision and began a dialogue. The human told the robot to stop. The robot stopped working on the apple task (changing its state back to *active*) and moved on to the burger, changing its state to *working* (Fig. 5a). Figure 5b shows the human's apple node status changed to *working* (after the robot stopped working), as the human chose to finish the apple task. Once the apple was placed, the status was changed to *done* for both agents. Likewise, after the burger was finished by the robot, the status was set to *done* for both agents.

Based on the experiment, we see that our architecture is able to dynamically allocate tasks in a human-robot team. The system allows a human and robot to negotiate to resolve collisions that arise during the task allocation in order to complete the joint task. The subset of our architecture that this experiment validates shows that our system would be able to dynamically allocate tasks between a human partner and a robot partner that involve sequencing and multiple ordering of execution hierarchical constraints.

6   Conclusions and Future Work

This paper proposed a control architecture that performs a set of distributive collaborative tasks between a human and robot as a team. Tasks were performed by following a hierarchical representation which is responsive to a changing environment. This architecture has the following contributions:

(1) The robot maintains its own state and the state of its collaborative human partner. A human intention system, designed as an augmentation to our previous robot architecture, continuously publishes a message containing the human intention status information for each object.

(2) This allows for agents to operate independently when all agents are working on non-overlapping tasks; however, when agents' goals overlap, a collision occurs on the task tree, and dialogue is used to resolve the collision. This allows one agent to finish the task and the other to move to a different task.

The OR node functionality is not included in the task tree for task due to the complexity of collision resolution. A collision may occur if the human and the robot go for any of the objects that are children of an OR node at the same time. Thus, if the agents choose different children, it would be difficult to detect a collision and begin a dialogue for resolution. This functionality will be implemented in this architecture in the future which will allow for human-robot collaboration for tasks with alternative paths of execution. Again, the system isn't flexible enough to deal with the human error after the collision detection. In addition, the current architecture for collaborative tasks can be extended to a multi-human-robot architecture for a more robust collaboration.

Acknowledgment. The authors would like to acknowledge the financial support of this work by Office of Naval Research (ONR) award #N00014-16-1-2312, N00014-14-1-0776.

References

1. Arkin, R.C., et al.: An ethological and emotional basis for human–robot interaction. Robot. Auton. Syst. **42**(3–4), 191–201 (2003)
2. Thrun, S., et al.: Probabilistic algorithms and the interactive museum tour-guide robot Minerva. Int. J. Robot. Res. **19**(11), 972–999 (2000)
3. Severinson-Eklundh, K., et al.: Social and collaborative aspects of interaction with a service robot. Robot. Auton. Syst. **42**(3–4), 223–234 (2003)
4. Hans, M., et al.: Robotic home assistant care-o-bot: past-present-future. IEEE (2002)

5. Ambrose, R., et al.: Robonaut: NASA's space humanoid. IEEE Intell. Syst. **15**(4), 57–63 (2000)
6. Khurshid, J., Bing-rong, H.: Military robots - a glimpse from today and tomorrow. In: ICARCV Control, Automation, Robotics and Vision Conference (2004)
7. Casper, J., Murphy, R.: Human-robot interactions during the robot-assisted urban search and rescue response at the world trade center. IEEE Trans. Syst. Man Cybern. Part B Cybern. **33**(3), 367–385 (2003)
8. Awais, M., Henrich, D.: Human-robot collaboration by intention recognition using probabilistic state machines. In: 19th International Workshop on Robotics in Alpe-Adria-Danube Region (RAAD 2010). IEEE, June 2010
9. Wang, Z. et al.: Recurrent convolutional networks based intention recognition for human-robot collaboration tasks. In: International Conference on Systems, Man, and Cybernetics (SMC) (2017)
10. Li, Y., Ge, S.S.: Human-robot collaboration based on motion intention estimation. IEEE/ASME Trans. Mechatron. **19**(3), 1007–1014 (2014)
11. Lasota, P.A., Shah, J.A.: Analyzing the effects of human-aware motion planning on close-proximity human–robot collaboration. Hum. Factors J. Hum. Factors Ergon.Soc. **57**(1), 21–33 (2015)
12. Luo, R.C., Huang, C.: Human-aware motion planning based on search and sampling approach. In: Workshop on Advanced Robotics and its Social Impacts (ARSO) (2016)
13. Navarro, S.E., et al.: Methods for safe human-robot-interaction using capacitive tactile proximity sensors. In: 2013 IEEE/RSJ International Conference on Intelligent Robots and Systems. IEEE, November 2013
14. Feil-Seifer, D., Matarić, M.: People-aware navigation for goal-oriented behavior involving a human partner. In: Proceedings of the International Conference on Development and Learning (ICDL), Frankfurt am Main, Germany, August 2011
15. Baraglia, J., et al.: Initiative in robot assistance during collaborative task execution (2016)
16. Hawkins, K.P. et al.: Probabilistic human action prediction and wait-sensitive planning for responsive human-robot collaboration. In: 2013 13th IEEE-RAS International Conference on Humanoid Robots (Humanoids), pp. 499–506, October 2013
17. Hawkins, K.P., et al.: Anticipating human actions for collaboration in the presence of task and sensor uncertainty. In: 2014 IEEE International Conference on Robotics and Automation (ICRA), pp. 2215–2222, May 2014
18. Blankenburg, J., et al.: A distributed control architecture for collaborative multi-robot task allocation. In: International Conference on Humanoid Robots, Birmingham, UK, November 2017
19. Quigley, M., et al. ROS: an open-source robot operating system. In Proceedings of the IEEE International Conference on Robotics and Automation (ICRA) Workshop on Open Source Robotics, Kobe, Japan, May 2009
20. Hoseini A., S.P., et al.: Handling ambiguous object recognition situations in a robotic environment via dynamic information fusion. In: Conference on Cognitive and Computational Aspects of Situation Management (CogSIMA), June 2018

A Human Factor Approach to HRI

Susanne Frennert[✉] [iD]

Faculty of Technology and Society, Malmö University, Malmö, Sweden
sussanne.frennert@mau.se

Abstract. In today's competitive marketplace, robotics and HRI is an exciting new paradigm for changing how work is done in organisations. Its potential success depends on how HRI fit to humans and other technologies in an organisation. The paper argues that the Human-Technology-Organisation framework may be used as an analytic tool to widen the understanding of prerequisites for successful development, implementation and deployment of HRI in organisations as well as for evaluations of existing HRI applications at work. This paper describes the Human-Technology-Organisation (HTO) framework, and ties it to HRI. It helps the reader to see HRI as a situated, local enactment involving diverse users, formal and informal rules and practices. Furthermore, it de-centers technology as the main agent of change. The aim of the paper is to provoke reflection and discussion about HRI, that through subtle interactions between humans, robots and organisations influence the quality of its development, implementation and deployment.

Keywords: HTO framework · Human factors · Human · HRI · Organisation

1 Introduction

HRI represents a technological revolution in the sense that it allows innovative applications in a host of areas: healthcare; education; entertainment; the defence industry; consumer market – to mention some. Efficient and successful adoption of robots are predicted to contribute to a range of benefits: as substitute in situations where humans are at significant risks (e.g. military, space, nuclear, rescue) and as supplement in situations/areas where increased efficiency and productivity is wanted (e.g. service industry, healthcare, logistics, agriculture). As a result, robotics and HRI is predicted to transform how human work is performed and develop new markets, new services, and new kind of value creation. Hence, human-robot interaction (HRI) need to be implemented and applied if it is to have positive impact on everyday working life. This may seem obvious, but there are numerous of examples of HRI applications that, while based on sound engineering, have limited uptake (Pearce et al. 2012). A fundamental problem is that HRI and technology adoption is essentially a socio-technical activity, as everyday HRI practices involve interaction and communication among humans and robots in complex infrastructures, social settings and organisations. Hence, HRI can't be treated as a separate technical issue, if the aim is successful application and deployment. People do not automatically adapt to a technical system or robots, they innovatively find ways to attain their goals (Suchman and Wynn 1984). These ways are

© Springer Nature Switzerland AG 2019
M. A. Salichs et al. (Eds.): ICSR 2019, LNAI 11876, pp. 311–321, 2019.
https://doi.org/10.1007/978-3-030-35888-4_29

not easily engineered by robots and technology but affected by organisational culture and social aspects (Cherns 1976). Consequently, HRI needs to be seen as arrangements and cooperation's of humans and robots in complex infrastructures and social settings/contexts. HRI might be playing important roles socially and politically as well as economically. Technological change may result in numerous challenges as for example unanticipated consequences and resistance.

In this paper, I present a human factor approach to HRI. The theoretical framework is meant to provide a conceptual direction that can be used for analytic purpose with the aim of identifying prerequisites for successful HRI application and implementation. The focal point is the application and deployment of HRI in organisations. My assumption is that the framework may help HRI developers reflect on the human, robot and organisational aspects of HRI. The framework is broad based, readily under-standable and easily translates into practice (Karltun and Eklund 2008). The motivation for writing this paper arise when reading the review of human-robot interaction: status and challenges (Sheridan 2016), the paper concludes that HRI research mainly focuses on innovation work, and subsequently the findings and results are moving targets rather than valid over time, detailed scientific conclusions. Hence, a theoretical perspective or theoretical lens can help to identify grounded questions and hypothesis, which are likely to generate findings of broad and generalized value. In this paper, I argue that HRI can benefit by being understood from a holistic systems perspective with the foci of enquiry on the interdependency between interactions and relations amongst humans and robots in organisations. It might ease the adoption and successful implementations of HRI applications. In the first part, I describe the human, technology and organisation (HTO) framework used within the field of human factors and ergonomics, and tie it to HRI. The second part describes the application of the HTO framework. In the third part, I provide an account of pre-conditions for applying the framework and its limitations.

2 The HTO Framework

When speaking about the HTO framework, it is important to note that the framework consist of three fundamentals: the human (H), technology (T) and organisation (O) plus the ongoing tangled interactions within and between these parts, that all are of equal importance (Eklund 2003; Berglund and Karltun 2007; Rollenhagen 1995; Eklund et al. 2014). The framework has its background in safety work and accident investi-gation. Especially with focus on the nuclear power industry and incidents during the 1980s. At that time errors were attributed to human factors and organisational short-comings such as leadership and work environment despite technical improvements that had reduced the number of incidents due to technical errors. It was realized the complexity of socio-technical systems and safety work therefore needed to include perspectives of people, technology and organisation in order to create safer workplaces (Eklund 2003). Over a period of time the HTO framework has become a meta-concept in Sweden (Berglund and Karltun 2007). It has been successfully applied during the last two decades in different contexts, in numerous constellations, and with different objectives (Karltun et al. 2014); mail distribution service (Karltun and Eklund 2008);

fork lift truck drivers (Solman 2002); meat cutters (Eklund et al. 2014); production planning and scheduling (Berglund and Karltun 2007). The use of the HTO-framework has moved beyond safety work and accident investigation to be applied for understanding further complex developments and prerequisites for innovations (Berglund and Karltun 2007; Schuh and Schwartz 2017). It is in regard to prerequisites that the HTO framework is likely to be beneficial in the field of HRI since it is not a reductive analysis method but considers a wide range of human, technology and organisational aspects. The HTO framework as an analytic tool might be helpful to (1) explain the values and roles of routines that emerge in an organisational context; (2) define how these routines will affect and be affected by an HRI application; (3); analyze and reflect up on what kind of technology and HRI application that is feasible to create the desired value; or/and (4) explore the value an HRI application creates or will create; (5) explore what kind of HRI application is viable in the organisation; and (6) capture the underlying phenomena the development team seeks to understand.

2.1 The Human

"H" in HTO stands for the human: her individual skills, background, expertise, weaknesses, motivation, relation to other colleagues, norms etc. The human can be analysed and described at any of the following four levels: biological; cognitive; psychological and/or social (Berglund and Karltun 2007). In HRI, the human can take on the role as supervisor, operator, mechanic, peer or bystander (Scholtz 2003). The tasks and expected performance of the human depends on its designated role in the HRI relation. As a supervisor, she might need to have an overview of the situation and understand the tasks the robots should carry out including interactions between robots and realize any deviations. As an operator, the human can either physically or remotely operate the robot. In these situations, the human brain needs to perceive, process and interpret the status of the robot and decide how to act in order to operate the robot. As a mechanic, the human is responsible for the physical and behavioural aspects of the robot platform. As a peer, the human collaborates with the robot as a team. As a bystander, the human co-exist in the same environment as the robot (ibid). Whatever role the human has in relation to a robot, the user experience is crucial. User experience is not an inherent feature of a robot but something that has to be carefully designed and evaluated, as Lindblom and Andersson (2016) draw attention to (Lindblom and Andreasson 2016). It concerns both functional requirements (usability) and emotional appeal (Hassenzahl and Tractinsky 2006). In other words, a robot need to serve some desired purpose to the user, be easy to use, be easy to learn how to use it as well as being effective to carry out certain tasks to achieve the users intended goals, and must be perceived as trustworthy and safe to use (Lindblom and Andreasson 2016). Research has shown that the user experience is not static but dynamic when deploying robots in a production environment (Wurhofer et al. 2015).

2.2 The Technology

"T" in HTO stands for technology: infrastructure, data transmission, data storage, hardware, software, laws, rules and standards, etc. Robots appear in various shapes and forms with different kind of functionalities (Frennert and Östlund 2014). Furthermore, they exist and are developed to exist in various environments and organisations with a wide variety of users. As a result, choices about robotic platforms, sensors, manipulators and software algorithms need to be made in each case when designing robots and HRI. For example, a mobile robot needs to know where it is localized and which paths to take, resources needed, and detecting obstacles in the environment when moving from A to B. The more complex the task-design for the robot is, the more complex the robotic hardware and software need to be. It is suggested that technology either can take on the role as a tool or as prosthesis: as a tool, it supports human abilities and as a prosthesis it enhances human abilities (Woods and Hollnagel 2005). In the case of robots, they can take on roles as tools or prosthesis but also as mentors or information sources (Goodrich and Schultz 2008). As a mentor, the robot is teaching or managing the human. As information source, the robot can autonomously collect information in environments which humans cannot or will not access such as in search and rescue operation or in war. Humans can on the other hand use the amassed information (ibid).

2.3 The Organisation

"O" in HTO stand for organisation and represent the elements of H in aggregation (Berglund and Karltun 2007). If the HTO framework is applied in a work setting, the "O" comprise how work is formally and informally organized e.g. what people do at work. Organisational work is coded by formal infrastructures (e.g. institutions, work hours, schedules, work design, laws and regulation) that make them recognizable entities but organisations and organisational work are also affected by organisational culture (e.g. prevailing discourses, needs, teamwork, leadership styles, co-evolving habits) and ideas which are circulated in everyday life. The practice of work is often characterized by social interactions, tacit abilities, mutual know-hows, experience based teamwork, circumstances and breakdowns even though, most organisations can be described by sequential workflows, tasks, and procedures (Hui et al. 2016; Suchman and Wynn 1984). These processes are important to make visible in order for the HRI to work successfully. Work needs to be viewed as situated activities (Suchman and Trigg 1992), i.e. work is affected by the social and technical context in which it is carried out.

2.4 Interactions

The ongoing interactions between the three elements (Human, Technology, and Organisation) result in continence transformation of the sociotechnical system, it is therefore never stable but more or less dynamic (Karltun et al. 2014). However, as mentioned before organisations are recognizable entities due to formal and informal infrastructures, which humans reproduces and that remains even though an individual leave the organisation. In 1960s Licklider proposed human technology symbiosis, which seems highly applicable even today. In HRI, the interaction and interdependent relationship between humans and robots can be co-extensive, co-evolutionary, co-action or co-dependent (Licklider 1960). Co-extensive, when the robot or robotic device becomes a human extension that stretches the human skills and capacities. Co-evolutionary, when the mutual interaction results in mutual evolution and adaption. Co-action, when robots and humans act together, humans change the technology and as a result everyday practice, work practices and habits changes. Co-dependence, when humans relay of technology or robots to carry out work tasks or everyday activities (ibid).

3   Application of the HTO Framework

The HTO framework was created as an analysis tool for reducing errors and unintended consequences and to increase productivity, enhance safety and comfort (Rollenhagen 1995; Eklund 2003; Karltun et al. 2014). In this paper, I suggest that the same conceptual framework may be used when designing HRI for work practices and assessing the deployment of HRI at work. The framework can either be viewed as a representation for system thinking regarding HRI or as an analytic approach for analyzing the relation between human and robots, and their interactions within an organisation. The ontology of the HTO framework is that realities are multiple, there are not one objective reality. People have different perspectives depending of their cognitive abilities, physical abilities and affective factors to their work situation as well as their role in the organisation. The assumption is that researchers and development teams require to be immersed in the organisational context in order to understand the local rules, meanings and language. HTO analysis often starts with broad research questions that becomes refined during the data analysis. In the following section, I will present broad research inquiries for each aspect in the HTO framework. The questions represent an attempt to present a variation and helpful balance of inquiries that may be useful to investigate, explore and reflect upon. It should be stressed that the aspects and related enquiries are neither exhaustive or mutually exclusive.

3.1   The Human Aspect

It helps to initially define and describe the potential user population. For this article, users are defined as people who have an interested in the use of HRI in working environments and organisations. The users can be the ones who are operating the robots but users are also the ones who buy the robots and/or maintains and installs the robotic platform. In organisations where robots already exist, the existing population of users may be analyzed. However, this is not enough if the goal is to attract a wide range of users. Hence, there might be a range of users to analyze; from the people who make decision to buy the robots to the people who are going to daily operate them as well as potential new employees, patients and family members. On particular interest when conducting user analysis are answers to the following questions:

Who are the users? What do they do at work? What are their jobs and tasks? What values and skills do they bring to do their job? Are they, the ones who decided to buy and deploy robots or the users who are faced with new working conditions without being able to affect their changing working situation? What is their prior experience with robots? Are the experts or novice users of similar technology? What are their expectations of interacting and working with robots? What reasons do they have for using the robot/robots? Will their job significantly change if they are to use robots?

Have the potential users been involved in the decision making of deploying robots? Do the users have high acceptance or lack of acceptance to change? Can their skill be transferred and how does it affect the HRI? How will the users learn to collaborate with robots?

The outcome of the user analysis may be presented as user profiles or personas. Personas are archetypes of actual users (to read more about personas in (Cooper 2004)). User profiles and personas may provide insights for the design process and decision-making process, as well as, for planning training, implementation, documentation and support.

Another critical dimension is to understand the users' line of work and everyday work tasks. What do they do? What are their intentions and goals? How do they perform their work tasks today? What is going on or is not going on at the work place? What problems do they encounter? What happens when the users have problems? How are their tasks related to other tasks that are carried out by other people or machines?

In workflow analysis, the process of work tasks is broken down into several tasks sequences, illustrating in flowcharts who does what in each step or sequence and the goals of each actor/robot (Bohgard et al. 2009). Preferable the workflow analysis should include if people are interrupted while doing the tasks, frequency of interruption, frequency of doing the tasks, difficulty, responsibility and pressures of doing the tasks and the time consumption. Workflow analysis can show how users really do a task or tasks, how the HRI works (if already employed) or where robots can be deployed. Workflow and task analysis are particularly useful to make robot developers aware of opportunities, interchanges and problems.

3.2   The Robot Aspect

Riek (2017) define robots as "physically embodied systems capable of enacting physical change in the world. They enact this change with effectors, which can move the robot, or objects in the environment. Robots typically use sensor data to make decisions. They can vary in their degree of autonomy, from fully autonomous to fully tele operated, through most modern systems have mixed initiative, or shared autonomy. More broadly, robotics technology includes affiliated systems, such as related sensors, algorithms for data processing, and so on" (Riek 2017). Robots can be in very different kind of organisations and be used by a variety of users. There are several problems that robots can encounter in working environments that so far has not been fully solved (Okamura et al. 2010). For example working environments are full of people, clutter and novel objects (Riek 2014). Robots need to have a cognitive capacity that enable them to adapt, predict, act and interact with humans and other robots in dynamic environments (Lindblom and Andreasson 2016; Okamura et al. 2010). Weiss et al. (2009) have suggested a USUS evaluation framework for Human-Robot Interaction (Weiss et al. 2009). The framework derives from HCI, HRI, psychology and sociology. It involves evaluating the time and effort it takes for the robot to carry out tasks, and how efficient the robot is at doing this (accuracy and time). Furthermore, USUS is a tool to evaluate the users' capability of learning to use the system and how the system is perceived by the users. The framework involves traditional usability metrics, social acceptance metrics, user experience metrics and societal impact metrics and the paper gives a detail account on methods to collect the data (ibid). In 2016, Lindblom and Andersson suggested that there are a high demand of incorporating UX methods and techniques in HRI and propose this as a solution to long-term success for socially interactive robots (Lindblom and Andreasson 2016). However, robots at work do not necessarily have to be sociable (Breazeal 2004). For example, surgical robots (the da Vinci surgical system) do not need to be sociable, they are only desired to enhance the effectiveness of a procedure by coupling information to action in the operating room to improve patient outcome. The robotic platform systems need to control and inform about current status and may work as a support and control tool in the organisation's areas of activity. Technical procedures are often closely linked to the direct production of the core business of current input and output, depending on the organisation's norms and values. Critical dimensions for successful deployment of robots are safety, reliability, capability, function and cost effectiveness (Riek 2017). When analysing the robot aspect, the following enquiries are of interest:

What does the robot do? How is the success rate of the tasks the robot carries out? What are the damage/hazards and amount of errors? In what speed does the robot carry out the tasks? With what effort and effectiveness? How does it work in relation to the users' expectations, norms and values? How does the robot adapt, learn, predict and act in the working environment? How does the robot adapt, learn, predict, act and interact with the users? What impact does the robot have on the human users and their working environment? How is the long-term engagement and robustness? How is the robot integrated with other technologies in the working environment? What are the costs and benefits compared to other solutions? What are the return of investments? By analysis of the feasibility, capability and functionality of the robot in its intended working environment, many situations may be encountered that might inform what kind of design decisions or deployment decisions that need to be made.

3.3 The Organisational Aspect

The organisational aspect needs to be put in foreground, if taking HRI as a focal point for designing for people and not merely for automation and replacement of people. HRI at work does not exist in isolation but is affected by a social, cultural and physical environment in which work takes place. Human work takes place within the context of specific actions (Suchman and Trigg 1992) and people finds innovative ways and means to achieve ends, goals and values. Organisational arrangements contain the formal elements of the organisation aimed at coordinating employee behaviour and the function of different parts. The formal elements are often written in the form of goals, strategy, administrative policies and procedures, administrative systems and ownership rights. Organisational objectives may be defined as planned positions or which result to be achieved. Organisational objectives pervade decision-making in the entire organisation, at all levels, and may be distinguished by official and operational goals, where the operational goals are considered to have a greater impact on the individual. Organisational strategy is closely linked to the operational goals but describes how to achieve the goals. Formal structures include the overall allocation of roles, administrative control, division of tasks and authority, which in turn affects communication within the organisation and how subsystems in the major system are correlated.

Administrative policy procedures include formal rules regarding how different tasks are to be performed. The formal policies and rules indicate the structures for how the organisation try to drive the behaviour of the employees in a desired direction. However, how the employees respond to the formal parts, depend on other factors such as social and cultural elements. Understanding the social dimension of organisations may help to make decisions about the design of the human-robot interaction and the deployment of robots in an organisation. How do the users interact with their co-workers? How quickly must they respond to each other? Are the users timed, tracked or evaluated on their performance at work? Are they under time pressure? Do they help each other easily if anyone encounter problems? Are the co-workers physically at the same place or how do they communicate/interact? Do they interact a lot as they work? Do they have open space office or individual rooms? Cultural factors such as how the users value their work, if they belong to a professional discipline with certain styles and values of interacting and working or do the user belong to the same socioeconomic group? What vocabulary and metaphors do they use? These factors are also critical to acknowledge and might affect the user experience and HRI deployment. The physical environment is also a critical dimension to consider. How much space do the users have to work with? Is there enough space to add a robot or should the robot replace currently used machines and equipment? Is the environment noisy? Does the noise interfere with the HRI? How is the indoor or outdoor temperature? Does it affect the robot negatively? How is the lightening? Does it affect the HRI? Are there any hazards in the environment for the human or the robot? Could robots be used to effectively make the working environment safer for humans, for example as suggested by Riek (2017) healthcare robots to be used to treat people with highly infectious diseases (Riek 2017)? Any element in the physical environment that can effectively downgrade the quality of the HRI experience is likely to have a negative impact on the deployment of robots in organisations. Identifying these in an early stage may be helpful to avoid design mistakes and unsuccessful deployment.

4 Methods

Once the objectives of the HTO analysis have been identified, various methods might be selected for the data analysis and collection e.g. interviews, focus groups, observations, data logs, incidents and accidents reports, system performance measurements, etc.

4.1 Pre-conditions

An understanding of HRI as sociotechnical systems requires both knowledge about robotics, technology and human behavior in organisations. It requires a team with multidisciplinary skills and perspectives. The theories of computer science, electrical engineering and mechanical engineering as well as cognitive science, social science, philosophy and other disciplines do not behave as pieces of a puzzle that could be joined together to form the real image of the prerequisites for successful development, implementation and deployment of HRI in organisations. Rather, with different purposes and materiality's, they produce different kinds and versions of HRI with different elements attached. This, on the other hand, doesn't mean that each of these disciplines should take its own path and ignore the others. This calls attention to the need for transdisciplinary efforts to facilitate the integration and synthesis of HTO knowledge towards a more complete understanding of the complexity of HRI at work and in organisations. With multidisciplinary skills, the development team might use the HTO framework to identify, reflect, theorize and generalize what the users wants and needs, what kind of HRI is technically feasible and viable within an organisation. The HTO approach might usefully be introduced to generate entirely new visions and alternative HRI applications and scenarios, that can re-orientate a HRI application or organisation around the people it serves. Thinking about the HTO aspects of HRI address the fundamental assumptions, values, norms, and believes on what makes employment, work and an organisation what it is, and shifts the perspective from an isolated robot or HRI application to a more system perspective. The HTO framework advise an explicit understanding of users, tasks, technology and environments/ organisations (Eklund et al. 2014; Eklund 2003; Karltun et al. 2014). The HTO framework can with advantage be used in an iterative process that moves from generating insights about different kind of stakeholders, users, tasks and technology in organisations, to ideation, prototyping and testing, to implementation and deployment.

4.2   Limitations

A limitation with the proposed HTO framework as an analytic tool is that it is time consuming. The researcher and development team need to spend time in the organisation. It can sometimes be difficult to access potential users since they may be busy or the organisation might be understaffed as at many hospitals and care organisations. While spending time in the working environment one might discover underlying problems that might not fall in line with the overall research agenda, project or development. On the other hand, spending time at the organisation with the users and the robots, may allow gaining a more complete picture and understanding of problems and areas of improvements. However, it is important to point out that developing robots for humans and deploying HRI is no exact science – there are a great variety. Sometimes it is impossible to say what is right or wrong, only if something is more or less good.

5   Conclusion

In this paper, I argue that HRI outcomes are determined by a whole complex of aspects: fixed robot-related aspects such as functionality and cognitive ability; human-related aspects such as motivation, expectations and skills, and the organisational approach to change including formal and informal structures. All these aspects affect each other, forming a sociotechnical system. This paper seeks to explain the HTO framework and suggests that the framework may be used as an analytic tool to widen the understanding of prerequisites for successful development, implementation and deployment of HRI in organisations as well as for evaluations of existing HRI applications at work. HRI is concerned with change not stability. Technology change as with HRI is not only about achieving business goals faster and simpler. HRI will fundamentally change how work is done in organisations; it will change contextual and relational factors of work; the relation to a discipline or an occupation; the relationship to co-workers; it will enable and/or constrain certain tasks and skills of the users; it will shape roles, identities and self-image of the users as well as in/off the organisation. The HTO framework does not describe what kind of HRI works or indicate best HRI practices but it might open up discussions about analysing HRI as whole sociotechnical systems, comprising human-, robot-, technology- and organisational aspects. It is hoped that the HTO framework may help to identify prerequisites for successful applications of HRI in organisations and give valuable insights to the design process and HRI deployment.

References

Berglund, M., Karltun, J.: Human, technological and organisational aspects influencing the production scheduling process. Int. J. Prod. Econ. **110**, 160–174 (2007)

Bohgard, M., Karlsson, S., Lovén, E., et al.: Work and technology on human terms: Prevent (2009)

Breazeal, C.L.: Designing Sociable Robots. MIT Press, Cambridge (2004)

Cherns, A.: The principles of sociotechnical design. Human Relat. **29**, 783–792 (1976)

Cooper, A.: The inmates are running the asylum: [Why high-tech products drive us crazy and how to restore the sanity. Sams, Indianapolis (2004)

Eklund, J.: An extended framework for humans, technology and organisation in interaction. In: Luczak, H., Zink, K.J. (eds.) Human Factors in Organisational Design and Management–VII, pp. 47–60. IEA Press, Santa Monica (2003)

Eklund, J., Karltun, J., Vogel, K.: Interactive research and HTO as an industry development model. ODAMNES **2014**, 337–342 (2014)

Frennert, S., Östlund, B.: Seven matters of concern of social robots and older people. Int. J. Soc. Robot. **6**, 299–310 (2014)

Goodrich, M.A., Schultz, A.C.: Human–robot interaction: a survey. Found. Trends Human Comput. Inter. **1**, 203–275 (2008)

Hassenzahl, M., Tractinsky, N.: User experience-a research agenda. Behav. Inf. Technol. **25**, 91–97 (2006)

Hui, A., Schatzki, T., Shove, E.: The Nexus of Practices: Connections, Constellations, Practitioners. Taylor & Francis, London (2016)

Karltun, A., Eklund, J.: Interactive research promoting a systems perspective in improving the work situation of 15,000 postmen. In: 40th Annual Conference of the Nordic Ergonomics Society Reykavik, Iceland, 11–13 August 2008

Karltun, A., Karltun, J., Berglund, M., et al.: HTO-a complementary ergonomics perspective. In: Human Factors in Organisational Design and Management–XI Nordic Ergonomics Society Annual Conference–46 (2014)

Licklider, J.C.: Man-computer symbiosis. IRE Trans. Human Factors Electron. **1**, 4–11 (1960)

Lindblom, J., Andreasson, R.: Current challenges for UX evaluation of human-robot interaction. In: Schlick, C., Trzcieliński, S. (eds.) Advances in Ergonomics of Manufacturing: Managing the Enterprise of the Future, pp. 267–277. Springer, Cham (2016). https://doi.org/10.1007/978-3-319-41697-7_24

Okamura, A.M., Mataric, M.J., Christensen, H.I.: Medical and health-care robotics. IEEE Robot. Autom. Mag. **17**, 26–37 (2010)

Pearce, A.J., Adair, B., Miller, K., et al.: Robotics to enable older adults to remain living at home. J. Aging Res. **2012**, 10 (2012)

Riek, L.D.: The social co-robotics problem space: six key challenges. In: Robotics Challenges and Vision (RCV2013) (2014)

Riek, L.D.: Healthcare robotics. Commun. ACM **60**, 68–78 (2017)

Rollenhagen, C.: MTO–en introduktion. Sambandet människa, teknik och organisation. Lund: Studentlitteratur (1995)

Scholtz, J.: Theory and evaluation of human robot interactions. In: 2003 Proceedings of the 36th Annual Hawaii International Conference on System Sciences, p. 10. IEEE (2003)

Schuh, G., Schwartz, M.: Prerequisites for the successful launch of enterprise social networks. In: Lödding, H., Riedel, R., Thoben, K.-D., von Cieminski, G., Kiritsis, D. (eds.) APMS 2017. IAICT, vol. 513, pp. 239–246. Springer, Cham (2017). https://doi.org/10.1007/978-3-319-66923-6_28

Sheridan, T.B.: Human–robot interaction: status and challenges. Hum. Factors **58**, 525–532 (2016)

Solman, K.N.: Analysis of interaction quality in human–machine systems: applications for forklifts. Appl. Ergon. **33**, 155–166 (2002)

Suchman, L., Wynn, E.: Procedures and problems in the office. Off. Technol. People **2**, 133–154 (1984)

Suchman, L.A., Trigg, R.H.: Understanding practice: video as a medium for reflection and design. *Design at work*. L. Erlbaum Associates Inc., pp. 65–90 (1992)

Weiss, A., Bernhaupt, R., Lankes, M., et al.: The USUS evaluation framework for human-robot interaction. In: AISB2009: Proceedings of the Symposium on New Frontiers in Human-Robot Interaction, pp. 11–26 (2009)

Woods, D.D., Hollnagel, E.: Joint Cognitive Systems: Foundations of Cognitive Systems Engineering. CRC Press, Boca Raton (2005)

Wurhofer, D., Meneweger, T., Fuchsberger, V., Tscheligi, M.: Deploying robots in a production environment: a study on temporal transitions of workers' experiences. In: Abascal, J., Barbosa, S., Fetter, M., Gross, T., Palanque, P., Winckler, M. (eds.) INTERACT 2015. LNCS, vol. 9298, pp. 203–220. Springer, Cham (2015). https://doi.org/10.1007/978-3-319-22698-9_14

Companion Transporter: A Co-worker in the Greenhouse

Alireza Nemati[1]([✉]) [iD], Dongjie Zhao[1] [iD], Wanyue Jiang[1] [iD],
and Shuzhi Sam Ge[1,2] [iD]

[1] Institute for Future (IFF), Qingdao University, Qingdao 266071, China
nemati@qdu.edu.cn
[2] Social Robotics Laboratory, National University of Singapore,
Singapore 117576, Singapore
samge@nus.edu.sg

Abstract. Demands to produce food is increasing every day in China, and greenhouses are a part of the solution to solve this problem. The tough condition, long working hours, and working alone in the small greenhouses, makes the work environment more unpleasant compare to many other work fields. In this paper, we present a smart robot for carrying the payloads in the greenhouses. Moreover, the robot is a companion robot and an assistant to the workers. The robot can socially interact with the workers, make conversation with them, answer to the work related questions, and receive orders through voice commands. Social interaction and communication with the robot, make more delightful work environment for the workers, who mostly work alone in a small greenhouse. Main brain of the robot is online and the robot have access to the server through the 4G network. The robot become more intelligent as working in the greenhouse without any need to become updated by the users. As well as reducing the mental pressure, the robot decrease the pressure of physical work by carrying the cargos and materials in the greenhouse. The aim of this project is to put a true co-worker in the small greenhouses.

Keywords: Small greenhouse · Transportation robot · Social interaction · Companion robot · Assistant robot

1 Introduction

The modern robots, which have been developed in the last decades, usually have complex mechanical and electrical structures [1]. At the first, most of the robots had been used for industrial purposes, therefore, they can be named as industrial robots. Soon the robots showed that they can become a partner for humans in addition of the conventional applications. This kind of robots are social robots, which are intelligent and have special abilities such as they are cooperative, socially interactive, they can learn, and have cognitive skills. Companion robots are most popular type of social robots have been involved in many different life aspects. They have become popular in the medical care, rehabilitation, therapy, education, daily services, and entertainment in the role of assistant, companion, waiter, and player [2, 3]. For example, some social

© Springer Nature Switzerland AG 2019
M. A. Salichs et al. (Eds.): ICSR 2019, LNAI 11876, pp. 322–331, 2019.
https://doi.org/10.1007/978-3-030-35888-4_30

robots are used to comfort and entertain lonely elders [4] and help the autistic patient to communicate through their emotions, to reduce their anxiety, and to improve their mood states [5]. The companion robots can be designed in different shapes. Humanoid robots are usually easier to be accepted by the user. The humanoid robots such as RoboThespian, Atlas, TOPIO, Nao, Pepper, Enon, which have a different sizes, have been considered as a good companion for children and adults [6–8]. Animals are the most important companion to humans. The animal shape robots, such as Aibo, Pleo, Carine, etc. are not only a robot toy, but also a companion friend [9, 10]. In addition of humanoid and animal shaped robots, some fancy shape robots, such as the Cozmo can create intelligent responses and show emotion [11, 12].

Most of the available companion robots cannot do labor works [13]. On the other hand, some types of robot always has been considered as a worker without any emotion capabilities, like the industrial arm robots or mobile robots such as AGVs. To complete the manufacturing process, the arm robots are automatic, programmable and capable of moving on two or more axes. Until now, the arm robots have typical applications such as welding, painting, assembly, picking, packaging, labeling, palletizing, product inspection, and testing [14–16]. The arm robots are mostly used more-or-less stationary, though the jointed arm and gripper assembly can move. Compared with arm robots, the AGV robots are not fixed to one location, they can move around in their work field and they have been designed to carry around some cargos. The AGV robots can be wheeled, tracked, biped, or legged [17].

Currently, the industrial arm robots or the AGVs work in the factories, offices, and restaurants and other similar locations. For example, a specific type of AGV robots work in the restaurants, as a waiter, and in some cases they have limited interaction with people [18]. However, most of the available waiter robots do not have advanced interaction with guests and they are just a mechanical machine with a certain task. Also for the arm robots, as there is a safe zone for the protection of the worker, it is not easy for the interaction to the workers, even for the cooperation arm robots, the interaction is not considered at the design stage. On the other hand, the interaction between users and robots is not strong in a factory or a restaurant, because the crowd's intensity is enough to meet the needs of communication between human users.

1.1 Greenhouse Environment

Unlike the factory environment, in some agricultural work fields such as greenhouses, workers usually work independently and have little chances for interaction with others. The large and modern greenhouses have been developed for decades, and are widely used in many countries especially in China. Currently, most of the greenhouses are being used for vegetable production or flower cultivation. The greenhouses that have built in the past years can be combined with the Internet of Things and advanced control system to make them more intelligent [19–21]. They can automatically control the shade, ventilation, cooling, heating, and fertigation. At the same time, with the development of agricultural machinery and equipment, many agricultural is being done by an intelligent machine. Taking vegetable cultivation as an example, in the recent years, a serious process from seed selection, seedling, transplanting to medium-term management and harvesting, needed a team of workers. However, in a modern greenhouse, this set of operations have been carried out by a single worker with the assistant of intelligent machines. In this process, the needs of labor for the independent greenhouse are reduced to a low level, and the worker's interaction is suppressed. Since all mechanical machines and robots have some effect on the quality of life of people in the work environment, it is worthwhile to add interactive modules to meet the interactive requirements in agricultural robots. Figure 1 depict some modern greenhouses for producing different plant.

Fig. 1. Some images of modern greenhouses for producing different products.

Demand for producing more food, result in rapid growth of small greenhouses. Local farmers in China, have started to convert their farms into the small greenhouses. The working conditions in that greenhouses are even harsher than a conventional one. The automation in the recently established small greenhouses is rare, and most of the tasks being done manually.

The most important thing, which makes a small greenhouse more unpleasant environment, is that most of the time, there is only one or two workers are working in a greenhouse, and major portion of labors in the small greenhouse in China are not young. In addition of physical strain, there is lots of mental pressure on the labor forces. Considering the hardships of working in a small greenhouse, it is necessary to find solutions to reduce the physical and mental pressure on the workers. Some pictures of typical small greenhouse in Qingdao, China has been presented in the Fig. 2.

Fig. 2. A typical small greenhouse in China.

2   The Solution

Transportation of materials and equipment is a major task within the greenhouses, especially during the planting and harvesting season. Currently, the material handling is being done manually or by employing conventional machines.

Most of available robots or AGVs in the market are not quite fit for conditions in the small greenhouses or they are extremely expensive for the local farmers.

The proposed robot can carry various materials, therefore, it can reduce the burden of labor works in the greenhouses. The appearance of our robot might be similar to the conventional AGVs, however, it completely different in the inside. The main purpose of the robot is to reduce the mental pressure on the workers in the work environment in addition of doing labor works.

Since most of the tasks are doing manually in the small greenhouses, the procedure is not very fast, hence, the robot may have much idle time before become fully loaded, or after bringing equipment to the worker.

During the idle time, the robot has a totally different role. When there is no task to do, instead of standing still or going back to a predefined spot, it becomes a companion robot. Through interaction with the workers, it reduces the mental pressure in the work environment, especially when only one person is working at the greenhouse. The details about proposed robot, in both mechanical structure and quality of interaction, has been discussed in the following sections.

3   Companion Transporter

3.1   Social Features

In this section, the social skills of the robot have been explained. As discussed before, the main goal of this project is to promote a robot from a machine doing the labor works, to a co-worker. The following points are the key features of our robot.

- Usually, it is convenient to identify the robots with a number. However, in the small greenhouses, not many robots works in the same area, so, we use actual name to identify the robots instead of the numbers.
- The robots are actually a companion robots with intelligent brain on an external server. They use 4G network to access the server. The simple and basic processing of data is being done by the robot, yet they do not have very powerful processing unit. Through the online engine, we can constantly keep the robots intelligence updated and make it smarter every day without any trouble for the robot operators.
- To increase the interaction of workers with the robot, a special compartment has been considered in the structure of the robot. They can put their meals or snacks in that box to keep it warm or cold. In this manner, the robot also play role as a waiter to the workers.
- The main method to send the orders to the robots is through voice commands. In addition, there are some control button on the robot, which can be used to dispatch the robots to a certain destination or give a specific command to it. Many workers in the small greenhouses cannot work with complicated machines. Hence, the voice command is most convenient method to command the robot.

3.2 Key Mechanical Features

Greenhouses, especially the small and traditional ones, have unique conditions compare to other industrial environments. Therefore, there are some special consideration in design of the transportation robot. In the following, most important features of the robot for the greenhouse have been presented.

- The greenhouses and the area around them are not flat or well-prepared, therefore, the robot should have the ability to move on the rough tracks.
- The temperature and humidity in the greenhouses are more extreme than most of industrial environment and water condensation is a usual phenomenon during the night.
- To use the space in the greenhouse more efficiently, the pathways are usually narrow. To adopt to this conditions, the structure of the robot is thin.
- Dust in the greenhouse, makes the environment more unpleasant. Therefore, the structure of the robot should prevent spreading the dust in the greenhouse.
- Eight ultrasonic sensors has been installed on the robot to avoid the collision to the obstacles. In many cases, there is not enough space to turn the obstacles. As a result, if an obstacle blocks the motion of robot, it should be removed manually.

3.3 The Robot Appearance

As the first step, we designed four different versions of the robot. In each version, we focused on a certain set of capabilities and features with different appearances. Some images of designed robot have been shown in the Fig. 3.

We had a few visit to the local greenhouses in Qingdao, China, and asked the opinion of some workers and owners on the appearance of the robot. We asked, which version of robot is more preferred to them. We took the opinion of 15 persons, 6 women and 9 men. Although 15 persons may not be large sample group, it can provide basic estimation of the workers preference on robot's appearance. The outcome results have been presented in Table 1.

Table 1. Acceptance rate of different versions of designed robot.

	Sample size (Persons)	Version A	Version B	Version C	Version D
Women	6	33%	0%	0%	67%
Men	9	33%	67%	0%	0%
Total	**15**	**33%**	**40%**	**0%**	**27%**

It is interesting that despite small size of our sample group, it clearly shows different taste of women and men on the figure of the robot. All the men preferred the version A or B (mostly B), version B looks more rugged and tougher, however, none of the women participants liked the version B. they mostly liked version D, which is more neutral.

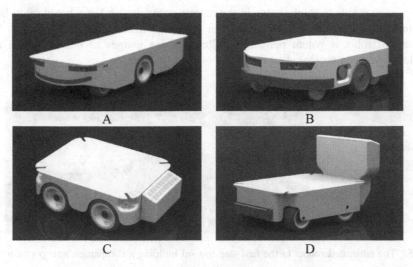

Fig. 3. Different designed robot platforms in the first step.

3.4 The First Prototype

Considering feedbacks from the survey, we applied some modification in our designs. The final version of the designed robot for the greenhouse has been predicted in the Fig. 4.

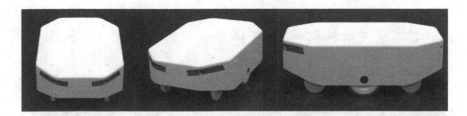

Fig. 4. The designed companion robot for transporting materials in the greenhouse

Since, building full size robot is time consuming and costly, we divided the whole project into two different stages. At the first stage, we built smaller samples. The first set of samples will be used mostly in the controlled environment for development purposes, and performing the tests. The robots have social skills of the final robot, however, their mechanical structure is not quite fit for harsh and rough environment of a small greenhouse. The final full size version will be made after accomplishing the tests and fulfilling the requirements of the social interaction.

The technical specification of the fabricated small samples are as follows. Size of the robot is about $50 \times 30 \times 13$ cm, it weighs less than 9 kg, and can carry payloads up to 25 kg with maximum speed of 1 m/s. The robot has 4 ultrasonic sensors in front and rear side to prevent collision with the obstacles and uses 2 additional ultrasonic sensors in each side to safely move in the narrow paths. It also has a novel multi body structure to easily maneuver on the uneven grounds while the payload is stable. The structure of robot is patent pending in China. Some images of the fabricated first samples have been presented in Fig. 5.

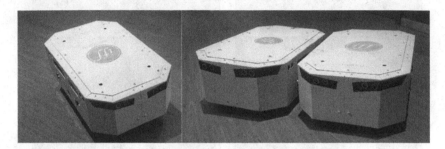

Fig. 5. The fabricated robots in the first step toward building a companion transporter robot.

After finishing primary test in the lab environment, we performed some test in the greenhouse to take the feedback of the workers on the interacting with the robot. The mechanical structure of robot is not quite fit for carrying payload in rough terrain, hence, our survey was mostly on the evaluation of the social interaction of the workers with the robot. It should mentioned that in the current stage, the robot is not completely smart and there is many room for improvement of the robot. Some pictures of the first prototypes in the greenhouse environment have been shown in Fig. 6.

Fig. 6. First prototypes of companion transporter in small greenhouse.

3.5 Assessment Tools and Results

We prepared a questionnaire, containing eight questions to evaluate the acceptance of a companion robot in the greenhouse environment. The opinion of 14 persons (6 women and 8 men) has been collected. The questions are design to investigate the willingness of workers to have cooperation with a robot and quality of the interaction. The answerers had been asked to rate their desire in response of each question from one to five. Five is the most desired and one is the least desired. Another type of analyzing result has been performed. Score 1 and 2 considered as low, score 3 as medium, and 4 and 5 have considered as high. No meaningful differences have been observed in answers between women and men. The questions and the answers in this survey have been listed in the Table 2.

The results of this survey shows workers cordially accept the robot in the greenhouse. Based on the answers on the question 1, the workers like to work with a robot in a same place. Answers to question 2 also provide a clear image that talking to a robot is pleasant to workers. Results from the question 3 shows that calling the robots by the names, instead of numbers, is also significantly acceptable to the workers.

Answers to the question 8 also illustrate that the workers are more comfortable to give the orders to the robot through voice commands compare to the conventional control buttons. It is mainly because most of the workers are not comfortable with advanced technological machines. We also prefer voice command, since, it provides more intimate interaction with the robot.

However, responses to the question 5 shows that the robot's design, appearance, and behavior should be in such a manner that increase the feeling of safety in the workers. Based on the feedbacks of question 7, small and medium size robots are more acceptable by the workers compare to the big size robots.

Big robots can carry larger payloads in the greenhouse, but, at the same time, they may seem hostile to workers. In addition, a small intelligent robot is more similar to a pet, therefore, it is more desirable to workers.

Table 2. Questions list and the collected result from the survey

Item	Question	Average (Std. Dev.)	Percentage of each answer		
			Low	Medium	High
1	How much do you like to work with a robot in a same place?	3.9 (0.8)	7	14	79
2	How much do you like to talk with a robot?	3.9 (0.7)	7	7	86
3	How much do you like to call the robot by name?	3.9 (1.0)	7	14	79
4	How much do you like the robot start a casual conversation with you?	3.9 (1.0)	14	7	79
5	How much do you feel safe a robot works around you?	3.2 (0.8)	14	64	21
6	How much time do you like the robot be around you?	3.2 (0.8)	14	57	29
7	Do you prefer a small size robot or big size robot?		Small (64)	Medium (36)	Big (0)
8	Do you like to send commands the robot, voice command or control button?	Control Button (29)	Not different (1)	Voice command (64)	Both (7)

The answers to the question six also shows that despite the great interest of the worker to interact with the robot, they still have some safety considerations back in their mind or keep the distance to robots.

4 Conclusion

The environment in the small greenhouses in China is more intense compare to other workplaces. The working hours are high, and most of the time the workers have to work alone in a greenhouse. In this paper we presented a smart robotic device to help the workers in the small greenhouses by carrying around the product and equipment. The presented robot is not only a device for transporting the payloads, but also, it improves the work environments by socially interacting with the workers. The mechanical structure of the robot is compatible with rough environment of a greenhouse. The low level processing of the voices, images, and data from different sensors is done by the robot. However, the intelligent brain of the robot is on an online server, to which the robot connect through a 4G network. The quality of the interaction between the robot and workers is comparable to available assistant software on the smartphones.

The workers give the orders, such as calling or dispatching the robot through voice commands. To make more personal connection between the robot and the workers, the robot identified with the names, instead of numbers.

We have divided this project into two stages. At the first stage, we mostly focused on the social skills of the robot and less on the mechanical structure. We designed a few versions of a small sample and asked opinion of 15 workers. Women workers mostly prefer a cheerful or neutral appearance for the robot, while men mostly selected the tough and rugged looking robot.

We fabricated two small prototypes. The samples are mostly used in the controlled environment to do the tests. We done basic tests in the greenhouse environment and investigate worker's feedback about working with a robot. They are highly interested to work with a robot in the greenhouse environment and talk with them. The workers prefer to interact with small and medium size robot and give the orders to the robots through voice commands. They also highly support the idea that robots start a conversation with them. However, they have mild concerns about safety of working near a robot and do not want the robot be around them all the time.

We hope a companion transporter robot makes the greenhouse environment more delightful by reducing both mental pressure and burden of the physical works.

References

1. Ge, S.S., Lewis, F.L.: Autonomous Mobile Robots: Sensing, Control, Decision Making and Applications. CRC Press, Boca Raton (2006)
2. Belpaeme, T., et al.: Social robots for education: a review. Sci. Robot. 3(21), p5954 (2018)
3. Li, M., et al.: Role playing learning for socially concomitant mobile robot navigation. CAAI Trans. Intell. Technol. 3(1), 49–58 (2018)

4. Conti, D., et al.: Robots in education and care of children with developmental disabilities: a study on acceptance by experienced and future professionals. Int. J. Soc. Robot. **9**(1), 51–62 (2017)
5. Pennisi, P., et al.: Autism and social robotics: a systematic review. Autism Res. **9**(2), 165–183 (2016)
6. Aaltonen, I., et al.: Hello pepper, may i tickle you?: children's and adults' responses to an entertainment robot at a shopping mall. In: Proceedings of the Companion of the 2017 ACM/IEEE International Conference on Human-Robot Interaction, pp. 53–54. ACM, Vienna (2017)
7. Pulido, J.C., et al.: Evaluating the child-robot interaction of the NAOTherapist platform in pediatric rehabilitation. Int. J. Soc. Robot. **9**(3), 343–358 (2017)
8. Verner, I.M., Polishuk, A., Krayner, N.: Science class with RoboThespian: using a robot teacher to make science fun and engage students. IEEE Robot. Autom. Mag. **23**(2), 74–80 (2016)
9. Kim, E.S., et al.: Social robots as embedded reinforcers of social behavior in children with autism. J. Autism Dev. Disord. **43**(5), 1038–1049 (2013)
10. Veloso, M.M., et al.: CMRoboBits: creating an intelligent AIBO robot. AI Mag. **27**(1), 67 (2006)
11. Kennington, C., Plane, S.: Symbol, conversational, and societal grounding with a toy robot. arXiv preprint arXiv:1709.10486 (2017)
12. Touretzky, D.S., Gardner-McCune, C.: Calypso for Cozmo: robotic AI for everyone. In: Proceedings of the 49th ACM Technical Symposium on Computer Science Education. ACM (2018)
13. Parks, J.A.: Lifting the burden of women's care work: should robots replace the "human touch"? Hypatia **25**(1), 100–120 (2010)
14. Dauth, W., et al.: German robots-the impact of industrial robots on workers (2017)
15. Bahrin, M.A.K., et al.: Industry 4.0: a review on industrial automation and robotic. Jurnal Teknologi **78**(6–13), 137–143 (2016)
16. Iqbal, J., et al.: Automating industrial tasks through mechatronic systems–a review of robotics in industrial perspective. Tehnički vjesnik **23**(3), 917–924 (2016)
17. Garcia, E., et al.: The evolution of robotics research. IEEE Robot. Autom. Mag. **14**(1), 90–103 (2007)
18. Cheong, A., et al.: Development of a robotic waiter system. IFAC-PapersOnLine **49**(21), 681–686 (2016)
19. Lan, Z., Ma, L.: Internet of things based farm greenhouse monitor and alarm management system, Google Patents (2014)
20. Dan, L., et al.: Intelligent agriculture greenhouse environment monitoring system based on IOT technology. In: 2015 International Conference on Intelligent Transportation, Big Data and Smart City. IEEE (2015)
21. Linlin, Q., et al.: Implementation of IOT-based greenhouse intelligent monitoring system. Trans. Chin. Soc. Agric. Mach. **46**(3), 261–267 (2015)

Proactive Intention Recognition for Joint Human-Robot Search and Rescue Missions Through Monte-Carlo Planning in POMDP Environments

Dimitri Ognibene[1]([⊠]) [iD], Lorenzo Mirante[1], and Letizia Marchegiani[2] [iD]

[1] School of Computer Science and Electronic Engineering, University of Essex, Colchester, UK
dimitri.ognibene@essex.ac.uk
[2] Department of Electronic Systems, Aalborg University, Aalborg, Denmark
lm@es.aau.dk

Abstract. Proactively perceiving others' intentions is a crucial skill to effectively interact in unstructured, dynamic and novel environments. This work proposes a first step towards embedding this skill in support robots for search and rescue missions. Predicting the responders' intentions, indeed, will enable exploration approaches which will identify and prioritise areas that are more relevant for the responder and, thus, for the task, leading to the development of safer, more robust and efficient joint exploration strategies. More specifically, this paper presents an active intention recognition paradigm to perceive, even under sensory constraints, not only the target's position but also the first responder's movements, which can provide information on his/her intentions (e.g. reaching the position where he/she expects the target to be). This mechanism is implemented by employing an extension of Monte-Carlo-based planning techniques for partially observable environments, where the reward function is augmented with an entropy reduction bonus. We test in simulation several configurations of reward augmentation, both information theoretic and not, as well as belief state approximations and obtain substantial improvements over the basic approach.

Keywords: Active vision · Active perception · Active intention recognition

1 Introduction

Humans are endowed with sophisticated social interactions skills that provide invaluable advantages. These are realised by implicit intention reading, through the interpretation of partners' sensorimotor coupling with the environment, or explicit communication [20,22]. The former modality can be advantageous for the 'acting' partners as it requires a lower cognitive load and allows focusing on the

© Springer Nature Switzerland AG 2019
M. A. Salichs et al. (Eds.): ICSR 2019, LNAI 11876, pp. 332–343, 2019.
https://doi.org/10.1007/978-3-030-35888-4_31

task at hand. However, the perceiving partner must gather and integrate information on several important factors like the presence, identity and configuration of any relevant affordances, as well as the pose of the partner and the trajectories of its effectors [18]. In complex and unstructured environments these skills have to heavily rely on proactive perception capabilities, as not all these elements may be immediately and simultaneously observable (e.g. being in another room, or occluded, out of the field of view or simply unattended), and require multiple steps to be sensed. This is one of the main issues impeding human robot collaboration in such environments as dense sensorisation of the environment necessary for passive perception is not viable, and current active perception strategies are still limited to single step 'myopic' proactive perception strategies [15, 19]. An important application domain for this skill is search-and-rescue missions where both risk for the first responders and time spent in localising a survivor must be optimized. Yet, fully automating even the riskiest and earliest phases of these tasks is still hindered by limited autonomous exploration algorithms. Human responders, indeed, rely not only on the flexibility of their perceptual skills, but also on non-verbal task knowledge gained by exploring multiple environments, which is difficult to transfer to a robot.

In this work we propose the use of active intention recognition (IR) paradigms to allow the robot to indirectly and naturally exploit first responders' knowledge and, thus, to improve its exploration performance. The intuition is that the responders may be able to more accurately guess the position of the target and start moving to reach it. Their initial movements, together with some partial information on the map (e.g. information on regions of interest), can be enough to estimate where the responders are directed and, thus, anticipate them to test the location and secure the path. We carry out our analysis in simulation assuming the use of a drone as the search-and-rescue robot of reference.

2   Background

Search and Rescue. Robot disaster responders are an important research target [13]. They aim to quickly locate and extract survivors. This has driven the study of the non-verbal interaction strategies adopted by human responders [2] and the development of collaborative navigation algorithms for groups of robots [4]. In this line of research we try to bridge these problems by enabling robots to more naturally understand and account for responders' intentions while finding computationally affordable solutions.

Planning in Partial Observable Conditions. Planning tasks are traditionally represented and addressed relying on *Markov Decision Processes* (MDP), as being a framework which allows for a neat problem formulation, while also accounting for the presence of uncertainty and control noise. Most commonly, in MDPs, the task is defined as finding a *policy* that maximizes the *expected cumulative discounted reward* given a representation of the environment in terms of

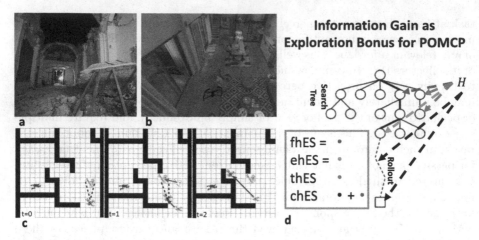

Fig. 1. (a) A real disaster condition. (b) A simulated environment view generated by AIRSIM [25] for testing our algorithm. The figure shows the drone, the responder and the target (*e.g.* a survivor in a disaster). The responder is supposed to be able to easily guess a good location where the target might be and slowly approach it. The drone enters the disaster zone from a different position, has initial knowledge of the entrance location of the responder and of a set of candidate areas where the target could be located. The drone, due to the complexity of the environment (*e.g.* occlusions), can see the target only when it is close to it. It must employ a policy that can take advantage of the presence of the responder (whose original position is known) to find the target as fast as possible. (c) A cartoon-like illustration of an example scenario. $t = 0$) the drone finds the first responder; $t = 1$) the drone observes the responder moving towards the room where the survivor is; $t = 2$) the drone anticipates the first responder and approaches the survivor room. (d) Information gain as exploration bonus for POMCP. The arrows represent where in the MCTS search three is computed the entropy used for the exploration bonus.

(i) a set of states and (ii) actions, (iii) a transition function describing the probability of reaching a certain state once an action is performed in a state, and a (iv) reward function describing the reward expected once an action is performed in a state. More realistic setups require to model noisy or missing sensory information. These problems are described extending MDPs to *Partially Observable MDP* (POMDP) [12], by providing an (v) observation function which describes the probability of obtaining a certain sensory input when the environment and the agent are in certain configurations. POMDP are particularly suitable to describe search-and-rescue environments, where the positions of the targets and the one of the responder are not necessarily known and they are detectable only when the robot is in their proximity. In this work, to approach these issues, we extend POMCPs, a Monte Carlo Tree Search (MCTS) algorithm for POMDP, which has been proposed in [26].

Intention Recognition (IR). IR supports natural, proactive collaboration between robots. Several algorithms have been proposed in the literature: some based on the idea of using pre-baked libraries of actions which suit a specific condition; others relying on the idea of inverse planning and the possibility of predicting the intentions of other agents, given a model of the environment which can be used to evaluate the effectiveness of a sequence of actions to achieve any possible goals [3,24]. This kind of approach leads to a more precise and flexible recognition process, but has a higher computational cost. Other approaches, particularly suitable for robotics applications, instead, employ the idea of IR as an inverse control task, where multiple parametrizable controllers are compared to explain others' behaviours [8,19].

Active Perception and Active Vision. Active Perception is the problem of actively controlling sensors to improve the speed and accuracy in the estimation of behaviourally relevant variables [17,27]. Its applications are numerous, spanning from inspection and localization, to object recognition and autonomous driving, and not only limited to robotics. Indeed, relevant efforts can be also be found in the neuroscience and cognitive science communities [10]. Different approaches have been proposed in the literature: *e.g.* methods based on neural models often trained by Reinforcement Learning (RL) [17,21,27], evolutionary algorithms [7], and information theoretic approaches [9,19].

Active Intention Recognition (AIR). Intention Recognition (IR) is a particularly challenging problem, as it needs to take into account the interactions among multiple elements (*e.g.* agents, affordances and effectors) which may not be known or observed simultaneously (*e.g.* while watching only the mouse running, we may not see the cheese, or not notice that a cat is running after the mouse). In unstructured and not instrumented environments, such as construction or disaster sites, or in general, when only few sensors with a limited receptive field are available, IR can be impossible to achieve if those sensors are not efficiently directed, so that they can perceive and track other agents, their effectors and the affordances they are interacting with. Active intention recognition (AIR) has been recently introduced as the problem of recognising the intentions of other agents, either humans or robots, when the sensing process can actively be controlled to deal with missing observations [18,19] or limited bandwidth [15]. AIR is formally defined as selecting the policy of sensor control which minimizes the final expected entropy on the state of the observed agent. Ognibene & Demiris in [19] presented an implementation of the concept on a humanoid robot, where IR is approached as an inverse control problem. The formulation used a mixture of Kalman filters to represent the robot's possible movements, assuming they were generated by one of multiple parametrizable linear controllers, and using a single-step myopic strategy based on a novel approximation of the information gain on the mixture selector variable. In [15] a similar method was employed to simultaneously recognize the complex activities of multiple actors, represented using Probabilistic Context Free Grammars.

In this work we extend [19] by: (a) closing the loop between social perception and interaction through the integration of AIR and action execution, aimed at the shared goal of finding the target (survivor); (b) relaxing the myopic constraint and considering multi-step policies.

3 Methods

Environment. The problem is described according to the POMDP formalism through transition, observation and reward functions. A termination function is also used, as adopted in other POMDP problems with Monte Carlo (MC) methods

Transition Function. The environment is static apart from the responder's movements. The transition function is, thus, defined by using a simple, deterministic, model of the drone's movements and a probabilistic model of the movements of the responder when searching and approaching the target. The state is composed of a 6 dimensional tuple, containing the position of the drone, the position of the responder and the one of the target. The responder either stays still with probability equal to p_{still} (to simulate a slower speed compared to the drone) either moves one step in the direction of the survivor location with $0.95(1-p_{still})$ or in random direction.

Observation Model. The observation model always provides the position of the drone without noise. The positions of the target and of the responder, instead, are available when they are in the same position of the drone.

Reward Function. The main objective for the system is to find the goal, which is the same objective of the responder. A reward equal to 1 is given when the drone finds the goal. AIR is auxiliary to the main collaborative objective and, thus, rewarding social interaction directly is not part of the problem description. Yet, as explained in the algorithm subsection, several forms of intrinsic reward [16] are employed to address several algorithmic limits in exploring large environments and in exploiting the information provided by the responder's movements.

End Function. End function stops both the real world simulation and the simulation inside the MC sampling algorithm when the drone is near the target.

Planner. The controller derives from the POMCP algorithm [26]. It integrates the planning with the state estimation processes by using the Monte Carlo simulation sampling to generate samples for the particle filter. POMCP has improved state-of-the-art performance in several tasks, and it has been already applied to social robotics in several instances [11]. POMCP uses a black-box generative model of the environment to estimate the action-observation sequences' values through repeated sampling. Each sampling iteration starts from a root node associated with the current sequence of observations h integrated in the belief state $b(h)$ with the initial 'prior' belief b_0. Then, POMCP builds a limited portion of the tree of the future actions and observations through the following steps:

(1) an initial state is sampled from the current belief state $b(h)$; (2) an action a is selected according to an action-selection strategy that balances exploration and exploitation; (3) an observation o is obtained defining a new history $h' = [h, a, o]$, the corresponding node is evaluated recursively if it is already in the search tree (going back to step 2), or is inserted into the search tree after getting a first estimate of its value by continuing the simulation using a predefined 'rollout' action selection policy until a certain depth d; and (4) update the statistics of the tree nodes by back-propagating the simulation results up to the root.

Modifications of POMCP. *I. Exploration Reward.* The default exploration strategy (**dES**) of POMCP algorithm [26] relies on the Upper Confidence Bound (UCB) exploration bonus [1] in action selection. In environments where most of the rewarding/punishing states are deeper in the search tree than maximum search depth applying MCTS planning based only on UCB for exploration can be problematic. In these contexts, MCTS algorithms may fail to estimate the value of observing informative cues and even prefer useless actions, as staying still at the entrance, because they never simulate long enough to reach the reward and, thus, fail to plan and observe such cues. In this specific task, the informative cues are the responders' movements, which inform on their intentions and goals [3,19,24] but can be noisy and expensive to acquire. Trying to identify those intentions requires finding and following the responder, which can be quite inefficient in several cases, *e.g.* when the drone is certain of the goal position or near to a candidate position, and approaching it directly would be faster than relying on the responder. Thus, while in previous works involving AIR [15,19] the expected information gain on the others' intentions was driving the robot behaviour, here *dealing with the trade-off between acquiring information about the responder and exploring autonomously* becomes an important part of the task. To address these issues, five other specific exploration strategies are tested that use an 'intrinsic' reward [5,16] to facilitate not only visiting new useful positions, but also the extraction of information from the human rescuer's presence: **1.** the responder observation reward (**rrES**), where a reward of 0.1 is added when the robot observes the responder; **2.** complete entropy (**chES**), at each step (both tree search and rollout) an intrinsic reward is added equal to $-0.2 \cdot H$ where H is the entropy (see Fig. 1d); **3.** search tree entropy (**thES**), like chES, but entropy is added only inside the search tree but not in the rollout avoiding the update of the filter; **4.** end search tree entropy (**ehES**), like shES, but entropy bonus is added only at the last step of the tree search, before the rollout phase. This makes the amount of bonus added independent from the number of search steps, factor that biases the other approaches; **5.** first step search tree entropy (**fhES**), where the bonus is added only after the first step of search in the tree. The effect of computing entropy only on the goal location (**gH**) like in [19], or on all the complete belief state (**bH**) is also tested for all the entropy based exploration strategies. This last variation exploits the structured form of the belief space containing the drone, the rescuer and the goal's location. This is motivated by the low variability of goals compared with the trajectories followed by the human responder to achieve them. Such variability induces a high entropy that may affect the planning algorithm. Entropy is directly computed from the belief state. Inside the search tree, filter and entropy are cached to speed up the algorithm.

We must note that using information gain instead of the reward for helper observation may be more computationally expensive but it avoids suboptimal behaviours, such as following the slower responder after the target location is known. Furthermore, the complex computations for information gain used in [19] are not necessary anymore as an expectation of the information gain will be provided by the backup phase of MCTS.

II. Rollout Policy. Together with a basic random rollout policy (**rRS**) that simply randomly samples actions during the rollout phase, five rollout strategies are developed which exploit additional task knowledge to reach a possible survivor position during the rollout. They differ in the way this position is selected: (1) **sample target rollout strategy** (**stRS**), which selects the survivor position of the current Monte-Carlo sample state[1] as the target position for the robot movement during the rollout; (2) **deterministic near target** (**dnRS**), which selects the nearest survivor position between the not visited ones as the objective of the robot's movement in the rollout; (3) **stochastic near target** (**snRS**), which selects one of the not visited targets as the target of the robot's movement with a probability inversely proportional to the distance from the drone; (4) **deterministic most probable target** (**dpRS**), which selects the not visited target which has the highest probability of containing the goal. This is based on the filter estimation computed during the simulation phase; (5) **stochastic most probable target** (**spRS**), which acts similarly to dpRS, but samples stochastically a not visited survivor location according to its probability of being the goal location. For all these five strategies, a new target is selected when the previous one is reached without finding the goal. Two policies for the actual *action selection* are adopted in combination with the above strategies for target selection: I. Best rollout action (**bRA**), which deterministically select the best action to reach the selected target, and II. Stochastic rollout action (**sRA**), which selects an action stochastically with a probability inversely proportional to the distance between the reached state and the selected target. To implement efficiently these modifications, the best actions to reach each target are precomputed.

III. State Estimation and Reconstruction. While the algorithm employed is inspired by the POMCP, it does not use a particle filter, instead it uses a complete discrete Bayesian filter (**cF**). This helps deal with the limited amount of information the robot has access to during the task and which may strongly affect the particle filter performance. The cF allows also for effective entropy computation as well, but still presents some limitations (for more details, see [6,14]). To decrease its computational cost we implement a truncated filter (**aF**), which, after each update, only maintains the $N_s = 20$ states with the highest

---

[1] POMCP samples a state from the initial belief state at the beginning of each iteration.

probability and zeroes the others[2]. Given that the movements are localized, *i.e.* only adjacent cells can be accessed from another cell, the filter update cost is limited. However, this approximation may lead to observation conditions which are wrongly estimated as impossible, *i.e.* to have zero probability (similarly to the particles impoverishment in particle filters). This happens when the robot either *i.* focuses all the probability on solely one target and finds it empty, or *ii.* observes the first responder in an unexpected position. In these conditions, a new belief state is re-sampled as follows:

I. When all the probability is focused on one false target, the belief is regenerated by simulating the first responder's behaviour starting from its last observation at time t_o and moving towards each of the non visited target locations l_g. The same probability $p_g(t_o)$, which was assigned to the corresponding targets at time t_o, is then assigned to each of these generated states x_g. If the first responder was never observed, then the behaviour is simulated from each possible starting condition l_s.

II. When the first responder is observed in a non-expected position l^*, a new element of the state x_g is generated for each of the non explored targets l_g. In this case the probability associated with that state is computed according to how efficient it is to visit l^* for the first responder from its previous location l_{old} before reaching the target location l_g, versus travelling directly towards l_g [23,24]. Thus $p(x_g) = p_g(t_o) \cdot c(l_{old}, l_g)/[c(l_{old}, l^*) + c(l^*, l_g)]$ where the $c(a, b)$ represents the cost of reaching b from a while following the optimal trajectory and its value is the same used to drive the rollout process.

Current implementation uses Python 3.6 and will be soon available online.

4   Results

Environments. We consider four environments: a small and a big squared environment, a cross-like environment, a building like maze as shown in Fig. 1 and big randomly generated environments of size 64×64 containing 6 rooms connected by corridors. The small environment [**SE**] is a 5×5 grid. The drone is initially positioned in the center and the responder is in one of 2 adjacent cells, but the drone does not know in which one of them. The target is positioned in one of the 4 corners. In total 8 equally probable initial conditions are possible, representing the initial belief state of the robot in this environment. The large environment [**LE**] is an 11×11 grid. Again the drone is initially positioned in the center and the responder is in one of 4 adjacent cells, but the drone is not informed of which of them. The target is positioned in one of the 16 cells in the 4 corners, 4 cell in square per corner. In total 64 equally probable initial conditions are possible, representing the initial belief state of the robot in this environment. The cross-like environment [**CE**] is not convex and, thus, more demanding. It is an 11×11 grid with the arms of the cross 5 cells wide where the drone and the responder start from same location, as in condition LE. The goals are located in

---

[2] Entropy is computed before this zeroing process.

Table 1. Performance with 1000 and 100 MC samples.

	1000 Samples				100 Samples			
	chES	rrES	thES	dfES	chES	rrES	thES	dfES
Success	0.85	0.88	0.54	**0.95**	**0.8**	0.63	0.25	0.63
Steps	7.96	8.43	1.033	**7.91**	**8.31**	9.12	11.58	9.74
RObs	31	37	148	10	20	24	29	13

Average behavior over 100 trials with 1000 MC samples for each step. **Success** is the average number of times the drone found the target before 16 steps. In the table, **Steps** is the average number of steps necessary to the drone to find the target (or 16 if it fails). RObs total number of times the drone met the responder before finding the target. Tests performed on the following variations of the architecture: **rrES** reward was given also when observing the responder (0.1) other than the target (1); **chES** reward contained an entropy bonus (−H * 0.2); **thES** reward contained an entropy bonus only during the search not during rollout (−H * 0.2); **dfES** Default, reward was given only reaching the target.

the corners of the ends of the cross arms. For the building-like environment we used a grid 15 × 15 with 4 rooms, each containing two possible target locations.

The result for the small environment with 1000 samples and max-depth-search = 14 (average on 100 trials) are reported in Table 1.

When computational resources are available the **dfES** default algorithm, not using any exploration bonus, gave the best performance. In this case, we must note that it performs better the trivial solution of navigating through the four corners which would have an expected number of steps $(2 + 7 + 11 + 15)/4 = 8.75$. This is true also for the chES and rrES. chES and rrES also observe the responder much more often than dfES; yet dfES performs better than them¿. This implies that dfES makes good use of the observations of the responder (both when it finds the responder in a cell and when it doesn't). We observe, without a statistical analysis, that the policy usually chosen by the dfES robot often consisted in (a) reaching a corner, (b) going back to the center if no target is observed, and (c) going to the next corner. This strategy may maximize the probability of encountering the responder, while not meeting it would decrease the probability of the target to be in that direction. Unexpectedly, the thES version of the system presents lower performance. We attribute this to the dependence of the exploration bonus on the length of the search tree branch.

Table 1 reports also the results when only MC 100 samples per step are performed. In this case the chES system is the most effective one, followed by rrES and dfES. chES is the least affected by the reduced number of samples. This suggest that using an entropy-based bonus may support exploration of environments when not enough time is available for construction of deep search tree.

With the big environment and 100 samples per action the best performance are achieved by the chES, which, in 50% of the trials, found the target in less than 40 steps (maximum steps allowed). thES achieved (28%), rrES 27 % and dfES 18%.

In Table 2 the results for the building like environment are reported when simulations are run for 100 MC samples. The results consistently favour the **ehES**,

Table 2. Performance with 100 MC samples in building like environment.

Approx	Rollout Pol	Rollout Act	Expl strategy	H	Steps	Time	Reward	Reward/time
FALSE	snRS	bRA	ehES	gH	1959	1483	76	0.051
TRUE	spRS	bRA	ehES	bH	1962	258	74	0.287
TRUE	dpRS	sRA	ehES	bH	2029	291	74	0.254
TRUE	dpRS	sRA	ehES	bH	2120	307	74	0.241
FALSE	dpRS	sRA	ehES	gH	2058	1583	74	0.047
FALSE	stRS	sRA	dfES	–	2148	331	69	0.208
TRUE	stRS	bRA	thES	bH	2431	344	42	0.122
TRUE	dnRS	sRA	thES	bH	2422	298	41	0.138
FALSE	stRS	bRA	thES	bH	2557	2006	40	0.020
FALSE	dnRS	sRA	thES	bH	2650	2026	34	0.017

Performance over 100 trials on the cross-like environment of the first best five, the most performing system without using entropy and the worst four configurations. No data collected for the **chES** due to its computational demands. **Approx** column define if the approximated belief state **aF** (True) or the complete **cF** one are tracked. **Rollout Pol** shows the rollout policy used. **Rollout Act** shows the Rollout action selection strategy used. **Expl Strategy** shows the Exploration Strategy employed **H** shows which entropy function was used to compute the exploration bonus, **steps** reports the number of steps in 100 trials, **time** computation time, **reward** total reward obtained and **reward/time** total reward over time, representing computational efficiency.

while the **thES** consistently show the worst performance. The performance of the best **dfES** are reported and are less effective than the configurations using **ehES**. The approximation does not appear to affect the performance, while yielding a substantial speed-up in the computation. Similar results have been obtained with the randomly generated bigger environments, but could not be reported for space reasons.

5   Conclusions and Future Work

Current result suggested that the idea of coupling a robot with a more expert but constrained human partner in the task of joint search for a target in an unknown environment may be promising. Future work will focus on optimizing the methods proposed, by integrating them with flexible SLAM algorithms, devising and testing alternative exploration bonus, employing realistic responders' models, considering additional collaborative tasks, such as verifying that the surrounding of the responder are safe.

References

1. Auer, P., Cesa-Bianchi, N., Fischer, P.: Finite-time analysis of the multiarmed bandit problem. Mach. Learn. **47**(2–3), 235–256 (2002). https://doi.org/10.1023/A:1013689704352

2. Bacim, F., Ragan, E.D., Stinson, C., et al.: Collaborative navigation in virtual search and rescue. In: 2012 IEEE Symposium on 3D User Interfaces (3DUI), pp. 187–188. IEEE (2012)
3. Baker, C.L., Jara-Ettinger, J., Saxe, R., Tenenbaum, J.B.: Rational quantitative attribution of beliefs, desires and percepts in human mentalizing. Nat. Hum. Behav. **1**(4), 0064 (2017)
4. Beck, Z., Teacy, L., Rogers, A., Jennings, N.R.: In: AAMAS (2016)
5. Bellemare, M.G., Srinivasan, S., Ostrovski, G., Schaul, T., Saxton, D., Munos, R.: Unifying count-based exploration and intrinsic motivation, June 2016. arXiv preprint arXiv:1606.01868
6. Boers, Y., Driessen, H., Bagchi, A., Mandal, P.: Particle filter based entropy. In: 2010 13th Conference on Information Fusion (FUSION), pp. 1–8. IEEE (2010)
7. de Croon, G.: Adaptive active vision. Ph.D. thesis, Universiteit Maastricht (2008)
8. Demiris, Y.: Prediction of intent in robotics and multi-agent systems. Cog. Proc. **8**(3), 151–158 (2007)
9. Denzler, J., Brown, C.: Information theoretic sensor data selection for active object recognition and state estimation. IEEE TPAMI **24**(2), 145–157 (2002)
10. Friston, K., Rigoli, F., Ognibene, D., Mathys, C., Fitzgerald, T., Pezzulo, G.: Active inference and epistemic value. Cogn. Neurosci. **6**, 1–28 (2015)
11. Goldhoorn, A., Garrell, A., Alquezar, R., Sanfeliu, A.: Continuous real time POMCP to find-and-follow people by a humanoid service robot. In: Humanoids 2014. IEEE (2014)
12. Kaelbling, L., Littman, M., Cassandra, A.: Planning and acting in partially observable stochastic domains. Artif. Intell. **101**(1), 99–134 (1998)
13. Kruijff, T., Linder, P., Gianni, P., Pizzoli, S., Pianese, C.: Rescue robots at earthquake-hit mirandola, italy: a field report. In: IEEE Safety, Security, and Rescue Robotics (2012)
14. Lauri, M., Ritala, R.: Planning for robotic exploration based on forward simulation. Robot. Auton. Syst. **83**, 15–31 (2016)
15. Lee, K., Ognibene, D., Chang, H.J., Kim, T.K., Demiris, Y.: Stare: spatio-temporal attention relocation for multiple structured activities detection. In: IEEE Transactions on Image Processing, vol. 24, no. 12, pp. 5916–5927 (2015)
16. Mirolli, G.B.M. (ed.): Intrinsically Motivated Learning in Natural and Artificial Systems. Springer, Heidelberg (2014). https://doi.org/10.1007/978-3-642-32375-1
17. Ognibene, D., Baldassare, G.: Ecological active vision: four bioinspired principles to integrate bottom-up and adaptive top-down attention tested with a simple camera-arm robot. In: IEEE Transactions on Autonomous Mental Development, vol. 7, no. 1, pp. 3–25 (2015)
18. Ognibene, D., Chinellato, E., Sarabia, M., Demiris, Y.: Contextual action recognition and target localization with an active allocation of attention on a humanoid robot. Bioinspiration Biomimetics **8**(3), 035002 (2013)
19. Ognibene, D., Demiris, Y.: Towards active event recognition. In: IJCAI, vol. 2013 (2013)
20. Ognibene, D., Giglia, G., Marchegiani, L., Rudrauf, D.: Implicit perception simplicity and explicit perception complexity in sensorimotor comunication. Phys. Life Rev. **28**, 36–38 (2019)
21. Paletta, L., Fritz, G., Seifert, C.: Q-learning of sequential attention for visual object recognition from informative local descriptors. In: Proceedings ICML 2005, p. 656 (2005)

22. Pezzulo, G., Donnarumma, F., Dindo, H., et al.: The body talks: sensorimotor communication and its brain and kinematic signatures. Phys. Life Rev. **28**, 1–21 (2019)
23. Ramirez, M., Geffner, H.: Goal recognition over POMDPs: Inferring the intention of a POMDP agent. In: IJCAI, Barcelona (2011)
24. Ramirez, M., Geffner, H.: Plan recognition as planning. In: IJCAI (2009)
25. Shah, S., Dey, D., Lovett, C., Kapoor, A.: AirSim: high-fidelity visual and physical simulation for autonomous vehicles. In: Field and Service Robotics (2017)
26. Silver, D., Veness, J.: Monte-Carlo planning in large POMDPs. In: 24th Advances in Neural Information Processing Systems, NIPS 2010, pp. 2164–2172 (2010)
27. Sprague, N., Ballard, D.: Eye movements for reward maximization. In: Advances in Neural Information Processing Systems 16, Cambridge (2004)

Game Approaches and Applications to HRI

Playing Rock-Paper-Scissors with RASA: A Case Study on Intention Prediction in Human-Robot Interactive Games

Ehsan Ahmadi, Ali Ghorbandaei Pour, Alireza Siamy,
Alireza Taheri[(⊠)], and Ali Meghdari

Social and Cognitive Robotics Laboratory,
Sharif University of Technology, Tehran, Iran
{artaheri,meghdari}@sharif.edu

Abstract. Interaction quality improvement in a social robotic platform can be achieved through intention detection/prediction of the user. In this research, we tried to study the effect of intention prediction during a human-robot game scenario. We used our humanoid robotic platform, RASA. Rock-Paper-Scissors was chosen as our game scenario. In the first step, a Leap Motion sensor and a Multilayer Perceptron Neural Network is used to detect the hand gesture of the human-player. On the next level, in order to study the intention prediction's effect on our human-robot gaming platform, we implemented two different playing strategies for RASA. One of the strategies was to play randomly, while the other one used Markov Chain model, to predict the next move. Then 32 players with the ages between 20 to 35 were asked to play Rock-Paper-Scissors with RASA for 20 rounds in each strategy mode. Participants did not know about the difference in the robot's decision-making strategy in each mode and the intelligence of each strategy modes as well as the Acceptance/Attractiveness of the robotic gaming platform were assessed quantitatively through a questionnaire. Finally, paired T-tests indicated a significant difference between the random playing strategy and the other strategy predicting players' intention during the game.

Keywords: Social robots · Intention prediction · Markov chain · Neural network · Human-Robot interactive games

1 Introduction

Playing interactive games is considered as an entertainment or even sometimes as an educational tool. Due to the recent improvement in the field of social robotics, robots can also take parts in some interactive games. Considering the importance of interactive games, different computer games and robotic platforms have been developed, invented or specialized for different purposes like education [1], therapy [2, 3], and fashion industry [4]. The common assumption is that human players prefer to interact with robots in the same way that they interact with other human players during an interactive game [5]. In this regard, intention detection and the ability of predicting other players' decisions during a game play can be valuable [6–9]. In [6], Variable-Order Markov is

© Springer Nature Switzerland AG 2019
M. A. Salichs et al. (Eds.): ICSR 2019, LNAI 11876, pp. 347–357, 2019.
https://doi.org/10.1007/978-3-030-35888-4_32

used to build a probabilistic model that is able to use the historic behavior of gamers and to predict their next actions. In another recent study [7], a teaching-learning-prediction model is presented for a robot to predict human intentions using wearable sensing information. Dermy et al. [8] described their software for predicting the intention of a user physically interacting with the humanoid robot iCub.

During the recent years, Social and Cognitive Robotics Laboratory at Sharif University of Technology, Iran have focused on robotic platforms for individuals with special needs [10–12]. Currently, we are working on development of a social robot called RASA for educating children with hearing problems [13]. One of our goals is to develop a human-robot interactive gaming platform for RASA with the ability of predicting human players' next move. To this end, the well-known children's game "Rock-Paper-Scissors" (RPS) is chosen for RASA, since it is easy to play (human players do not need any tool or major training), and it can be played by a wide range of ages, and even by children with hearing problems. Due to the sequential nature, Rock-Paper-Scissors is not a completely random game and even for amateur players, the results from previous rounds are important in decision making process [14]. Some of the studies on intention detection in Rock-Paper-Scissors are based on analysis of physical or biometric data from the player [15, 16]. In these methods, prediction is not based on the history of the game. However, we would like to "predict" the player's intention based the previous rounds results. This might lead to a more pleasant game since there is always a chance for the player to defeat the robot, while it is not purely random.

This paper presents an initial attempt to have an interactive human-robot gaming platform for intention prediction studies on RASA. The platform used in this research, consists of a Leap Motion sensor to get the hand gestures of the player, then the players hand gesture is recognized through a Multilayer Perceptron Neural Network. Then, a Markov Chain model is used to predict players next hand gesture, and finally, RASA exerts the robot's reaction by implementing the proper hand gestures. Our hypothesis is: "using intention prediction during our gameplay with RASA would lead to a high socially acceptable human-robot interaction". In this regard, the acceptance and attractiveness of the setup, interaction quality during the game, and legitimacy of our hypothesis were assessed during a pilot study.

2   Robotic System

2.1   Leap Motion Controller

In this study, we have used Leap Motion Controller as an input device to capture human hands gestures. The effective range of the Leap Motion Controller approximately is a spherical cap with radius of 600 mm above the center of the device with a field of view of about 150° [17]. Leap Motion Controller tracks hands and arms and distinguishes right hand from left hand. In addition, it measures and computes the position and orientation of the palm, distance between finger bones' joints, and the direction of each bone in fingers and the position of the fingertips of the hand for each frame. The sensor's software development kit assumes 4 bones in each finger. The beginning and the end point position of each bone is available.

2.2   RASA, the Humanoid Robot

We have used on of our robotic platforms called RASA as our humanoid robot for the HRI procedure. RASA is designed and manufactured in the Center of Excellence in Design, Robotics, and Automation (CEDRA) at Sharif University of Technology [13]. RASA is 110 cm tall and has 32° of freedom (DOF). There are 13 DOFs in each arm, and 3 DOFs in the neck of the robot. Using a display screen as the face for facial expression make the interactions richer. Figure 1 shows RASA and its hand gestures.

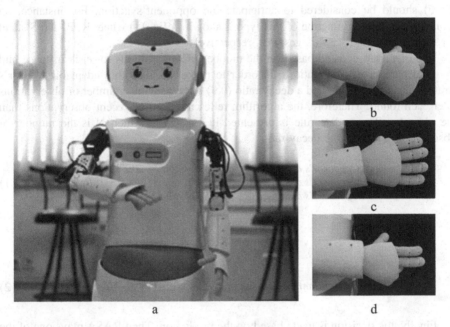

Fig. 1. (a) RASA humanoid robot. (b) rock sign, (c) paper sign, and (d) scissors sign represented by RASA respectively.

3   Methodology

3.1   Hand Gesture Recognition Using Artificial Neural Network

A Multi-Layer Perceptron (MLP) neural network is used to classify the rock, paper, and scissors gestures from the raw data which is captured by the Leap Motion Controller. The MLP takes 14-element input vector fully connected to 5 neurons at the first layer with ReLU activation function, and has 3 neurons with sigmoid activation functions at the last layer. To train the MLP, an inclusive training dataset including 450 features vectors is gathered. Each features vector contains 14 inner products of normalized direction of successive bones of each finger.

3.2   Intention Prediction Algorithm

As a robot, to win a sequential game with arbitrary choices like Rock-Paper-Scissor in a fare game without cheating, the robot needs to analyses the history of human's actions for predicting his/her next action. To this end, we used the Markov Chain model [18] as a stochastic tool to predict the human's next action. If the probabilities of all actions are equal, the next action will be taken using a uniform random distribution; for example, this state occurs at the first round where the robot have no history of the opponent's behavior.

State of the game at each round is a tuple of robot's action and the user's action. Since there are three states for each action, it is obvious that the total number of possible states are 9. Therefore, 9 discrete probability distribution functions (PDF) should be considered to anticipate the opponent's action. For instance, an arbitrary distribution function of this type is shown in Eq. (1) where R, P, and S stand for rock, paper, and scissors gestures, respectively.

The PDFs are updated based on the number of observations for each instance and the total number of observations. In order to make the algorithm adaptable to user's strategy changes, we applied a decay ratio (0.9) to all previous number of observations after each round. Therefore, the algorithm relies more on its recent observations than the old ones. The update rule is presented in Eq. (2) in which N is the number of observations and e is the decay ratio.

$$
\begin{aligned}
P(\text{Opponent's action} &= \text{``}P\text{''} \mid \text{previous state} = \text{``}PS\text{''}) = 0.4 \\
P(\text{Opponent's action} &= \text{``}S\text{''} \mid \text{previous state} = \text{``}PS\text{''}) = 0.1 \\
P(\text{Opponent's action} &= \text{``}R\text{''} \mid \text{previous state} = \text{``}PS\text{''}) = 0.5
\end{aligned}
\tag{1}
$$

$$
N_i^{new} = e \times N_i^{old} + N_i^{last}
$$

$$
P(\text{Opponent's action} \mid \text{previous state}) = \frac{N_i}{\sum_{i=1}^{3} N_i}
\tag{2}
$$

Finally, the decision is made based on the prediction. Then RASA plays one of the pre-recorded hand gestures of the type: rock, paper, or scissors. Since the mechanical response of the robot is slower than the user's, the chosen gesture is shown on a screen to insure the opponent that the action is generated spontaneously and RASA is not cheating.

3.3   Experimental Setup and Participants

Each participant was asked to play the Rock-Paper-Scissors game with the robot in two modes after a short introduction presented by the RASA robot about the game session and rules. The two mentioned modes (including "mode a" and "mode b") referred to the robot's strategies in making decisions in replying the participants. In "mode a", the robot uses the random strategy in selecting/showing its actions; while in "mode b", RASA made decisions and performed the game based on the presented Markov Chain model. Half of the subjects were randomly selected to play "mode a" first, and then "mode b", and the other half did vice versa (i.e. counterbalanced condition). It should be noted that the participants were not informed of the robot's exact strategy/technique for its decision making during each mode and they were just told when each mode finished; instead, a questionnaire was provided to ask the subjects to rate and compare the possible differences between the robot's two strategies in playing the game. The number of the rounds in each mode was 20 and the whole process for each participant took about 10 min. The game sessions were held at the Social and Cognitive Robotics Lab., Sharif University of Technology, Iran.

We invited 32 participants (22 males and 10 females) to take part in playing the Rock-Paper-Scissors game with the RASA robot. The mean age and standard deviation of the subjects were 27 and 5 years, respectively.

3.4   Assessment Tool

We provided the following questionnaire (Table 1) and asked the subjects to fill in it after the game session. Based on the results observed during the games (e.g. the number of robot's wins, draws, and loses) in modes a and b, and the participants viewpoints, it is studied whether there is a significant difference between the performance of the robot in the random and Markov Chain-based strategy and a possible correlation between the questionnaire results and the robot's performances.

Table 1. The questionnaire provided in this study to collect the participants' viewpoints regarding the robot's performance.

Overall Viewpoints about the HRI game		
No.	Questions	Answer: 1 2 3 4 5
1	I find the robotic-assisted game pleasant	
2	I find the robot enjoyable	
3	How understandable was the actions of the RASA robot during the RPS game?	
4	I believe that the time duration of the game was unusual. *(inverse question)*	
5	In each of the game's round, I tried to beat the robot	

Comparison Questions		
No.	Questions	1st Mode: 1 2 3 4 5	2nd Mode: 1 2 3 4 5
6	How intelligent was the robot's decisions in playing the Rock- Paper- Scissors game?		
7	Which algorithm do you prefer to be used by the robot to continue playing the game?	*First or Second?*	

4   Results and Discussion

4.1   Hand Gesture Recognition Results

In the training phase of the neural network for hand gesture recognition, we used 80% of our training data set for the training procedure and the remaining as our test data. We used K-fold cross-validation of 10 for the training dataset in the training process. The training method was Adam algorithm which is based on the Stochastic Gradient Descent (SGD). We indicated that the gesture recognition's result for this network on its test data was 93% and the standard deviation was 11% which is fairly admissible to be used in our experimental conditions. Now, the MLP is ready to be used in the RPS game operation as the gesture recognition algorithm. The outputs of the MLP would send to the next stage (i.e. the prediction algorithm) as an input. It should be noted that regarding the recognition of hand gestures, although the presented algorithm could handle the situations of this study, for real life applications, perhaps more robust and real-time hand gesture detection is needed which is investigated in [19].

4.2   Human-Robot Interaction Results

A sample snapshot of the designed HRI game is shown in Fig. 2a. We consider the points +1, 0, and −1 for the win, draw, and lost situations in each round, respectively. Therefore, we can define the "score" parameter in each set to be the number of robot's wins minus the number of its losses. The positive, zero, and negative scores are equivalent to the robot's overall performance of win, draw, and lost. One may interest to see different details of each rounds' results for the both used algorithms; however, considering that there is not enough room to present all of the figures in this paper, we selected three graphs which is described in the following.

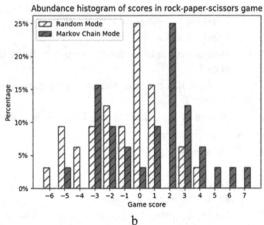

a   b

Fig. 2.   (a) The RASA robot during the RPS game. (b) The histogram of the robot's scores in the Markov Chain mode and random mode (positive, zero, and negative game scores indicate the robot's wins, draws, and losses, respectively).

As the first graph of the robot's performance during the game sessions, Fig. 2b shows the histogram of the robot's scores in this study in both modes. By performing paired T-tests (Table 2) on the observed results in the two modes, it is indicated that in the current situation of this study (i.e. the number of participants and the small sample set of games), the robot's mean scores as well as its overall results in the Markov Chain mode are significantly higher than the random mode (p-values < 0.05) which shows that the robot became a smarter opponent in mode b which makes the HRI more appealing. As it can be seen in Fig. 2b, in 16 out of 32 sets, the participants beat the robot with the random strategy. The most frequent observed result in the random mode is the score of zero (i.e. the overall result of draw) and interestingly, it seems that the random mode's bar graphs somewhat looks like a normal distribution around zero which is the most likely prediction come to mind due to the random nature of the used algorithm. On the other hand, our participants could not easily beat the robot during the Markov Chain mode and in 21 out of 32 games (66%), they lost the game to RASA. An interesting observation in this study was that only in 5 out of 32 performed pair games, the overall results of the random strategy is higher than the smart strategy (e.g. for participant #6, the random strategy drew while the smart strategy lost the game to the human opponent).

Table 2. The results of the paired T-tests on the robot's scores (i.e. mode a verses mode b).

Item *(possible range)*	Mean *(SD)*		T-Value	P-Value
	Markov Chain-based strategy	Random strategy		
Score *(−20 to 20)*	1.09 (2.82)	−0.81 (2.66)	2.78	**0.007**
Overall Result *(−1 to 1)*	0.375 (0.907)	−0.219 (0.870)	2.67	**0.010**

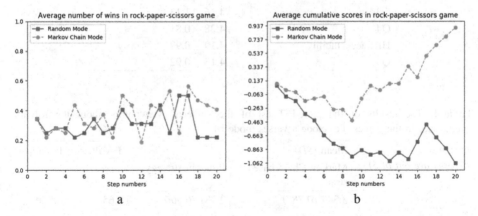

Fig. 3. The histogram of the robot's scores in the Markov Chain mode and random mode (positive, zero, and negative game scores indicate the robot's wins, draws, and losses, respectively).

In Fig. 3a, the average number of the wins for the robot in each round are presented for both modes. Qualitatively, we can observe that in the second half of the games (i.e. rounds 11–20), the difference between the average scores of the robot in the smart mode and the equivalent number in the random mode is higher than the similar difference in the first half of the game. We believe that this probably happened due to the ability of the Markov Chain model in intention prediction of the users based on the history of their movements and the model performed more powerful as the rounds continued and its database got richer. In Fig. 3b, another perspective of the mentioned observation is presented. It can be seen that during our experiments, the average cumulative scores of the Markov Chain model has approached the mean score of +1 (robot's win) while the equivalent number for the random mode has tended to −1 (robot's lost). While it may not been considered as a big difference between the strategies' performance, it can show us that the robot is a stronger/smarter opponent when it uses Markov Chain strategy.

Regarding the participants' viewpoints of the robot-assisted interactive game, the results of the filled questionnaire are presented in Table 3. As a preliminary estimate of the developed HRI's acceptability, the mean average of Questions #1 to #4 is 4.19 out of 5 which indicates that the developed HRI was highly acceptable and enjoyable for the users while they involved in doing the game's tasks quite serious (Question #5). The overall Cronbach's alpha (Q1–Q4) is the acceptable value of 0.74 while each Cronbach's alpha regarding Q1 to Q4 are 0.60, 0.62, 0.67, and 0.79, respectively.

Table 3. The mean and standard deviation (SD) of Questions #1 to #5 of the assessment tool.

Question # *(Scores are out of 5)*	Mean	Standard deviation
Q1	3.84	1.06
Q2	4.47	0.84
Q3	4.16	1.13
Q4	4.28	0.81
HRI acceptability	**4.19**	**0.99**
Q5	4.13	0.92

Table 4. The results of the paired T-test of the subjects' viewpoints about the robot's intelligence in the games (i.e. mode a verses mode b).

Question # *(Scores are out of 5)*	Mean *(SD)*		T-Value	P-Value
	Markov Chain-based strategy	Random strategy		
Q6	3.344 *(0.787)*	2.781 *(0.906)*	2.65	**0.010**

In order to investigate whether there is a significant difference between the participants' viewpoints about the robot's intelligence during each game mode, a paired T-test was conducted on the results of Question #6 (in "mode a" and "mode b"). As it is shown in Table 4, the p-value is less than 0.05 which means that regarding the subjects' opinions in our experiments, the mean score of the robot's intelligence in the Markov Chain-based algorithm was significantly higher than the random strategy mode. Without having a previous knowledge about the used strategies, the participants sensed that the performance of the robot in one mode is more intelligent than the other mode. This finding alongside the other questions' scores is also in line with the confirmation of the hypothesis of this study that intention prediction in playing Rock-Paper-Scissors makes the robot quite attractive, intelligent, and even a stronger opponent for the users which would lead to a more socially acceptable HRI. Finally, after calculating the correlations between the robot's scores and the results of Question #6, we observed that the Pearson coefficient (r) is 0.34 (p-value = 0.006) which indicates a positive correlation between the participants' viewpoints of the robot's intelligence and the scores they got in the games. As it is mentioned, the real aim of using intention prediction is to improve human-robot game playing more natural and pleasurable. We believe that this is doable when the robot is also trying to predict the opponent's next move as other people do. It should be noted that intention prediction does not lead an opponent who always wins. As in [20], it is shown that loosing at times on purpose increases engagement of children and makes educational tasks more fun. Due to the combinatorial random-strategic nature of the RPS game, both of the players have appropriate chance to win the game and using the prediction strategies by the robot does not guarantee the robot's win.

5   Conclusion

In this paper, we presented a social robotic setup to play Rock-Paper-Scissors while the robot is trying to predict the intention of its opponent during the gameplay. Although RPS is not considered as a solved game, the analysis of the results from previous rounds can improve the chance of winning. We had two strategies ahead, one was playing randomly and the other was using an algorithm for player's intention prediction. Among different intention prediction methods, we used a probabilistic model (Markov Chain) using the results from gameplay history for prediction. Nonetheless, this also leave an acceptable chance for the opponent to win the robot. Our assumption was that playing with a platform equipped to intention prediction system can be highly enjoyable. In the prediction module, a Markov Chain model is implemented to memorize the information about transitions of game states. Each game state contains both the actions of the user and the robot at every round. After conduction experimental tests with 32 persons, the results coming from both the gameplay scores and the surveys shows that Markov Chain based strategy reaches reasonable high rate of wins comparing to the random strategy. The results also revealed that participants attribute high scores in smartness, attractiveness, and acceptance of the robot who is equipped to a smart algorithm.

As the main limitation of this study, the combinatorial random-strategic nature of the RPS game makes it difficult to make big/strong claims about the findings of this study; and generalizing them to the other situations needs recruiting more participants and performing more rounds in the games in future studies. In addition, other prediction approaches such as learning based, or ensemble methods could be implemented on the robot to evaluate their effectiveness. Moreover, it can be mentioned that in normal communication, the task is not that always well-defined; i.e. the intention prediction cannot be made by getting real-life sequences of the 3 gestures that are used in RPS. There are various adversarial games which could be selected as a case study to investigate other dimensions of intention detection in human-robot games.

Acknowledgement. This research was supported by the "Dr. Ali Akbar Siasi Research Grant Award". We also appreciate the Iranian National Science Foundation (INSF) for their complementary support of the Social & Cognitive Robotics Laboratory (http://en.insf.org/).

References

1. Belpaeme, T., Kennedy, J., Ramachandran, A., Scassellati, B., Tanaka, F.: Social robots for education: a review. Sci. Robot. **3**(21), 5954 (2018)
2. Alhaddad, A.Y., Javed, H., Connor, O., Banire, B., Al Thani, D., Cabibihan, J.J.: Robotic trains as an educational and therapeutic tool for autism spectrum disorder intervention. In: International Conference on Robotics and Education RiE 2017, pp. 249–262. Springer, Cham (2018). https://doi.org/10.1007/978-3-319-97085-1_25
3. Taheri, A., Meghdari, A., Alemi, M., Pouretemad, H.R.: Clinical interventions of social humanoid robots in the treatment of a pair of high-and low-functioning autistic Iranian twins. Scientia Iranica. Trans. B Mech. Eng. **25**(3), 1197–1214 (2018)
4. Alemi, M., et al.: RoMa: a hi-tech robotic mannequin for the fashion industry. In: International Conference on Social Robotics. ICSR 2017. LNCS, pp. 209–219. Springer, Cham (2017). https://doi.org/10.1007/978-3-319-70022-9_21
5. Taheri, A., et al.: Virtual social toys: a novel concept to bring inanimate dolls to life. In: Ge, S.S., Cabibihan, J.-J., Salichs, Miguel A., Broadbent, E., He, H., Wagner, Alan R., Castro-González, Á. (eds.) ICSR 2018. LNCS (LNAI), vol. 11357, pp. 286–296. Springer, Cham (2018). https://doi.org/10.1007/978-3-030-05204-1_28
6. Baldominos Gómez, A., Albacete García, E., Marrero, I., Saez Achaerandio, Y.: Real-time prediction of gamers behavior using variable order Markov and big data technology: a case of study (2016)
7. Wang, W., Li, R., Chen, Y., Jia, Y.: Human intention prediction in human-robot collaborative tasks. In: Companion of the 2018 ACM/IEEE International Conference on Human-Robot Interaction, pp. 279–280. ACM, March 2018
8. Dermy, O., Paraschos, A., Ewerton, M., Peters, J., Charpillet, F., Ivaldi, S.: Prediction of intention during interaction with iCub with probabilistic movement primitives. Front. Robot. AI **4**, 45 (2017)
9. Dermy, O., Charpillet, F., Ivaldi, S.: Multi-modal intention prediction with probabilistic movement primitives. In: Human Friendly Robotics, pp. 181–196. Springer, Cham (2019). https://doi.org/10.1007/978-3-319-89327-3_14
10. Taheri, A., Meghdari, A., Alemi, M., Pouretemad, H.: Teaching music to children with autism: a social robotics challenge. Sci. Iranica **26**(1), 40–58 (2019)
11. Meghdari, A., Alemi, M., Pour, A.G., Taheri, A.: Spontaneous human-robot emotional interaction through facial expressions. In: International Conference on Social Robotics, pp. 351–361. Springer, Cham (2016). https://doi.org/10.1007/978-3-319-47437-3_34
12. Meghdari, A., Behzadipour, S., Abedi, M.: Employing a novel Gait pattern generator on a social humanoid robot. Sci. Iranica **26**, 2154–2166 (2019). https://doi.org/10.24200/sci.2019.21358. (Special Issue Dedicated to Professor Abolhassan Vafai)

13. Zakipour, M., Meghdari, A., Alemi, M.: *RASA*: a low-cost upper-torso social robot acting as a sign language teaching assistant. In: Agah, A., Cabibihan, J.-J., Howard, A.M., Salichs, Miguel A., He, H. (eds.) ICSR 2016. LNCS (LNAI), vol. 9979, pp. 630–639. Springer, Cham (2016). https://doi.org/10.1007/978-3-319-47437-3_62
14. Walker, D., Walker, G.: The official rock paper scissors strategy guide. Simon and Schuster (2004)
15. Jang, G., Choi, Y., Qu, Z.: Rock-paper-scissors prediction experiments using muscle activations. In: 2012 IEEE/RSJ International Conference on Intelligent Robots and Systems, pp. 5133–5134. IEEE (2012)
16. Katsuki, Y., Yamakawa, Y., Ishikawa, M.: High-speed human/robot hand interaction system. In: Proceedings of the Tenth Annual ACM/IEEE International Conference on Human-Robot Interaction Extended Abstracts, pp. 117–118. ACM (March 2015)
17. Weichert, F., Bachmann, D., Rudak, B., Fisseler, D.: Analysis of the accuracy and robustness of the leap motion controller. Sensors **13**(5), 6380–6393 (2013)
18. Rozanov, Y.A.: Markov random fields. In: Rozanov, Y.A. (ed.) Markov Random Fields, pp. 55–102. Springer, New York (1982). https://doi.org/10.1007/978-1-4613-8190-7_2
19. Betancourt, A., Morerio, P., Marcenaro, L., Barakova, E., Rauterberg, M., Regazzoni, C.: Towards a unified framework for hand-based methods in first person vision. In: 2015 IEEE International Conference on Multimedia & Expo Workshops (ICMEW), pp. 1–6. IEEE, June 2015
20. Barakova, E.I., De Haas, M., Kuijpers, W., Irigoyen, N., Betancourt, A.: Socially grounded game strategy enhances bonding and perceived smartness of a humanoid robot. Connection Sci. **30**(1), 81–98 (2018)

Virtual or Physical? Social Robots Teaching a Fictional Language Through a Role-Playing Game Inspired by *Game of Thrones*

Hassan Ali, Shreyans Bhansali, Ilay Köksal, Matthias Möller,
Theresa Pekarek-Rosin, Sachin Sharma, Ann-Katrin Thebille, Julian Tobergte,
Sören Hübner, Aleksej Logacjov, Ozan Özdemir, Jose Rodriguez Parra,
Mariela Sanchez, Nambiar Shruti Surendrakumar, Tayfun Alpay[✉],
Sascha Griffiths, Stefan Heinrich, Erik Strahl, Cornelius Weber,
and Stefan Wermter

Knowledge Technology, Department of Informatics, Universität Hamburg,
Vogt-Kölln-Str. 30, 22527 Hamburg, Germany
`PHRI1819-extended@informatik.uni-hamburg.de`

Abstract. In recent years, there has been an increased interest in the role of social agents as language teachers. Our experiment was designed to investigate whether a physical agent in form of a social robot provides a better language-learning experience than a virtual agent. We evaluated the interactions regarding enjoyment, immersion, and vocabulary retention. The 55 participants who took part in our study learned 5 phrases of the fictional language *High Valyrian* from the TV show *Game of Thrones*. For the evaluation, questions from the Almere model, the Godspeed questionnaire and the User Engagement Scale were used as well as a number of custom questions. Our findings include statistically significant results regarding enjoyment ($p = 0.008$) and immersion ($p = 0.023$) for participants with little or no prior experience with social robots. In addition, we found that the participants were able to retain the *High Valyrian* phrases equally well for both conditions.

Keywords: Language learning · Social robot · Virtual agent ·
Role-play · Fictional language

1 Introduction

Research into technology-enhanced language learning has shown that technology can facilitate communication, reduce anxiety, encourage discussions and lead to an overall increase in learning motivation [1]. However, the effectiveness of language teaching is often dependent on the ability to raise and maintain the interest and enthusiasm of the student, which is easier with a teacher conducting the lessons [2]. Therefore, an embodied agent, for instance a robot, may positively influence how people learn.

© Springer Nature Switzerland AG 2019
M. A. Salichs et al. (Eds.): ICSR 2019, LNAI 11876, pp. 358–367, 2019.
https://doi.org/10.1007/978-3-030-35888-4_33

In our research, we aim to investigate the impact of having a social robot as a language teacher. We conducted a user study which directly compared interacting with a robot and a virtual agent of the same appearance and capabilities. Seeing how most people are already accustomed to learning a language with the aid of technology, the virtual agent, which is a virtual version of the robot on a screen, is necessary to measure the effect of the physical agent. We focused on three hypotheses:

1. People enjoy interacting with a physical agent more than with a virtual agent.
2. People have a more immersive interaction with a physical agent than with a virtual agent in a role-playing scenario.
3. People learn better when interacting with a physical agent than with a virtual agent.

Since role-playing is an often deployed and well-received method in language teaching to facilitate engagement [3], we decided to model our interaction in the frame of a role-playing scenario as well. We decided on teaching a fictional language to eliminate any bias caused by prior knowledge of the language in international study participants. The fictional language of our choice was *High Valyrian* from the TV show *Game of Thrones*, which currently boasts over 1 million learners on the language learning platform *Duolingo*[1], making it more popular than naturally evolved languages like Hawaiian (537k learners) or Navajo (311k learners).

2   Social Agents as Second Language Teachers

Human-Robot Interaction (HRI) experiments, which revolve around teaching a language, often benefit from using artificial languages. *Toki Pona* is an artificial language with a small vocabulary size (~120 words), which was taught to children between the ages of ten and eleven through a dialogue-based interaction with the iCat social robot [4]. Especially in international environments where almost every language could potentially be spoken, creating or using an existing artificial language not only limits bias but also minimizes ambiguity in natural language understanding [5]. We decided on teaching the language *High Valyrian*, which was originally created for the *A Song of Ice and Fire* fantasy book series written by George R. R. Martin and further developed in the context of the famous television series *Game of Thrones*. In addition to the benefits of any fictional language (e.g. similarity to revitalized languages like Hebrew or constructed languages like Esperanto [6]), our intention with selecting *High Valyrian* was using the popularity and interest surrounding the start of the final season of the show to recruit a large number of participants.

One major advantage of one-on-one tutoring is the possible adaptation to the skills of a student by the teacher. A study on the effective role of teachers revealed that enjoyment is highly related to the classroom practices, engaging the

---

[1] https://www.duolingo.com/courses (accessed 21/08/2019).

students, and a positive attitude [7]. The effect of a personalized experience with a social agent in language tutoring scenarios has been explored in studies like [8], where an adaptive response algorithm provided children (three to five years old) with tailored verbal and non-verbal feedback. Even though no significant difference was recorded in regard to learning gains, the long-term valence showed a significant difference in favor of the personalized robot. Thus, we designed our social agent with a focus on facilitating enjoyment and enthusiasm in the adult learner, while providing a personalized learning experience. Additionally, the physical presence of a robot tutor has been shown to have a positive influence on the cognitive learning gains of participants in a game-play scenario [10].

In addition to the teacher's behavior, the setting also plays an important role in learning a foreign language. It has been shown that the use of games, more specifically role-playing games, in language education supports communication and social interaction due to an increase in immersion [3,9]. To improve the learning experience in our study, we designed a role-playing scenario which was simple enough to be easily explained to participants unfamiliar with *Game of Thrones* while still capturing the spirit of the show.

3   Methodology

For our study, we used the Neuro-Inspired COmpanion (NICO), which is a humanoid robot developed at the University of Hamburg as a novel open-source neuro-cognitive research platform [11]. It is equipped with sensors, motors, stereo cameras, and facial expression capabilities to feature human-like perception and interaction. For the sake of the experiment, a virtual version of NICO was built using the Godot[2] game engine. With the thought of unifying the two experimental conditions, the appearance, dialogue, and non-verbal communication of the virtual NICO were designed to be as identical to the physical robot as possible (Fig. 1). The participant can interact with the virtual NICO via external speakers, a mouse, an external microphone, and a screen-mounted camera. Grasping real objects (either a bottle or a cup) to present them to the agent was substituted by moving a mouse pointer to the virtual object and clicking it.

3.1   Proposed System

In our experiment, the participant interacts with the social agent mainly through spoken dialogue. Each interactive session with the social agent follows a typical three-phase design [12]:

1. **Presentation:** The participant is welcomed to the role-playing scenario, in which they play an ambassador who is being prepared for a meeting with the Khaleesi[3] by her counselor NICO.

---

[2] https://godotengine.org/ (accessed 21/08/2019).
[3] A popular character from *Game of Thrones* speaking *High Valyrian*.

Fig. 1. Experimental setup of the two conditions: the physical robot on the left and virtual agent on the right. Participants sit at the table in front of the respective agent.

2. **Practice**: 5 phrases consisting of greeting, introduction, presenting two objects (a wine bottle and a golden cup) as gifts to the Khaleesi, and farewell are taught utilizing a simple version of spaced repetition.
3. **Production**: As a final step of the preparation, NICO pretends to be the Khaleesi in order to practice for the imminent meeting. The participant is prompted to recall the taught phrases to test their retention.

The moment the participant steps into the experiment room, the role-playing scenario is initiated and NICO stays in character throughout the whole interaction. We dressed both the physical robot and the virtual agent in the appropriate style for *Game of Thrones* (Fig. 1). NICO plays a counselor to the Khaleesi, teaching the participant the *High Valyrian* phrases necessary to navigate the court as an ambassador from a distant land, who might not know the proper etiquette and protocol.

The conversation is modeled through a Hierarchical State Machine control architecture using SMACH[4] for the internal structure and ROS[5] for communicating data. For a lively and human-like experience, the system is enhanced by features like gestures, face tracking, pointing at objects, and object manipulation. Figure 2 shows a snippet of the state machine when teaching the name of an object in the practice phase. The depicted states are repeated for each phrase (Table 1) and define the interaction flow.

Phrases spoken by NICO are generated with a speech synthesizer built using Amazon Polly[6]. The Text-to-Speech system supports monolingual (only English or *High Valyrian*) and bilingual (mixed) phrases. To recognize the participant's utterances of *High Valyrian*, an Automatic Speech Recognition (ASR) system has been built on top of DOCKS [13]. The system achieved a precision of 0.81, a recall rate of 0.66, and an F1 score of 0.73.

---

[4] http://wiki.ros.org/smach (accessed 21/08/2019).
[5] http://www.ros.org/ (accessed 21/08/2019).
[6] https://aws.amazon.com/polly/ (accessed 21/08/2019).

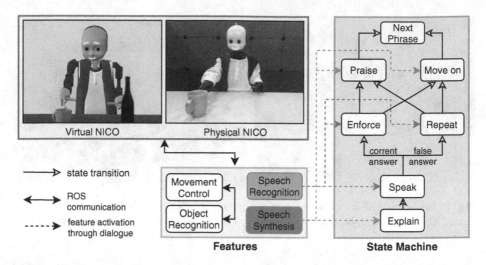

Fig. 2. The interaction flow while teaching an object name in the practice phase. The red and blue arrows show in which states speech recognition or speech synthesis is used. (1) NICO says the phrase ("Explain") and points at the object. (2) The participant repeats it ("Speak"). (3) The "Enforce" state ensures an equal number of repetitions among all participants. (4) NICO provides motivational feedback depending on the correctness of the participant's answer ("Praise"\"Move on") before proceeding to the next phrase. (Color figure online)

Table 1. The *High Valyrian* phrases taught during the interaction with their English translation. *: shortened from "Mother of Dragons", one of the titles for the Khaleesi in the show. **: translates as "coming from the waves", the title given to the participant.

Rytsas, mhysa.	Iksan pelone.	Averilla\Aeksion maghan.	Ilas daria.
Hello, mother*.	I am pelone**.	I bring wine\a golden cup.	Farewell, my queen.

To achieve an immersive conversation, NICO has to be able to show awareness to the surroundings and interact with them. For example, NICO should be able to look and point at an object simultaneously when teaching its name (Fig. 2). To be able to perform such gestures, NICO needs to be able to detect the positions of the objects on the table in front of it. While the object has a fixed position in the virtual environment, Darknet CNN (YOLOv3-416) [14] is used to detect the objects for the physical robot. The positions are then mapped to the closest match in a previously recorded data set in order to efficiently generate correct joint movements.

3.2 Experimental Procedure

59 participants, recruited through flyers around town and the University of Hamburg, took part in the experiment, of which 4 samples had to be excluded due

to their insufficient English skills, leaving a total of 55 participants (21 female, 34 male). 70.9% reported little or no prior experience with social robots, while 76.4% had used a language learning application before. Before the experiment, 63.7% reported being comfortable with the idea of interacting with a robot in an educational context. The majority of the participants were native German speakers between the ages of 18 and 29.

The experimental procedure consisted of two interactions, one with the physical and one with the virtual NICO, as part of a within-subject design, with a number of questionnaires in between. The informed consent of each participant was acquired before the start of the experiment. First, they were asked to fill out a questionnaire inquiring their experience with language learning applications, social robots, and their preference regarding real or virtual teachers in a language learning context. The order of the interaction with the two agents was randomized for each participant while keeping an equal number of samples for each condition.

After each interaction, the participants were asked to fill in a questionnaire which was composed of (1) the Godspeed questionnaire [15], measuring anthropomorphism, animacy, likeability, perceived intelligence, and perceived safety, (2) the perceived enjoyment and usefulness scale of the Almere Model [16], and (3) the User Engagement Scale (UES) [17] which measures perceived usability, aesthetic appeal and focused attention. An additional post-experiment questionnaire contained some demographic questions regarding age, gender, the participant's familiarity with the role-playing scenario, and lastly, their preference for one of the two conditions. Afterward, we briefly interviewed each participant to gain further insight into the reasons behind their preference of one agent over the other.

While NICO itself interacted autonomously with the participants, the interaction was supervised by two researchers hidden behind a wall, who were responsible for evaluating the accuracy of the ASR system and, in case of system errors, operated a Wizard of Oz interface for a seamless flow of the experiment. It was generally triggered due to microphone failures caused by noise and unintelligible speech (coughing, sneezing, etc.) with a failure rate of 3.6% per condition.

4   Results

According to our hypotheses we expect (1) increased enjoyment, (2) increased learnability and (3) increased immersion when interacting with the physical agent. For the evaluation of the results of the 5-point semantic differential scales of the Godspeed questionnaires and the 5-point Likert scales of the Almere Model and the UES, a Mann-Whitney-U test was used with an expected α value of 0.05.

4.1   User Experience

While the results of the Godspeed questionnaires proved to be partially inconclusive for our pool of participants, we found statistically significant results

$(p < 0.05)$ for both enjoyment and immersion in the subgroup of participants, who had no or little prior experience with social robots $(n = 39)$.

Enjoyment: Comparing the score of the perceived enjoyment scale of the Almere model shows that participants with little or no experience with robots experienced higher enjoyment while interacting with the robot. They perceive the robot as more enjoyable, more fascinating and less boring than the virtual agent. There was no significant difference in the perceived usefulness of the agents (Table 2), even though the virtual agent scored slightly higher in that regard.

Table 2. The individual items of the Perceived Enjoyment scale. For the subgroup of participants with no or little prior experience with robots $(n = 39)$, the analysis of the Perceived Enjoyment scale of the Almere model shows a significantly higher mean for the robot $(p < 0.05)$. While the Virtual Agent scores higher in regard to Perceived Usefulness, the difference is not statistically significant. *: reverse-scored.

Item (Almere)	Robot	Virtual	p
Enjoyable	3.95 ± 0.89	3.53 ± 0.86	0.014
Fascinating	4.05 ± 0.86	3.28 ± 0.99	<0.001
Boring*	4.26 ± 0.79	3.69 ± 1.10	0.011

Scale (Almere)	Robot	Virtual	p
Perceived Enjoyment	3.80 ± 0.75	3.41 ± 0.71	0.008
Perceived Usefulness	3.00 ± 1.00	3.09 ± 0.88	0.379

For the entire pool of participants $(n = 55)$, the Godspeed questionnaires showed a significant difference in anthropomorphism $(p = 0.03)$ and a tendency of animacy $(p = 0.08)$ in favor of the robot, especially for the participants who interacted with the robot after interacting with the virtual agent. Regarding the likeability, perceived intelligence and perceived safety of the two agents, no significant differences $(p > 0.05)$ could be discerned, which indicates that both agents were perceived as equally likeable $(M_R = 4.03 \pm 0.83, M_V = 4.01 \pm 0.63)$, and competent $(M_R = 3.57 \pm 0.63, M_V = 3.61 \pm 0.55)$. Participants felt equally safe $(M_R = 2.33 \pm 1.04, M_V = 2.44 \pm 0.91)$ regardless of the observed condition. In general, the robot seems to be perceived as more enjoyable and people seem to be more willing to attribute human-like qualities to the physical NICO.

Regardless of the condition, the second interaction was enjoyed less by the participants, with a measurable decrease in the perceived likeability $(p = 0.038)$, friendliness $(p = 0.009)$, and kindness $(p = 0.003)$ of the agent. This could be linked to a growing familiarity, as anxiety $(p = 0.003)$, agitation $(p < 0.001)$, surprise $(p < 0.001)$ and confusion $(p = 0.023)$ also decreased for the second interaction. The fact that the enjoyment decreased regardless of the condition shows that a similar enough design was accomplished.

Immersion: The results of the user engagement scale (UES) show that the robot was generally perceived as more aesthetically appealing ($p = 0.012$) than the virtual agent, while there was no measurable difference for Focused Attention, Perceived Usability, and Reward Factor ($p > 0.05$). However, participants with little or no experience with robots ($n = 39$) were more immersed and therefore more attentive while interacting with the robot. They also found the robot more appealing (Table 3). The subgroup of participants who were familiar with *Game of Thrones* ($n = 23$), more frequently "lost themselves in the experience" when interacting with the robot ($p = 0.03$), tended to find the robot more "aesthetically appealing" ($p = 0.09$) and more "appealing to the senses" ($p = 0.03$). They were in agreement that the experiment and the subsequent role-playing scenario fit the series well.

Table 3. The subgroup of participants familiar with *Game of Thrones* ($n = 23$) more frequently "lost themselves in the experience" while interacting with the robot. Participants with minimal experience with robots ($n = 39$) perceived the robot as more attentive, aesthetically appealing and the interaction as more rewarding.

Item (UES)	Robot	Virtual	p
Lost themselves	3.17 ± 0.65	2.70 ± 0.93	0.035
Aesthetically appealing	2.70 ± 1.11	2.26 ± 0.86	0.090
Appealing to the senses	3.17 ± 1.07	2.70 ± 0.82	0.034

Scale (UES)	Robot	Virtual	p
Focused Attention	3.50 ± 0.89	3.12 ± 0.96	0.023
Perceived Usability	2.79 ± 0.93	2.79 ± 0.81	0.500
Aesthetic Appeal	3.04 ± 0.88	2.62 ± 0.90	0.017
Reward Factor	3.92 ± 0.71	3.63 ± 0.92	0.088

4.2   Language Retention

While there was only little difference in the retention rate after the first interaction with both the robot (48.5%) and the virtual agent (43.9%), participants on average were able to recall more phrases with the use of the hint system ($R = 34.6\%$, $V = 30.7\%$) than without ($R = 13.9\%$, $V = 12.2\%$).

When interacting with the robot, participants who described themselves as comfortable while interacting with robots used for educational purposes performed better with regards to retention and learnability than participants who did not. This group of participants ($n = 35$) used a lower number of hints, while still performing significantly better ($p = 0.002$) than those that explicitly reported themselves as not comfortable ($n = 8$). This implies that a positive predisposition towards robots might be necessary to achieve better learning results with social robots.

In the post-experiment interviews, some participants pointed out that it was difficult to recall the newly learned phrases in the practice phase because it was only taught through dialogue, which could explain the overall low retention rate. They specifically mentioned visual clues or written hints as possible improvements. Due to the physical limitations of the robot, and thus the virtual agent, additional assistance could not be given in our case, but further improving the teaching methods could lead to a higher retention rate.

5 Conclusion

In this paper, we have investigated the impact of having a physical robot as a language teacher, compared to interacting with its virtual counterpart on a computer screen. We started with our three hypotheses measuring the enjoyment, immersion, and retention of the participant and in order to compare them, we built a language tutor to teach a handful of *High Valyrian* words and phrases to our participants. Teaching a fictional language gave us the opportunity to make the role-playing scenario interesting, helping the participants immerse themselves in the interactions and enjoy the experience.

Analyzing the results of our user study shows that the perceived enjoyment is significantly higher in the physical condition for the subgroup of participants who report little or no experience with robots. These participants are also significantly more attentive while interacting with the robot, hence, they are more immersed during the interaction with the robot. There is no significant difference between the two conditions regarding how much has been learned, which mirrors the results of previous similar studies comparing robots and virtual agents in a language teaching scenario [18]. However, the evaluation of our results strongly suggests that the physical robot as a language teacher facilitates a better learning experience for the participant. One reason, in particular, could be the physical presence of the robot which prompts people to devote themselves more to the learning process. Another reason could be that robots are usually not devices present in our daily lives, which could foster curiosity and focused attention.

Future work could entail using a different scenario that is specifically tailored to learning. The three-phase structure we used is sufficiently flexible to be used for other teaching scenarios. Moreover, a different environmental setup may enhance the user experience even more.

Overall, our results show that interacting with a robot as a language teacher is already perceived positively. Improvements in making robots more human-like, more interactive, and more intelligent can certainly pave a way for robots as language teachers in the perceivable future.

References

1. Yang, S., Chen, Y.-J.: Technology-enhanced language learning: a case study. Comput. Hum. Behav. **23**(1), 860–879 (2007)
2. Lucardie, D.: The impact of fun and enjoyment on adult's learning. Procedia Soc. Behav. Sci. **142**, 439–446 (2014)
3. Livingstone, C.: Role Play in Language Learning, 1st edn. Longman, Harlow (1983)

4. Saerbeck, M., Schut, T., Bartneck, C., Janse, M.D.: Expressive robots in education: varying the degree of social supportive behavior of a robotic tutor. In: Proceedings of the 28th International Conference on Human Factors in Computing, pp. 1613–1622. ACM, New York (2010)
5. Mubin, O., Bartneck, C., Feijs, L.: What you say is not what you get: arguing for artificial languages instead of natural languages in human robot speech interaction. In: Spoken Dialogue and HRI Workshop at IEEE (RO-MAN), Japan (2009)
6. Adams, M.: From Elvish to Klingon: Exploring Invented Languages, 1st edn. Oxford University Press, Oxford (2011)
7. Dewaele, J.M., Witney, J., Saito, K., Dewaele, L.: Foreign language enjoyment and anxiety: the effect of teacher and learner variables. Lang. Teach. Res. **22**(6), 676–697 (2018)
8. Gordon, G., et al.: Affective personalization of a social robot tutor for children's second language skills. In: Proceedings of the 30th AAAI Conference on Artificial Intelligence (AAAI 2016), pp. 3951–3957. ACM, New York (2016)
9. Peterson, M.: Massively multiplayer online role-playing games as arenas for second language learning. Comput. Assist. Lang. Learn. **23**(5), 429–439 (2010)
10. Leyzberg, D., Scassellati, B., Spaulding, S., Toneva, M.: The physical presence of a robot tutor increases cognitive learning gains. In: 34th Annual Conference of the Cognitive Science Society, Japan, pp. 1882–1887 (2012)
11. Kerzel, M., Strahl, E., Magg, S., Navarro-Guerrero, N., Heinrich, S., Wermter, S.: NICO - Neuro-Inspired COmpanion: a developmental humanoid robot platform for multimodal interaction. In: 26th Proceedings of the IEEE International Symposium on Robot and Human Interactive Communication (RO-MAN), Portugal, pp. 113–120 (2017)
12. Akalin, N., Uluer, P., Kose, H., Ince, G.: Humanoid robots communication with participants using sign language: an interaction based sign language game. In: Proceedings of the IEEE Workshop on Advanced Robotics and its Social Impacts, Japan, pp. 181–186. IEEE (2013)
13. Twiefel, J., Baumann, T., Heinrich, S., Wermter, S.: Improving domain-independent cloud-based speech recognition with domain-dependent phonetic post-processing. In: Proceedings of the 28th AAAI Conference on Artificial Intelligence (AAAI 2014), pp. 1529–1535. AAAI Press (2014)
14. Redmon, J., Divvala, S., Girshick, R., Farhadi, A.: You only look once: Unified, real-time object detection. In: Proceedings of the IEEE Conference on Computer Vision and Pattern Recognition, pp. 779–788 (2016)
15. Bartneck, C., Croft, E., Kulic, D.: Measurement Instruments for the anthropomorphism, animacy, likeability, perceived intelligence, and perceived safety of robots. Int. J. Soc. Robot. **1**(1), 71–81 (2009)
16. Heerink, M., Kröse, B., Evers, V., Wielinga, B.: Assessing acceptance of assistive social agent technology by older adults: the Almere model. Int. J. Soc. Robot. **2**(4), 361–375 (2010)
17. O'Brien, H., Cairns, P., Hall, M.: A practical approach to measuring user engagement with the refined user engagement scale (UES) and new UES short form. Int. J. Hum. Comput. Stud. **112**, 28–39 (2018)
18. Rosenthal-von der Pütten, A.M., Straßmann, C., Krämer, N.C.: Robots or agents – neither helps you more or less during second language acquisition. In: Traum, D., Swartout, W., Khooshabeh, P., Kopp, S., Scherer, S., Leuski, A. (eds.) IVA 2016. LNCS (LNAI), vol. 10011, pp. 256–268. Springer, Cham (2016). https://doi.org/10.1007/978-3-319-47665-0_23

Stackelberg Punishment
and Bully-Proofing Autonomous Vehicles

Matt Cooper[(✉)], Jun Ki Lee, Jacob Beck, Joshua D. Fishman, Michael Gillett,
Zoë Papakipos, Aaron Zhang, Jerome Ramos, Aansh Shah,
and Michael L. Littman

Brown University, Providence, RI 02912, USA
matthew_cooper@alumni.brown.edu
https://cs.brown.edu

Abstract. Mutually beneficial behavior in repeated games can be enforced via the threat of punishment, as enshrined in game theory's well-known "folk theorem." There is a cost, however, to a player for generating these disincentives. In this work, we seek to minimize this cost by computing a "Stackelberg punishment," in which the player selects a behavior that sufficiently punishes the other player while maximizing its own score under the assumption that the other player will adopt a best response. This idea generalizes the concept of a Stackelberg equilibrium. Known efficient algorithms for computing a Stackelberg equilibrium can be adapted to efficiently produce a Stackelberg punishment. We demonstrate an application of this idea in an experiment involving a virtual autonomous vehicle and human participants. We find that a self-driving car with a Stackelberg punishment policy discourages human drivers from bullying in a driving scenario requiring social negotiation.

Keywords: Algorithmic game theory · Autonomous driving ·
Behavior and control · Human-agent interaction · Social robots

1 Introduction

Driving is an inherently social activity, and it will remain so as long as human drivers share the road with autonomous vehicles. The social nature of driving introduces several problems that are often overlooked in self-driving car (SDC) research. An effective SDC will have to account for the variance in human driving styles and preferences [1], as well as varying norms [4] and laws [2] in different parts of the world. Additionally, SDCs will have to navigate the many nuanced "corner cases" of driving that require complex social negotiation.

Current planning algorithms for self-driving cars are hard-coded and programmed to be cautious. Caution is important for safety, but single-minded caution can make it impossible to complete required driving tasks. For example, to merge onto a busy highway, a driver must stick the car's nose out and encourage other drivers to slow down [5]. Furthermore, human drivers can take

M. A. Salichs et al. (Eds.): ICSR 2019, LNAI 11876, pp. 368–377, 2019.
https://doi.org/10.1007/978-3-030-35888-4_34

advantage of overly-cautious SDCs by driving aggressively, effectively bullying SDCs by forcing them to yield when they should otherwise have the right of way. Such behavior has been noted as a possible impediment to mainstream adoption of SDCs [3,13].

In this work, we explore a computational game theoretic approach that might be useful in these scenarios. In particular, we examine the idea of using a strategy that adaptively discourages anti-social behavior while remaining safe. Our proposed strategy has the overall structure of the "folk theorem" of repeated games—stabilize mutually beneficial behavior with the threat of punishment in later rounds of play [11]. However, unrestricted punishment could include unsafe behavior like intentionally crashing into the opponent's car. We propose using a punishment strategy that only restricts the opponent's utility to some safe target level while maximizing the utility of the agent. With analogy to a Stackelberg equilibrium, which is the strategy with maximum utility when paired with the opponent's best response, we call such a strategy a *Stackelberg punishment*.

A Stackelberg punishment can be computed efficiently in several classes of games for which efficient Stackelberg equilibria algorithms exist. We demonstrate the concept deployed in a simple but strategically relevant driving scenario of negotiating right of way on a one-lane bridge.

In the first part of this paper, we discuss efficient algorithms for computing Stackelberg punishment. In the second part, we describe an application of a Stackelberg punishment to solving the SDC bullying problem and demonstrate its efficacy in an experiment with human participants.

2   Tree-Based Games

We define a tree-based alternating-move two-player game as a tuple $\langle S, A, B, I, F, s_r, T, R \rangle$. Here, S is a set of states with $A \subseteq S$ being the subset of states where the first player (the leader) has control, $B \subseteq S$ being the subset of states where the second player (the follower) has control, and $F \subseteq S$ being the subset of states that are final states (leaves), ending the decision process. The sets A, B, and F partition S. The initial state s_r is the root of the tree. The set I is the set of actions available at each state with the transition function $T : S \times I \rightarrow S$ returning the next state reached from non-final state $s \in S \setminus F$ when action i is selected. The state space forms a tree in that each state can be reached by only one path from the root. The pair $R(s) = (\alpha, \beta)$ is the reward values obtained by the players when state $s \in F$ is reached.

A policy $\pi(s, i)$ maps each non-final state $s \in S \setminus F$ and action i to the probability that action i is taken in that state. We can define the value of a policy π from state $s \in S \setminus F$ as

$$V^\pi(s) = \sum_i \pi(s, i) V^\pi(T(s, i)),$$

where $V^\pi(s) = R(s)$ for $s \in F$. That is, $V^\pi(s)$ represents the payoff pair for the two players if they adopt the joint (stochastic stationary Markov) strategy π.

The leader makes the selection in the $\mathcal{A}$ states and the follower makes the selection in the $\mathcal{B}$ states. Given a policy π_A defined on the states in $\mathcal{A}$ and a policy π_B defined on the states in $\mathcal{B}$, we write $\pi = (\pi_A, \pi_B)$ to represent the policy $\pi(s, i) = \pi_A(s, i)$ if $s \in \mathcal{A}$ and $\pi_B(s, i)$ if $s \in \mathcal{B}$.

For policies for the two players, π_A and π_B, we can write $V_A(\pi_A, \pi_B)$ and $V_B(\pi_A, \pi_B)$ representing the expected payoffs to the two players when these policies are executed:

$$(V_A(\pi_A, \pi_B), V_B(\pi_A, \pi_B)) = V^\pi(s_r).$$

Given such a tree-based game and a policy π_A, we call a policy π_B a *best response* if, for all π'_B, $V_B(\pi_A, \pi_B) \geq V_B(\pi_A, \pi'_B)$. That is, the follower cannot improve its value by adopting a different policy. We write $\pi_B = M(\pi_A)$ for the best response to π_A.

In this setting, a Stackelberg equilibrium policy for the leader is

$$\underset{\pi_A}{\operatorname{argmax}} V_A(\pi_A, M(\pi_A)).$$

That is, assuming the follower will adopt a best response to whatever the leader elects to do, the leader behaves so as to maximize its reward.

Letchford and Conitzer [7] introduced an efficient algorithm for computing Stackelberg equilibria in tree-based games. In a tree with n leaves and m internal nodes, their approach runs in time $O(mn^2)$. The algorithm works by determining, for each state s, a set of payoff pairs that can be obtained through some choice of π_A and a best response π_B. Since the objective is to find a policy π_A that maximizes reward for the leader, we need only maintain the points of this set that maximize reward for the leader for each possible value obtained by the follower.

The algorithm represents the set via a finite set of payoff points $P(s)$ and a finite set of line segments $L(s)$ connecting some subset of the points in $P(s)$. It builds up the representation for a state s out of the representation computed for the children of s. At the leaves of the tree, the representation is simply the rewards at the leaves.

For a state s where the leader selects the action, the representation is computed by noting that the leader can choose any child of s, therefore any of the achievable payoffs at any of the children of s are also achievable. However, the leader can also probabilistically select any of its children. This translates into line segments where one endpoint comes from the representation of one child node and the other endpoint comes from the representation of a different child node. This set is sufficient for capturing the representation of the set of possible values at s, but it may include some unnecessary lines (or even points). These extra bits of representation can be removed or ignored, as we are ultimately only concerned with the points with maximum value for the leader.

For a state s where the follower selects the action, the follower will select the action that gives it the highest value, assuming it has adopted a best response policy. For an action i, we compute σ_i to be the lowest value for which one should be willing to tolerate selecting i over the alternatives. To compute this value, we assume the leader will make the alternatives maximally unattractive. We then modify the points and lines representing the child's values to reflect this preference. Once that modification is completed, every value for every child can be achieved at s.

Once the set of points and lines needed to represent the achievable values at the root s_r are computed, the point with the largest value for the leader can be returned as the value of the Stackelberg equilibrium for the tree. (Computing the policy itself involves unrolling this computation in reverse order and is detailed in the original paper.)

A single change is all that is needed to adapt the algorithm to produce a Stackelberg punishment—the strategy must also result in an expected reward for the follower that does not exceed θ:

$$\underset{\pi_A : V_B(\pi_A, M(\pi_A)) \leq \theta}{\operatorname{argmax}} V_A(\pi_A, M(\pi_A)).$$

That is, the leader maximizes its reward against a best responding follower while holding the follower's value to a cap of θ. It follows that the leader cannot improve its value without the follower's value rising above θ.

Our algorithm for computing a Stackelberg punishment is a simple extension over the Stackelberg equilibrium solution. In particular, it finds the point on the line segments that maximizes the leader's value subject to the follower's value being below θ. For lines that fall completely below θ in terms of their follower values, we need only check the endpoints to see which is largest for the leader. For lines that span θ in terms of their follower values, we need to check the intersection point with θ as well as the endpoint that falls below θ. This calculation does not increase the overall complexity over that of computing the Stackelberg equilibrium.

3   Other Models

The game representation in which transitions form a general graph, payoffs can occur at any node, and actions can have stochastic effects has also been called a simple stochastic game [6] or an alternating Markov game [9]. The difference between a stochastic game [12] and an alternating stochastic game is that actions are selected non-simultaneously in an alternating stochastic game.

Since a Stackelberg equilibrium is a Stackelberg punishment with $\theta = \infty$, computing a Stackelberg punishment is at least as hard as computing a Stackelberg equilibrium. Letchford and Conitzer [7] provide complexity results for a variety of Stackelberg equilibrium problems, showing that allowing stochastic transitions, simultaneous actions, or DAG-structured transition functions results in an NP-hard problem. As such, we should not expect efficient algorithms for computing Stackelberg punishment in these other game models.

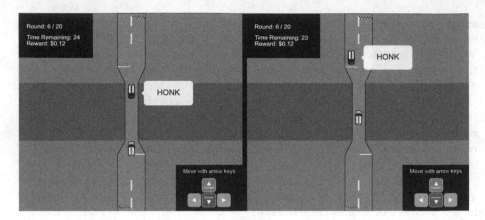

Fig. 1. The SDC uses its horn to indicate its internal state. For example, in this sequence, the human driver forces the SDC (in cooperative mode) off the back of the bridge. The SDC honks to indicate that it considers itself to have been bullied and will retaliate on the next round.

4   User Study

Our motivation for studying Stackelberg punishment is as a component of an algorithm that can work productively with people. We conducted an experiment to assess the efficacy of this idea in a simple SDC-inspired game that requires social negotiation.

The scenario we used consists of a one-lane bridge fed from both ends by a 2-lane road (Fig. 1). When two cars arrive on opposite sides of the bridge at roughly the same time, right-of-way rules dictate that the car closer to the bridge should cross, while the further car should wait. However, the further car has the opportunity to "bully" the closer car by crossing the bridge first, forcing the closer car to wait. In this case, a self-driving car that is hard coded to be cautious would be forced to back off the bridge, yielding to the human bully to avoid a collision, despite having the right of way.

Our experiment takes the form of an online game in which a virtual self-driving car (controlled by our algorithm) starts on one side of the bridge, displayed at the top of the screen, and a human-controlled car starts on the other side, shown at the bottom. On each turn, a player can move one position forward, stay in place, or move one position backward. The human participants control their own car's actions using the arrow keys on their keyboard.

Human participants were sourced online through Amazon Mechanical Turk and were rewarded monetarily based on how quickly they got to the other side of the bridge. The reward for each episode was $0.13, minus $0.01 for every two seconds before the user reached the goal. This structure was designed to encourage participants to finish quickly while still receiving a fair wage for their time (around $15/hour). We limited our study to participants from the US to ensure that all participants had experience with similar driving laws and norms. Other demographic information was not collected.

Participants were placed into either a control group or an experimental group, and each participant completed 20 episodes of the game. At the start of each episode, one car begins noticeably closer to the bridge than the other (controlled so that each participant has an equal number of "close" and "far" starts.) We consider the closer-starting car to always have the right of way in terms of crossing the bridge first.

In response to the human participant's behavior in prior episodes, the SDC follows either a hard-coded "cautious" policy or a Stackelberg punishment-based policy. The policy-switching logic will be explained in Sect. 4.3.

4.1 Stackelberg Punishment Policy

We computed a Stackelberg punishment policy on a simplified game with four abstract positions for each car (*start, before-bridge, on-bridge, finish*), resulting in a total of 16 distinct arrangements of the cars. On each decision round, one car could move forward, backward, or stay in place. We built a tree-based game over these arrangements with a maximum depth of 20 (10 decision rounds for each player). The resulting tree has 2,621,437 nodes and 1,572,862 leaves. Payoffs were computed using the same scheme as for the interactive game, $0.13 minus $0.01 for each step it takes to reach the finish. Each step in this abstracted game corresponds to two seconds of gameplay in the interactive game.

The result of running the algorithm on the abstracted game is shown in Fig. 2. It produces no more than 11 line segments in any one node. Three behaviors for the SDC emerge, *block* ($\theta < 0.10$), *bully* ($0.10 \leq \theta < 0.12$), and *yield* ($\theta \geq 0.12$), by setting θ to different values. In the *bully* case, the SDC always crosses the bridge first, regardless of starting position, as quickly as possible. This behavior is analogous to the human driver's bullying behavior. The *block* strategy also takes the bridge first regardless of starting position, but drives slowly while on the bridge. Doing so decreases the reward for both players by forcing the human player to wait longer while the SDC crosses the bridge. To achieve more severe punishments, the *block* strategy waits on the bridge for more time steps before proceeding to the finish line. The *yield* strategy causes the SDC to let the human driver take the bridge first. For θ values other than those labeled in the figure, the SDC would behave according to a stochastic mixture of the pure strategies on either side of it.

In our experiments, we used the strategy resulting from setting $\theta = \$0.02$, which results in a Stackelberg punishment in which the SDC blocks the human driver for 9 steps (18 s) before proceeding. Note that the Stackelberg equilibrium strategy is for the SDC to always bully (maximizing the leader's payoff), and the minimax punishment for the game is to block the human car indefinitely (minimizing the follower's payoff). Our Stackelberg punishment strategy strikes a more humane balance between these extremes.

4.2   Control Group

In the control group, the SDC is controlled by a naïve, cautious policy: If the SDC starts farther away from the bridge than does the human driver, it will wait until the human driver passes the bridge before proceeding. If the SDC starts closer to the bridge, it will try to cross the bridge, but will back off to avoid a collision if the human driver takes the bridge. We say the human has "bullied" the SDC if either (1) the human forces the SDC to back off the bridge and finishes first on a round where the SDC had the right of way, or (2) if the human blocks the SDC from finishing within the round time limit (26 s). We hypothesized that once participants in the control group discover that they can force the SDC to yield to them, they will bully the SDC at every opportunity to maximize their monetary reward.

4.3   Experimental Group

In the experimental group, the SDC is controlled by a policy that can be in one of two driving modes, determined by a computational version of the folk theorem [8, 10]. In *cooperative* mode, the SDC is hard coded to follow right-of-way rules and avoid collisions (as in the control group). In *punishing* mode, the SDC selects actions according to a computed Stackelberg punishment policy that limits the human driver's reward. Informally, the resulting policy is: go to the start of the bridge and drive forward slowly (to block the human driver) until enough time has passed that the participant's final reward cannot be above the imposed limit ($\theta = \$0.02$), then finish crossing the bridge.

We also use a horn to signal the SDC's state to the human driver. In cooperative mode, the SDC will honk while it is being bullied. In punishing mode, the SDC will honk the entire round (Fig. 1). Anecdotally, we found honking to be an important signaling device. Without it, the human participants did not understand the motivation behind the SDC's reactive behavior. To our knowledge, this work is the first research that explores the use of the horn as a social signaling device for autonomous vehicles. Further experimentation is necessary to decorrelate the effects of honking from the effects of the adaptive policy, but exit survey responses (discussed in the Results section) suggest that participants' decision-making was mainly affected by the adaptive policy.

The SDC selects its mode based on the human driver's behavior in the previous round, tit-for-tat style. If the human driver obeys right-of-way rules, the SDC uses its cooperative mode in the following round. If the participant bullies the SDC, it switches to punishing mode in the following round. This tit-for-tat strategy provides the necessary incentives to cooperate with the SDC. Other response strategies could be used, but this is left to future work. We hypothesized that participants in the experimental group who bully the SDC at first will learn to treat the SDC fairly over the course of multiple episodes, as bullying will cause our adaptive policy to restrict the participant's subsequent reward.

To test this hypothesis, we compared occurrences of bullying between a control group of 18 participants and an experimental group of 37 participants.

(We assigned fewer participants to the control group because pilot testing suggested that their behavior would have lower variability than the experimental group).

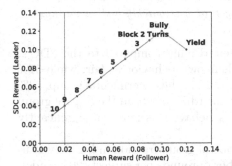

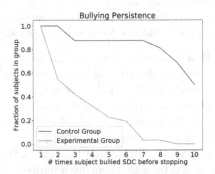

Fig. 2. The Stackelberg punishment payoffs for our one-lane bridge game. Labels are a verbal description of the policy at that point. Different line colors indicate that they are separate line segments. The red vertical line indicates a θ of \$0.02. (Color figure online)

Fig. 3. The relative dropoff in the number of times participants bullied the SDC, by group. Participants in the experimental group bullied far fewer times before stopping, signaling that our Stackelberg punishment policy effectively encourages drivers to behave fairly.

4.4 Results

In both the experimental and control groups, around 15% of participants never bullied. Since the conditions look exactly the same up until the first occurrence of bullying (punishing mode is never triggered), we only consider data from participants in both groups who bullied at least once, leaving 31 and 16 participants in the experimental and control groups, respectively.

Of these participants, Fig. 3 shows the dropoff in the fraction who bully more than a given number of rounds. Most participants in the experimental group stop bullying after just a few initial rounds in which they experience punishment, while participants in the control group bully many more times.

The first takeaway from the control group is that human bullying of SDCs does occur. Once participants in the control group realized that the SDC would yield to them even when they did not have the right of way, they tended to take advantage of that fact at every opportunity, despite understanding it was unfair. In a post-experiment survey, control group participants commented:

Once I realized that the other car would reverse as soon as I crossed the line, I used it to my advantage. I would go no matter what so that I could cross the finish line faster.

Since the other car was completely submissive, I just did whatever was in my own best interests to 'win' the game.

In the post-experiment survey for the experimental group, participants expressed that the adaptive policy stopped them from bullying:

At first it made me more aggressive, since I noticed I could easily barge my way through to get a bit of extra cash. However it only took one time for me to realize anything I gained by doing that was quickly lost in the next round as the car went agonizingly slow.

When asked to rate the fairness of their driving compared to the SDC's, only 32% of the control group described their own behavior as fair, while 91% described the SDC's behavior as fair. In contrast, in the experimental group, 73% of subjects described their own behavior as fair (different from the control group at $p < .005$), and 85% described the SDC's behavior as fair (not significantly different from the control group).

It is worth noting that the reason the control group fraction in Fig. 3 eventually dips is because there are a limited number of rounds per subject (20 rounds), and it usually takes subjects a few rounds to "discover" that bullying is possible (that is, that the SDC will back off the bridge to let them pass). We expect that if the number of rounds were considerably larger, the fraction of control group participants who bully would remain high for an indefinite number of rounds, and the experimental group would drop to zero.

To quantitatively evaluate the results, we looked at how the adaptive policy influences drivers after their first exposure to the punishing mode. Participants in the experimental group face an SDC in punishing mode in the round immediately following their first occurrence of bullying, so we compared the fraction of subjects in both groups that bully only once to the fraction that bully more than once. We use a Fisher Exact Test with an alpha level of 0.05 to determine statistical significance. Table 1 shows the categorical data from our experiments. The result of the Fisher Exact Test gives a p value of 0.0016, meaning that the adaptive Stackelberg punishment policy significantly reduced repeat bullying.

Table 1. The contingency table for bullying as a function of participant group.

	Control	Experimental
Bullied only once	0	14
Bullied more than once	16	17

5   Conclusion

Research on self-driving cars has historically focused on the hard technical problems of perception, planning and control. Social interaction between autonomous vehicles and human drivers has been largely overlooked, but has major implications for the mainstream adoption of self-driving technology.

In this paper, we explored "right-of-way bullying"—a social problem that could hinder the effectiveness of self-driving cars. Through an online experiment with human subjects, we showed that such bullying does occur in a simplified driving scenario. By adopting an adaptive driving policy based on a novel Stackelberg punishment formulation, we showed how to significantly decrease repeat occurrences of bullying and encourage pro-social driving behavior.

Future work should explore how Stackelberg punishment could interact with hard-coded safety features in a production self-driving car. In addition, the solution algorithm needs to be made considerably more efficient to scale to more complex social behaviors with finer-grained states and actions.

We hope that this work can be a foundation for further investigation of autonomous driving as an inherently social problem that necessitates novel technological, behavioral and sociological solutions.

References

1. Basu, C., Yang, Q., Hungerman, D., Singhal, M., Dragan, A.D.: Do you want your autonomous car to drive like you? In: ACM/IEEE International Conference on Human-Robot Interaction, pp. 417–425 (2017)
2. Brodsky, J.S.: Autonomous vehicle regulation: how an uncertain legal landscape may hit the brakes on self-driving cars. Berkeley Technol. Law J. **31**, 851–878 (2016)
3. Brooks, R.: Unexpected consequences of self driving cars (2017). http://rodney brooks.com/unexpected-consequences-of-self-driving-cars/
4. Bruce, A.: Planning for human-robot interaction: representing time and human intention. Ph.D. thesis, Thesis, Robotics Institute, Carnegie Mellon University (2005)
5. Chesterman, S.: Do driverless cars dream of electric sheep? SSRN (2016). SSRN. https://ssrn.com/abstract=2833701 or https://doi.org/10.2139/ssrn.2833701
6. Condon, A.: The complexity of stochastic games. Inf. Comput. **96**(2), 203–224 (1992)
7. Letchford, J., Conitzer, V.: Computing optimal strategies to commit to in extensive-form games. In: Proceedings of the 11th ACM Conference on Electronic Commerce, pp. 83–92. ACM (2010)
8. Littman, M.L., Stone, P.: A polynomial-time Nash equilibrium algorithm for repeated games. Decis. Support Syst. **39**(1), 55–66 (2005)
9. Littman, M.L.: Algorithms for sequential decision making. Ph.D. thesis, Department of Computer Science, Brown University, February 1996. Technical report CS-96-09
10. Munoz de Cote, E., Littman, M.L.: A polynomial-time Nash equilibrium algorithm for repeated stochastic games. In: 24th Conference on Uncertainty in Artificial Intelligence (UAI 2008) (2008)
11. Osborne, M.J., Rubinstein, A.: A Course in Game Theory. The MIT Press, Cambridge (1994)
12. Shapley, L.: Stochastic games. Proc. Nat. Acad. Sci. U.S.A. **39**, 1095–1100 (1953)
13. Tennant, C., Howard, S., Franks, B., Bauer, M.W.: Autonomous vehicles: negotiating a place on the road (2016). http://www.lse.ac.uk/website-archive/newsAnd Media/PDF/AVs-negociating-a-place-on-the-road-1110.pdf

Gesture Cues in Navigational Robots

Investigating the Effects of Honesty on People's Perceptions and Performance in a Navigational Game

Joey A. F. Verhoeven and Peter A. M. Ruijten[✉]

Eindhoven University of Technology, Eindhoven, The Netherlands
j.a.f.verhoeven@student.tue.nl, p.a.m.ruijten@tue.nl

Abstract. As robots have become better in tasks such as motion planning and obstacle avoidance, they will soon face a new challenge: sharing a physical space with humans. This challenge means that robots and humans need to be able to interpret what the other is doing at the moment, and predict what will happen in the near future. In the current study we tested whether people would learn from a robot's navigation behavior while playing a navigational game. The robot was either honest or dishonest in showing its navigational intentions. Results showed differences in people's understanding of the robot's behavior, the perceived human-likeness of the robot, and performance in the game. People also improved their performance throughout the dishonest rounds. These findings can be used in the design of robots that need to function effectively in mixed human-robot environments.

Keywords: Perceived message understanding · Anthropomorphism · Mental models · Robot navigation

1 Introduction

In recent history robots have become better in tasks such as motion planning and obstacle avoidance, making them able to perform various types of tasks at different locations [11]. As a consequence, robots are starting to share their physical space with humans, meaning that they need to be able to work together with humans [5]. This challenges the robot's social capabilities, as it has to adapt to human conventions [14]. More specifically, they need to have capabilities that allow them to build up a mutual understanding between itself and a person [7]. If this mutual understanding exists, robots and humans will be able to interpret what the other is doing at the moment, and predict what will happen in the near future [10].

Such a mutual understanding would prevent humans and robots from colliding into each other or following inefficient routes, and as such gives us a better sense of how to design and develop robots that operate in a mixed human-robot environment. In order for a human observer to be able to predict what a robot will do in the near future, its behavior needs to be adaptable and easily

© Springer Nature Switzerland AG 2019
M. A. Salichs et al. (Eds.): ICSR 2019, LNAI 11876, pp. 378–387, 2019.
https://doi.org/10.1007/978-3-030-35888-4_35

understandable [16]. The display of navigational cues is a way for robots to communicate their behavioral intention towards humans. These navigational cues could be indicated through different modalities. Cues can be described as short prompts that have the potential to communicate information [3], and they can be either implicit or explicit [16]. Implicit cues are mostly unconsciously communicating information during an interaction, for example an emotional undertone during a conversation. Explicit cues more clearly communicate information, for example the distance people keep between them to signal the level of intimacy of their interaction.

An example of an explicit cue for navigation is using gestures, in which the body of the robot is used to indicate a direction by pointing the front of the robot in the intended direction [18]. An advantage of using gestures is that they provide visual feed-forward information that is suitable for navigational behavior and is intuitive from a human perspective [1]. In addition, intuitive gestures may increase a robot's perceived human-likeness, which is one of the most critical aspects of human-robot interaction [6]. A disadvantage of using gestures is that the robot needs a clear front, but in most cases this will be the side of the robot that is moving forward.

These navigational cues allow people to build a mental representation of the robot. A mental representation, or mental model, is a conceptual framework that helps people to predict and coordinate in dynamic environments [9]. Having a correct mental model of a robot suggests that the user can accurately predict that robot's next actions. The set of actions that need to be performed or have been performed to reach a certain goal show a robot's intention [2], and understanding those intentions is important for building a mental model. Having an incorrect or incomplete mental model of a robot suggests that the user's expectation may be violated, and people need to adapt their behavior accordingly [4], thereby decreasing the effectiveness of the interaction with the robot. If we aim to improve people's understanding of a robot's behavior, we should thus focus on gaining insights about how these mental models are formed, used, and adapted based on experiences people have with a robot.

A common method for obtaining whether people have a correct mental model of a robot is to measure their so-called Perceived Message Understanding (PMU), which covers both the extent to which people understand the robot, and whether they believe the robot understands them [8]. The higher a person's PMU is, the more correct their mental model of a robot will be. We expect that a person's PMU of a robot will increase with experience with that robot. If that robot will then perform behavior that is unexpected, this would cause a drop in PMU.

1.1 Research Aims

The aim of the current study is to investigate the extent to which people's mental models of a robot are adapted based on its behavior. We expect that people's understanding of the robot's behavior will increase with experience and that this understanding will drop if the robot shows surprising behavior. In addition, this surprising behavior is expected to be perceived as more human-like than predicted behavior. Based on earlier work that showed that perceived human-likeness varies while people get more experience with a robot [17], we expect a similar pattern to occur. Finally, we expect that people are better able to predict a robot's behavior if they have a more accurate mental model of the robot.

These expectations were tested in a navigational game in which people had to recognize and understand the behavioral intention of a humanoid robot. The robot indicated its next move by turning its body towards the direction it would take. The goal of the person was to reach a target location on a grid without colliding with the robot.

2   Method

2.1   Participants and Design

Fifty-seven participants (29 males and 28 females, $M_{age} = 23.3$, $SD_{age} = 2.9$, Range 19 to 30) participated in a study with a 1×2 (Robot Behavior: Honest vs. Dishonest) within-subjects design. In the Honest condition, the robot showed behavior that was consistent with its navigational cue. In the Dishonest condition, the behavior did not match the navigational cue.

Each participant played ten rounds in a navigational game in which they competed against a robot. This game was adapted from earlier work on social cues in robot navigation [15]. In each round, the participant had to reach a target location in as few steps as possible, while not colliding with the robot. The game was played on a 3.6 by 3.6 m grid with tiles of 60×60 cm. The tiles were indicated with numbers (1–6) and letters (A–F), resulting in a chessboard-like setup (see Fig. 1). The participant and the robot each had a different starting position, and they could move one tile on each turn. If the participant would be on a tile where the robot stepped into, they would lose the round. The dependent measures were participants' Performance, Perceived Message Understanding, and Anthropomorphism. Each of these measures were collected during and right after every round.

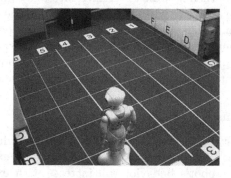

Fig. 1. Overview of the setup of the grid with the Pepper robot, the tiles, and the labels of the tiles in numbers and letters.

2.2   Materials and Procedure

The humanoid robot Pepper from Aldebaran Softbank Robotics was used. Unknown to participants, Pepper had a predefined location and path in each round. Pepper always took five steps to reach its goal, and participants also could reach theirs in a minimal number of five steps. Prior to entering the lab, participants provided informed consent. They next received a brief introduction of the rules of the game. The first round was a practice round, in which the participant was able to get familiar with the game, Pepper and the environment. During this round no cue was displayed and collision with Pepper was highly unlikely (see Fig. 2).

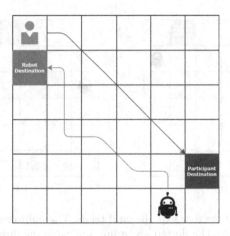

Fig. 2. Visualization of the practice trial. The green line indicates the path the robot took. The blue line indicates one of the shortest possible routes for the participant without colliding with the robot. (Color figure online)

Next, participants played 8 rounds of the game in two blocks of four, see Fig. 3. During the first block of four rounds, the robot indicated its next move honestly, as shown by the solid green lines in Fig. 3. During the second block of 4 rounds, the indication provided by the robot was mirrored on the vertical axis facing the front of the robot, as shown by the dotted green lines in Fig. 3. For example, if the robot would state that it would go diagonally left, it would go diagonally right instead.

All four trials were used twice, once for the Honest and once for the Dishonest condition. To prevent participants from recognizing the rounds, we rotated them 90 degrees between the two conditions. The order and rotation of the boards was counterbalanced.

The final round of each block was a critical trial that was used to investigate whether the participant had learned how the robot indicated its next step (see Fig. 4). In this trial, the participant and the robot started next to each other at the tiles on the edge of the grid. The participant only had to move forward

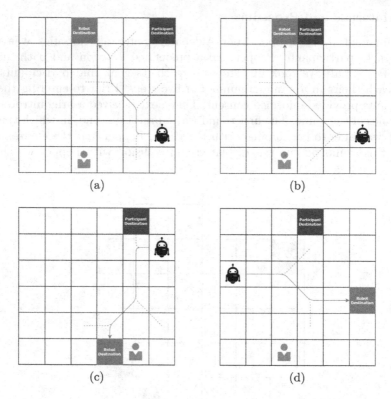

Fig. 3. Visualization of the four experimental trials. The unbroken green line indicates the path the robot took. The dotted green line indicates the direction the robot gave in the Dishonest rounds. (Color figure online)

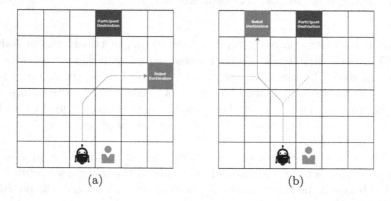

Fig. 4. Visualization of the two critical trials, with (a) the critical trial in the Honest block and (b) the critical trial in the Dishonest block. The unbroken green line indicates the path the robot took. The dotted green line indicates the direction the robot gave in the Dishonest round. (Color figure online)

to reach the goal in the least number of steps. However, after the first step the robot indicated that its next movement would be diagonally onto the path of the participant. If the participant understood the navigational indication in the Honest trials, they would move out of the robot's way. If they would understand the navigational indication in the Dishonest trials, they would know that the robot moved in the mirrored direction of what was indicated.

After each round, participants completed several scales: a 6-item scale measuring Perceived Message Understanding (PMU, $\alpha = 0.79$) adapted from [8], and a 7-item scale measuring Anthropomorphism ($\alpha = 0.85$) adapted from [19]. Both concepts were measured on 5-item scales.

At the end of the experiment, participants completed demographic questions, were debriefed about the goals of the experiment, and were compensated with either €5 or course credits. The experiment took about 30 min to complete.

3   Results

3.1   Perceived Message Understanding

To investigate whether participants' understanding of the behavior of the robot increased over time, we performed two regression analyses (one on the Honest rounds, one on the Dishonest rounds) with round number as predictor and Perceived Message Understanding as dependent variable.

No relation between round and PMU was found for the Honest rounds ($\beta = .03$, $p = 0.58$), nor for the Dishonest rounds ($\beta = .06$, $p = 0.34$). As can be seen in Fig. 5a, however, a clear difference in PMU was found between the Honest ($M = 3.97$, $SD = 0.60$) and Dishonest rounds ($M = 3.11$, $SD = 0.77$), $t(56) = 9.64$, $p < 0.001$, Cohen's $d = 1.25$. It appears that PMU remains constant throughout the Honest and Dishonest rounds, but drops significantly the moment the robot starts to provide wrong indications of its next move.

3.2   Anthropomorphism

To investigate whether participants' perceived human-likeness of the robot would decrease over time, we performed two regression analyses with round number as predictor and Anthropomorphism as dependent variable. The first analysis was performed on the Honest rounds, the second one on the Dishonest rounds.

No relation between round and Anthropomorphism was found for the Honest rounds ($\beta = -.08$, $p = 0.16$), nor for the Dishonest rounds ($\beta = -.06$, $p = 0.33$). As can be seen in Fig. 5b, however, a difference in Anthropomorphism was found between the Honest ($M = 2.16$, $SD = 0.73$) and Dishonest rounds ($M = 2.24$, $SD = 0.79$), $t(56) = -2.04$, $p = 0.05$, Cohen's $d = 0.10$. It appears that Anthropomorphism remains fairly constant throughout the Honest and Dishonest rounds, but increases significantly the moment the robot starts to provide wrong indications of its next move.

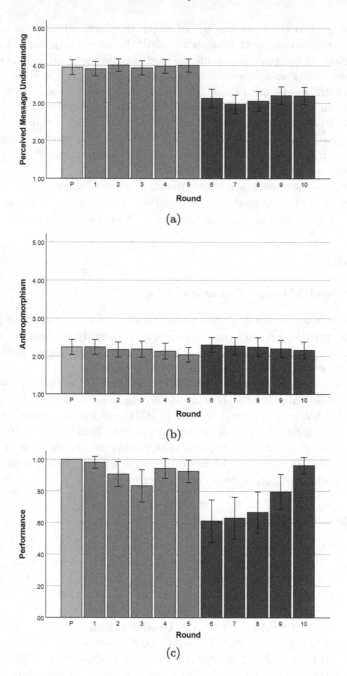

Fig. 5. Average scores of (a) Perceived Message Understanding and (b) Anthropomorphism, and (c) participants' Performance in each of the rounds. The yellow bar indicates the Practice round, the green bars indicate the Honest rounds, and the red bars indicate the Dishonest rounds. Whiskers represent 95% confidence intervals. (Color figure online)

3.3 Performance

To investigate whether participants' performed better in the game over time, we performed two regression analyses with round number as predictor and Performance as dependent variable. The first analysis was performed on the Honest rounds, the second one on the Dishonest rounds.

No relation between round and Performance was found for the Honest rounds ($\beta = -.04$, $p = 0.53$), but such a relation did exist for the Dishonest rounds ($\beta = .28$, $p < 0.001$). As can be seen in Fig. 5c, most participants were able to win the rounds in the first half of the game. After a steep drop when the robot starts being dishonest, participants drastically improve their performance in the second half of the game. This also led to a difference in Performance between the Honest ($M = 0.92$, $SD = 0.13$) and Dishonest rounds ($M = 0.73$, $SD = 0.14$), $t(54) = 6.92$, $p < 0.001$, Cohen's $d = 1.38$. It appears that Performance remains fairly constant throughout the Honest rounds, and after dropping drastically it significantly increases throughout the Dishonest rounds.

4 Discussion

The current study investigated whether people adapt their mental model of a robot based on its behavior. People played a navigational game in which the robot indicated its next move by rotating its body. For the first half of the rounds, the robot indicated its direction honestly. For the second half, it indicated a direction that was mirrored to its actual direction. We expected that people's understanding of the robot's behavior would increase with experience and that this understanding would drop when the robot showed surprising behavior.

Results indicated clear differences in people's understanding of the robot's behavior, the perceived human-likeness of the robot, and people's performance in the game, between the honest and dishonest rounds. Moreover, people significantly improved their performance throughout the dishonest rounds. None of the other trends within the honest or dishonest rounds were significant.

We expected that both PMU and perceived human-likeness would change throughout both the honest and dishonest blocks, but no such trend was found. One possible explanation for this could be that the game was too short to allow people to really get used to the navigational behavior of the robot. Many people seemed focused on reaching their target location more than they were focusing on the robot. Earlier work on dynamic perceptions of robots [13] indicated that these perceptions go through different stages. A short interaction with a robot is described as a context in which people apply existing mental models to the robot, and they are only able to adapt their mental models at a later stage. It could well be the case that in the current study, this stage was not reached.

Participants did show an increase in their performance throughout the dishonest rounds. It should be noted however that successfully evading the robot or winning the game does not always mean that the robot's navigational movement was correctly anticipated. Successfully evading the robot could still be achieved by just moving away from the robot. Though almost all participants tried to move towards their goal, some of them ignored the goal and just tried to move away from the robot while observing its movements.

Finally, a significant difference was found on all dependent measures between the last of the honest rounds and the first of the dishonest ones. Participants suddenly understood the (behavior of the) robot less well, they perceived it as more human-like, and they performed significantly worse in the game. These effects were independent of which experimental trial was applied, so it was clearly the behavior of the robot that caused this effect. Earlier work showed that surprise can make people curious about a robot's behavior, encouraging them to seek information [12]. This may explain why performance drops so drastically when the robot in the current study started being dishonest. When people seek information about a robot's behavior, they start exploring its capabilities and may be less focused on performing well in the game.

4.1 Limitations and Future Work

People played an interactive game in which they and a robot took one step at a time. This does not fully resemble an environment in which humans and robots share physical spaces. As a result, people's behavior in the current study could have been different from how they would behave in a more dynamic environment. Future work should investigate people's responses in a less static context.

The study was performed with a Pepper robot, which has a human-like morphology. Many robots that will be applied in dynamic environments may have a more machine-like appearance and have mostly functional roles (e.g., vacuum cleaners, baggage handlers). People's mental models of such robots may differ from those of their more social counterparts. It is worthwhile to extend the current work into different types of robots and test whether similar effects occur.

The goal of this study was to investigate how people anticipate future actions of a robot when it uses gestures to indicate its navigational intention. Results of this study can be used in the design of robots that need to function effectively in mixed human-robot environments. We hope that the current work can be used to encourage creators and developers to design robots that are more social and intuitive for humans in mixed human-robot environments.

References

1. Ajoudani, A., Zanchettin, A.M., Ivaldi, S., Albu-Schäffer, A., Kosuge, K., Khatib, O.: Progress and prospects of the human-robot collaboration. Auton. Robots **42**(5), 957–975 (2018). https://doi.org/10.1007/s10514-017-9677-2
2. Bauer, A., Wollherr, D., Buss, M.: Human-robot collaboration: a survey. Int. J. Humanoid Rob. **05**(01), 47–66 (2008). https://doi.org/10.1142/S0219843608001303
3. Breazeal, C., Kidd, C.D., Thomaz, A.L., Hoffman, G., Berlin, M.: Effects of nonverbal communication on efficiency and robustness in human-robot teamwork. In: 2005 IEEE/RSJ International Conference on Intelligent Robots and Systems, pp. 708–713, August 2005. https://doi.org/10.1109/IROS.2005.1545011

4. Campo, S., Cameron, K.A., Brossard, D., Frazer, M.S.: Social norms and expectancy violation theories: assessing the effectiveness of health communication campaigns. Commun. Monogr. **71**(4), 448–470 (2004). https://doi.org/10.1080/0363452042000307498
5. Christensen, H.I., Pacchierotti, E.: Embodied social interaction for robots. In: AISB 2005, pp. 40–45 (2005)
6. Duffy, B.R.: Anthropomorphism and the social robot. Robot. Auton. Syst. **42**(3), 177–190 (2003). https://doi.org/10.1016/S0921-8890(02)00374-3
7. Fong, T., Nourbakhsh, I., Dautenhahn, K.: A survey of socially interactive robots. Robot. Auton. Syst. **42**(3), 143–166 (2003). https://doi.org/10.1016/S0921-8890(02)00372-X
8. Harms, P.C., Biocca, P.F.: Internal consistency and reliability of the networked minds measure of social presence (2004). http://cogprints.org/7026/1/Harms_04_reliability_validity_social_presence_(Biocca).pdf
9. Kiesler, S., Goetz, J.: Mental models of robotic assistants (2002). https://doi.org/10.1145/506443.506491
10. Klein, G., Feltovich, P.J., Bradshaw, J.M., Woods, D.D.: Common ground and coordination in joint activity. Organ. Simul. **53**, 139–184 (2005). https://doi.org/10.1002/0471739448.ch6
11. Kruse, T., Pandey, A.K., Alami, R., Kirsch, A.: Human-aware robot navigation: a survey. Robot. Auton. Syst. **61**(12), 1726–1743 (2013). https://doi.org/10.1016/j.robot.2013.05.007
12. Law, E., et al.: A wizard-of-oz study of curiosity in human-robot interaction. In: 2017 26th IEEE International Symposium on Robot and Human Interactive Communication (RO-MAN), pp. 607–614. IEEE (2017). https://doi.org/10.1109/ROMAN.2017.8172365
13. Lemaignan, S., Fink, J., Dillenbourg, P.: The dynamics of anthropomorphism in robotics. In: Proceedings of the 2014 ACM/IEEE International Conference on Human-Robot Interaction, HRI 2014, pp. 226–227. ACM, New York (2014). https://doi.org/10.1145/2559636.2559814
14. Mumm, J., Mutlu, B.: Human-robot proxemics: physical and psychological distancing in human-robot interaction. In: Proceedings of the 6th International Conference on Human-Robot Interaction, HRI 2011, pp. 331–338. ACM, New York (2011). https://doi.org/10.1145/1957656.1957786
15. Neggers, M.M.E., Ruijten, P.A.M., Cuijpers, R.H., IJsselsteijn, W.A.: Investigating the efficiency and understandability of directional cues in robot navigation. In: RO-MAN 2019 (2019, submitted)
16. Rios-Martinez, J., Spalanzani, A., Laugier, C.: From proxemics theory to socially-aware navigation: a survey. Int. J. Soc. Robot. **7**(2), 137–153 (2015). https://doi.org/10.1007/s12369-014-0251-1
17. Ruijten, P.A.M., Cuijpers, R.H.: Dynamic perceptions of human-likeness while interacting with a social robot. In: Proceedings of the Companion of the 2017 ACM/IEEE International Conference on Human-Robot Interaction, HRI 2017, pp. 273–274. ACM, New York (2017). https://doi.org/10.1145/3029798.3038361
18. Saulnier, P., Sharlin, E., Greenberg, S.: Exploring minimal nonverbal interruption in HRI. In: 2011 RO-MAN, pp. 79–86. IEEE (2011). https://doi.org/10.1109/ROMAN.2011.6005257
19. Waytz, A., Morewedge, C.K., Epley, N., Monteleone, G., Gao, J.H., Cacioppo, J.T.: Making sense by making sentient: effectance motivation increases anthropomorphism. J. Pers. Soc. Psychol. **99**(3), 410–435 (2010). https://doi.org/10.1037/a0020240

Hand Gesture Based Gameplay with a Smoothie Maker Game Using Myo Armband

Sudhir Sharma$^{(\boxtimes)}$, Volker Steuber, and Farshid Amirabdollahian

University of Hertfordshire, Hatfield AL10 9AB, UK
{s.sharma25,v.steuber,f.amirabdollahian2}@herts.ac.uk
https://www.herts.ac.uk

Abstract. Serious games have the potential to guide the relearning process via encouraging and motivating meaningful interaction. This paper focused on assessing the feasibility of gameplay by performing hand gestures using an off the shelf myoelectric armband to make smoothies in a functional game. The game was designed in Unity3D and interfaced with the wireless Myo Armband as an input device for performing the tasks in game. Based on earlier work on feasibility of incorporating machine-learning based gesture recognition, cylindrical, spherical, and tripod grasps were incorporated into the game. Smoothie Maker game was designed with two versions Game-A & Game-B. Participants, ($n = 20$), were randomly assigned to an AB or BA group which differs in order of gameplay for the two games. After playing each game, participants offered their insights using the Intrinsic Motivation Inventory (IMI).

The results featured multiple parameters including score, time to pick, idle time, as well as gesture recognition accuracy for both game versions. Most outcomes indicated that games A and B did not have a statistically significant difference, but when comparing using gesture accuracy, the two game differed slightly with statistical significance. Analysis of the qualitative IMI survey did not provide a significant difference between the two game versions.

Conclusions are drawn from our findings towards improving the games and their recognition accuracy, highlighted for our future work.

Keywords: Serious games · Hand gestures · Smoothie maker game · Virtual reality

1   Introduction

The popularity of serious games is growing in various fields such as military, health, security, safety and general education due to its potential to enhance training outcomes. Serious games are those games which have its primary purpose to learn, train and educate rather than entertainment which becomes secondary [12]. In a rehabilitation context, these games have a potential to assist

---

University of Hertfordshire.

© Springer Nature Switzerland AG 2019
M. A. Salichs et al. (Eds.): ICSR 2019, LNAI 11876, pp. 388–398, 2019.
https://doi.org/10.1007/978-3-030-35888-4_36

self-mediated training as well as training in clinics as they could be an engaging and motivating medium which allows the user to move in and interact with objects in a virtual environment [2]. Serious games have the potential for increasing user interaction with rehabilitation exercises needed to improve the functionality of the affected part after stroke [6].

Serious games are one of the most appropriate interaction mediums for a practice environment requiring repetitive movements [14]. The repetitive activity that is non-specific to functional tasks appears to be less effective [11]. Rehabilitation therapies can be easily designed through serious games in a more natural way using movements required for daily living tasks (ADL) can be easily imitated through serious games. The effectiveness of ADL-focused therapy in improving patient performance in ADL is well established [7].

In our earlier work, we used eleven games that were designed for stroke rehabilitation, to motivate patients to practice at their own home using a robotic glove [3]. While the results from this study were supportive of technology-mediated home rehabilitation [10], one of the limitations identified was that glove was tethered to the PC thus restricting the patient to move freely, while also obstructing the fingertips. The current study considers the feasibility of using wireless wearable electromyography sensors to address the above issues. We also intend to utilise myoelectric signals frequently captured as a source of benchmark closely linked to the status of neuro-recovery.

In the current study, the Smoothie Maker game was developed on the basis of elementary movements necessary to perform daily living tasks such as forearm pronation/supination, and versatile grasping. Grasping is one of the essential activities in our daily life enabling us to interact with our environment and aid our personal independence. Prior to deployment in clinical evaluation, research presented here aims at feasibility of gameplay using hand gestures obtained from sensing muscular contractions of the forearm, and its influence on game usability and player performance compared between a virtual and an embedded reality game version.

One element of this evaluation relates to whether a real object is a necessity to perform rehabilitation games when gestures are identified using electromyography. Our earlier work with kinematic measures obtained from the robotic glove worn on the hand and wrist showed that presence of objects did not have a significant impact in recognition accuracy obtained from healthy participants and stroke patients [9]. Thus the question here is mainly to verify if EMG sensing offers the same affordances.

2 Background

Humans utilise their hands to accomplish various tasks via gestures. Human-computer interaction utilising hand gestures for interaction with devices and applications has been completely changed. Hand gestures are traditionally captured using image analysis algorithms, but different techniques are being explored to improve recognition accuracy and resilience.

2.1 Support Vector Machine (SVM)

Support Vector Machine (SVM) is a popular approach [5] in supervised machine learning which is used to identify a useful pattern in myoelectric signals. It is a potent and reliable technique for data classification and regression. SVM is based on the concept of decision planes that define decision boundaries. The SVM algorithms finds the boundary with the largest possible margin around it. It segregates the two classes with the best hyperplanes. Tavakolan et al. used SVM for pattern classification of surface electromyography signals of four forearm muscles in order to classify eight hand gestures. They concluded that it was feasible to identify gestures using the four locally placed electrodes [15]. Similarly, Wang et al. used linear discriminant analysis to achieve an average accuracy of around 98% in detecting 8 hand gestures using two electrodes placed on the forearm [17]. Our study focuses on using SVM with a commercially off the self device, the Myo armband from Thalmic labs, in detecting a number of hand grasp gestures and incorporating them into functional gameplay for rehabilitation objectives.

2.2 Feature Extraction

Data was captured by placing the armband on the forearm making direct contact with skin. Data was collected at 200 Hz sampling rate and logged into CSV files. Features were selected using $N = 40$ Waveform Length (WL) equation. The choice of N is due to research by [16] that showed 200 ms of data is sufficient to detect intention in muscle EMG. The complete process of feature extraction and detecting hand gestures has mentioned in our earlier studies [4,13]. The preliminary study intended to assess if myoelectric sensing could be a reliable tool for interacting with games. Results supported utility of this sensor in interaction via games, leading to current study.

2.3 Myo Armband and Hand Gestures

In the published preliminary study [13] five different types of hand gestures Cylindrical, Spherical, Tripod, Lateral Pinch and Hook depicted in Fig. 1. The study was conducted in four phases: Familiarisation, Training-1, Dumbbell exercises and Training-2 with 20 healthy participants. During the two training phases, each participant performed 5 hand gestures, each gesture was performed in 5 iterations. Each iteration lasted 5 s and consisted of 5 repetitions of each gesture, visually guided to last a second each. The logged data was recorded into CSV (Comma- Separated Values) files at a rate of 200 Hz. In order to compare grasps before and after the fatiguing exercise, we used SVM (Support Vector Machine), using the capability to judge grasp accuracy for each phase. By comparing the grasp accuracy pre and post exercise, we found that muscular fatigue can negatively impact on gesture accuracy.

Fig. 1. Myo armband and hand gestures

3   Proposed Approach

Hand gesture based gameplay for Smoothie Maker game consisted of performance of different types of hand gestures performed for grasping to pick fruits in the game shown by block diagram in Fig. 2. Three most reliable hand gestures Cylindrical, Spherical and Tripod were selected from previous study [13] and were Incorporated into the game. These main gestures were further classified into 10 different sub-gestures which allow for grasping a range of fruits incorporated into the game.

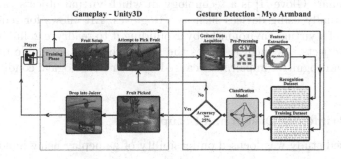

Fig. 2. Configuration of hand gesture detection system with unity3d to create hand gesture based gameplay for smoothie maker game

The system was built by integration of Unity3d interface and myoelectric signals utilisation for interaction with Smoothie Maker game. The game required picking different fruits in the game. While participant perform the required hand gesture to pick the fruit, simultaneously the myo device records myoelectric signals for the current gesture performed. The preliminary study suggested the length of data recorded for each gesture to be 2.5 s training data and 1 s recognition data [13]. As the game involved a training phase to capture the training data, game play itself did not suffer long waits and could flow in an acceptable manner. In order to facilitate game play, if a player performed a desired gesture with an accuracy greater than 25%, their gesture was accepted and would result in a game action, e.g. pick up of a fruit. However, any produced gestures with an accuracy value less than this margin required a repetition of the gesture before the game could progress to the next task.

The gesture accuracy data was exchanged between Unity3d and Myo arm-band through implementation of a TCP (Transmission Control Protocol) inter-face. The game could trigger the myo to record and stop recording, while a parallel process in game could assess the accuracy of gestures detected. This approach was used due to secession of support for the myo armband via the parent company Thalmic Lab.

4   Materials and Methods

Most machine mediated therapies benefit from an interactive paradigm to sup-port a patient interaction with the machine. Although many may not identify the interaction mediated via the graphical interface as virtual reality (VR), the con-text of interaction is increasingly focusing on presentation of real daily activities. This is often supported by clinicians and within the co-creation principles [8]. In recent years VR technology is enhanced with embedded reality tools. Embedded Reality (ER) allows for linking VR to the real world better, by providing a tool that enables exploring the VR with multiple senses such as touch, hearing and so on that are anchored to the real world. An example of this type of world is Rapael Smart Glove [1] is a technology in which virtual objects can be con-trolled externally using devices such as VR gloves. ER allows for reducing the complexity of a virtual environment by grounding it to reality, e.g. linking it with real-world objects. As such, it makes the approach more accessible to patients suffering from cognitive impairment caused by their neurological conditions such as stroke [6].

4.1   Experimental Design and Setup

The proposed study was focused on feasibility of gameplay using hand gestures and its influence on game usability and player performance comparing between VR and ER game sharing a fixed interface, the smoothie maker game. Exper-iment was designed with two sessions in which participants play Game-A and Game-B. Participants were randomly assigned into AB or BA groups, which dictates the order of gameplay, game A before game B, or vice versa. After play-ing each game, participants were asked to fill out a questionnaire based on their experience of the gameplay.

Table 1. Statistics of demographic data

Gender	Participants	Mean(Age)	Std deviation(Age)
Male	17	30.94	4.6699
Female	3	34	3.4641

The experiment protocol was approved by the University of Hertfordshire's ethics committee under the approval number COM/PGR/UH/03268. A total number of 20 participants consented to take part in the study with their demographics presented in summary Table 1. Each participant took part in a 45 min session sitting in front of a 21-inch display with Myo Armband placed on the forearm of their dominant hand.

4.2   Embedded Reality (Game-A) and Virtual Reality (Game-B)

Smoothie Maker game was designed as an interactive Virtual Reality (VR) game, which was then played as an embedded reality (ER) game referenced as Game-A and also as a fully virtual (VR) game referenced here as Game-B. The main difference between Game-A and Game-B was that in Game-A participants performed each gesture using decorative fruits whereas in Game-B gestures were performed just by imagining to grasp the decorative fruits. Participant did notice the difference between Game-A and Game-B while performing the gestures using real fruit or without fruit.

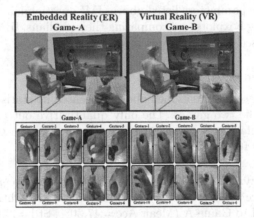

Fig. 3. (Top left) In Game-A Gesture performed with decorative fruit (Carrot), (Top right) Game-B Gesture performed by pretending to hold a fruit. (Bottom left) Training-1 for Game-A with ER environment, (Bottom right) Training-2 for Game-B with imagined poses

In the current study, we were concerned about the feasibility of gameplay using hand gestures to utilise the game in a rehabilitation context in our next studies. For each game there was a specific training session (Fig. 3). During the Training-1 phase, we asked participants to grab the fruit displayed on the screen from a real tray on the table containing some decorative fruits and hold it for 2.5 s in Game-A. In Game-B participants performed gestures without fruits, just by pretending to grasp the fruit shown on screen and holding it for 2.5 s. Similarly during recognition phase participants performed all the gestures in the same way but the duration to hold the fruit in hand was 1 s, to allow for a more seamless gameplay. Recognition of gestures was done using an SVM classification which outputs a *GestureAccuracy*.

5   Results

After the completion of each session gameplay data was recorded and saved into CSV files and useful parameters were saved for further analysis. The quantitative parameters included *GestureAccuracy*, *Scores* from gameplay, Number of *FruitsPicked*, *FruitPickTime* and *PickIdleTime* which captures time between successful picks, and *SmoothiePourTime* which reflects on time taken to serve the drinks. All the game parameters were compared between Game-A & B using boxplots, comparing between games and between different participants. Qualitative data included the questionnaire from Intrinsic Motivation Inventory (IMI) to measure players perceptions of intrinsic motivation in the game. IMI refers to the internal feelings of enjoyment and interest of the player while playing a game. These feelings are produced without any desire and are naturally produced by enjoyment and being interested in the game.

Gestures accuracy and game parameters were analysed by using repeated measures ANOVA. One-way ANOVA test was conducted to compare the means for the quantitative parameters listed above. IMI questionnaire survey data was analysed by plotting boxplots and comparing their medians. IBM SPSS Statistics version 25.0 was used for the analysis reflected here.

5.1   Quantitative Results

All quantitative outcomes mentioned above presented no statistically significant differences across the two games. The only quantitative outcome with statistically significant difference between the two groups was the *GestureAccuracy* parameter which is further detailed here.

Gesture Accuracy. Gesture accuracy varied slightly between the two games. Game-B (Mean Acc = 52.38%, Std = 29.030 ± 0.70) had slightly higher gesture accuracy compared to Game-A (Mean Acc = 47.30%, Std = 27.502 ± 0.663) and this difference was statistically significant in a one-way ANOVA ($p < 0.005$). Figure 4 present the difference between different gesture accuracies detected across the two game versions. When each gesture was compared between the two games, all three grasps showed better accuracies for Game-B, with Tripod and Spherical showing statistically significant differences using a one-way ANOVA test applied to each gesture category.

5.2   Qualitative Results

Results obtained from the IMI questionnaires can be viewed as the median of the five categories in Fig. 5. Mann-Whitney U-Test did could not reject the null hypothesis of different responses between the two games. Participants enjoyed playing the games (Enjoyment median of 6 points) and perceived playing the games as their own choice and felt competent in playing both games. Participants were slightly more relaxed in Game-A comparable to Game-B but this difference was not statistically significant. Both games seem to have attributed the same amount of effort.

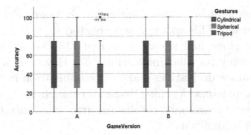

Fig. 4. Tripod and Spherical grasps have better means for Game-B compared to Game-A, with statistically significant differences

6   Analysis and Discussion

The *Smoothie Maker* game was designed on the basis of incorporating elementary grasps necessary to perform daily living tasks into a playful and fun interaction. The game is operated using multiple grasps as well as arm movement and pronation and supination of the forearm.

Results from this study compared the two game versions, virtual and embedded reality games, and provided comparable quantitative and qualitative results for each version. The only statistically significant parameter that varied to a slight difference across the two versions was the *GestureAccuracy* measured

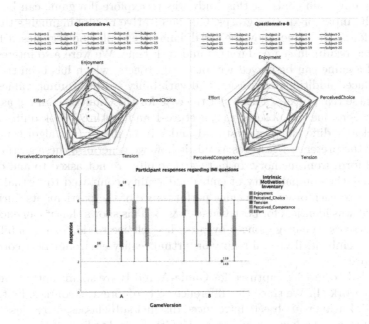

Fig. 5. IMI questionnaire survey plotted into boxplots showing participants enjoyed playing both games

using the SVM assessment of gestures. Interestingly Game-B had a slightly better recognition accuracy. This was not an expected finding as our earlier study with a mechatronic glove had shown that real objects assisted in improving the recognition accuracy for machine learning [9]. However, we have started to examine different feature derivatives and their combination in training the SVM model and different machine learning techniques such as Convolutional Neural Networks and our preliminary results confirm substantially better gesture accuracy for gesture recognition.

Looking deeper into current findings, one potential cause for the observation here is that in current study, training for Game-A is performed using a number of fruits that are grasped using one of the three main grasp categories, tripod, cylindrical and spherical. However, the actual training values for a real banana and a real carrot for example are not necessarily very similar, although classed as a cylindrical grasp. We pose that due to generalising these different grasps into one of the three categories, we have confused the SVM by offering distinct and different sub-classes as a class with the same character. It is possible that when a pretend grasp is performed, due to recall of a pose, there is a degree of variability in the reproduced grasp that brings the sub-classes closer towards the main class, so for example a pretend grasp for a banana and a carrot is more cylindrical than the actual grasps performed with a curved banana and conical carrot (as depicted in Fig. 3. We intend to further explore this theory in our next paper where training values are used to discriminate the sub-class rather than main class, and will report results in our future work.

One of our main goals for this study was to explore if a game can be played using EMG input predicting grasps. Our qualitative results highlights that participants found the game enjoyable and did manage to play both games, achieving comparable results in score, duration and pick time. We were also interested to explore if a game can be played without real objects, which has been the case.

Introduced additional confusion and variability to the training values gathered by these real objects. This is not the case for the Game-B training as shown in Fig. 3 where one can observe that gesture-1 and gesture-7 look quite similar, and are clearly different from gesture-1 and 7 in Game-A. Our algorithm works better for the pretended gestures as this is how we generalise these gestures into a recalled form from memory. In fact participants are not asked to and demonstrated that the compatibility of embedded reality compared to virtual reality was similar to each other. The game performance of the participants during the experiment was identical for both Game-A & B. This shows that it can encourage stroke survivors to engage longer by providing choice to do their rehabilitation exercises in embedded virtual reality or virtual reality environment according to their interest.

Recorded accuracies captured for Game-A and B are significantly lower than our earlier work [4]. We trace the difference to two potential sources: first, training the SVM using real objects introduced distinct sub-classes into a class, affecting recognition accuracy; second, we used TCP channel to link the game interface with the Myo device. This created a slight delay between visual and performed grasp, which brought the two components out of sync with a maximum of 1s delay, but unfortunately this delay is not a fixed 1s for all performed cases. We have now re-programmed our EMG signal capture to work continuously, but use timestamps to synchronise the visual and performance data.

7   Conclusion and Future Work

In this study, the Smoothie Maker game is presented two different modes of training's to train hand gestures used in performing in-game tasks. We observed that training with real objects had a small knock-on effect on gesture recognition accuracy, potentially due to introducing more variation, as distinct subclasses, into the training data. Lack of real objects allowed the pretend grasps to generalise better under their class groups, which highlights a new exploration area for our future studies. We intend to look at grasp memory, comparing training and recognition with sub-classes, to training with imagined grasps. Our hypothesis is that pretend grasp can utilise extrinsic characteristics of grasp poses, while embedded reality grasps will have more clear intrinsic qualities.

Here our main aim was to explore if a game can be played with the Myo armband using electromyography, and if there were distinct differences between embedded and virtual interactions in game. Our findings affirm enjoyment and also shows similar game performance data, leading to our next step in utilising the game in a rehabilitation context in our next studies.

References

1. Rapael Smart Glove This smart glove speeds rehabilitation of stroke patients. https://www.forbes.com/sites/jenniferhicks/2015/11/08/thissmartglovespeedsrehabilitationofstrokepatients/595eeb3566b0
2. AlMousa, M., Al-Khalifa, H.S., AlSobayel, H.: Requirements elicitation and prototyping of a fully immersive virtual reality gaming system for upper limb stroke rehabilitation in Saudi Arabia. Mob. Inf. Syst. **2017** (2017)
3. Amirabdollahian, F., et al.: Design, development and deployment of a hand/wrist exoskeleton for home-based rehabilitation after stroke - script project. Robotica **32**(8), 1331–1346 (2014). https://doi.org/10.1017/S0263574714002288
4. Amirabdollahian, F., Walters, M.L.: Application of support vector machines in detecting hand grasp gestures using a commercially off the shelf wireless myoelectric armband. In: 2017 International Conference on Rehabilitation Robotics (ICORR), pp. 111–115, July 2017. https://doi.org/10.1109/ICORR.2017.8009231
5. Hsu, C.W., Chang, C.C., Lin, C.J.: A practical guide to support vector classification. Technical report, Department of Computer Science, National Taiwan University (2003). http://www.csie.ntu.edu.tw/~cjlin/papers.html
6. Jack, D., et al.: Virtual reality-enhanced stroke rehabilitation. IEEE Trans. Neural Syst. Rehabil. Eng. **9**(3), 308–318 (2001). https://doi.org/10.1109/7333.948460
7. Kristensen, H.K., Persson, D., Nygren, C., Boll, M., Matzen, P.: Evaluation of evidence within occupational therapy in stroke rehabilitation. Scand. J. Occup. Ther. **18**(1), 11–25 (2011)

8. Laver, K., George, S., Thomas, S., Deutsch, J.E., Crotty, M.: Virtual reality for stroke rehabilitation. Stroke **43**(2), e20–e21 (2012). https://doi.org/10.1161/STROKEAHA.111.642439. http://stroke.ahajournals.org/content/43/2/e20

9. Leon, B., et al.: Grasps recognition and evaluation of stroke patients for supporting rehabilitation therapy. BioMed Res. Int. **2014** (2014)

10. Nijenhuis, S.M., et al.: Feasibility study into self-administered training at home using an arm and hand device with motivational gaming environment in chronic stroke. J. Neuroeng. Rehabil. **12**(1), 89 (2015)

11. Nudo, R.: Adaptive plasticity in motor cortex: implications for rehabilitation after brain injury. J. Rehabil. Med. **35**, 7–10 (2003). Official journal of the UEMS European Board of Physical and Rehabilitation Medicine

12. Michael, D.R., Chen, S.L.: Serious Games: Games that Educate, Train, and Inform (2006)

13. Sharma, S., Steuber, V., Amirabdollahian, F.: Assessing the impact of muscular fatigue on myoelectric signals using myo armband. In: 2019 12th International Conference on Advances in Computer-Human Interactions (ACHI), pp. 159–164. IARIA (2019)

14. da Silva Cameirão, M., Bermúdez i Badia, S., Duarte, E., Verschure, P.F.: Virtual reality based rehabilitation speeds up functional recovery of the upper extremities after stroke: a randomized controlled pilot study in the acute phase of stroke using the rehabilitation gaming system. Restorative Neurol. Neurosci. **29**(5), 287–298 (2011)

15. Tavakolan, M., Xiao, Z.G., Menon, C.: A preliminary investigation assessing the viability of classifying hand postures in seniors. Biomed. Eng. Online **10**(1), 1 (2011)

16. Valls-Solé, J., Rothwell, J.C., Goulart, F., Cossu, G., Muñoz, E.: Patterned ballistic movements triggered by a startle in healthy humans. J. Physiol. **516**(3), 931–938 (1999). https://doi.org/10.1111/j.1469-7793.1999.0931u.x

17. Wang, N., Chen, Y., Zhang, X.: The recognition of multi-finger prehensile postures using LDA. Biomed. Signal Process. Control **8**(6), 706–712 (2013)

The Impact of a Robot Game Partner
When Studying Deception During
a Card Game

David-Octavian Iacob$^{(\boxtimes)}$ and Adriana Tapus

Autonomous Systems and Robotics Lab, U2IS, ENSTA Paris,
Institut Polytechnique de Paris,
828 Boulevard des Maréchaux, 91120 Palaiseau, France
{david-octavian.iacob,adriana.tapus}@ensta-paris.fr

Abstract. Our previous work in detecting deception in HRI was based
on research findings from the psychology of inter-human interactions.
Nonetheless, these conclusions may or may not be directly applied in
HRI, as humans may not behave similarly when deceiving a robot. This
paper studies the differences between human physiological manifestations
during a deception card game scenario when playing it with a human or
a robot partner. Our results show the existence of significant differences
between the participants' skin conductance, eye openness, and head pose
when playing the game with a robot partner compared to when playing the game with a human partner. These results will then be used to
improve the ability of robots to detect deception in HRI.

Keywords: Robotics · Deception · Physiology

1 Introduction

Social Robotics [2,3] focuses on improving the ability of robots to naturally
and efficiently interact with humans. In order to do so, robots must be able to
understand the verbal and nonverbal messages sent by their interlocutors. In our
research [1], we focus on the nonverbal components, which are crucial parts of
the communication, especially since a lack of comprehension of these components
could make the robots significantly easier to deceive.

According to [4], humans react in line with previous experiences with communications, even when having an agent or a robot interlocutor. Moreover, the
authors also concluded that if one of the communication partner lacks some of
the basic abilities for interaction and communication, such as social perspective
taking, the result could be the impossibility to achieve proper communication
between the partners. Such an ability is understanding when being deceived by
the interlocutor, at least up to some extent, and lacking it could significantly
impair the quality of the communication.

On top of reducing the quality of the communication, the lack of the ability to
detect deception is particularly problematic for Socially Assistive Robots (SAR)

© Springer Nature Switzerland AG 2019
M. A. Salichs et al. (Eds.): ICSR 2019, LNAI 11876, pp. 399–409, 2019.
https://doi.org/10.1007/978-3-030-35888-4_37

[5], used in the process of physiological or psychological rehabilitation [6–8]. The latter sometimes attempt to deceive the former [9] in order to avoid following the medical recommendations that are part of the rehabilitation process. Therefore, SARs could be unable to perform their tasks due to their inability to detect deception.

One of the state-of-the-art techniques in deception detection is the polygraph-based approach [10]. This technique has been developed and refined by psychologists and has been used for decades by investigators, prosecutors, and law enforcement forces, using **humans** as interrogators. Therefore, if we apply similar techniques in HRI, we have no guarantee they will work, simply because the entity asking the questions is a robot instead of a human.

In this work, we have designed a card game that entices players to deceive their game partners and that each participant plays twice, once with a robot game partner and once with a human game partner. We investigate **the differences between the physiological manifestations** that the participants exhibit when playing the game with the robot partner and with the human partner. In particular, we are measuring the participants' heart rate, skin conductance, as well as their head position and orientation and their eye openness.

The paper is structured as follows: Sect. 2 discusses the techniques that can be used in order to detect deception and how the results can be influenced by the nature of the interlocutor, Sect. 3 presents the experimental setup, Sect. 4 describes the methodology used for data acquisition and analysis, Sect. 5 discusses our results, and finally Sect. 6 concludes our paper.

2 Deception and Physiological Signals

2.1 Deception Detection Techniques

The polygraph [10] is by far the most accurate way to detect deception in inter-human interactions based on physiological manifestations, with a reliability of 81% to 91% according to the latest research [11]. It measures, with high accuracy, various physiological parameters, such as Galvanic Skin Response (GSR) [10, 12], the heart rate, and blood pressure [10,13] or respiratory rate [10]. These measurements are collected by invasive means, in very rigorous conditions and setups, which makes traditional polygraphs inappropriate for detecting deception in HRI.

Therefore, we decided to focus on **noninvasive and minimally-invasive measurement techniques**, while using a polygraph-based approach. In particular, we are using a RGB video camera and a wireless, portable sensor armband. They allow us to evaluate various physiological measurements without compromising the quality of the interaction and without limiting the mobility and dexterity of the human in any significant way. Moreover, such measurement techniques can be easily integrated or are already part of robotic platforms. On the downside, the noninvasive and minimally invasive measurement techniques offer less precise and accurate measurements, therefore reducing the ability to detect deception. Also, such noninvasive techniques that rely on video cameras have already been used to detect deception in inter-human interaction scenarios [21].

2.2 Interacting with Robots

Researchers have already studied, to some extent, the behaviour, reactions, and physiological manifestations of human users when interacting with a robot or even virtual partners, in some cases comparing them with similar inter-human interactions. For example, the authors in [14] have studied the heart and electro-dermal activity of human users when interacting with human and virtual agents, finding that heart inter-beat intervals were shorter when interacting with virtual agents instead of human agents. Moreover, in [15] the human arousal was analysed by measuring the GSR, electrocardiography, and cortisol levels of the participants in order to understand the effect of a robot initiated touch on the stress level of participants. Even though past research [15] had shown that humans physiological or subjective stress responses could decrease when participants were being briefly touched on their arm, they concluded that there was no such decrease when the participants were touched by a robot.

In one of our past research conducted in a lab setting, we investigated the human physiological responses to various HRI scenarios by monitoring the GSR [16,17], facial temperature [16,17] and blink rates [17]. In both interaction scenarios (a Jenga game [16] played with either a robot or a human and a variation of the Stroop test [18] played with or without robot's assistance), the number of GSR peaks was significantly higher when interacting with a robot with respect to the control conditions (human game partner [16] or the absence of the robot [17]). Moreover, the blink rate was significantly higher when playing the Stroop game while being assisted by a robot than when playing it alone [17].

In this work, we compare the values of several physiological parameters (i.e., heart rate, GSR, eye openness, head position) in the particular context of interaction scenarios that have the main purpose of enticing the participants to deceive their interlocutors. To the best of our knowledge, no other research had directly compared the values of these parameters during identical human-human and human-robot interaction scenarios similar to the one we have designed.

3   Experimental Setup

We designed an experiment consisting of a card game played by the participant with both a human and a robot partner. The objective of the participant was to deceive their game partner during half of the game rounds and be honest during the other half of the game rounds, scoring a point for each round where they were successful. The participant also had to fill in a post-experiment questionnaire, in order to evaluate their perception of the experiment. Their predilection to lie was established using an Eysenck Personality Questionnaire (EPQ) [19], using the Lie (EPQ-L) dimension.

The physiological manifestations of the participant were monitored using both a high-definition RGB camera, as well as a wireless sensor armband, shown in Fig. 2, that was being placed on the participant's left arm during the experiment.

3.1 The Card Game

The participant sat down at a table, in front of the game partner. Two decks of cards, shown on the left side of Fig. 1, were placed on the table. On the left, there was a deck of 32 large cards with pictures of objects, persons, or animals, with a text caption naming the main entity depicted in the picture. On the right, there was a deck of 8 small cards, half red and half green, randomly shuffled and facing down. The colour of the card instructed the player whether to be honest (green) or deceitful (red) during that round. In the middle, there was a small box used to discard the used cards and a sheet of paper containing the game instructions.

Fig. 1. The two decks of cards (left) and the game setup (right) (Color figure online)

As the experiment started, the game partner (human or a Softbank Pepper robot) explained the game rules to the participant. Then, the first 8 rounds of the game started. Even though the robot was shorter than the human when both were standing up, we made sure that their heads were placed at the same height for this experiment. The human game partner was sitting down, while the robot was standing up, therefore eliminating any source of bias induced by the position of the game partner's head and/or eyes. The experimental setup can be observed on the right of Fig. 1.

At each round, the player chose one of the 32 picture cards from the left side deck, then drew the top card from the small deck on the right. The game partner then tried to guess what was depicted in the chosen image card. The human or robot partner asked 5 questions that the participant had to answer with *YES* or *NO* and guessed an image based on these answers. If the participant had drawn a green card, then their objective was to answer these questions truthfully, so their partner guessed the right image card. Otherwise, if the participant had drawn a red card, their objective was to mislead their game partner.

At the end of the round, after the game partner tried to guess the chosen image, the participant showed their partner their two current cards. If the participant was supposed to be honest and their partner had guessed the correct image, then the participant won a point. Similarly, if they were supposed to be deceitful and their partner had guessed the wrong image, the participant also won a point. Otherwise, the participant did not win any point for that round.

After the 8 rounds were complete, the participant was notified about the outcome of the game. If they had scored 4 points or more, they won a marshmallow or a candy. Moreover, if they scored the maximum score of 8 points, they also had a chance to win a 50€gift card, based on the results of a lottery organised with all the participants who had obtained the maximum score.

3.2 Questionnaires

Two questionnaires were given to the participants: the EPQ (short, revised version) and a post-experimental questionnaire. The short version of the revised EPQ [19], comprised of 48 questions, was used to establish the Lie (EPQ-L) dimension of a participant's personality, on a scale from 0 to 12, therefore allowing us to know to what extent they were willing to lie.

The post-experimental questionnaire was handed to the participant after the experiment was over and consisted of 12 questions, such as: *Did you like playing the game?*, *Did you find it stressful to answer the questions during the rounds where you had to lie?*, and *Do you think your game partner knew when you were deceiving him?*.

3.3 Participants

25 participants took part in this experiment, all having a background in Technical Sciences. All of them have played the game twice, with the robot and with the human partner. They were distributed into two equal groups: 13 (robot partner first) and 12 (human partner first). They were distributed in these two groups based on their EPQ-L score and their gender as evenly as possible:

- **robot first**: 11 male, 2 female, 6.15 average EPQ-L
- **human first**: 10 male, 2 female, 6.42 average EPQ-L.

4   Data Analysis

4.1   Hardware and Measurements

Two main sensors are used to record and analyse the physiological manifestations of the participant during the game: a Logitech C920 video camera, providing HD (1280×720) output at 30 Hz and a custom-built, ROS-compatible wireless sensor armband, measuring the participant's heart rate and GSR. The video camera is placed on a fixed tripod, right in front of the participant, on the other side of the table, while the armband is placed on the participant's left upper arm, with the heart rate sensor being placed on the participant's wrist, and the GSR sensors on the index and the little finger. The armband, displayed in Fig. 2, was designed to be as minimally cumbersome and invasive as possible and to allow the participants to easily use both their hands throughout the game. They both communicate with the computer used by the experimenter to supervise the experiment.

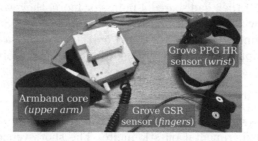

Fig. 2. The wireless sensor armband

The sensors used to measure the GSR and heart rate are both provided by Grove. The heart rate sensor is optical, using an LED and an optical sensor to detect blood flow, and has a sampling frequency of 1 Hz, computing the heart rate every second based on the previous measurements. The GSR sensor is analog, therefore not limiting the sampling frequency. The data streams (video, HR, and GSR) are being acquired using ROS packages and then processed using a program developed in C++ using ROS and OpenCV. The software then uses the DLib Face Tracker [20] to track 68 facial landmark points in the RGB frame. The application also monitors the video stream during the experiment, the evolution of the HR and GSR and allows the experimenter to control the robot during the games played with a robot partner.

Based on the facial landmark points detected using the DLib Face Tracker, several facial features are being extracted: **eye openness** (the vertical distance between the eyelids, in pixels), **head position and size** (horizontal and vertical position in the frame and head width and height, in pixels) and **head orientation** (estimated face pitch, roll and yaw). Each set of variables, whether raw or computed, is logged to an individual stamped CSV (Comma Separated Variable) file, at a frequency of 20...30 Hz (depending on the CPU load). Each CSV file is later used for post-experimental processing and analysis.

4.2   Analysis Procedure

The logged data is analysed post-experimentally, using Scilab and MATLAB scripts that process the CSV log files. Manual annotations register the key moments of the game (beginning and end of each interval), as well as the whether the participant was deceitful or honest during each round. The annotations are used for data segmentation, so the evolution of each parameter can be correlated to the objective of the participant. All the data was annotated by one of the authors, while the recordings of 4 random participants have been chosen for annotation by a second rater. The Cohen's kappa coefficient for inter-rater agreement had a value of $\kappa = 0.938$, which corresponds to almost perfect agreement.

For a given participant and evaluated parameter, we define 9 analysis intervals: **the reference interval** (the phase during which the game partner explains the rules to the participant) and **8 game round intervals**, each of them between the moment when the participant is asked to choose an image card and the moment when they are notified if they won a point during the round. For each of these intervals, we compute the **average value**, the **standard deviation** and the **slope** of a linear interpolation of the data samples in the interval. Then, for each of the 8 game round intervals, we compute the relative values (average, standard deviation and slope) with respect to the reference interval. The relative values are then stored in a new set of .csv files, where they are correlated with the participant's objective during each round (help or deceive their game partner).

5   Results

5.1   Statistical Correlations

We have established a series of correlations between the head position and orientation and the nature of the game partner, that can be resumed in Table 1. Here, the $\tilde{H}$ and $\tilde{R}$ columns represent the median values of the given measure relative to the reference interval when playing the game with a human and robot partner, respectively. All the data tested with the ANOVA test and the t-test was normally distributed, while the data tested with the Kruskal-Wallis test was not.

Table 1. Head position and orientation vs. nature of the game partner

Parameter	Measure	Test	p-value	$\tilde{H}$	$\tilde{R}$
Head x	std. dev.	t-test	$1.02 * 10^{-12}$	$2.71 * 10^{-1}$	$4.90 * 10^{-1}$
Head y	std. dev.	t-test	$3.61 * 10^{-16}$	$1.32 * 10^{-1}$	$2.27 * 10^{-1}$
Head width	std. dev.	Kruskal-Wallis	$4.01 * 10^{-9}$	$5.11 * 10^{-1}$	$0.40 * 10^{-1}$
Head height	std. dev.	ANOVA	$7.58 * 10^{-6}$	$4.97 * 10^{-1}$	$0.50 * 10^{-1}$
Head roll	average	ANOVA	$1.31 * 10^{-2}$	$3.05 * 10^{-2}$	$1.12 * 10^{-2}$
Head pan	std. dev.	ANOVA	$3.33 * 10^{-6}$	$-2.48 * 10^{-2}$	$3.34 * 10^{-2}$
Head tilt	std. dev.	ANOVA	$1.31 * 10^{-4}$	$-0.80 * 10^{-2}$	$4.17 * 10^{-2}$

As our results show, the participants have moved their heads more both in the horizontal and vertical planes when playing the game with the robot partner compared to the human partner. The participants' head pan and tilt also varied more when playing the game **with a robot partner** compared to a human partner, these results being in line with the variations observed with respect to the head x and y positions. However, their head width and height varied more when playing the game **with a human partner**, which implies that their interaction distance also varied more when playing the game **with the human partner** than with the robot partner. On top of that, their average head roll was also higher when playing the game **with a human game partner**.

The data in Table 2 shows the correlations found between the evolution of the participants' skin conductance and eye openness and the nature of their interlocutor, with the same conventions used in Table 1. The analysis of the results shows that the participants had exhibited a higher skin conductance (therefore a lower skin resistance) relative to the baseline interval when playing the game **with a human partner** compared to playing the game with a robot partner. A higher skin conductance (or a lower skin resistance) is usually associated to an increased level of sweating. This reaction can be a consequence of an increased stress level when playing the game with a human partner.

Moreover, the slope of the linear interpolation of the skin conductance was **lower when playing the game with a robot partner**, which means that their skin conductance was more constant during the games played with a robot.

Table 2. Physiological manifestations vs. the nature of the game partner

Parameter	Measure	Test	p-value	$\check{H}$	$\check{R}$
Skin conductance	average	t-test	$2.81 * 10^{-22}$	$2.16 * 10^{-1}$	$2.04 * 10^{-1}$
Skin conductance	slope	t-test	$3.48 * 10^{-6}$	$7.51 * 10^{-4}$	$2.20 * 10^{-5}$
Eye openness	average	t-test	$1.63 * 10^{-3}$	$-1.15 * 10^{-2}$	$-1.34 * 10^{-2}$
Eye openness	std. dev.	ANOVA	$1.42 * 10^{-2}$	$7.80 * 10^{-3}$	$2.25 * 10^{-3}$

The participants average eye openness was also higher when playing the game **with a human partner**, as well as the standard deviation of the same physiological parameter. This means that their eyelids were more open and also that they blinked more often when playing the game with a human partner than with a robot partner. No statistically significant correlations were found between the participants' heart rate and the nature of their game partner.

5.2   Questionnaire-Based Evaluation

The answers to the post-experimental questionnaire were analysed in order to understand their perception of the game and of their game partner, as well as their desire to win their rewards. The participants' answers are on a Likert scale from 1 to 7, where 1 corresponds to "Strongly disagree", 7 corresponds to "Strongly agree" and 4 to "Neutral". The list of questions comprised in the post-experimental questionnaire is the following:

1. Did you like playing the game?
2. Would you like to play the game again?
3. Did you find it difficult to play the game?
4. Did you want to win the marshmallow or candy?
5. Did you want to get the maximum score, so you can have a chance to win the gift card?
6. Did you find it difficult to answer the questions when you had to tell the truth?
7. Did you find it difficult to answer the questions when you had to lie?
8. Were you frustrated during the rounds when you had to tell the truth?
9. Were you frustrated during the rounds when you had to lie?
10. Were you stressed during the rounds when you had to tell the truth?
11. Were you stressed during the rounds when you had to lie?
12. Do you think your game partner knew when you were deceiving him?

Overall, the participants enjoyed playing the game, with an average of **5.74**, were motivated to get the maximum score (**5.80**) and did not find the game difficult (**2.42**). Their perceived stress level was also low (**3.12** overall, with **2.56** for the rounds when they were honest and **3.68** for the deceitful ones).

We also studied if there are any statistically significant differences between their answers after playing the game with a robot game partner and their answers after playing the game with a human game partner, we have observed that the only significant difference was found with respect to question number 3 (*Did you find it difficult to play the game?*). Participants have found it more difficult to play the game with a robot partner than with a human partner, with an average value of **2.76** and **2.08** respectively, with a p-value of $4.79 * 10^{-2}$. The data was analysed with the Wilcoxon rank sum test.

Participants also reported an increased stress level when playing the game with a robot partner compared to a human, with averages of **3.26** and **2.98**, respectively. The difference was more notable during the rounds when participants were honest, with an average of **2.88** and **2.24**, respectively. Albeit not proven to be statistically significant, these values confirm the theory that the participants' higher skin conductance when playing the game with a robot can be justified by an increased stress level.

6 Conclusions

The purpose of this research was to study the physiological response induced by a robot game partner during an interaction scenario where humans would be enticed to lie while playing a card game. We tried to understand if there are statistically significant differences in the physiological manifestations of the participants when playing the game with a robot compared to the scenario where the same game is played with a human. Moreover, we analysed their perception of the stress, difficulty and frustration levels in each game scenario.

We have found statistically significant correlations between the nature of the game partner (human or robot) and the relative skin conductance, the relative eye openness, and the relative head position and orientation of the participants. The physiological parameters we have analysed are also monitored when trying to detect deception in inter-human interactions, proving therefore that the nature of the interaction (inter-human vs. human-robot) has an impact on the ability to detect deception using polygraph-based approaches and that the nature of the interlocutor (human or robot) needs to be taken into account when detecting deception.

In future research, we plan on analysing the correlations between the physiological manifestations we monitor and deception during the rounds where the participants are enticed to lie, and then comparing them to the impact of the game partner's nature in the same game scenario.

References

1. Iacob, D.O., Tapus, A.: First attempts in deception detection in HRI by using thermal and RGB-D cameras. In: RO-MAN (2018)
2. Duffy, B.R.: Fundamental issues in social robotics. Int. Rev. Inf. Ethics (2006)
3. Hegel, F., Gieselmann, S., Peters, A., Holthaus, P., Wrede, B.: Towards a typology of meaningful signals and cues in social robotics. In: RO-MAN (2011)
4. Krämer, N.C., von der Pütten, A., Eimler, S.: Human-agent and human-robot interaction theory: similarities to and differences from human-human interaction. In: Zacarias, M., de Oliveira, J.V. (eds.) Human-Computer Interaction: The Agency Perspective. SCI, vol. 396, pp. 215–240. Springer, Heidelberg (2012). https://doi.org/10.1007/978-3-642-25691-2_9
5. Feil-Seifer, D., Mataric, M.: Socially assistive robots. In: ICORR (2005)
6. Malik, N.A., Hanapiah, F.A., Rahman, R.A.A., Yussof, H.: Emergence of socially assistive robotics in rehabilitation for children with cerebral palsy: a review. Int. J. Adv. Robot. Syst. **13**(3), 135 (2016)
7. Mataric, M., Tapus, A., Winstein, C., Eriksson, J.: Socially assistive robotics for stroke and mild TBI rehabilitation. Adv. Technol. Rehabil. **145**, 249–262 (2009)
8. Tapus, A., Mataric, M.J.: Socially assistive robotic music therapist for mantaining attention of older adults with cognitive impairments. In: ICORR (2009)
9. Matarić, M., Eriksson, J., Feil-Seifer, D., Winstein, C.: Socially assistive robotics for post-stroke rehabilitation. J. NeuroEng. Rehabil. **4**(1), 5 (2007)
10. Horvath, F., Reid, J.: The reliability of polygraph examiner diagnosis of truth and deception. J. Crim. Law Criminol. **62**, 276 (1971)
11. Gaggioli, A.: Beyond the truth machine: emerging technologies for lie detection. Cyberpsychol. Behav. Soc. Netw. **21**(2), 144–144 (2018)
12. Hossain, M.Z., Gedeon, T., Sankaranarayana, R.: Observer's galvanic skin response for discriminating real from fake smiles. In: The 27th Australasian Conference on Information Systems (2016)
13. Reid, J.E.: Simulated blood pressure responses in lie-detector tests and a method for their detection. J. Crim. Law Criminol. **36**, 201 (1945)
14. Poore, J., Webb, A., Hays, M.J., Trimmer, M.: Emulating sociality: a comparison study of physiological signals from human and virtual social interactions. In: Society for Cognitive and Affective Neuroscience (2012)
15. Willemse, C.J.A.M., Toet, A., van Erp, J.B.F.: Affective and behavioral responses to robot-initiated social touch: toward understanding the opportunities and limitations of physical contact in human-robot interaction. Front. ICT **4**, 12 (2017)
16. Agrigoroaie, R., Cruz Maya, A., Tapus, A.: "Oh! I am so sorry!": understanding user physiological variation while spoiling a game task. In: IEEE/RSJ International Conference on Intelligent Robots and Systems (IROS) (2018)
17. Agrigoroaie, R., Tapus, A.: Cognitive performance and physiological response analysis. Int. J. Soc. Robot. (2019)
18. Stroop, J.: Studies of interference in serial verbal reactions. J. Exploratory Psychol. **18**(6), 643 (1935)

19. Eysenck, S.B.G., Eysenck, H.J., Barrett, P.: A revised version of the psychoticism scale. Pers. Individ. Differ. **6**(1), 21–29 (1985)

20. King, D.E.: Dlib-ml: a machine learning toolkit. J. Mach. Learn. Res. **10**, 1755–1758 (2009)

21. Bouma, H., Burghouts, G., den Hollander, R., et al.: Measuring cues for stand-off deception detection based on full-body non-verbal features in body-worn cameras. In: SPIE Security + Defence (2016)

I'm Not Playing Anymore! A Study Comparing Perceptions of Robot and Human Cheating Behavior

Kerstin Haring[1](✉)(iD), Kristin Nye[2], Ryan Darby[2], Elizabeth Phillips[2], Ewart de Visser[2](iD), and Chad Tossell[2](iD)

[1] University of Denver, Denver, CO, USA
`kerstin.haring@du.edu`
[2] United States Air Force Academy, Colorado Springs, CO, USA
`{elizabeth.phillips,ewart.devisser,chad.tossell}@usafa.edu`

Abstract. Cheating is a universally salient and disliked behavior. Previous research has shown that a cheating robot dramatically increases perception of its perceived agency. However, this original research did not directly compare human cheating to robot cheating. We examined whether the human and the robot were evaluated differently in terms of reactionary behaviors as well as attribution of mental states and perception of competence, warmth, agency, and capabilities to experience. This study was able to partially recreate the previous study findings [10] showing that participants were highly socially engaged with the cheating robot and showing hostile reactions to the cheating action of the robot. In contrast, these reactions were not observed for the human condition. Additionally, play interactions with the robot were rated as more discomforting compared to the experience with the human player. Finally, it was found that the robot was perceived as less warm, competent, agentic, and able to experience than the human. This result could be attributed primarily due to the inherent human-like difference in agents. Several implications of this study are discussed with respect to the design of robot behavior and human social norms.

Keywords: Human-robot interaction · Social robots · Robot perception · Robot behavior

1 Introduction

Previous studies have shown that the perception of agency in a robot can be investigated using the social dynamics of cheating [13,15]. The initial study [13] investigated which robot behavior variations result in attributions of mental

This research is supported by the Air Force Office of Scientific Research under grant number 16RT0881. The views expressed in this article reflect those of the authors and may or may not reflect those of the USAF Academy, United States Air Force, and United States Government.

M. A. Salichs et al. (Eds.): ICSR 2019, LNAI 11876, pp. 410–419, 2019.
https://doi.org/10.1007/978-3-030-35888-4_38

states and intentionality to the robot. Results showed that the robot announcing its (cheated) win verbally was interpreted as a malfunction. The robot displaying the (cheated) gesture to win was perceived as cheating and showed an increase in social engagement, greater attributions of mental states to the robot and the robot being perceived as more agentic. These results were obtained by observation of participant behaviors and written responses towards a Nico robot. A follow-up study using a Nao robot investigated the possible explanations for the greater attribution of agency [10]. The study included four conditions in which the robot would cheat to win when it lost, cheat to tie when it lost, cheat to tie when it won, and cheat to lose when it won. It was shown that the cheat to win when lost condition was significantly more salient for participants recognizing the cheating action and was the significantly least to be considered fair and honest compared to all other conditions. This study however did not replicate the findings of higher agency for a cheating robot. This could have been due to the initially high attribution of agency towards the Nao robot used in this study as opposed to the Nico robot. Other studies have shown that when the perceived agency of highly humanoid robots are initially high no significantly changes occur before, during and after an interaction [7]. The research to date has shown that humans do indeed have a cheating detector which is triggered by the most adversarial type of cheating; the robot cheating to win when it lost, as opposed to the stipulated additional motion of cheating action [13]. It has been proposed that humans tend to detect cheating against them as a means of self-preservation [3], that this capability is independent of age or cognitive capacity, that the detection is performed automatically and effortlessly [16], and aids in identifying individuals that cheat against the person [17]. This seems to also apply to robots, supported by the experimental results of the robot in the cheating to win condition [10]. Few studies so far have investigated the difference between a human and a robot agent in the same study setting. It is possible however that people are more open to show their immediate reactions towards the robots based on previous research. For example, a previous study found that people are willing to disclose more information to a virtual agent than to a human [11]. This leads to hypothesis H1: The reactions towards a robot cheating is stronger and more immediate than a human cheating. Given the salience of the adversarial and least pro-social cheating to win condition in prior research [10], this research recreates in part the cheating condition in which the robots changes its gesture to win and then announces its win. This study directly compares the reactions to and perceptions of competence, warmth, discomfort, agency, and experience of cheating for a human and a robot in more detail. Even though people seem to be somewhat more lenient towards robots than algorithms, we hypothesized that humans will be evaluated more favorably than robots when compared directly. Our second hypothesis (H2) was therefore as follows: The perception of the agent in the robot condition is lower for all perception measurements than in the human condition.

2 Methodology

2.1 Participants

We recruited 38 participants from the US Air Force Academy in Colorado. Three participants were excluded due to incomplete data and robot malfunctions, leaving 20 in the robot condition, and 15 in the human condition. The age range of all participants was between 17 and 24 in the participant pool. This resulted in a median age of participants of 20.5. Of the participants, 16 were female, 2 did not identify their gender, and 20 were male. Participants were recruited through the academy's participant recruitment Sona System. Participants were reimbursed for their time trough extra credit as stated in their participating course syllabi.

2.2 Robot Platform

This study used the Aldebaran Nao robot. The Nao robot is a humanlike robot with an ABOT score of 45.92 out of a 100 [12]. This made Nao one of the more humanlike robots available for research and did account for its perceived intelligence and agency at some level [19]. A custom python code from a previous study [10] was used as wizard-of-oz control for the robot.

2.3 Experimental Setup

The study consisted of two conditions, robot and human agent, in which both agents displayed the exact same behavior at a prior specified time in the study. When the agent lost, it cheated to win by changing its hand gesture (i.e., rock, paper, or scissors, see Fig. 1) after the throw and announced the (unjust) outcome verbally ("I win"). The human condition followed the same protocol as the robot condition. The human confederate was always the same person, male, and of the same age group as the participants. The confederate followed the same protocol as the robot with the gestures matching the robot's as shown in Fig. 1. The confederate was instructed to make gesture decisions in the moment to act and play the game naturally. The confederate then cheated in the same fashion as the robot did, twice via visible gesture change between rounds 11 and 20.

2.4 Procedure

Participants were asked to play 30 rounds of rock, paper, scissors with the Nao robot in a wizard-of-oz design using the same code as presented in [10]. The robot started the study by introducing itself as "Chris" and demonstrating the three different gestures. The robot did not explain the rules of the game as it was assumed to be widely known. None of the participants did not have knowledge of the game and all proceeded to start playing after the robot announced: "Let's play". The robot raised and lowered its right hand three times, declared the respective notion "Rock", "Paper", "Scissors", and on the fourth time said "Shoot", displaying its randomly pre-determined gesture. In the non-cheating

Fig. 1. The experimental set-up with the human cheating confederate experimental set-up on the left and the robot cheating confederate condition on the right, including Nao's rock, paper, and scissors gestures as used in this and the previous study [10].

phase, the robot then declared its win "Yes, I win", its loss "Aw, you win", and a draw "We have tied this round". In the cheating phase, the robot visibly changed its initially thrown gesture to a winning gesture before announcing it won. These were the same utterances as emitted in Short et al. [13] and Litou et al. [10]. The initial and last ten rounds of the study were designated as the non-cheating portion of the study (rounds 1–10 and 21–30). Only between rounds 11 and 20, the robot cheated a total of two times. Given that the gestures of the participant could not be anticipated, the cheating occurred at the first two occasions in which the robot could cheat to win and the rest of the gameplay proceeded in a regular fashion. If there were was no opportunity to cheat to win (e.g. robot wins all rounds 11–20), the cheat would happen at the first two occasions and the game would proceed for more than 30 rounds. This did not occur in the present study. To minimize operator influence on the game outcome and potential operator errors or wrong timings, the robot was programmed to automatically account for the cheating phase. A human operator was remotely observing the participant's gestures via camera and input this information. The robot used this input to declare it's win, loss, or draw on the non-cheating phases of the study and to cheat and declare it's win in the cheating phase.

Previous research established that gesture changes in the cheating part should be clear and visible in order to have the intended effect [10]. The movements were designed to be slow and pronounced enough that the gesture change was visible. All gestures were randomly created before the study and repeated in the same order for each participant to ensure consistency across participants in the robot condition. In the human condition, the experimenter made his decisions about the gesture to throw on the spot to ensure a natural gameplay interaction. The cheating was incorporated at the exact same time (between rounds 11 and 20) as the robot. The experimenter also always changed his gesture from a loss to a win.

2.5 Measures

Participant behaviors and utterances were collected for each condition. Participants were asked to fill out a post-experiment questionnaire rating participants' perceptions of the robot's or human's competence, warmth, discomfort (scale 1

– not at all to 7 – very much so) [2], agency, and experience (scale 1 – not at all
to 5 – very much) [7]. Agency perception included items asking if the robot has
the capability to memorize, plan, independently execute actions, and exercise
self control. Experience perception included items of the robot being able to feel
pleasure, pain, fear, and emotions. An open comment section was also included
in the questionnaire.

3   Results

Hypothesis testing was performed using Welch's unequal variances t-test to
determine whether there were significant differences between the means of the
two conditions for each concept measured. The Welch's t-test was used due to
unequal sample sizes.

Table 1. The accumulated behavioral observations and participant's reactions to the
human and robot cheating action.

Behavioral observation	Human	Robot	Verbal responses	Human	Robot
Smile	12	13	No (you don't)	0	8
Laugh	0	17	He is cheating	0	6
Cheating back	0	14	What? or Wait! What?	0	4
Startle response	0	11	Utterance: hm?	0	2
Head shake	0	7	This robot, man	0	1
Surprise	0	5	Lies!	0	1
Refusing to play	0	4	This was blatant buddy	0	1

3.1   Behavioral Observations and Open-Ended Responses

Given the opportunity to comment on the agent's behavior, 60% of the participants in the robot and 33.3% in the human condition chose to comment on
the behaviors. The comments in the human condition included that the experimenter was professional, and that "[the experimenter] did not completely play
to the rules of the game but he was not aggressive and still very friendly". For
the robot however, comments included confusion to why the robot cheated, that
it was easy for the robot to cheat, and the lack of capabilities to play anything
besides rock, paper, scissors. The behavioral observation (see Table 1) show a
high social engagement with the robot, and not with the human agent. Table 1
describes the reactions to the cheating action. These behaviors have to be seen
in the context of participants displaying some degree of boredom playing with
the robot for the first 10 rounds. Other comments towards the robot's cheating
action included statements like: "This is just like babysitting" "Chris, I don't
appreciate it" "Right, this is killing me (laugh)".

3.2 Perceived Discomfort, Competence, and Warmth

Significant differences were found between the robot and the human for perceived discomfort experienced (see Fig. 2). Discomfort ratings for the two groups differed significantly according to Welch's t-test, $t(27.5) = -7.72$, $p < .001$, Cohen's $d = -2.38$. The 95% confidence interval is between 1.33 and 2.3 on the 1–7 rating scale.

Significant differences were found between the robot and the human for perceived competence (see Fig. 2). Competence ratings for the two groups differed significantly according to Welch's t-test, $t(31.9) = -5.44$, $p < .001$, Cohen's $d = -1.83$. The 95% confidence interval is between 1.31 and 2.88 on the 1–7 rating scale.

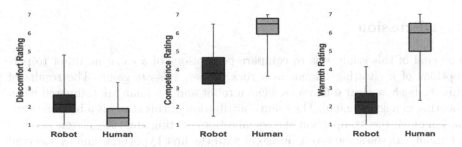

Fig. 2. A boxplot showing the Interquartile Range (IQR) of the perceived discomfort rating. The horizontal lines inside the boxes are the median, the Whiskers shows Minimum and Maximum values. The agent has an effect on the perceived discomfort rating, the competence rating, and on the perceived warmth rating with the human condition seeming to have more variability.

Significant differences were found between the robot and the human for perceived warmth experienced (see Fig. 2). Warmth ratings for the two groups differed significantly according to Welch's t-test, $t(21.7) = -7.61$, $p < .001$, Cohen's $d = -2.78$. The 95% confidence interval is between 2.88 and 4.0 on the 1–7 rating scale.

3.3 Perceived Agency and Experience

Significant differences were found between the robot and the human for perceived capability of agency (see Fig. 3). Agency ratings for the two groups differed significantly according to Welch's t-test, $t(27.5) = -7.72$, $p < .001$, Cohen's $d = -2.83$. The 95% confidence interval is between 1.33 and 2.3 on the 1–5 rating scale. These results support the second researchers' hypothesis.

Significant differences were found between the robot and the human for perceived capability of experience (see Fig. 3). Experience ratings for the two groups differed significantly according to Welch's t-test, $t(20.3) = -11.7$, $p < .001$, Cohen's $d = -4.34$. The 95% confidence interval is between 2.52 and 3.61 on the 1–5 rating scale. These results support the researchers' second hypothesis.

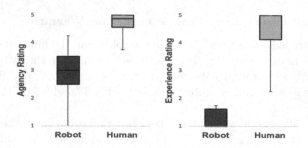

Fig. 3. The perceived agency and experience rating. The agent seems to have an effect on the perceived agency rating with the robot condition seeming to have more variability. The agent seems to have an effect on the perceived experience rating.

4   Discussion

The goal of this study was to compare perceptions of a cheating robot to perceptions of a cheating human in a rock, paper, scissors game. The results of this study show clear differences when a robot and a human are compared when cheating in a social game. The main contribution of this study is a baseline evaluation of a direct comparison of a social robot cheating and the differences when a human acts the same way. Consistent with the first hypothesis and as observed in the previously conducted studies, participants showed high social engagement with the robot in the cheating to win condition with the robot [10]. They also showed immediate and emotional reactions towards the cheating robot and even made unfavorable character attributions to the cheating robot [13].

In direct comparison, participants simply smiled when the human experimenter cheated and then continued on with the gameplay. No utterances or statements were made during the study in the human condition. The reactions towards robot stand in stark contrast with the reaction towards the human player. Participants showed a range of different reactions ranging from smiles and laughter, to startle responses showing pronounced changes in expression, to participants refusing to continue to play, insulting the robot, and often vehemently stating "No! You didn't!" when the robot falsely announces "Yes, I win". It was also observed that participants, up to the point where the robot started cheating after round 10, seemed relatively unengaged or even bored by the interaction with the robot. The participants often opposed the cheating actions of the robot explicitly but not the human, which may have caused a higher rating of interaction discomfort for the robot. Even though participants displayed amusement and surprise when the robot cheated, they did not seem comfortable of the action itself directed towards them. Despite the salient behavioral reactions towards the robot, the human was rated significantly higher than the robot for competence, warmth, agency, experience which is in line with the second hypothesis. With regard to the second hypothesis, these results have to be carefully interpreted as two different agents are expected to be perceived differently. Like all perception, social perception reflects evolutionary pressures [4].

It therefore was an expected result that the human has significantly higher ratings along the universal dimensions of social cognition: warmth and competence. This also is in line with prior research showing machine systems and robots as less competent. Warmth is a dimension traditionally not attributed with machines, however it is a dimension that could potentially contribute to the evaluation of social robots and the interactions with them. The human interaction in this study was with a human adult, traditionally able and shown to have full capabilities for agency and experience [5], the perception of the human were expected to reach the upper limit of the rating scales. This did happen for perceived agency ($M = 4.71$, $SD = .41$) and respective perceived experience ($M = 4.45$, $SD = .91$) in this study. For the robot, perceived agency seemed to be quite high for a robot ($M = 2.9$, $SD = 0.94$, with other studies showing rating which are roughly equivalent of perceived agency ratings with $M \approx 1.5$ [14]), especially when compared to the experience ratings, which showed to be extremely low ($M = 1.38$, $SD = .5$). This might display that the robot behavior, in this case cheating, does influence the robot's perceived intentionality of its actions however make it literally "robot-like" when it comes to its perceived capabilities to experience. With the current state-of-the-art robots and research examining robot behaviors and how they ought to be perceived as intentional actions [18], it can only be speculated to why a robot's cheating behavior is perceived different from a human's. One hypothesis is that robots might be subject to a different set of social norms than humans are. Breaking social norms can result in formal punishments (e.g. fines for littering) or informal punishment (e.g. being shunned by other social agents). Some sort of informal punishment happened in this study by the participants refusing to continue the game with the robot after it cheated, however this was not observed for the human. One reason could be that especially machines, like robots, are expected to "play by the rules", even if those rules for robots are mostly not as clear as the general social norms people structure their lives around [8]. With social norms tied to behavioral expectations, people's expectation towards robots might be biased [6] and acting outside those expectations, as done here by cheating, result in strong reactions. However, the actions would need to be perceived as intentional.

Cheating in a game was highly salient. Other studies found that a robot littering was not recognized as intentional but an accidental action (even though it was intentional for purposes of the experiment [9]). In this study, there was no expectation of the robot actually having the capability of correctly disposing of trash. Cheating, by contrast, might be a very specific norm violation. Social norms often refer to the unwritten rules of behaviors that are considered acceptable within a group. Cheating, however, can be a very explicit and provocative violation. Also, cheating might be given special consideration because it is a direct hostile action against the participant, gaining an unfair advantage at their expense. In other words, cheating might be so salient because humans attribute it as intentional behavior. Previous research has shown that intentionality is the key to attributing human likeness to robotic agents [1]. This not necessarily the case with other types of norm violating behaviors. A previous study found that for certain norm-violating behaviors such as littering or jumping the line, people did not attribute higher mental states to robots performing these violations. The authors concluded that people may consider these types of violations as unintentional for robotic agents [9].

This study had several limitations. First and mainly, a robot and a human behavior were compared directly, hence significant changes in the perceptions of the respective behaviors were expected and the results should be interpreted with this limitation in mind. A future study should include a comparison that compares the behaviors of humans and robots while playing rock-paper-scissors without any cheating behavior. Second, the technology itself still poses challenges in terms of reaction times to human behaviors and interactions with the human. The robot acted quite slow at some points which could have additionally influenced the perception. Further, it is not quite clear if cheating is a special case of a social norm violation and what social mechanisms are at play when social robot make errors, intentionally cheat, or violate social norms. Building on to the current data in this study, additional conditions implementing a social norm violation as well as a baseline comparison of a neutral interaction would likely give additional insights about potential distinctions. Generally, additional research with different robot types is needed to examine and clarify the respective concepts for robot actions that are perceived as intentional.

5 Conclusion

People react to robot actions and perceive their actions differently compared to humans. In particular, the robots were likely perceived as intentional which elicited immediate and explicit responses from the human participants when it cheated. In contrast, humans were not as explicit when fellow humans cheated in the same task. Given robots can be attributed as agentic when cheating, designing future robotic systems should take this into account.

References

1. Abubshait, A., Wiese, E.: You look human, but act like a machine: agent appearance and behavior modulate different aspects of human-robot interaction. Front. Psychol. **8**, 1393 (2017)
2. Carpinella, C.M., Wyman, A.B., Perez, M.A., Stroessner, S.J.: The robotic social attributes scale (RoSAS): development and validation. In: Proceedings of the 2017 ACM/IEEE International Conference on Human-Robot Interaction, pp. 254–262. ACM (2017)
3. Cosmides, L., Tooby, J.: Cognitive adaptations for social exchange. Adap. Mind: Evol. Psychol. Gener. Cult. **163**, 163–228 (1992)
4. Fiske, S.T., Cuddy, A.J., Glick, P.: Universal dimensions of social cognition: warmth and competence. Trends Cogn. Sci. **11**(2), 77–83 (2007)
5. Gray, K., Young, L., Waytz, A.: Mind perception is the essence of morality. Psychol. Inq. **23**(2), 101–124 (2012)

6. Haring, K.S., Watanabe, K., Velonaki, M., Tossell, C.C., Finomore, V.: FFAB–
   the form function attribution bias in human-robot interaction. IEEE Trans. Cogn.
   Dev. Syst. **10**(4), 843–851 (2018)
7. Haring, K.S., Watanabe, K., Silvera-Tawil, D., Velonaki, M., Takahashi, T.:
   Changes in perception of a small humanoid robot. In: 2015 6th International Conference on Automation, Robotics and Applications (ICARA), pp. 83–89. IEEE
   (2015)
8. Jackson, R.B., Wen, R., Williams, T.: Tact in noncompliance: the need for prag-
   matically apt responses to unethical commands (2019)
9. Korman, J., Harrison, A., McCurry, M., Trafton, G.: Beyond programming: can
   robots' norm-violating actions elicit mental state attributions? In: 2019 14th
   ACM/IEEE International Conference on Human-Robot Interaction (HRI), pp.
   530–531. IEEE (2019)
10. Litoiu, A., Ullman, D., Kim, J., Scassellati, B.: Evidence that robots trigger a
    cheating detector in humans. In: Proceedings of the Tenth Annual ACM/IEEE
    International Conference on Human-Robot Interaction, pp. 165–172. ACM (2015)
11. Lucas, G.M., Gratch, J., King, A., Morency, L.P.: It's only a computer: virtual
    humans increase willingness to disclose. Comput. Hum. Behav. **37**, 94–100 (2014)
12. Phillips, E., Zhao, X., Ullman, D., Malle, B.F.: What is human-like?: decomposing
    robots' human-like appearance using the anthropomorphic robot (abot) database.
    In: Proceedings of the 2018 ACM/IEEE International Conference on Human-Robot
    Interaction, pp. 105–113. ACM (2018)
13. Short, E., Hart, J., Vu, M., Scassellati, B.: No fair!! an interaction with a cheat-
    ing robot. In: 2010 5th ACM/IEEE International Conference on Human-Robot
    Interaction (HRI), pp. 219–226. IEEE (2010)
14. Stafford, R.Q., MacDonald, B.A., Jayawardena, C., Wegner, D.M., Broadbent, E.:
    Does the robot have a mind? Mind perception and attitudes towards robots predict
    use of an eldercare robot. Int. J. Soc. Robot. **6**(1), 17–32 (2014)
15. Ullman, D., Leite, L., Phillips, J., Kim-Cohen, J., Scassellati, B.: Smart human,
    smarter robot: how cheating affects perceptions of social agency. In: Proceedings
    of the Annual Meeting of the Cognitive Science Society, vol. 36 (2014)
16. Van Lier, J., Revlin, R., De Neys, W.: Detecting cheaters without thinking: testing
    the automaticity of the cheater detection module. PLoS ONE **8**(1), e53827 (2013)
17. Verplaetse, J., Vanneste, S., Braeckman, J.: You can judge a book by its cover:
    the sequel.: a kernel of truth in predictive cheating detection. Evol. Hum. Behav.
    28(4), 260–271 (2007)
18. Wiese, E., Metta, G., Wykowska, A.: Robots as intentional agents: using neurosci-
    entific methods to make robots appear more social. Front. Psychol. **8**, 1663 (2017)
19. Zhao, X.: Rethinking anthropomorphism: the antecedents, unexpected conse-
    quences, and potential remedy for perceiving machines as human-like. In: Sym-
    posium submitted to Proceedings of the Association for Consumer Research (in
    press)

Applications in Health Domain

Getting Acquainted for a Long-Term Child-Robot Interaction

Mike Ligthart[1] , Mark. A. Neerincx[2,3] , and Koen V. Hindriks[1]([⊠])

[1] Vrije Universiteit Amsterdam, Amsterdam, The Netherlands
{m.e.u.ligthart,k.v.hindriks}@vu.nl
[2] Delft University of Technology, Delft, The Netherlands
[3] TNO Soesterberg, Soesterberg, The Netherlands
m.a.neerincx@tudelft.nl

Abstract. We are developing a social robot that should autonomously interact long-term with pediatric oncology patients. The child and the robot need to get acquainted with one another before a long-term interaction can take place. We designed five interaction design patterns and two sets of robot behaviors to structure a getting acquainted interaction. We discuss the results of a user study (N = 75, 8–11 y.o.) evaluating these patterns and robot behaviors. Specifically, we are exploring whether the children successfully got acquainted with the robot and to what extent the children bonded with the robot.

Results show that children effectively picked up how to talk to the robot. This is important, because the better the performance the more comfortable the children are, the more socially attractive the robot is, and the more intimate the conversation gets. The evaluation furthermore revealed that it is important for children, in order to get familiar with the robot, to have shared interests with the robot. Finally, most children did initiate a bond with the robot.

Keywords: Child-robot interaction · Getting acquainted · Bonding

1 Introduction

We are developing a social robot companion for children with cancer. The goal is to reduce medical traumatic stress. The robot can offer event-oriented support, in the form of a concrete intervention during a potential traumatic event. However, our primary research focus lies on providing *prolonged social support*. The goal

This work is part of the Hero project and is supported by the research program 'Technology for Oncology' (grand number 15198), which is financed by the Netherlands Organization for Scientific Research (NWO), the Dutch Cancer Society (KWF Kankerbestrijding), the TKI Life Sciences & Health, ASolutions, Brocacef, and the Cancer Health Coach. The research consortium consists of the Vrije Universiteit Amsterdam, Delft University of Technology, Princess Máxima Center, Centrum Wiskunde & Informatica (CWI), and the University Medical Centers Amsterdam UMC.

© Springer Nature Switzerland AG 2019
M. A. Salichs et al. (Eds.): ICSR 2019, LNAI 11876, pp. 423–433, 2019.
https://doi.org/10.1007/978-3-030-35888-4_39

is not only to keep up the effectiveness of an intervention after the novelty effect wears off. It's also about offering consistent social support throughout the whole treatment process. By being there, especially when parents cannot (e.g. during radiation therapy), and forming a bond, the robot can potentially achieve those goals.

However, we are not there yet. First the robot needs to be able to form and maintain a bond with a child. In this paper we focus on the very beginning, the child and the robot getting acquainted. Not only does the child gets familiar with the robot during this first encounter. It is also the first opportunity for the robot to learn things about the child that it can use in future interactions. Finally, like with people, first impressions matter. It is also the moment that determines if, and to what extend, a bond is formed.

We designed five interaction design patterns and two sets of robot behaviors to structure the getting acquainted interaction. We evaluated the performance of the interaction design with a user study (N = 75 school children, 8–11 y.o.) on three aspects. The robot getting acquainted with the child, the child getting acquainted with the robot, and the bonding between the child and the robot. In past work we discussed whether the robot got acquainted with the child. Results show that the interaction design effectively allowed the robot to elicit children to self-disclose and process those self-disclosures to form a user model of the children [12]. In this paper we evaluate whether the child got acquainted with the robot as well and whether a child-robot bond is initiated.

2   Related Work

Enabling robots to engage long-term and repeatedly with the same user is one of the main challenges within HRI research. Although we are not quite there yet, there is an increasing body of work that gives us insights into how to design and evaluate these long-term interactions [10].

2.1   Long-Term Bonding

In order for the social robot companion to bond with the children it at least needs to safeguard the continuity of the interaction [3,4], personalize the interaction [10], and deepen the bond [4]. Safeguarding the continuity is mostly about recognizing, recalling, and referring to relevant information about the child, previous conversations, and shared activities. Personalizing is about adapting the robot's behavior and interaction content to the child's preferences and interests [13]. Deepening the bond is about presenting novel interaction content over time [3,10] and adapting the intimacy level accordingly [5].

2.2   Getting Acquainted

Before the robot can personalize or safeguard the continuity of the interaction the robot needs to get enough information about the child. And before a bond can be deepened it must be formed first. In other words, a getting acquainted interaction needs to happen before anything else.

When people get acquainted they typically engage in an unstructured conversation where various topics are seemingly discussed freely [8]. However, under the surface there are a lot of implicit social norms and mechanisms that shape the relationship formation process [14]. Sharing personal information, a process often referred to as 'self-disclosure', is one important mechanism [1,16]. Getting acquainted, and forming a bond, does not work if the partner does not self-disclose as well [6]. Research shows that reciprocity is not only important between people, but also between people and artificial agents [5].

The discussed research forms the foundation for our interaction design. The goal is not to imitate how people get acquainted, but to facilitate this process to the best of the robot's ability. In the next section the interaction design is discussed in more detail.

3 The Getting Acquainted Interaction

We have formulated three goals for the getting acquainted interaction. The robot needs to get acquainted with the child, the child must be able to get acquainted with the robot, and the bonding process needs to be initiated.

3.1 The Robot Gets Acquainted with the Child

What we mean with "the robot gets acquainted with the child" is enabling the robot to collect enough information about the child to facilitate a long-term interaction. We have designed robot behaviors that on the one hand elicit children to self-disclose, but on the other hand keep that process manageable for the robot to process it autonomously [12]. All our designs and evaluations do not rely on the Wizard-of-Oz approach.

The main interaction modality is speech. To keep it feasible we apply quite some structure to the conversation. The challenge is to keep the conversation from feeling too restrictive. In our interaction design the robot has the initiative, controls the turn-taking, and asks the children questions about their hobbies and interests.

Children are first prompted to give a concise answer by using closed-ended questions. For example, "would you rather dance or play football?". These constrained questions are followed by an open question that allows children to elaborate themselves. For example, "why is France your favorite holiday destination?". This keeps the conversation from turning into an interrogation. Note that the robot only processes the closed-ended questions. For the open questions, the robot only uses speech activity detection to take the turn back when the child finished answering.

Children have two speech attempts to get their answer across. If the second attempt fails as well, the robot switches to the touch modality. The robot lists all answers possibilities and the child can press a button on the robot's feet to lock in an answer (see Fig. 1). Although children do not have the opportunity to ask questions, the robot shares fictional anecdotes about itself and its own hobbies and interests to reciprocate the self-disclosures of children.

Besides conversational elements we also designed two behavior profiles for the robot. The profiles are relatively less and more energetic in nature. Details can be found in Ligthart et al. [12]. Originally these profiles were meant to result in a matching effect, and stimulate self-disclosure elicitation, for introvert and extravert children respectively. Results show however that all children self-disclosed more to a robot with the less energetic behavior profile [12].

3.2   The Child Gets Acquainted with the Robot

A second goal is the child getting acquainted with the robot. This goal is achieved when three sub-goals are met. Firstly, the child needs to learn how to effectively communicate with the robot. At the start of the getting acquainted interaction the robot demonstrates to the child how to talk to it and offers a practise question. We are interested in the performance of the children making themselves understood by the robot, what and why mistakes were made, and what the influence is of those mistakes are on the outcome of the interaction.

The second sub-goal is managing the expectations of the children. Research shows that inappropriate expectations can reduce the effectiveness of the social support offered by the robot [11]. The design did not include explicit behaviors to manage the expectations. The getting acquainted interaction as a whole is meant to be an accurate representation of what children can expect from future interactions.

The third sub-goal is that the child gets familiar with the robot [9]. This means that the child knows something about the robot and its interests after the interaction. The robot disclosed several personal anecdotes about its hobbies and interests. We are interested in what the children can remember about the robot.

3.3   Child-Robot Bonding

For this last goal we follow the steps taken by Vittengl and Holt (2000) closely. They studied bonding between dyads of children during a short getting acquainted interaction [16]. In their study they followed Baumeister and Leary's work on relationship formation, who established that an increase of positive affect is indicative of bonding [2]. In their study, Vittengl and Holt, established that positive affect increase also occurs when children form a bond. They furthermore found that self-disclosure and social attraction between partners was predictive of the positive affect change [16]. We replicated their set-up, but instead, study child-robot dyads.

Fig. 1. Child getting acquainted with the Nao robot.

4   Method

4.1   Participants and Experimental Design

75 children (45 girls and 30 boys), between 8 and 11 years old, completed the experiment. The experiment had a 2×2 between-subject design with the personality of the children (introverts vs. extraverts) and the two robot behavioral (lower vs. higher energy) as independent variables. However, the evaluation discussed in this paper was done across all child-robot dyads independent of condition.

4.2   Set-Up, Procedure, and Materials

The experiment was approved by the ethics review board of our institution. Children interacted one-by-one with the robot for 15 min in an empty classroom at their school (see Fig. 1). Each interaction was recorded on video. After the interaction the children filled in a questionnaire and were interviewed in a separate room.

A Nao robot (see Fig. 1) was used in the experiment. The robot was controlled by a rule-based artificial cognitive agent implemented in the cognitive agent programming language GOAL [7]. The rules were based on the interaction design pattern defined in Ligthart et al. [12]. The agent followed a predefined conversation script, containing the following topics: sports, leisure activities, books, pets, seasons, colors, holidays, and television.

4.3   Measures and Instruments

Each speech recognition error was logged together with the most probable cause. We investigated the relationship between all speech recognition errors and the outcome of the interaction. The included outcome measures are the amount and

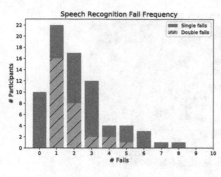

(a) Speech recognition fails

(b) Reasons for speech recognition fails

Fig. 2. How much trouble do children have talking to the robot and why?

intimacy of children's self-disclosures, the perceived comfort, social attraction, and positive affect change.

All conversations between participant and robot were transcribed to text. Using the transcripts of the open questions we calculated the *amount* of statements self-disclosed by the children and how *intimate* those self-disclosures where. See Ligthart et al. for a detailed discussion of these measures [12]. Perceived comfort was measured using a custom-made 3-item 5-point Likert-scale. Social attraction and positive affect change are introduced below.

To assess whether children got familiar with the robot we asked them during the exit-interview to recall the topics they discussed with the robots and whether they could recall the favorite tv-series of the robot. We also asked them if they shared interests with the robot.

For researching bond formation we have used the same measures for self-disclosure, social attraction, and affect as Vittengl and Holt [16]. The only difference is that we used the Dutch version of the measures. To measure *perceived self-disclosure* participants were asked to indicate how much they disclosed about 10 different topics. *Social attraction* is a self-report measure used to capture the social attraction of the participants towards the robot. It is heavily based on the social attraction subscale of the Interpersonal Attraction Scale. The Positive and Negative Affect Schedule (PANAS) was used to measure *positive affect* before and after the interaction with the robot.

5   Results

5.1   Child Getting Acquainted with Robot

There were 986 speech recognition attempts. 266 times (27%) the attempt failed. We assigned a reason to each failed attempt. 80% of the fails were due to something the participant did (see Fig. 2b). For example, speaking too soft. In the remaining 20% of the cases the participants followed protocol, but the speech recognition failed nonetheless.

The robot asked ten questions. In Fig. 2a the frequency of participants who failed with zero or more questions are displayed by the blue non-hatched bars. Each participant had two speech attempts before switching to the touch modality. The orange hatched bars show the frequency of participants that failed two speech attempts on one or multiple occasions.

To assess whether there is a relationship between the failed speech recognition attempts (regardless of cause) and the outcome of the interaction a Pearson's product-moment correlation was run. The included outcome measures are the amount and intimacy of self-disclosures, perceived comfort, social attraction, and positive affect change. The results are shown in Table 1.

Table 1. Pearson's correlation results of failed speech recognition attempts with several interaction outcome measures.

Amount of SD	Intimacy of SD	Perceived comfort	Social attraction	Positive affect
−.063	−.303**	−.298**	−.241*	−.077

** Correlation is significant at the 0.01 level (2-tailed).
* Correlation is significant at the 0.05 level (2-tailed).

The robot and the child discussed 8 different topics. On average children recalled 3 ± 1 topics with a maximum of 4 topics. 33 (40%) children mentioned they had similar interests as the robot. A Mann-Whitney U test was run to determine if there were differences in amount of topics recalled by the children between those we felt had similar interests and those who did not. Median topic recall scores were not significantly different between both groups (3.00 vs. 3.00), $U = 637$, $z = -.101$, $p = .920$.

37 (49%) children recalled the favorite tv-program of the robot (Pokemon). 21 (.68) children who felt had similar interests as the robot correctly recalled it's favorite tv-program, compared to 16 (.36) children who felt no similarity. A chi-square test of homogeneity showed that these proportions where statistically significantly different, $p = .007$.

5.2 Child-Robot Bonding

The positive affect scores from before and after the interaction were compared. Of the 72 included[1] participants, 48 reported a higher positive affect afterwards, 19 reported a lower positive affect, and 5 reported no difference. A Wilcoxon signed-rank test determined that there was a statistically significant median increase (.35) in positive affect from before (3.40) to after (3.75) the interaction with the robot, $z = 4.55$, $p < .0005$.

A number of things stood out while exploring as to why a smaller, but sizable, portion of the participants had a decrease in positive effect. No statistical differences for positive affect change were observed for age, extraversion, and robot

---

[1] 3 participants showed signs of an extremity bias, where they maxed out every rating. These data points were deemed unreliable and were excluded.

behavior where observed. This was different for gender. An independent t-test was run to determine if there were differences in positive affect change between boys and girls. Girls ($.35 \pm .40$) have a statistically higher positive affect change than boys ($.15 \pm .45$), $t(70) = 2.00$, $p = .049$, $d = .48$. The 19 cases of decreased positive affect represents $1/3$ of the boys in the sample, compared to $1/5$ of the girls. The top 90-percentile contains 10 girls versus 3 boys.

Finally, a multiple regression analysis was run to predict a positive affect change from self-disclosure and the social attractiveness of the robot. The multiple regression model statistically significantly predicted a positive affect change, $F(2, 74) = 4.340$, $p = .017$, $adj R^2 = .108$. Only the perceived degree of self-disclosure added statistically significantly to the prediction, $p = .022$.

6   Discussion

6.1   Child Getting Acquainted with Robot

Knowing how to communicate with the robot is a first step for starting a relationship. The robot offered a tutorial at the start of the getting acquainted interaction. Results show that the majority of children (86%) make no to only two mistakes.

Because this part of the study was not in the form of a controlled experiment, we cannot make causal claims about the effect of the tutorial on the mistakes. However, we did observe a high amount of self-correcting behavior among the participants. For example, when the Nao starts listening it beeps and when children spoke before the beep (too early) they would repeat their answer after the beep. This behavior prevented a lot of mistakes. Furthermore, when asked to explain how to talk to the robot, almost all the children mentioned they had to speak loud and clear. This makes it likely that the tutorial had a positive effect on the performance of the children.

Although the overall performance was good, mistakes were made, and some children consistently made the same mistakes. The most prominent mistake was speaking too softly, followed by speaking before the robot was ready. These mistakes can probably be reduced by using a more state-of-the-art speech recognition system. Children being too verbose or saying unexpected things are more tricky to deal with. Improving the conversation management could support the children even more. For example, when the robot detects a verbose answer it could give the child the feedback to be more concise.

These improvements are necessary because the results show that there is a negative relationship between the amount of recognition errors and how comfortable the children feel in the conversation and how socially attractive the robot is. It is plausible that children either blame themselves or the robot (or both) for the mistakes. Furthermore, a negative relationship was found between the amount of errors and how intimate the children's self-disclosures were. No significant relationship was found with the amount of self-disclosures and positive affect change. This suggests that on the short term it does not prevent the robot from getting acquainted with the child and children forming a bond. However, it might have consequences on the long-term, because children initiate a more shallow relationship.

Finally, we also evaluated whether the children got familiar with the robot. We did this by asking what children could recall from their conversation with the robot. Children seem to recall at most four different conversational topics. Experiencing a shared interest with the robot did not influence their recall ability for topics. However, it did influence their ability to remember specific details. Children who felt they shared interests with the robot were more successful in recalling its favorite TV-show. It is important to note that this analysis was done for only one topic.

6.2   Child-Robot Bonding

In our user study we have studied child-robot bonding in a similar fashion as Vittengl and Holt, who studied bonding within child-child dyads [16]. The results first of all show a positive affect increase for most children. This is indicative of forming a bond [2]. More importantly, the results show the same mechanism as with child-child bond formation, namely mutual self-disclosure [16], is steering the bonding process. However, in contrast with Vittengl and Holt's study, we did not find that social attraction was of influence. A novelty effect might have affected the scoring of social attraction.

Most participants took the first step to initiate a bond with the robot. There is however a smaller, but sizable, portion of the participant that did not bond with the robot. The results show a medium sized effect of gender on positive affect change. The majority of the stronger 'bonders' with the robot are girls and a larger part of those who do not seem to bond with the robot are boys. This could be because girls have been found to be more accepting of human-like social robots [15].

7   Conclusion

We have designed robot behaviors meant to facilitate a getting acquainted interaction between children and the robot. We have run a user study ($N = 75$, 8–11 y.o.) to evaluate that design. We explored whether the children got acquainted with the robot by investigating whether children learned how to communicate with the robot and whether they got more familiar with the robot. By including a 'how to communicate with me' tutorial, children seem to efficiently pick up on how to communicate with the robot. The recurrency of mistakes is low and the children self-correct themselves often preventing speech recognition failures.

Improvements in speech recognition technology and conversation management will lower recognition failures even further, and eventually pave the way for a less restrictive conversation. Improvements are beneficial, because the lower the amount of failures, the more comfortable and intimate the conversation gets and the more socially attractive the robot is.

Preliminary results show that having shared interests is beneficial for recalling specific details about the robot. To find common ground the robot should explore a diverse range of interests, hobbies, and other topics, during the getting acquainted interaction. It is also a useful personalization strategy for future interactions.

We, furthermore, explored whether children bonded with the robot by investigating the changes in positive affect. For most children a bond was initiated with the robot. Just like with other children, mutual self-disclosure is an important factor for bonding with a robot. It were mostly girls who showed the strongest increases in positive affect. On the other end, a larger portion of the boys showed a decrease in positive affect, inhibiting bonding. This reinforces the importance of further personalization.

In this explorative evaluation we establish that our interaction design for an autonomous social robot is on the right track for facilitating a getting acquainted interaction. More importantly, we identified a number of clear leads to improve our design. The next steps are to improve, extend (e.g. hold multiple conversations), and properly validate the interaction design, so that the robot can truly contribute to the social support of pediatric oncology patients.

References

1. Altman, I., Taylor, D.: Social Penetration Theory. Holt, Rinehart & Winston, New York (1973)
2. Baumeister, R.F., Leary, M.R.: The need to belong: desire for interpersonal attachments as a fundamental human motivation. Psychol. Bull. **117**(3), 497–529 (1995)
3. Baxter, P., Belpaeme, T., Cañamero, L., Cosi, P., Demiris, Y., Enescu, V.: Long-term human-robot interaction with young users. In: Proceedings of the ACM/IEEE Human-Robot Interaction Conference (2011)
4. Belpaeme, T., et al.: Multimodal child-robot interaction: building social bonds. J. Hum. Robot Interact. **1**(2), 33–53 (2013)
5. Burger, F., Broekens, J., Neerincx, M.A.: Fostering relatedness between children and virtual agents through reciprocal self-disclosure. In: Bosse, T., Bredeweg, B. (eds.) BNAIC 2016. CCIS, vol. 765, pp. 137–154. Springer, Cham (2017). https://doi.org/10.1007/978-3-319-67468-1_10
6. Ehrlich, H.J., Graeven, D.B.: Reciprocal self-disclosure in a dyad. J. Exp. Soc. Psychol. **7**(4), 389–400 (1971)
7. Hindriks, K.V.: Programming rational agents in GOAL. In: El Fallah Seghrouchni, A., Dix, J., Dastani, M., Bordini, R.H. (eds.) Multi-Agent Programming, pp. 119–157. Springer, Boston, MA (2009). https://doi.org/10.1007/978-0-387-89299-3_4
8. Ickes, W.: A basic paradigm for the study of unstructured dyadic interaction. New Dir. Methodol. Soc. Behav. Sci. (1983)
9. Kruijff-Korbayová, I., et al.: Young users' perception of a social robot displaying familiarity and eliciting disclosure. Social Robotics. LNCS (LNAI), vol. 9388, pp. 380–389. Springer, Cham (2015). https://doi.org/10.1007/978-3-319-25554-5_38
10. Leite, I., Martinho, C., Paiva, A.: Social robots for long-term interaction: a survey. Int. J. Social Robot. **5**(2), 291–308 (2013)

11. Ligthart, M., Henkemans, O.B., Hindriks, K., Neerincx, M.A.: Expectation management in child-robot interaction. In: 2017 26th IEEE International Symposium on Robot and Human Interactive Communication (RO-MAN), pp. 916–921 (2017)
12. Ligthart, M., Fernhout, T., Neerincx, M.A., van Bindsbergen, K.L.A., Grootenhuis, M.A., Hindriks, K.V.: A child and a robot getting acquainted - interaction design for eliciting self-disclosure. In: Proceedings of the 18th International Conference on Autonomous Agents and MultiAgent Systems, AAMAS 2019, pp. 61–70. International Foundation for Autonomous Agents and Multiagent Systems (2019)
13. Rossi, S., Ferland, F., Tapus, A.: User profiling and behavioral adaptation for HRI: a survey. Pattern Recogn. Lett. **99**, 3–12 (2017)
14. Svennevig, J.: Getting Acquainted in Conversation: A Study of Initial Interactions, vol. 64. John Benjamins Publishing, Amsterdam (2000)
15. Tung, F.-W.: Influence of gender and age on the attitudes of children towards humanoid robots. In: Jacko, J.A. (ed.) HCI 2011. LNCS, vol. 6764, pp. 637–646. Springer, Heidelberg (2011). https://doi.org/10.1007/978-3-642-21619-0_76
16. Vittengl, J.R., Holt, C.S.: Getting acquainted: the relationship of self-disclosure and social attraction to positive affect. J. Soc. Pers. Relat. **17**(1), 53–66 (2000)

Use of Robotics in the German Healthcare Sector

Application Scenarios - Drivers and Barriers – Time Savings

Marija Radic[1(✉)], Agnes Vosen[1], and Birgit Graf[2]

[1] Fraunhofer Center for International Management and Knowledge Economy IMW, Neumarkt 9-19, 04109 Leipzig, Germany
marija.radic@imw.fraunhofer.de
[2] Fraunhofer Institute for Manufacturing Engineering and Automation IPA, Nobelstraße 12, 70569 Stuttgart, Germany

Abstract. Assistance robots have a large potential to support patients and staff in outpatient and inpatient settings. Despite the need and large potential, the diffusion of robotic applications in the German healthcare sector is only slowly picking up pace. The objective of this study is to shed some light on the reasons and identify measures that support involved stakeholders in closing this gap in the upcoming years. Using an online survey, we addressed more than 150 clinics and nursing service providers throughout Germany with respect to the benefit of different robot application scenarios, drivers and barriers for the introduction of service robots in healthcare settings as well as estimated time savings. Concerning possible application areas, disinfection and cleaning robots are currently perceived to have the highest benefit, whereas the value of robots to support personal hygiene is considered rather low. The greatest drivers for using robot assistants in healthcare settings are their potential to save time for the staff as well as to increase employer attractiveness and higher efficiency in processes. The most frequently cited barriers are financing, data protection, legal obstacles and the importance of human contact. For three selected scenarios: assistance robots as guides, lifting robots and activation and communication robots, we further asked for the expected time savings. The results show differences between clinics as well as inpatient and outpatient nursing services. In order to accelerate the diffusion of robot assistants in Germany, several implications have to be considered: Acceptance and experience are positively correlated i.e. from a political standpoint, research programs are needed to support joint development of robot assistants by research, industry and end users. Legal and financial barriers should be reduced. For manufacturers, creating testing possibilities and close interaction with potential users for the identification of adequate scenarios and clarifying legal questions could prove to be beneficial in terms of a higher acceptance in the market.

Keywords: Assistance robots · Social acceptance · Clinic · Elderly care

© Springer Nature Switzerland AG 2019
M. A. Salichs et al. (Eds.): ICSR 2019, LNAI 11876, pp. 434–442, 2019.
https://doi.org/10.1007/978-3-030-35888-4_40

1   Introduction

Both demographic change and the shortage of skilled workers are exerting pressure on nursing services and hospitals as well as on the entire healthcare system - creating an urgent need for new patient-centric and cost intelligent solutions. One promising approach is the use of robotics. Scientific advisory groups in Asia, Europe and the US have targeted healthcare robotics as a key means of improving healthcare in the 21st century. Different groups such as the National Science Foundation (USA) and the European Commission have developed roadmaps to accelerate the development of a healthcare robotics economy [1].

Several studies focus on the general acceptance of robotics and its potential in healthcare. Meyer [2] e.g. interviewed 110 senior citizens, 50 nursing service employees and managers and 32 engineers and experts. On the one hand, a quantitative survey was conducted to determine the degree of approval for the use of service robotics in well-defined application fields. On the other hand, qualitative input was drawn from 20 interviews with elderly people between 70 and 87 years of age. One result of the study is that the spontaneous acceptance among older people is relatively high if the robot relieves and supports them during physically exhausting work (such as vacuuming and cleaning the floor, mowing the lawn, lifting heavy objects and bringing them to a specific place, etc.). Both the individual benefit of the robotic solution and the usability are important. However, based on the empirical results, the use of these technologies should not replace human labor. Another more recent study from 2017 conducted interviews and focus groups with 27 experts from the hospital, rehabilitation, inpatient and outpatient care sectors and the home sector [3]. The study concludes that there is great potential in the increased use of robotic assistance systems, but there is a need to shape several external conditions: Research funding as well as an orientation of research to people's needs play an important role. On the other hand, an information culture must be created for dealing with robots, and the financing question needs to be resolved.

Several studies have found that employees are much more critical of the use of robots than older people are [4, 5]. Both elderly people and caregivers show enthusiasm and interest in robots. Caregivers, however, have issues to share their workplace with the robots to some extent [6]. Hebensberg et al. [7] investigated which functions robots could take over in geriatric care. "Fetch and carry" tasks, entertainment and information as well as support during physically demanding tasks are regarded as particularly desirable.

Despite rising growth numbers in the United States and Asia, the diffusion of healthcare robotics in Germany has been only limited [8, 9]. Empirical evidence on the gap between the needs and the actual diffusion is rather scare.

The objective of this study is thus to get a better understanding of the reasons and identify measures that support involved stakeholders in closing this gap Specifically, the study focuses on the benefits and experiences of different application scenarios in healthcare, drivers and barriers for the introduction of robots in healthcare settings and the economic question of estimated time savings.

2   Empirical Study

2.1   Methodology

The data was generated based on an online survey of clinics and nursing service providers in Germany between October and December 2018. The specific target groups were executives in the organizations that have a direct or indirect impact on potential investment decisions around robotics i.e. managing directors, commercial managers and nursing supervisors. The participants answered questions on the benefits of different application scenarios, time saving as well as drivers and barriers for the adoption of robotics in the healthcare market. The participants can be divided into three subgroups: inpatient care, outpatient care and clinics, without distinguishing between public and private institutions. Inpatient care refers exclusively to nursing homes and similar institutions while clinics addresses the inpatient care in clinics. Outpatient care represents ambulatory care.

Overall, 162 executives participated in the study. Around one quarter of the respondents came from the hospital sector, three quarters from the nursing service sector.

Figure 1 shows that the percentage of institutions with 10–50 or 50–100 employees is highest. However, outpatient care has mostly between 10–50 employees. Participants in inpatient care usually run a much larger facility between 50–250 employees. In our survey, clinics usually have a size of over 500 employees. The sample is statistically not representative in terms of regions and size of the organizations.

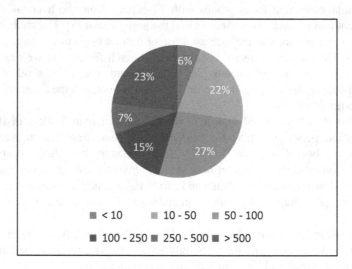

Fig. 1. Size of the participating organization in number of employees, n = 162

2.2   Added Value of Different Robotic Application Scenarios

In order to identify the perceived benefit of different application scenarios, we asked the participants whether the benefit of an application scenario was low, medium or high (Fig. 2).

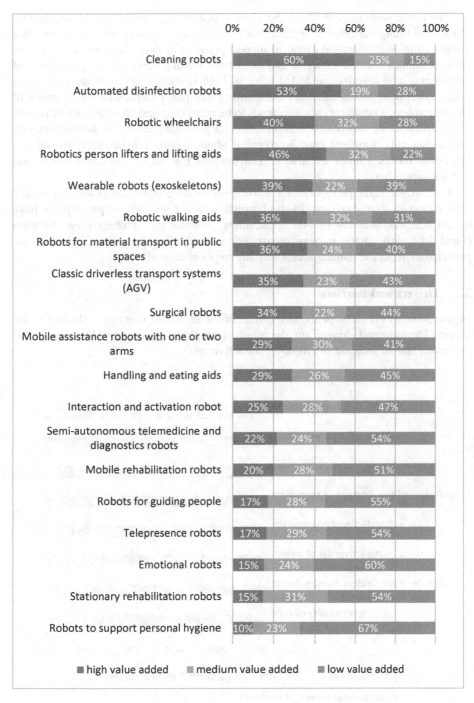

Fig. 2. Added value of the scenarios, n = 162

The participants in general see the greatest benefit in cleaning robots, disinfection robots and lifting aids. Robot applications that have a low perceived benefit are robot guides, emotional robots and robots to support personal hygiene. In terms of differences between clinics and the inpatient and outpatient nursing services, the percentage of participants who describe the added value as high is always well over ten percentage points lower in outpatient care than in the other participant groups, with the exception of cleaning robots. Outpatient care thus tends to be more skeptical about the use of robots.

Outpatient care sees little benefit in robots for personal guidance as well as handling and eating aids. Inpatient care is skeptical about mobile rehabilitation robots and emotional robots. Clinics are also critical towards the use of emotional robots and telepresence robots.

Overall, the participants from the nursing sector have significantly less experience with robots in everyday care. In the hospital sector, 6 to 28% of participants have experience with different robotic applications, whereas the numbers range between 0 and 14% only in the nursing sector. For several robotic scenarios, none of the participants from the nursing sector has any experience at all.

2.3   Drivers and Barriers

Figure 3 shows the participants' assessment of the drivers of robotics in the healthcare sector. The strongest drivers are the relief of employees, a higher efficiency in the processes and an increase in employer attractiveness.

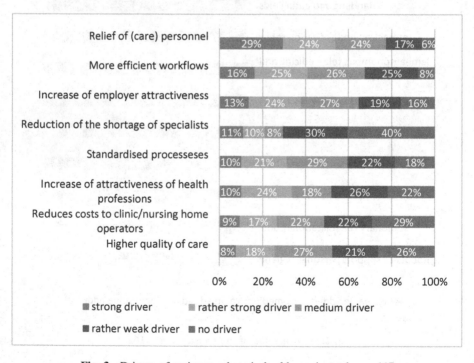

Fig. 3. Drivers of assistant robots in healthcare in total, n = 117

In terms of the three different subgroups, two interesting results emerge. In the inpatient care sector, the relief of (nursing) personnel is as a major advantage: 60% see this as a rather strong or strong driver. By comparison, this number lies at around 40% in outpatient care.

Clinics seem to have a slightly different focus. The higher quality of care for the patient and the standardization of processes as well as the lower costs for the clinic are the dominant drivers. The reduction of the shortage of specialists does not seem to be a main driver. This may be due to the fact that robots are not intended to replace skilled personnel, but to support and relieve them in their work.

Interestingly, the greatest advantages for the clinic are precisely the drivers that are least important for the nursing service providers – and vice versa.

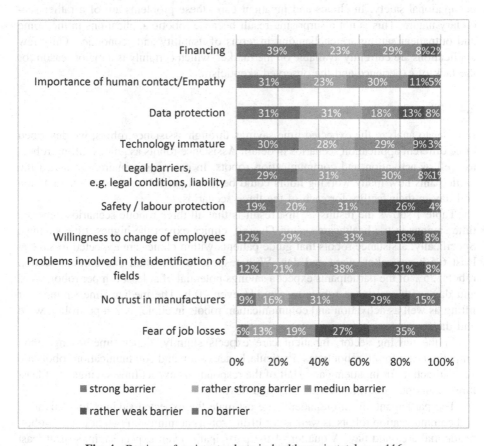

Fig. 4. Barriers of assistant robots in healthcare in total, n = 116

Figure 4 shows the results for the barriers towards robotics in healthcare. The first impressive result is that the barriers for robotics in healthcare are assessed to be very high. The four most frequently cited barriers are financing, data protection, legal barriers and the importance of human contact. More than 50% of the participants see them as rather strong or strong barriers. Fear of job losses might be seen as least important, as robots are designed to support the caregivers and not to take over the tasks on their own.

In terms of subgroups, the barriers are assessed to be much higher in the nursing sector than in clinics. The issue of financing dominates in nursing services with 45% and is described as a major obstacle, whereas in clinics financing ranks third with relatively low 17% of respondents stating it to be a barrier. Within the group of respondents from the nursing sector, participants from outpatient care have the greatest concerns. More than 70% of the participants see the four largest obstacles as rather strong or strong barriers and they differ significantly from those mentioned by the clinic or the inpatient nursing staff: no trust in the manufacturer, difficulties with the identification of adequate application scenarios, immature technologies and safety or occupational safety. In clinics and inpatient care, these problems are of a rather secondary nature. This is not a surprising result because robotic applications in the home and outpatient setting are challenging in terms of usability and economics. Only few applications are currently available on the market, which certainly is a major reason for the lack of experience and the observed skepticism.

2.4 Time Savings

In order to analyze the expected time savings through assistance robots, we described three different application scenarios in detail: Assistance robots as guides, lifting robots as well as activation and communication robots. In our questionnaire, we asked the participants how many working hours could be saved per robot, ward/residential area and day in their facility for each of the three scenarios.

Table 1 shows the results. A first result is that all three robotic scenarios generate time savings in the healthcare sector. Overall, clinics expect the highest time savings. Specifically, assistance robots that guide patients within clinics are expected to save at least 6.5 h per robot, ward and day. With respect to activation and communication robots, 25% of the participants expect a savings potential of at least 8 h per robot, ward and day, with assistance robots as a guide even 10 h. The median time savings for lifting as well as activation and communication robots in clinics is 2 h per robot, ward and day.

In the nursing sector, inpatient care expects slightly higher time savings than outpatient care for all robot types. Particularly activation and communication robots are very attractive for inpatient care. Half of the respondents expect time savings of at least three hours per robot, residential area and day.

The participants from outpatient care estimate the expected savings for activation and communication robots as well as for lifting robots at minimum two hours per robot, residential area and day. A quarter of the participants even expect savings of at least 7.5 h.

Table 1. Estimated time savings of different robotic applications in clinics and nursing services

Median time saving per robot/station/day	Outpatient care	Inpatient care	Clinic
Assistant robot as guide, n = 103	0 h	1 h	6.5 h
Lifting robot, n = 105	2 h	2 h	2 h
Activation and communication robot, n = 103	2 h	3 h	2 h

3 Conclusion

The survey shows that there is need for various application scenarios for assistance robots in the German healthcare sector associated with beneficial effects for residents, patients and staff. The highest value is currently attributed to robot applications that physically relieve staff and do not involve social interaction. Examples are cleaning, disinfection, transport, or lifting robots. This is in line with the top drivers of robotic applications identified in the study: The reduction of workload for the staff, an increase in employer attractiveness and a higher efficiency in processes are the dominant motives to introduce robotic applications in the participating organizations. Interestingly, the top rated scenarios are the ones where experience levels are highest and commercial products already exist. The lowest rated scenarios on the other hand are applications, which are still in the research and development phase. This implies that acceptance and experience are positively correlated.

All three presented robotic applications – a robot guide, lifting robot and activation and communication robot – are associated with time savings. In clinics, robot guides are expected to create the largest time savings. In nursing services, lifting and activation robots could help to relieve staff.

The obstacles to introduce robotic applications are still significant. More than 50% of the participants describe four barriers specifically as large or rather large: Financing, data protection, legal obstacles, and the importance of human contact. Outpatient care is the sector that is most skeptical about robot applications. This is not a surprising result in view of the fact that there are hardly any commercial products available. This in turn is a result of challenges in the outpatient setting with respect to logistical and economic factors.

Summarizing, several consequences arise from the results of this study. Additional projects should look into the test of existing solutions allowing end users to gain experiences with potentials but also limits of applying robotics solutions in health care. From a political standpoint, the result that 'acceptance follows experience' implies that research projects need to be set up and disseminated widely where researchers, robot manufacturers and end users jointly develop new robotic applications tailored to end user needs. This holds specifically for the outpatient sector, which currently has only little experience with robotic applications and where most applications are in their early development phase. In addition, three major obstacles need to be resolved in the future: financing incentives for end users including the legal framework for financing as well as adequate legal frameworks in terms of data protection and occupational health and safety.

For robot manufacturers, our results show that creating user experience is essential for acceptance and that robotic applications focusing on relieving staff physically currently have higher acceptance than robots with social interaction. Robot manufacturers could help overcome the mentioned obstacles by taking on a consulting role and supporting clinics and nursing service providers in jointly identifying adequate applications and providing advice on data protection, data security and occupational safety.

SPONSORED BY THE

Federal Ministry
of Education
and Research

Acknowledgment. The project is sponsored by the German Federal Ministry of Education and Research (Förderkennzeichen: 16SV7871K).

References

1. Robotic Business Review. https://www.roboticsbusinessreview.com/health-medical/healthc are-robotics-current-market-trends-and-future-opportunities. Accessed 20 June 2019
2. Meyer, S.: Mein Freund der Roboter: Servicerobotik für ältere Menschen. Eine Antwort auf den demografischen Wandel? VDE-Verlag, Berlin und Offenbach (2011)
3. Klein, G., Klein, B., Schlömer, F., Roßberg, H., Röhrich, K., Baumgarten, S.: Robotik in der Gesundheitswirtschaft. medhochzwei, Heidelberg (2017)
4. Broadbent, E., Tamagawa, R., Kerse, N., Knock, B., Patience, A., MacDonald, B.: Retirement home staff and residents' preferences for healthcare robots. In: The 18th IEEE International Symposium on Robot and Human Interactive Communication Toyama, Japan, 27 September–2 October (2009)
5. Broadbent, E., et al.: Attitudes towards health-care robots in a retirement village. Australas. J. Ageing **31**(2), 115–120 (2012)
6. Hebesberger, D., Koertner, T., Gisinger, C., Pripfl, J.: A long-term autonomous robot at a care hospital: a mixed methods study on social acceptance and experiences of staff and older adults. Int. J. Social Robot. **9**(3), 417–429 (2017)
7. Hebesberger, D., Körtner, T., Pripfl, J., Gisinger, C., Hanheide, M.: What do staff in eldercare want a robot for? An assessment of potential tasks and user requirements for a long-term deployment. In: IROS Workshop on "Bridging User Needs to Deployed Applications of Service Robots (2015)
8. International Federation of Robotics. https://ifr.org/ifr-press-releases/news/summary-outlook-on-world-robotics-report-2019-by-ifr. Accessed 20 June 2019
9. Medizin und Elektronik. https://www.medizin-und-elektronik.de/medizin-40-iot/artikel/1490 49. Accessed 20 June 2019

In Their Own Words: A Companion Robot for Detecting the Emotional State of Persons with Parkinson's Disease

Andrew Valenti[✉][iD], Meia Chita-Tegmark[iD], Michael Gold, Theresa Law, and Matthias Scheutz[iD]

Human-Robot Interaction Laboratory, Tufts University,
200 Boston Ave., Medford, MA 02155, USA
{andrew.valenti,mihaela.chita_tegmark,michael.gold,
theresa.law,matthias.scheutz}@tufts.edu
https://hrilab.tufts.edu

Abstract. In typical human interactions emotional states are communicated via a variety of modalities such as auditory (through speech), visual (through facial expressions) and kinesthetic (through gestures). However, one or more modalities might be compromised in some situations, as in the case of facial masking in Parkinson's disease (PD). In these cases, we need to focus the communication and detection of emotions on the reliable modalities, by inferring emotions from what is being said, and compensate for the modalities that are problematic, by having another agent (e.g., a robot) provide the missing facial expressions. We describe the initial development stage of a robot companion that can assist the communication and detection of emotions in interactions where some modalities are totally or partially compromised. Such is the case for people living with Parkinson's disease.

Our approach is based on a Latent Dirichlet Allocation topic model as a principled way to extract features from speech based on a trained classifier that can be linked to measures of emotion. The trained model is integrated into a robotic cognitive architecture to perform real-time, continuous speech detection of positive, negative, or neutral emotional valence that is expressed through the facial features of a humanoid robot. To evaluate the integrated system, we conducted a human-robot interaction experiment in which the robot credibly detected and displayed emotions as it listened to utterances spoken by a confederate. The utterance were directly extracted from interviews with people with Parkinson's Disease. The encouraging results will form the basis for further developments of finer prediction models to be employed in a companion robot for persons with PD.

Keywords: Affective computing · Topic modeling · Parkinson's disease · Human-robot interaction · Assistive technologies

© Springer Nature Switzerland AG 2019
M. A. Salichs et al. (Eds.): ICSR 2019, LNAI 11876, pp. 443–452, 2019.
https://doi.org/10.1007/978-3-030-35888-4_41

1   Introduction

Humans are good at estimating affect in terms of valence and arousal from facial expressions of other humans and from their voice. However, in some situations, facial expressions or affect in the voice are either not available or not reliable. For example, one symptom of Parkinson's disease (PD), a neurodegenerative disorder, is facial masking (hypomimia) which arises from diminished control of one's facial and vocal expression. Facial masking can lead to dissociation between one's inner emotional state and outward facial appearance (e.g., looking angry when one is not). Given that facial and vocal expressiveness can sometimes be a problematic channel for communicating emotion, as in the case of people with PD, an alternative channel for detecting emotion is verbal communication: the words a person uses in their verbal or written speech.

In this paper, we further develop the model we reported on in [19] to automatically detect the emotional content of a speaker's utterances continuously and in real-time. The model described in this paper also uses Latent Dirichlet Allocation (LDA) as the basis for an unsupervised learning system, which is trained to extract topic probabilities from a collection of written documents. When an unseen sentence is presented to the model, it finds the document's topic probabilities and uses them as a set of features. We then use a Multi-Layer Perceptron (MLP) classifier to associate these features with training data labeled according to emotion valence (neutral, positive or negative).

This paper proceeds as follows. In the *Related Work* section, we talk about the approaches that have been used for emotion recognition and sentiment analysis in general and to evaluate the emotional state of persons with PD. In the *Methods* section we described the text data that we used and the approach we took for obtaining emotional content ratings. We also describe how we trained and tested the computational model for detecting the emotional content. In the *Results and Validation* section, we explain the human-robot interaction experiment we ran to validate the model. The results of the study suggest that when embedded in the robot, participants recognized the connection between the robot's emotion expressions and the speaker's utterances more when the robot emoted based on the model's predictions than when the robot emoted randomly. Finally, in the *Discussion* and *Conclusion* sections, we discuss the advantages, disadvantages, and limitations of this approach and the potential for embedding the model in emotion-detecting assistive conversation tools.

1.1   Related Work

Emotion recognition often refers to the techniques used to detect emotion from facial expression and speech. Rather than recognizing emotions as belonging to discrete and often binary categories (e.g., positive, negative), emotion recognition attempts to infer a set of emotion labels such as happiness or satisfaction, both of which fall under the positive category. Conversely, sentiment analysis usually refers to the techniques used to infer the binary emotional polarity of a person as they interact with a text or a document, rather than determining the specific human emotion. However, sentiment analysis approaches may also attempt to classify additional emotion labels.

Existing approaches to emotion recognition and sentiment analysis fall broadly into three categories: statistical, natural language processing (NLP), and a combination of the two [4]. The challenge for the statistical approach is to find document features which will be sufficiently discriminating so that a classifier can separate the document into the desired sentiment categories. Deriving these features from the speech signal directly as in [12,13] has the advantage of using both affect in the voice and in the content; however, this assumes an intact vocal channel which is not always the case, as we will subsequently discuss. Regardless of the modality, the challenge for the researcher is to discover a set of discriminative features and it is often difficult to discover these features *a priori*. As a result, features are often found through experimentation using various selection methods such as information gain [8], principal component analysis for speech, and manually selected emotion keywords for text [5]. In these cases, feature selection is tied to a particular database which may result in poor generalization. A *principled* way for feature selection would overcome these limitations by utilizing features that operate at a higher level of abstraction, one that is common across text or speech datasets. For example, Shah [12] used Latent Topic Models to extract emotionally-salient features from speech.

NLP approaches include the use of sentiment lexicons to associate words in a document with a sentiment 'score' [7,14,16]. Balahur [2] analyzes the syntactic structure of the text and consults domain-specific data banks to capture and store the structure and semantics of events in the text, and use it to predict the emotional responses triggered by a chain of actions. In either of these approaches, language-specific knowledge and hand-crafted lexicons are required for the NLP techniques to be successful. The NLP has a limitation similar to that of the statistical approaches: different types of text (e.g., blogs, newspaper articles, movie reviews, tweets) require specialized methods [1,10] and cannot be generalized. Finally, some approaches to sentiment analysis combine NLP and statistical approaches. Pang and Lee [9] train several classifiers using features extracted from the text using NLP tools; additional examples of the hybrid approach can be found in [3].

There are models of affect and arousal that rely on facial expression and affect in the voice; for a review, see [3]. These approaches have traditionally employed modalities such as physiology, facial expressions, and intonation. However, given that facial and vocal expressiveness is a problematic channel for communicating emotional states in people with PD, researchers have proposed that a more accurate channel might be verbal communication: the words a person uses in their verbal or written speech [6]. To detect and characterize the emotional content of communications from individuals with PD, the prevalent approach employed so far has been to use a sentiment lexicon such as LIWC [7]. However, in [19], we showed that LIWC did not categorize two categories of emotion (positive, negative) contained in a document as well as a topic modeling approach when the word count approached that of the average sentence, i.e., 13 words.

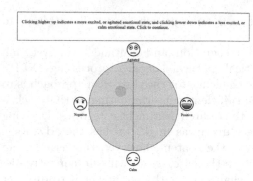

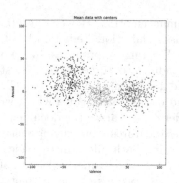

Fig. 1. Human-labeling of text. At a mouse-click (valence, arousal) coordinates of the cursor and the elapsed time are recorded.

Fig. 2. k-means clustering identified center-points of the three classes: negative (blue), neutral (green), and positive (red) (Color figure online)

2   Methods

2.1   Materials

Our model was trained on the individual sentences drawn from 448 documents with an average word count of 258 words, the largest containing 1,732 and the smallest, 2 [19]. The documents were constructed from selected interview transcripts from 106 male and female participants with PD, living in the community, who participated in a study [17] which asked them to recall two types of experiences they had during the past week: a frustrating one and an enjoyable one. The robot running the model could then be expected to accurately predict emotion from utterances spoken in a similar contextual domain.

We used the interview documents to collect ratings of the emotional content (i.e., valence and arousal) for each sentence of the document; 2,781 sentences in total were evaluated. A subset of these sentence evaluations were used as the training targets for the model. We collected this data using Amazon Mechanical Turk (AMT). AMT workers used a Web-based application we created to indicate their perceived emotion contained in text content (see Fig. 1). The Web application is described in detail elsewhere [19]. To ensure high-quality of the training data, we only used those sentences for which at least 70% of the raters agreed on the label for valence (positive or negative). This represented 996 sentences. For the current study, we use emotional valence alone for model prediction. In prior research using this same dataset [18], we showed that humans had more difficulty inferring arousal than valence, reducing the sentences for which there was agreement on arousal by one-third, to approximately 600.

2.2   Model Design

We used the model design described in our prior work [19] which consists of two processing steps: (i) extract the topic probabilities from each document

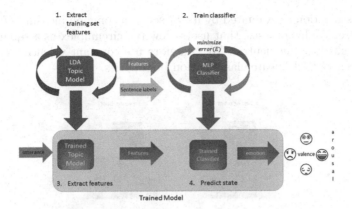

Fig. 3. Affective prediction model. (1) The LDA model is trained to extract features from the interview documents (2) For each document's sentence, its topic probabilities (features) are extracted and, along with its emotion target, is used to train the classifier (3) Features are extracted from the utterance by the trained LDA model, and (4) presented to the trained classifier to predict its emotional state

in the set (items 1 and 3 in Fig. 3), and (ii) use these features to predict the emotion valence of individual sentences as yet unseen by the model (items 2 and 4 in Fig. 3). Training of the LDA model and the classifier (items 1 and 2 in Fig. 3) was done outside of the robotic architecture and the results saved to files. These were subsequently used to initialize the predictor component in the robotic cognitive architecture; in principle, training could also take place in the architecture.

We trained the LDA topic model to generate vectors with 100 features. We used a stable, widely-used implementation of the MLP classifier from Scikit-learn [11] configured with two hidden layers and 50 artificial neurons to associate the features produced by the trained LDA model with the training targets collected from the human workers. Further detail on the model design and parameter selection is given in [19]. As previously mentioned, predicting both valence and arousal simultaneously proved problematic because there were relatively few training examples in which there was high agreement for both valence and arousal in the same sentence. For the initial phase of the investigation, we chose to predict valence only as the state where there was high agreement among the human raters and had many more training examples. To allow the robot to credibly mimic basic human facial affect, we made the assumption that a three classes of emotional states would be needed: neutral, positive, and negative.

Using k-means clustering of the (x, y) data we collected from the AMT study, we found three classification center points on the circumplex diagram, Fig. 2. This classification gives valence scores of -100 to -10 as negative, -10 to 25 as neutral, and 25 to 100 as positive. Upon model evaluation, we found that classification by constant valence scores of -100 to -24 as negative, -24 to 24 as neutral, and 24 to 100 as positive give the most predictive ranges to use for classification as evaluated by its F_1 score, a common measure of classifier performance. We hypothesize that users view the circumplex as a square graph, with the center as true neutral. We therefore use constant valence values away from the center to delineate classification boundaries.

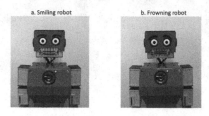

Fig. 4. Robo Motio's Reddy robot. (a) Smiling (b) Frowning

3   Emotional Pipeline Architecture

We embedded the trained model as a Java component called the topicModel in our robotic cognitive architecture. The component receives a text utterance from the large vocabulary automated speech recognizer (LVASR), extracts its topic probabilities and gives these as features to the trained classifier which makes a prediction as to the current emotional state (this corresponds to items 3 and 4 in Fig. 3). The prediction $\{0, 1, 2\}$ is then mapped onto a goal predicate string as $\{0 : neutral, 1 : frown, 2 : smile\}$ and sends the goal predicates representing desired affective states to the Goal Manager. This prediction model will eventually be developed to generate finer emotional states.

Here, we are using Robo Motio's Reddy robot (see Fig. 4). We defined action primitives for 'smile', 'frown', and 'neutral' which correspond to the robot's facial motors moving to produce the corresponding affect. The action script checks to see if the goal predicate created a smile, frown, or neutral goal, and performs the proper action primitive. Through this pipeline our robot can change its facial expression to match the affect it believes is contained in the spoken utterance.

4   Results and Validation

When evaluating valence, the trained LDA model was used to extract 100 features for each of the 1,069 sentences in the training set obtained from the AMT workers. Then, the classifier was trained to associate the feature vectors with the values $\{neutral = 0, negative = 1, positive = 2\}$ for the emotion valence. We used Scikit Learn's *GridSearchCV* parameter sweep for tuning the MLP hyper-parameters and ran a 10-fold cross validation to evaluate the model's expected performance. There were 445 examples of neutral affect, 226 examples of negative affect, and 398 examples of positive affect in our training set. We evaluated

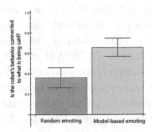

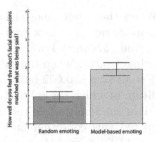

Fig. 5. Participants first watched the video and then answered the question: "Is the robot's behavior connected to what is being said?" (*yes/no*)

Fig. 6. Participants answered the question: "How well do you feel the robot's facial expressions matched what was being said?" (5-point Likert scale from *Not at all* to *Always*)

the model performance using the F_1 score weighted by the support for each class, and found $F_1 = 0.45$ where chance level is 0.33. We observed that when the model misclassified emotion, it tended toward classifying it as neutral or positive. In a model of emotion for persons with PD, a bias towards neutral or positive rather than negative affect is desirable given that it has been shown [15] that PD persons often become depressed when are judged to have negative affect when they do not.

4.1 Model Validation

To validate our emotional pipeline, we conducted a study for which we recorded videos of a person talking to the camera accompanied by a robot. The person in the video was a male actor who interpreted one of the interviews produced by a person with Parkinson's Disease, that was set aside from the dataset used to train the model. The interview contained an account of one enjoyable and one frustrating experience from the previous week. The actor reproduced the facial masking and affectless tone typical of Parkinson's Disease. The robot either used the model to emote based on what the person was saying or emoted randomly. Each participant saw just one of these two conditions.

A total of 54 participants completed the study on Amazon Mechanical Turk and passed our attention checks (44.4% Female, Age Range: 21–69 years, *Mean* age = 35.02 years, *SD* = 10.53). Participants first watched the video and then answered questions about it: "Is the robot's behavior connected to what is being said?" (*yes/no*), "How well do you feel the robot's facial expressions matched what was being said?" (5-point Likert scale from *Not at all* to *Always*). When the robot emoted based on what the person was saying, using the model, 65.5% of the participants indicated the that robot's behavior was connected to what was being said, significantly more than when the robot emoted randomly, 36%, $\chi^2 = 4.685, p = 0.03$ (see Fig. 5).

When the robot emoted based on what the person was saying, the mean participant rating of how well the robot's facial expressions matched what was being said ($Mean = 1.93, SD = 1.25$) was significantly different than the mean participant rating when the robot emoted randomly ($Mean = 0.96, SD = 0.93$), $t(52) = 3.187, p = 0.002$ (see Fig. 6). As an additional control, we also created a condition in which the robot did not emote at all but rather turned its head left and right randomly while the actor was speaking. An additional 25 participants completed this condition and passed our attention checks (48% Female, Age Range: 22–62 years, $Mean$ age $= 35.72$ years, $SD = 9.75$). Significantly fewer participants (24%) saw a connection between the robot's behavior and what the actor said, $\chi^2 = 9.307, p = 0.002$.

To further explore the effects of timing we also recorded one video in which the robot used the model for emoting but the emoting was done with an average delay of 5 s. A total of 26 participants completed this condition and passed our attention checks (46% Female, Age Range: 24–51 years, $Mean$ age $= 31.96$ years, $SD = 7.32$). When the robot emoted with delay only 50% (chance level) of the participants indicated that there was a connection between the robot's behavior and what the actor was saying, not significantly different from when the robot emoted randomly $\tilde{\chi}^2 = 1.018, p = 0.313$. Also, there was no significant difference in how well the facial expressions matched what was being said between delayed emoting ($Mean = 1.415, SD = 1.180$) and random emoting, $t(47) = 1.508, p = 0.138$.

5 Discussion

Our study shows that when the robot emoted based on the model's predictions, participants recognized the connection between the robot's emotion expressions and what was being said more so than when the robot emoted randomly. Additionally, proper timing made a big difference, suggesting that in order to have the desired effect the system needs to run fast and emoting has to happen based on short chunks of speech. This further shows that other approaches such as LIWC, which might need longer chunks of text for correctly predicting emotions, would not be appropriate for embedding in an assistive robotic system meant to emote in real-time based on the person's speech content.

While this suggest that the model can be used to appropriately generate a neutral, smile, or frown affect, future work is needed to be able to automatically detect emotional content with more resolution, moving beyond these three coarse levels of valence: neutral, negative and positive. Ideally the model could be improved to be able to detect various degrees of positivity or negativity and calm or arousal. Additionally, our training and testing dataset was comparatively small. We used 448 transcripts to train the LDA model and 1,069 sentences to train the classifier, a limited amount of data compared to typical machine learning endeavors which may have thousands of training examples available. We are in the process of collecting additional labeled training examples using AMT for the purpose of developing the model's ability to predict additional emotional states beyond positive and negative. Furthermore, in order to generalize the test results to a domain beyond that described in [17], additional training documents from more general domains will have to be used.

6 Conclusion

We developed and evaluated an automated method for inferring the emotional valence in the continuous speech of a person with PD and embedded it in our robotic cognitive architecture. In our earlier research, we hypothesized that such a tool equipped with the ability to accurately and immediately provide feedback on the emotion content of a conversation is not only beneficial for improving the social interaction with the PD patient, it can improve the quality of life in the home. Since human emotion is communicated via multiple modalities, and through different channels, e.g., voice, facial expressions, gestures, situating such a tool in a robot that appropriately controls the robot's facial motors could compensate for the problematic visual modality of communicating emotion. We found encouraging results that showed participants in our study connected the robot's facial expressions to what was being said. Once enhanced with finer prediction resolution, a family member/caregiver could use this as a way to infer the emotional state of a person with PD. The device's technology is not restricted to the domain of PD patients; it should be able to generalize and serve as an intelligent agent useful for monitoring the emotional content of the interaction between any two parties, providing real-time feedback on the emotion valence and arousal as the interaction unfolds.

Acknowledgements. The work is supported by the Center for Scientific Review under Grant No.: R01-NAG21152 and the National Science Foundation under Grant No.: IIS-1316809.

References

1. Balahur, A.: Sentiment analysis in social media texts. In: Proceedings of the 4th Workshop on Computational Approaches to Subjectivity, Sentiment and Social Media Analysis, pp. 120–128 (2013)
2. Balahur, A., Hermida, J.M., Montoyo, A.: Building and exploiting emotinet, a knowledge base for emotion detection based on the appraisal theory model. IEEE Trans. Affect. Comput. 3(1), 88–101 (2011)
3. Calvo, R.A., D'Mello, S.: Affect detection: an interdisciplinary review of models, methods, and their applications. IEEE Trans. Affect. Comput. 1(1), 18–37 (2010). https://doi.org/10.1109/T-AFFC.2010.1
4. Cambria, E.: Affective computing and sentiment analysis. IEEE Intell. Syst. 31(2), 102–107 (2016). https://doi.org/10.1109/MIS.2016.31
5. Chuang, Z.J., Wu, C.H.: Multi-modal emotion recognition from speech and text. Int. J. Comput. Linguist. Chin. Lang. Proces. 9(2), 45–62 (2004). Special Issue on New Trends of Speech and Language Processing

6. DeGroat, E., Lyons, K.D., Tickle-Degnen, L.: Verbal content during favorite activity interview as a window into the identity of people with Parkinson's disease. Occup. Ther. J. Res. Occup. Participation Health **26**(2) (2006)

7. Hutto, C., Gilbert, E.: VADER: a parsimonious rule-based model for sentiment analysis of social media text. In: International AAAI Conference on Web and Social Media (2014)

8. Mower, E., Mataric, M.J., Narayanan, S.: A framework for automatic human emotion classification using emotion profiles. IEEE Trans. Audio Speech Lang. Process. **19**(5), 1057–1070 (2011). https://doi.org/10.1109/TASL.2010.2076804

9. Pang, B., Lee, L., Vaithyanathan, S.: Thumbs up?: Sentiment classification using machine learning techniques. In: Proceedings of the ACL-02 Conference on Empirical Methods in Natural Language Processing - Volume 10, EMNLP 2002, pp. 79–86. Association for Computational Linguistics, Stroudsburg (2002). https://doi.org/10.3115/1118693.1118704

10. Pang, B., Lee, L., et al.: Opinion mining and sentiment analysis. Found. Trends® Inf. Retrieval **2**(1–2), 1–135 (2008)

11. Pedregosa, F., et al.: Scikit-learn: machine learning in Python. J. Mach. Learn. Res. **12**, 2825–2830 (2011)

12. Shah, M., Miao, L., Chakrabarti, C., Spanias, A.: A speech emotion recognition framework based on latent dirichlet allocation: algorithm and FPGA implementation. In: 2013 IEEE International Conference on Acoustics, Speech and Signal Processing, pp. 2553–2557, May 2013. https://doi.org/10.1109/ICASSP.2013.6638116

13. Shah, M., Chakrabarti, C., Spanias, A.: Within and cross-corpus speech emotion recognition using latent topic model-based features. EURASIP J. Audio Speech Music Process. **2015**(1), 4 (2015). https://doi.org/10.1186/s13636-014-0049-y

14. Svetlana, K., Xiaodan, Z., Saif, M.: Sentiment analysis of short informal texts. J. Artif. Intell. Res. **50**, 723–762 (2014)

15. Takahashi, K., Tickle-Degnen, L., Coster, W.J., Latham, N.K.: Expressive behavior in Parkinson's disease as a function of interview context. Am. J. Occup. Ther. **64**(3), 484–495 (2010)

16. Tausczik, Y.R., Pennebaker, J.W.: The psychological meaning of words: LIWC and computerized text analysis methods. J. Lang. Soc. Psychol. **29**(1), 24–54 (2010). https://doi.org/10.1177/0261927X09351676

17. Tickle-Degnen, L., Ellis, T., Saint-Hilaire, M., Thomas, C., Wagenaar, R.C.: Self-management rehabilitation and health-related quality of life in Parkinson's disease: a randomized controlled trial. Mov. Disord. **25**, 194–204 (2010)

18. Valenti, A.P., Chita-Tegmark, M., Law, T., Bock, A.W., Oosterveld, B., Scheutz, M.: Using topic modeling to infer emotional state: when your face and tone of voice don't say it all: inferring emotional state from word semantics and conversational topics. In: Workshop on Cognitive Architectures for HRI: Embodied Models of Situated Natural Language Interactions at AAMAS 2019, Montreal, Canada, May 2019

19. Valenti, A.P., Chita-Tegmark, M., Tickle-Degnen, L., Bock, A.W., Scheutz, M.J.: Using topic modeling to infer the emotional state of people living with Parkinson's disease. Assistive Technol., 1–10 (2019). https://doi.org/10.1080/10400435.2019.1623342

Train with Me: A Study Comparing a Socially Assistive Robot and a Virtual Agent for a Rehabilitation Task

Valentina Vasco[1(✉)], Cesco Willemse[2(✉)], Pauline Chevalier[2],
Davide De Tommaso[2], Valerio Gower[3], Furio Gramatica[3],
Vadim Tikhanoff[1], Ugo Pattacini[1], Giorgio Metta[1],
and Agnieszka Wykowska[2]

[1] iCub, Istituto Italiano di Tecnologia (IIT),
Via San Quirico 19D, 16163 Genoa, Italy
{valentina.vasco,vadim.tikhanoff,ugo.pattacini,
giorgio.metta}@iit.it

[2] Social Cognition in Human-Robot Interaction, Istituto Italiano di Tecnologia
(IIT), Via Enrico Melen 83, 16153 Genoa, Italy
{cesco.willemse,pauline.chevalier,davide.detommaso,
agnieszka.wykowska}@iit.it

[3] IRCCS Fondazione Don Carlo Gnocchi,
Via Capecelatro 66, 20148 Milan, Italy
{vgower,fgramatica}@dongnocchi.it

Abstract. Long-term motor deficits affect approximately two thirds of stroke survivors, reducing their quality of life. An effective rehabilitation therapy requires intense and repetitive training, which is resource demanding. Virtual Agents (VAs) and Socially Assistive Robots (SARs) offer high intensity, repetitive and reproducible therapy and are thus both promising as rehabilitation tools. In this paper, we compare a SAR and a VA during a rehabilitation task in terms of users' engagement and movement performance, while leveraging neuroscientific methods to investigate potential differences at the neural level. Results show that our participants' performance on the exercise was higher with a SAR than with a VA, which was especially clear under conditions of decreased perceptual information. Our participants reported higher levels of engagement with the SAR. Taken together, we provide evidence that SARs are a favorable alternative to VAs as rehabilitation tools.

Keywords: Socially assistive robot · Virtual agent · Embodiment

1 Introduction

According to the World Health Organization (WHO), 15 million people suffer stroke worldwide yearly and, among the survivors, approximately 75% exhibit persistent upper extremity deficits, as limb weakness and impairment of grasping movements [1].

V. Vasco and C. Willemse—Contributed equally to this manuscript.

M. A. Salichs et al. (Eds.): ICSR 2019, LNAI 11876, pp. 453–463, 2019.
https://doi.org/10.1007/978-3-030-35888-4_42

A substantial number of activities of daily living involve the use of the upper limbs and thus such disabilities can severely affect the quality of life.

Intensive and repetitive therapeutic training can significantly reduce motor impairment and lead to a partial or complete motion recovery, as patients re-learn the kinetic movements of the affected limbs [2]. However, such rehabilitation process requires supervision of trained professionals, with a consequent increase of the workload of therapists, whose number is not sufficient to accommodate such needs, both in and (especially) out of the clinic. Innovative solutions could be adopted to efficiently and effectively respond to this demand, with the aim of augmenting current care standards while allowing for greater flexibility of both patients and therapists. An area of active research is that of Virtual Agents (VA), which simulate a physiotherapist in a virtual environment: therapy costs can be reduced as patients can perform the exercises off site (e.g. in their home) and the "gamified" training activity improves their motivation and engagement, with the potential of high deployability and low maintenance [4]. Socially Assistive Robots (SAR) have also recently emerged, with the focus of aiding humans through social interaction, rather than offering only physical support [3]: a SAR guides the user in accomplishing a task through non-contact feedback, encouragement and constant monitoring. Both solutions have the potential of delivering high intensity and repetitive therapy, while providing a reliable and reproducible way to measure improvements in performance. With respect to a VA, a SAR offers physical embodiment and presence, which can positively affect the patient's motivation in terms of persuasion and attraction [5], but also performance (e.g. persistence in performing the exercise [4]).

Previous research has demonstrated the efficacy of social robots in a number of domains, including elderly care [5], daily activities [17], physical therapy [4, 6] and stroke rehabilitation [7]. On the other hand, virtual agents have been shown to provide a viable alternative in the same domains [8, 9]. Therefore the question of whether to implement a robotic or a virtual agent remains open. Several works directly compare the effect of a SAR and a VA on the user. Schneider et al. [4] analyze data from previous studies to investigate the effect of an embodied robot (the SoftBank Robotics Nao) on users' motivation, compared to a video of a human performing the exercise. Results show that participants training with a robot exercise significantly longer than with a virtual partner and that the robot elicits at least the same motivational effect as the VA. Fasola et al. [5] evaluate the role of physical embodiment by comparing the effect of a robot (the BlueSky Robotics Bandit) to its virtual counterpart. The study shows a strong user preference for physical robot embodiment over the virtual counterpart. Results are further confirmed in [6], which shows a dependence on the use of an embodied agent, as opposed to a simulated agent, when assessing adherence to a physical therapy. A complete review can be found in [10].

In general, previous works show that the physical embodiment and presence of a robot are beneficial to user interaction, in terms of persuasiveness and task performance. In this paper, we compare a SAR and its virtual version displayed on a screen during a typical motor rehabilitation task, consisting of a left shoulder abduction, while the real and the virtual agent monitor, assist and encourage the participants. The aim of the study is to investigate whether participants respond differently to a session with the robot and its virtual version in terms of task performance and engagement. We also adopt neuroscientific methods to investigate the potential differences that occur at neural level.

2   The Framework

In this paper, we used the humanoid robot R1 [12] and developed its virtual version within the simulation environment Gazebo. The devised framework, shown in Fig. 1, consists of a set of modules interconnected on a YARP network and is detailed in the next Sections.

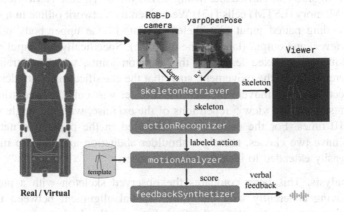

Fig. 1. The devised framework.

2.1   3D Skeleton Acquisition

yarpOpenPose estimates human poses based on *OpenPose* [11], an open-source library for real-time multi-person 2D pose estimation. The pipeline processes an RGB image and outputs a list of 2D keypoints for each person found in the image, achieving high accuracy and speed regardless of the number of people present in the image. *skeletonRetriever* combines the 2D locations of the keypoints with the depth provided by the camera to reconstruct keypoints in 3D fashion, using the classical pinhole camera model.

2.2   Motion Evaluation and Feedback

The motion evaluation technique is based on two interconnected layers: an action recognition layer (i.e. *actionRecognizer*), which classifies the skeleton data in a pre-defined temporal interval, and a subsequent motion analysis layer (i.e. *motionAnalyzer*), which further analyzes the skeleton joints if the action predicted has the same label as that of the exercise to perform (i.e. *abduction*). A feedback synthesizer layer (i.e. *feedbackSynthetizer*) finally transforms the numeric analysis into a verbal feedback with instructions to improve the execution of the exercise.

Action Recognition. This layer aims at preventing an erroneous analysis when the motion repertoire includes a high number of exercises, which can be very similar to each other (for example abduction and rotation of the shoulder have common moving joints). In such case, modeling the exercise as a set of interconnected static/dynamic joints is not feasible as covering all the possible joint configurations would be very complex and prone to errors. Furthermore, random movements can not be modeled *a-priori* and would thus lead to wrong analysis.

Action recognition is carried out using a Recurrent Neural Network with Long Short-Term Memory (LSTM) cells [13]. We trained the network offline in a supervised fashion, providing paired input (2D skeleton joints of the upper body provided by *skeletonRetriever*) and output (label of the exercise). Specifically, the input consists of temporal sequences of fixed length of the skeleton joints, which, at training time, include different parts of the movement, such that the classification is not dependent on a specific section of the movement. The training set was collected recording from a frontal and a side camera view 5 repetitions of the exercise, with the single movement performed 10 times. For the experiments presented in the paper, the network was designed to have two classes, namely a shoulder abduction and random movements, but can be easily extended to include more exercises.

Motion Analysis. This layer compares the observed skeleton with a pre-recorded template moving coherently with the robot. Spatial alignment between the two is achieved using the roto-translational offset between the bodies, extracted by the shoulders and the hips 3D positions. Temporal alignment is also achieved applying Dynamic Time Warping (DTW) to the 3D joint positions to extract the optimal warping path w between candidate and template joints. We then compute the error in position ε between each component of candidate c and template skeletons t in a predefined temporal window, as following:

$$\varepsilon_i = \sum_{k=0}^{N} (c_i(w_k) - t_i(w_k)),$$

with $i = \{x, y, z\}$ and N indicating the joint component and the temporal window's length. Positive (negative) tails in the error distribution reflect a c with a higher (lower) range of motion than t and are identified applying a threshold $\bar{\gamma}$ to the skewness γ:

$$\gamma_i = E\left[\left(\frac{\varepsilon_i - \mu_i}{\sigma_i}\right)^3\right] > \bar{\gamma}(< -\bar{\gamma}),$$

with (μ_i, σ_i) being the distribution mean and standard deviation.

Finally, we evaluate the speed performing the Fourier transform of each component of the joints under analysis in the defined temporal window. A difference in frequency can be related to a difference in speed, reflecting a skeleton moving slower (faster) than the template if positive (negative).

Based on the detected errors, each participant is associated to a score in a range of [0, 1], with 0 indicating a completely wrong movement and 1 a movement performed perfectly. Values in the middle reflect an error in speed or in position.

Verbal Feedback. This layer is responsible for providing a real-time verbal feedback to the participants, according to the strategy summarized in Table 1.

Table 1. Verbal feedback.

Detected error	Score	Verbal feedback
Action not recognized	0.0	Please put more effort
$df > 0$ (< 0)	0.5	Move the left arm faster (slower)
$\varepsilon_x > 0$ (< 0)	0.5	Move the left arm more on the left (on the right)
$\varepsilon_y > 0$ (< 0)	0.5	Move the left arm further up (further down)
$\varepsilon_z > 0$ (< 0)	0.5	Move the left arm backward (forward)
–	1.0	You are moving very well

3 Experimental Design

We used convergent methods to systematically validate the framework and to compare user engagement with an embodied (SAR) versus the virtual version (VA) of R1 whilst doing the exercise. We investigated self-reported engagement as well as performance measures under different conditions: observation, visible imitation, and occluded imitation. During the observation phase, participants merely observed the agent demonstrating the abduction movement. This condition was primarily used to establish baseline electroencephalography (EEG). During the visible imitation condition, participants executed the movement together with the robot, much like in a realistic rehabilitation exercise scenario, during which verbal feedback was provided by the agent at two moments. Finally, during the occluded imitation condition, the arm of the robot was removed from the view whilst the participant attempted to continue the movement in synchrony with the agent. To enhance the effects of absence of information, verbal feedback was not provided in this condition. We employed this condition for two reasons. First, this allowed us to measure real-life performance in situations where perceptual information processing is further from perfect, but more importantly, this allowed us to examine how well the movement was maintained in mental representation as a measure of engagement.

3.1 Materials

To compare the engagement between the SAR and VA, we measured self-reported engagement (questionnaires), a collection of performance metrics, and EEG.

Self-report Questionnaires. We used a 10-item questionnaire to evaluate the participant's engagement with the experiment, adapted from the previous literature [14, 15].

The items were scored on 7-point Likert-scale (1 – "not at all", 7 – "very much"), see Table 2 for the items.

Table 2. Self-report questionnaire item completed after the SAR and VA sessions.

Nr	Item question	Nr	Item question
1	How engaging was the interaction?	6	I was so involved in the interaction that I lost track of time.
2	How relaxing was the experience?	7	Overall, to what extent do you think you were able to engage with R1?
3	How exciting was the experience?	8	Overall, to what extent would you say that you liked R1?
4	How completely were your senses engaged?	9	To what extent do you feel you have developed a relationship with R1?
5	The experience caused real feelings and emotions for me	10	How engaged do you think R1 was with you?

Performance Metrics. As a more objective indication of engagement, we compared the following metrics of the participant's arm movements during the imitation and occlusion conditions against the template. *Hand position:* The cross-correlation between the participant's hand position (X & Y) and the template for each condition to determine the delay between the two signals. We corrected the lag between the two signals and computed their correlation coefficients *Amplitude:* The euclidean distance between the participant's and the template's mean peak to peak vertical distance. *Feedback:* Mean participant scores as outlined in Table 1.

EEG. We recorded EEG to examine the potential of recording human neuronal activity in naturalistic human-robot interaction – as opposed to typical lab-based psychology experiments during which participants are explicitly asked to sit still and observe well-controlled stimuli on a screen. More specifically, we examined the mu-rhythm, which is typically observed on electrodes placed over the sensorimotor cortex under rest. Mu-rhythm (typically 8–13 Hz) has been initially observed as being suppressed under execution of motion, but later studies also showed mu-suppression for mere observation [16]. We examined how mu suppression changes between conditions of observation of movement and executing movement. Specifically, this served as a manipulation check to see if performance differences could not be attributed to differential motion processing. To these means, we used a 16-channel setup (BrainProducts ActiCap and V-Amp) in which 15 active electrodes were positioned on the scalp covering the midline. We registered horizontal and vertical eye movements with three dedicated electrodes.

3.2   Participants and Procedure

Sixteen participants took part (age M = 23.0, S.D. = 2.81, 7 males). After giving informed consent, we fitted them with the EEG equipment, gave task instructions, and gave them ear plugs to wear (to attenuate background and actuator noise). This study was approved by the local Ethics Committee (Comitato Etico Regione Liguria).

The experimental procedure was as follows (cf. Fig. 2). Whilst sat on a chair, participants first only observed R1 executing the abduction movement (observation), after which they would be asked to do the movement together (visible imitation). Then, R1's arm would be occluded by an experimenter placing a panel in front of the robot's shoulder joint with the SAR, or by presenting a virtual panel on the screen (occluded imitation). Each of these conditions lasted for eight arm movements and the total sequence was repeated six times to increase statistical power. Next, participants completed a questionnaire about their engagement during the previous session and repeated this entire procedure with the VA if they started with the SAR, or with the SAR if they started with the VA (test order was counterbalanced between participants).

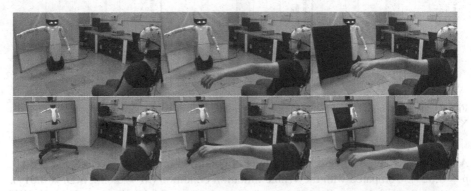

Fig. 2. The experimental scenarios during observation, visible imitation and occluded imitation (first, second and third column) for embodied (first row) and virtual agent (second row).

4   Results

4.1   Self-report Questionnaires

We found a significant difference in self-reported user engagement between the SAR and VA, $t(15) = 4.37$, $p < .001$. These data showed that the interaction with the SAR was more positively rated (M = 43.8, S.D. = 12.2) than with the VA (M = 33.9, SD = 13.1). This pattern was also observed when we analyzed items individually with Wilcoxon signed-rank tests, except for items 2, 5, and 6; $ps \geq .39$.

4.2   Performance Metrics

The performance metrics below were subjected to 2 (agent; SAR, VA) X 2 (condition; visible imitation, occluded imitation) repeated-measures ANOVAs.

Hand Position. For both the X and Y-positions, we found main effects of agent (X: $F(1, 15) = 34.9$, $p < .001$, Y: $F(1, 15) = 41.8$, $p < .001$. Participants had better performance with the SAR) and of condition (X: $F(1, 15) = 43.7$, $p < .001$, Y: $F(1,$

15) = 28.0, $p < .001$. Performance was better during the visible imitation condition than during occlusion). More critically, we also found and interaction effect of agent and condition (X: $F(1, 15) = 31.9, p < .001$. Y: $F(1, 15) = 28.0, p < .001$). For the visible imitation condition, there was no significant difference between the embodied and the virtual agent. However, during the occluded imitation condition, participants performed better with the embodied agent than with the virtual one (X and Y: $ps < .001$). Further, with the virtual agent, the imitation phase was better performed than the occlusion phase (X and Y: $ps < .001$), whereas no significant difference was found between the imitation and occlusion phase for the embodied agent (see Fig. 3).

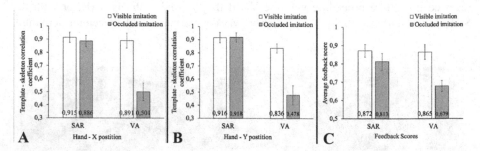

Fig. 3. A: Correlation coefficients between the participants and the template for the left hand's X-position and **B:** Y-position. **C:** Average feedback scores per condition. Error bars: ±1 SE.

Amplitude. Here, we found a main effect of condition in X-position ($F(1, 15) = 5.80$, $p = 0.029$). Compared with the visible imitation condition (M = 0.038, S.D. = 0.019), the deviation of the amplitudes from the template was higher in occluded imitation condition (M = 0.042, S.D. = 0.020) in the X-position. No significant effects were observed in Y-position.

Feedback Scores. We found a main effect of condition, $F(1, 15) = 29.3, p < .001$. Participants performed worse when the robot's arm was occluded compared to visible imitation. There was no main effect of agent ($p = .14$), but an agent x condition interaction effect emerged; $F(1, 15) = 7.70, p = .014$. Paired samples t-tests revealed that whereas performance was worse during occlusion for both agents (SAR $p = .016$, VA $p < .001$), participants performed 13.4% better (cf. Fig. 3) when the SAR was occluded compared with the VA occlusion, $t(15) = 2.77, p = .014$. There was no difference in performance between the agents during the visible imitation condition ($p = .90$). Taken together, the performance metrics demonstrate that participants performed the exercise better, and were thus more engaged, with the SAR than with the VA, especially when hindered perception is taken into account.

4.3   EEG

The EEG data were filtered (IIR Butterworth, 0.5 Hz–80 Hz 24 dB/oct, 50 Hz notch) before carrying out a Gratton and Coles ocular correction. These data were then segmented, and other artifacts were rejected semi-automatically. We then carried out a Fast

Fourier Transformation. For analysis we exported mean activity (μV) between 8.0–13.0 Hz and calculated the average value of the electrodes where mu-rhythm is typically observed, C3/C4. On these data, we conducted a 2 (agent: SAR, VA) X 3 (condition: observation, imitation, occlusion) repeated measures ANOVA. We excluded one participant from the analyses because the mu-rhythm was not observed in the individual data.

We found a main effect of condition, $F(2, 26) = 11.4$, $p < .001$. Post hoc comparisons revealed that with both agents more mu-rhythm was evoked during the observation phase than during the imitation phase ($p < .001$) and than during the occlusion phase ($p = .003$). Mu-rhythm during visible imitation did not differ significantly between visible imitation and occluded imitation ($p = .37$). We found no main effect of agent nor an interaction effect. See Fig. 4 for scalp distributions of mu-rhythm.

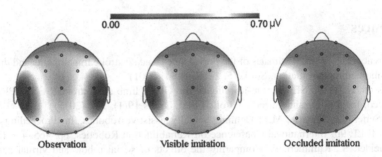

Fig. 4. Power (μV) and scalp distribution of mu-rhythm (8.0–13.0 Hz) in the three different conditions, collapsed across both agents.

5 Discussion

In summary, our questionnaire and performance data both show that engagement was higher with the SAR compared with the VA. The EEG data confirm that mu-suppression with an artificial agent shows a similar pattern as often observed for human movements, whilst demonstrating the feasibility of future mu-rhythm studies in more naturalistic setting than well-controlled experiments with static stimuli. Moreover, mu-rhythm was indeed equally suppressed for both agents between the visible imitation and occluded imitation conditions, so the performance results cannot be attributed to differences in motor activity *per se*.

Our results support the idea that a SAR as rehabilitation tool improves both participants' engagement and performance, if compared to a VA. This is in line with previous research [4–6, 10], but uniquely, the current study expands on the literature by combining questionnaire data with (1) direct performance metrics, (2) assessing the mental representation of the interacting agent by subtracting perceptual information from the scenario (occlusion condition) and (3) using EEG to check that the findings can not be attributed to different motion processing. Furthermore, we used structured repetition of trials to increase reliability of our measures.

Importantly, although the rehabilitation task proposed was quite easy, the level of engagement with the SAR was already significantly higher than with a VA. We plan to design a more complex setup with the participant having to touch the agent's hand, which also navigates towards him/her. Such task requires a deeper level of interaction and thus might further enhance the user's engagement with the real robot.

In conclusion, we propose that a robot's physical presence engages humans in exercise more compared to screen-based animations. Robot's presence increases motivation leading to better performance, potentially aiding in a faster recovery.

Acknowledgments. This project is funded by the Joint Lab between IIT and Fondazione Don Carlo Gnocchi Onlus and by the Minded Program - Marie Skłodowska-Curie grant agreement No. 754490 (fellowship awarded to Pauline Chevalier). The authors thank Nina Hinz and Serena Marchesi for their assistance with data collection.

References

1. Lawrence, E.S., et al.: Estimates of the prevalence of acute stroke impairments and disability in a multiethnic population. Stroke **5**, 1279–1284 (2001)
2. Carlsson, H., et al.: SENSory re-learning of the UPPer limb after stroke (SENSUPP): study protocol for a pilot randomized controlled trial. Trials **19**(1), 229 (2018)
3. Feil-Seifer, D., Mataric, M.J.: Defining socially assistive robotics. In: Proceedings of the 2005 IEEE 9th International Conference on Rehabilitation Robotics, pp. 465–468 (2005)
4. Schneider, S., Kummert, F.: Comparing the effects of social robots and virtual agents on exercising motivation. In: Ge, S.S. (ed.) ICSR 2018. LNCS (LNAI), vol. 11357, pp. 451–461. Springer, Cham (2018). https://doi.org/10.1007/978-3-030-05204-1_44
5. Fasola, J., Mataric, M.: Comparing physical and virtual embodiment in a socially assistive robot exercise coach for the elderly. Technical report, CRES–11–003 (2011)
6. Brooks, D., Chen, Y., Howard, A.: Simulation versus embodied agents: does either induce better human adherence to physical therapy exercise? In: Proceedings of the IEEE International Conference on Biomedical Robotics and Biomechatronics, pp. 1715–1720 (2012)
7. Mataric, M., et al.: Socially assistive robotics for stroke and mild TBI rehabilitation. Stud. Health Technol. Inform. **145**, 249–262 (2009)
8. Fiol-Roig, G., et al.: The intelligent butler: a virtual agent for disabled and elderly people assistance. In: Corchado, J.M., Rodríguez, S., Llinas, J., Molina, J.M. (eds.) International Symposium on Distributed Computing and Artificial Intelligence 2008. Advances in Soft Computing, vol. 50, pp. 375–384. Springer, Heidelberg (2008). https://doi.org/10.1007/978-3-540-85863-8_44
9. Arip, E.S.M., et al.: Virtual reality rehabilitation for stroke patients: recent review and research issues. AIP Conf. Proc. **1905**, 050007 (2017). https://doi.org/10.1063/1.5012226
10. Li, J.: The benefit of being physically present: a survey of experimental works comparing copresent robots, telepresent robots and virtual agents. Int. J. Hum Comput Stud. **77**, 23–37 (2015)
11. Cao, Z., et al.: OpenPose: realtime multi-person 2D pose estimation using Part Affinity Fields, arXiv preprint arXiv:1812.08008 (2018)

12. Parmiggiani, A., et al.: The design and validation of the R1 personal humanoid. In: 2017 IEEE/RSJ International Conference on Intelligent Robots and Systems (IROS), pp. 674–680 (2017)
13. Chevalier, G.: LSTMs for human activity recognition (2016). https://github.com/guillaume-chevalier/LSTM-Human-Activity-Recognition
14. Sidner, C.L., et al.: Explorations in engagement for humans and robots. Artif. Intell. **166**(1–2), 140–164 (2005)
15. Hall, J., et al.: Perception of own and robot engagement in human–robot interactions and their dependence on robotics knowledge. Rob. Auton. Syst. **62**(3), 392–399 (2014)
16. Hobson, H.M., Bishop, V.M.: The interpretation of mu suppression as an index of mirror neuron activity: past, present and future. Roy. Soc. Open Sci. **4**(3) (2017)
17. Rossi, S., et al.: Socially assistive robot for providing recommendations: comparing a humanoid robot with a mobile application. Int. J. Soc. Rob. **10**, 265–278 (2018)

User Testing of Cognitive Training Games for People with Mild Cognitive Impairment: Design Implications

Mikaela Law[ID], Ho Seok Ahn[ID], Bruce MacDonald[ID],
Dina-Sara Vasjakovic[ID], JongYoon Lim, Min Ho Lee,
Craig Sutherland[ID], Kathy Peri, Ngaire Kerse[ID],
and Elizabeth Broadbent[(✉)][ID]

Centre for Automation and Robotic Engineering Science (CARES),
The University of Auckland, Auckland, New Zealand
{m.law, hsahn, b.macdonald, jy.lim, mlee242,
cj.sutherland, k.peri, n.kerse,
e.broadbent}@auckland.ac.nz,
dvaj001@aucklanduni.ac.nz

Abstract. Mild cognitive impairment (MCI) occurs in older adults whose cognitive decline is greater than in normal aging, and it is a risk-factor for dementia. Cognitive training through games is a potential way to protect against further decline and delay the onset of dementia. This study investigated the usability and acceptability of a set of cognitive games for people with MCI when delivered on a robotic interface. 10 older adults played a set of cognitive games delivered on a robot with a touchscreen. Participants evaluated their experience through questionnaires. Observations of their interaction with the robot were also conducted by the researchers and experts in aged care to get further insight into the usability of these games. Findings demonstrated that both the users and experts believed the games to have potential to improve cognition in people with MCI. However, there were many functional issues with the robot that needed improvement including technical difficulties, problems with understanding the robot's speech and language, and problems for the older adult in using the touchscreen to complete the games. This study highlights design considerations for cognitive games for older adults on robotic devices.

Keywords: Mild cognitive impairment · Cognitive training · Robots · Elderly

1 Introduction

Dementia is a progressive disease that transfers through different clinical stages [1]. One of the earliest stages of dementia is mild cognitive impairment (MCI), which refers to cognitive decline that is greater than for normal aging, but does not yet meet the criteria for dementia [2]. MCI presents as mild impairments in one's memory, thinking and executive functioning and can have mild effects on one's daily activities [1]. Although MCI does not always lead to dementia, it is a risk factor and therefore it is important to stop or delay the transition in these patients.

© Springer Nature Switzerland AG 2019
M. A. Salichs et al. (Eds.): ICSR 2019, LNAI 11876, pp. 464–473, 2019.
https://doi.org/10.1007/978-3-030-35888-4_43

One possible way to help delay the transition from MCI to dementia is through participation in complex mental activities, such as cognitive training and cognitive games [3, 4]. There has been a proliferation of the development of these games targeted specifically towards patients with existing MCI or dementia [5]. These games may be able to maximize current function and reduce the risk of both further cognitive decline and the onset of dementia. This could allow patients with MCI to retain their cognitive abilities and remain independent for longer.

Many systematic reviews and meta-analyses have found that cognitive games can have benefits in many aspects of the lives of those with MCI. For example, cognitive games have been found to improve cognitive functions including working memory [6], reasoning skills [7], attention and learning [8], as well as lead to improvements in psychosocial functioning including reductions in anxiety and depression [8, 9]. One systematic review by Gates and colleagues [3] found overall moderate to large effects of cognitive training in MCI on memory related outcomes and global cognitive measures with computer-based games having the largest effects, however the review stated that further trials were a priority.

Recently, it has been postulated that cognitive games could be more effective if they were presented via a robotic interface. Robots could make these games more accessible and improve users' motivation. For example, one study showed that users reported higher motivation to complete the cognitive intervention when it was presented on a LEGO robot, rather than on a tablet [10]. There have already been a variety of homecare robots designed for people with MCI, including Irobiq and Cafero, that have cognitive training programmed into the robot, alongside other features [11].

As well as these service robots with multiple functions, robots have been designed purely for the delivery of cognitive training. For example, the Bandit robot was developed to increase user's motivation to complete cognitive stimulation therapy for MCI [12]. This robot encouraged users to complete a series of brain games, presented on a different screen. The participants enjoyed completing the games and interacted more with the games when the robot was present versus absent. This study demonstrates that a robot could increase the motivation of users to complete cognitive training.

Another study by Kim et al. [4] found that elderly who completed robot-assisted cognitive training had a reduction in age-related thinning of the cerebral cortex compared to a control group who did not receive any cognitive training. The robot-assisted training group also showed better results than traditional paper and pen cognitive interventions, demonstrating that the use of robots as the platform for cognitive training could be further beneficial. The authors propose that the robotic interface could be more effective because it increases participants' motivation to complete the games, it can include games with physical exercise components, and lastly because the novelty of the robot could promote more brain activation.

Ahn and colleagues [13] conducted a usability study on brain games that were implemented on a healthcare service robot (iRobiS) to investigate feedback from older adults. Older adults who tested these games reported that they were usable and reported positive feedback. Lastly, Tangibot was designed to make cognitive games more appealing to users with cognitive impairment [14]. This robot uses tangible paddles, rather than a touch screen and is designed for use by people with further cognitive decline. User feedback has shown that those with MCI found the games on Tangibot engaging and enjoyable [14]. More research is still needed to determine the usability and acceptability of these robots for patients with MCI.

This project is part of a five-year project with an overall aim to develop a homecare robot to be used in the home of patients with MCI. The current study aimed to obtain qualitative and quantitative feedback from both older adults and experts in aged care about the acceptability and usability of cognitive games for MCI presented on a robot interface. Feedback gained from the study will be used to further develop the games so that they can be implemented in the final homecare robot design.

2   Method

2.1   Study Design

This study used both a quantitative (questionnaires) and qualitative (semi-structured interviews and observations) design to gather feedback from both users and observers of a series of cognitive training games delivered on a robot interface. Ethics approval was obtained by University of Auckland Human Participants Ethics Committee.

2.2   Sample

A sample of 10 older adults (6 female, 4 male; age range 75–101 years) were recruited via convenience sampling. Participants were included if they had no or mild cognitive impairment, were able to read and write clearly on both paper and on a screen and were English speaking. All 10 participants either identified as New Zealand European or European. The highest educational qualification obtained by nine of the participants was high school, however, one participant had completed a University degree.

2.3   Procedure

Participants were recruited from Selwyn Village. Interested participants were assessed using the Montreal Cognitive Assessment (MOCA) for degree of mental impairment [15]. This brief assessment tool is used to detect any cognitive impairment a patient may have in a variety of cognitive domains. Potential participants were included in the study if they had no to mild cognitive impairment. Those who met the inclusion criteria for the study were given further information on the study and invited to attend one to three sessions at the village where they would complete series of cognitive training games on a robot and provide feedback on their experiences. Each session lasted approximately one hour.

At the first session, participants completed written informed consent and completed a baseline questionnaire, which asked participants about their gender, age, highest educational qualification and ethnicity. In each session, participants completed part of a cognitive training exercise developed at Ewha Women's University, Korea, and translated into English. These exercises were presented as games that were designed to test the cognitive skills of the participant and activate their brain. These games were presented to the participant via a robot with a large touchscreen shown in Fig. 1. The robot has the ability to move its neck for simple expressions (two degrees of freedom), and has one camera, a touchscreen and a speaker to interact with users.

(a) Dressing game   (b) Cooking game

Fig. 1. Photos of the cognitive games robot displaying the (a) dressing game and (b) cooking game.

For this study, two animated cartoon games were presented to the participants via the touchscreen on the robot. In the first game, the dressing game, the robot presented an outfit that the child on the screen would like to be dressed in. The participant had to remember the outfit and then after a brief wait, select the correct clothing from a series of options (for example, red trousers, a yellow shirt and a blue shoes). In the second game, the cooking game, participants had to remember a meal and select the correct ingredients and cooking style (for example, chicken cooked in a fry pan and boiled pumpkin). To complete both of these games, participants had to follow the instructions provided by the robot and use the touchscreen to complete their actions. Each game had 10 levels which increased in difficulty as they progressed. Each level took around 10 min to complete and included several games.

During the sessions, participants were introduced to one of the two games and asked to complete as many levels as they could, starting from level one. If the participants found level one of the game too easy, they could skip the second level and move to a more difficult level. Levels increased in difficulty by adding more items to remember, such as more items of clothing, or clothing with different patterns. At the end of each session, participants completed a questionnaire about their experiences and were given a $10 voucher as an appreciation for their time.

2.4   Measures

Participant Questionnaires
At the end of each session, participants were provided with a short and simple questionnaire that assessed their opinions and acceptance of the games they had just completed. The researcher asked the questions verbally if required. The first part of this question included asking the participants to rate the difficulty of the games on a scale of

1 (easy) to 3 (difficult), the speed of the games progress and speech from a scale of 1 (slow) to 3 (fast), how difficult it was to understand the rules of the game and the robots pronunciation on a scale of 1 (easy) to 3 (difficult), how satisfied they were with the game overall, the writing on the screen and the images on a scale from 1 (satisfied) to 3 (dissatisfied) and lastly how much they would like to play the game in the future on a scale of 1 (very much) to 3 (not very much). The questionnaire also included some open-ended questions asking about the advantages and disadvantages of playing the games and a section for overall comments on the games they had completed.

Researcher Observations

The participants' interaction with the robot was observed live by the researcher using an observation schedule. Some of the session were also video recorded so that a second researcher could observe the videos for inter-rater reliability. The researchers were asked to comment on whether the participant could follow the instructions easily, whether the participant was able to solve the levels by themselves, what made the participants struggle to complete the levels of the game, which levels the participants showed excitement or interest about, and which levels the participants seemed bored or annoyed with.

Expert Observations

Two experts in aged care (one caregiver and one nursing assistant) were also invited to attend a session in order to gain their opinions of the games. Each expert attended one session and observed a participant completing the dressing game. No experts were available to observe the cooking game. The experts were asked to complete the same observation schedule that the researcher completed, during the session. After the participant had completed their session, the experts also completed a semi-structured interview about the games they had observed in order to gain further insight into their opinions. Experts were asked to comment on the content of the game, how helpful they thought it would be for someone with MCI, how easy or difficult the game would be for someone with MCI, how the games could be improved and any likes or dislikes that they had. These responses were recorded using an audio-recorder and then transcribed by the researcher.

Statistical Analysis

The quantitative data from the participant questionnaires was analysed to find the mean values for each question. The participants' responses to the open-ended questions, the observations by both the researcher and experts and the transcribed expert interviews were coded using thematic analysis by two independent researchers to identify key themes. Triangulation then occurred with the two researchers discussing differences until agreement was reached for interrater reliability.

3   Results

3.1   Overview of the Sessions

Out of the 10 participants, four attended one session, three attended two sessions and the last three attended three sessions. Participants played the dressing game in the first two sessions, and the cooking game in the third session. Reasons for not continuing after the first session included; hospitalization (n = 1), aversion towards the robot (n = 1) and not seeing much point in the games (n = 2).

All 10 participants tried at least the first three levels of the dressing game, but only two completed all 10 levels. For the dressing game, participants completed four levels on average per one-hour session. Only six of the participants attempted the cooking game. However, this game had a few technical errors and most participants were unable to progress past the first level before the game crashed. Only two participants were able to move onto level two, where the game then crashed. Therefore, the data on the cooking game is limited by these technical difficulties.

3.2 Participant Questionnaires

Means and standard deviations for answers to the quantitative questions are provided in Table 1. For the dressing game, most people rated the difficulty of the games was easy to medium. The speed was rated as moderate and not too slow or fast, while the speed of the speech was rated as slightly fast. For understanding the robot, the responses were mixed with some saying it was easy to understand while others saying it was difficult. However, most thought the rules of the game were easy to understand, with only a few saying they were difficult. Almost everyone was satisfied with the pictures and the writing on the screen. Most participants were satisfied overall with the game, with only two saying they were dissatisfied. Finally, it was very mixed among the group of whether they would like to play the game again.

Table 1. Means and standard deviations for the participants' quantitative questions.

Item	Dressing, $n = 10$	Cooking, $n = 6$
Difficulty (1 = easy, 3 = difficult)	$M = 1.70, SD = 0.67$	$M = 1.83, SD = 0.75$
Speed of game (1 = slow, 3 = fast)	$M = 2.05, SD = 0.37$	$M = 1.67, SD = 0.82$
Speed of speech (1 = slow, 3 = fast)	$M = 2.20, SD = 0.35$	$M = 2.00, SD = 0.63$
Understanding of Robot's pronunciation (1 = easy, 3 = hard)	$M = 1.90, SD = 0.97$	$M = 2.33, SD = 0.82$
Understanding of rules (1 = easy, 3 = hard)	$M = 1.65, SD = 0.82$	$M = 2.50, SD = 0.84$
Satisfaction with pictures (1 = satisfied, 3 = dissatisfied)	$M = 1.20, SD = 0.42$	$M = 1.00, SD = 0.00$
Satisfaction with writing (1 = satisfied, 3 = dissatisfied)	$M = 1.15, SD = 0.34$	$M = 1.33, SD = 0.82$
Overall satisfaction (1 = satisfied, 3 = dissatisfied)	$M = 1.50, SD = 0.85$	$M = 1.33, SD = 0.52$
Would they play again (1 = very much, 3 = not much)	$M = 1.95, SD = 0.83$	$M = 2.00, SD = 0.89$
Maximum level reached	$M = 5.44, SD = 2.11$	$M = 1.33, SD = 0.47$

For the cooking game, most rated the level of difficulty as easy to moderate with one person saying that it was difficult. However, most said that the game was too slow. The robot's speech was rated moderately difficult to understand and most thought that the rules of the game were difficult to understand. Every participant stated that they were satisfied with the pictures, and all but one participant were satisfied with the writing on the screen. Most participants were satisfied with the game overall, and results were mixed among the group regarding whether or not they would like to play the game again.

In the open-ended questions of the dressing game, the two themes of advantages of the game and issues with the game were identified. The most common advantages identified were that the game stimulated and engaged their mind, made them focus on the present and concentrate as well as use their short-term memory. For example, participants mentioned that "the game was good to keep the brain engaged" and they "made me concentrate and use my short-term memory." However, participants also mentioned a variety of issues with the games such as; the games as being repetitive, boring and not very interesting. A few participants noted that they did not see a point or purpose to the game with one participant mentioning, "I don't see a lot of point in the game, apart from memory, but I think there must be a better way of training the brain." Participants said that the robot's speech and language were hard to understand.

For the cooking game the same two themes were identified; advantages and issues with the game. Under the advantages theme, the participants mentioned that the game made them engage their brains. For example, one participant said that the game "was an encouraging game that made me stop and think." One participant mentioned that the cooking game was more challenging than the dressing game. However, they had many issues understanding the game instructions, and said that the instructions were very unclear and they were confused about what was required. In addition, the participants mentioned that the text was too small which made it difficult to read the writing. Participants found the game repetitive and boring and they found similar problems as the dressing game in regards to the robot speech and pronunciation. For example, one participant mentioned, "the game is quite repetitive which makes it boring."

3.3 Observations

The two researchers who watched the participants' interaction with the games reported a series of issues with the usability of games. One of the main issues observed was that participants had difficulty understanding the instructions for the game and many missed important instructions which hindered their later performance in the game. The researchers mentioned, "he couldn't understand the robot's instructions - stating they are very unclear and he didn't know what to do." The biggest barrier to the game was that participants had difficulty with the touch screen sensitivity and finger pressure. They had problems dragging the outfits in the dressing game and that impacted their ability to complete the games. Some participants had so much difficulty with the dragging, that they ran out of time in the levels, or were so frustrated that they forgot what the game was originally asking. For example, one researcher stated, "her frustration was stemming from the screen sensitivity and not being able to move the clothes on the screen. She would attempt to move them multiple times and would not give up, however, after a while the game ran out of time." One participant mentioned to the researcher that the dragging hurt their finger by the end of the session. Another main issue was that participants had problems understanding the pronunciation/accent of the robot as well as encountered difficulties with the language the robot used. Lastly, some of the participants found the games quite boring and repetitive and lost interest very quickly.

3.4 Expert Interviews

The expert interviews revealed three key themes; benefits of the games, issues with the games and suggested improvements. For the benefits, the experts mentioned that the overall concepts behind the game were beneficial and suitable for people with MCI. They thought that the content and graphics were good for stimulating the mind and improving memory with one expert stating, "I think the content was good. My initial impression was that it was an engaging game." However, the experts also mentioned a variety of issues that impacted the functionality of the game. In particular, problems with the language and robot pronunciation impacted the participants' ability to complete the levels. The experts also thought that the game was too complex by requiring the participants to remember the instructions as well as how to use the touch screen at the same time. Suggestions from the experts to improve the game included; that the items should be touched to select them rather than dragged across the screen, especially as this age group is not used to using touch screens. The experts mentioned removing the negative reinforcement from the robot which sounded patronizing and taunting. One expert suggested, "having more positive reinforcements when the person makes a correct choice, such as 'yay, that's right', because there appears to be significantly more negative comments."

4 Discussion

This study aimed to evaluate the usability and acceptability of a set of cognitive training games designed for people with MCI that were presented on a robotic interface. The users themselves provided mixed feedback on the games with some stating the games were useful and other stating they saw no point in the games. They thought the content of the games was good for stimulating their mind and improving their memory, but they also reported a variety of issues which affected their experience of the games. In particular they mentioned that the games were a repetitive, the speech and language of the robot was difficult to understand and the instructions for the games were unclear.

The observations from the researchers and experts were in line with these comments. Although the experts thought that the games would be good to stimulate the brains of people with MCI, they reported that there were many problems with the functionality of the games that needed to be improved. In particular, they observed difficulties with understanding the instructions, which could be both due to the complexity of instructions as well as the language used by the robot. The games were translated from Korean to English, so it may be that the translation process was imperfect which led to problems understanding the instructions.

One of the main issues brought up by both experts and researchers during their observations, was the difficulties for the older adults in using the touchscreen. The users had trouble dragging items using the touchscreen, and difficulties with the sensitivity of the pressure applied. This led to frustration with the games and inability to complete levels. A previous study with games on a robot demonstrated similar difficulties with older adults using touchscreens and suggested instead using more tangible interactions, such as paddles [10]. However, another study showed that older adults with dementia were able to use a touch-screen independently [16]. Therefore, researchers need to be aware of possible difficulties with touch screen sensitivity, and possibly allow items to be simply touched rather than dragged. This is an important design consideration for cognitive training games for older adults with MCI.

This study was limited by the small sample size and the fact that users only completed one to three sessions of the games. Nevertheless, even five users can be enough to find major issues during usability testing [17], and in this study sufficient feedback was obtained for useful recommendations to be made. The study was also limited by the technical difficulties with the cooking game, which led to participant frustration and could have reduced their motivation to play the games. However, that is critical feedback for the developers of the games.

Overall, both the older adults and experts in aged care believed that the cognitive games delivered on a robot interface could be useful for patients with MCI to stimulate their minds and improve their memory. The study identified many functional problems with the robot that made the games difficult to use and decreased motivation in the users, including the language and speech of the robot, and the touch screen sensitivity. These identified issues can now be improved in later iterations of the cognitive games.

The main design recommendations from this study are that cognitive training games delivered on robotic interfaces for people with MCI need to: (1) use language and pronunciation appropriate for the culture of the users, (2) have touch screen interactions that do not demand too much dexterity for an older person, (3) give feedback that is positively reinforcing, (4) use large text, and (5) have very simple instructions. Consideration should also be given to use the robot platform to increase emotional engagement and make the games interesting.

Funding. This study was supported by the Ministry of Trade, Industry & Energy (MOTIE, Korea) under Industrial Technology Innovation Program (No. 10063300).

References

1. Gauthier, S., et al.: Mild cognitive impairment. Lancet **367**(9518), 1262–1270 (2006)
2. Petersen, R.C.: Mild cognitive impairment. CONTINUUM Lifelong Learning in Neurology **22**(2 Dementia), 404 (2016)
3. Gates, N.J., Sachdev, P.S., Singh, M.A.F., Valenzuela, M.: Cognitive and memory training in adults at risk of dementia: a systematic review. BMC Geriatr. **11**(1), 55 (2011)

4. Kim, G.H., et al.: Structural brain changes after traditional and robot-assisted multi-domain cognitive training in community-dwelling healthy elderly. PLoS ONE **10**(4), e0123251 (2015)
5. McCallum, S., Boletsis, C.: Dementia games: a literature review of dementia-related serious games. In: Ma, M., Oliveira, M.F., Petersen, S., Hauge, J.B. (eds.) SGDA 2013. LNCS, vol. 8101, pp. 15–27. Springer, Heidelberg (2013). https://doi.org/10.1007/978-3-642-40790-1_2
6. Belleville, S.: Cognitive training for persons with mild cognitive impairment. Int. Psychogeriatr. **20**(1), 57–66 (2008)
7. Klimova, B.: Computer-based cognitive training in aging. Frontiers Aging Neurosci. **8**, 313 (2016)
8. Hill, N.T., Mowszowski, L., Naismith, S.L., Chadwick, V.L., Valenzuela, M., Lampit, A.: Computerized cognitive training in older adults with mild cognitive impairment or dementia: a systematic review and meta-analysis. Am. J. Psychiatry **174**(4), 329–340 (2016)
9. García-Casal, J.A., Loizeau, A., Csipke, E., Franco-Martín, M., Perea-Bartolomé, M.V., Orrell, M.: Computer-based cognitive interventions for people living with dementia: a systematic literature review and meta-analysis. Aging Ment. Health **21**(5), 454–467 (2017)
10. Lopez-Samaniego, L., Garcia-Zapirain, B., Mendez-Zorrilla, A.: Memory and accurate processing brain rehabilitation for the elderly: LEGO robot and iPad case study. Biomed. Mater. Eng. **24**(6), 3549–3556 (2014)
11. Broadbent, E., et al.: Robots in older people's homes to improve medication adherence and quality of life: a randomised cross-over trial. In: Beetz, M., Johnston, B., Williams, M.-A. (eds.) ICSR 2014. LNCS (LNAI), vol. 8755, pp. 64–73. Springer, Cham (2014). https://doi.org/10.1007/978-3-319-11973-1_7
12. Tapus, A., Vieru, A.-M.: Robot cognitive stimulation for the elderly. In: Ferrández Vicente, J.M., Álvarez Sánchez, J.R., de la Paz López, F., Toledo Moreo, F.J. (eds.) IWINAC 2013. LNCS, vol. 7930, pp. 94–102. Springer, Heidelberg (2013). https://doi.org/10.1007/978-3-642-38637-4_10
13. Ahn, H.S., Santos, M.P.G., Wadhwa, C., MacDonald, B.: Development of brain training games for a healthcare service robot for older people. In: Beetz, M., Johnston, B., Williams, M.-A. (eds.) ICSR 2014. LNCS (LNAI), vol. 8755, pp. 1–10. Springer, Cham (2014). https://doi.org/10.1007/978-3-319-11973-1_1
14. Garcia-Sanjuan, F., Jaen, J., Nacher, V.: Tangibot: a tangible-mediated robot to support cognitive games for ageing people, a usability study. Pervasive Mob. Comput. **34**, 91–105 (2017)
15. Nasreddine, Z.S., et al.: The montreal cognitive assessment, MoCA: a brief screening tool for mild cognitive impairment. J. Am. Geriatr. Soc. **53**(4), 695–699 (2005)
16. Astell, A.J., et al.: Does familiarity affect the enjoyment of touchscreen games for people with dementia? Int. J. Med. Inf. **91**, e8 (2016)
17. Virzi, R.A.: Refining the test phase of usability evaluation: how many subjects is enough? Human Fact. **34**(4), 457–468 (1992)

Robot-Assisted Therapy for the Severe Form of Autism: Challenges and Recommendations

Zhansaule Telisheva[1], Aizada Turarova[1], Aida Zhanatkyzy[1],
Galiya Abylkasymova[2], and Anara Sandygulova[1(✉)]

[1] Department of Robotics, Nazarbayev University, Kabanbay Batyr Ave 53,
Nur-Sultan, Kazakhstan
anara.sandygulova@nu.edu.kz
[2] Republican Children's Rehabilitation Center, University Medical Center,
Turan Ave 36, Nur-Sultan, Kazakhstan

Abstract. This paper presents an exploratory study consisting of a series of Robot-Mediated Therapy (RMT) sessions utilizing a humanoid NAO robot with five children with a severe form of autism for two weeks. The focus on RMT for children with low-functioning autism (LFA) was motivated by a relative neglect of Robot-Assisted Therapy efforts to address additional challenges facing individuals with LFA such as impairments of language and intellectual ability. Children aged 4–8 years old attended six 15-min sessions that included different types of applications programmed on the robot. The cumulative results obtained from the observations and interviews of the participants' parents did not demonstrate significant progress in their social skills. Also, this paper explains the challenges and provides recommendations for further improvements of patient-centered interaction design in the area of RMT tailored for children with a severe form of autism.

Keywords: Robot-Mediated Therapy · Robot-Assisted Therapy · Robot-Enhanced Therapy · Severe Autism Spectrum Disorder (ASD) · Low-functioning Autism · NAO robot

1 Introduction

Recent years have seen an increase in the amount of research works that investigate RMT applications for children with Autism Spectrum Disorder [1–3]. However, most research has focused on individuals with high-functioning autism (HFA), rather than on individuals with low-functioning autism (LFA). Severe or low-functioning autism can be much more debilitating and challenging than other types of autism due to combined effects of cognitive and linguistic impairments making it virtually impossible for a child with severe autism (and her family) to function well in typical settings ranging from school to hospital settings [4].

© Springer Nature Switzerland AG 2019
M. A. Salichs et al. (Eds.): ICSR 2019, LNAI 11876, pp. 474–483, 2019.
https://doi.org/10.1007/978-3-030-35888-4_44

Better understanding of the additional impairments and individual differences are required to provide appropriate robot-mediated interventions.

Severe autism is usually diagnosed as Level 3 Autism Spectrum Disorder. LFA is extremely challenging and may include aggression and other difficult behaviors. Most people with severe autism never gain meaningful use of spoken language but might gain the ability to communicate through signs, picture boards, or other means [5]. Their reaction to the environment is aggravated and differs in a way of manifestation. For instance, they might unexpectedly and vigorously move around the room with load vocal spurts, and in parallel, rapid decline in mood as well as obscure interest in sharp objects characteristically distinguish the severe form of ASD from the mild and moderate. In addition to the above-mentioned features of the acute autism category, the children have a lack of interaction with strangers and often do not speak at all [6].

There are numerous exploratory studies that demonstrate the possible use of a robot with people with ASD. However, studies exclusively targeting the severe form of autism are rare. Thus, this paper presents a study that aims to explore the challenges of the RMT for such children, discusses our qualitative data, and offers suggestions for future work. The nature of the study is exploratory therapy sessions, which were repeated six times for two weeks (three sessions per week) with five children. Each session began by greeting the child and lasted for approximately fifteen minutes. We developed a set of applications: "Dances", "Transports", "Emotions", "Animals" and "Storytelling" in two local languages.

2   Related Work

With the popularity of commercially-available socially interactive robots, it is increasingly important to investigate their effect on children with LFA since most research on Robot-Assisted Therapy have relatively neglected this form of autism in comparison to HFA.

The study conducted by Boccanfuso et al. [7] reported that although their only nonverbal participant (out of six participants) did not make any significant gains in communication or speech, some fundamental imitation and attention skills were improved throughout a 6-week robot-assisted intervention with a low-cost kinematically simple Charlie robot.

Another recent study by Zorcec et al. [8] provided a case study with a humanoid robot KASPAR. They have revealed the observational analysis of the behavior of two young children with a severe form of autism during a one-year trial. The intervention was targeted at improvising the therapeutic and educational gains of the children while using a humanoid robot. Their findings demonstrate that children enjoy interaction, gain new knowledge and improve their communication, initiative and proactivity.

Tapus et al. [9] investigated whether autistic children show more social engagement towards the NAO robot or to a human partner in a motor imitation task via conducting four single-subject experiments. Three children with a moderate level of autism and one child with a severe form aged from 2–6 years participated in a 4-week study with two intervention sessions per day (one dyadic with either a robot or a human and another triadic with either a robot or a human and the experimenter). Results were mixed and showed that the level of the autism affected the results, since the child with a severe form rejected participation in the sessions with the human. Overall, they suggest that interaction with the NAO robot is more attractive and useful for children with LFA.

Duquette et al. (2008) compared a mobile robot to a human mediator for imitative play with an exploratory study with four children with LFA. Imitation of body movements and of familiar actions were higher for two children paired with a human mediator, but shared attention (visual contact, physical proximity) and imitation of facial expressions (such as smile) were higher for two children paired with the robot.

The study by Robins et al. [10] conducted a long-term therapy with three ASD children using the KASPAR humanoid robot, where two of them had a severe form of autism, while the third child had a moderate form of autism. The paper is a part of AuRoRa project. The first child did not speak and had a loss of attention span. She participated in all sessions and had noticeable improvements such as improvement in eye contact with the robot and even tried to imitate the robot's movements. The second child showed a great interest to the robot and regularly attended sessions. He progressed with the eye gaze as he often touched and explored robot's eyes. After several weeks he started to share his excitement with the teacher by asking her (non-verbally) to join the game. This study demonstrated the utility of the robot-assisted therapy with LFA.

When comparing twins (LFA and HFA) in the study by Taheri et al. [11], no change was reported for the social skills of the low-functioning twin, but his stereotyped behaviors decreased during the 12-session robot-assisted group-games program.

3   Method

The study was conducted at Republican Children's Rehabilitation Center which provides a 21-day hospitalization for children and their parents on voluntarily basis. We recruited five families whose children were diagnosed with a severe form of ASD. The recruited children were from 4 to 8 years old. This research was approved by the ethics committees of the university and the center.

3.1   Procedure

Each session lasted for approximately 15 min. At the beginning of each session, the robot greeted the children, then started applications such as dancing, storytelling and demonstrations of emotions. At the end of each session, the robot said goodbye to them. Due to unexpected health issues, some of the children were unable to participate in all six sessions.

Fig. 1. The experimental setup

3.2 Experimental Setup

The study took place in a small sensory room at the rehabilitation center. The sensory room was suitable for our study in such a way that it did not contain any distracting toys, pictures or a lot of furniture. The NAO robot was placed on the floor in order for the children to interact with it easily. The whole therapy session was recorded by a web camera, and the robot's behaviors were controlled by one of the researchers in the room (Fig. 1).

4 Behaviors

The following behaviors were implemented and adapted to two local languages:

- *"Dances"*: we implemented three robot dance animations, which were launched upon a particular body part of the robot was touched (head, left and right feet). The robot danced with different body movements for each song such as "Mummy", "Little spider" and "Clocks". This application was similar to a music or dance therapy where a child was encouraged to dance and repeat the movements after the robot. The goal of this application was to improve children's ability to imitate.
- *"Emotions"*: this application targets joint attention by exercising child's ability to pay joint attention at the pictures placed on the left side and on the right side of the robot. In addition, the purpose of this application was also

to learn and encourage the child to imitate emotions (such as happy, bored, sad, surprised, interested) that were displayed by the robot (with a sound) and children on the pictures. Each emotional state was accompanied with a photograph of a familiar situation so that the child could refer to his or her emotional state in a similar situation. For each emotion, the robot was pointing to a photo and was telling what it felt. For example, the robot demonstrated a bored animation and said that it felt bored waiting for a bus. Then, the robot pointed with its arm movement at the picture with a bus stop, said that it felt bored waiting for a bus at a bus stop like the one on the picture and demonstrated a bored animation again. Finally, the robot pointed with its arm movement and also turned its head to simulate eye gaze to a picture with a bored child first and then to a picture with a bus stop, firstly saying that children usually feel bored waiting for a bus like the child on the picture and at a bus stop like the one on the picture.

- *"Transport"*: we created four robot demonstrations of four types of transport (a car, a motorcycle, an airplane, and a boat) accompanied with a distinctive transport sound. The child was encouraged to repeat the demonstration, and each animation was repeated in a random order. This application purpose was to improve imitation skills.
- *"Animals"*: this one is similar to the "Transports", but instead of transports, the robot demonstrated four animated behaviors of animals such as gorilla, mouse, elephant, and horse with sounds and asked the child to guess and repeat.
- *"Storytelling" game*: NAO robot told two fairy tales, "The bun" and "The turnip" in Kazakh and Russian languages using animated movements. Each story lasted around 3–4 min.

4.1   Participants

Participant 1: gender: male, age: 8 years old. The participant has a severe form of ASD, ADOS-2 is 9. He responds to his name only after several attempts. He does not speak at all, and he often flaps his hands, jumps and screams. Although he does not speak, he can follow instructions and sometimes use gestures to ask for help. In addition, he has a strong attachment to his father.

Participant 2: gender: male, age: 5 years old. The child has stereotypic behavior which is expressed by active hand movements and use of vocalization. His ADOS-2 test score is 9. He sometimes may not respond to his name, and he does not speak. However, he is able to follow instructions. Also, he may show aggression when he has to wait for a long time.

Participant 3: gender: male, age: 4 years old. The child is very passive and does not react to surroundings much, and he can easily get tired. According to his ADOS-2 test score, which is 7, he also has a severe form of ASD. Also, the participant shows aggressive behavior when someone tells him that its forbidden or not allowed behavior. However, he can understand basic instructions and follows them.

Participant 4: gender: female, age: 5 years old. This child is very active. She usually does not sit in one place for a long time, and likes walking around and touching everything, tasting and biting. Her ADOS-2 test score is 9. Her movements are sometimes clumsy and limited as she interacts with other people. Her eye contact is good, but she does not concentrate on the robot during the sessions. Also, she showed some sudden movements towards the robot, and she could unexpectedly scream or change her behavior and facial expression, and become aggressive.

Participant 5: gender: male, age: 4 years old. This participant, with the comparative score 8 of ADOS-2 test, pronounces only specific memorized words, as his whole speech is delayed. Most of the time he expresses his emotions only by prolonged shouts. He has weak eye gaze and his anxiety from the surroundings can lead to quick mood changes.

5   Results

We conducted two semi-structured interviews with each of the parents (after the first session and after the last session) asking the following questions:

- **To what extent does the child maintain eye contact, tactile contact?** The first participant's parent said that there were some stereotypic behaviors of the child including hand flapping, screaming and anxiety. He does not respond to his name very quickly. The child maintains tactile contact well. The second child maintains eye contact only for a few seconds. He has stereotypic behaviors such as vocalization and moving hands very actively and does not speak. However, he can follow given instructions. Also, if he waits for something for a long time, he becomes aggressive. The third participant is not communicable and does not follow instructions as his parent noted. He does not make any eye contact with people and usually uses only single words to communicate. The forth child does not maintain eye contact with new people. She maintains eye contact only with close relatives. She used to behave very stereotypically as any other children with ASD. However, with many years of treatments, she managed to get rid of them. The fifth child can look at the person or an object for a long time, but he does not maintain an exact eye contact. Also, according to his mother, he has terrifying shriek that does not mean anything but he can express it at any time.
- **Parents' opinion about RMT as a therapy for their children.** The parent of the first participant liked this new approach and was eager for his child to try it. As the parent of the second child has not seen this therapy for children with autism, he was interested in it, and supportive of the idea. The parent of the third participant thought that this kind of approach was new, interesting and very unusual for them. Also, she noted that it would be very good if the usage of the robot for children with ASD could improve their communication with people. The parent of the forth child liked the robot because her child got in contact with the robot very easily. She considered it

to be a huge progress in her child's communication skills, because she usually does not interact with others much. The robot was also liked by the parent of the fifth participant and most especially by the child. He even asked his mother to buy a robot. In addition, this child, even if he could not express his thoughts with the speech, had a strong affection to the robot's movements.

- **What she could compare her child's attitude to the robot with? Was his/her reaction similar to getting new toys or seeing animals?** The first child, in general, is not interested in toys or animals. Therefore, his reaction could not be compared to them. However, the child showed some aggression towards the robot in a way that he wanted it to fall. The second participant was afraid of the robot, and did not react much. The third child avoids interaction with animals at all and does not have any favourite kinds of toys. However, he really paid attention to the robot. The forth child liked the robot, and therefore, she got on well with it. This was unusual, because she often looks at animals from some distance, but in this case, she immediately reacted to the robot and started playing with it. The parent of the fifth participant could not really compare the robot with anything.
- **Have the parents noticed any changes in their child's behaviour after each session? Overall?** In general, there was not much difference, because the first child was more interested just in robot's movements while it was dancing, rather than interacting, communicating with it or following its instructions. The second parent noted that there was not much improvement in his behavior because he did not want to interact with the robot at all, and stayed close to his mother. However, he showed some aggression towards the robot as he hit the robot's head. Overall, the parent of the third child liked that her child had a good eye contact with the robot because, usually, he does not look at people's eyes. He really enjoyed the robot dancing Gangnam Style, as he was eagerly asking to turn it on again by pronouncing its name. As it was mentioned, the parent of the forth participant admitted that the child did not hesitate to enter the room and interact with the robot, even though there were other people in the room. She is usually afraid of entering new places. Also, usually, she cannot concentrate and listen to fairy tales till the end. However, during our therapy sessions she sat patiently and listened to two fairy tales "The bun" and "The turnip". The parent of the fifth participant was impressed because after several sessions the child started to follow some movements after the robot.
- **Parents' suggestions or recommendations to improve the therapy?** In general, the first child's parent liked the idea and wished for more positive results. The parent of the second participant suggested to make games, songs and dances more familiar to the children in order for them to be able to be engaged and interested more in it. The third child's parent suggested to create more active games such as dancing in order to encourage the children to move more and to make the interaction more interesting. The parent of the fourth participant advised to create more engaging games to grab children's attention, and also to make them more concentrated on the robot. The parent of the fifth child said that the stories are little bit boring for children with

a severe form of ASD because they do not understand and can not follow verbal instructions so they rather need more repetitive actions by the robot.

6 Discussion

Overall, the parents were very positive about their experience of the RMT for their children. Since the main goal of this research is to include diverse forms of autism for RMT, it is important to discuss limitations and lessons learned for future work improvement:

- Challenging nature of LFA: the chronological age of these children does not match their age of development and their parents compared their children to being around 6–12 months old. Another challenge was that they do demonstrate aggression, stereotypical behaviors in the form of screaming or sensory search. It also happened during this study. It was also difficult to communicate with the participants of this study as they do not comply with instructions or respond in any way.
- In relation to the procedure and the duration of each session, we chose to have 15-min sessions with changing number of applications each time. Of course we could implement more applications and have longer sessions to address this limitation. For the future, the number of sessions with the robot could be increased and the application to the robot could be expanded with dances and games adapted to children's preferences. For instance, some might get upset with sharp movements or loud noises of the robot, some may become bored from the "Storytelling" game. Also, one of the participants was sensitive to loud noises, while the participant 4 only liked to listen and watch the "Gangnam Style" dance.
- Parents' presence positively contributed to child's interaction with the robot, as children may feel shy or fearful with new people or environment. Some parents stopped attending the therapy sessions after realizing that their children were fine with the robot, while for others the presence of the parent was required. One of the participants was close to her mother and she refused to follow instructions suggested by the robot without her. She also showed aggression towards the robot: she started to scream and shake hands as her mother left the room.
- Interviewing parents: due to a challenging nature of LFA, apart from observations and other metrics, it is important to talk to children's caregivers as they are the ones who can notice even slight differences in their children's typical behaviour. Due to specific conditions of every child, their parents are sometimes the most qualifying respondents who can spot and report these differences. However, asking appropriate questions at the right time is difficult, but researchers could consider administering a questionnaire to parents after every session. Our current interviews are not informative as the questions are too general, so future work should address this limitation.

- Presence of robot operator (researcher). The presence of a robot operator in the room along with the therapist (assistant) and the parent is justified by the following reasons. First reason is in the case of technical problems with the robot. After two-three hours of continuous use, the robot would stop working properly. To minimize the risk, we put the robot into a sleeping mode after every child. But the presence of a robot operator is important to resolve such kind of problems.
- Assistance. As reported in Wood et al. [12], providing assistants is quite normal as children might need help from their parents, therapists or researchers. Due to varying abilities, some children might need assistance to learn how to interact with the robot. But it is important to give children a few seconds before helping them, especially during latter sessions, for an opportunity to do it by themselves.
- For a quick and easy setup we used one RGB web camera as children and parents can feel uncomfortable with the presence of too many cameras. Also, it would be time-consuming to assemble a complex setup on a daily basis, as after each day we had to disassemble the setup.
  Throughout this experience, the ideal setup included 2 NAO robots, two laptops, Wi-Fi router and printed pictures for the games. The second robot was used as a backup. Since we frequently encountered problems with the robot, we needed to be able to switch from one robot to another as fast as possible. As a consequence, presence of the researchers in the room was unavoidable.
- The child-robot interaction using the humanoid NAO robot was the main robotic platform of this experimental work as we believe humanoid robots could bring an additional advantage (such as nonverbal social cues) in comparison to other robot embodiments.

7   Conclusion

This paper demonstrates the effect of Robot-Mediated Therapy on children with the severe form of Autism Spectrum Disorder. As it can be noticed from the qualitative data, those children did not show any specific improvements in their behaviors and communication skills. The robot could not maintain children's attention for a long time, although there were one-two successful attempts. Some children showed aggression towards the robot. Different games affected these children in different ways, such as if a storytelling was interesting for one child, it made other children bored, also some of them liked dancing with the robot, while others did not enjoy the dancing. Such kinds of observations reveal that the applications need to be diversified and improved in order to meet the challenges of LFA. In addition, for future research works, before starting the actual therapy sessions, it would be more useful if the children's stereotypic behaviors, things they like and their preferences were identified and adopted to the applications.

Acknowledgement. We would like to express our gratitude to the administration and staff of the Republican Children's Rehabilitation Center for their immense help to conduct these research experiments.

References

1. Dautenhahn, K.: Robots as social actors: aurora and the case of autism. In: Proceedings CT99, The Third International Cognitive Technology Conference, August, San Francisco, vol. 359, p. 374 (1999)
2. Richardson, K., et al.: Robot enhanced therapy for children with autism (dream): a social model of autism. IEEE Technol. Soc. Mag. **37**(1), 30–39 (2018)
3. Tleubayev, B., Zhexenova, Z., Zhakenova, A., Sandygulova, A.: Robot-assisted therapy for children with ADHD and ASD: a pilot study. In: Proceedings of the 2019 2nd International Conference on Service Robotics Technologies, pp. 58–62. ACM (2019)
4. Boucher, J., Mayes, A., Bigham, S.: Memory, language and intellectual ability in low-functioning autism (2008)
5. Morrier, M.J., et al.: Brief report: relationship between ADOS-2, module 4 calibrated severity scores (CSS) and social and non-social standardized assessment measures in adult males with autism spectrum disorder (ASD). J. Autism Dev. Disord. **47**(12), 4018–4024 (2017)
6. Ousley, O., Cermak, T.: Autism spectrum disorder: defining dimensions and subgroups. Current Dev. Disord. Rep. **1**(1), 20–28 (2014)
7. Boccanfuso, L., Scarborough, S., Abramson, R.K., Hall, A.V., Wright, H.H., O'Kane, J.M.: A low-cost socially assistive robot and robot-assisted intervention for children with autism spectrum disorder: field trials and lessons learned. Auton. Rob. **41**(3), 637–655 (2017)
8. Zorcec, T., Robins, B., Dautenhahn, K.: Getting engaged: assisted play with a humanoid robot kaspar for children with severe autism. In: Kalajdziski, S., Ackovska, N. (eds.) ICT 2018. CCIS, vol. 940, pp. 198–207. Springer, Cham (2018). https://doi.org/10.1007/978-3-030-00825-3_17
9. Tapus, A., et al.: Children with autism social engagement in interaction with nao, an imitative robot: a series of single case experiments. Interact. Stud. **13**(3), 315–347 (2012)
10. Robins, B., Dautenhahn, K., Dickerson, P.: From isolation to communication: a case study evaluation of robot assisted play for children with autism with a minimally expressive humanoid robot. In: Second International Conferences on Advances in Computer-Human Interactions, pp. 205–211. IEEE (2009)
11. Taheri, A., Meghdari, A., Alemi, M., Pouretemad, H.: Human-robot interaction in autism treatment: a case study on three pairs of autistic children as twins, siblings, and classmates. Int. J. Social Robot. **10**(1), 93–113 (2018)
12. Wood, L.J., Robins, B., Lakatos, G., Syrdal, D.S., Zaraki, A., Dautenhahn, K.: Developing a protocol and experimental setup for using a humanoid robot to assist children with autism to develop visual perspective taking skills. Paladyn J. Behav. Rob. **10**(1), 167–179 (2019)

Toward Robot-Assisted Psychosocial Intervention for Children with Autism Spectrum Disorder (ASD)

Vasiliki Holeva[1], Vasiliki-Aliki Nikopoulou[1], Maria Papadopoulou[2],
Eleni Vrochidou[3], George A. Papakostas[3],
and Vassilis G. Kaburlasos[3(✉)]

[1] 1st Psychiatric Clinic, Papageorgiou General Hospital,
Aristotle University of Thessaloniki, 56403 Thessaloniki, Greece
vholeva@yahoo.gr, v.a.nikopoulou@gmail.com
[2] Division of Child Neurology and Metabolic Disorders,
4th Department of Pediatrics, Papageorgiou General Hospital,
Aristotle University of Thessaloniki, 56403 Thessaloniki, Greece
mtpapado@gmail.com
[3] HUman-MAchines INteraction Laboratory (HUMAIN-Lab),
International Hellenic University, Agios Loukas, 65404 Kavala, Greece
{evrochid, gpapak, vgkabs}@teiemt.gr

Abstract. The effectiveness of social robots in education is typically demonstrated, circumstantially, involving small samples of students [1]. Our interest here is in special education in Greece regarding Autism Spectrum Disorder (ASD) involving large samples of children students. Following a recent work review, this paper reports the specifications of a protocol for testing the effectiveness of robot (NAO)-based treatment of ASD children compared to conventional human (therapist)-based treatment. The proposed protocol has been developed by the collaboration of a clinical scientific team with a technical scientific team. The modular structure of the aforementioned protocol allows for implementing parametrically a number of tools and/or theories such as the theory-of-mind account from psychology; moreover, the engagement of the innovative Lattice Computing (LC) information processing paradigm is considered here toward making the robot more autonomous. This paper focuses on the methodological and design details of the proposed intervention protocol that is underway; the corresponding results will be reported in a future publication.

Keywords: Social robots · Autism spectrum disorders · Human-robot interaction · Psychological intervention · Protocol design · Robot-assisted therapy

1 Introduction

Children with ASD suffer from communication deficits, lack of social interaction and motivation [2]. A lack of motivation can diminish the ability to learn and improve social skills. Several treatments are being used to tackle symptoms of ASD and

© Springer Nature Switzerland AG 2019
M. A. Salichs et al. (Eds.): ICSR 2019, LNAI 11876, pp. 484–493, 2019.
https://doi.org/10.1007/978-3-030-35888-4_45

improve social functioning, everyday living abilities and learning disabilities, but, still, a single cure for ASD does not exist. Treatment requirements combined with children's difficulties make it hard to elicit and maintain engagement of children during therapeutic sessions. Moreover, due to the nature of the disorder and the large variations in the symptoms, no single approach can be established as the most efficient, since a therapeutic model may work for one child but not for another [3].

Social robots have been used in psychosocial interventions for children suffering from ASD disorders with promising results [4], as they seem to increase their social engagement and enable social cues with a simplicity that is essential for kids with ASD to accept and understand. Children with ASD are attracted to robots, possibly because they seem to adjust better interacting with the robot's predictable and repeated mode of action [5]. Moreover, since children with ASD cannot relate with others, they seem to prefer to relate to robots instead of humans [6]. On top of that, robots allow for a multisensory interaction in a controlled and reproducible learning environment, and for a personalized application of intervention techniques. Several reviews have been conducted addressing the results of robot-assisted therapy in the ASD population. Diehl et al. [7] conducted a review of relevant studies showing promising results but with little clinical value. Pessini et al. [8] evaluated the feasibility of robot-mediated therapeutic approaches and concluded that ASD subjects often performed better with a robot rather than with a human partner. Robinson et al. [9] studied randomized controlled trials (RCTs) using social robots to deliver psychosocial interventions to children with ASD, to conclude that robot-assisted interventions "appear to have positive outcomes, although studies with larger samples and longer follow-ups are needed to build confidence in the strength and sustained maintenance of these effects".

Therefore, the next step in the field is to include robots in clinical trials with larger samples and strict methodology and not limit their use to specific game scenarios or to a single symptom. The expansion of robots' involvement during therapy sessions is dependent upon sophisticated technological designs reinforcing robot autonomy. Adhering to this path, the current protocol is designed to target an adequate sample in a randomized and blind fashion to minimize biases and to enable the researchers to determine the intervention's lasting effect after a 6-month follow-up period.

In this work we present an experimental design for evaluating the effects of a socially assistive robot (NAO) in a therapeutic setting with 80 children with ASD interacting with the robot which behaves as an assistant therapist. The intervention is designed as an attempt to target the autism core symptom of impaired social communication, to modify challenging behaviours or teach adaptive behaviours of daily activities, through the application of theory-of-mind principles and behavioural techniques [10]. In this project the role of the robot is crucial as it participates in every session and in all therapeutic scenarios. The proposed methodology contributes towards the design of therapeutic interventions for children with ASD as part of a national project entitled "Social Robots as Tools in Special Education" [11]. This study aims at providing a robust methodology to further investigate the strengths and weaknesses of robot-assisted therapy, adding to the research field of ASD. The goals of the study are (1) to explore potential differences in a comparative analysis between a robot-assisted intervention group and a human-assisted control group that receives intervention by humans only and (2) to determine the contribution of social robots to therapeutic interventions with children diagnosed with ASD.

The rest of the paper is organized as follows: In Sect. 2 the proposed methodology is presented. The screening and diagnostic tools that are used and the role of the robot are described in Sect. 3. Section 4 concludes with the expected outcomes and the contribution of this work.

2 Methodology

In order to develop a robust protocol design, a multidisciplinary team of experts was put together to identify the intervention's requirements. The group was composed of one neuropediatrician, one pediatrician, a clinical psychologist, a neuropsychologist, a child psychologist, three special needs' educators, a speech therapist, a physiotherapist, an ergotherapist and a technical team including engineers and computer scientists. The technical team provided support to the clinical team who established the specifications. After several focus group sessions, four main topics were identified; namely, safety requirements, robot's autonomy, task selection and procedure. A manual was developed, so all Therapists/Educators (T/E) could apply the same method, so as to avoid methodological inconsistencies and to produce comparable results.

2.1 Safety Requirements

Social robot NAO is selected to carry out the proposed methodology. The design and the functionalities of the selected robot are crucial for the effectiveness of the therapy. Children with ASD may be more receptive towards certain features. However, the suitability of NAO for ASD therapy is already established [12]. NAO has a friendly visual engaging appearance, without being over-stimulated. It has no sharp edges, ropes or cables and brightness of the displayed colors can be adjusted.

Children in general can be uncontrollably impulsive. Thus, it is highly possible to touch the robot and hurt both themselves and the robot. For safety reasons, the robot is programmed to move in a smooth way. The distance between the robot and the child needs to be optimal in a way that the child could not reach easily for the robot, yet close enough so as the robot's capability for voice recognition is intact. This distance is experimentally estimated between 15 to 50 cm. If, however, an algorithm requires movement of the robot, then the technical team members need to address the movement in a way to avoid any potential damage to the robot. The clinical team needs to interfere when a child attempts to touch the robot whenever he/she is not supposed to.

2.2 Robot's Autonomy

Robot-assisted therapy up-to-date, mainly consider passive or remote-controlled robots. Robots need to become more autonomous, mainly to reduce the burden on therapists and be able to provide, in long terms, stable and consistent therapeutic interventions. Functionality of the robot is therefore a main issue. Functionality is interpreted in terms of *autonomy* and *adaptivity*.

Autonomy means that the robot is able to execute a sequence of desired actions without the interference of the technician. The therapist needs to be able to press a button to lead the robot to expected behaviours such as guiding the session. This semi-autonomous robotic behaviour is desired when it comes to children with ASD since therapists cannot be replaced completely, as a most effective judge of children's psychological/emotional state.

Adaptivity means that the robot allows different functionalities for different children. Adaptivity gives to the robots the emotional intelligence they lack, thereby providing a progressive growth in the complexity of the interaction according to the development/responses of the child. In a way, robots have something in common with children suffering from autism; they have difficulties understanding peoples' emotions or social cues. In this work, one of the biggest challenges was to program the robot in order to be able to understand the child's emotion and to respond accordingly.

To make NAO's behaviour more natural to the child, the robot was programmed to translate specific linguistic cues (i.e. words or phrases that reveal sympathy, empathy, encouragement etc.) to emotions and to react accordingly, meeting the child's individual needs. The supervision by the T/E is considered necessary. When needed, the T/E should intervene in a calm way, not sharply interrupting the child-robot interaction. Previous research [13] has shown that children could develop signs of distress during the session either due to their emotional state or due to robot malfunctions. For the intervention scenarios to be performed smoothly the robot should respond physically or verbally in some basic orders coming from the T/E, to resolve potential problems arising during the intervention. A methodology was developed and presented in [14] intending to serve the latter purpose; contribute towards the design of therapeutic interventions for children with ASD where speech is the basic communication channel. Trigger words to regulate a conversation and guide the therapeutic activities are represented by Interval Numbers (INs). A classification model is then adopted to recognize the trigger words. This method is especially designed to be a computationally inexpensive tool used in conjunction with the robots' build-in speech recognition engine. Clinical professionals chose eight trigger-words that use more often during the session (Table 1). If by any chance the robot's battery runs out or other technical problems arise, the robot informs the child: "I like your company a lot, but I have to rest".

2.3   Task Selection and Logs

Based on the theory of mind [15] and applied behaviour analysis (ABA) principles [16] combined with cognitive-behavioural techniques [10], the tasks selected for the intervention aim at addressing social, cognitive and behavioural issues related to ASD. The tasks were selected in a way to meet the following requirements:

- Being in accordance with standard therapeutic methods.
- Providing individualized treatment, i.e. being suitable and adaptable to each child's development and personal needs.
- Being easy to apply all of them (or partially) with the aim of the robot.

Table 1. Trigger words controlling robot's behaviour.

Trigger word	Robot's behaviour
Follow me	The robot follows the T/E (when the robot is needed to follow the T/E away from the child)
Well done	The robot applauds and empowers the child saying "you did it, wow" having his eyes changing colour (when the child has completed a task successfully)
Again	The robot utters an interjection ("Hmmm") showing uncertainty and says "I am not sure, let's try one more time"
Break	The robot stops whatever it's doing and says "we need some time to relax". This is used when the child looks tired, performs stereotypical movements without stopping, does not participate in the scheduled tasks, lacks eye contact for a significant amount of time or does not respond to the T/E cues
Change	The robot stops whatever it is doing and says: "let's do something different". This phrase is used as a transition signal to the next task
Attention	The robot says: "this is not safe, I am going" and moves to the relaxation space. This phrase will be used by the T/E when the child moves aggressively towards the robot and the T/E perceives a possible danger or when the child abuses toys or other therapeutic elements
Stop	The robot pauses and says "I am upset; I need some time to relax". This is used when the child meltdowns, has a tantrum, is aggressive or dysphoric
Over	The robot enters the sleep mode. This phrase is used if the T/E realizes the existence of other technical problems that the robot itself cannot recognize

The robot will be facilitated with the appropriate algorithms for recording valuable information during each session, in real time. This is very useful for the therapist, since it is not needed to record the entire session and to gather the needed information later, which is time-consuming and tiring. The information collected by the robot (logs) for each task are summarized in Table 2.

Recognizing children's responses requires the use of the speech recognition algorithm provided by the robot. The built-in microphone of the robot needs to make a quality voice recording. The recording room should be equipped with a special wall lining to meet the minimum acoustic specifications to eliminate all noises (electronic noise, sound reflection noise, noise from the robot parts etc.).

Table 2. Tasks and robot's logs.

Task	Logs
Interaction	Eye contact time, verbal communication, spontaneous communication, communication by gestures
Joint attention	Time spent on targeted tasks, correct response and speed response
Memory task	Number of correct answers, concentration time
Imitation	Accuracy of movement, correct repetitions
Sequence	Following rules, waiting time before acting

The speaker should speak as loud and as clear as possible, ideally in the direction of the built-in microphones of the robot (e.g. in NAO the microphones are placed in the front). The robot's voice needs to be adjusted, in speed and intensity, so as to be easily understood and attributed to a natural human speaker.

For logs coming from image processing, the robot uses its built-in camera. The camera must be set to maximum image quality. The robot must be mounted on a stable surface and not move while taking frames that will be processed. The room must be properly illuminated and there should be no light source opposite the camera lens or any reflective surfaces (e.g. mirrors, windows, water bottle, etc.). Ideally, and since all recordings will be made in the same room, the camera can be adjusted according to the lighting conditions of the room. As far as the angle of reception is concerned, the child should be within the robot camera's range, ideally facing the camera.

2.4 Procedure

A randomized double-blind experiment has been designed. At least eighty children, aged 2–12 years, diagnosed with ASD will be included in the study. They will be randomly assigned to two groups; a social robot-assisted therapy group (NAO group) and a psychosocial human-assisted intervention group (control group). The experiments will take place in two specialized centers: the pediatric clinic at Papageorgiou General Hospital in Thessaloniki, Greece and the Learning Disabilities center "Praxis" in Kavala, Greece.

NAO will be programmed and employed as a robotic assistant to the T/E in the NAO group to perform various scenarios during up to 21 intervention sessions. These sessions are aimed at instructing the children about social skills e.g. empathy, behaviour control skills e.g. self-regulation and cognitive skills e.g. joint attention, memory and imitation. The same intervention will be conducted by the T/E alone on the control group. If the child's cognitive and emotional development permits, the robot will have a significant role functioning in higher levels of autonomy during the session, while remaining under the supervision of the T/E. Otherwise, the robot's role will vary accordingly. In some scenarios it will participate only as a social facilitator and in others as an assistant therapist.

Inclusion criteria for the selected children are the following: ages 2–12 years, confirmed ASD diagnosis, IQ over 70, Greek-language comprehension, CARS-2 from 30 to 37, ADI-R: social interaction ≥ 10, communication ≥ 8 (when verbal ability present) or ≥ 7 (verbal ability absent), stereotypic behaviour ≥ 3 and parents/caregivers written informed consent. The children will be assessed at baseline, at the end of the intervention and two months later by an independent "blind" assessor. The results of the study will be disseminated to the families of children with ASD and clinicians with a specific interest in children with special needs.

3 Tools

As ASD are characterized by diagnostic heterogeneity, both groups would undergo cognitive and psychological evaluations to determine areas of strengths and weaknesses and to appropriately match across groups and conditions. Each participant will be assessed through the appropriate screening measures and by means of two questionnaires measuring strengths, difficulties and satisfaction. Parents/caregivers will undergo a semi-structured interview. The tools that are going to be used are:

- Wechsler Preschool and Primary Scale of Intelligence [17],
- Wechsler Intelligence Scale for Children [18],
- Childhood Autism Rating Scale [19],
- Autism Diagnostic Interview, revised [20],
- Developmental Neuropsychological Assessment [21],
- Acchenbach System of Empirically Based Assessment [22],
- Strengths and Difficulties Questionnaire [23],
- a semi-structured parent interview and
- a satisfaction scale, created for the project.

3.1 The Steps of the Intervention

The proposed intervention protocol consists of seven steps, described in Table 3. It is probable that children with ASD may have problems following all steps. For this reason, the T/E could intervene and change the flow of the steps in favour of the child's emotional well-being. There is a quick shift in the scenarios to keep the child interested. Depending on child's attention abilities, each session could last 30 to 45 min. At the end of each session the therapist gives a synopsis to the parents of how the intervention went and a short task as homework in order to retain the benefits of the session.

3.2 The Robot's Role

In the robot-assisted therapy, the robot is used as a tool to help the child embed social skills. For the child with ASD it is important to be encouraged so as to feel rewarded whenever he/she achieves a goal [24]. In our case, positive feedback from the robot is considered beneficial. For this reason, the robot encourages the child through sensory rewards; lighting the eyes, clapping hands, saying encouraging words or playing music, whenever this is considered necessary.

The role of the robot includes locomotion. Locomotion makes the robot more interactive rather than a passive tool. Moreover, it adds the feature of moving around, allowing for more sophisticated scenarios. Sensors such as press buttons on the robot, provide the children with more control. This may recant the autonomy requirement, yet, it makes the child more engaged since the ability of choice given to them by pressing different buttons, would lead to different consequences. As a parallel task, the robot will collect real-time information regarding the session (Table 2). For the requirement of information logging, proper algorithms are developed; machine vision algorithms to recognize actions and gestures/emotions, and speech recognition algorithms to recognize answers and emotions.

Table 3. The intervention protocol.

Step	Description
1. Free play	The robot welcomes the child and invites him/her to start playing in the provided area. During the play the robot empowers the child
2. Role playing-symbolic play	The robot asks the child age-appropriate questions to empower symbolic play
3. Cognitive training	First the therapist will perform the exercises with the child, and the robot will repeat them to determine if the child could generalize what he/she has taught to a new context • Mimics: the children perform gross motor imitation tasks managed by the robot only with different levels of difficulty • Joint Attention: During a game of treasure hunt, the robot guides the child's attention to find the desired object. The child follows the direction of the robot's gaze • Memory: The robot instructs the child how to play the game and responds accordingly if the choice was successful or unsuccessful • False belief task: The robot helps the child understand other person's beliefs by reading to the child specific stories and asking specific questions
4. Empathy training	The robot helps the child to improve emotion recognition, facial expression decoding, and appropriate response, through a game of "guess how I feel"
5. Behaviour training	The robot involves the child in behaviour training targeting self-care, daily activities, anger expression and anxiety management by social stories
6. Tablet (Serious games)	The robot instructs the child how to play some serious games in a tablet
7. Relaxation (3 levels)	The robot teaches the child some relaxation techniques. T/E and child follow the instructions

4 Expected Outcomes and Conclusions

In this work we present an experimental protocol for evaluating the effects of a socially assistive robot involving children with ASD in a real-world therapeutic setting. The children will interact with the robot which will behave as an assistant therapist. The proposed intervention protocol is designed by a team of experts, integrating diverse sources of knowledge and skill, based on the theory of mind and ABA principles combined with cognitive-behavioural techniques. When a robotic application involves humans, then non-numerical data may emerge such as words. In the latter context, the LC paradigm has been proposed for rigorous modeling based on numerical and/or non-numerical data [5]. LC models will be developed for application in a future work toward making the social robot more intelligent. The expected outcomes of the proposed methodology are to evaluate the effectiveness of robot-assisted psychosocial intervention for children with ASD, and to explore the robots' ability to function in a semi-autonomous way. It may also be possible to distinguish the children who had the more efficient interaction with the robot and identify the factors that contributed towards it. Upon the conclusion of the study it is expected to be able to better define the requirements needed for robots in order to be effective in clinical or therapeutic settings. Close collaboration with parents will help children generalize the skills learned during intervention and will highlight the impact of the intervention in children's daily life. This work is designed to point out the beneficiary effects of social robots on ASD and to investigate in future work this hypothesis over a large sample of children for an extended period of therapeutic sessions.

Acknowledgment. This research has been co-financed by the European Union and Greek natal ionfunds through the Operational Program Competitiveness, Entrepreneurship and Innovation, under the call RESEARCH – CREATE – INNOVATE (project code: T1EDK-00929).

References

1. Pedersen, B.K.M.K., Larsen, J.C., Nielsen, J.: The effect of commercially available educational robotics: a systematic review. In: Merdan, M., Lepuschitz, W., Koppensteiner, G., Balogh, R., Obdržálek, D. (eds.) RiE 2019. AISC, vol. 1023, pp. 14–27. Springer, Cham (2020). https://doi.org/10.1007/978-3-030-26945-6_2
2. Battle, D.E.: Diagnostic and statistical manual of mental disorders (DSM). CoDAS **25**, 191–192 (2013)
3. Cabibihan, J.J., Javed, H., Ang, M., Aljunied, S.M.: Why Robots? A survey on the roles and benefits of social robots in the therapy of children with autism. Int. J. Soc. Robot. (2013). https://doi.org/10.1007/s12369-013-0202-2
4. Huijnen, C.A.G.J., Lexis, M.A.S., Jansens, R., de Witte, L.P.: Mapping robots to therapy and educational objectives for children with autism spectrum disorder. J. Autism Dev. Disord. (2016). https://doi.org/10.1007/s10803-016-2740-6
5. Kaburlasos, V.G., Vrochidou, E.: Social robots for pedagogical rehabilitation: trends and novel modeling principles. In: Global, I. (ed.) Cyber-Physical Systems for Social Applications, pp. 1–12 (2019)
6. Richardson, K., et al.: Robot enhanced therapy for children with autism (DREAM): a social model of autism. IEEE Technol. Soc. Mag. **37**, 30–39 (2018). https://doi.org/10.1109/MTS.2018.2795096
7. Diehl, J.J., Schmitt, L.M., Villano, M., Crowell, C.R.: The clinical use of robots for individuals with autism spectrum disorders: a critical review (2012). https://doi.org/10.1016/j.rasd.2011.05.006
8. Pennisi, P., et al.: Autism and social robotics: a systematic review (2016). https://doi.org/10.1002/aur.1527
9. Robinson, N.L., Cottier, T.V., Kavanagh, D.J.: Psychosocial health interventions by social robots: systematic review of randomized controlled trials. J. Med. Internet Res. **21**, e13203 (2019)
10. Attwood, T., Scarpa, A.: Modifications of cognitive-behavioral therapy for children and adolescents with high-functioning ASD and their common difficulties. In: Scarpa, A., Williams White, S., Attwood, T. (eds.) CBT for Children and Adolescents with High-Functioning Autism Spectrum Disorders, pp. 27–44, 329 p. Guilford Press, New York (2013)
11. Social Robots as Tools in Special Education. http://www.koiro3e.eu/

12. Kaburlasos, V.G., Dardani, C., Dimitrova, M., Amanatiadis, A.: Multi-robot engagement in special education: a preliminary study in autism. In: 2018 IEEE International Conference on Consumer Electronics, ICCE 2018 (2018). https://doi.org/10.1109/ICCE.2018.8326267
13. Bharatharaj, J., Huang, L., Al-Jumaily, A., Mohan, R.E., Krägeloh, C.: Sociopsychological and physiological effects of a robot-assisted therapy for children with autism. Int. J. Adv. Robot. Syst. (2017). https://doi.org/10.1177/1729881417736895
14. Lytridis, C., et al.: Audio signal recognition based on internals' numbers (INs) classification techniques. In: 10th International Conference on Information, Intelligence, Systems and Applications (IISA 2019) (2019)
15. Baron-Cohen, S.: Theory of mind and autism: a review. Int. Rev. Res. Ment. Retard. **23**, 169–184 (2000)
16. Lovaas, O.I.: Behavioral treatment and normal educational and intellectual functioning in young autistic children. J. Consult. Clin. Psychol. (1987)
17. Wechsler, D.: Wechsler Preschool and Primay Scale of Intelligence - Third Edition (WPPSI-III) Technical and Interpretive Manual. Psychological Corporation, San Antonio (2002)
18. Weiss, L.G., Locke, V., Pan, T., Harris, J.G., Saklofske, D.H., Prifitera, A.: Wechsler intelligence scale for children—fifth edition. In: WISC-V (2019). https://doi.org/10.1016/b978-0-12-815744-2.00005-7
19. Schopler, E., Van Bourgondien, M.E., Wellman, G.J., Love, S.R.: The Childhood Autism Rating Scale, 2nd edn. West Psychological Services, Los Angeles (2010)
20. Le Couteur, A., Lord, C., Rutter, M.: The autism diagnostic interview- revised (2003)
21. Korkman, M., Kirk, U., Kemp, S.: Design and purpose of the NEPSY-II. In: The NEPSY (2007)
22. Achenbach, T.: Manual for the ASEBA School-Age Forms & Profiles An Integrated System of Multi-informant Assessment. Research Center for Children (2007)
23. Goodman, R.: The strengths and difficulties questionnaire: a research note. J. Child Psychol. Psychiatry Allied Discip. (1997). https://doi.org/10.1111/j.1469-7610.1997.tb01545.x
24. Robins, B., Otero, N., Ferrari, E., Dautenhahn, K.: Eliciting requirements for a robotic toy for children with autism - results from user panels. In: Proceedings - IEEE International Workshop on Robot and Human Interactive Communication (2007). https://doi.org/10.1109/ROMAN.2007.4415061

Adding a Context: Will It Influence Human-Robot Interaction of People Living with Dementia?

Jorien Hendrix$^{(\boxtimes)}$, Yuan Feng, Marieke van Otterdijk,
and Emilia Barakova

Eindhoven University of Technology, De Rondom 70,
5612 AP Eindhoven, The Netherlands
{j.hendrix, m.t.h.v.otterdijk}@student.tue.nl,
{y.feng, e.i.barakova}@tue.nl

Abstract. Improving the quality of life of people with dementia in long-term care facilities is very important and can be achieved by designing engaging activities for the residents. The introduction of social robots for people with dementia has already proven its benefits, and we expected that adding contextual cues to this interaction would enhance the positive engagement of these individuals. A total of five participants took part in a comparison study in which they engaged in a free-play session with the robot PLEO and in a free-play session with the robot PLEO within a jungle-themed context. The gaze and arm/hand behaviors of the participants were measured and were used to determine the level of their engagement. Contrary to our expectations, we found a significant decrease in engagement for the sessions where the context was added to the interaction. Our explanation of this result is that the added cues increased the threshold to interact with the robot, but the elderly were still engaged as spectators.

Keywords: People with dementia · Social robots · Contextual design · Multi-sensory stimulation · Engagement · Human-robot interaction

1 Introduction

Dementia is a progressive disease that affects the memory, ability to pay attention and the communication skills of a person [1]. The World Alzheimer Report [17] predicts that the amount of people with dementia by 2030 will be 66 million and by 2050 this will be almost doubled to 115 million. As there currently is no cure found for dementia, it is important to improve the quality of life of the people who are living with dementia [8]. Despite their various losses, many people with dementia rate their overall quality of life as good or excellent, yet improving the quality of life of this group of people has been identified as the number one priority of dementia treatment [12]. In order to improve the quality of life of the individuals who are living with dementia, it is necessary to understand their needs. The research of Cadieux et al. [3] makes a systemic review of the needs of people with dementia who live in a long-term care facility.

© Springer Nature Switzerland AG 2019
M. A. Salichs et al. (Eds.): ICSR 2019, LNAI 11876, pp. 494–504, 2019.
https://doi.org/10.1007/978-3-030-35888-4_46

They identified nineteen needs from which the needs for individual activities, individual care, and social needs were proven to be the most important ones.

One way to fulfill the needs of being involved in sociable interactions and providing meaningful and stimulating individual activities is by introducing Social Assistive Robots (SARs) in the long-term care facilities. Research from Huschilt and Clune [9] shows that the use of SARs enhances the quality of life of people with dementia and supports caregivers. SARs were designed to interact with people and to create a sense of companionship [2]. These social robots can increase the engagement of people with dementia in activities and stimulates conversation between residents, not only about the robot but also about family, previous pets, and life experiences [19].

A recent study from Feng et al. [6, 7] designed a multi-sensory installation for people with dementia, which included interaction with a physical sheep robot. The interaction was part of an augmented reality platform on which virtual sheep were approaching when the physical sheep was being stroked. The study showed that the overall installation, together with the robot, provoked positive emotions, increased social bonding and, helped to enhance alertness and communication for the residents of a long-term care facility. This indicated that it positively impacted the quality of life of the residents. The main assumption in this study was that multi-sensory stimulation, that includes human-robot interaction, will increase the engagement that results in positive experiences. Looking closely at the experiment, the multi-sensory stimulation provides a lot of context to the interaction – the large screen shows sheep in natural environment, and physically stroking the robotic sheep caused virtual sheep to approach. Therefore, it is worth investigating whether the added context in the interaction, and not the multi-sensory stimulation is the reason for the positive outcomes for elderly.

Related studies used solely a social robot, which showed a similar effect on the elderly [14, 21]. The work of Salam and Chetouani [20] however, showed the impact of context: the mental and/or emotional states of the users and their engagement varied depending on the context of the interaction. Context can be included in different ways. We questioned what the impact of adding contextual cues within the robot environment is on the positive engagement of the elderly with dementia.

We believe context could contribute to a more immersive and engaging play experience through enabling visual clues of what the role of robot is and how to interact. This makes the users more situation-aware and creates a more natural start for the interaction sessions. Additionally, people with dementia often need vibrant and high-contrast color to help compensate low visual ability as well as maintain their interests and encourage curiosity during the interaction process.

This is why we used the social robot PLEO in combination with a jungle-themed environment. A total of five elderly, all diagnosed with dementia, participated in two free-play sessions with the robot. One of the sessions was with, and one without the contextual environment. The nonverbal behavior and the conversations during the sessions were analyzed to determine the engagement of the participants.

2 Related Work

2.1 Use of Social Robots in Dementia Care

Social robots could be a good addition to dementia care, as they provide a sense of companionship, and therefore, may satisfy the social needs of the elderly [9]. Multiple studies have introduced social robots to people with dementia and have studied their interaction and their impact on these individuals. The study of Tapus et al. [22] showed that the use of social robots in dementia care is very promising, as they proved that the use of an embodied social robot, instead of a computer interface, improved and sustained the overall performance of people with dementia on a memory task. Additionally, according to Mordoch et al. [13], there is initial evidence that the use of therapeutic robots increases the engagement of people with dementia with each other. Moreover, social robots such as PARO, AIBO, and NeCoRo, were shown to have a calming effect on people with dementia and provided a feeling of companionship and joy [13]. Animal Assisted Therapy (AAT), had similar effects. Animals were also shown to induce feelings of companionship and happiness [18]. The study of Roger et al. [18] compared AAT to the use of a robotic dog and showed that the use of this robot decreased loneliness in people with dementia. They also showed that, even though people with dementia often realized that the robot was mimicking an animal, they still felt engaged with the robot and wanted to care for it. Additionally, in a study with the robotic seal PARO, it was shown that the robot had direct (interaction with robot) as well as indirect (engaged with others) effects on the engagement of people with dementia, which would increase over time. The interaction with the seal increased the engagement with both the environment and other people [19].

From the studies above, we can conclude that using social robots in dementia care can improve the engagement of the elderly. However, the studies mentioned above have only studied the engagement of a person living with dementia and a social robot. Whether the engagement of the activity with the robot can be enhanced by adding another cue to the activity has not been investigated.

2.2 Measuring Engagement in Dementia

The inactivity of residents in a nursing home is often very high, due to their inability to find and access activities and the little amount of offered activities at the nursing home [5]. When residents are actively engaged in activities, it can improve their well-being and decrease their depression [11]. Therefore, the engagement of a person with dementia is an important indicator of their quality of life [4].

There are different methods to measure the engagement of people with dementia. Often its measurement relies only on the observation of the behavior, and the Behavioral and Psychological Symptoms of Dementia (BPSD) are not taken into account. The study of Perugia et al. [15] showed that the quantity of a movement could be used to measure the engagement of a person with dementia. The study of Cohen-Mansfield et al. [5] the engagement was measured through observation based on rating scales called, Observational Assessment of Engagement (OME). The focus of the OME is on observing the attention, attitude, and duration of the activity.

Perugia et al. [16] designed an Ethnographic and Laban-Inspired Coding System of Engagement (ELICSE) which can be used to measure the engagement of people with dementia. This coding scheme was designed for people with dementia involved in physical and social interaction. In this coding scheme, head-, torso- and arm/hand behaviors are included. These behaviors are directed to certain elements such as the partner, game, facilitator, or to the robot. Additionally, the study of Wada et al. [23] looked at expression, gaze and conversation behaviors which were related to the robot or the staff. Lastly, the study of Takayanagi et al. [21] considered talking, touching, and the emotional expression of the participant in relation to the staff member, the robot, or a stuffed animal.

From these studies, we can conclude that the choice of behaviors to take into account, depends on the experimental setup, therefore in Sect. 3 we propose a modification of the scheme of Perugia et al. to our experimental setup. Most studies considered the quantity of the head-, arm/hand behaviors, and talk.

3   Method

3.1   Participants

This study was conducted at a long-term care facility for people with dementia in Eindhoven, the Netherlands, Vitalis Berckelhof. At this facility, there are a total of 24 residents with different stages and forms of dementia living. A total of five participants were recruited and participated in two sessions. Inclusion criteria for the study were: (a) an established diagnosis of dementia, (b) being residential to the long-term care facility, (c) availability during the research period and (d) a positive recommendation by the staff. Additionally, the guardian of each participant provided informed consent regarding the participation.

In a previous study by Feng et al. [6], the Mini-Mental State Examination (MMSE) was determined for each patient. A lower score on the MMSE represents a higher level of cognitive impairment. The collected demographics of the participants are shown in Table 1.

Table 1. Demographics of the participants. The types of dementia were distinguished in Alzheimer's Dementia (AD), Vascular Dementia (VD) or Mixed Dementia (MD)

Participants	Gender	Age	Type of dementia	Phase of dementia	MMSE score
P1	F	94	MD	Moderate	12
P2	F	84	MD	Moderate	11
P3	M	80	AD	Mild	22
P4	F	82	MD	Severe	9
P5	F	85	AD	Moderate	18

3.2   Setting

The sessions were executed on Wednesday or Friday morning between 10:00 and 13:00 in the hallway of the residential home. This place was chosen as it is a neutral space at the facility and it provided fewer distractions than other places at the facility, especially during the morning activities. The conditions for both the free-play session with PLEO (session A) and the free-play session with PLEO within a jungle-themed environment (session B) were controlled, so that the experimental conditions were similar, except for the provided stimulus. The participant was asked to take place behind a table and the robot was placed on the table. For both, people in a wheelchair and people sitting in a chair, it was made sure that they could reach the robot easily. The researcher took place next to the participant (Fig. 1).

Fig. 1. User evaluation study with two settings in Vitalis: (A) the free-play session with PLEO; (B) the free-play session with PLEO in the jungle-themed environment

3.3   Design and Materials

The PLEO Robot. During this study, the animatronic dinosaur, PLEO was used (Fig. 2). PLEO, designed by the company Innvo Labs, has multiple different sensors and is able to learn from its environment. PLEO was chosen as it can distinguish different types of touch, it has camera-based vision, and it has the ability to express human-like emotions such as, happiness and grumpiness [11]. During this research PLEO was in its second life stage called; socialization development. This means that it was not able to walk but, was exploring its environment and expressed basic needs such as hunger and tiredness [10]. The participants were able to feed PLEO using the leaf accessory.

The Design. This research will compare the engagement of people with dementia in two sessions. During session A, only the social robot PLEO was used. The participants were free to interact with the robot and to explore what the abilities of PLEO were. In session B, the environment was adapted to the robot (Fig. 1). As PLEO is an animatronic dinosaur, the direct environment of the activity was transformed into a jungle. With the use of jungle-themed music[1] the atmosphere of being in a jungle was

---

[1] https://brandonfiechter.bandcamp.com/.

recreated. Additionally, a jungle-themed play mat covered the table and some trees were put on the mat. This transformed the area into a small jungle in which the participant was able to interact with PLEO (Fig. 2).

Fig. 2. The jungle-themed context with PLEO

3.4 Procedure

Before the study took place, the legal guardians of the residents were asked to provide consent about the participation of the study. At the same time, they provided consent allowing the research sessions to be filmed. A resident, recommended by the staff of the facility, was invited to take part in the research by the researcher. The participants were free to interact with the robot for a maximum of 20 min. The researcher could terminate the sessions earlier when the participants were too distracted, not interested in the robot or indicated that they were done. At the start of each session, the researcher suggested a few interactions, such as petting the robot or feeding it, to show what PLEO's abilities were.

During the sessions, the researcher asked some questions regarding the interaction with the robot. These questions were used to spark some new interest in the robot when the participant did not know what to do anymore and, to retrieve additional insights about the interest of the participant and the robot.

Participants P1, P2, and P3 interacted during the first session solely with PLEO, the contextual cues were added in the second session one week later. Participants P4 and P5 participated first with the added contextual cues; a week later they followed the sessions with solely PLEO. Due to limited time and availability of the participants, there were only two participants who started with session B and three participants who started with session A.

3.5 Data Analysis

All sessions were filmed, in which the participant and the robot were clearly visible. These videos were used to determine the engagement of each participant. This was done by coding the videos based on an adapted version of the coding scheme proposed by Perugia et al. [16], which excluded the torso movement. This change was made based on pre-experiment observations that users rarely shift their torso among the other testing agents; therefore, few data could be generalized to provide useful information to understand the engagement situations.

The behavior of the gaze and the arm/hands were observed. The scored direction of the gaze was: towards the robot, towards the contextual environment, towards the researcher or none. The scored direction of the arm/hands were; manipulating the robot, manipulating the contextual environment, positive signs of affection, and none.

Analysis of the Engagement. For session A, with the robot, we define engagement as the total sum of the percentages of the gaze towards the robot, manipulating the robot and positive signs of affection using the arm/hands, from each session. For session B, with the robot and the added contextual cues, we also add the gaze towards the contextual environment and manipulating the contextual environment to this sum (Table 2).

Table 2. Engagement for session A and B. Engagement is the sum of the percentages of each variable for each session

Behavior	Engagement session A		
Gaze	Towards robot		
Arm/hands	Manipulate robot	Positive signs of affection	
Behavior	Engagement session B		
Gaze	Towards robot	Towards context	
Arm/hands	Manipulate robot	Positive signs of affection	Manipulate context

4 Results

The videos from the sessions were coded using The Observer XT version 14. The results from this were analyzed using the IBM SPSS Statistics version 25. A paired samples t-test, with an alpha level of .05, was used to compare the total engagement of people living with dementia when interacting with a robot (session A) and when interacting with a robot in a contextual environment (session B) with a total of five individuals. There was a significant difference in the engagement between session A (M = 105.02, SD = 30.23) and session B (M = 81.07, SD = 23.97) with the conditions; $t(4) = 6.81$, $p = .002$.

Figure 3 shows the distribution of the measured engagement in the sum of the percentages of the gaze (100%) and arm/hand behaviors (100%), of session A and B.

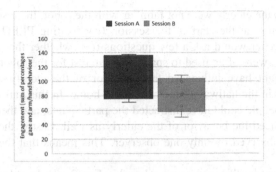

Fig. 3. The distribution of the engagement to experiment stimulus of session A and B displayed as the sum of the percentages of the gaze and arm/hand behaviours related to the robot and context

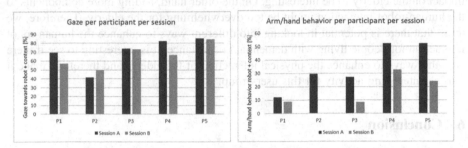

Fig. 4. The total gaze behavior (left) and arm/hand behavior per participant per session (right)

5 Discussion

Previous studies have shown that the introduction of social robots can increase the engagement of people who are living with dementia, which positively influences their quality of life. In this study, we compared two free-play sessions with the PLEO robot, one without (A) and one with (B) added contextual cues.

From this study, we saw that the overall engagement of each participant was higher in session A than in session B (Fig. 3). For each participant the arm/hand behavior decreased when the contextual cues were added (session B). However, the gaze duration increased for participant P2, and for participants P3 and P5 it only decreased by less than 1% in session B (Fig. 4). Therefore, we can assume that adding a context to a human-robot interaction makes it more interesting to look at the behaving robot and its environment, but it can increase the threshold to interact with the robot. This might be because there is too much going on at the same time or it was not clear to the participants what they should be doing.

The study has several limitations. The main limitation is the small sample size, since we could test with only five participants in two sessions. Other limitations concern the validity of the sessions as follows. One researcher was present during every session. The role of the researcher was to support the elderly during their interaction with the robot. As the elderly were not familiar with the robot, the researcher proposed a possible interaction at the start of the session (e.g. petting PLEO) and during the session, the researcher would ask a few questions (e.g. whether they liked the robot). As these questions were often used to spark new interest for the robot, the direction of the researcher might have influenced the behavior of the elderly. Additionally, all sessions took part in the hallway of the residential home. In this hallway many people passed by, these people could have distracted the participants, and therefore the setting could have influenced the behavior of the elderly as well. Lastly, the behavior of the participants was observed by only one observer. This means that the coded behavior could be biased.

The context used for this study, as displayed in Fig. 2, was based on the LiveNature installation from Feng et al. [6]. Yet, as the contextual cues that we introduced were not interactive (as in the experiment reported in [6]), and the contextual environment was rather small, this could have influenced the results as it might not have had enough impact on the elderly to be interesting. On the other hand, adding more components to the human-robot interaction might be too overwhelming for the elderly. Therefore, we think that there is potential in looking into different ways to enhance the human-robot interaction for people living with dementia. For instance, it is interesting to see if there are other ways to enhance the physical interaction of the elderly and therefore, make it into an interesting activity for this user group.

6 Conclusion

To ensure a higher quality of life for persons with dementia, a long-term care facility should be able to offer engaging activities to their residents. Previous studies have already shown that activity that includes a social robot engages the residents. We wanted to see if adding contextual cues to this human-robot interaction would enhance the engagement of the elderly. We compared the engagement of five elderly with dementia in a free-play session with a social robot, with and without added contextual cues. The results of our evaluation show that adding a contextual environment to the human-robot interaction decreased the interaction of the elderly. However, the gaze duration towards the activity of some participants only slightly decreased or even increased with the added contextual cues. This would imply that adding a contextual environment is interesting for the elderly to look at but does not invite them to interact with the robot. We think future research should include other ways to enhance the engagement through interaction for people with dementia.

Acknowledgements. We would like to thank all of the participants and the staff at Vitalis for being so kind and helpful. Additionally, we would like to thank M. Hendrix for their contribution to this research.

References

1. Alzheimer's association: What Is Dementia? https://www.alz.org/alzheimers-dementia/what-is-dementia
2. Breazeal, C., Dautenhahn, K., Kanda, T.: Social robotics. In: Siciliano, B., Khatib, O. (eds.) Springer Handbook of Robotics, pp. 1935–1972. Springer, Cham (2016). https://doi.org/10.1007/978-3-319-32552-1_72
3. Cadieux, M.A., et al.: Needs of people with dementia in long-term care: a systematic review. Am. J. Alzheimers Dis. Other Demen. **28**(8), 723–733 (2013). https://doi.org/10.1177/1533317513500840
4. Cohen-Mansfield, J., et al.: Engagement in persons with dementia: the concept and its measurement. Am. J. Geriatr. Psychiatry (2009). https://doi.org/10.1097/JGP.0b013e31818f3a52
5. Cohen-Mansfield, J.: The underlying meaning of stimuli: impact on engagement of persons with dementia. Psychiatry Res. **177**(1–2), 216–222 (2010). https://doi.org/10.1016/j.psychres.2009.02.010
6. Feng, Y., et al.: Closer to nature: multi-sensory engagement in interactive nature experience for seniors with dementia. In: Proceedings of the Sixth International Symposium Chinese, CHI, pp. 49–56 (2019). https://doi.org/10.1145/3202667.3202674
7. Feng, Y., Yu, S., van de Mortel, D., Barakova, E., Hu, J., Rauterberg, M.: LiveNature. In: Proceedings of the 2019 on Designing Interactive Systems Conference - DIS 2019 (2019). https://doi.org/10.1145/3322276.3322331
8. Howe, E.: Improving the quality of life in patients with Alzheimer's disease. Psychiatry (Edgmont) **5**(8), 51–56 (2008)
9. Huschilt, J., Clune, L.: The use of socially assistive robots for dementia care. J. Gerontol. Nurs. **38**(10), 15–19 (2012). https://doi.org/10.3928/00989134-20120911-02
10. Innvo Labs: PLEOworld. https://www.pleoworld.com/pleo_rb/eng/lifeform.php
11. Kolanowski, A.: Factors that relate to activity engagement in nursing home residents. Am. J. Alzheimers Dis. Other Demen. **21**(1), 15–22 (2006). https://doi.org/10.1177/153331750602100109
12. Longsdon, R.G.: Evidence-based interventions to improve quality of life for individuals with dementia. Alzheimers Care Today **8**(4), 309–318 (2007)
13. Mordoch, E.: Use of social commitment robots in the care of elderly people with dementia: a literature review. Maturitas **74**(1), 14–20 (2013)
14. Perugia, G., et al.: Modelling engagement in dementia through behaviour. Contribution for socially interactive robotics. In: IEEE International Conference on Rehabilitation Robotics, pp. 1112–1117 (2017). https://doi.org/10.1109/ICORR.2017.8009398
15. Perugia, G.: Quantity of movement as a measure of engagement for dementia: the influence of motivational disorders. Am. J. Alzheimers Dis. Other Demen. **33**(2), 112–121 (2018). https://doi.org/10.1177/1533317517739700
16. Perugia, G., et al.: Understanding engagement in dementia through behavior. The Ethographic and Laban-inspired Coding System of Engagement (ELICSE) and the Evidence-based Model of Engagement-related Behavior (EMODEB). Front. Psychol. **9**, 1–18 (2018). https://doi.org/10.3389/fpsyg.2018.00690
17. Prince, M., Jackson, J.: World Alzheimer Report (2009)
18. Roger, K.: Social commitment robots and dementia. Can. J. Aging **31**(1), 87–94 (2012). https://doi.org/10.1017/S0714980811000663

19. Šabanovic, S., et al.: PARO robot affects diverse interaction modalities in group sensory therapy for older adults with dementia. In: IEEE International Conference on Rehabilitation Robotics (2013). https://doi.org/10.1109/ICORR.2013.6650427
20. Salam, H., Chetouani, M.: A multi-level context-based modeling of engagement in human-robot interaction. In: 11th IEEE International Conference and Workshop on Automatic Face and Gesture Recognition, vol. 3, pp. 1–6 (2015). https://doi.org/10.1109/fg.2015.7284845
21. Takayanagi, K., et al.: Comparison of verbal and emotional responses of elderly people with mild/moderate dementia and those with severe dementia in responses to seal robot, PARO. Front. Aging Neurosci. 6, 1–5 (2014). https://doi.org/10.3389/fnagi.2014.00257
22. Tapus, A., et al.: The role of physical embodiment of a therapist robot for individuals with cognitive impairments. In: IEEE International Workshop on Robot and Human Interactive Communication, pp. 103–107 (2009). https://doi.org/10.1109/ROMAN.2009.5326211
23. Wada, K., et al.: Development and preliminary evaluation of a caregiver's manual for robot therapy using the therapeutic seal robot PARO. In: IEEE International Workshop on Robot and Human Interactive Communication, pp. 533–538 (2010). https://doi.org/10.1109/ROMAN.2010.5598615

Evaluating the Emotional Valence of Affective Sounds for Child-Robot Interaction

Silvia Rossi[1]([✉]), Elena Dell'Aquila[1,2], and Benedetta Bucci[1]

[1] Department of Electrical Engineering and Information Technologies,
University of Naples Federico II, Naples, Italy
{silvia.rossi,elena.dellaquila}@unina.it
[2] CRDC Tecnologie, Naples, Italy

Abstract. Social Assistive Robots are starting to be widely used in paediatric health-care environments. In this domain, the development of effective strategies to keep the children engaged during the interaction with a social robot is still an open research area. On this subject, some approaches are investigating the combination of distraction strategies, as used in human-human interaction, and the display of emotional behaviours. In this study, we presented the results of a pilot study aimed to evaluate with children the valence of emotional behaviours enhanced with non-verbal sounds. The objective is to endow the NAO robot with emotional-like sounds, selected from a set of para-linguistic behaviours validated by valence. Results show that children aged 3–8 years perceive the robot's behaviours and the related selected emotional semantic free sounds in terms of different degrees of arousal, valence and dominance: while valence and dominance are clearly perceived by the children, arousal is more difficult to distinguish.

Keywords: Para-verbal sounds · Emotional behaviour · User study

1 Introduction

Social robots hold significant potential to support children in health-care contexts [4]. They have been used and tested especially with the main purposes to reduce discomfort, pain or anxiety, to provide entertainment and distraction [10]. In this paper, we present the results of an experimental study that is part of a larger research conducted in the paediatric emergency department of the San Salvatore hospital in Italy. One of the main objectives of the research study at the hospital is to expose the little patients, aged 3–8 years, to a distraction procedure from the impending medical treatment with the help of a robot. The NAO robot has been programmed to use cognitive-behavioural strategies age-appropriate with the little patients while a nurse assesses the patient's needs. The robot emotional behaviours, while supporting the distraction strategies, are also fundamental for the children engagement with the robot itself [27].

© Springer Nature Switzerland AG 2019
M. A. Salichs et al. (Eds.): ICSR 2019, LNAI 11876, pp. 505–514, 2019.
https://doi.org/10.1007/978-3-030-35888-4_47

Hence, the distraction procedure will be associated, in a controlled way, to a number of negative or positive valence emotions so to explore their impact on the engagement experienced by the little patients.

In a previous work [20], we compared different non-verbal interaction modalities to display emotions with the same robot. Such modalities were used in isolation and combined together in a coherent or incoherent way. Results showed that the voice channel was the most reliable, with respect to the others, for the correct recognition of the intended displayed emotion, also in the case of an incoherent combination of modalities. Moreover, there is a large literature that provides clear evidence that complex emotional auditory stimuli elicit intensive emotional reactions on behavioural, physiological, and on neuronal levels, similarly as the traditionally used complex visual emotional scenes [26]. Yet, non-verbal emotional sounds seem to be the auditory equivalent of emotional face expressions [24]. The ability to convey emotions is considered one of the key aspect of the interaction between humans and robots [19,21], and the use of para-linguistic vocalisations to express emotional state is a relatively under-investigated research area [30]. Hence, the primary objective of this preliminary study is to assess the way children perceive emotional behaviours displayed by NAO - in terms of positive and negative valence, high and low arousal, and high and low dominance - rather than their ability to guess, recognise and label them. This is the first step to further investigate the psycho-social and emotional impact of those emotional responses during the interaction between the little patients and NAO at the Emergency Department. Indeed, this represents a crucial step to effectively develop and implement a tailored intervention with NAO in such a sensitive context.

With regard to the valence dimension and the dominance dimension, result shows that children are able to make a clear distinction between behaviours eliciting pleasant and unpleasant emotional state, and between behaviours eliciting the feeling of being in control and dominated. Instead, the arousal dimension does not show such a clear distinction between behaviours, suggesting that the emotional behaviours displayed by NAO do not elicit sufficiently distinctive feelings associated to the arousal dimension, or that the representation used for the evaluation was not sufficiently clear to children.

2   Background and Related Works

Recent research has reviewed the role of social robots to help children in health-care contexts and has highlighted that they hold the potential to effectively assist children [5]. This review identify 73 studies that explored the use of a social robot in children health-care; robots were used in the role of companion, teacher, coach, and to connect children to school. In these studies, the main target populations are children with disabilities, impairments, diabetes, and who require hospitalisation. Some of the key findings show that social robots can help to reduce anxiety, anger and depression in children with cancer [1], are able to motivate children with cerebral palsy to engage in exercises so improving physical functioning [8]. What emerges is that the communication of emotions plays a crucial role within the human-robot interaction and it is able to render an artificial partner a good companion for humans [14], especially when this involves children.

In this work, we are interested in how children perceive and respond to affective communication using para-linguistic vocalisations expressed by the NAO robot, which potential has not been investigated sufficiently yet, also in combination with other communication modalities [30]. In the current state of the art on the use of semantic free utterances (SFU) in social human interaction [30], it seems that social robots are unable to leverage the power of natural language. SFU concern a variety of methods that allow robots to express and communicate through sounds and vocalisations not involving semantic content and language dependence. We are specifically interested in para-verbal vocalisations that we have shaped in order to reproduce natural human language. Researches have shown that the emotional content, depending on the shape and functionality of the robot, can be carried out by means of different modalities, such as facial gestures, poses, gaze, and body language. SFU research applied to social HRI has received very little attention in comparison to those modalities of expression, especially in regards to para-verbal utterances.

Studies using NAO robot for expressing emotions, mainly including adults, have been primarily based on participants' ability to recognise and interpret the emotional states. Recently researchers have started to examine the integration of emotional expressions from different modalities [28]. Results show that incongruous emotional signals from the body and voice of humanoid robots may influence the ability to identify and interpret the robot's emotional state. The quality of the emotion decoding in the users is an expression of combined factors; by combining different communication modalities, the subjects see a more intense emotion than when presented separately [29]. Indeed, the voice seems to be a reliable channel for the correct recognition of the intended displayed emotion also in the case of an incoherent combination of different modalities [20].

In our work, we are interested in the use of para-verbal sounds, in combination with simple gestures and eye-colours to express a range of emotions. More specifically, we aim to explore how the use of para-verbal vocalisations is perceived rather than recognised in child-robot interaction. This area of research has remained fundamentally unexplored, as there has not been a significant investigation on how children interpret semantic free utterances, especially in real-life scenarios, such as in contextual settings [30].

3   Emotional Model

The conceptual framework that we have adopted for exploring and understanding how children assess, discern, and describe emotional behaviours during their interaction with the NAO humanoid robot, takes inspiration from the dimensional approach of emotion. In this perspective, individuals do not experience and distinguish emotions as isolated entities, but they rather conceive them as overlapping experiences. Each and every subjective emotional experience is the consequence of a combination of three independent dimensions, that organise emotional responses interpreted as representing a particular emotion, which are: pleasure/valence (positive-negative), arousal/activation (low-high), and dominance/control (low-high) [22]. Valence, arousal, and dominance were introduced by Mehrabian and Russell [16] as three independent emotional dimensions to describe people's state of feeling. These three dimensions are respectively related to the triad: feeling, thinking and acting; of affective, cognitive and conative responses. Valence is intended as a continuum range from extreme unhappiness to extreme happiness, or also from satisfaction to dissatisfaction. Arousal is conceived as a mental activity and is described as a continuum range from excitement to calm, or also from stimulation to relaxation. Dominance is the feelings of having control and the extent to which a person feels restricted or influential in his/her behaviour, and it is described by using a continuum range from dominance to submissiveness. The authors mentioned the noun 'relaxation' as an indicator for all three dimensions pleasure, arousal and dominance.

In this study, we propose sixteen behaviours eliciting certain emotional states by taking inspiration from the six basic emotions (anger, disgust, fear, happiness, sadness, and surprise) known after the work by Ekman and Friesen [6] and other variations used in several research studies with robots [7,20]. To be consistent with the dimensional model presented above, such emotional states have been selected according to the mapping of the terms used as markers for the emotions identified by the three dimensions, i.e., valence, arousal, and dominance.

Although the recognition of emotions is facilitated by the availability of different sensory channels, it has been shown that the voice is particularly powerful for decoding a person's emotional state [11]. Moreover, the theories of appraisal have highlighted how the vocal expression of emotions is determined by the combined action of arousal and valence [12]. Studies [2,17] have identified and recognised as primary dimensions supporting the perception of human speech pitch (frequency), volume (intensity), and articulation (rate of speaking). The investigation of vocalic quality expressing specific emotions has produced consistent results. For example, while joy is characterised by increased pitch, volume, and articulation, sadness by decreased pitch and articulation.

3.1 Experimental Design

The robot used for our experimentation is the NAO T14 V4 robot model. In this work, emotional behaviours are mainly conveyed by using different para-verbal communication. This is defined as emotional sounds and feedback vocalisations, as words without a standard orthography, semantic content or language dependence [30]. Aldebaran library does not have vocalisations to be used. Indeed, some vocalisation is only associated with complex robot's behaviours, but in this case, there was not the possibility to modulate pitch and speed. Examples of these signals are laughter, breathing, sounds such as "Eeh weeh", "Yea!" (see Table 1). These sounds were mainly recorded by us and then adjusted with respect to their tone and frequency. We have then assigned emotion-labelling

Table 1. The considered affective sounds with a transcription of the vocalizations

N	Vocalization	Tone volume and frequency	Label
1	*Grrrr*	High and intense	Anger
2	*Argh*	High and intense	Frustration
3	*Eh oh*	High and acute	Fear and alarm
4	*Eeeeek*	High and acute	Scare
5	*Eww*	Normal	Dislike
6	*Yuck*	Normal	Disgust
7	*Eeh weeh*	Low tone, modest intensity, slow rhythm	Despair
8	*Waah waaaaah*	Low tone, modest intensity, slow rhythm	Crying
9	*Lalalalala*	Medium speech speed and pitch range	Light-hearted
10	*Whistling*	Medium high frequency	Delight
11	*Ya hahaha*	High tone, wide and full voice, high intensity and quite modulated	Enthusiasm
12	*Hihihihihihi*	High tone, wide and full voice, high intensity and quite modulated	Joy
13	*Hahahahahaha*	High tone, wide and full voice, high intensity and quite modulated	Amusement
14	*Yea!*	High and intense	Triumph
15	*Hewa*	Low and mild	Relaxation
16	*Ahh ahh*	Low and mild	Relief
17	*Haya name is NAO*	Medium low	Warming up

adjectives for each of the sixteen behaviours (that were confirmed at the end of the experimental phase) by taking into account both the expected perceived valence, arousal, and dominance, and the identified theoretical framework. Indeed, our aim is to specifically investigate how children perceive the emotional behaviours displayed by NAO in terms of positive and negative valence and high or low arousal and dominance, rather than their ability to name the emotions.

We have identified the vocalisations associated with the 16 emotional behaviours according to the aforementioned studies and complemented them with the modalities of the poses/gestures and the eye colour[1]. In detail, we identified 8 unpleasant emotional behaviours that were intended to score low on the valence scale, and 8 pleasant emotional behaviours that intended to obtain high scores on the valence scale. As previously highlighted, we are interested in investigating how children perceive semantic free utterances in real-life scenarios, thus we have designed the NAO vocalisations in order to reproduce natural

---

[1] The selected para-linguistic sounds are available for download at http://prisca.unina.it/demo/EmotionSounds.rar.

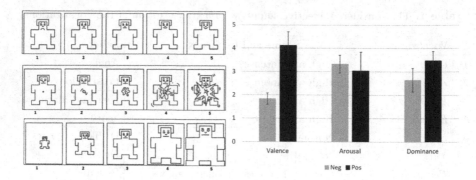

Fig. 1. Self-Assessment Manikin [3] (left), average results for positive and negative valence sounds (right)

human language that is familiar to children [30]. For eye colour, we took inspiration from the colour model by Plutchik [18]. In detail, we used red eyes for Anger, Frustration, Fear, Scare, Dislike, Disgust, Despair, and Crying; green for Light-hearted, Delight, Enthusiasm, Joy, Amusement, and Triumph; Blue for Relaxation, Relief, and Warming up. Poses and simple gestures associated to the different emotional behaviours have been designed according to the studies on the physical expression of emotion, especially related to closeness or openness and symmetry of body limb and relative orientation of body parts [9]: (1) Arms slightly closed toward the chest and head straight for Anger and Frustration; (2) Arms closed toward the chest and head inclined toward the left for Fear, Scare, and Dislike; (3) Right arm half-bent toward the head and head down inclined toward the right for Disgust; (4) Arms slightly open and head down shaking for Despair and Crying; (5) Arms open and head straight for Light-hearted, Delight, Relaxation, Relief, and Warming up; (6) Arms open and head up for Enthusiasm, Joy, Amusement, Triumph.

3.2   Self-Assessment Manikin Scale

Participants in the study were asked to rate the robot behaviours varying in emotional content by using the Self-Assessment Manikin (SAM), a non-verbal pictorial assessment scale developed to measure emotional responses [3] (see Fig. 1 (left)). The SAM contains five images for each of the three emotional dimensions: valence (from positive to negative), arousal (from high to low), and perceptions of dominance (from low to high) that participants used to provide ratings. Figure 1 (left) shows the SAM with valence, arousal, and dominance scales on the top, middle, and bottom rows, respectively. On the SAM the valence dimension ranges from positive (smiling, happy figure) to negative (frowning, unhappy figure); the arousal dimension ranges from excited (wide-eyed figure) to relaxed (sleepy, eyes closed figure), and also by the intensity of arousal ranging from high (figure representing an explosive-like burst) to low (figure representing

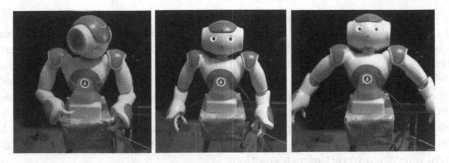

Fig. 2. Three snapshots taken during the emotional behaviour Alarm (on the left), Relax (in the centre), and Joy (on the right)

a small pinprick); finally the dominance dimension ranges from being in control or dominated (figure changes in the size from small to large).

3.3 Procedure

The preliminary study explored emotional reactions in the participants which were randomly exposed to a set of behaviours varying in emotional content displayed by NAO. The study was conducted in a neutral/home setting (not in the hospital context) with children not needing medical treatments. Data was collected from multiple age groups (3–8 years old). We had a total of 25 participants, 11 male and 14 female children. Parental consent was requested before the experiment was conducted. All participants answered the SAM questionnaire at the end of each of the emotional interactions displayed by NAO (see Fig. 2). At the end of the session, a semi-structured interview was administered in order to further explore motivations beyond their responses.

In the first phase of the study, the participants were familiarised with the scale before the actual experimental procedure. Each participant was exposed to a set of 5 pictures (OASIS) [13] containing pleasant, unpleasant, and neutral stimuli in random order. Each picture was presented for a few seconds after which the participant was asked to complete the form with the manikins. After that, a random subset of the emotional behaviours described above, at least eight behaviours, was presented to each participant. Children were asked to rate from 1 to 5 each dimension of valence, arousal and dominance. In some cases, participants asked to see the behaviour another time to be sure of his/her assessment. We explored emotional reactions in children to determine whether the different behaviours showed by the robot elicit similar patterns of reactivity in terms of valence, arousal and dominance.

4   Results

In order to assess the reliability for the three dimensions of the scale, we calculated the reliability coefficient (Cronbach alfa) for each dimension according to the procedure presented in [15], to take into account the sparse acquisition of data, as described above. Reliability coefficients are 0.70, 0.37 and 0.75 for valence, arousal and dominance, respectively. Valence and dominance demonstrate a good internal consistency and robustness of the scale, while Arousal presents a weak level of internal consistency, suggesting that the 16 emotional behaviours may not elicit sufficiently distinctive feelings associated to the arousal dimension, or that the manikin representation was not sufficiently clear to subjects. The difficulty of interpreting the arousal dimension of emotional states is also discussed in [25] showing that children around the age of 7 use valence as main dimension to distinguish emotions.

An independent-samples t-test was conducted to compare responses on the two sets of robot's behaviours. There was a significant difference ($p < 0.001$) in the scores for the perceived positive emotions ($M = 4.11$, $SD = 0.59$) and the perceived negative emotions ($M = 1.83$, $SD = 0.23$).

Regarding the arousal dimension, we do not have such a clear distinction. Indeed, by performing an independent-samples t-test to compare responses on the two sets of robot's behaviours, we did not find a significant difference ($p = 0.38$) in the scores for the arousal associated to the perceived positive emotions ($M = 3.03$, $SD = 0.80$) and perceived negative emotions ($M = 3.32$, $SD = 0.38$). The only notable difference is that with negative perceived emotions the arousal is more concentrated around the central part of the scale, while for the emotions perceived as positive is more spread.

For the dominance scale, behaviours perceived as positive score above the theoretical mean of the scale (3), while behaviours perceived as negative score below the theoretical mean of the scale. An independent-samples t-test was conducted to compare responses on the two sets of robot's behaviours. There was a significant difference ($p < 0.05$) in the scores for perceived positive emotions ($M = 3.47$, $SD = 0.39$) and perceived negative emotions ($M = 2.64$, $SD = 0.50$). Results are summarised in Fig. 1 (right).

Results clearly show that the valence of the identified behaviours was correctly perceived by the children, while the perceived average arousal, in the case of positive and negative emotions, are very similar with an high variability. The results for the dominance dimension associated to the different displayed emotional behaviours, will be analysed and evaluated in relation to the results obtained with the large sample of children at the Hospital San Salvatore. Children will interact with NAO following a structured distraction procedure to verify to what extent these dimensions impact on the reactions, decisions and on discomfort management. Indeed, in line with the literature, valence and arousal are conceived as indicators of affect; dominance is considered to be a more cognitive component of emotions [23].

5   Conclusions

In this paper, we have investigated how emotional behaviours expressed by NAO employing para-verbal communication cues are perceived in terms of negative and positive valence and high or low level of arousal. We have presented a preliminary study conducted in a neutral setting involving children not in the need of medical treatment. The group of children aged between 3 and 8 have clearly identified two groups of emotional behaviours characterised by negative and positive valence and by a different degree of experienced dominance (although, in the average, near to the neutral case). Results of the study show that valence and dominance provide different information of individual's emotional categorisation, highlighting the richness of considering different levels of analysis for a more detailed understanding of person perception. Indeed, children were not able to clearly identify emotional behaviours eliciting positive and negative emotional perceptions for the arousal dimension, suggesting that it is not sufficiently distinct as dimension of the emotional behaviours displayed by the selected paralinguistic sounds or that the manikin scale was not easily interpreted by the children in the study.

In the next step of the study, NAO will be endowed with the two identified different sets of emotional behaviours (i.e., with positive and negative valence). We are interested in understanding whether, and to what extent, the exposure to pleasant and unpleasant emotional states displayed by NAO impact on children emotional responses and coping strategies in order to manage distress, fear and worry before a medical treatment.

References

1. Alemi, M., Ghanbarzadeh, A., Meghdari, A., Moghadam, L.J.: Clinical application of a humanoid robot in pediatric cancer interventions. Int. J. Soc. Robot. **8**(5), 743–759 (2016)
2. Anolli, L., Ciceri, R.: The voice of deception: vocal strategies of naive and able liars. J. Nonverbal Behav. **21**(4), 259–284 (1997)
3. Bradley, M.M., Lang, P.J.: Measuring emotion: the self-assessment manikin and the semantic differential. J. Behav. Ther. Exp. Psychiatry **25**(1), 49–59 (1994)
4. Breazeal, C.: Social robots for health applications. In: Annual International Conference of the IEEE Engineering in Medicine and Biology Society, pp. 5368–5371. IEEE (2011)
5. Dawe, J., Sutherland, C., Barco, A., Broadbent, E.: Can social robots help children in healthcare contexts? A scoping review. BMJ Paediatr. Open **3**(1), e000371 (2019)
6. Ekman, P., Friesen, W.: Emotion facial action coding system (EM-FACS). University of California, San Francisco (1984)
7. Erden, M.S.: Emotional postures for the humanoid-robot Nao. Int. J. Soc. Robot. **5**(4), 441–456 (2013)
8. Fridin, M., Belokopytov, M.: Robotics agent coacher for CP motor function (RAC CP Fun). Robotica **32**(8), 1265–1279 (2014)
9. Harrigan, J.A.: Proxemics, kinesics, and gaze. In: The New Handbook of Methods in Nonverbal Behavior Research, pp. 137–198 (2005)
10. Jeong, S., Logan, D.E., Goodwin, M.S., et al.: A social robot to mitigate stress, anxiety, and pain in hospital pediatric care. In: Proceedings of HRI - Extended Abstracts, pp. 103–104. ACM (2015)

11. Jürgens, R., Fischer, J., Schacht, A.: Hot speech and exploding bombs: autonomic arousal during emotion classification of prosodic utterances and affective sounds. Front. Psychol. **9**, 228 (2018)
12. Klasmeyer, G., Sendlmeier, W.F.: The classification of different phonation types in emotional and neutral speech. Int. J. Speech Lang. Law **4**(1), 104–124 (2013)
13. Kurdi, B., Lozano, S., Banaji, M.R.: Introducing the open affective standardized image set (OASIS). Behav. Res. Methods **49**(2), 457–470 (2017)
14. Libin, A.V., Libin, E.V.: Person-robot interactions from the robopsychologists' point of view: the robotic psychology and robotherapy approach. Proc. IEEE **92**(11), 1789–1803 (2004)
15. Lopez, M.: Estimation of Cronbach's alpha for sparse datasets. In: Proceedings of the 20th Annual Conference of the National Advisory Committee on Computing Qualifications (NACCQ), pp. 151–155 (2007)
16. Mehrabian, A., Russell, J.A.: An Approach to Environmental Psychology. MIT Press, Cambridge (1974)
17. Pittman, J., Scherer, K., Lewis, M., Haviland-Jones, J.: Vocal expression and communication of emotions. In: Handbook of Emotions, pp. 185–197 (1993)
18. Plutchik, R.: The nature of emotions: human emotions have deep evolutionary roots, a fact that may explain their complexity and provide tools for clinical practice. Am. Sci. **89**(4), 344–350 (2001)
19. Rossi, S., Cimmino, T., Matarese, M., Raiano, M.: Coherent and incoherent robot emotional behavior for humorous and engaging recommendations. In: 28th IEEE RO-MAN, October 2019
20. Rossi, S., Ruocco, M.: Better alone than in bad company: Effects of incoherent non-verbal emotional cues for a humanoid robot. Interac. Stud. (2019, to appear)
21. Rossi, S., Staffa, M., Tamburro, A.: Socially assistive robot for providing recommendations: comparing a humanoid robot with a mobile application. Int. J. Soc. Robot. **10**(2), 265–278 (2018)
22. Russell, J.A., Barrett, L.F.: Core affect, prototypical emotional episodes, and other things called emotion: dissecting the elephant. J. Pers. Soc. Psychol. **76**(5), 805 (1999)
23. Russell, J.A., Ward, L.M., Pratt, G.: Affective quality attributed to environments: a factor analytic study. Environ. Behav. **13**(3), 259–288 (1981)
24. Sauter, D.A., Eimer, M.: Rapid detection of emotion from human vocalizations. J. Cogn. Neurosci. **22**(3), 474–481 (2010)
25. Simoës-Perlant, A., Lemercier, C., Pêcher, C., Benintendi-Medjaoued, S.: Mood self-assessment in children from the age of 7. Euro. J. Psychol. **14**(3), 599 (2018)
26. Soares, A.P., Pinheiro, A.P., Costa, A., Frade, C.S., Comesaña, M., Pureza, R.: Affective auditory stimuli: adaptation of the international affective digitized sounds for European Portuguese. Behav. Res. Meth. **45**(4), 1168–1181 (2013)
27. Tielman, M., Neerincx, M., Meyer, J.J., Looije, R.: Adaptive emotional expression in robot-child interaction. In: Proceedings of HRI, pp. 407–414. ACM (2014)
28. Tsiourti, C., Weiss, A., Wac, K., Vincze, M.: Multimodal integration of emotional signals from voice, body, and context: effects of (in) congruence on emotion recognition and attitudes towards robots. Int. J. Soc. Robot. **11**, 555–573 (2019)
29. Yilmazyildiz, S., Henderickx, D., Vanderborght, B., Verhelst, W., Soetens, E., Lefeber, D.: Multi-modal emotion expression for affective human-robot interaction. In: Proceedings of the Workshop on Affective Social Speech Signals (2013)
30. Yilmazyildiz, S., Read, R., Belpeame, T., Verhelst, W.: Review of semantic-free utterances in social human-robot interaction. Int. J. Hum. Comput. Interact. **32**(1), 63–85 (2016)

Robostress, a New Approach to Understanding Robot Usage, Technology, and Stress

Kimmo J. Vänni[1(✉)], Sirpa E. Salin[1], John-John Cabibihan[2], and Takayuki Kanda[3]

[1] Tampere University of Applied Sciences, Kuntokatu 3, 33520 Tampere, Finland
{kimmo.vanni, sirpa.salin}@tamk.fi
[2] Qatar University, Doha 2713, Qatar
john.cabibihan@qu.edu.qa
[3] Kyoto University, Kyoto, Japan
kanda@i.kyoto-u.ac.jp

Abstract. Robostress is a user's perceived or measured stress in relation to the use of interactive physical robots. It is an offshoot from technostress where a user perceives experience of stress when using technologies. We explored robostress and the related variables. The methods consisted of a cross-sectional survey conducted in Finland, Qatar and Japan among university students and staff members ($n = 60$). The survey data was analyzed with descriptive statistics and a Pearson Correlation Test. The results presented that people perceived stress when or if using the robots and the concept of robostress exists. The reasons for robostress were lack of time and technical knowledge, but the experience of technical devices and applications mitigate robostress.

Keywords: Robostress · Technostress · Robots · Productivity · Attitude

1 Introduction

The use of Information and Communications Technologies (ICT)-enabled technologies has increased during the last twenty years. Much recently, smart phones and Voice over Internet Protocol (VOIP) applications, such as Skype and Messenger, offer possibilities to be available anytime and anywhere. The new digital trend seems to favour the use of artificial intelligent (AI), like software bots and service robotics, automation and virtual technologies. According to Viola [1] AI and robotics will be the most relevant drivers of economic and productivity growth in the near future. Chakravorti et al. [2] reported that digital technologies could affect 50% of the world's economy and may displace routine jobs, and thus increase social inequities. Mühleisen [3] reported that digital technology will spread further, and people should not only adopt but also adapt to new technologies. However, the rapid implementation of AI and robotics may lead to changes in occupations and may foster workers to learn new digital skills to be employed [4]. Stacey et al. [5] argued that the workforce would be more diverse in the future and inequality among ICT-skilled and unskilled workers will grow. Tarafdar et al. [6] and Ragu-Nathan et al. [7] have reported that use of technology causes low job

© Springer Nature Switzerland AG 2019
M. A. Salichs et al. (Eds.): ICSR 2019, LNAI 11876, pp. 515–524, 2019.
https://doi.org/10.1007/978-3-030-35888-4_48

satisfaction and organisational commitment, decreased productivity and poor innova-tion capacity. Stacey et al. [5] have reported that digitalisation of work may increase work-related stress.

1.1   Background

Even if the AI and robotics are crucial for economics, they may have mixed effects on workers' job tasks, productivity and perceived stress level. There are few studies available that discuss the association between e.g. the use of industrial robots and stress [8] or medical robots and stress [9]. Also, some studies are available regarding e.g. stress detection in human-robot co-operation [10] but a number of studies regarding the association between interactive robots and stress is still limited. However, Dang and Tapus [11] have reported that social robots can be used to help people coping with stress, but their viewpoint is how robots could be used as tools.

The impact of social and service robots on employees' health and on an organi-sation's productivity is an emerging societal issue. The European Union has suggested that Member States initiate the development and usage of AI and robotics, and as a result many Member States have heeded the call through the proposals of various AI and robotics strategies [12]. The future of work is AI and robot-assisted and the use of all kinds of digital devices will be essential.

The pace of development of ICT-enabled technologies such as robotics is rapid, which may hamper organizations' psychosocial working environment and exacerbate workers' emotional and cognitive load [13]. In addition, Thomée et al. [14] have reported that ICT use was associated with sleep disturbances, reduced performance, and may contain risk factors for mental wellbeing among young adults. One indicator of that mechanism may be the increase of sick leave rates due to mental disorders which have increased rapidly [15]. In practice, workers and especially managers, directors and other top-level officers are always available and expected to react to any request [16]. A potential dilemma in the near future is on how organizations are going to implement robots and how people learn to use them without an excessive amount of cognitive load. Studies show that in some cases ICT-enabled technologies at work may cause stress and decreased productivity, but employees have no other options than use them [17]. According to Thomée et al. [14] a desirable approach would be to support the healthy use of ICT-enabled technologies, since ICT is an essential part of people's daily life everywhere. Tarafdar et al. [6] stated that facilitation and organisations' support are the key issues. It has been argued that organisations should have digital culture and clear ideas how to use technology [18].

Technostress is the key term to understand the robot related stress (robostress). Technostress was introduced for the first time more than three decades ago by Brod [19] and it describes a user's perceived or measured stress reactions in relation to the use of technical devices [7, 20, 21] or the Internet [22]. According to Owusu-ansah et al. [23], technostress is becoming a new challenge for organisations.

Ragu-Nathan et al. [7] have identified five technostressors: (1) a demand to work faster and longer because of available digital tools, (2) a blurred boundary between the work and private life, (3) a lack of IT skills, (4) the fear of losing one's job due to technology, (5) the changes in the organization due to new technology. All these stressors are relevant for robots as well.

Hampton et al. [24] explored the use of social media, mobile phones, and the Internet and found that use of social media were able to cause stress for some but not for all. Sethi et al. [25] reported that perceived stress was common among information system professionals but the causes for stress were long working hours and customers' requirements. According to Maier [26] the technostressors are user and environment related and an environment can mitigate or exacerbate technostress [6, 27]. Earlier studies have reported that a user's age, gender, earlier experience of technology and the user's personality might have an influence on perceived technostressors [7, 28]. Men were more prone to technostress than women and increasing age, good education, and high computer confidence may mitigate technostress [7].

This study perceives robostress as a hyponym of technostress and aims to explore the perceived stress due to the use of robots in comparison with stress due to use of smart phones and application software. As far as we know, robostress has not been earlier defined and therefore we follow the definition of technostress and conclude that robostress describes a user's perceived or measured stress in relation to the use of interactive physical robots, whereas technostress is mainly related to computers, mobile phones and application software.

2 Methods

The study was based on a cross-sectional survey questionnaire conducted in Finland, Qatar, and Japan. The number of respondents was 60 and their mean age was 41.2 (Md 41.0, SD 12.2). Among these, 34 were female and 26 male. The country of residence of 42 respondents was from Finland, 12 was from Japan and 6 from Qatar. Twenty-six respondents were students or trainee and the rest of them (34) had an occupational position such as researcher, lecturer, professor and director. The respondents were chosen among academia and according the criteria that they had basic knowledge on social and assistive robots (physical entities) and those application domains. The disciplines of the respondents were robotics and/or health sciences. Because the numbers of respondents from countries differed a lot, we did not compare those in between.

2.1 Survey Data

Data on the perceived robostress was based on the questions: "Do you think that you are stressed when you are using robots?" and "Do you think that you would be stressed if you should learn to use robots?". We also asked the respondents to evaluate the reasons that may cause or exacerbate mental stress for them. The questionnaire also included questions regarding the perceived work ability and productivity, ease of using devices and applications, experience on technology and robots, awareness of terms technostress and robostress, as well as an open-ended question where the respondents were able to comment technostress and robostress. The response options were mainly on a five-point Likert scale, excluding work ability, productivity and perceived stress questions where a ten-point scale was used (1 = low, 10 = high) and awareness of terms technostress and robostress where three-point scale was used (1 = not at all, 3 = quite well). The quantitative survey results were analysed with statistical software package (SPSS 25, IBM Corp, NY, USA).

2.2 Statistical and Qualitative Analyses

There was a three-step process for the statistical and qualitative analyses. First, data was analysed with descriptive statistics and mean values and standard deviations were assessed. Regarding the variables, Chi-square ($\chi 2$) test was performed and p-values were assessed with the 95% confidence intervals (95% CI). Second, Pearson Correlation Tests were performed. Third, open-ended questions were analysed.

3   Results

3.1   Survey

Among the study participants, the mean of perceived work ability was 8.18 (SD 1.75) and a perceived productivity 7.52 (SD 1.55). A perceived stress levels due to use of robots was 3.25 (SD 2.10), due to use of smart phone and computer 2.72 (SD 2.02) and due to application software 2.52 (SD 1.94), respectively, in a ten-point Likert scale. We asked if the respondents were stressed when using robots and if they should learn to use robots. About half of the subjects (N = 31) were not or a little stressed when using robots and about 67% of them (N = 40) if they should learn to use robots. However, respondents were not stressed when using smart phones or computers. Only 8% perceived stress to some extent and the rest 52% had no or a little stress. The result regarding the use of application software was comparable to the use of computers and only 13% perceived stress.

Results showed that the mean regarding technostress was 1.68 (SD 0.70) and robostress 1.27 (SD 0.52) in a three-point Likert scale. Among the participants, 27 (45%) did not know technostress and 46 (77%) robostress. However, a correlation coefficient between the awareness of technostress and robostress was 0.61 (P < 0.01). The respondents have been aware of robots in average about 4.1 years (SD 5.0) and had 22.6 years (SD 8.2) experience on the use of technology. However, a correlation coefficient between these factors was poor and non-significant −0.057 (P = 0.664). The experience of technology and robots in relation to their age showed that respondents had experience of technology about a half of their life (Mn 0.55, SD = 0.13) and on robots about a tenth (Mn 0.12, SD 0.16). The younger had higher relative shares compared to older respondents.

Table 1 shows an association between perceived stress when using robots and years of being aware of robots. The results showed that awareness of robots may mitigate robot-related stress (R = −0.333, P = 0.009).

Table 1. Correlations between robostress and awareness of technology (N = 60)

		Perceived stress when using robots	Perceived stress if should learn to use robots	Experience on use of technology	Years aware of robots
Perceived stress	R	1	.218	.182	−.333**
when using robots	Sig.		.095	.165	.009
Perceived stress if	R	.218	1	−.017	−.135
should learn to use robots	Sig.	.095		.897	.303

**p < 0.01; *p < 0.05

Table 2 shows that there also were significant associations between robots at work and perceived work ability (R = 0.296, P < 0.05) and perceived productivity (R = 0.315, P < 0.05). Of participants 38 (63%) replied that robots were able to help them at work at least to some extent, and 22 (37%) perceived that not. The corresponding figures regarding smart phones and computers as well as application software were as follows 56 (93%) and 4 (7%).

Table 2. Correlations between work ability, productivity and robot's and devices' help at work (N = 60)

		Robots help at work	Smart phone and/or computers help at work	Application software help at work	Perceived work ability	Perceived productivity
Robots	R	1	−.286*	−.122	.296*	.315*
help at work	Sig.		.027	.355	.022	.014
Perceived	R	.296*	.127	.052	1	.622**
work ability	Sig.	.022	.334	.692		.000

**p < 0.01; *p < 0.05

We explored the reasons for a perceived stress level due to use of robots and tested the following variables presented in Table 3. The most prevalent reasons for perceived robostress seem to be a lack of technical knowledge (R = 0.399, P < 0.01) and too many devices to use during a day (R = 0.455, P < 0.01).

Table 4 shows that perceived stress due to use of robots has significant associations between easiness to use technical devices (R = 0.425, P < 0.01) and applications (R = 0.510, P < 0.01). This means that respondents who had difficulties to use technical devices and applications perceived high stress due to use of robots.

Table 3. Correlations between perceived stress and some factors (N = 60)

		Lack of time to learn to use robots	Lack of tech. knowledge	Poor user interfaces	Lack of time to learn to use new apps	Too many devices to use during a day	Too many applications to use during a day	Lack of time to do anything new	Too many things to do during free time
Perceived stress due to use of robots	R	.366**	.399**	.278*	.392**	.455**	.340**	.130	.231
	Sig.	.004	.002	.032	.002	.000	.008	.322	.076
Perceived stress due to use of smart phone etc.	R	−.063	.049	−.049	−.020	.215	.236	.249	.329*
	Sig.	.635	.707	.710	.880	.102	.070	.055	.010
Perceived stress due to use of application software	R	.023	.138	.043	.083	.375**	.409**	.313*	.342**
	Sig.	.861	.293	.745	.530	.003	.001	.015	.008

**p < 0.01; *p < 0.05

Table 4. Correlations between perceived stress and easiness to use devices and applications (N = 60)

		Easiness to use technical devices	Easiness to use applications
Perceived stress due to use of robots	R	.425**	.510**
	Sig.	.001	.000
Perceived stress level due to use of smart phones etc.	R	−.046	−.008
	Sig.	.726	.951
Perceived stress due to use of application	R	.163	.143
	Sig.	.215	.274

**p < 0.01; *p < 0.05

3.2   Open-Ended Question

Fifteen of the respondents wrote about their thoughts in the open question. Their responses were distilled into 53 statements, none of which were against robots or technology in general.

Many respondents considered the use of technology from the perspective of increased opportunities. Robots are already used in physical rehabilitation, but not as much as they should. They mentioned remote rehabilitation as an important area in which robots should be used much more.

Respondents also stated technology as increasing possibilities for remote work. More kinds of work are possible remotely, which allows workers to focus more on their work rather than commuting. The goal is to use new technologies to enable working regardless of time or place.

The daily use of technology was seen as obvious and something whose opportunities should be harnessed. Some respondents felt that perceived stress is caused by insufficient time to learn and test new technology at the workplace. The introduction of new technology was also seen as educational and something that may ease work in the future. The use of technology in health sector saves time and makes working with patients less hectic. Respondents wanted to learn how to work with robots in a correct and controlled way. Another way of reducing perceived stress was seen as being interested in technology and being eager to learn more. One respondent expressed these thoughts in the following way: "Technology and robotics are making the world more efficient, but humans still need time to learn new things and to adopt new practices."

Respondents also wrote about the obstacles they face in using technology. Even if they themselves were positive and eager to use new technology, their interest could fade if their colleagues were only interested in looking for faults in the new devices. It was stressful to teach a person who had never used a robot before. They were also concerned with the blurring of the line between work and leisure.

Respondents expected usability from robots and the design of them should be based on individual needs. Adopting a new device can be difficult at first, as it can take time to re-learn how to use previously familiar functions. The users' positive attitudes and willingness to examine and use robots is of crucial importance.

Some respondents had never heard of the concepts of technostress or robostress before and did not understand them. Some wrote that they had no experience of using robots but would be interested in trying them in e.g., teaching.

4 Discussion

This study showed that the main reasons for perceived robostress were lack of time and knowledge to learn to use robots. That kind connections were not found regarding perceived stress due to use of smart phones, computers or application software because the respondents were familiar with them. Another reason for perceived robostress may be that the greatest part of respondents had only a short-time experience or no experience on robots and use of robots may still be challenging. The results showed in general that respondents who had experience of technology did not perceive technostress or robostress. The terms and definition of technostress and robostress were not well-known. The respondents who are working with technology and robots were more aware of terms than other respondents.

There are some studies available which discuss ICT and technostress but a number of studies regarding robostress is limited. The negative consequences of technostress have been reported [7] and according to Owusu-ansah et al. [23] the symptoms are both mental and physical including e.g., anxiety, technophobia, mental fatigue, perfectionism, headaches, insomnia, lack of rest and high blood pressure. Although, there are no studies available related to robostress, we can assume that the negative consequences may be similar.

This study showed a significant positive association between perceived productivity and robots' ability to help at work. Also, a high positive correlation was found regarding perceived work ability and productivity [29]. Even if, some studies addressed that the excessive use of technology may hamper productivity and cause technostress in some cases, there might be mechanisms that inhibit the negative influences of technology on employees' health and organisations' productivity [26].

Robots are a relevant part of our future and an open-ended question presented that respondents were positive towards robots at work. Overall, the development of ICT-enabled technologies have been found useful and positive from the business point of view. Companies, which exploit digital tools and communication, are productive and agile to adopt changes. In addition, employees, especially digital natives, consider that AI, robotics and ICT overall at work are basic issues and do not affect one's work negatively.

The decision-makers should take into account that implementation of robots at work places requires an approach [30] and time resources for learning to use them for avoiding robostress and productivity loss. It could be concluded that the strategy to mitigate and avoid perceived robostress, would be first to use other technical devices and applications. Therefore, we conclude the concept of robostress is needed even if the concept of technostress can be used as well.

The nature of the study was explorative and tried to find new information regarding robostress and the related variables. Even if, the results are promising and were able to report some variables related to robostress, we have to take into account some limitations or the study. First, the survey was conducted among academia and number of respondents was limited. Second, the respondents perceived their stress levels, work ability and productivity. In addition, robots are quite new devices for many respondents even if they should have basic knowledge on social and assistive robots, and some of them had only a short experience or no experience on robots. Therefore, some respondents may reply how they may consider if they should use robots instead of replying how they really consider when they are using robots. Regardless the limitations, the study showed that people perceive stress when or if using the robots and the concept of robostress exists.

References

1. Viola, R.: Artificial intelligence (AI) and robotics will be a key driver of economic and productivity growth in the future. The Parliament Magazine (2017). https://www.theparliamentmagazine.eu/printpdf/6255
2. Chakravorti, B., Bhalla, A., Chaturvedi, R.S.: 60 Countries' digital competitiveness, indexed. Harvard Bus. Rev (2017). https://hbr.org/2017/07/60-countries-digital-competitiveness-indexed
3. Mühleisen, M.: The long and short of the digital revolution. Finan. Dev. **55**(2), 4–8 (2018)
4. Furman, J., Seamans, R.: AI and the Economy. NBER Working Paper Series. Working Paper 24689. National Bureau of Economics Research. Cambridge, US (2018). http://www.nber.org/papers/w24689
5. Stacey, N., Ellwood, P., Bradbrook, S., Reynolds, J., Williams, H., Lye, D.: Foresight on new and emerging occupational safety and health risks associated with digitalisation by 2025. European Agency for Safety and Health at Work, Luxemburg (2018)
6. Tarafdar, M., Tu, Q., Ragu-Nathan, T.S.: Impact of technostress on end-user satisfaction and performance. J. Manag. Inf. Syst. **27**(3), 303–334 (2010)

7. Ragu-Nathan, T.S., Tarafdar, M., Ragu-Nathan, B.S., Qiang, T.: The consequences of technostress for end users in organizations: conceptual development and empirical validation. Inf. Syst. Res. **1**(4), 417–433 (2008)
8. Arai, T., Kato, R., Fujita, M.: Assessment of operator stress induced by robot collaboration in assembly. CIRP Ann. Manufact. Technol. **59**(1), 5–8 (2010)
9. Taniguchi, K., et al.: Method for objectively evaluating psychological stress resulting when humans interact with robots. In: Advances in Human-Robot Interaction (2009)
10. Sims, J., Vashishtha, D., Rani, P., Brackin, R., Sarkar, N.: Stress detection for implicit human-robot co-operation. In: Proceedings of the 5th Biannual World Automation Congress, pp. 567–572 (2002)
11. Dang, T.-H., Tapus, A.: Coping with stress using social robots as emotion-oriented tool: potential factors discovered from stress game experiment. In: Herrmann, G., Pearson, M.J., Lenz, A., Bremner, P., Spiers, A., Leonards, U. (eds.) ICSR 2013. LNCS (LNAI), vol. 8239, pp. 160–169. Springer, Cham (2013). https://doi.org/10.1007/978-3-319-02675-6_16
12. European Commission: Artificial Intelligence for Europe. European Commission, Brussels (2018). https://ec.europa.eu/transparency/regdoc/rep/1/2018/EN/COM-2018–237-F1-EN-MAIN-PART-1.PDF
13. Stacey, N., Ellwood, P., Bradbrook, S., Reynolds, J., Williams, H.: Key trends and drivers of change in information and communication technologies and work location. European Agency for Safety and Health at Work, Luxemburg (2017). http://www.wtec.org/robotics/report/05-Industrial.pdf
14. Thomée, S., Härenstam, A., Hagberg, M.: Computer use and stress, sleep disturbances, and symptoms of depression among young adults – a prospective cohort study. BMC Psychiatry **12**, 176 (2012)
15. Salomonsson, S., Hedman-Lagerlöf, E., Öst, L.-G.: Sickness absence: a systematic review and meta-analysis of psychological treatments for individuals on sick leave due to common mental disorders. Psychol. Med. **48**(12), 1954–1996 (2018)
16. Bordi, L., Okkonen, J., Mäkiniemi, J.-P., Heikkilä-Tammi, K.: Communication in the digital work environment: implications for Wellbeing at work. Nord. J. Working Life Stud. **8**(3), 29–48 (2018)
17. Ayyagari, R., Grover, V., Purvis, R.: Technostress: technological antecedents and implications. MIS Q. **35**(4), 831–858 (2011)
18. Tech Data: Is "technostress" making workers less productive? (2018). https://www.techdatanewsflash.co.uk/trendingit/is-technostress-making-workers-less-productive/376
19. Brod, C.: Techno Stress: The Human Cost of the Computer Revolution. Addison-Wesley, Reading (1984)
20. Berg, M., Arnetz, B.B., Liden, S., Eneroth, P., Kallner, A.: Technostress. A psychophysiological study of employees with VDU-associated skin complaints. J. Occup. Med. **34**(7), 698–701 (1992)
21. Weil, M., Rosen, L.: Techno Stress: Coping with Technology @Work @Home @Play. Wiley, New York (1997)
22. Hudiburg, R.A.: Assessing and managing technostress (1996). http://www.una.edu/psychology/alakslk.html
23. Owusu-Ansah, S., Azasoo, J., Adu, I.: Understanding the effects of technostress on the performance of banking staff. Int. J. Bus. Continuity Risk Manag. **6**(3), 222–237 (2016)
24. Hampton, K.N., Rainie, L., Lu, W., Shin, I., Purcell, K.: Social media and the cost of caring. Pew Research Center, Washington, DC (2014). https://www.pewresearch.org/wp-content/uploads/sites/9/2015/01/PI_Social-media-and-stress_0115151.pdf
25. Sethi, V., King, R., Campbell Quick, J.: What causes stress in information system professionals? Commun. ACM **47**(3), 99–102 (2004)

26. Maeir, C.: Technostress. Theoretical foundation and empirical evidence. Ph.D. Dissertation, University of Bamberg, Germany (2014)
27. Wang, K., Shu, Q., Tu, Q.: Technostress under different organizational environments: an empirical investigation. Comput. Hum. Behav. **24**(6), 3002–3013 (2008)
28. Bakker, A., Boyd, C., Dollard, M., Gillespie, N., Winefield, A., Stough, C.: The role of personality in the job demands-resources model: a study of Australian academic staff. Career Dev. Int. **15**(7), 22–636 (2010)
29. Vänni, K., et al.: The Presenteeism Scale as a measure of productivity loss. Occup. Med. (Lond.) **68**(8), 512–518 (2018)
30. Ge, S.S.: Social robotics: integrating advances in engineering and computer science. In: Proceedings of Electrical Engineering/Electronics, Computer, Telecommunications and Information Technology International Conference, pp. 9–12 (2007)

Robots at Home and at Public Spaces

Now I Need Help! Passing Doors and Using Elevators as an Assistance Requiring Robot

Jonathan Liebner$^{(\boxtimes)}$ [iD], Andrea Scheidig[iD], and Horst-Michael Gross[iD]

Neuroinformatics and Cognitive Robotics Lab, Ilmenau University of Technology,
PF 100565, 98684 Ilmenau, Germany
{jonathan.liebner,fg-nikr}@tu-ilmenau.de

Abstract. The ability to handle closed doors and elevators would extend the applicability of Socially Assistive Robots (SAR) enormously. In this paper, we present a new approach which integrates uninstructed persons as helpers to open doors and to call and operate elevators. The current implementation status of these two abilities into a robotic application developed for real-world scenarios together with first experimental results obtained are presented below.

1 Introduction

Socially Assistive Robots (SAR) can already be found in lots of applications in everyday life, e.g. to fulfill transport or inspection tasks or to guide persons in shopping centers [1] or in rehabilitation centers [2]. But indeed, the amount of applications is restricted by the incapability of almost all robots to open closed doors and to operate elevators. This capability requires a technical upgrade of doors, elevators and robots as demonstrated in [3], or alternatively it requires the usage of a robot with integrated manipulator to be active by itself. Both approaches are barely practicable, because the upgrade is time and cost consuming and, moreover, the skills of cost-intensive manipulators to open doors are still underdeveloped.

An alternative approach is the integration of persons as helpers to open doors or to call and to operate elevators for our Assistance Requiring Robot (ARR). So the ARR has to find bystanders, to speak to and to motivate them for assistance. This approach is tracked in the ongoing research project FRAME ("Elevator Usage and Room Access for Robots Assisted by Human Helpers" running from 2017–2020), and investigated in different environments, an office, a production and a clinic building. So, in FRAME several challenges are investigated, e.g. the identification of situations demanding assistance, the robust detection and tracking of persons in everyday poses, the estimation of the willingness to support the ARR, the re-identification of helpers, an user-centered navigation in

This research and development project is funded by the German Federal Ministry of Education and Research (BMBF) within FRAME (16SV7829K).

M. A. Salichs et al. (Eds.): ICSR 2019, LNAI 11876, pp. 527–537, 2019.
https://doi.org/10.1007/978-3-030-35888-4_49

narrow environments as like elevators, and a human-robot-interaction to convey the concrete actions.

In this paper, especially the identification of situations that demand an assistance, the handling of closed doors, and the use of elevators, together with a suitable user-centered navigation are to be introduced. The methods used for person tracking and for human-robot interaction are presented in [4–6], respectively.

The remainder of this paper is organized as follows: Sect. 2 discusses related work in the field of human assisted robotic applications. In Sect. 3 typical procedures to drive through a door and to use an elevator assisted by a human helper will be introduced. Based on this, Sect. 4 presents the robot prototype that is used in FRAME with the used sensors, the essential human-robot interaction and navigation skills required to operate autonomously in challenging real-world environments, like an office building. Methods used for identification and handling of assistance demanding situations are introduced in Sect. 5. Using these functionalities in Sect. 6, the results of first functional tests with 20 non-instructed persons are discussed. Sect. 7 gives an outlook on pending long term user studies in an office building.

2   Related Work

SARs, explicitely using human assistance to fulfill a task that they can not do alone, are still rare to find. Similar to FRAME the group of Manuela Veloso already developed the Collaborative Robots (2009–2015) [7] to investigate human assisted SAR transport tasks in an office building. Different to FRAME they mainly investigated probabilistic planning mechanisms of where and when to look for help and integrated persons instructed to help. [8] Used the tasks of traversing doors and operating elevators, too, but in a simplified form to investigate social actions as subplans in motion control of a SAR. The explicit help from passers to reach a goal in downtown of Munich was used by the outdoor robot IURO of the Technical University Munich [9].

Also the FP-7 project HOBBIT [10] addressed the assistance of a SAR as mutual care in households with residents. Further, in 2015 it was demonstrated that the conversational but immobile robot hitchBOT can do hitch-hike tours, getting help by strangers. Children are needed in [11] to fill a sociable trash box (STB). The STB tries to receive attention by moving towards the trash or using intentional stance. The authors also evaluated the interaction distance which is an important metric for our AAR.

A main contribution of this paper in the context of FRAME is the **identification of need for assistance**. Especially closed doors and elevators have to be detected and to be integrated in motion planning. There are different approaches to detect doors and their features like the opening direction and the opening angle, e.g. by analyzing the local obstacle map [12,13]. Further approaches take the geometric relations in image and depth data into account, e.g. [14]. [12] assumes that all objects (like doors or walls) have the same color, which is not suitable for our scenario. Therefore, [14] computes the vanishing point of the image based on line segments. Especially in the rooms of the production building of our project this approach would fail due to lots of shelves standing in front of walls. Detecting doors by observing objects over time (like [13]) is only successful, if the robot would be able to observe every door open and closed which is not really promising in any building with lots of doors.

There are less approaches to estimate the opening state of elevator doors like [15], which uses an approach based on opening states of doors or [16], which estimates the possibility to drive into the elevator. In FRAME, we need a fast way to classify the elevator door state as described in Sect. 5.

An **user-centered motion planning** is also important in environments where persons and a robot move close, as like at doors or for and in elevators. That's why based on the Dynamic Window Approach (DWA), which is the mostly used approach for motion planning, a personal space has to be considered [17]. Personal space also means, that to initiate an interaction a robot has to approach a person from the front [18] and has to choose appropriate movement parameters, like velocity or acceleration, which also will improve the person's acceptance [19]. The Evolutionary Motion Planner, developed in our group [20], a more versatile motion planner than the DWA, both enabling the optimization of motion command sequences under various combinations of criteria, is also used in FRAME.

3   Procedures to Handle Closed Doors and Elevators

In the following, the phases of door passing and elevator use of a typical ARR are outlined, implemented as a state-based training application (see Sect. 4), and tested in a series of functional tests with users (see Sect. 6).

The need for passing doors and use of elevators results from the task of the robot, e.g. a transport task in a multi-level building. This is also the context of FRAME, the transport of mail and material between rooms in the building, at first between secretariats in an office building and later in a production and a clinic building. The procedure is as follows: The mobile robot receives a concrete transport task in one secretariat to yield to another. For this task, it determines its best way [3], with the need to handle possible doors and evaluators.

In the following, the exemplarily described interactions integrate voice outputs, GUIs and LED-color representations at the robot's head described in [6].

3.1   Closed Doors

When the robot approaches a door, closed or not enough open to pass, it recognizes its state and drives to a waiting position beside this door. This position has to be chosen allowing to recognize a changing of the opening state or opening angle of the door, caused by persons. Also the waiting position has to guarantee a good look for persons in the surroundings, which will be rated according their willingness to help and consequently asked for help, e.g. by "Could you help me to pass the door, please?" together with a blinking of the head LEDs to enhance the peripheral attention (see Sect. 4.1). In the current implementation, persons in a distance of approx. 10 m will be sensed but will be addressed not until an interaction distance of 3 m is achieved (see Sect.5). In the next stage of expansion, an active search for helpers, instead of waiting alone, is supposed to be integrated.

If the person comes to the robot, it repeats its request when the person stands in front of it and requests a confirmation to help by touching the display. By doing this the person becomes the short-term helper of the robot. Then the helper opens the door and as soon as the robot senses an opening angle enough to pass trough, it says "I am starting to drive.", changes its display and LED color and moves on. When the robot is passing the door threshold, it thanks for help, e.g. by "Thank you, have a nice day." while continuing its way to the goal without stopping. Should the helper open the door not wide enough to pass or blocks the passage by itself, the robot points out "The door is not wide enough open." Should the helper leave before ending the assistance, the robot waits at its waiting position for the next person to ask for help.

3.2   Elevator Use

When the Assistance Requiring Robot (ARR) approaches an elevator, the same procedure to move to a waiting position as that from doors takes place. If the ARR has a helper, it says "Please call the elevator and keep the door open for me. When I'm in the elevator please press button for floor 2." So, the helper has to call the elevator and also has to ensure, that the door keeps open while the ARR drives into the elevator, e.g. by pressing the elevator call button repeatedly. Should the door close before the robot is at the threshold, it keeps outside and asks the helper to open the door again.

Depending on the goal of the helper, s/he can also use the elevator or leave it after assistance. Should the ARR be alone in the elevator, it moves in front of the door to realise a speedy leaving after reaching the desired floor level. Should the ARR be not alone in the elevator, shortly before reaching the desired level, it says to the bystanders "At the next stop I want to leave. Please make room infront of the door." After reaching the desired level, the SAR continues its way to the goal.

4   Assistance Requiring Robot

4.1   Mobile Robot

Using a differential drive, our mobile robot can reach a driving speed up to 1.4 m/s. To sense the environment two SICK laser range finders cover a 360° field of view in addition to two ASUS depth cameras facing in front and reverse driving direction. Immediate contacts with obstacles can be detected with the safety edges which are directly connected to the robot's motor. A panoramic camera system and a Kinect2 (mounted in our robot head) are

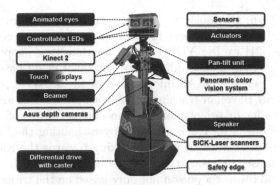

Fig. 1. Our mobile robot platform; grey: sensors, white: actuators

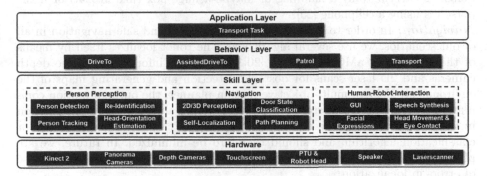

Fig. 2. Hierachichal system architecture; the intelligence to pass doors and elevators with assistance of humans is part of the AssistedDriveTo-Behavior

used for person perception. As we are challenged with the need of assistance by uninstructed persons, two touch displays are mounted for input of the person. For communication with people, we can use a speaker and our robot head with animated eyes and controllable LEDs to achieve a natural human robot interaction.

4.2 System Architecture

In our scenario described in Sect. 3 the mobile robot is facing multiple challenges in order to fulfill his tasks. Therefore we developed a complex system that can be separated in different layers (consisting of different modules) which are shown in Fig. 2.

(1) Hardware Layer: Our mobile robot is equipped with different sensors and actuators for obstacle avoidance, human robot interaction or person perception which are mounted on a SCITOS platform (see Fig. 1). Details of the hardware layer are described in Sect. 4.

(2) Skill Layer: The skill layer realizes the basic functions our mobile robot needs to fulfill our requirements for the door pass and elevator ride.

Person Perception: Obviously the person perception is a crucial skill for our application. Besides detecting legs in laser scans based on generic distance-invariant features [21] we use YOLOv3 [22] for detecting people on images of the panoramic camera system. Additionally, the point cloud based detector [23] is used for person perception. All information of the separate perception modules are fused in our Bayesian tracking framework [5] which is also able to track attributes like gender or orientation. In the current phase of the project we choose our helper out of all tracked people by estimating the interest in being assistive via their trajectories. A person walking towards the robot is probably more willing to assist our robot than a person going away. In future, we will classify if we should contact a person not only based on the trajectory by adding more information like head orientation. Furthermore, we want to classify if a person is carrying only a handbag or maybe a huge box (like in [24]) or if the person is using a cellphone [25].

Navigation: In order to achieve a socially accepted and safe navigation in all of our scenarios, we use several algorithms. The robot localizes itself by means of the well known aMCL approach [20]. We use 3D information of the depth cameras and 2D laser scans for obstacle detection and generating maps of the environment. Using a multi-objective motion planner, the optimal motion command is computed. Our system ensures that we are always at the right position in the map. Small errors in the localized pose (≥ 20 cm) can influence our door classification algorithm and should therefore be minimized. In future, we are planning to use door detection algorithms to update the local door pose in case of errors in localization.

Our mobile robot is challenged in various situations during the assistance of people as the distance between the robot and the person is very small. Usually the robot would not intrude the personal space of the people but due to the limited space in our scenario, we still need to ensure a socially acceptable navigation. The classification of door states is a major part of the navigation to empower our mobile robot to detect the need for assistance at closed doors.

Human-Robot-Interaction: Our robot is equipped with multiple devices to interact with humans. The two touch interfaces at the front and the back of the robot are used to show several information about the needed assistance and additionally to get touch inputs used as feedback. Furthermore, the robot head can show various emotions via animated eyes and generate attention with RGB-LEDs. It is mounted on a pan and tilt unit to be able to always look at the person that is supposed to assist the mobile robot. Every information will also be spoken by a speech synthesis software in realtime.

(3) Behavior Layer: Each behavior uses several modules of the skill layer in order to achieve its task often realised as state machines which coordinate the use of all needed skills. In addition, each behavior is able to use the other behaviors of this layer. The main behaviors used in our application are the *AssistedDriveTo* (driving around with the assistance of people for closed door and elevator use) and the *Transport* (coordinating the route of the robot).

(4) Application Layer: Our application is the interface for the users to send the robot to several offices. In each office the mailbox mounted on our mobile platform can be filled with additional post and be send to other offices in the building.

5 Functional Requirements

Requirements For Door Passes

In order to pass a door in any scenario, we labeled the position of doors in the environment of our mobile robot. On top of the knowledge about door positions, the door state needs to be classified. We analyze the door opening angle in order to decide if a door is sufficiently opened for our mobile robot to pass it. This classification needs to be very fast as the angle can change all over sudden. By applying a probabilistic hough transform as described in [26] on the local laser map, we are searching for the door line. In case we found the door segment, the opening angle is computed and the door state is classified via a threshold (see Fig. 3). If the door is not visible in the laser map due to occlusions, the state will remain unknown.

During navigation, we check if there is a closed door in the next 5 m around the robot that we need to pass. In case of an opened door we can just drive through, if it is closed or not wide open the robot needs to look for a person to assist it by opening the door. During the assistance of a helper, the door state classification is more difficult as the person will always partially (or fully!) occlude the door in the laser scan (see Fig. 3b) resulting in a failure if the door line cannot be detected anymore. As this will only happen when the helper blocks the path to the door center and therefore blocking our path to pass the door, the robot will ask the person to make more room.

In future, we are looking into utilize semantic segmentation to detect doors in color images and 3D point clouds instead of manual labeling. The big advantage of the semantic segmentation is that the robot will also be able to estimate the opening direction via the location of the segmented door hinges and therefore enable the robot to autonomously add all surrounding doors to its navigation map. The door state classification only needs around 5ms, and the tracking results are published with 5 Hz, which allows the robot to react on all fast changes of the environment.

Requirements For Elevator Use

To identify the support need for elevator use the robot needs to use information of our topological path planning algorithm across multiple levels as presented in [27]. The different areas (so-called nodes) in each floor are connected via gateways and build a graph structure which is used for global path planning. The graph structure is handmade and needs to be created only once. At the moment, the position of all elevator doors is labeled manually, in future they will be automatically labeled using a classification algorithm for this task. The local path planning is based on the cost map containing local obstacles. Every time we are choosing a gateway to a different floor, we need to use an elevator and, therefore, the mobile robot will start to search for a helper.

(a) Robot in front of closed door   (b) Person is blocking laser beams by standing in front of robot

Fig. 3. Door state classification; yellow: labeled door line, blue: detected door line, green: detection area, red: classified state and opening angle (Color figure online)

As the complexity of assistance is higher during an elevator ride than a door pass, our mobile robot needs to adapt to a lot more of possible actions of the selected helper. For example it is crucial in some elevators that the robot enters first due to the limited space in the elevator. Therefore, we do not only observe if the door is held open but also continuously check the position of all tracked people around the robot and within the elevator. If anyone enters the elevator before the robot, it will immediately stop and ask the person to leave the elevator. An instruction repetition will be done when the elevator door closes again (e.g. because the helper did not held it open the entire time).

As our robot can ride the elevator alone as soon as the helper chose the right floor, we are always observing the current floor by evaluating the acceleration sensors. If the helper leaves the elevator in a different floor than our target floor, we just wait for another person to enter the elevator (or check if there is someone else in the elevator) and then ask the new person to assist our mobile robot. If the elevator is moving and no person is present in the elevator, the robot know it is riding alone and can already drive in front of the door. If the elevator is starting to brake for another floor (which is not our target floor), it leaves its position in front of the door to enable people to enter the elevator. Evaluating the acceleration sensors enables the mobile robot to react fast to changes in the environment.

6   User Tests with Technical Benchmarking

To assure that all our skills and behaviors are working as planned, we performed functional tests with 20 non-instructed persons in January 2019. The half of them had to assist our mobile robot during a door pass and the other half during an elevator ride. They were sent to a specific secretariat on a way passing our robot waiting at a closed door or in front of an elevator. After being contacted by the robot, the people assisted it based on the instructions given by our system.

This functional test proved that our system is able to pass doors and ride elevators with the assistance of people. On the one hand, this was evaluated from social sciences perspective, and on the other hand we performed a technical benchmark to determine the performance of our system.

For the evaluation, we chose a bunch of performance measures including:

- Mileage (How far did the robot drive autonomously?)
- Duration of assistance (How long did people assist our mobile robot?)
- Interaction count (With how many people did the robot interact?)
- Success rate (How many approached people are helping?)
- Termination rate (How many people aborted the assistance?)
- Fail rate (How often did our system fail to pass a door or ride an elevator?)
- Waiting time (How long did the robot wait until he could pass the barrier?)
- Instruction count (How many instructions were needed for a successful pass?)
- Ignorance count (Did people ignore the robot? How did they ignore it?)
- Non-intended helper behavior (Did people behave in an non intended way?)
- Trajectories of selected helper (How often did the tracker lose the helper?)
- Human-Robot-Interaction (What are typical trajectories close to the robot?)

As some performance measures are not suitable for the fixed setup of the functional test (like waiting time or interaction count), we only evaluated a subset of them. The average assistance duration for an elevator ride was 92 s, for passing a door 27 s. During those functional tests, our mobile robot was not ready to ride the elevator alone. Therefore, the needed assistance duration is now lower, and we expect more people to be willing to assist if the duration is as low as possible.

As already described in Sect. 5, our mobile robot is challenged with a very small interaction distance to the selected helper. During the functional test, the average distance between the helper and the robot was around 1 m only. Despite this small distance and the need of disturbing the personal space of the helper, no person felt uncomfortable during the assistance.

In ongoing tests we are comparing how the robot is able to obtain help in the all scenarios. We already determined the need of different approach behaviors based on the target audience. In an office building of a technical university the potential helpers are trying to test the limitations of our system while in other scenarios the people might be more willing to just follow the instructions of the AAR.

7   Conclusion and Outlook

In this paper, we presented a new approach integrating uninstructed persons as helpers to open doors and to call and operate elevators. This allows our mobile robot to operate in entire buildings consisting of multiple floors and aisles with doors without the need of any technical change of the building. Using a fast door state classification and person tracker, we obtained a real-time application which is able to react to fast changes in the environment. This will be proven in long term tests in different scenarios of FRAME.

Besides detecting doors autonomously, our mobile robot will also start to actively search for people to assist in future. This will result in a huge decrease of the waiting time in less frequented areas of the building.

References

1. Gross, H.M., et al.: TOOMAS: interactive shopping guide robots in everyday use - final implementation and experiences from long-term field trials. In: IEEE/RSJ Proceedings of IROS, pp. 2005–2012 (2009)
2. Gross, H.M., et al.: Mobile robot companion for walking training of stroke patients in clinical post-stroke rehabilitation. In: IEEE International Conference on Robotics and Automation (ICRA), pp. 1028–1035 (2017)
3. Stricker, R., et al.: Konrad and suse, two robots guiding visitors in a university building. In: Autonomous Mobile Systems (AMS), pp. 49–58 (2012)
4. Breuers, S., Beyer, L., Rafi, U., Leibe, B.: Detection-tracking for efficient person analysis: the detta pipeline. In: IEEE/RSJ Proceedings of IROS, pp. 48–52 (2018)
5. Wengefeld, T., Mueller, S., Lewandowski, B., Gross, H.M.: Probabilistic framework for tracking people on mobile platforms. In: IEEE Proceedings of RO-MAN (2019)
6. v.d. Grinten, T., Mueller, S., Westhoven, M., Wischniewski, S., Scheidig, A., Gross, H.M.: Designing an expressive head for a help requesting socially assistive robot. In: Submitted to HFR (2019)
7. Veloso, M., Biswas, J., Coltin, B., Rosenthal, S.: Cobots: robust symbiotic autonomous mobile service robots. In: Proceedings of IJCAI, pp. 4423–4429 (2015)
8. Nardi, L., Iocchi, L.: Representation and execution of social plans through human-robot collaboration. In: Proceedings of ICSR (2014)
9. Weiss, A., et al.: The interactive urban robot: user-centered development and final field trial. Paladyn J. Behav. Robot. 6(1), 42–46 (2015)
10. Fischinger, D.: Hobbit, a care robot supporting independent living at home. Robot. Auton. Syst. 75, 60–78 (2016)
11. Yamaji, Y., Miyake, T., Yoshiike, Y., De Silva, P.R.S., Okada, M.: STB: child-dependent sociable trash box. Int. J. Soc. Robot. 3(4), 359–370 (2011)
12. Anguelov, D.E.A.: Detecting and modeling doors with mobile robots. In: IEEE Proceedings of ICRA, pp. 3777–3784 (2004)
13. Nieuwenhuisen, M.E.A.: Improving indoor navigation of autonomous robots. In: IEEE Proceedings of ICRA (2010)
14. Sekkal, R., Pasteau, F., Babel, M., Brun, B., Leplumey, I.: Simple monocular door detection and tracking. In: IEEE Proceedings of ICIP (2013)
15. Yang, X.E.A.: Context-based indoor object detection as an aid to blind persons. In: Proceedings of the 18th International Conference on Multimedia (2010)
16. Niechwiadowicz, K., Khan, Z.: Robot based logistics system for hospitals-survey. In: IDT Workshop (2008)
17. Weinrich, C., Volkhardt, M., Einhorn, E., Gross, H.M.: Prediction of human collision avoidance behavior by lifelong learning for socially compliant robot navigation. In: IEEE Proceedings of ICRA, pp. 376–381 (2013)
18. Ishiguro, H.E.A.: Development of an interactive humanoid robot "robovie". In: IEEE Proceedings of ICRA (2003)

19. Kruse, T.E.A.: Human-aware robot navigation: a survey. Robot. Auton. Syst. **61**, 1726–1743 (2013)
20. Müller, S., Trinh, T.Q., Gross, H.-M.: Local real-time motion planning using evolutionary optimization. In: Gao, Y., Fallah, S., Jin, Y., Lekakou, C. (eds.) TAROS 2017. LNCS (LNAI), vol. 10454, pp. 211–221. Springer, Cham (2017). https://doi.org/10.1007/978-3-319-64107-2_17
21. Weinrich, C., Wengefeld, T., Schroeter, C., Gross, H.M.: People detection and distinction of their walking aids in 2D laser range data based on generic distance-invariant features. In: IEEE Proceedings of RO-MAN, pp. 767–773 (2014)
22. Redmon, J., Farhadi, A.: Yolov3: an incremental improvement. arXiv (2018)
23. Lewandowski, B., Liebner, J., Wengefeld, T., Müller, S., Gross, H.M.: A fast and robust 3D person detector and posture estimator for mobile robotic applications. In: IEEE Proceedings of ICRA (2019)
24. Liu, W., Xia, T., Wan, J., Zhang, Y., Li, J.: RGB-D based multi-attribute people search in intelligent visual surveillance. In: Schoeffmann, K., Merialdo, B., Hauptmann, A.G., Ngo, C.-W., Andreopoulos, Y., Breiteneder, C. (eds.) MMM 2012. LNCS, vol. 7131, pp. 750–760. Springer, Heidelberg (2012). https://doi.org/10.1007/978-3-642-27355-1_79
25. Redmon, J., Farhadi, A.: Yolov3: an incremental improvement (2018). http://arxiv.org/abs/1804.02767
26. Matas, J., Galambos, C., Kittler, J.: Robust detection of lines using the progressive probabilistic hough transform. CVIU **78**(1), 119–137 (2000)
27. Stricker, R., et al.: Interactive mobile robots guiding visitors in a university building. In: IEEE Proceedings of RO-MAN, pp. 695–700. IEEE (2012)

Mobile Assistive Robot in an Inclusive Space: An Introduction to the MARIS Project

Yesenia Aquilina, Michael A. Saliba$^{(\boxtimes)}$ ⓘ, and Simon G. Fabri ⓘ

University of Malta, Msida MSD 2080, Malta
michael.saliba@um.edu.mt

Abstract. Elderly or infirm persons who live alone may encounter difficulties in carrying out the instrumental activities of daily living. Often such persons who would prefer to live independently are forced to rely on outside assistance from family, friends, or social workers, or possibly even to leave their homes. A potential approach to address this social issue involves the use of an assistive robot to provide help within the home. However the challenges involved in achieving a satisfactory robot design for reliable operation within the typically unstructured domestic environment remain difficult to meet. To date, attempts reported in the literature to mitigate this problem by developing a more amenable home environment – a robot-inclusive space – remain sparse and preliminary. In this work, a new systematic engineering approach is taken to address this problem. A structured data collection exercise has been carried out with samples of older adults and of associated allied healthcare professionals to first identify those regular tasks within the home that are typically problematic for the elderly. These tasks are then analyzed to extract those specific steps, movements and performance skills that could benefit from facilitation through a combined approach of environment-redesign and robot assistance. A new conceptual design for a robot-inclusive kitchen has been generated, and an associated prototype six-degree-of-freedom tele-operated domestic robot has been designed and constructed.

Keywords: Domestic robot · Robot-inclusive space · Assisted living

1 Introduction

Over the last several decades, a steady growth has been observed in the older adult (OA) population, and as life expectancy increases more seniors are living alone in their own house [1]. The OAs living alone however are an at-risk group, and due to frailty and/or health problems often experience difficulties in performing the basic activities of daily living (ADLs, e.g. bathing, transferring), and/or the instrumental activities of daily living (IADLs, e.g. telephone use, food preparation). This often leads to dependence of the OA on outside help from family, friends, or social workers, and/or ultimately to relocation of the OA to a nursing or rest home. However, surveys have consistently shown that the majority of OAs would prefer to remain in their own homes and communities-at-large as they age, rather than moving to a retirement home [2, 3].

M. A. Salichs et al. (Eds.): ICSR 2019, LNAI 11876, pp. 538–547, 2019.
https://doi.org/10.1007/978-3-030-35888-4_50

Many researchers are working on new robotic assistive technologies that can help the OA with simple tasks required to continue living independently at home, which would otherwise be carried out by a caregiver (e.g. [4, 5]). However, the dynamic and highly unpredictable nature of everyday living spaces presents a challenge for an assistive robot that must work efficiently and safely around people. Thus, practical and widely capable assistive robots still remain an unmet promise, despite the significant advances made in associated sensor and control technologies.

A key realization is that one of the root causes of this problem involves the fact that in the traditional (and intuitive) domestic robot scenario, the robot must adapt to an environment which was not designed for it. To address this issue, the general concept of universal design of the environment, normally understood to indicate accessibility to all people regardless of age, disability or other factors, was extended in [6] to include accessibility to robots. This holistic approach has been explored by a small number of other research teams (e.g. [7–10]), and has led to the definition of the robot-inclusive space (RIS) [11, 12]. The results so far however have been mainly conceptual and/or very exploratory, and a lot of work remains to be done to bring the concept to a successful and wide demonstration, and ultimately to application and general use.

The end objective of this work is to take a more extensive and structured approach to address this problem, by exploring in a systematic manner how the home environment can be designed/converted to be amenable to use by both humans and robot(s), and then to evaluate the concept by developing a test environment and an associated early prototype robotic device for domestic support. The overall project (and the robot) have been given the acronym MARIS – *Mobile Assistive Robot in an Inclusive Space*.

The MARIS project is intended to be an ongoing research activity within the Robotic Systems Laboratory (RSL), of the Department of Mechanical Engineering at the University of Malta. This paper gives a summary of the results that have been achieved in the first phase of this project, mainly (1) the targeted and empirically derived understanding, analytical description, and categorization of the needs and preferences of OAs who live independently; (2) an early concept design for a robot-inclusive kitchen that is derived from the empirical and analytical results; and (3) the development, simulation and evaluation of a first prototype of an assistive robot capable of functioning within this space. Items (2) and (3) are addressed only very briefly in this introductory report.

2 Data Collection, Analysis and Interpretation

2.1 Objectives of the Data Collection Process

Various studies in the literature have investigated and/or reviewed the problems with independence faced by OAs, and the potential for acceptance of robotic assistants by OAs. In [13], a survey of 44 OAs who lived independently indicated that the tasks that presented the most difficulties involved cleaning (e.g. laundry, washing dishes), outdoor work (e.g. gardening), and home upkeep (e.g. air conditioner maintenance, replacing a light bulb). In [14], a literature survey as well as a focus group based study carried out on 113 participants (41 OAs, 40 professional caregivers, and 32 informal caregivers) indicated that the main areas of difficulty involved activities related to mobility, self-care and social isolation, although no single activity could be identified as the main threat to independence. A literature survey carried out in [15] concluded that users' characteristics such as age, needs and experience with technology/robots play a crucial role in the user's acceptance and preferences for a robot assistant. These results for robot acceptance were in general consistent with the results of a Euro-barometer survey taken across the EU member states, which showed that demographic attributes such as older age and lower education level tended to negatively affect acceptance. An extensive literature review in [16] found that acceptance of robots by OAs, is likely to be better if robots use humanlike communication and if they meet the users' emotional, psychological, social and environmental needs.

The above important works, and other similar studies, have served to determine those activities and preferences of OAs that require focus, however the results obtained to date remain mainly qualitative and generic. In the present work, the objective of the data collection exercise is to obtain more specific and detailed information on the actual tasks and movements that OAs encounter difficulties with, with the aim of applying the analyzed results to the design of a RIS, and of an associated assistive robot. A boundary that was set in this research was to target only those OAs who have no difficulties with the basic ADLs (i.e. whose potential difficulties lie only with their performance of IADLs), and who have no cognitive impairment. The data collection exercise also aims to acquire specific information on preferred appearance, level of autonomy, and size of an assistant robot, within the local population, and also information about whether they would be willing to make changes to their home to accommodate a robot.

2.2 Method

The original intended approach to the data collection involved the acquisition of data exclusively from OAs, with participants to be recruited from among the elderly who are active in various community centres. However a pilot survey conducted on ten OAs revealed problems with this approach, in that (1) the OAs from this demographic tend not to have significant problems with performing IADLs; and (2) in spite of the requisite information and consent forms, the OAs were reticent to give detailed and truthful answers to survey questions being posed by researchers who they are unfamiliar with.

The approach was therefore modified to recruit OAs only from among relatives and friends of the core research team, or where a friend or acquaintance of a team member could serve as intermediary; and to acquire data also from allied health care professionals (AHCPs), in this case occupational therapists and physiotherapists who work with OAs. Thus two versions of a survey questionnaire were prepared, one targeting the OAs and the other the AHCPs. Each version was divided into three parts, with Part 1 addressing demographic and classification data; Part 2 addressing difficulties and assistance requirements with IADLs; and Part 3 addressing preferences with regard to assistive robots and willingness to make changes in the home.

Part 1 of the OA questionnaire collected data on gender, age, marital status, living companions (if any), availability of family or friends' assistance and frequency of the assistance, community services used, health problems, whether assistance is needed for

ADLs and/or IADLs, and experience with technologies such as mobile phones, computers, or other electronic devices. Part 1 of the AHCP questionnaire collected data on AHCP gender, age, education, occupation, place of work, and years of experience; as well as general information about their patients: ages, health problems, ADL/IADL abilities, family/friends assistance, and experience with technologies.

Part 2 first inquired whether the OAs experience lack of hand dexterity; or weak muscles in their hands, forearms and shoulders. The survey then examined the difficulties that OAs encounter when they perform 23 important day-to-day activities, chosen from the Assessment of Motor and Process Skills (AMPS), Task Challenge Hierarchy [17] (a list of tasks through which an occupational therapist can assess the OA's functional status). The activities chosen cover five different domains of function (responsibility for own medication, telephone use, meal preparation, housekeeping and laundry) from the Lawton-Brody IADL Scale [18], which is an instrument used to assess a person's independent living skills. The list of performance skills was based on the motor skills that occupational therapists use in the AMPS evaluation [19] and the classification of manipulation activities in everyday activities defined in [11].

Parts 2 and 3 of the questionnaire were almost identical across the two versions (apart from necessary differences in syntax), except that the OA version used 3-point Likert scales in Part 2 where applicable, while the AHCP version used 5-point scales. For the OAs, the questionnaire was filled by the researcher (or person known and trusted by the OA) in an interview setting at the OA's home. For the AHCPs, the survey respondents and responses were solicited over e-mail through the director of a local long-term care facility: selected AHCPs all had experience and ongoing work with outpatients who live independently, and the survey questions addressed issues pertaining to these outpatients. The data collection was conducted in Malta during early 2018.

2.3 Participants

In total, seventeen OAs were interviewed, having ages in the 60s (23.5%), 70s (35.3%) and 80s (41.2%), with 82.4% of the respondents being female. The respondents suffered from the following health conditions: arthritis (58.8%), chronic heart failure (29.4%) and fractures (23.5%). Almost half the OAs were married (47.1%), closely followed by widows (35.3%), widowers (11.8%) and single (5.9%). Just over half of the OAs (52.9%) lived alone, with the rest living either with their spouse or family member. Most of the participants (93.8%) required assistance, mainly with IADLs, which is to be expected since the OAs participating in this survey were ones who were able to perform their ADLs. The community service mostly used was Home Help Services (35.3%), with 29.4% of the OAs hiring private helpers to assist them with housekeeping. Other commonly used community services were Telecare + (23.5%), CommCare (17.6%) and Meals on Wheels (17.6%) [20].

Meanwhile, twenty-two AHCPs (50% occupational therapists and 50% physiotherapists) took part in this study, having between one and twenty-five years of experience (Mean = 9.4 years, SD = 8.8 years). The participants surveyed mainly interact with people who are over 60 years old having health conditions such as arthritis (90.9%), post-stroke (77.3%), chronic heart failure (77.3%) and fractures (72.7%). The majority of respondents (63.6%) stated that OAs who live independently at home mainly require assistance with IADLs and 90.9% said that the majority of OAs have family members or friends to assist them with these activities. However, the required assistance depends on the severity of the disease, which impacts not only the OAs' quality of life but also that of their family or friends.

From the interviews carried out with the OAs, 94.1% said that they used mobile phones, closely followed by electronic appliances (88.2%). The use of computers was less common with a rate of 52.9%. This was observed to be quite similar to the responses given by the AHCPs, in that among the OAs, the use of mobile phones and electronic appliances is more popular than the use of computers. Most of the AHCPs (90.9%) stated that the majority of the OAs they interact with have experience using electronic appliances, while 68.2% said that the OAs have experience using mobile phones. Meanwhile, only 9.1% of the AHCPs thought that the majority of the OAs have experience using computers.

2.4 Results and Analysis on IADL Assistance

The responses obtained from both the OAs and the AHCPs for Part 2 of the survey were analyzed using SPSS Statistics Software [21]. Due to the higher robustness of the AHCP data (larger sample size, smaller error bars, higher consistency in the responses) it was later decided to base the decisions on the designs of the RIS and the robot on the results from these data, and these are summarized herein.

The responses to the first inquiry of Part 2 (see Sect. 2.2 above) were subjected to the Friedman statistical test, and demonstrated a significant difference between the two mean scores ($Q = 5.444$, $P = 0.02$), i.e. that the AHCPs were more likely to encounter OAs who suffer from weak muscles in hands, forearms and shoulders, than OAs who suffer from reduced hand dexterity. The mean rating scores for the assistance needs queried are shown in Fig. 1 in order of decreasing importance, and the frequencies of encountering OAs with the queried performance skills problems are shown in Fig. 2.

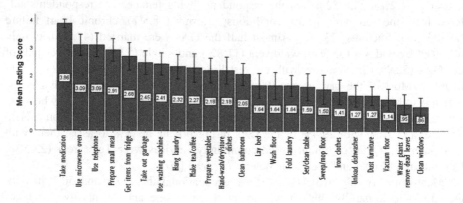

Fig. 1. Importance of assistance in IADLs according to AHCPs (Error bars: 95% CI)

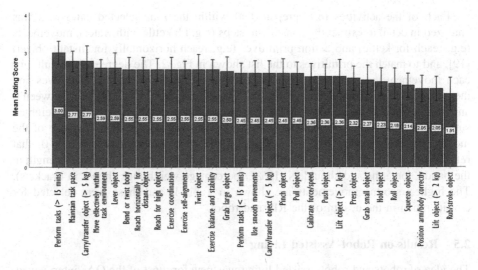

Fig. 2. Frequency AHCPs interact with OAs having the above problems during task execution (Error bars: 95% CI)

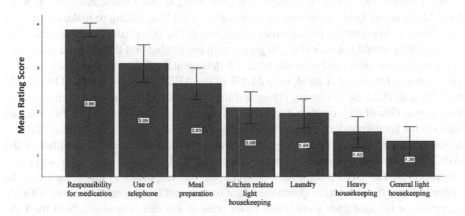

Fig. 3. Importance of categories of IADLs based on AHCP responses (Error bars: 95% CI)

The IADLs shown in Fig. 1 were grouped into seven categories: Responsibility for Medication, Use of Telephone, Meal Preparation, Kitchen-Related Housekeeping, General Light Housekeeping, Heavy Housekeeping and Laundry. The latter five categories were identified as unidimensional constructs extracted from a number of related activities: in each case the Cronbach's alpha was measured to verify an adequate internal consistency. The relative importance of the seven categories are shown in Fig. 3. In each case the mean rating score was obtained by averaging the rating scores given to the activities included in that category. The four highest ranked categories were selected for further analysis, as drivers for the RIS and robot design.

Each of the activities (e.g. prepare tea) within the four selected categories was analyzed in detail to extract the constituent steps (e.g. fill kettle with water), movements (e.g. reach for kettle) and action primitives (e.g. reach horizontally for distant object) [19], and to match the primitives to the list shown in Fig. 2. The degree of difficulty for each movement was extracted from the number of constituent action primitives and their associated degrees of difficulty (from Fig. 2), normalized to a fraction between 0 and 1. The priority score for each movement was then obtained through a weighted sum of this normalized difficulty (60%), the normalized degree of occurrence of the movement across all the selected activities (30%), and a binary score (1 or 0) that reflects whether or not the movement requires a relatively significant muscle strength in the hands, forearms and shoulders (10%), (percentage weightings shown in brackets). The highest scoring movements are shown in Table 1, and these were selected for consideration in the design of the RIS and robot.

2.5   Results on Robot-Assisted Living

The idea of robots and robot-assisted living was new for most of the OAs interviewed. However, once the concept and potential benefits were explained, the majority were hesitant but intrigued by the idea, especially if the robot is able to do tasks they can no longer perform, thus allowing them to continue living in their home independently. In fact, 70.6% of the OAs interviewed said that they would be willing to make changes to their home to improve the performance of the robot. The others, despite liking the idea, said that they would not be willing to go through the trouble and the required costs, and some were also concerned with the potential detrimental effect on the aesthetics of the environment. On the other hand, only 31.8% of the AHCPs thought that the OAs would be willing to make the necessary changes if they understood the purpose of the robot in their home. One of the common concerns was that the majority of the OAs they interact with do not have knowledge regarding robots and thus are unable to understand the use of the robot and the need to change their environment. Additionally, a number of the AHCP respondents commented on the reluctance of OAs to change their ways and environment. The large discrepancy between the two responses in this regard may be either because the OAs were questioned face to face and felt the need to agree with the surveyor, or because they were really more open to the idea. However, both the OAs and the AHCPs pointed out various important concerns which should be considered during the design of both the environment and the robot.

Table 1. Selected movements and their scores.

Movement	Score	Movement	Score	Movement	Score
Carry object	0.479	Open drawer/cupboard/appliance	0.388	Pour liquid	0.360
Open Tupperware-type container	0.427	Remove kettle lid	0.386	Turn on tap	0.357
Open dustbin	0.426	Reach for object	0.383	Cut/slice	0.354
Open medication bottle	0.402	Open bottle	0.380	Open can	0.352
Open store-bought container	0.397	Remove whistle cap	0.371	Open jar	0.349

With regard to the robot design, 52.9% (31.8%) of the OAs (AHCPs) interviewed preferred a machine-like robot; 23.5% (50%) preferred a robot with human traits; and 23.5% (18.2%) preferred a humanoid robot. A smaller robot was preferred by 70.6% (63.6%) of the OAs (AHCPs). With regard to level of autonomy, 47.1% (68.2%) of the OAs (AHCPs) preferred a semi-autonomous robot; 29.4% (13.6%) preferred a tele-operated robot; and 23.5% (18.2%) preferred a fully autonomous robot.

3 Prototype Development

3.1 Introduction to the Design of the Robot-Inclusive Space

The context selected for the first prototype RIS design was the kitchen, since this space is compatible with all the movements given in Table 1. Since all of these movements involve access and manipulation, the design effort focused on placing/modifying/selecting objects so that they are easy to reach, grasp and move; and on modifying activities such that they can be carried out with a single, low dexterity manipulator [11]. A concomitant objective was that the kitchen environment should also be functional, safe and aesthetically pleasing for human use (even in the absence of a robot).

A list of 27 individual steps, selected from the IADLs of Fig. 1, and containing movements from Table 1, was drawn up (e.g. throw away unwanted items; add water; cut sandwich). Each step was decomposed into its constituent movements, and a function means table [22] was used to brainstorm different concepts in which the environment could be modified to assist the robot. Morphological charts were used to formulate alternative methods to accomplish each step, and solution selection was based on established universal design guidelines for robots (e.g. [23]). The designs and/or selections address room layout, as well as various other details (e.g. door handles, utensils).

3.2 Introduction to MARIS, the Assistive Robot

The product design specifications for the robot included minimization of the degrees-of-freedom (DOFs); ability to reach standard countertop heights, as well as lower and higher cabinets; ability to handle standard or RIS re-designed kitchen objects; untethered operation; height shorter than an average person; and safe operation. A conceptual design approach similar to that of the RIS was taken. Ultimately the 6-DOF kinematic configuration of Fig. 4(a) was selected, and the embodiment and detailed designs, as well as a failure mode and effects analysis, were carried out. Commercially available items (3-DOF omni-directional mobile base, linear actuator spine, stepper motor for the 1-DOF wrist joint, and 2-jaw parallel gripper) were employed in the design. Tele-operated control was opted for in this first prototype, and a commercially available wireless controller was used. System control was built around an Arduino platform. System power was supplied by two 12 V sealed lead acid batteries. The constructed robot can lift a bottle weighing 2 kg, or a plate (from the rim) weighing 0.5 kg. It has a maximum horizontal linear ground speed of 0.25 m/s, a vertical stroke length of 0.8 m with speed 0.014 m/s, and a wrist rotation speed of 14.25°/s. In the fully extended position and at full load it can withstand a maximum angle of tilt of 12.25°, and has a vertical deflection of 3.16 mm at the gripper.

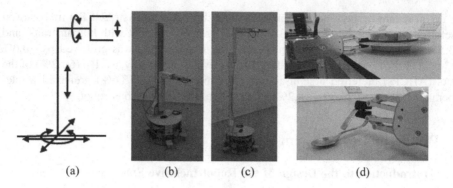

Fig. 4. (a) MARIS kinematic configuration; (b) MARIS (retracted); (c) MARIS (extended); (d) conceptual elements of the RIS (top: wide rimmed plate; bottom: custom spoon handle)

The MARIS prototype is shown in Fig. 4(b) and (c). Figure 4(d) shows two conceptual elements of the RIS being handled by the robot.

4   Conclusion

Preliminary simulations of MARIS within a fully furnished robot-inclusive kitchen have been carried out in SketchUp with MSPhysics [24], and this exercise has indicated that it is possible to achieve a functional and aesthetically pleasing kitchen in which an appropriately designed domestic robot can operate. In a post project-phase evaluation exercise, a sample of 18 AHCPs have received favourably the new concept and system, although some have re-expressed concern on the actual willingness of OAs to implement changes in their home. Current work is focused on improving the RIS, on developing simple and low cost suggestions to convert typical kitchens to RIS, and on upgrading MARIS to more autonomous control.

Funding. The research work disclosed in this publication is partially funded by the Endeavour Scholarship Scheme (Malta). Scholarships are part-financed by the European Union - European Social Fund (ESF) - Operational Programme II – Cohesion Policy 2014–2020 *"Investing in human capital to create more opportunities and promote the well-being of society"*.

References

1. Reher, D., Requena, M.: Living alone in later life: a global perspective. Popul. Dev. Rev. **44**(3), 427–454 (2018)
2. Mitzner, T.L., Chen, T.L., Kemp, C.C., Rogers, W.A.: Identifying the potential for robotics to assist older adults in different living environments. Int. J. Soc. Robot. **6**, 213–227 (2014)
3. Smarr, C., Fausset, C.B., Rogers, W.A.: Understanding the potential for robot assistance for older adults in the home environment. Georgia Institute of Technology, Human Factors and Aging Laboratory, Technical Report HFA-TR-1102 (2011)

4. Kittmann, R., Fröhlich, T., Schäfer, J., Reiser, U., Weißhardt, F., Haug, A.: Let me introduce myself: I am Care-O-bot 4, a gentleman robot. In: Diefenbach, S., Henze, N., Pielot, M. (eds.) Mensch und Computer 2015 – Proceedings, pp. 223–232. De Gruyter Oldenbourg, Berlin (2015). https://dl.gi.de/handle/20.500.12116/7892

5. Ventura, R., Basiri, M., Mateus, A., Garcia, J., Miraldo, P., Santos, P.: A domestic assistive robot developed through robot competitions. In: IJCAI Workshop on Autonomous Mobile Service Robots, New York (2016)

6. Matsuhira, N., Hirokawa, J., Ogawa, H., Wada, T.: Universal design with robots toward the wide use of robots in daily life environment. In: Advances in Service Robotics, InTech, China, pp. 149–160 (2008)

7. Tan, N., Mohan, R.E., Watanabe, A.: Toward a framework for robot-inclusive environments. Autom. Constr. **69**, 68–78 (2016)

8. Ohara, K., et al.: Visual mark for robot manipulation and its RT-middleware. Adv. Robot. **22**, 633–655 (2008)

9. Tsuji, T., Mozos, O.M., Chae, H., Pyo, Y., Kusaka, K.: An informationally structured room for robotic assistance. Sensors **15**(4), 9438–9465 (2015)

10. Sandoval, E.B., Sosa, R., Montiel, M.: Robot-Ergonomics: a proposal for a framework in HRI. In: Proceedings of the ACM/IEEE International Conference on Human-Robot Interaction, Chicago, IL, pp. 233–234 (2018)

11. Mohan, R.E., Rojas, N., Seah, S., Sosa, R.: Design principles for robot-inclusive spaces. In: International Conference on Engineering Design, Seoul, Korea (2013)

12. Elara, M.R., Rojas, N., Sosa, R.: Robot inclusive space challenge: a design initiative. In: Proceedings of the IEEE Conference on Robotics, Automation and Mechatronics, Manila, Philippines (2013)

13. Fausset, C.B., Kelly, A.J., Rogers, W.A., Fisk, A.D.: Challenges to aging in place: understanding home maintenance difficulties. J. Hous. Elderly **25**(2), 125–141 (2011)

14. Bedaf, S.: Which activities threaten independent living of elderly when becoming problematic; inspiration for meaningful service robot functionality. Disabil. Rehabil. Assistive Technol. **9**(6), 445–452 (2014)

15. Broadbent, E., Stafford, R., MacDonald, B.: Acceptance of healthcare robots for the older population: review and future directions. Int. J. Social Robot. **1**, 319–330 (2009)

16. Whelan, S., Murphy, K., Barrett, E., Krusche, C., Santorelli, A., Casey, D.: Factors affecting the acceptability of social robots by older adults including people with dementia or cognitive impairment: a literature review. Int. J. Social Robot. **10**, 643–668 (2018)

17. Fisher, A., Jones, K.: Assessment of Motor and Process Skills, vol. 2, User Manual (7th edn.). Three Star Press, Fort Collins Co. (2012)

18. Lawton, M.P., Brody, E.M.: Assessment of older people: self-maintaining and instrumental activities of daily living. The Gerontologist **9**(3), 179–186 (1969)

19. Fisher, A., Jones, K.: Assessment of Motor and Process Skills, vol. 1, Development, Standardization, and Administration Manual (7th edn.). Three Star Press, Fort Collins Co. (2010)

20. Malta Government Active Aging Services. https://activeageing.gov.mt/Elderly-and-Community%20Care-Services-Information/Pages/default.aspx. Accessed 25 June 2019

21. IBM, SPSS Statistics Software (2017)

22. Roozenburg, N.F.M., Eekels, J.: Product Design: Fundamentals and Methods. Wiley, New York (1995)

23. Matsuhira, N., Hirokawa, J., Ogawa, H., Wada, T.: Universal design with robots for the wide use of robots - core concept for interaction design between robots and environment. In: Proceedings of the ICROS-SICE International Joint Conference, Fukuoka, Japan (2009)

24. Trimble Inc., SketchUp and MSPhysics. https://www.sketchup.com/ and https://extensions.sketchup.com/en/content/msphysics. Accessed 27 June 2019

Should a Robot Guide Like a Human? A Qualitative Four-Phase Study of a Shopping Mall Robot

Päivi Heikkilä[1]([✉]), Hanna Lammi[1], Marketta Niemelä[1],
Kathleen Belhassein[2,3], Guillaume Sarthou[2], Antti Tammela[1],
Aurélie Clodic[2], and Rachid Alami[2]

[1] VTT Technical Research Centre of Finland Ltd, Tampere, Finland
{paivi.heikkila,hanna.lammi,marketta.niemela,antti.tammela}@vtt.fi
[2] LAAS-CNRS, Univ. Toulouse, CNRS, Toulouse, France
{kathleen.belhassein,guillaume.sarthou,aurelie.clodic,
rachid.alami}@laas.fr
[3] CLLE, Univ. Toulouse, CNRS, UT2J, Toulouse, France

Abstract. Providing guidance to customers in a shopping mall is a suitable task for a social service robot. To be useful for customers, the guidance needs to be intuitive and effective. We conducted a four-phase qualitative study to explore what kind of guidance customers need in a shopping mall, which characteristics make human guidance intuitive and effective there, and what aspects of the guidance should be applied to a social robot. We first interviewed staff working at the information booth of a shopping mall and videotaped demonstrated guidance situations. In a human-human guidance study, ten students conducted seven way-finding tasks each to ask guidance from a human guide. We replicated the study setup to study guidance situations with a social service robot with eight students and four tasks. The robot was controlled using Wizard of Oz technique. The characteristics that make human guidance intuitive and effective, such as estimation of the distance to the destination, appropriate use of landmarks and pointing gestures, appear to have the same impact when a humanoid robot gives the guidance. Based on the results, we identified nine design implications for a social guidance robot in a shopping mall.

Keywords: Shopping mall robot · Robot guidance · Design implications · Multi-phased study · Social robots

1 Introduction

Providing information and guidance is a suitable task to a social service robot in a public place such as a shopping mall [19]. Various robots have been tested in offering guidance to mall or store visitors either by route explanation and pointing, or escorting the customer to the target location [4,5,7,9,10,20]. Guidance

© Springer Nature Switzerland AG 2019
M. A. Salichs et al. (Eds.): ICSR 2019, LNAI 11876, pp. 548–557, 2019.
https://doi.org/10.1007/978-3-030-35888-4_51

is one of the most desired task for a robot among shopping mall customers and even mall managers, who are aware of the customer's challenges in way-finding in their malls [14,19].

As a guidance facility, compared to mall maps, a robot has some clear advantages. It is a physical device able to move in the same space as humans, and humanoid robots have bodily characteristics that are intuitive to understand by humans: *"A robot can naturally explain a route by pointing like a human, looking in the same direction as the person is looking, and using such reference terms as 'this way.'"* [10].

Robot guidance as a form of social interaction between a robot and a human has not been studied much. This is related to perceived usefulness and usability of the robot but also to how the robot should behave in its role as a guide. For instance, in our earlier workshop with shopping mall customers one finding was that a mall robot should not behave as if it was in the position of a human. The robot should not refer to itself as human, for instance, saying "in my view" or "personally I think" [14]. But to what extent a robot guide should mimic a human guide, and how do people perceive a robot as a guide?

In this paper, we report a four-phase study of human guidance and robot guidance. The aim of the study was to understand how a humanoid robot should give guidance in an intuitive and effective way in a shopping mall. We studied this by first gaining understanding of the effective ways to give guidance by human guides and applied the results to guidance behavior of a humanoid robot. Our study questions are:

1. What characteristics of human guidance should be applied to a humanoid robot?
2. What are the design implications for guidance behavior for a social robot?

The study was part of the Multi-Modal Mall Entertainment Robot (MuMMER) project, which develops a socially interactive shopping mall robot with Softbank Robotics' Pepper as the robot platform [8]. The robot is intended to provide customer service that complements and extends the current info booth service (i.e. guidance, information and entertainment service). The project's main study site is a large shopping mall Ideapark approximately 30 km from one of the largest cities in Finland. The mall consists of approx. 200 shops and stores of mainly fashion and leisure equipment. The customers are of all ages from families to older adults. In 2018, there were more than 19 000 visitors per day in the mall in average[1].

2   Related Work

In the literature, providing guidance is defined as a particular kind of spatial description called "route description" or "route directions". [11] defined it as a

---

[1] https://www.kauppakeskusyhdistys.fi/media/kauppakeskusjulkaisu/2018-kauppakeskusjulkaisu.pdf (in Finnish).

set of routes segment, each connecting two important points and explained in a chronological way. The way in which humans communicate spatial knowledge through the route description has been extensively studied both verbally and textually. This has allowed identifying invariants as well as good practices to ensure the success of the task in both urban and interior environments. Through five experiments, Allen [1] identified three basic practices as important for communicating knowledge about routes. They can be summarized as follows: (a) respect the spatiotemporal order, (b) concentrate on the information about the points of choice and (c) use landmarks that the listener can easily identify. This use of reference marks has been called critical information by Tversky in [22] after highlighting that 91% of the guidance contains additional information (landmarks) to the only actions of reorientation and directions [21], which confirms the results of [6]. Using the terms of [12], guides usually used landmarks when the target places were no longer in the *Vista* place (being within sight) but in the *Environmental* space (being reachable through locomotion). In accordance with [22], using landmarks typically occurs when the explained action is a change of direction. In addition, the importance of landmarks and their choice based on salient features during a route description is described in [16].

The choice of the route to explain may have an impact on its understanding and memorization: Morales in [13] argued that the choice is based more on its complexity (the number of stages that compose it) than on its length. The types and frequency of gestures used during route descriptions have been studied in [2]: pointing gestures have been found more frequent than other types of gestures, and their stages to be successful have been highlighted by [24] in the context of collaborative virtual environments.

Many robot guides have been developed based on guidance tasks in a shopping mall. [10] focused on aspects of communication, including user recognition and dialogue history. [17] used a "skeletal" description containing minimal information sets and chose to use only deictic gestures because of their clarity. [19] were interested in the types of questions asked from a robot guide and in the data needed to answer these questions. They also focused on engagement and the reasons why interaction between a human and a robot guide might not start.

3   Methods and Participants

The research consisted of four parts carried out during the research project (2016–2018, Fig. 1): a preliminary interview, a pilot study on human guidance giving, a human-human guidance study and a robot-human guidance study.

First, the preliminary one-hour interview was conducted with a person working at the information booth of the shopping mall to understand what kind of guidance related questions customers ask and how the information workers give guidance. We arranged the interview at the information booth and focused on typical questions from customers and challenging places to guide. We also observed two real situations of guidance giving during the interview. Based on this data, we generated and carried out five example guidance-giving situations and video recorded them.

Fig. 1. The study was carried out in four phases during two years.

Second, we carried out a pilot study on human guidance giving in a future location of the mall robot [3]. Based on the preliminary interview, we created a list of 15 locations and items to buy that customers typically ask for receiving guidance and which are located in different parts of the mall. Two researchers asked the questions of two persons working at the information booth, who were instructed to give guidance as they would normally do. The situations were video recorded and the guides were briefly interviewed after the sessions.

Third, the human-human guidance study was conducted with 10 volunteer student participants who were not very familiar with the venue. Each participant completed seven way-finding tasks based on the preliminary interviews. The tasks included only locations (e.g. a pharmacy) or a product to buy (e.g. a suitcase), and the participants asked them with their own words. They were also encouraged to ask clarification or further guidance if needed. The tasks included:

1. an easy warm-up task
2. a complex location to guide
3. a product that can be found in several shops
4. two locations in the same question
5. two persons asking guidance to find a place to have lunch together
6. one participant asking guidance and another one interrupting
7. any location or item that participants wanted to ask (preferably according to their real needs if any).

After asking guidance, the participants went to the actual locations and took a photo of the location. We interviewed the participants briefly between the tasks and checked the photos to validate whether they had found the right place. In addition, they all participated in a short individual interview at the end of the study session. After the session, we had a group discussion and revealed them the purpose of the study. They had an opportunity to ask further questions and share their feelings about having a social robot as a guide in the mall. The same person working at the information booth of the shopping mall acted as a guide in all of the sessions. She was asked to give guidance the same way as in typical customer service situation. The sessions were audio recorded and videotaped.

Fourth, the robot-human guidance study replicated the study setting of a human-human guidance study in a slightly smaller scale with 8 volunteer students and 4 guidance tasks for each participant. The tasks were similar to the first four tasks of the human-human study. The findings of the earlier study were used in designing the guidance behavior (dialogues and gestures) for the robot. In addition, as part of the dialogue, we tested how participants reacted to personal greetings, e.g. "How has your morning been?". We chose Wizard of Oz (WOz) technique to control the robot, as an autonomous version that is developed in the research project was not yet stable enough to be used. The wizard was an experienced researcher who stood two meters away from the robot partly behind a pillar and posters covering the computer, not to be too visible to the participants. He controlled the robot to turn, point into appropriate directions and respond with ready-made parts of a dialogue with shortcuts in a WOz interface. In addition, he could write short free-form sentences for the robot to say aloud. Similar to the human-human study, the participants went to the actual locations and took a photo of the location. They were interviewed briefly between the tasks and as a group in the end of the study session. The WOz set-up was revealed to them only after the study. The WOz simulation was found convincing by the participants as none of them had realized the human wizard.

The student participants were recruited through university student email lists and they represented different fields of studies. Most of them had visited the shopping mall a couple of times. Participants who had visited the shopping mall more than once a month were not included. In the human-human study, 6/10 of the participants were female with the mean age of 29 years, ranging from 21 years to 41 years. In the robot-human study 5/8 of the participants were female with the mean age of 34 years, ranging from 24 years to 61 years. The four persons working at the information booth who participated in the first three phases of the study were female and had worked in the mall from a few months to six years.

The study was carried out in compliance with the EU General Data Protection Regulation (GDPR). All participants filled in an informed consent form before participation. The participants were reimbursed with two movie tickets.

The data of the parts of the study were analyzed qualitatively. In this paper, we focus mainly on the data of the interviews. Based on the analysis, we propose design implications for guidance behavior of a social robot.

4   Results

4.1   Effective Human Guidance

According to preliminary interviews, typical guidance related questions include specific shops, items to buy, type of the shops (e.g. shoe shops) and recommendations, especially for restaurants. The staff giving guidance highlighted that equality between shops is very important for them, and thus they aim at telling the customer all the options (e.g. all four shoe shops and shops including shoes) or asking further questions of the needs or preferences of the customer (e.g. what kind of food would you like to have for lunch). They do not give direct recommendations, even though they had personal favorites. In addition, they never say that they do not know the response, but always try to help the customer.

The human-human guidance study revealed means to give guidance in an intuitive and effective way. Even though we designed the guidance tasks to be challenging locations, the participants found all locations according to the guidance given to them. Only one task was such that one of the participants did not find the place easily and needed to use the information board of the shopping center to get further guidance to the location. He was confused because the guide told him the instructions without emphasizing that the location was very close.

Even though the participants found the places relatively easily, the interviews revealed aspects that helped them recalling the instructions or feeling sure that they are on the right route to the location. This was important especially in cases when the location was far away. In general, the participants appreciated short instructions with clear structure accompanied with gestures for pointing the main directions. When the guide gave an estimation of the distance to the location, such as it locating very near or in the very end of the corridor, the participants felt themselves more confident in finding the place. In the cases when they had received instructions to two locations at once, the pointed directions and rough estimations of the distance helped them to recall the instructions to the second location. The instructions were easier to recall, if the guide had used an expression that connected the places together, such as the other destination being located in the totally opposite direction than the first one.

For the places not in sight, the guides typically used landmarks to make the destination and the turnings needed easier to locate. For example, a particular cafe was regularly used as a landmark because it was located at a crossing of two aisles. These results confirm what was highlighted by [21]. The most effective landmarks for the participants were familiar brands having clear signs, confirming the salient features as criteria presented by [16]. One or two landmarks in one guidance dialogue seemed to be a maximum number to be easily recalled.

4.2 Characteristics of Human Guidance Applied to a Social Robot

Based on the results related to effective human guidance, we designed the guidance behavior of the robot to include characteristics that helped the participants to recall the guidance instructions and find the places easily. To make the guidance feel intuitive, we followed the typical structure of giving guidance that the guiding personnel used. One of the guides had a pattern to repeat the location that was asked by the customer first, and we adopted the same confirmation for our robot. In case of a robot, it is crucial that the customer knows that the robot has recognized the destination asked. After that, the robot was designed to give a general remark of the destination first (e.g. it is very close). We regarded this as important for the robot, to give a customer an overall image of the destination first and thus a possibility to orientate to the exact directions.

In the robot-human study, the same characteristics that helped the customers when they were interacting with human guide were found effective also with a robot guide. The participants found the pointing gestures particularly helpful. Similar to the interaction with a human guide, they valued short and structured instructions, estimation of the distance to the destination, and appropriate use of landmarks.

The differences to a human guide were not found in the guidance itself, but in the small talk before that. All the participants liked the polite and friendly greetings and way of talking of the robot. They commented that they liked the way the robot looked at them, which made them feel that it is focusing on them and ready to help. However, some felt awkward if the robot asked a personal question in the start of the interaction, such as "How has your morning been?" One participant commented that it feels stupid to tell about your day to a robot, because a robot cannot be truly interested in that.

In general, the participants felt communication with the robot rather natural. The robot initiating the interaction made the situation feel natural and the robot repeating the asked destination confirmed that the robot has understood the questions correctly. The only problems were related to the WOz setup. As the researcher controlling the robot needed to simultaneously manage several aspects of the communication (such as the parts of each guidance dialogue and pointing of directions), the communication was not perfectly smooth and unintentional breaks occurred during the guidance. This made it more difficult for participants to follow the instructions and also know when the interaction ended.

Human-like gestures and way of communication was liked, but a couple of participants commented that besides giving guidance like a human, the robot could use its robotic features and abilities. Unlike a human, a robot could give for example an exact distance to the destination or it could use the tablet in complementing its speech. Naturally, exact distances or tablet use could also confuse users and should be tested before adoption.

4.3   Design Implications for Guidance Behavior of a Social Robot

Based on the results of our multi-phased study, we propose nine implications for designing the guidance behavior of a social robot.

1. **Help to start the interaction:** Use speech and gaze to receive the attention of the user. Start interaction by friendly greeting and offering help.
2. **Confirm the asked location:** Before giving guidance, ensure that the request is understood.
3. **Give short instructions:** Short instructions are easier to understand and recall.
4. **Have a clear structure of the instructions with natural rhythm of speech:** Clearly structured instructions without long breaks or too fast proceeding help following the instructions and recalling the main points later.
5. **Inform distance to the asked location:** Give an overall image of the location with an estimation whether it is close or further away.
6. **Use gestures (pointing at directions):** Helps both initial understanding and recalling the instructions later.

7. **Use landmarks when appropriate:** Salient landmarks as well as ones located in the crossings of aisles are helpful. However, include only 1–2 landmarks in one guidance case.
8. **Ensure equality between retails:** Instead of personal recommendation, try finding out the preferences of the customer.
9. **Stay flexible:** Give the customer a possibility to ask for repeating an instruction or to interrupt the situation. When the response includes several options, the customer should be able to ask further questions (e.g. which is the closest option). If the robot cannot answer a question, it could advice the customer to continue the case with the personnel of the mall.

5   Discussion

The aim of our research was to find out how we should design a social service robot to give guidance in an intuitive and effective way in a shopping mall. Based on our multi-phased study, we identified design implications and explored whether a humanoid robot should guide like a human.

According to our results, the participants felt human-like guidance behavior intuitive and the characteristics used by a human guide were effective in robot-human interaction. Our findings are in line with the principles introduced by Allen [1], emphasizing the clear structure of guidance as well as a chose of landmarks so that the customer can find the points of interest quickly and easily. Thus, the requirements and expectations of a route description by a robot do not seem to differ from a human-human guidance. However, asking additional personal questions ("How your morning has been?") was felt suitable for a human only. It seems that even though the structure of the communication and the aspects of making the guidance easy to understand and recall, seem to be applicable to humanoid robots, the robot should not pretend to be a human or replicate the human behavior besides functional aspects of it. This supports our earlier findings that a mall robot should not behave as if it were in the position of a human [14]. However, the result might be different in a study that would focus on e.g. free communication with a robot instead of functional task, such as guidance.

The limitations of this study include a small sample size and practical problems with the WOz setup. External validity is high as the guidance studies were carried out in the field, in an actual shopping mall with realistic way-finding tasks. However, the results cannot be directly generalized to all customer groups or other shopping malls. The participants were students, who do not make a representative sample of the mall customer population. For instance, student participants might have a more positive attitude towards a robot guide than the mall customers in average, which would make them willing to listen to the robot's advice more carefully than an average customer would. In some earlier human-robot interaction studies in the MuMMER project, we have recruited participants in the field [15]. However, this was not possible for this study due to the study setting, which required the participants to commit for 2–3 h to the study. Therefore, we have to be cautious when drawing conclusions from the results. Furthermore, we assume the attitudes to the human-like behavior of robots to be strongly dependent on the cultural context, and thus it would be interesting to extend the study also to other cultures.

Our results have been used in developing software components for the robot that will be deployed in the shopping mall in the end of the research project. The components include software for route search and the guidance explanations generation [18] and planning of the positioning of the human and the robot so that they have a common perspective while pointing [23]. During the deployment, we will extend our research to more realistic guidance situations with the autonomous robot.

6   Conclusions

In this paper, we presented a four-phased qualitative study to explore which means make human guidance intuitive and effective, and whether the means have the same impact in guidance given by a humanoid service robot. We proposed nine design implications and discussed whether a robot should guide like a human. Our results give practical insights to human-robot interaction designers and contribute to the literature of robot guidance as a form of social interaction.

Acknowledgements. We thank Olivier Canévet for creating a Wizard of Oz user interface which we used in this study and Petri Tikka for giving technical support. We also thank Ideapark for their cooperation and the volunteer participants of the study. This work has been supported by the European Union's Horizon 2020 research and innovation program under grant agreement No. 688147 (MuMMER project).

References

1. Allen, G.L.: Principles and practices for communicating route knowledge. Appl. Cogn. Psychol. **14**(4), 333–359 (2000)
2. Allen, G.L.: Gestures accompanying verbal route directions: do they point to a new avenue for examining spatial representation? Spat. Cogn. Comput. **3**(4), 259–268 (2003)
3. Belhassein, K., et al.: Human-Human Guidance Study. Technical-report hal-01719730, LAAS-CNRS, CLLE, VTT (2017)
4. Brscic, D., Ikeda, T., Kanda, T.: Do you need help? A robot providing information to people who behave atypically. IEEE Trans. Robot. **33**(2), 500–506 (2017)
5. Clodic, A., et al.: Rackham: an interactive robot-guide. In: 15th IEEE RO-MAN (2006)
6. Denis, M.: The description of routes: a cognitive approach to the production of spatial discourse. Cahiers de Psychologie Cognitive **16**, 409–458 (1997)
7. Díaz, M., Paillacho, D., Angulo, C., Torres, O., González, J., Albo-Canals, J.: A week-long study on robot-visitors spatial relationships during guidance in a sciences museum. In: 9th ACM/IEEE International Conference on HRI, pp. 152–153 (2014)
8. Foster, M.E., et al.: The MuMMER project: engaging human-robot interaction in real-world public spaces. In: Agah, A., Cabibihan, J.-J., Howard, A.M., Salichs, M.A., He, H. (eds.) ICSR 2016. LNCS (LNAI), vol. 9979, pp. 753–763. Springer, Cham (2016). https://doi.org/10.1007/978-3-319-47437-3_74

9. Gross, H., et al.: TOOMAS: interactive shopping guide robots in everyday use - final implementation and experiences from long-term field trials. In: 2009 IEEE/RSJ IROS, pp. 2005–2012 (2009)

10. Kanda, T., et al.: A communication robot in a shopping mall. IEEE Trans. Rob. **26**(5), 897–913 (2010). https://doi.org/10.1109/TRO.2010.2062550

11. Kopp, S., et al.: Trading spaces: how humans and humanoids use speech and gesture to give directions. In: Nishida, T. (ed.) Conversational Informatics: An Engineering Approach. Wiley Series in Agent Technology, pp. 133–160. Wiley, Chichester (2007)

12. Montello, D.R.: Scale and multiple psychologies of space. In: Frank, A.U., Campari, I. (eds.) COSIT 1993. LNCS, vol. 716, pp. 312–321. Springer, Heidelberg (1993). https://doi.org/10.1007/3-540-57207-4_21

13. Morales, Y., Satake, S., Kanda, T., Hagita, N.: Building a model of the environment from a route perspective for human-robot interaction. Int. J. Soc. Robot. **7**(2), 165–181 (2015)

14. Niemelä, M., Heikkilä, P., Lammi, H., Oksman, V.: A social robot in a shopping mall: studies on acceptance and stakeholder expectations. In: Korn, O. (ed.) Social Robots: Technological, Societal and Ethical Aspects of Human-Robot Interaction. HIS, pp. 119–144. Springer, Cham (2019). https://doi.org/10.1007/978-3-030-17107-0_7

15. Niemelä, M., Arvola, A., Aaltonen, I.: Monitoring the acceptance of a social service robot in a shopping mall: first results. In: Proceedings of the Companion of the 2017 ACM/IEEE HRI. ACM (2017)

16. Nothegger, C., Winter, S., Raubal, M.: Selection of salient features for route directions. Spat. Cogn. Comput. **4**(2), 113–136 (2004)

17. Okuno, Y., et al.: Providing route directions: design of robot's utterance, gesture, and timing. In: 4th ACM/IEEE International Conference on HRI (2009)

18. Sarthou, G., Clodic, A., Alami, R.: Semantic spatial representation: a unique representation of an environment based on an ontology for robotic applications. In: Proceedings of the Combined Workshop SpLU-RoboNLP, pp. 50–60. Association for Computational Linguistics (2019)

19. Satake, S., Nakatani, K., Hayashi, K., Kanda, T., Imai, M.: What should we know to develop an information robot? PeerJ Comput. Sci. **1**, e8 (2015)

20. Triebel, R.: SPENCER: a socially aware service robot for passenger guidance and help in busy airports. In: Wettergreen, D.S., Barfoot, T.D. (eds.) Field and Service Robotics. STAR, vol. 113, pp. 607–622. Springer, Cham (2016). https://doi.org/10.1007/978-3-319-27702-8_40

21. Tversky, B., Lee, P.U.: How space structures language. In: Freksa, C., Habel, C., Wender, K.F. (eds.) Spatial Cognition: An Interdisciplinary Approach to Representing. LNCS (LNAI), vol. 1404, pp. 157–175. Springer, Heidelberg (1998). https://doi.org/10.1007/3-540-69342-4_8

22. Tversky, B., Lee, P.U.: Pictorial and verbal tools for conveying routes. In: Freksa, C., Mark, D.M. (eds.) COSIT 1999. LNCS, vol. 1661, pp. 51–64. Springer, Heidelberg (1999). https://doi.org/10.1007/3-540-48384-5_4

23. Waldhart, J., Clodic, A., Alami, R.: Planning human and robot placements for shared visual perspective. In: Workshop on Robotic Co-workers 4.0 in IEEE/RSJ International Conference on Intelligent Robots and Systems (IROS) (2018)

24. Wong, N., Gutwin, C.: Where are you pointing? The accuracy of deictic pointing in CVEs. In: Proceedings of the SIGCHI Conference on Human Factors in Computing Systems, pp. 1029–1038. ACM Press (2010)

Identifying Social Context Factors Relevant for a Robotic Elderly Assistant

Birgit Lugrin[1]([✉]), Astrid Rosenthal-von der Pütten[2], and Svenja Hahn[1]

[1] Human-Computer Interaction, University of Wuerzburg, Wuerzburg, Germany
birgit.lugrin@uni-wuerzburg.de
http://www.mi.uni-wuerzburg.de
[2] iTec Chair for Individual and Technology, RWTH Aachen University,
52078 Aachen, Germany
arvdp@humtec.rwth-aachen.de
http://www.itec.rwth-aachen.de

Abstract. Social robots are envisioned to support elderly people in their daily lives. To interact in a socially competent way with its users a Robotic Elderly Assistant (REA), just as any other social robot, should consider the full *social context* of the situation in which it is interacting. In this paper, we investigate how to identify important factors that are relevant to distinguish social situations. Our study aims at determining social context factors that are important for a REA to consider when deciding when and how to deliver a message. Therefore, we describe the creation of video-based stimuli that were used in an interview study with senior users (n = 8). Our results suggest that the content of the message and certain factors of the social situation are important for the decisions of elderly users. They can serve as a basis for future studies that will further investigate social context modelling.

Keywords: Social robot · Elderly assistant · Social context

1 Motivation

One of the major areas of application for social robots lies in the domain of elderly care, with a number of projects, such as the European projects SERA, COMPANIONABLE, or Accompany, which investigate assistive robots as social companions (see [3] for a summary). These robots are envisioned to support elderly users in their daily life, often with the aim to enable them to live in their private homes for a longer time. Special attention should be paid to the design of those systems. While supporting self-dependent living is the goal of companion robots, their implementation into elderly users' homes might backfire in case they evoke feeling of loss of control over their lives in the users, or feelings of embarrassment because of uncertainty how to interact with or operate the social robot.

In the domain of elderly care, useful use cases include physical support as well as cognitive support [4]. A task that is often reported for Robotic Elderly

M. A. Salichs et al. (Eds.): ICSR 2019, LNAI 11876, pp. 558–567, 2019.
https://doi.org/10.1007/978-3-030-35888-4_52

Assistants (REA) is to remind their users to take their prescribed medication, to not forget private or doctors' appointments, and remind them of health routines such as drinking water (e.g., [2]). Such a "robot calendar" has been evaluated as a useful application by older adults [8]. To execute its reminder tasks reliably and in a socially acceptable manner, a REA has to be embedded in an intelligent environment. In order to interact with humans in a shared environment it is crucial for any kind of agent, including social robots, to have an extensive and consistent representation of contextual knowledge. Abowd et al. [1] define context as *"any information that can be used to characterize the situation of an entity. An entity is a person, place, or object that is considered relevant to the interaction between a user and an application, including the user and applications themselves"*. To interact in a socially competent way, the full *social context* has to be considered by a REA. The notion of social context is gaining increasing interest in various domains, such as multimedia, computer vision or robotics [7]. Riek and Robinson [7] describe the challenges and opportunities of such socially intelligent agents, and break down social context to the influencing factors situational context, social roles, social norms and cultural conventions.

The situational context for instance comprises the physical place, a set of actions, a particular social occasion, time of day, and so forth. The situational context guides and determines to a great extend human behavior. Other people situated in (or entering) this context and their relationship to the subject of interest, i.e. the social roles they might take on in this situation, also have great influence. Riek and Robinson offered the example that a person's behavior when dining in the company's cafeteria will most likely change to be more formal when the president of the company decides to sit next to this person. Some features of the situational context (place, time, occasion) will provide information on what social norms have to be followed and thus which "standard, customary, or ideal form of behavior to which individuals in a social group try to conform." [5]. These rules for adequate behavior can be highly different not only regarding situational features, but also in different groups (e.g., classmates, colleagues, family, best friends) and especially between different cultures. The judgment of a social situation comes naturally to humans, without considerable cognitive effort. For example, a person who needs to deliver a message to another person only needs to have a glance at the receiver of the message, other people in the room, a snip of their conversation, nonverbal behavior, social distance to each other, etc. to decide how to behave socially adequate in this situation. Such a judgment is not a trivial task for a robot. To build a model of social context that can help a robot to reason about the situation, we need to understand how people would decide in a given situation and why, which information is taken into account, and which information is ignored. Then, in a second step, we need to know what (elderly) people would like the robot to do in the situation. This is supported by Broadbent et al. [4] who point out that a proper assessment of the needs and expectations of the human user in specific situations and then matching the robot's role, appearance and behaviour to these needs, might help increase the acceptance of a healthcare robot.

Already providing context information to users without actually implementing these abilities into a REA proofs to be beneficial. Xu et al. [9] found that elderly users rate a robot as being more acceptable (in terms of intention to use, adaptability, trust, social influence, and sociability) when more information about its own social context (in terms of the user's social relations, the robot's technical details, and labor costs in elderly care) is provided. However, providing humans with context information about the "content" a robot is able to deliver (e.g., the services it can provide, the behaviors it will show) will not be enough because still the robot will provide this content in social situation and if the behavior is not adapted to the specific context features, it will likely be misplaced and bothersome or just not acceptable. Work in other areas of technology development has shown that ignoring content in favor of context can improve success of that technology [10]. Analysing context cannot be done while ignoring the user him- or herself [4] since characteristics of the user also determines his or her membership in groups, relationship to other people and so forth. Age is especially relevant, since we categorize people naturally in age groups accompanied by rules how to behave in front of this group and in interaction with group members. Thus, we have to take into account that younger and older users will presumably prefer different robotic behavior. This has been shown in a number of studies comparing younger and older adults evaluations of robotic behaviors [6,11]. These works highlight the need for empirical studies with the target age group and not to rely on theory-based approaches or on the transfer of findings from other age groups or convenience samples.

2   Approach

The rational behind our endeavour is to build a computational model of social context for a Robotic Elderly Assistant (REA). For such a model, we need to break down the complex social situation into discrete and measurable social context factors and their parameters, e.g. number of people present, their relationship status, social distance, the topic of conversation, the categories of objects that are currently used. These context factors and their parameters serve on the one hand to distinguish different types of situational context within the modelling of social context. On the other hand, this information is used (a) to determine reasoning on appropriate actions for the REA and (b) to decide how exactly these actions should be executed in an socially acceptable manner that suites the situational context at hand.

In order to obtain helpful information to further define social context for a REA, a couple of considerations have to be taken into account. First and foremost, it is very difficult for elderly people to state what they would like such a robot to do, as they simply have no experience with them and potential expectations or apprehensions might not meet the scope of our endeavour. However, having a fully functional REA that is able to demonstrate its abilities to the elderly users in different social context situations is a very time consuming task, if not impossible at the current state. Thus, **videos of different social situations** and a robot that should interact therein are a very good compromise

[12]. Other difficulties might arise by conducting online studies for technical reasons, such as obsolete browser settings, or physical reasons such as difficulties to read instructions from screens or type answers on a keyboard. Therefore, **in situ studies** with an experimenter to help where necessary is essential in this domain. Even during a live study, filling in questionnaires might be too difficult as the situation described (living with a robot) could be too novel to put oneself in. Therefore, **interviews** with the elderly participants are conducted to enable the experimenter to give hints or explanations where necessary.

2.1 Creation of Stimuli

In order to identify important aspects of different social situations that could be integrated into a computational model for an REA, different situations with varying social context factors are needed. For our endeavour, we created eight situations that are likely to be observed in this environment but cover a range of different types of context, while keeping other factors consistent (e.g., place and daytime): a birthday party, two friends playing a card game, two friends chatting about the good old times, two people being engaged in different independent things, a medical situation, an advice for a school report, an argument, and a situation with only one person reading a book.

Fig. 1. Scenes with different social context factors (left to right: card game, birthday party, interaction with caregiver)

All situations are embedded in a use case to support the imagination of participants. An elderly person, Rosa, is living in an elderly care home, where she is supported by her REA. All other persons are acquaintances of hers such as grand children, a caregiver, or other inhabitants of the elderly care home.

The scenarios were designed to contain many alternations in the other persons' age (and thereby age difference to the main person Rosa), number of people involved in a scene, objects that specify the scene (e.g. cake or playing cards on the table, work cloth), presence or absence of a conversation, and emotional displays. Figure 1 shows examples of these situations as recorded for our videos. In our fictive use case the task of the robot is to deliver messages and appointment reminders to its owner. To investigate the impact of their content, two messages types (delicate/non-delicate) and two appointment types (urgent/not urgent) were created. To illustrate that the robot is about to deliver a message/appointment reminder to its owner, for each situation a sequence with the robot approaching and opening a door was added to the videos subsequently showing the different social situations. Since in human-human-communication a few seconds are usually sufficient to judge a situation, the scenes of the different context situations lasted for 10 s each.

2.2 Interview Guidelines

The first question was a binary choice on the participants' general opinion whether the robot should deliver the message/reminder or not. Based on this choice, we wanted to know why they thought so and what features of the situation were the decisive factor. In case they decided that the message/reminder should be delivered, we asked the participant how the robot should deliver it. In case, they did not want the message to be delivered, we asked what the robot should do instead. In general, the interviewer should provide as little input as possible. Only in cases where the conversation got stuck, hints are provided that help the interviewee give the situation a second thought, e.g. "If you reconsider the situation, was your decision based on the persons involved?", or "If the robot should deliver the message would you like it to read it out loud?". Although interviews are video recorded for later analysis, the interviewer wrote down the answers of the participant to create pauses between the questions and sessions.

2.3 Feasibility Test

To ensure that the recorded videos with the different social context situations, the selected messages for the robot to deliver, and the questions prepared for the interviewer match the understanding and abilities of our target user group, a pre-study with three female participants (mean age = 81 years) was conducted. According to their comments and our impressions, the study material was refined. The short video clips in the pre-study showing the social context situation in which the robot needs to act were 10 s in length. Participants stated that this was too short to grasp the situation. This might be due to an decrease in speed of information processing that comes with age. Thus, videos were edited again to result in clips of 20 to 25 s each. Some of these eight videos recorded to exemplify different social context situations, were identified to be too similar to each other. Therefore, three videos were not used in the final study. The final videos were: (1) a birthday party, (2) two friends playing a card game, (3) a medical situation, (4) an argument, and (5) a situation with only one person reading a book.

Also the content of messages that the robot should deliver were adapted. For example, we designed a message containing the results of a medical test as being delicate. However, the elderly participants found the privacy level of this message quite normal to be shared in an elderly home, even during social situations. Thus, a message from the elderly care management was created that contained a reprimand for not fulfilling her duties in housekeeping again. The final messages were as follows:

- **Message delicate:** The care home manager wants to speak to you. She said you forgot again to do your assigned housekeeping tasks.
- **Message non-delicate:** Your daughter Bianca has send a message that she and your grand daughter will come to visit you next Friday.
- **Appointment urgent:** You have an important appointment with your doctor today at 2 pm. Your post surgery bandage has to be changed urgently.
- **Appointment non-urgent:** Tomorrow you are all going to the museum. Meeting point is the entrance hall at 10 am.

The number of messages and appointments was kept constant, as the pre-study revealed that the content thereof was of high relevance for the decisions of the elderly participants. The interviewer guideline was adapted to contain more reminders, for example, of what the current message was, and more structured questions were added to be asked in case the participant did not know how to respond.

3   Interview Study

3.1   Participants and Procedure

To investigate how elderly users judge different social situations, what are the factors that played a role in this judgement and what they would like a social robot to do in this situation, we conducted semi-structured interviews. Eight participants (mean age = 75; 5 female, 3 male) of a supported living home took part. One participant (female) did not feel well and we had to stop the interview before the intended end. Her answers until then were nevertheless analysed for our results.

The interviews took place with each participant individually in their personal flat within the supported living establishment. In the beginning, the manager of the elderly care home introduced the interviewer to the participant in order to get them acquainted and to build a friendly and professional basis. The interviewer explained the scope of the study, the background on social robots for elderly assistance, and that they were going to be videotaped. Before the interviews, participants were given an instruction sheet that contained pictures and information about our use case (e.g. Pepper the social robot, Rosa the owner of the robot, her grand children, her friends at the elderly care home). Then an introduction video with the robot was shown for the participants to understand that the robot needs to deliver a message to its owner and therefore has to judge the current situation the owner is in. For each video, participants were reminded of the process and then the current message was read out loudly and given in written form to them on a record card. Then they were asked to watch the video that was played on a laptop placed in front of them. After watching the video, the experimenter interviewed the participant according to her interview guidelines. The last steps were repeated for either both messages (delicate/non-delicate) or both appointments (urgent/non-urgent) for each of the five social

564   B. Lugrin et al.

situations. In that vein, each participant gave his or her opinion ten times (four participants saw all videos with urgent and non-urgent reminders; four participants saw all videos with delicate and non-delicate messages). After the last interview, the participant was thanked and filled in a data privacy statement. During the whole time participants were given enough time to ask further questions. The whole session lasted between 30 and 50 min per participant. For later analysis the videos of the interviews were transcribed.

3.2 Results and Discussion

Delivery of Message/Reminder. Regarding the first question, whether the message/reminder should be delivered, both the message type and the social situation were important (see Figs. 2 and 3).

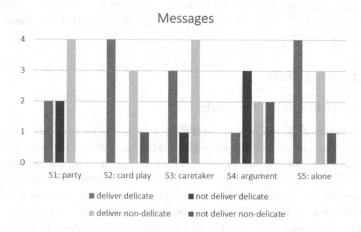

Fig. 2. Total number of times participants (did not) want(ed) messages to be delivered.

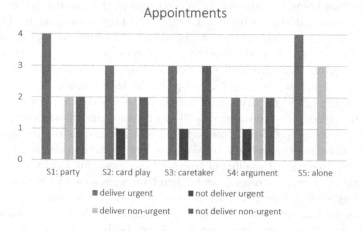

Fig. 3. Total number of times participants (did not) want(ed) appointments to be delivered.

Generally, the four participants evaluating the different messages (delicate/non-delicate) decided that messages should rather be delivered ($n = 30$; 14 times for the delicate message, 16 times for the non-delicate message) then not delivered ($n = 10$; 6 times for the delicate message, 4 times for the non-delicate message). The only exception is situation 4, an argument between the owner of the robot and her grandchild, in which messages should rather not be delivered. It seems that older adults rather want to receive their messages right away except in the case where they are in a highly negative emotional situation where delivering a message is misplaced.

For appointment reminders, the type of appointment is more crucial for the decision. While the urgent appointment should mainly be delivered (16 times delivery, 3 times no delivery), the non-urgent appointment should only be delivered in half of the situations (9 times delivery, 9 times no delivery). This means that especially for non-urgent reminders social robots needs to pay attention to the situation since delivering the reminder might more easily be perceived as unnecessary in that specific situation, and thus bothersome.

Identifying Social Context Factors. In the second question following each video, participants should indicate reasons why they think the message or reminder should be delivered or not. We qualitatively analysed the participants' answers in order to identify possible situational context factors that we can study in more detail in upcoming studies. The interview answers support what we discussed in the motivation section of this paper. When humans decide whether or not to deliver a message this happens in a split-second without cognitive effort. Hence, we might not have cognitive access to the different bits of information that were the basis for this decision. In this regard, people did not clearly mention factors that we assumed were important for the decision such as the presence of other people, the content of the conversation, and so forth. Their judgements were rarely motivated by what we argued to be situational factors, but were very personal judgements often based on interpersonal relationships. For instance, participants mentioned that frequently "for me personally it is (not) okay to interrupt a party" (no interruption: because celebrating is too important in that age; interruption: because celebration can be continued after message), and they "do not mind when other people (family, care personnel) hear that message" (because they have less privacy anyway in a care home; because it might be beneficial if others hear the message/reminder and could also remind the person or help with the message). Interrupting within the argument was justified with the statement "sometimes it is good when someone interrupts an argument". Additionally, the interviews revealed that the valence of the message seemed to be an important factor. Several participants mentioned that the visit of a relative is a very positive, and thus important, event and can therefore be shared at any time and with other people. Socially delicate information (like not attending to one's duties) was judged as mildly unpleasant if mentioned in front of others but that depended on the people in the room. For instance, family members and staff were okay to hear the messages. Important to us was that participants' views on delicate/non-delicate information and privacy concerns deviated from what we expected. The pre-study showed that, in contrast to our assumption, elderly inhabitants would not like to have medical information about them overheard, they actually regarded this as normal in their environment. In the main study, we also expected participants to be more selective about delivering the delicate message, but it was rather seen as social information that can be discussed with family members, friends or care personnel. Also, in some cases the fear of not being able to understand the robot due to background noise, or of fearing to not remember the message after the current social situation played a role during the decisions.

How to Deliver the Message/What to Do Instead. Regarding the question how the message/reminder should be delivered, is was overall most desirable that the message was read out aloud. Delivering a written information was mainly mentioned to serve as an additional reminder, or this option was mentioned linked to certain pre-conditions such as the presence of strangers or if the message was of an intimate nature. In cases participants decided that the message/appointment reminder should not be delivered, they wished the robot wait until the ongoing social situation was over or that the REA should ask for permission whether it is allowed to speak.

4   Conclusion and Future Work

With the ultimate goal to build a computational model of social context for a Robotic Elderly Assistant (REA), we conducted an interview study with elderly participants who reported their ideas on a fictive use case with a REA that helps its owner in a supported living home by reminding her on appointments and delivering messages. Therefore videos with different social situations were created. Our results suggest that both, the type of message/appointment as well as the social situation were important for the judgements of our participants, but also other factors such as the background noise, or the own ability to concentrate. They also highlight the need for a very structured and guided approach to gain elderly peoples' assessment suitable for a technical implementation. We expected to receive information on which visual or interaction information people use for making decisions in order to extract factors that can easily be modelled. This was obviously not the granularity of information people are consciously considering. This insight helps us to generate more higher-level social factors and their parameters such as relationship status of interactants and social rules [7]. The insights of the present study allow us to conduct further studies where the ideas mentioned by participants will be used as predefined answers from which future participants can choose how important or unimportant they rate them regarding their decision making.

Acknowledgements. We thank the inhabitants and staff of the Elisenstift in Schillingsfuerst for their help in recording the videos. We thank Thomas Zatloukal for his help in organizing the interviews and establishing contact with the participants, and the inhabitants of the elderly care home of Arbeiterwohlfahrt Wuerzburg for taking part in the interviews.

References

1. Abowd, G.D., Dey, A.K., Brown, P.J., Davies, N., Smith, M., Steggles, P.: Towards a better understanding of context and context-awareness. In: Gellersen, H.-W. (ed.) HUC 1999. LNCS, vol. 1707, pp. 304–307. Springer, Heidelberg (1999). https://doi.org/10.1007/3-540-48157-5_29
2. Bartl, A., Bosch, S., Brandt, M., Dittrich, M., Lugrin, B.: The influence of a social robot's persona on how it is perceived and accepted by elderly users. In: Agah, A., Cabibihan, J.-J., Howard, A.M., Salichs, M.A., He, H. (eds.) ICSR 2016. LNCS (LNAI), vol. 9979, pp. 681–691. Springer, Cham (2016). https://doi.org/10.1007/978-3-319-47437-3_67
3. Böhle, K., Pfadenhauer, M.: Social robots call for social sciences. Sci. Technol. Innov. Stud. 10(1), 3–10 (2014). http://www.sti-studies.de/ojs/index.php/sti/article/view/160/123
4. Broadbent, E., Stafford, R., MacDonald, B.: Acceptance of healthcare robots for the older population: review and future directions. Int. J. Soc. Robot. 1(4), 319 (2009). https://doi.org/10.1007/s12369-009-0030-6
5. Burke, M.A., Young, P., Jackson, M.: Norms, Customs, and Conventions. Handbook for Social Economics. Elsevier, Amsterdam (2010)
6. Hammer, S., Lugrin, B., Bogomolov, S., Janowski, K., André, E.: Investigating politeness strategies and their persuasiveness for a robotic elderly assistant. In: Meschtscherjakov, A., De Ruyter, B., Fuchsberger, V., Murer, M., Tscheligi, M. (eds.) PERSUASIVE 2016. LNCS, vol. 9638, pp. 315–326. Springer, Cham (2016). https://doi.org/10.1007/978-3-319-31510-2_27
7. Riek, L.D., Robinson, P.: Challenges and opportunities in building socially intelligent machines [social sciences]. IEEE Signal Process. Mag. 28(3), 146–149 (2011). https://doi.org/10.1109/MSP.2011.940412
8. Mast, M., et al.: User-centered design of a dynamic-autonomy remote interaction concept for manipulation-capable robots to assist elderly people in the home. J. Hum.-Robot Interact. 1(1), 96–118 (2012). https://doi.org/10.5898/JHRI.1.1.Mast
9. Xu, Q., et al.: The role of social context in human-robot interaction. In: Khalid, H.M. (ed.) 2012 Southeast Asian Network of Ergonomics Societies Conference (SEANES). IEEE, Piscataway, NJ (2012). https://doi.org/10.1109/SEANES.2012.6299594
10. Jain, R., Sinha, P.: Content without context is meaningless. In: Proceedings of the 18th ACM International Conference on Multimedia, Firenze, Italy, pp. 1259–1268. ACM (2010). https://doi.org/10.1145/1873951.1874199
11. Rosenthal-von der Pütten, A.M., Bock, N., Brockmann, K.: Not your cup of tea? How interacting with a robot can increase perceived self-efficacy in HRI. In: Mutlu, B., Tscheligi, M. (eds.) Proceedings of the 2017 ACMIEEE International Conference on Human-Robot Interaction. ACM, New York, NY (2017). https://doi.org/10.1145/2909824.3020251
12. Woods, S., Walters, M., Koay, K.L., Dautenhahn, K.: Comparing human robot interaction scenarios using live and video based methods: towards a novel methodological approach. In: 9th IEEE International Workshop on Advanced Motion Control, pp. 750–755 (2006). https://doi.org/10.1109/AMC.2006.1631754

Improving the Interaction of Older Adults with a Socially Assistive Table Setting Robot

Samuel Olatunji[✉], Noa Markfeld, Dana Gutman, Shai Givati,
Vardit Sarne-Fleischmann, Tal Oron-Gilad, and Yael Edan

Ben-Gurion University of the Negev, Beer-Sheva, Israel
olatunji@post.bgu.ac.il

Abstract. This study provides user-studies aimed at exploring factors influencing the interaction between older adults and a robotic table setting assistant. The influence of level of automation (LOA) and level of transparency (LOT) on the quality of the interaction was considered. Results revealed that the interaction effect of LOA and LOT significantly influenced the interaction. A low LOA which required the user to control some of the actions of the robot influenced the older adults to participate more in the interaction when the LOT was high (more information) compared to situations with low LOT (less information) and high LOA (more robot autonomy). Even though, the higher LOA influenced more fluency in the interaction, the lower LOA encouraged a more collaborative form of interaction which is a priority in the design of robotic aids for older adult users. The results provide some insights into shared control designs which accommodates the preferences of the older adult users as they interact with robotic aids such as the table setting robot used in this study.

Keywords: Shared control · Levels of automation · Transparency · Collaborative robots · Human-robot interaction

1 Introduction

Robots with improved capabilities are advancing into prominent roles while assisting older adults in performing daily living tasks such as cleaning, dressing, feeding (Honig et al. 2018; Shishehgar et al. 2018). This has to be done with careful consideration for the strong desire of these older adults to maintain a certain level of autonomy while performing their daily living tasks, even if the robot provides the help they require (Wu et al. 2016). Furthermore, the robot's involvement should not drive the older adult to boredom, sedentariness or loss of skills relevant to daily living due to prolonged inactivity (Beer et al. 2014). A possible solution is shared control where the user preferences are adequately considered as the robot's role and actions are being defined during the interaction design. This ensures that the older adults are not deprived of the independence they desire (Zwijsen et al. 2011).

This study, proposes a shared control strategy using levels of automation (LOA) which refers to the degree to which the robot would perform particular functions in its defined role of assisting the user in a specific task (Parasuraman et al. 2008). The aim is to ensure high quality collaboration between the older adult and the robot in

© Springer Nature Switzerland AG 2019
M. A. Salichs et al. (Eds.): ICSR 2019, LNAI 11876, pp. 568–577, 2019.
https://doi.org/10.1007/978-3-030-35888-4_53

accomplishing desired tasks, without undermining the autonomy, preferences and satisfaction of the older adult.

To ensure transparency of the robot's role at all times, the LOA implementation is reflected in the ways through which the users interact with the robots. Transparency in this context is the degree of task-related information provided by the robot to the older adults to keep them aware of its state, actions and intentions of the robot (Chen et al. 2018). The content of this information provided by the robot can be graded according to the detail, quantity and type of information as mirrored in Endsley's situation awareness (SA) study (Endsley 1995) and Chen et al.'s SA-based Transparency model (Chen et al. 2014). It is essential that the level of transparency (LOT) of the information being presented to the older adults conforms with their perceptual and cognitive peculiarities such as the processing and interpretation of the information provided by the robot (Smarr et al. 2014; Mitzner et al. 2015; Feingold Polak et al. 2018). Existing studies reveal that the information presented to the users significantly influences their comprehension of the robot's behavior, performance and limitations (Dzindolet et al. 2003; Lyons 2013; Chen et al. 2014). This information facilitates the users' knowledge of the automation connected to the task (Endsley 2017). This affects the users' understanding of their role and that of the robot in any given interaction (Lyons 2013; Chen et al. 2014; Doran et al. 2017; Hellström and Bensch 2018).

Some studies explored the presentation of information through various technological aids such as digital mobile applications, webpages, rehabilitation equipment, and other facilities through which older adults would interact with their environment (Cen/Cenelec 2002; Fisk et al. 2009; Mitzner et al. 2015). These studies, provided recommendations which served as design guidelines for information presented in various modes such as visual, audial or haptic information. These recommendations are not specific to information presented by robots to the older adults. They are general guidelines recommended to aid usability as older adults interact with technological devices. It was therefore recommended in those studies that more user studies should be conducted in specific robot-assistance domains such physical support, social interaction, safety monitoring, cognitive stimulation and rehabilitation (Cen/Cenelec 2002; Fisk et al. 2009; Mitzner et al. 2015; Van Wynsberghe 2016). Through such studies, suitable design parameters could be identified that would meet the needs of the older adults in specific applications such as the table setting robot application on which this study is focused.

The aforementioned studies have explored individual effects of LOA or LOT separately in different domains. But this has not been examined in the use of socially assistive robots for older people. LOA, as a control strategy, tends to improve the collaboration between the user and the robot by sufficiently keeping the user in the loop. This is critical in older adults' interaction with robots in order to avoid inactiveness. LOT, as an information presentation strategy, also tends to improve the awareness of the user during the interaction. This is also critical for the older adults to ensure that they are constantly carried along in the interaction. We therefore hypothesize that exploring some LOA and LOT options in robot-assisted tasks could increase the engagement and satisfaction of the older adults as they interact with the robots. The current study aims to explore how LOA and LOT influences the quality of interaction (QoI) between the older adults and the assistive robot in a shared task of table setting.

The QoI is a construct in this paper which entails the fluency, understanding, engagement and comfortability during the interaction.

2 Methods

2.1 Overview

A table setting task performed by a robotic arm was used as the case study. The robot had to pick up a plate, a cup, a fork and a knife and to place them at preset positions on the table. The user operated the robot in two levels of automation. In the high LOA condition, the robot operated autonomously. The user could only start and stop the robot's operation by pressing a specific button. In the low LOA condition, the user could still start and stop the robot, but the robot required the user's consent before setting each item. The robot asked the user through a GUI which item to bring and the user was required to respond before the robot could continue its operation.

Two conditions utilizing different levels of transparency (LOT) were compared for two different levels of the robot's automation: high and low (Table 1). Information was given by the robot in visual form through a GUI on an adjacent screen where the LOT manipulated (Fig. 1). The two conditions differed by the amount of details provided by the robot. The low level of information included text messages that specified the status of the robot by indicating **what** it was doing (e.g. bringing a plate, putting a fork, etc.), while the high level of information included also the **reason** for this status (i.e. I'm bringing the plate since you asked me, etc.)

Table 1. Experimental conditions.

LOT	LOA	
	Low	High
Low	Condition 1 – LL User instructs the robot using the GUI and receives information about **what** the robot is doing in each stage	Condition 3 – LH Robot operates automatically. In each stage user receives information about **what** the robot is doing
High	Condition 2 – HL User instructs the robot using the GUI and receives information about what the robot is doing and the reason for it in each stage	Condition 4 – HH Robot operates automatically. In each stage user receives information about **what** the robot is doing and the **reason** for it

2.2 Apparatus

A KUKA LBR iiwa 14 R820 7 degrees of freedom robotic arm equipped with a pneumatic gripper was used (Fig. 1). The tasks were programmed using python and executed on the ROS (Schaefer 2015) platform.

In order to instruct the robot and to present the information received by the robot a graphical user interface (GUI) was used on a PC screen, which was located on a desk to the left of the user (see Fig. 1).

Fig. 1. A participant using the GUI to instruct the robot.

2.3   Participants

Fourteen older adults (8 Females, 6 Males) aged 62–82 (mean 69.8) participated in the study. Participants were recruited through an advertisement which was publicized electronically. They were healthy individuals with no physical disability who came independently to the lab. Each participant completed the study separately at different timeslots, so there was no contact between participants.

2.4   Experimental Design

The experiment was set with a mixed between and within subject design with the LOA modes as the between subject variable, and the LOT as the within subject variable.

Participants were assigned randomly to one of the two LOA conditions. All participants completed the same table setting task for both levels of transparency. The order of the two tasks was counterbalanced between participants, to accommodate for potential bias of learning effects, boredom or fatigue.

2.5   Performance Measures

Initially, participants completed a pre-test questionnaire which included the following: demographic information, and a subset of questions from the Technology Adoption Propensity (TAP) index (Ratchford and Barnhart 2012) to assess their level of experience with technology and from the Negative Attitude toward Robots Scale (NARS) (Syrdal et al. 2009) to assess their level of anxiety towards robots.

Objective measures that were collected during each session are interaction-related variables such as fluency, engagement, understanding and comfortability. Subjective measures were assessed via questionnaires. Participants completed a short post-session questionnaire after each session and a final questionnaire at the end of the two sessions to evaluate subjective measures. The post-session questionnaire used 5-point Likert scales with 5 representing "Strongly agree" and 1 representing "Strongly disagree". The final questionnaire related to the difference between both sessions.

2.6   Analysis

A two-tailed General Linear Mixed Model (GLMM) analysis was performed to evaluate for a positive or negative effect of the independent variables. The user ID was included as a random effect to account for individual differences. LOA and LOT were utilized as fixed factors while all objective and subjective variables representing 'Quality of Interaction' (QoC) were used as dependent variables.

3   Results

3.1   Demographics and Attitude Towards Technology

There was an equal distribution of participants within the two groups. On a scale of 1 (strongly disagree) to 5 (strongly agree), the TAP index reveals that most of the participants are optimistic about technology providing more control and flexibility in life (*mean = 3.86, SD = 1.17*). It was also observed that over 75% of the participants like to learn the use of new technology (*mean = 3.93, SD = 1.07*) and feel comfortable communicating with robots (*mean = 3.43, SD = 1.50*). The majority (80%) did not have negative feelings about situations in which they have to interact with a robot (*mean = 4.14, SD = 0.86*).

3.2   Quality of Interaction

A two-way ANOVA was run to find out if there was a significant difference between the LOA-LOT manipulation as conditions ($F(3, 22) = 2.35, p = 0.033$). The effect of the manipulation was significant on the robot's idle time ($F(3, 22) = 4.91, p = 0.009$), functional delay ($F(3, 22) = 21.22, p < 0.001$), human idle time ($F(3, 22) = 3.03, p = 0.005$), the gaze on the robot ($F(3, 22) = 3.97, p = 0.021$), perception of safety ($F(3, 22) = 3.22, p = 0.042$) and overall interaction time ($F(3, 22) = 5.31, p = 0.007$). The effect of the manipulation was not significant on the gaze on the GUI where the robot provided feedback ($F(3, 22) = 2.01, p = 0.142$). More details of the components of the quality of interaction are presented below.

3.3   Fluency

Fluency was represented by the idle time of the robot, functional delay and overall time spent on the task. The LOA was significant on the robot's idle time (*mean = 122.54, SD = 59.70, $F(1, 24) = 9.97, p = 0.004$*) with the high LOA (*mean = 88.85, SD = 2.48*) having a lower robot idle time compared to low LOA (*mean 156.21, SD = 70.38*). The LOT was not significant as a main effect but there was a significant effect in the interaction between the LOA and LOT ($F(4, 24) = 44.2, p < 0.001$) as depicted in Fig. 2. In terms of delay (*mean = 12.86, SD = 13.87*), the LOA was significant ($F(1, 24) = 14.48, p = 0.001$). The low LOA had more delays (*mean = 20.85, SD = 15.99*) than high LOA *(mean = 4.87, SD = 13.87)*. The LOT was not significant *(F(1, 24) = 2.04, p = 0.17)*. There was also no interaction effect of the LOA and LOT on the delays *(F(1, 24) = 1.49, p = 0.23)*. The duration of the experiment with low LOA *(mean = 239.21, SD = 74.41)* were longer than that with high LOA *(mean = 158.53, SD = 66.17)*. This was also statistically significant *(mean = 198.53, SD = 66.17, F(1, 24) = 15.42, p = 0.001)*. The results therefore suggest that high LOA influenced more fluency in the interaction than low LOA.

3.4   Engagement

The duration of the gaze on the robot was significantly affected by LOA *(mean = 155.64, SD = 34.51, p = 0.006)*. Participants in low LOA *(mean = 175.57, SD = 34.77)* gazed on the robot more than participants in high LOA *(mean = 135.71, SD = 20.22)*. The interaction between LOA and LOT on the time participants gazed on the robot was significant *(F(1,24) = 7.83, p = 0.01)*. Participants in low LOA *(mean = 35.50, SD = 17.81)* were also more significantly focused on the GUI *(mean = 27.01, SD = 19.60, p = 0.037)* than participants in high LOA *(mean = 18.643, SD = 18.10)*. The interaction between LOA and LOT was significant regarding the focus on GUI *(F(1, 24) = 4.48, p = 0.045)*. The effect of LOA on the human's active time was also significant *(mean = 16.39, SD = 16.62, p < 0.001)* with low LOA *(mean = 31.07, SD = 10.47)* keeping the human more active than the high LOA *(mean = 1.71, SD = 0.82)*. There was an interaction effect between the LOA and LOT *(F(1, 24) = 47.28, p < 0.001)*.

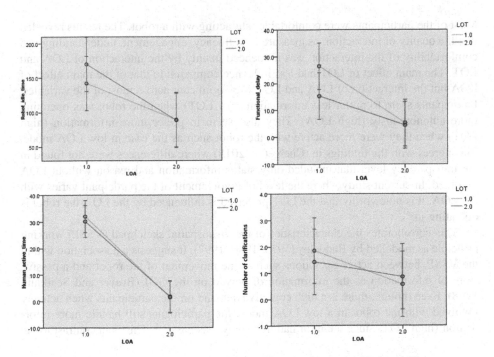

Fig. 2. Interaction effect of LOA and LOT on various some QoI variables

3.5 Understanding

There was no significant difference in the number of clarifications made by the participants during the interaction (*mean = 1.18, SD = 1.59, p = 0.124*) as a result of the LOA manipulation. The participants seemed to understand the status of the interaction and actions of the robot in both LOA and LOT modes (*F(1, 24) = 2.27, p = 0.15*). Only a few participants asked for clarification at the low LOA (*mean = 1.64, SD = 1.95*) and high LOA modes (*mean = 0.71, SD = 0.99*). However, in terms of reaction time of the participants as the robot interacted with them, the LOA was significant (*mean = 12.86, SD = 13.87, p = 0.001*). The participants spent more time observing and processing the information the robot was presenting to them as consent in the low LOA (*mean = 20.85, SD = 15.99*) compared to the high LOA (*mean = 4.87, SD = 13.87*).

3.6 Comfortability

The effect of the LOA and LOT did not influence the heart rate of the participants. But it was also not significant on the comfortability of the participants with regards to their perception of safety of the robot (*mean = 2.54, SD = 0.58, p = 0.48*). However, it was observed that participants in low LOA moved much closer to the robot which represented more comfortability with it than participants in high LOA which sat further away from the robot.

4 Discussion and Conclusion

Most of the participants were comfortable interacting with a robot. The results revealed that the quality of interaction, as measured via fluency, engagement, understanding and comfortability of the interaction was influenced mainly by the interaction of LOA and LOT. The main effect of LOT had less influence compared to that of the main effect of LOA but the interaction of LOA and LOT was significant across most of the variables. Participants seem to prefer less information (low LOT) when the robot was operating more autonomously (high LOA). They also seem to prefer more information (high LOT) when they were more active with the robot such as the case in low LOA mode. This agrees with the findings in (Chen et al. 2018) where differences were not found in the transparency level that included only status information and reason without LOA involved. In current study where the level of involvement of the participant varies with the LOA, it is noteworthy that the LOT preferred is influenced by the LOA the robot is operating in.

This corroborates the characteristics of the visuospatial sketchpad (VSSP) working principle as modelled by Baddeley (1975, 1986, 1997). It suggests a dissociation within the VSSP, between active operations such as the movement of the robot and a passive store of information as the information displayed on the GUI (Bruyer and Scailquin 1998). Even though, there is a high cognitive demand on the participants when actively involved with the robot in a low LOA mode, the participants still handle more information (high LOT) since the information display was passive. This is in contrast to the scenario where the robot was more autonomous (high LOA), with less cognitive demand on the participant.

Future research should advance a longitudinal study, to increase familiarity with the robot operation and overcome the suspected naivety effect (Shah and Wiken 2011; Kirchner and Alempijevic 2012) of the older adults with the robot. We expect that the more the older adults get familiar with the operation of the robot, their level of trust in the robot may change and thus cause a change in their LOT demands as well.

According to the participants' recommendations more awareness might be improved through voice feedback. This possibility is also supported by the suggestion of (Sobczak-Edmans *et al.* 2016) indicating that some form of verbal representation of information supports visual representations. This should be explored in future work to improve the shared control of the older adult with the table setting robot.

Previous research in human robot collaboration discovered the effectiveness of coordination in team performance as presented in (Shah and Wiken 2011). Our work further presents the potential of LOA in improving quality of interaction. This is reflected in the various objective measures taken for engagement, fluency, degree of involvement and comfortability with the robot where the LOA effect was significant. The low LOA enabled the participant to interact more with the robot by selecting the specific item that the robot should pick up and the order of arrangement. This inspired greater collaboration with the robot. It enhanced the concept of shared control where the user is more involved in the decisions and control of the robot's operations. This is very critical to ensure that the older adult keeps active so as not to lose skills or functionality of the muscles (Wu et al. 2014). This corresponds with the "use it or lose it" logic presented by (Katzman 1995) in their study of older adult lifestyle.

Most studies which included some form of adaptive coordination to improve the collaboration between the robot and the user (Huang et al. 2015; Someshwar and Edan 2017) tried to reduce the completion time of the task. There was a trade off in this current study regarding degree of involvement and time to complete task i.e., at a higher degree of user involvement, more time was spent to complete the task. It is noteworthy that the focus for the target population is to ensure user involvement to avoid idleness and other negative outcomes of sedentariness and not speed. Moreover, most participants expressed enjoyment, and pleasure as they interacted with the robot, which suggests other reasons for the longer interactive time. This can therefore be considered as a positive outcome of the interaction and a favorable contribution to improve shared control in human-robot interaction scenarios such as this.

Acknowledgments. This research was supported by the EU funded Innovative Training Network (ITN) in the Marie Skłodowska-Curie People Programme (Horizon2020): SOCRATES (Social Cognitive Robotics in a European Society training research network), grant agreement number 721619 and by the Ministry of Science Fund, grant agreement number 47897. Partial support was provided by Ben-Gurion University of the Negev through the Helmsley Charitable Trust, the Agricultural, Biological and Cognitive Robotics Initiative, the Marcus Endowment Fund, the Center for Digital Innovation research fund, the Rabbi W. Gunther Plaut Chair in Manufacturing Engineering and the George Shrut Chair in Human Performance Management.

References

Baddeley, A.D., et al.: Imagery and visual working memory. In: Rabbitt, P.M.A., Domic, S. (eds.) Attention and Performance V. Academic Press, London (1975)

Baddeley, A.D.: Working Memory. Issue 11 O. Oxford University Press, Oxford (1986). Issue 11 O. Clarendon Press

Baddeley, A.D.: Human Memory: Theory and Practice, Revised edn. Psychology Press Ltd., Taylor and Francis Group, New York (1997)

Beer, J.M., Fisk, A.D., Rogers, W.A.: Toward a framework for levels of robot autonomy in human-robot interaction. J. Hum.-Robot Interact. 3(2), 74 (2014). https://doi.org/10.5898/JHRI.3.2.Beer

Bruyer, R., Scailquin, J.C.: The visuospatial sketchpad for mental images: testing the multicomponent model of working memory. Acta Psychol. 98(1), 17–36 (1998). https://doi.org/10.1016/S0001-6918(97)00053-X

Cen/Cenelec. Guidelines for standards developers to address the needs of older persons and persons with disabilities, Edition 1, January 2002, CEN/CENELE (January), p. 31. (2002). ftp://cencenelec.eu/CENELEC/Guides/CENCLC/6_CENCLCGuide6.pdf

Chen, J.Y.C., et al.: Situation Awareness – Based Agent Transparency (No. ARL-TR-6905) (2014)

Chen, J.Y.C.: Situation awareness-based agent transparency and human-autonomy teaming effectiveness. Theoret. Issues Ergon. Sci. 19(3), 259–282 (2018). https://doi.org/10.1080/1463922X.2017.1315750

Doran, D., Schulz, S., Besold, T.R.: What does explainable AI really mean? a new conceptualization of perspectives (2017). http://arxiv.org/abs/1710.00794

Dzindolet, M.T., et al.: The role of trust in automation reliance. Int. J. Hum. Comput. Stud. 58(6), 697–718 (2003). https://doi.org/10.1016/S1071-5819(03)00038-7

Endsley, M.R.: Toward a theory of situation awareness in dynamic systems. Hum. Factors: J. Hum. Factors Ergon. Soc. 37(1), 32–64 (1995). https://doi.org/10.1518/001872095779049543

Endsley, M.R.: From here to autonomy. Hum. Factors 59(1), 5–27 (2017). https://doi.org/10.1177/0018720816681350

Feingold Polak, R., et al.: Differences between young and old users when interacting with a humanoid robot. In: Companion of the 2018 ACM/IEEE International Conference on Human-Robot Interaction - HRI 2018, New York, New York, USA, pp. 107–108. ACM Press (2018). https://doi.org/10.1145/3173386.3177046

Fisk, A.D., et al.: Designing for older adults. Geogr. J. (2009). https://doi.org/10.1201/9781420080681

Hellström, T., Bensch, S.: Understandable robots - what, why, and how. Paladyn, J. Behav. Robot 9, 110–123 (2018)

Honig, S.S., et al: Towards socially aware person-following robots. IEEE Trans. Cogn. Dev. Syst. p. 1 (2018). https://doi.org/10.1109/TCDS.2018.2825641

Huang, C.-M., Cakmak, M., Mutlu, B.: Adaptive coordination strategies for human-robot handovers. Designing Gaze Cues for Social Robots View project CoSTAR View project Adaptive Coordination Strategies for Human-Robot Handovers. In: 2015 Robotics, Science and Systems Conference (2015). https://doi.org/10.15607/RSS.2015.XI.031

Katzman, R.: Can late life social or leisure activities delay the onset of dementia? J. Am. Geriatr. Soc. 43(5), 583–584 (1995). https://doi.org/10.1111/j.1532-5415.1995.tb06112.x

Kirchner, N., Alempijevic, A.: A robot centric perspective on the HRI paradigm. J. Hum.-Robot Interact. 1(2), 135–157 (2012). https://doi.org/10.5898/JHRI.1.2.Kirchner

Lyons, J.B.: Being transparent about transparency : a model for human-robot interaction. In: Trust and Autonomous Systems: Papers from the 2013 AAAI Spring Symposium, pp. 48–53 (2013)

Mitzner, T.L., et al: Adult's perceptual abilities.pdf. In: The Cambridge Handbook of Applied Perception Research, pp. 1051–1079 (2015)

Parasuraman, R., Sheridan, T.B., Wickens, C.D.: Situation awareness, mental workload, and trust in automation: viable, empirically supported cognitive engineering constructs. J. Cogn. Eng. Decis. Making 2(2), 140–160 (2008). https://doi.org/10.1518/155534308X284417

Ratchford, M., Barnhart, M.: Development and validation of the technology adoption propensity (TAP) index. J. Bus. Res. 65(8), 1209–1215 (2012). https://doi.org/10.1016/j.jbusres.2011. 07.001

Schaefer, K.E.: Programming robots with ROS a practical introduction to the robot operating system. J. Chem. Inf. Model. (2015). https://doi.org/10.1017/CBO9781107415324.004

Shah, J., Wiken, J.: Improved human-robot team performance using Chaski, a human-inspired plan execution system. Artif. Intell. 29–36 (2011). https://www.researchgate.net/publication/ 221473232_Improved_human-robot_team_performance_using_Chaski_a_human-inspired_ plan_execution_system

Shishehgar, M., Kerr, D., Blake, J.: A systematic review of research into how robotic technology can help older people. Smart Health (2018). https://doi.org/10.1016/j.smhl.2018.03.002

Smarr, C.A.: Domestic robots for older adults: attitudes, preferences, and potential. Int. J. Soc. Robot. 6(2), 229–247 (2014). https://doi.org/10.1007/s12369-013-0220-0

Sobczak-Edmans, M.: Temporal dynamics of visual working memory. NeuroImage 124, 1021– 1030 (2016). https://doi.org/10.1016/j.neuroimage.2015.09.038

Someshwar, R., Edan, Y.: Givers & receivers perceive handover tasks differently: implications for human-robot collaborative system design (2017). ArXiv http://arxiv.org/abs/1708.06207. Accessed 7 Apr 2019

Syrdal, D.S., et al: The negative attitudes towards robots scale and reactions to robot behaviour in a live human-robot interaction study. In: 23rd Convention of the Society for the Study of Artificial Intelligence and Simulation of Behaviour, AISB, pp. 109–115. (2009). https://doi. org/10.1.1.159.9791

Wu, Y.-H.: Acceptance of an assistive robot in older adults: a mixed-method study of human-robot interaction over a 1-month period in the Living Lab setting. Clin. Interv. Aging 9, 801– 811 (2014). https://doi.org/10.2147/CIA.S56435

Wu, Y.-H.: The attitudes and perceptions of older adults with mild cognitive impairment toward an assistive robot. J. Appl. Gerontol. 35(1), 3–17 (2016). https://doi.org/10.1177/ 0733464813515092

Van Wynsberghe, A.: Service robots, care ethics, and design. Ethics Inf. Technol. 18(4) (2016). https://doi.org/10.1007/s10676-016-9409-x

Zwijsen, S.A., Niemeijer, A.R., Hertogh, C.M.P.M.: Ethics of using assistive technology in the care for community-dwelling elderly people: an overview of the literature. Aging Ment. Health 15(4), 419–427 (2011). https://doi.org/10.1080/13607863.2010.543662

Towards Socially Acceptable, Human-Aware Robot Navigation

Noelia Fernández Coleto$^{(\boxtimes)}$, Eduardo Ruiz Ramírez, Frederik Haarslev, and Leon Bodenhagen

SDU Robotics, Maersk Mc-Kinney Moller Insitute,
University of Southern Denmark, Odense, Denmark
fernandezcoletonoelia@gmail.com, {err,fh,lebo}@mmmi.sdu.dk

Abstract. The introduction of service robots to our daily life requires adaptation of the current navigation strategies. In the presence of humans, robots must be designed to ensure their safety and comfort. This paper proposes a layered costmap architecture that incorporates social norms to generate trajectories compatible with human preferences. The implemented framework creates a social abstraction of the environment – in the form of an occupancy grid – to plan human-friendly paths. It employs information about individuals in the scene to model their personal spaces. In addition, it uses predicted human trajectories to improve the efficiency and legibility of the robot trajectory. Different simulation scenarios resembling everyday situations have been used to evaluate the proposed framework. The results of the experiments have demonstrated its ability to behave according to social conventions. Furthermore, the navigation system was assessed in real life experiments where it was proved capable of following similar paths to those performed by humans.

Keywords: Socially acceptable navigation · HRI · Personal space

1 Introduction

The introduction of service robots in our daily life is growing day by day; hence, the need for intelligent mobile robots to be able to navigate in dynamic environments where the presence of humans is expected. Furthermore, a robot should not only carry out its tasks efficiently but also in a human-friendly way, adapting its behavior according to social conventions. During the last years researchers have developed different approaches to human-aware navigation; a commonly used strategy is based on the generation of a social map that models human space according to social conventions and interaction among individuals, using as a reference the studies presented by Hall [4] and Kendon et al. [5].

Papadakis et al. [8] proposed a method based on the use of non-stationary, skew-normal probability density functions for describing the social zones related to single individuals as well as associations among humans. The experiments carried out have proven the correct interpersonal spaces modeling of their proposed

© Springer Nature Switzerland AG 2019
M. A. Salichs et al. (Eds.): ICSR 2019, LNAI 11876, pp. 578–587, 2019.
https://doi.org/10.1007/978-3-030-35888-4_54

method; however, it entails the human interacting with the robot which is inadequate in some situations. A similar method was suggested by Charalampous et al. [3]. In addition, the approach presented by Vega et al. [11] proposed a human aware navigation strategy which uses an adaptive spatial density function to cluster groups of people according to their spatial arrangement and the environment. It uses also affordance spaces for defining potential activity spaces. The major drawback of this approach is that it assumes a static environment which can lead to an erratic robot navigation. Truong and Ngo [9] presented a solution that models group formations and human-object interactions, using social force models and the reciprocal velocity obstacle model. Experiments conducted in simulation and in an office environment demonstrate smooth operation in the presence of static or moving obstacles.

Kruse et al. [7] studied human behaviors in a path crossing situation in order to generate similar trajectories for robots. They use a linear projection of the human path based on his velocity to describe the context according to the human movement. Although the experiments demonstrated that the robot could perform distinct trajectories by velocity adaptation and waiting behavior, it has been only evaluated for the crossing scenario in simulation. On the other hand, the work in [6] uses predicted human trajectories and a social cost function to plan collision-free paths that take social constraints into account. It has been proven that it can generate consistent paths which respect to social conventions. However, the proposed method is only concerned with following a given trajectory, it does not perform any collision avoidance for unexpected obstacles, furthermore, the use of several descriptive costmaps involve a high computational cost if it would be utilized constantly during the navigation.

In order to equip the robot with a description of the situation, including information about individual personal spaces, possible groups arrangements, and future conflictive areas, this work proposes the development of three costmap layers as plugins for the current ROS Navigation Stack. This allows usage independence between layers and an easy implementation on systems using ROS as architecture. Each developed layer was individually tested under different circumstances to ensure it was capable of creating appropriate costmaps. Simulation and real life experiments were performed and their results were evaluated.

2   Methodology

The costmap layers developed in this work are explained in the following subsections. These layers work in combination with the default static, obstacle and inflation layers provided by ROS [1].

2.1   Human Layer

The *Human Layer* takes into account static humans in the environment. To ensure that the robot keeps a comfortable distance, a mixture of Gaussian distributions is used to calculate the cost of each cell around the human position.

Fig. 1. Left: Path generated using only *Human Layer*. Right: Path generated using both *Human Layer* and *Proxemics Layer*. (Color figure online)

In order to achieve a distribution capable of adapting different shapes, five parameters that can be dynamically reconfigured were defined. Three of those parameters define the variance to model the distribution at the front, back and sides. Additionally, two thresholds were used to define the limits of the distribution. The first threshold was in charge of modeling the inner part of the distribution. It establishes the highest cost to the area surrounding the human. Likewise, the second threshold, models the outer part of the distribution, the cost of each cell will correspond to the cost of the Gaussian distribution until it reaches this second threshold, then the cost will be considered as free space. This approach allows to efficiently modify the used shape depending on the situation.

2.2   Proxemics Layer

The *Proxemics Layer* considers arrangements formed by static persons interacting in groups. This paper proposes a two step strategy to model groups formations. The first step groups the people in clusters according to the Euclidean distance between each of them. This assumes that two or more people that are in a close distance to each other, will be interacting. The next step is to model the space surrounding the group. The method proposed considers a polygon, which vertices are each person in the group. The edges of the polygon obtained are represented in the costmap with the highest cost possible. In the case that the group only have two members, a line connecting them is used. The fact that only the edges of the polygon are represented in the costmap significantly reduces the memory and computational costs required.

The combination of both *Human Layer* and *Proxemics Layer* has an outstanding performance. In Fig. 1, the green arrows represent the pose of four persons that seem to be having a conversation. The green line represents the global path plan between the robot and its goal. In the first case (Fig. 1a) only the *Human Layer* was used, therefore the robot moved through the group. On Fig. 1b, both layers were used, hence the path generated goes around the group, avoiding interfering with interpersonal interactions.

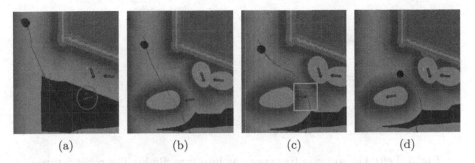

Fig. 2. (a) First trajectory generated. Orange circle represents the dynamic human (b) Master grid Costmap (c) New trajectory (d) Following new trajectory (Color figure online)

2.3 Prediction Layer

The *Prediction Layer* was created to determine possible regions that the robot and dynamic humans might share in the future. It estimates the robot and humans poses through a time period. The robot pose estimation is based on the point in the path generated by the global planner that the robot would reach every second, following its current velocity. On the other hand, the human estimation is based on a linear assumption, considering the actual and the previous pose and the time interval between them. For all the estimated poses it is found the shortest distance (collision point) between the robot and the human pose. The collision point is compared with a previous one, if any, and then if it is under a threshold it is considered into the costmap, modeling the region around the point using a mixture of Gaussian distributions, similarly to the one in the *Human Layer*. The estimation is performed every second, which is the global path update rate. As an example, a simulation experiment in which two humans are having a conversation, and a third person is walking, was considered (Fig. 2). The arrows and the green line represent the poses and the robot global path respectively. First, a global path was generated. The orange circle in Fig. 2a highlights the moving person. The collision point is determined using this path and the information from the moving person. The area enclosing the collision point is modeled using an Eggshape (Fig. 2b). Here, as the current path crossed a forbidden zone, it needed to be recalculated. Afterwards, a new path which considers the future estimation is calculated (Fig. 2c), even though it overlaps with the current human position (yellow square). Finally, the robot follows the planned trajectory avoiding the collision with the human (Fig. 2d).

2.4 ROS Implementation

As mentioned in the Introduction, there were created costmap plugins (one for each layer) following the shapes and procedures previously explained. Those plugins were loaded in the move_base node which calculates the velocity commands needed to move the robot to the designated goal taking into account

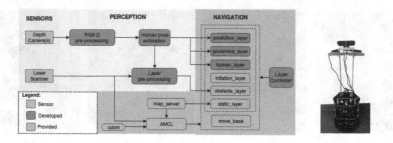

Fig. 3. Left: The software framework architecture. Right: The robot setup

the information of the Layered Costmaps. The implemented software framework architecture (Fig. 3) allows the replacement of modules with other similar ones, providing high versatility and convenience. The perception system comprised all the modules needed to extract relevant information from the cameras and the laser scanner. This includes a RGB-D pre-processing in charge of synchronizing the data captured by the cameras in order to provide the people detector a full FOV image. The perception system involves also the laser pre-processing module and filters out the scanner data corresponding to detected moving humans; therefore, they are not represented in the costmap created by the obstacle layer. Additionally, the navigation system was in charge of moving the robot to the desired position, it used the data obtained by the perception system. As part of this system, a layer controller was developed to determine which layers should be used. In crowded and narrow spaces, the proposed layered architecture could generate a particularly restrictive costmap, leading the robot to consider the desired goal as inaccessible. Using the layer controller, when the navigation system fails to find a path, it will disable the *Proxemics Layer* and the path planner will try to reach the goal again using the new generated costmap.

3   Experimental Results

The set of metrics given in [10] served as a basis to define the evaluation strategy used. Two kinds of metrics were used: *Objective metrics*, which measures the efficiency of the robot navigation (generated path length, navigation time and mission completion, number of times the robot successfully reaches the goal without colliding) and *subjective metrics*, which evaluates the robot trajectory according to social norms (minimum distance to human and number of times the robot performs a social space invasion).

Two approaches have been taken to evaluate the software framework according to the metrics exposed above, experiments in a simulated environment and in a real life setup. For the experiments the robot needed to navigate using the layered costmaps developed in this work. Besides, for comparison reasons, the navigation system using the default layered costmap offered by ROS was evaluated on both setups under the same circumstances.

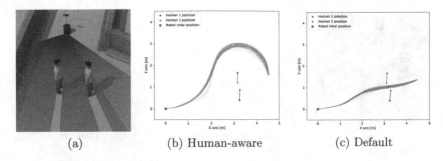

(a)   (b) Human-aware   (c) Default

Fig. 4. Simulated scene (a) for experiment 1 and paths generated by the human-aware (b) or default (c) planner. Mean poses of persons represented by arrows.

3.1 Simulation Experiments

A Turtlebot 2 model was implemented in Gazebo to provide simulated sensor information to the ROS system. A generic laser scanner model was placed at the center front of the robot, and a generic RGB-D camera (represented in Gazebo as a Kinect) was placed in the robot center at a height of 1.05 m and a horizontal FOV of 180°. Human models poses were obtained from the models' information provided by Gazebo; hence, there was not applied any perception algorithm.

Two different experiments scenarios were considered. These scenarios were selected having in mind relevant situations where the robot should demonstrate a human-friendly behaviour. A total of 30 repetitions are run for each experiment, where human positions and orientations are randomly modified to resemble a realistic human scenario.

Experiment 1. Consisted of two static humans having a conversation (Fig. 4a). The paths followed in each repetition by the human-aware navigation system and the default navigation system can be seen in Fig. 4c. This illustration shows the robot's trajectory for each repetition. The humans are represented by an arrow whose location, and direction depends on the mean value of their detected positions and orientations.

Table 1 displays the mean value and standard deviations for the evaluation metrics proposed. As might be expected, the human-aware mobile robot traveled a longer distance and needed more time to reach the goal. The default navigation system provided by ROS interrupted the conversation in all the repetitions, whereas the proposed method respected the group and kept longer distances.

Experiment 2. In this experiment, there are three humans involved, two humans are having a conversation, and a third human is moving (Fig. 5a). The desired goal was selected in order to replicate a crossing situation, where the human path and the robot trajectory might concur. From the trajectories followed by the robot (Fig. 5c), it can be appreciated how the human-aware navigation system prevented the collision by navigating through the initial position

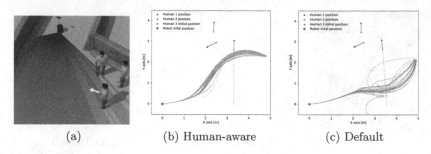

Fig. 5. Simulated scene (a) for experiment 2 and paths generated by the human-aware (b) or default (c) planner. Mean poses of persons represented by arrows. (Color figure online)

of the dynamic human (pink arrow); in contrast paths generated by the default path planner coincided with the human forcing the robot to modify the trajectory abruptly, or even colliding. The Human-Aware navigation system reached the goal without any trouble. On the other hand, the default approach collided with the human a total of eight times out of 30. Table 1 only shows evaluated data from successful repetitions.

3.2 Real Life Experiments

In addition to the Turtlebot, a Hokuyo URG-04LX laser scanner was placed in the same position as the simulation. Two Intel RealSense D435 cameras were placed at the same height as in the simulated setup and separated by 18.5 cm. They were positioned with a pitch rotation of $-20°$ in order to focus on people's upper body. Additionally a yaw rotation was applied to each of the cameras in order to have a merged horizontal FOV of approximately 135° (Fig. 3). The human pose estimation was done using OpenPose [2]. The detected keypoints were projected to 3D by looking up the coordinates in the RGB-D point cloud.

Table 1. Results for simulation experiments (standard deviations in brackets).

Planner	Objective metrics			Subjective metrics			
	Path length [m]	Time [s]	Mission completed	Min distance [m]			Social space invasions
				H1	H2	H3	
Experiment 1, n = 30							
Human-aware	6.764 (0.114)	22.055 (0.495)	100%	1.610 (0.059)	1.083 (0.033)	-	0%
Default	4.715 (0.014)	12.345 (0.182)	100%	0.636 (0.041)	0.638 (0.046)	-	100%
Experiment 2, n = 30							
Human-aware	8.518 (0.095)	16.178 (0.428)	100%	1.001 (0.049)	1.814 (0.076)	0.872 (0.066)	-
Default	5.876 (0.194)	16.958 (2.711)	73.33%	3.099 (0.196)	3.031 (0.204)	0.402 (0.166)	-

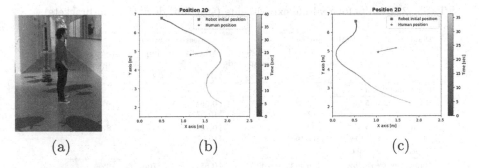

Fig. 6. The setup (a) for the real life experiment 1 and example trajectories for the proposed (b) and default (c) planner.

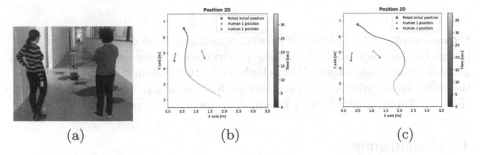

Fig. 7. The setup (a) for the real life experiment 2 and example trajectories for the proposed (b) and default (c) planner.

The orientation of each detected person was calculated by projecting the two shoulder keypoints to the floor plane, and calculating the vector orthogonal to the line between the two points. The detected neck keypoint was chosen as the position of the person. All system processing including neural network computations were done on a Jetson TX2.

A total of six repetitions were run per experiment. In this case, the humans taking part in the experiment were static since the perception system used is not able to extract an adequate number of pose estimations from a moving human.

Experiment 1. It involves a human standing in the middle of a corridor, looking at the paintings in the wall. The robot should transverse the hall without interrupting the human's activity. In Fig. 6, it can be observed one of the repetitions carried out for the proposed navigation systems and the default navigation system provided by ROS. Red arrows depict the mean detected human position and orientation calculated using the information from the perception system during the corresponding repetition. As might be expected, the human-aware system moved behind the person; in contrast, the default system crossed in front of him, interrupting the activity. A comparison between the proposed approach and the default navigation system can be found in Table 2.

Table 2. Results for real life experiments (standard deviations in brackets).

Planner	Objective metrics			Subjective metrics		
	Path length [m]	Time [s]	Mission completed	Min distance [m]		Social space invasions
				H1	H2	
Experiment 1, n = 6						
Human-aware	5.531 (0.113)	44.388 (2.445)	100%	0.961 (0.072)	-	0%
Default	5.324 (0.147)	44.722 (7.158)	100%	0.700 (0.073)	-	83.33%
Experiment 2, n = 6						
Human-aware	5.459 (0.101)	46.111 (10.432)	100%	0.854 (0.055)	1.708 (0.142)	0%
Default	5.216 (0.092)	40.333 (2.880)	100%	0.661 (0.453)	0.661 (0.453)	83.33%

Experiment 2. It involves two persons standing in front of the robot (Fig. 7a). In this case, humans might be having a conversation, therefore the robot should avoid to cross between them. The default navigation system (Fig. 7b) interrupted the conversation, whereas the proposed method behaves in a human-friendly way (Fig. 7c). Table 2 shows further information about this experiment.

4   Conclusions

The paper in hand proposed an integrated navigation system which enables a mobile robot to behave according to social conventions and generates socially acceptable trajectories in a human populated environment. The layered costmap suggested, have been integrated into the current version of ROS navigation stack. Therefore, it can be easily added to any navigation system based on ROS while maintaining the advantages of the local and global path planners. Moreover, the layers have been developed having in mind the memory and computational costs associated with each costmap. The *Proxemic Layer* only represents the edges of a polygon since its combination with the *Human Layer* provides adequate information about the scenario, reducing the computational effort.

While other studies proposed solutions that are only applicable under certain circumstances, the suggested approach demonstrates how a detailed layered costmap is more versatile, and it can be used in a broader range of situations. Its capability of respecting personal spaces and group formations, as well as avoiding conflictive regions, has been proven not only in simulation but also in real life experiments. In particular, the results obtained in simulation verify that in order to achieve suitable trajectories, a comprehensive layered costmap is needed. Furthermore, the evaluation in real life experiments demonstrates the correct performance of the method and its feasibility.

Future improvements involve the use of a robust and reliable perception system, capable of detecting the poses of multiple of humans. This would allow the evaluation of the method in complex constellations of persons. Furthermore, the persons orientation can be taken into account in the group formation determined by the *Proxemics Layer*. Besides, the performance of the *Prediction Layer* could be assessed using real life experiments.

Acknowledgment. This work was supported by the project Health-CAT, funded by the European Fund for regional development.

References

1. ROS navigation stack (2007). http://wiki.ros.org/navigation
2. Cao, Z., Simon, T., Wei, S., Sheikh, Y.: Realtime multi-person 2D pose estimation using part affinity fields. CoRR abs/1611.08050 (2016)
3. Charalampous, K., Kostavelis, I., Gasteratos, A.: Robot navigation in large-scale social maps: an action recognition approach. Expert Syst. Appl. **66**, 261–273 (2016)
4. Hall, E.T.: The hidden dimension (1966)
5. Kendon, A.: Conducting Interaction: Patterns of Behavior in Focused Encounters. Studies in Interactional Sociolinguistics (1990)
6. Kollmitz, M., Hsiao, K., Gaa, J., Burgard, W.: Time dependent planning on a layered social cost map for human-aware robot navigation. In: European Conference on Mobile Robots (2015)
7. Kruse, T., Basili, P., Glasauer, S., Kirsch, A.: Legible robot navigation in the proximity of moving humans. In: IEEE Works on Advanced Robotics and its Social Impacts (2012)
8. Papadakis, P., Rives, P., Spalanzani, A.: Adaptive spacing in human-robot interactions. In: IEEE/RSJ International Conference on Intelligent Robots and Systems (2014)
9. Truong, X., Ngo, T.D.: Toward socially aware robot navigation in dynamic and crowded environments: a proactive social motion model. IEEE Trans. Autom. Sci. Eng. **14**(4), 1743–1760 (2017)
10. Vasquez, D., Okal, B., Arras, K.O.: Inverse reinforcement learning algorithms and features for robot navigation in crowds: an experimental comparison. In: IEEE/RSJ International Conference on Intelligent Robots and Systems (2014)
11. Vega, A., Manso, L.J., Macharet, D.G., Bustos, P., Núñez, P.: Socially aware robot navigation system in human-populated and interactive environments based on an adaptive spatial density function and space affordances. Pattern Recognit. Lett. **118**, 72–84 (2019)

Safe Human-Robot Interaction Through Crowd Contact Video Analysis

Fernando Garcia[(✉)], Alexandre Mazel[(✉)], and Arturo Cruz Maya[(✉)]

Softbank Robotics Europe, Paris, France
{ferran.garcia,amazel,arturo.cruzmaya}@softbankrobotics.com

Abstract. This work proposes a contact management approach using Pepper robot, which focuses on safety constraints for navigation through cluttered environments. Firstly, we conduct an analytical study to identify the most common undesired physical contacts between humans in crowded scenes. Based on that, a set of recommendations for robot reaction is provided. Special emphasis is given to contact detection and reaction by proposing a sensorless detection method and different body compliance strategies, respectively, that match the safety guidelines proposed. Finally, an experimental validation is conducted in a controlled environment and through user studies.

Keywords: Social robots · pHRI · Contact management · Humanoid

1 Introduction

Historically, robots have been deployed in controlled environments such as automotive industry or scientific facilities within research labs. However, with the shift to human-centered applications, the number of robots placed in public or domestic areas has dramatically increased in the last years; healthcare, personal assistance, education or entertainment are some of the main fields of adoption.

In order to be successfully deployed in human environments, social robots must be able to move through cluttered scenes while preserving safety. However, ensuring a contactless navigation under all kinds of circumstances might be extremely complex if we consider the limitations in perceptive hardware present on budget robots. Specifically, cluttered environments, occlusions and variability in lighting conditions could prevent safety perception-based systems to engage properly. Therefore, when deploying a platform in the wild, expected or unexpected physical contacts will likely take place.

Safety contributions that focus on personal robots by targeting the design principles that minimize risks of injury are numerous [6,11], providing in some cases qualitative assessment of the challenges involved in the evaluation of user

This work has received funding from the European Union's Horizon 2020 framework programme for research and innovation under the ICT No. 779942 (CROWDBOT).

M. A. Salichs et al. (Eds.): ICSR 2019, LNAI 11876, pp. 588–598, 2019.
https://doi.org/10.1007/978-3-030-35888-4_55

comfort and acceptability [9], also at the psychological level. More recently, [7] sets a classification for human-centered safety strategies; pre-control and post-control approaches, motion planning with human-based constraints and motion prediction. However, most of the work concerned with improving pHRI is typically focused on the limitation of motion as well as velocity or energy [5]. These constraints provide a strong motivation for the study of post-collision control safety methods targeting personal humanoid robots.

In this work, we focus on identification of undesired contacts with the goal to propose suitable robot responses that allow us to mitigate potential hazards in a crowded scenario. Moreover, implementation and evaluation of such reaction strategies allow identifying the most appropriate human-like behaviour for enabling social tasks such as human compliant navigation, shared control navigation or robot guidance. Specifically, we present two main contributions:

1. An undesired human physical contact taxonomy in crowded environments and the most common upper-body contact areas to provide a set of safety guidelines for humanoid robots deployed in crowded environments.
2. A sensorless contact detection approach using z-score on motor torque that allows to implement and validate the reaction strategies proposed earlier.

2   Data Analysis

In order to propose a taxonomy of undesired physical contacts and identify the most common body areas where an anthropomorphic robot platform and a human could potentially collide, a video analysis was conducted. However, the current crowd datasets available such as WorldExpo'10 or PEdesTrian Attribute [2], among others, do not provide annotations about human contacts. In addition, no software is available to automatize this process. In consequence, 60 min of crowd recordings (minimum resolution of 800×600) were analyzed and manually annotated. The recordings include different situations, geographical variability and crowd density of commuters, congested events such as demonstrations or concerts, and conventional scenarios such as crosswalks. The samples were classified as *restricted/dense*, *very dense* and *jammed* scenarios with a maximum of 3 people per squared meter (p/m^2) as seen in Fig. 1.

2.1   Contact Taxonomy

In [12], a contact taxonomy between humans and robots is established defining a categorization that includes *pinch* and *impact* as possible contact types. Based

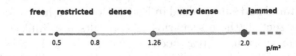

Fig. 1. Categorization of the crowd density levels [8]

on the results from the video analysis (see Fig. 2), our observations match and extend it by proposing three contact types; *clamp/pinch*, *impact* and *push*, with its corresponding particular reaction (see Fig. 3):

Impact. The occurrence of this type of contact is characterized by a significant difference in speed between two human bodies before colliding, typically coming from opposite directions. It will result in a sudden disturbance of the limb or body motion.

Push. It takes place when a continuous exerted force causes a body to move aside by complying to it, under two different circumstances: when the contact between the two bodies is at a low speed, or when the vector of motion of the two bodies is very similar. Eventually, this disturbance generates a progressive motion in the body or limb.

Clamp. This type of contact occurs when a body part is constrained in between the movement of a second body. This can be due to the active movement of two parts that constrain the space, or one part against a steady body.

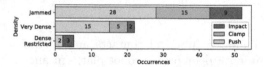

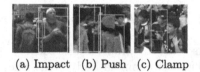

(a) Impact (b) Push (c) Clamp

Fig. 2. Undesired human to human contact events based on the density scenarios evaluated.

Fig. 3. Samples of contact types during data analysis annotation.

Results show that the quantity of events registered is directly related with density of the crowd, which reproduces the findings reported in [10]. *Impacts* in *restricted* scenarios represent a high rate (60%) while in *jammed* contexts are much lower (17.3%). Short-term contacts or *impacts*, are likely to happen with a low crowd density due to the increment of interpersonal space and motion flow. In contrast, long-term contacts (*pushing* and *clamping*) are common in dense crowds due to the homogeneous motion flow and little interpersonal space.

2.2   Contact Areas

During the video analysis, several contact points along the human body were identified, annotated and summarized in Fig. 4. However, due to the high number of occlusions present in these scenarios, the results are limited to the upper-body areas, from waist up. Areas such as shoulders, back, chest, elbows and hands shown the highest degree of implication. Having identified the areas of

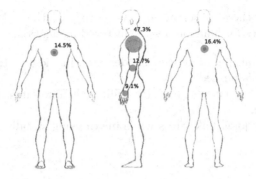

Fig. 4. Human upper-body contact areas in a crowded scenario sized by occurrences.

the human body contained between neck and waist, which are more likely to collide, we hypothesize the same zones of undesired pHRI for the Pepper robot acknowledging the difference of height; 120 cm vs 175 cm (average human height).

In addition, specific areas show a contact likeliness with other areas due to the proximity of the body parts when humans share similar body orientation; this is the case of shoulder to shoulder, elbow to shoulder and chest to back contacts. Moreover, it is observed that anticipatory reactions motivated to protect a body area mitigating an impact are correlated to high densities of people since they take place in *very dense* and *jammed* scenarios.

3   Safety Guidelines for Personal Robots

According to the assessment presented, some safety requirements would need to be ensured if an anthropomorphic robot is deployed in a crowded scenario. These considerations can be divided in design and operation principles. Part of these suggestions can be found in several international standards: *ISO 12100 Safety of machinery* and *ISO 10218 Robots and robotic devices* specifies basic terminology, principles and a methodology for achieving safety in the design of machinery, that can be partially applied to personal robots. *ISO 21260* provides mechanical safety data for physical contacts between moving machinery and people. But more recently, *ISO 13482* specifies requirements for the inherently safe design, protective measures for use of personal care robots.

However, none of the previous standards establish appropriate robot behaviours while operating in dynamic environments. In such scenarios, safety must be ensured with minimum constraints to the system autonomy. In consequence, some of the main capabilities that personal robots should exhibit while moving between humans are kinematic configuration adaptability or joint compliance depending on external forces, with the goal of minimizing them.

According to these observations, we propose the following hierarchy behaviour principles for humanoid safe cluttered navigation:

1. Location compliance if no obstacle is detected in the direction of the motion when the robot is pushed.
2. Body posture compliance or backdrivability when no safe robot displacement can be achieved.
3. Minimization of joint/link stress while maximizing stability.

4   Approach

The approach proposed in this section detects and isolates the link whose surface has the contact with an obstacle. Then, the contact type is classified as *push* or *impact* event, and a proper reaction is triggered by modifying the joint position according to the principles stated in Sect. 3.

4.1   Contact Detection

Social robots actively deployed in the human environment are not usually equipped with torque sensors in their joints, making the collision detection a complex task. Several approaches have been proposed in order to detect contacts based on expected position tracking errors [1], using the momentum-based residual signal [3] or Extended Kalman Filters. We propose a cost efficient approach that detects the direction of the contact force and its intensity when the robot remains steady. Such strategy is based on the standard score value (z-score) of joint torque (τ) estimations computed from the mechanical parameters of the motor.

However, there are undesired effects of the joint mechanism that penalize the torque transmission from the motor τ_M to the link τ_L such as friction and backlash, and can not be neglected when computing the torque load τ_l. Then, considering a classical robot dynamic model:

$$\tau_l = M(q)\ddot{q} + C(q,\dot{q}) + \tau_f + \tau_B - \tau_{ext} \tag{1}$$

$M(q)$ is the robot inertia matrix and C combines centrifugal, gravity effects and Coriolis term. Finally, τ_B represents the joint torque due to backlash, τ_f is the friction torque and τ_{ext} is the external joint torque. Because of τ_B, τ_l may experiment a high variability.

The standard score is the signed number of standard deviations by which a value, in this case external torque, is above the mean of what is being observed. Observed values above the mean have positive standard scores, while values below the mean have negative standard scores. The standard score is a dimensionless quantity obtained by subtracting the population mean μ from an individual raw score X and then dividing the difference by the population standard deviation σ. A positive detection is acquired when the condition shown in Eq. (2) is satisfied, being c a predefined constant threshold.

$$\left|\tau_N - \frac{1}{N-1}\sum_{i=0}^{N-1}\tau_i\right| > c \cdot \frac{1}{N-1}\sum_{i=0}^{N-1}(\tau_i - \mu_\tau)^2 \tag{2}$$

Then, the equation system shown in (3) will identify the direction of the force applied to the surface of a specific link L. For instance, if we consider the torso, 1 will represent a frontal collision and -1 a collision from the rear.

$$s_L(\tau) = \begin{cases} 1, & \text{if } \tau_N > \mu_{\tau N-1} \\ -1, & \text{if } \tau_N \leq \mu_{\tau N-1} \end{cases} \tag{3}$$

The non-smooth activation of this approach is suitable for our particular case, since it is robust to the non-linearity effects induced by backlash or friction. In order to isolate the body link involved in a collision, this approach is run for neck, hip and knee joints. According to the evidence collected in Sect. 2, the most common type of undesired contacts between humans when moving within a crowd are *impacting* (short-term) and *pushing* (long-term). Here, a simplified approach for differentiating these two contact types is accomplished by looking at the continuity of τ applied to the joint j along a given number of time-steps.

4.2   Reaction

Location Compliance. All robot joints obey a specific rotation dimension; roll, pitch or yaw, and can be used to estimate the direction of the force over the robot's surface. In order to determine the resulting direction of the motion to be transmitted to the wheels, two components are needed: τ_{ext} estimated from Eq. 1, and the joint angle error θ_ϵ between the position sensed (θ_s) and the commanded (θ_c) which indicates the force direction acting on the robot's surface [4]. Then, the function f would translate a positive θ_ϵ as a front force direction (90°), and the negative as a rear one ($-90°$), depending on the joint. Finally, the velocity V_m shown in Eq. 4 can be formalized, and will describe the direction and the magnitude of the force to be transmitted to the wheels.

$$V_m = \left(\tau_{ext}, f(\theta_s - \theta_c)\right) \tag{4}$$

As can be seen in Fig. 5, the knee pitch joint is used to estimate the forward/backward displacement and the hip roll for lateral ones.

If a pressure is exercised on the body surface of the robot, the corresponding motion is encoded within the x-axis when it is identified as a front/rear force direction, and in the y-axis when comes from the sides. Any combination of the previous motions can be acquired by merging the two V_m.

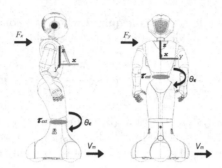

Fig. 5. Estimation of V_m using the knee (front/rear forces) and hip roll (lateral ones).

Body Compliance. According to the results presented in Sect. 2.2, one of the most exposed human body areas to undesired physical contacts are the arms. As a reaction, it is natural for a human to tilt the torso laterally in the same direction of the pressure detected so that the contact is suppressed. Likewise, bouncing towards the front or the rear, in case the contact is on the chest or the back of the person.

The reaction described is implemented by exploiting the high resolution of the joint sensor position and the free motion gap provided by the backlash, resulting in the compliance of the knee pitch and hip roll of Pepper. Considering the discrepancy θ_ϵ between the position sensed by the magnetic rotary encoder θ_s and the position achieved previously by the actuator θ_c, the discrepancy can be used to update θ_c towards the direction of the angle error as $\theta_\epsilon = \theta_s - \theta_c$.

5   Experiments and Results

Deploying a humanoid robot in an unsupervised crowded environment to analyze potential collisions expose several ethical concerns. In addition, robots still generate a great deal of expectation since they are not available for the general public yet. And thus, the novelty effect would likely constrain the human behaviour around the platform becoming an inappropriate test-bed for validation. Therefore, the experimental scenario of this work has been divided into two different parts; a controlled environment study where the detection strategy as well as the reaction approaches described in Sect. 4.2 are validated; and a user study where the base compliance approach is tested with humans.

In the first case, the tests took place in a controlled environment of 150 cm width with a 40 cm tall fence where Pepper was deployed to simulate a reduced mobility environment. In the second case, the user experiments were carried out in a rehabilitation centre under supervision of a medical team. Four patients with different conditions performed a 30 min long activity. The robot was pushed from the back to transmit the user's movement intention to the base compliance approach described in Sect. 4.2 (see Fig. 6).

Fig. 6. User experiments in a rehab centre and a controlled environment.

The next sections show the results and discussion of the contact detection strategy (Sect. 4.1), the contact classification, and the two compliance approaches of Sect. 4.2 structured with the hierarchy presented in Sect. 3.

5.1 Contact Detection and Classification

As can be seen in Fig. 7, Pepper's hip original torque signal (top) shows 3 different areas of perturbation present around 2 s, 3.5 s and 5 s, corresponding to front impact, back impact and intentional disturbances. Then, when the torque values, which are previously smoothed, exceed the threshold due to a rapid raise (impact), a pulse 1 or −1 is generated.

In addition, around 3 s a variability in the torque after a collision is produced; when the robot recovers its original position (4 s), the resistance to keep the platform steady might be higher or lower due to the position of the gear teeth within the joint. Therefore, certain degree of robustness after collision and when facing disturbances (from 4.5 s to 6.5 s) is achieved. In consequence, the collision detection approach proposed in this work allows to mitigate two main drawbacks when dealing with budget platforms: the shakiness of the robot during the wheelbase motion and the hysteresis when recovering the kinematic configuration. The collision detection algorithm generates a positive detection only when a sudden raise in the torque values monitored takes place. If no impact is detected, the system will always be reactive to *push* contacts. In the contrary, when an impact is detected *push* events are inhibited, as can be seen in Fig. 8.

5.2 Compliance Reaction

When the base compliance behaviour (1st principle) is disturbed by an obstacle within the safety area and the force over the surface of the robot is still present, the system is able to perform a transition to a more appropriate behaviour. Such transitions allow additional force contact minimization by complying in the direction of the force with a suitable joint (2nd principle). Eventually, if the force ceases, the joint affected returns to its original position, see Fig. 9.

The force applied over the y-axis around 1.5 s creates a reaction in the base position. Due to the holonomic nature of Pepper's locomotion system, the front left wheel engages intermittently as the tracking shows. When an obstacle is

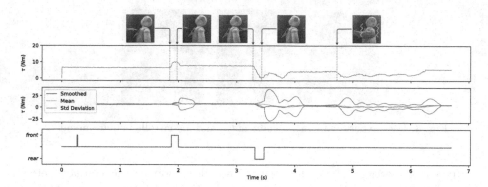

Fig. 7. Contact detection in Pepper's torso using z-score method on the hip joint torque (top). The approach registers the contact direction (bottom) with robustness against hysteresis and backlash effects (middle).

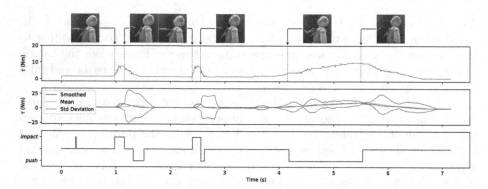

Fig. 8. Hip contact detection classification. *Push* (4 s) and *impact* (1 s and 2.5 s) events.

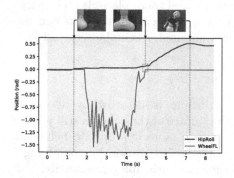

Fig. 9. Transition from position compliance (wheelbase) to body compliance, when an obstacle is detected (red box). (Color figure online)

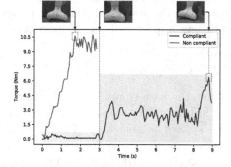

Fig. 10. Hip roll torque when a force is applied on the robot y-axis. Green/blue areas define wheelbase and hip actuation. (Color figure online)

within the safety area (<0.3 m), the wheelbase brakes to avoid a collision and transitions to a body compliance strategy through a compliant hip joint.

In usual conditions, during a continuous contact event over the surface of the robot, the system reacts with the required torque in order to keep the joint affected as close as possible to the requested position. In fact, if the force contact is great enough, Pepper's wheel is lifted and the system becomes unstable. However, when the compliance approach is activated, the joint torque is minimized as can be seen in Fig. 10 by moving the base and torso towards the direction of the force (3rd principle). As a result, the robot becomes more stable over time (red boxes). However, due to the kinematic configuration resulting from the motion in both cases, with and without the compliance activated, the instability points vary. In the first case (7 s), the hip is flexed to the maximum, displacing the centre of mass towards one side. In contrast, the robot remains completely still when the compliance control is not activated.

6 Conclusions and Future Work

In this work, a crowd contact taxonomy is presented (Sect. 2.1) together with identification of the most common human body areas and its contact rate (Sect. 2.2). Based on it, we have provided a hierarchy of behaviours principles and its implementation for personal robot deployment in human scenarios. However, these results are limited by the exclusion of other possible undesired contact types that could take place in a physical human-robot interaction such as dragging, pinching or scrapping. These events have not been spotted during the video analysis and would require other type of studies to help assessing suitable robot reactions to enhance the previous recommendations.

Moreover, the cost-effective sensorless contact detection method based on the z-score computation presented, has shown robustness to hysteresis and backlash; both undesired effects very present in budget platforms. However, this detection approach may show a limited performance when contacts occur during a commanded joint displacement. On the other side, benefits of the reaction implementations in terms of stability and joint stress mitigation have been shown. However, an evaluation of these strategies for people's safety, comfort and human-likeliness, remains as future work.

References

1. Bolotnikova, A., Courtois, S., Kheddar, A.: Contact observer for humanoid robot pepper based on tracking joint position discrepancies. In: RO-MAN: Robot and Human Interactive Communication (2018)
2. Deng, Y., Luo, P., Loy, C.C., Tang, X.: Pedestrian attribute recognition at far distance. In: Proceedings of the 22nd ACM International Conference on Multimedia, pp. 789–792. ACM (2014)
3. Flacco, F., Kheddar, A.: Contact detection and physical interaction for low cost personal robots. In: RO-MAN (2017)

4. Garcia, F., Kumar Pandey, A., Fattal, C.: Wait for me! towards socially assistive walk companions. In: 14th ACM/IEEE International Conference on Human Robot Interaction. 2nd Workshop on Social Robots in Therapy and Care (2019)
5. Haddadin, S., Albu-Schaffer, A., Hirzinger, G.: The role of the robot mass and velocity in physical human-robot interaction-part i: non-constrained blunt impacts. In: Robotics and Automation, ICRA, pp. 1331–1338. IEEE (2008)
6. Iwata, H., Sugano, S.: Design of human symbiotic robot twendy-one. In: 2009 IEEE International Conference on Robotics and Automation, pp. 580–586. IEEE (2009)
7. Lasota, P.A., Fong, T., Shah, J.A., et al.: A survey of methods for safe human-robot interaction. Found. Trends® Robot. 5(4), 261–349 (2017)
8. Polus, A., Schofer, J.L., Ushpiz, A.: Pedestrian flow and level of service. J. Transp. Eng. 109(1), 46–56 (1983)
9. Salem, M., Lakatos, G., Amirabdollahian, F., Dautenhahn, K.: Towards safe and trustworthy social robots: ethical challenges and practical issues. In: Tapus, A., André, E., Martin, J.C., Ferland, F., Ammi, M. (eds.) Social Robotics. LNCS (LNAI), vol. 9388, pp. 584–593. Springer, Cham (2015). https://doi.org/10.1007/978-3-319-25554-5_58
10. Sarmady, S., Haron, F., Talib, A.Z.H.: Modeling groups of pedestrians in least effort crowd movements using cellular automata. In: 2009 Third Asia International Conference on Modelling & Simulation, pp. 520–525. IEEE (2009)
11. Tadele, T.S., de Vries, T., Stramigioli, S.: The safety of domestic robotics: a survey of various safety-related publications. IEEE Robot. Autom. Mag. 21(3), 134–142 (2014)
12. Vasic, M., Billard, A.: Safety issues in human-robot interactions. In: 2013 IEEE International Conference on Robotics and Automation (ICRA), pp. 197–204 (2013)

Robots in Education

A Robot Math Tutor that Gives Feedback

Koen V. Hindriks[1(✉)] and Sander Liebens[2]

[1] Faculty of Science, Vrije Universiteit Amsterdam, Amsterdam, The Netherlands
k.v.hindriks@vu.nl
[2] Department of Computing Science, Delft, The Netherlands
sander.liebens@gmail.com

Abstract. We report on the exploratory design and study of a robot math tutor that can provide feedback on specific errors made by children solving basic addition and subtraction problems up to 100. We discuss two interaction design patterns, one for speech recognition of answers when children think aloud, and one for providing error-specific feedback. We evaluate our design patterns and whether our feedback mechanism motivates children and improves their performance at primary schools with children ($N = 41$) aged 7–9. We did not find any motivational or learning effects of our feedback mechanism but lessons learnt include that the robot can execute our interaction design patterns autonomously, and advanced algorithms for error classification and adaptation to children's performance levels in our feedback mechanism are needed.

1 Introduction

Feedback is one of the most powerful influences on learning and achievement [4]. In this paper we present the design of and evaluate a social robot that can provide error-specific feedback on answers to math problems. We focus on the domain of addition and subtraction, for sums and differences up to 100. Children aged 7–8 are being introduced to these problems with the aim to be able to fluently add and subtract two-digit numbers. We deploy a social robot to provide additional training to children aged 8–9 at school to help children to learn to automate the strategies they use for adding and subtracting numbers.

Social robot tutors have recently become more popular in elementary schools, for example, to teach language and mathematics skills. Children are motivated to work with social robots. Their physical presence compares favourably with other tutoring technologies (e.g., using games on tablets) as it appears to increase cognitive and affective outcomes [2, 10]. We briefly discuss a few related studies that use social robots to teach mathematics. [5] combines a variety of 30 different arithmetic tasks with an engaging game in which children aged 9–10 have to imitate the gestures a Nao robot performs and finds evidence that suggests that challenging children more helps them reach higher problem levels. [3] studies the effects of a Darwin robot as a tutor for children aged 13–18 that were asked to complete algebra problems. They find that the use of verbal engagement (instead of only nonverbal cues) enhances test performance most on these problems. [7]

© Springer Nature Switzerland AG 2019
M. A. Salichs et al. (Eds.): ICSR 2019, LNAI 11876, pp. 601–610, 2019.
https://doi.org/10.1007/978-3-030-35888-4_56

compares the effects of a Nao robot executing a social versus an a-social tutoring strategy with children learning about prime numbers. Their results suggest that a physical robot leads to improved learning but also may lead a child to pay more attention to the robot's social behaviour than the lesson content. In these studies, no effort is made to identify the type of error that is made and no detailed feedback on how to correct that NBT is provided so the child can learn how to avoid it next time, which is the focus of the work reported on here.

Feedback is information about how you are doing in your efforts to reach a goal [4,11,17]. We build on the conceptual model proposed in [4] to design a feedback mechanism that the robot can use to help a child understand what kind of error it made (if it did) in how it produced an answer to a math problem. According to [4], feedback directed to the self is the least effective, while self regulated feedback and feedback about the process of a task are most powerful in terms of mastery of tasks. Immediate feedback, moreover, gives better results than feedback that is delayed [14,17].

The main idea we explore in this paper is that the robot not only automatically detects a mistake but also identifies what kind of mistake has been made and explains how to avoid this mistake next time. The robot uses speech to interact with the children and we present an interaction design pattern to handle the typical thinking aloud behaviour of these children. We also design a feedback mechanism and compare task performance, affection, and the interaction with the robot of a control group that did not receive feedback with a feedback group that received explicit feedback on mistakes made from the robot. We hypothesise that (i) the score on math problems is higher for children that receive feedback from the robot, and that (ii) children that receive feedback like the robot more.

The paper is organised as follows. Section 2 introduces our robot interaction design and Sect. 3 our feedback mechanism. Sections 4, 5, and 6, present method, results, and discussion of our study. Section 7 concludes the paper.

2 Interaction Design

We designed a robot math tutor called Pixel that is able to teach children how to perform the basic operations addition and subtraction up to 100.[1] At the start of a session, Pixel introduces itself and welcomes the child, after which it explains that it is going to pose some addition and subtraction problems which the child has already been practising with for some time in the classroom. This strategy of explaining a subject before engaging in it has been shown to be an effective teaching strategy [12,15]. The robot has been programmed to select problems from seven different categories (cycling through these categories).[2]

---

[1] This is task CCSS.MATH.CONTENT.2.NBT.B.5 in the Common Core Standard for Grade 2 (age 7–8) http://www.corestandards.org/Math/Content/2/NBT/B/5/.

[2] The following 7 categories are used: "Passing tens" (e.g., $7 + 6$), "Adding tens and units" (e.g., $37 + 31$), "Adding tens and units, passing tens" (e.g., $67 + 14$), "Through tens" (e.g., $12 - 5$), "Remove tens and add later" (e.g., $53 - 2$), "Tens minus tens and units" (e.g., $38 - 17$), and "Tens and units, through tens" (e.g., $46 - 18$).

Providing an Answer. During a pilot, we found that children may engage in thinking aloud while trying to compute an answer. This poses a problem for the robot when it starts listening for an answer. It is hard for the robot to identify exactly which of the numbers a child mentions is supposed to be the answer. To deal with this issue, we developed an interaction design pattern (see Table 1) called *Touch-Based Speech Activation* for providing an answer to the robot [6].

Table 1. Interaction design pattern: Touch-Based Speech Activation

Problem	When asked to answer a question by a robot, children may engage in thinking aloud while trying to compute the answer to the question. Children's speech while thinking aloud is harder to recognise as speech volume, for example, is varied more. Both the longer and more complicated speech produced (instead of providing only the answer) and the variation in speech parameters complicates the natural language understanding, in particular the identification of the answer
Principle	We do not want to restrict children in the way they compute an answer, and allow them to engage in thinking aloud and other interaction (e.g. asking another child sitting next to them). Instead, to provide an answer, a child is asked to indicate it is ready and focused to provide an answer.
Solution	A child is asked to indicate that it thinks it knows the answer to a question by means of a touch sensor. Touching the sensor will activate speech recognition and the robot will then listen for an answer for a specified period of time

We used the feet bumper sensors of the Nao robot to activate speech recognition and used a window of 3 seconds to listen for an answer. Note that the interaction pattern is quite generic and can be used for any type of question, and only requires a robot with a touch sensor. Because we did not use any visual support e.g. using a tablet for displaying the question and children sometimes fail to understand or memorise the question (or simply want to be reassured they answer the right question), we found it also useful to provide them with a touch mechanism for asking the robot to repeat a question. We enabled children to ask the robot to repeat a question by pressing buttons on the robot's head.

Rewards. To motivate children, rewards are provided if the correct answer is given. Rewards have been implemented by randomly having the robot say one of four compliments while displaying a rotating rainbow colour pattern using the LEDs in the robot's eyes. The four texts we used are "Great job! That indeed is the correct answer!", "Correct again! You're doing great!", "You're the best! That is the correct answer!", and "Yes, correct! Let's go for the next one!". The rewards are not part of the feedback mechanism discussed below and used to motivate all children (whether or not they receive extensive feedback or not from the robot). At the end of a session, the robot also informs the child how many exercises were answered correctly in the first try, thanks the child for paying attention and completing the exercises with the robot, and, as a final reward, first teaches the child how to perform the short *Chu Chu Wa* dance and then invites the child to perform it together.[3]

3   Feedback Targeting the Type of Mistake Made

One of the simplest feedback mechanisms only informs the child whether the answer it provided was right or wrong. We used this mechanism for children in the control group in our study to provide feedback on each answer. After providing an incorrect answer in a first attempt, children always were invited to try a second time. If in a second attempt a child also failed to provide the right answer, the robot would indicate this and provide the right answer for the current problem. In case of a good answer a reward (see above) is provided.

A second, more elaborate mechanism that we used with the feedback (test) group in our study is based on the model of [4]. The mechanism we propose is based on the "How are we going?" question and aims to provide feedback at the process level of this model. We have made these choices as feedback is effective when it consists of information about progress, and/or about how to proceed [4]. Speech is used to provide verbal feedback, inspired by [15] who argue that a dialog in teaching is more effective. The main aim of our feedback mechanism is to help children understand *what* they did wrong by providing relevant feedback on the specific error that most likely was made. See the algorithm discussed below for detecting the type of error made for details. If the kind of error made is identified by this algorithm, feedback is adapted specifically to this error to explain what went wrong and to help the child understand how it can correct its mistake. If the algorithm cannot classify the error type, the robot will indicate the answer is wrong the first attempt but after a second attempt will explain how to compute the correct answer using the jump strategy [1].

Detecting Errors in Answers to Math Problems. In order to give specific feedback, the robot should be able to diagnose what kind of error is made when a child provides an incorrect answer. The literature provides some insight into the types of errors that are made when children use the jump and/or split strategy [1], but does not detail how to mechanically detect such errors. We therefore have taken a pragmatic approach and implemented an algorithm to detect some of the errors in the addition or subtraction domain that are easy to detect. This would suit the purpose of evaluating our feedback mechanism assuming these errors occur frequently enough. We have included the following four commonly made errors: (i) "missing the last step", e.g., $7+5 = 7+3 = 10$, forgetting to add 2, (ii) "visualising a number incorrectly", e.g., switching numbers and use 83 instead of 38, (iii) the "split and add error", e.g. $32 - 14 = 22$, by first subtracting 10 from 30, then subtracting 2 from 4, because the other way around seems impossible, and (iv) "using the wrong operator", e.g., $7 + 5 = 7 - 5 = 2$.

---

[3] See https://www.youtube.com/watch?v=3T5cPaZIW8M for a video of the dance.

Table 2. Interaction Design Pattern: Feedback Targeting Specific Error

Problem	Children make a variety of errors when answering math problems, in e.g., the addition and subtraction domain. Feedback is more effective if it can target the error made more specifically
Principle	We want to provide feedback that specifically focuses on the type of error a child makes. The robot should be able to explain *what* went wrong to help the child understand its mistake but also allow a child to correct the error to learn from it.
Solution	An algorithm is used to classify the type of error a child makes when answering math problems. Feedback is designed to specifically explain what the child did wrong to help the child understand how to fix the error in a step-by-step fashion. If the type of error cannot be classified, simply provide feedback that the answer is incorrect. In any case, allow the child to retry and provide an answer to the same problem again. If an incorrect answer is provided for the second time, indicate this and have the robot explain how the correct answer can be computed

For each of the four errors the algorithm can detect, different feedback is designed. For "missing a step", the child is told which step it may have missed. For "wrongly visualising a number", the child is told it may have switched numbers and how to fix that. For "split and add error", the child is told it may have switched units in the different numbers. And, finally, for "using the wrong operator", the child is told it may have used the wrong operator and which operator should have been used in the problem.

Pilot. A primary school teacher was asked to assess the wording used by the robot and whether children could understand the feedback. This resulted in a few changes to the wording used. A pilot with a small group of children at a day care centre confirmed that children could understand the robot's feedback.

4   Method

4.1   Design

We used a between-subject study design. The independent variable is the feedback provided (only indicating whether answer is correct or not, or also providing error-specific feedback). The dependent variables are the test results of the math problems (amount of correct answers, ranging from 0 to 20) and the PANAS scores (sum of the weights, ranging from -40 to 40). The interaction design patterns were implemented across all conditions. All the interactions that were included in the experiment were used to evaluate these patterns.

4.2   Participants

A total of 41 children aged 7–9 ($M = 8.17$), 23 male and 18 female, from two primary schools in The Netherlands participated (20 children from one school, 21 from the other). We obtained approval from the Ethics Committee and consent of the children's parents beforehand. Children were split into a feedback and control group with on average the same level of math performance using the results of a test of 20 math problems administered in class before the experiment and an average math grade provided by the teacher. The feedback group consisted of 13 boys and 7 girls and the control group of 10 boys and 11 girls.

4.3   Materials

A human-like Nao robot (V5) from SoftBank Robotics was used, with a standard laptop to control it. Three different paper-and-pencil tests with 20 math questions each were used as pre- and post-tests. A small survey of 5 open and 6 Likert-scale (5-point) questions about math and robots in general, and about their math session with the robot was used. The survey for the feedback group had two additional questions about the feedback from the robot. We used the PANAS form to measure affection [16]. Finally, an observation sheet was used for notes by the experimenter.

4.4   Procedure

A week before the individual sessions with the robot, all children took part in an hour-long class in which the robot was introduced. At the end of this class they were asked to complete a math pre-test. During the math sessions, the robot was standing on a table, within reach of the child sitting in front of it. A brief explanation of the session was given before a training session was started to make the child familiar with how to interact with and answer math problems posed by the robot. Help was provided when needed. The training session was repeated only once for a child who could not complete it without repeated assistance. After the training session, children also completed a PANAS form. The first session took about 45 min with 20 min in which the robot asked children to answer math problems. All children were told by the robot whether the answer was correct or not, but the feedback group also received detailed feedback on the type of mistake that was made, if the robot could identify it. All exercises with given answers of the first session were stored in a database. A week later children participated in a second session of about 30 min which did not include training, with again 20 min of math problems. In this session the robot selected math problems from categories in which a child made (more) mistakes than other categories during the first session. After each math session, children were asked to complete a PANAS form and a short survey. After the second math session children completed a first math post-test. Two weeks later, children completed a second post-test.

5   Results

The control group completed 638 in the first and 515 math problems in the second session, whereas the feedback group completed 477 in the first and 420 in the second session. Children in the control group completed significantly more questions ($M = 30.4$) in the first than in the second session ($M = 24.5$, $t(20) = 4,353$, $p = 0,0003$). No difference was found in the feedback group ($M = 23.9$ questions in the first and $M = 21.0$ in the second session). Using One-Way ANOVA, we find that the control group completed significantly more exercises in the first session than the feedback group ($F(1, 39) = 7,321$, $p = 0.010$) but no difference was found in the second session ($F(1, 39) = 1,679$, $p = 0.203$).

The control group gave 254 incorrect answers (including repeated tries) for 164 questions (25.7%) in the first and 261 incorrect answers for 157 questions (30.5%) in the second session. The feedback group gave 221 incorrect answers for 143 questions (30.0%) in the first and 219 incorrect answers for 139 questions (33.1%) in the second session. All mistakes that could be identified by our detection algorithm as fitting in one of the error categories we defined were identified as such and all categories occurred at least once but our algorithm was only able to recognise 15 out of 254 incorrect answers given by the feedback group in the first session and 12 out of 219 in the second session. Most of the mistakes made thus could not be classified by the algorithm, often because, for example, answers given seemed 'random' and any pattern was hard to detect. Upon the given feedback, 44.4% of the time children were able to produce a correct answer. Because feedback was also given to children who gave incorrect answers after a second try, feedback was given 158 times (35.9%) in total in both sessions.

We did not find any significantly different results on the three math tests that were taken before and after the experiment between the control and feedback group. The results of the first math test were not significantly different from the second ($p = 0.316$), and those of the second were also not significantly different from the last one ($p = 0.630$). Similarly, we used Mixed ANOVA to analyse the PANAS scores of the children, but did not find any significant differences between the feedback and the control group nor between sessions.

Children needed to get used to the interaction mechanism that we designed, although they hardly ever (5 out of 3994 times) forgot to press the feet before telling the robot their answer. The main issues were that children provided their answer too late and the speech-to-text module sometimes failed. Children provided an answer too late, more in the first than the second session (2.51 times on average versus 0.66, a significant difference, $t(49) = 2.94$, $p = 0.005$, with 3 children who had more issues in this regard but only in the first session). The robot misinterpreted in the first session on average 3, 4 correct answers per child, significantly more often than the 1, 7 answers that were incorrectly transcribed to text in the second session ($t(80) = 2.67$, $p = 0.009$). Children also learned to ask the robot to repeat a math problem by touching the robot's head more in the second (10.6) than the first session (6.8, $t(75) = -3.28$, $p = 0.002$).

Children indicated in the survey that they liked working with the robot and that they felt they learned something from the robot. Only in the control group, we found a significant increase in rating of the statement "I think Pixel [i.e. the robot] has taught me something", with an average of $M = 3.81$ out of 5 after the first session versus $M = 4.19$ after the second session ($t(20) = 2.36$, $p = 0.029$).

6   Discussion

Our detection algorithm was only able to classify a few of the many mistakes that children made, limiting the feedback that children received from the robot. Although theory has identified several categories of commonly made mistakes, many of the mistakes we found in practice did not fit into these categories and another approach is needed to handle these. We found evidence that suggests that feedback is more appreciated by children who have more difficulty with math problems and appreciate the fact that the robot put no time pressure on providing an answer. Children who perform well at math sometimes got impatient with the robot that explained them things they already know.

We could not establish any learning effects by means of the math tests children completed before and after the experiment. We thus found no evidence to support our hypothesis that feedback provided by a robot improves performance on math problems. This may have been partly due to the high scores on the pre-test completed before the experiment leaving little room for improvement in the other tests but equally likely is that a few sessions with a robot are insufficient to find any learning effects on math questions. Although most children indicated that the robot improved their math skills and that they learnt from the robot, a few said that the robot did not teach them anything new. Some of the better performing children also said it took the robot too long to provide feedback, and they would have preferred to be able to move on to the next question quicker.

The PANAS results also do not support our hypothesis that a robot that provides more feedback is liked more. Interestingly, however, some children said they liked working with the robot better than doing math on a tablet because the robot did not use a timer as the tablet apps do. The tablet apps for math force children to produce answers quickly while the robot gave children as much time as they needed. Teachers at the schools that participated also were very enthusiastic about the use of a robot math tutor.

Children need time to learn how to interact with a robot, which became clear from the two sessions in which children's interaction with the robot significantly improved: in the second session children were quicker to provide the robot with an answer, they asked the robot more often to repeat the question by touching its head, and they learnt how to talk to the robot when providing their answers to it. Some of the students were shy and had trouble communicating with the robot at first, but this improved in the second session. The robot's misunderstandings were frustrating, and children indicated after the sessions that the robot should listen better to their answers. Issues with speech recognition remain a big issue in child-robot interaction [8]. Overall, however, we can say that the combination of speech and touch created a robust interaction mechanism as all children were able to successfully complete the sessions without any intervention from the researcher who was present.

Limitations. Our results indicate that a few sessions over a two week period are insufficient to measure any learning effects of the robot on the children's performance on math problems. It seems hard to ascribe any effects specifically to the robot when the teacher spends much more time teaching the children.

7   Conclusion

Our approach to identify specific errors in addition and subtraction problems, as was to be expected, has turned out to be somewhat naive. We have overestimated the frequency of occurrence of the types of problems our algorithm is able to detect. Moreover, our method does not detect the strategy used by a child to solve the problem. Even though it is not clear from the literature whether feedback is best given using the same strategy as the child uses, we are also unable to do this. One important lesson of our work therefore is that there is a need for more detailed knowledge about which errors children make in the addition and subtraction (and other) domain(s) and how we can detect these and the strategies children use in this domain. As [1] indicates, there is still much to learn about this domain and this is still the case even though some progress has been made more recently in the automated diagnosis of subtraction bugs [9].

It is hard to assess the effectiveness of our feedback approach given the low frequency of addition and subtraction errors that the robot was able to detect. We did not find any evidence to support our hypothesis that feedback improves children's performance in the addition and subtraction domain. One issue, unrelated to the robot here, is that the children in our study already did quite well on the problems we presented. We also did not find any evidence that feedback increases affection towards the robot math tutor. We did receive very positive comments from children on learning with the robot though.

The interaction mechanism was robust and the robot was able to execute our interaction design patterns autonomously. Children were always able to complete a session without any need for human intervention. We found that the interaction with the robot in the second session improved compared to the first. With regards to our first Touch-Based Speech Activation pattern, fewer children were late in providing an answer and the robot made fewer speech recognition mistakes. Children needed some time but overall were able to quickly learn how to interact with the robot. With regards to our second Feedback pattern, it appears that differences in children's performance also should be reflected more in the feedback mechanism. Children that perform better, for example, become impatient when they have to listen to the rather long feedback of the robot in case of an error and should be able to proceed quicker to the next problem. It would also be interesting to adapt the problem level to the performance level of a child [13].

Finally, we have focused on verbal feedback and only used non-verbal rewards (LEDs, dance) but non-verbal behaviour can also be used to give feedback. The integration of such behaviour, e.g., using nodding or head shaking to steer a child in the right direction [12], may be an interesting direction for future work.

References

1. Beishuizen, M.: Mental strategies and materials or models for addition and subtraction up to 100 in Dutch second grades. J. Res. Math. Educ. **24**(4), 294–323 (1993)
2. Belpaeme, T., Kennedy, J., Ramachandran, A., Scassellati, B., Tanaka, F.: Social robots for education: a review. Sci. Roboti. **3**(21), eaat5954 (2018)
3. Brown, L., Howard, A.M.: Engaging children in math education using a socially interactive humanoid robot. In: 2013 13th IEEE-RAS International Conference on Humanoid Robots (Humanoids), pp. 183–188, October 2013
4. Hattie, J., Timperley, H.: Review of educational the power of feedback. Rev. Educ. Res. **77**(1), 81–112 (2007)
5. Janssen, J.B., van der Wal, C.C., Neerincx, M.A., Looije, R.: Motivating children to learn arithmetic with an adaptive robot game. In: Mutlu, B., Bartneck, C., Ham, J., Evers, V., Kanda, T. (eds.) ICSR 2011. LNCS (LNAI), vol. 7072, pp. 153–162. Springer, Heidelberg (2011). https://doi.org/10.1007/978-3-642-25504-5_16
6. Kahn, P.H., et al..: Design patterns for sociality in human-robot interaction. In: Proceedings of the International Conference on Human Robot Interaction, pp. 97–104. ACM (2008)
7. Kennedy, J., Baxter, P., Belpaeme, T.: The robot who tried too hard: social behaviour of a robot tutor can negatively affect child learning. In: Proceedings of the International Conference on Human-Robot Interaction, vol. 801, pp. 67–74 (2015)
8. Kennedy, J., et al.: Child speech recognition in human-robot interaction: evaluations and recommendations. In: Proceedings of the International Conference on Human-Robot Interaction, pp. 82–90. ACM (2017)
9. Lee, J., Corter, J.E.: Diagnosis of subtraction bugs using Bayesian networks. Appl. Psychol. Meas. **35**(1), 27–47 (2011)
10. Mubin, O., Stevens, C.J., Shahid, S., Al Mahmud, A., Dong, J.J.: A review of the applicability of robots in education. J. Tech. Educ. Learn. **1**(209–0015), 13 (2013)
11. Norcini, J.: The power of feedback. Med. Educ. **44**(1), 16–17 (2010)
12. Saerbeck, M., Schut, T., Bartneck, C., Janse, M.D.: Expressive robots in education: varying the degree of social supportive behavior of a robotic tutor. In: Proceedings on Human Factors in Computing Systems (SIGCHI), pp. 1613–1622. ACM (2010)
13. Schadenberg, B.R., Neerincx, M.A., Cnossen, F., Looije, R.: Personalising game difficulty to keep children motivated to play with a social robot: a Bayesian approach. Cogn. Syst. Res. **43**, 222–231 (2017)
14. Singh, R., et al.: Feedback during web-based homework: the role of hints. In: Biswas, G., Bull, S., Kay, J., Mitrovic, A. (eds.) AIED 2011. LNCS (LNAI), vol. 6738, pp. 328–336. Springer, Heidelberg (2011). https://doi.org/10.1007/978-3-642-21869-9_43
15. Tiberius, R.G., Billson, J.M.: The social context of teaching and learning. New Dir. Teach. Learn. **1991**(45), 67–86 (1991)
16. Watson, D., Clark, L.A., Tellegen, A.: Development and validation of brief measures of positive and negative affect: the PANAS scales. J. Pers. Soc. Psychol. **54**(6), 1063 (1988)
17. Wiggins, G.: 7 Keys to Effective Feedback. Educ. leadersh. **70**(1), 10–16 (2012)

Natural Teaching of Robot-Assisted Rearranging Exercises for Cognitive Training

Antonio Andriella[(✉)], Alejandro Suárez-Hernández, Javier Segovia-Aguas, Carme Torras, and Guillem Alenyà

Institut de Robòtica i Informàtica Industrial, CSIC-UPC,
C/Llorens i Artigas 4-6, 08028 Barcelona, Spain
{aandriella,asuarez,jsegovia,torras,galenya}@iri.upc.edu

Abstract. Social Assistive Robots are a powerful tool to be used in patients' cognitive training. The purpose of this study is to evaluate a new methodology to enable caregivers to teach cognitive exercises to the robot in an easy and natural way. We build upon our existing framework, in which a robot is employed to provide encouragement and hints while a patient is physically playing a cognitive exercise. In this paper, we focus on empowering the caregiver to easily teach new board exercises to the robot by providing positive examples.

The proposed learning method has two main advantages (i) the teaching procedure is human-friendly (ii) the produced exercise rules are human-understandable. The learning algorithm is validated in 6 exercises with different characteristics, correctly identifying and representing the rules from a few examples.

Keywords: SAR · Robotic assisted exercises · Natural teaching

1 Introduction

The increase in life expectancy is one of the most important achievements of the 21st century. However, ageing and age-related diseases are a mounting challenge for families, social, economic and healthcare systems [15]. One of the biggest challenges of the modern world associated with the ageing population is dementia [13]. According to the Word Health Organization the number of people with dementia will rise from 50 mil in 2018 to 82 mil in 2030, and more than 150 mil in 2050 [1].

This project has received funding from the European Union's Horizon 2020 research and innovation programme under the Marie Sklodowska-Curie grant agreement SOCRATES MSCA-ITN-721619, by the Spanish Ministry of Science and Innovation HuMoUR TIN2017-90086-R, and by the Spanish State Research Agency through the María de Maeztu Seal of Excellence to IRI (MDM-2016-0656).

© Springer Nature Switzerland AG 2019
M. A. Salichs et al. (Eds.): ICSR 2019, LNAI 11876, pp. 611–621, 2019.
https://doi.org/10.1007/978-3-030-35888-4_57

(a) First loop of interaction   (b) Second loop of interaction

Fig. 1. Illustrative images. (a) A caregiver sets the patient's mental and physical impairment and the robot's initial behaviour. (b) The robot assists the patient while he is playing the cognitive exercise. Frames from the video in https://youtu.be/zqcLSdl0UcE.

Currently there is no treatment available to cure dementia or to modify the progression of the disease [7]. The limited efficacy of the pharmacological therapies is the reason to explain the arising interest for non-pharmacological interventions for dementia patients. The non-pharmacologic intervention aims to enhance or at least maintain the individual's cognitive function, enabling to address behavioural symptoms that often exist in people affected by dementia, such as depression [7]. These interventions can be divided into four categories outlined by [9]: holistic techniques, brief psychotherapy, cognitive methods, and alternative methods. In our project, we focus on cognitive therapies, specifically on Cognitive Training (CT) exercises. CT is one of those activities that seeks, through repetitive practice, to train specific cognitive processes via standardized exercises [6].

Socially Assistive Robotics (SAR) is a branch of Robotics that aims to endow robots with the capability to aid people through individual social assistance, rather than physical, in convalescence, rehabilitation, and training [16]. Robots not only can be available twenty-four hours a day, but they may also help with the growing shortage of personnel support and, moreover, ease the workload of human therapists. Research has already shown that SAR can help improve the quality of life for older adults and bridge the gap when human assistance is not available [20].

In this paper, we extend our previous work [4] in which a SAR is employed by a caregiver to provide encouragement and motivation, through speech and gesture, to a patient while he is playing a cognitive exercise. There, two main loops of interaction are proposed. In the first one, the caregiver sets the patient's cognitive and physical impairment and the initial preferences on the robot's behaviour (see Fig. 1a). In the second one, the robot, given the caregiver's settings, provides assistance to the user through encouragements and hints based on his performance (See Fig. 1b).

Most of the current works in SAR are focused on the second loop of interaction (robot - final user) in which the robot, partially or entirely replaces the caregiver's role [2]. On the contrary, we target our attention to the first loop as we envisage a central role for the caregiver.

In previous work [4], the caregiver could provide information about the patient with the intent to personalize the robot's behaviour (see Fig. 1a). However, she/he could not extend the repertoire of exercises. Programming a robot, in fact, is a tedious process that requires a considerable amount of technical expertise. With that in mind, the practice of configuring new exercises is exclusive to the competent personnel and this represent a limitation in reality.

In this paper, we present a way to equip the caregiver with an easy and natural human-like approach to teach new exercises simply by playing them. From few moves taught by the caregiver, the robot is able to learn the rules of the new exercise. This enables the robot to monitor patients who perform this same exercise. Furthermore, the learned rules are available in first-order language. This provides an explainable and intuitive way of understanding what the system has learned, since rules can be easily translated to natural language.

The proposed exercises are inspired by the Syndrom Kurztest [17], and they have been thought specifically to combine cognitive and motor functions on visuomotor skills like grasping and manipulation [11]. Six different exercises are defined: sorting odd numbers in ascending order, sorting numbers in ascending and descending order, an exercise where position within the board matters, composing a word, and sorting letters in alphabetical ascending order.

The main contributions of this paper are: (1) a friendly method of teaching board exercises using natural interactions; and (2) a learning algorithm that produces human-understandable rules.

We believe the proposed paper is a step further in the direction to provide non-expert people, and in particular therapists, with easy-to-use methods where exercises can be programmed through playing examples, and directly represent exercise rules into an explainable symbolic high-level language such as STRIPS [12].

2   Related Work

In the last decade, a lot of effort has been put in developing robotic systems programmable from non-experts.

Graphical programming and user-friendly interface have been developed to provide non-experts with a way to understand and program without investing much time in learning. Pieska *et al.* [18] present an interesting review about the state of the art on user-friendly interface for robots and in their work they develop a platform suitable for both programming experts and people with no robot programming skill. The platform is based on a set of ready-made plugins, whose plugins can be connected through a graphical interface to generate a robot program.

There are also a few attempts to introduce user-friendly programming to Robotic Operating System (ROS)-based systems. Crick *et al.* [10] introduce rosbridge, a middleware abstraction layer to enable ROS accessible to programmers that are not them-self roboticists. Tiddi *et al.* [23] develop a user interface

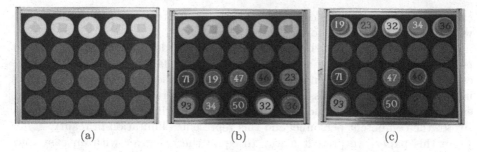

Fig. 2. (a) Empty Board: goal row in white, storage rows in blue. (b) Tokens randomly placed in the storage rows from the caregiver. (c) Tokens moved in the goal row in ascending order from the caregiver. (Color figure online)

for assisting non-expert users to design complex robot behaviours and control robotic systems based on ROS. Zubrycky *et al.* [24] present a graphical programming interface called Robokol, based on ROS and Snap, that enables non-technical professionals to program robots and internet-of-things devices.

In the field of education robots, there are also examples of introducing easy interfaces to program robots. One of the most well-known is *Choregraphe*, a graphical environment developed by Aldebaran Robotics for programming their humanoid robot, NAO [19]. *Choregraphe* enables non-experts to create robot behaviours using a Box library. It contains from high-level (walking, dancing, etc) to low level robot's functionalities (sensors, LEDs, etc) that can be assembled and linked based on user's own need to create a custom robot's behaviour. All these approaches have in common the idea of a graphical interface to link basic behaviours. On the contrary, we propose to use simple real demonstrations.

Real demonstrations have been used before to teach physical tasks using Learning by Demonstration techniques [5]. This approach has been extensively used in the literature for learning low-level robot motions [8], and also for incrementally learning assembly tasks [22]. In our work, we are not interested in teaching the motion trajectories but the logical rules of the exercise from a few user's gameplay demonstrations.

3   Method

A practical system ought to be naturally programmable by caregivers and practitioners. Thus, we propose that the caregiver shows the robot some successful runs of the exercise, and then let the robot discover the underlying rules. The board exercise is of the form of several tokens arranged (see Fig. 2b) in the **storage rows** (see blue cells in Fig. 2a) that have to be displaced to the **goal row** (see white cells of Fig. 2a) based on rules taught by the therapist (see Fig. 2c). This setup is very flexible, as the tokens can be labelled with numbers, letters or symbols, allowing the generation of multiple exercises. In this paper, we have used 6 different exercises to show the generality of the approach. We will present them in Sect. 4.

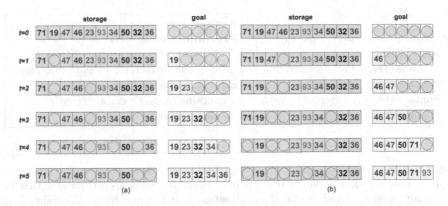

Fig. 3. Example of two traces or play-outs, provided by a caregiver to teach the "ascending order" exercise. Both traces are meant to demonstrate the same exercise. In (a) the caregiver teaches how to sort the five smallest numbers while in (b) he teaches how to sort the five largest numbers. In both traces, the initial token position ($t = 0$) is random. Later steps ($t > 0$) show the progress of the caregiver in the current trace.

3.1 Perception

The most common approach is to use computer vision to monitor the changes in the environment [14]. However, from our experience in real environments, simple vision algorithms able to run embedded in common robots are not reliable enough in natural environments. Furthermore, most of the current robotic platforms are equipped with only one camera that is generally located in their head, thus if the camera is used to detect the board state then, for instance, it cannot be used to monitor the user's affective behaviour.

For this reason, we built an electronic board based on RFID technology. Each token is univocally identified with an ID. The board consists of 20 Grove - NFC boards one for each board cell, 3 Adafruit TCA9548A, 1 to 8 I2C multiplexers, and 1 Arduino Nano. The Grove NFC has a highly integrated transceiver module PN532 which handles contact-less communication at 13.56MHz. Finally, Grove NFC is controlled using I2C communication protocol.

Using this board we have experienced no errors in detecting the tokens and in creating reliable traces. A trace is a sequence of valid pick-and-place actions in which the demonstrator moves tokens from one location to another one (see Fig. 3). For each timestamp t, our driver records the current move as a triplet ($token\_id, orig, dest$). It is worth to be mentioned that although the board is capable to detect more than one move at the same time, in this context we don't allow the demonstrator to teach more than one move at a time.

Action: move-v19-t1($from$, to) Precondition: $to = l_{11} \wedge$ contains($from, v_{19}$) $\wedge$ empty(to) Effect: $\neg$ contains($from, v_{19}$)$\wedge$ contains(to, v_{19}) $\wedge$ empty($from$)$\wedge$ $\neg$ empty(to)	Action: move-v23-t2($from$, to) Precondition: $to = l_{12} \wedge$ contains($from, v_{23}$) $\wedge$ empty(to)$\wedge$ $\exists v'$ (contains($l11, v'$) $\wedge$ less-than(v', v_{23})) Effect: $\neg$ contains($from, v_{23}$)$\wedge$ contains(to, v_{23}) $\wedge$ empty($from$)$\wedge$ $\neg$ empty(to)
(a)	(b)

Fig. 4. (a) the action for moving token v_{19} (the token with value 19) as the first move requires that the destination is the top left corner (location l_{11}); (b) the action for allocating token v_{23} requires that the destination is at location l_{12} (at the right of the top left corner) and that there is a token at location l_{11} with lower numeric value.

3.2 Actions and Rules

In every board scenario, all 10 tokens are distributed among the storage and goal cells. The particular arrangement conforms the current *state* of the exercise. The state is described in terms of propositional variables (e.g. when contains (l_{ij}, A) is true, it means that token A is in the cell (i, j)). An action is defined as a 2-tuple ⟨*precondition, effect*⟩, where *precondition* is a logic formula that must hold in the current state for the action to be applicable, and *effect* is a set of variable assignments that modify the current state. The exercise's *rules* determine the set of applicable actions for each state, while the inapplicable actions are those against the rules. Therefore, learning the rules of an exercise reduces to learn the preconditions of the different actions.

Rules are expressed in terms of observable features that describe the characteristics of individual tokens (e.g. *odd*) or pairs of tokens (e.g. *less-than*). These features aim at being generic enough to provide the capability of defining interesting cognitive exercises. For a particular exercise, the rules involve only a subset of these features, while the rest are distractors. Since exercises require only 5 movements, it is possible that up to 5 tokens are irrelevant, or that exercises have more than one correct solution (e.g. sorting 5 tokens out of 10 in ascending order). The fact that tokens can be randomly arranged in the initial state adds extra complexity, so learning the rules must generalize over any input order.

Once rules are learned, they can be used for validating actions performed by the patients. In validation, the robot checks if the preconditions of the applied action are met in the previous state. If not, the patient is informed the action performed is invalid and the movement is undone by the robot.

As a means to give intuition about actions and rules, let us consider the board setting from Fig. 2b and the exercise of sorting tokens with numbers in ascending order. Figure 4 shows 2 out of the 30 actions that are needed to solve the exercise. Notice how the preconditions are quite different from each other and are in direct correspondence with the rules of the exercise. The first movement must be moving one of the 6 tokens (19-23-32-34-36-46) with lowest value to

Fig. 5. A user teaching a new exercise to the robot.

the top left corner cell. Further movements must fill successively the rest of the goal row with tokens making sure that the cells at their left have lower numeric values. Our next section outlines how our method is capable of learning such rules from exercise traces.

3.3 Learning Method

Our learning method infers the precondition of all actions from exercise traces given by the caregiver (Fig. 5). An action has the form move-*value-timestep* (*from*, *to*), where *value* is the value of the token associated to the action, *timestep* is the move index in the sequence of moves in which the action is meant to be executed, *from* is the source cell parameter and *to* is the destination parameter. Since every exercise has 10 tokens and solutions require 5 time steps, problems will consist of learning preconditions of up to 50 pick-and-place actions.

The input is a set of traces or examples provided by the caregiver. Initially, we include all possible restrictions in all of the 50 actions' preconditions. Therefore, actions are initially inapplicable because some propositional variables interfere (e.g. the preconditions require that a token is in multiple locations at the same time). Our method then uses the available traces to progressively relax the preconditions, leaving them just restrictive enough so they can be used to explain the transitions of all the given traces. This is done via symbolic planning with Madagascar [21], in a way that is reminiscent of the approach taken and detailed by Aineto *et al.* [3]. Namely, we pose a planning problem in which the goal is to relax the preconditions in order to validate all the given traces.

Exercises like the *odd ascending* (introduced later in Sect. 4) do not need to use the whole set of actions, because many actions cannot ever be executed (like those actions for moving tokens with even numbers) and will not show up in any trace. Other exercises, like placing any sequence of 5 tokens in ascending order with no parity constraints, have many solutions and, thus, require more traces to learn the rules. Overall, the lower the complexity, the easier it is to learn the rules.

Figure 3 shows two example traces that can be used to learn the rules of an ascending sorting exercise. These two traces serve to discard some of the irrelevant features (e.g. the initial position of the tokens). When exposed to enough traces, our learner infers the rules depicted in Fig. 4.

4   Experiments

We set up our system to gather exercise traces and learn human-understandable rules from them using the board presented in Sect. 3.1. We used 6 self-described exercises as a proof of concept: (i) sorting five odd numbers in ascending order; (ii) sorting five numbers in ascending order; (iii) sorting five numbers in descending order, (iv) moving first storage row to goal row, (v) spell "CURIE" word choosing 5 of 10 available letters, and (vi) sorting five letters in lexicographical order. Exercises from (i) to (iv) use tokens with integer values, while exercises (v) and (vi) used tokens with letters.

4.1   Trace Generation for New Exercises

In order to learn new exercises, we need to extract traces such as those from Fig. 3. When an exercise is being demonstrated via traces, we transform the information from perception into symbolic states. Transitions between states are the result of actions taken by the caregiver. The number of required traces to learn the ground truth of the exercise will depend on the intrinsic complexity of exercise and solution space.

The minimum number of traces required to demonstrate an exercise depends on its complexity. Exercises (i) and (v), only require **2 traces** where all tokens are in different initial locations, as only one solution is possible. Exercises (ii), (iii) and (vi) need **12 traces** that summarize all the possible ways of sorting 5 pieces out of 10. Finally, exercise (iv)'s rules only involve locations, so we have to observe all 10 tokens moving from every column in the first storage row to the goal row, and this can be done with **10 traces**. Experimentally, we found that only expert users are able to provide this minimum number of demonstrations. Interestingly, our system can use all the traces that are provided, even if they are not the most informative ones.

Additionally, our system provides an interface to decide beforehand which features are relevant for learning the next exercise (for example, an exercise may not require the *less-than* feature). When used, it reduces drastically the number of traces that are needed.

Figure 6a gives an intuition on how the system's actions progress over time, as more and more traces are demonstrated. This plot is associated with the exercise (ii). When a few traces are shown, the system deduces overly restrictive rules. As more traces are shown, the system relaxes the preconditions and comes up with the correct set of rules.

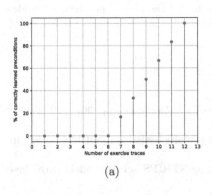

Action: move-v23-t2($from$, to)
Inferred rules:
  Destination (to) goal is cell l_{12}
  Source ($from$) contains token v_{23}
  Destination (to) is empty
  Location l_{11} token is less than 23.
Descriptive text:
  In the second movement, if the token
  marked with number 23 is in its
  original position then has to moved
  to the goal cell 2 only if it is empty
  and the token in cell 1 is less than 23.

(a)   (b)

Fig. 6. (a) percentage of correctly learned rules for exercise (ii) given the number of traces demonstrated by the caregiver (this is the percentage of actions whose precondition matches exactly the ground truth of the exercise); (b) rule from Fig. 4b (belonging to exercise (ii)) explained in natural language, as output by our system.

4.2 Human Readable Rules

Figure 6b shows an example of the underlying rules behind an action in exercise (ii). We describe the method to generate human-understandable rules with a particular example: from the learned rules (Fig. 4b) an intermediate explanation is generated; using this intermediate representation, a complete sentence can be assembled. These rules can be displayed in natural language, so the caregiver can easily understand them.

Space restrictions do not allow to show all the generated rules. In terms of time, computing the complete set of rules and explanations for this kind of exercises take less than 2 s in an average computer.

5 Conclusions and Future Work

The main contribution of this paper lies in proposing an approach to teach a robot new exercises through human demonstrations. The proposed method enables non-technical professionals, such as caregivers and therapists, to program new cognitive exercises to a robotic system, that can afterwards administer the exercise. Notably, the learned rules are easily readable and explainable because they can be expressed in logic language using well-understood features such as order relationships.

In the future, we will extend the current learning algorithm to cope with more complex rules. We would like to explore further its ability to generalize from examples, and reduce the number of traces needed to learn the rules.

Acknowledgements. Authors would like to thank Patrick Grosch, Sergi Hernandez and Alejandro López for assembling and programming the electronic board. Thanks to Nofar Sinai (http://www.vikkiacademy.com/) for allowing us to use some frames of the SOCRATES video.

References

1. Alzheimer's disease facts and figures. Alzheimer's & Dementia, pp. 367–429, March 2018
2. Abdi, J., et al.: Scoping review on the use of socially assistive robot technology in elderly care. BMJ Open **8**(2), 18815 (2018)
3. Aineto, D., Jiménez, S., Onaindia, E.: Learning STRIPS action models with classical planning. In: ICAPS (2018)
4. Andriella, A., et al.: Deciding the different robot roles for patient cognitive training. Int. J. Hum Comput Stud. **117**, 20–29 (2018)
5. Argall, B.D., et al.: A survey of robot learning from demonstration. Rob. Autonom. Syst. **57**(5), 469–483 (2009)
6. Bahar-Fuchs, A., et al.: Tailored and adaptive computerized cognitive training in older adults at risk for dementia: a randomized controlled trial. J. Alzheimers Dis. **60**(3), 889–911 (2017)
7. Berg-Weger, M., Stewart, D.B.: Non-pharmacologic interventions for persons with dementia. Mo. Med. **114**(2), 116–119 (2017)
8. Calinon, S.: Learning from demonstration (programming by demonstration). In: Encyclopedia of Robotics, pp. 1–8 (2018)
9. Cammisuli, D.M., et al.: Non-pharmacological interventions for people with Alzheimer's disease: a critical review of the scientific literature from the last ten years. Eur. Geriatr. Med. **7**(1), 57–64 (2016)
10. Crick, C., Jay, G., Osentoski, S., Pitzer, B., Jenkins, O.C.: Rosbridge: ROS for Non-ROS users. In: Christensen, H.I., Khatib, O. (eds.) Robotics Research. STAR, vol. 100, pp. 493–504. Springer, Cham (2017). https://doi.org/10.1007/978-3-319-29363-9_28
11. De Boer, C., et al.: Thinking-while-moving exercises may improve cognition in elderly with mild cognitive deficits: a proof-of-principle study. Dement. Geriatr. Cogn. Disord. Extra **8**(2), 248–258 (2018)
12. Fikes, R., Nilsson, N.: BLACKBOX: a new approach to the application of theorem proving to problem solving. Artif. Intell. J. **2**, 189–208 (1971)
13. Irwin, K., et al.: Healthy aging and dementia: two roads diverging in midlife? (2018)
14. Leo, M., et al.: Computer vision for assistive technologies. Comput. Vis. Image Underst. **154**, 1–15 (2017)
15. Lunenfeld, B., Stratton, P.: The clinical consequences of an ageing world and preventive strategies. Best Pract. Res. Clin. Obstet. Gynaecol. **27**(5), 643–659 (2013)
16. Matarić, M.J., Scassellati, B.: Socially assistive robotics. In: Siciliano, B., Khatib, O. (eds.) Springer Handbook of Robotics, pp. 1973–1994. Springer, Cham (2016). https://doi.org/10.1007/978-3-319-32552-1_73
17. Overall, J.E., Schaltenbrand, R.: The SKT neuropsychological test battery. J. Geriatr. Psychiatry Neurol. **5**(0891–9887), 220–227 (1992)
18. Pieskä, S., Pieskäa, J., Saukko, O.: Towards easier human-robot interaction to help inexperienced operators in SMEs. In: 3rd IEEE International Conference on CogInfoCom 2012 - Proceedings, pp. 333–338 (2012)

19. Pot, E., et al.: Choregraphe: a graphical tool for humanoid robot programming. In: Proceedings - IEEE International Workshop on RO-MAN, pp. 46–51 (2009)
20. Pu, L., et al.: The effectiveness of social robots for older adults: a systematic review and meta-analysis of randomized controlled studies (2019)
21. Rintanen, J.: Madagascar: scalable planning with SAT. In: Proceedings of the 8th International Planning Competition (2014)
22. Savarimuthu, T.R., et al.: Teaching a robot the semantics of assembly tasks. IEEE Trans. Syst. Man Cybern. Syst., 670–692 (2018)
23. Tiddi, I., et al.: A user-friendly interface to control ROS robotic platforms. In: CEUR Workshop Proceedings, vol. 2180 (2018)
24. Zubrycki, I., Kolesiński, M., Granosik, G.: Graphical programming interface for enabling non-technical professionals to program robots and internet-of-things devices. Adv. Comput. Intell. **10306**, 620–631 (2017)

A Digital Wooden Tabletop Maze
for Estimation of Cognitive Capabilities
in Children

Seethu M. Christopher[1]([✉]), Corrie C. Urlings[2],
Henri van den Bongarth[3], Karien M. Coppens[2], Petra P. M. Hurks[4],
Lex Borghans[2], and Rico Möckel[1]

[1] Faculty of Science and Engineering, Maastricht University,
Maastricht, The Netherlands
seethu.christopher@maastrichtuniversity.nl
[2] School of Business and Economics, Maastricht University,
Maastricht, The Netherlands
[3] IDEE, Maastricht University, Maastricht, The Netherlands
[4] Faculty of Psychology and Neuroscience,
Maastricht University, Maastricht, The Netherlands

Abstract. Standardized tests play an important role in assessing a child's cognitive capabilities. The results of such tests are used e.g. in schools and kindergartens to analyze and support the development of the tested child. Unfortunately, with classical standardized tests often only limited information on a child's behavior can be documented even by a professional observer. Obtaining detailed information would require automated data recording procedures. Also, standardized tests typically rely on well-controlled and thus rather artificial environments. As a result, young children age (e.g. with an age below 7) might not be able to fully understand the test instructions, feel uncomfortable being tested outside their natural environment, and thus test results become less relevant. Computer-based stealth-assessments that e.g. use a gaming environment to be fun and to hide the assessment from children might present a valid alternative. However, for children of lower age computer-based tests are not easily applicable due to technological boundaries. In this paper we thus explore an alternative approach: physical game devices with a look and feel similar to toys typically provided to children of their age group but that embed the electronics required for computer-based stealth testing. As a result, the game device – in our case a wooden tabletop maze – combines advantages of standardized computer-free and computer-based assessments. The device allows for stealth assessments in less structured environments without creating technological boundaries for the children.

Keywords: Intelligent games design · Digital toy · Cognitive assessments · Digital maze · Serious games

M. A. Salichs et al. (Eds.): ICSR 2019, LNAI 11876, pp. 622–632, 2019.
https://doi.org/10.1007/978-3-030-35888-4_58

1 Introduction

Cognitive assessments are useful to monitor a child's cognitive development [1, 2]. The field of psychology knows a variety of standardized tests targeting a variety of cognitive aspects. The Porteus Maze test [3] for instance is a nonverbal intelligence test developed to estimate psychological planning capacity and inhibition of a participant [4]. The Mazes subtest in WPPSI-R is another widely used test for assessing cognitive development of young children [5]. During these tests, children are confronted with mazes of varying complexity and instructed to solve as many mazes as possible within a given time. For this, children must trace through the mazes printed on paper with a pencil.

A key challenge with such standardized tests is that they rely on a professional observer to document the behavior of the participating children. A detailed recording of all potentially relevant behavioral information becomes not only impossible but also sometimes unreliable [6]. For instance to reach a high score in the Porteus Maze test, children are asked to solve mazes as efficiently as possible – by avoiding crossing maze lines, going into dead ends, without moving backwards, and lifting the pencil. The professional observer must record these features from the solved paper mazes by hand and calculate the final score. There might also be inconsistencies in the final score due to the complex scoring procedures, interrater reliability and administration difficulties [7]. Other potentially valuable information, like for instance at which maze position and for how long a child stopped drawing because the child planned the next actions, gets lost. Another criticism of standardized tests is that they require structured environments and are typically used under well-controlled conditions. Standardized tests thus can be stressful if the child has to leave his/her well-known environment or boring [8]. As a result, the child's motivation to participate in the test might drop and impact the test results [9].

To allow for maintaining high engagement of children during tests, to reduce the work load of testing professionals and to increase measurement accuracies, computer-based tests using game environments can present a valuable alternative to standardized pencil-and-paper tests [10]. Such computer-based tests have the additional advantage that they allow for collecting large amounts of detailed data in real-time. However, computer-based tests also always test a child's ability to adapt to and to handle the computer environment. In addition, computer-based tests cannot fully reassemble the interaction with and perception of natural environments. As a result, computer-based tests are often not suitable for young children for instance because of underdeveloped fine motor skills.

A better alternative might be to allow young children to play with tangible physical devices, as children naturally do during the continuous development of their skills [11]. Automated data collection then can be implemented e.g. by observing the participating child through computer vision. We for instance developed a setup where participants can play a game of Ludo using a physical game board. The game state was automatically captured through computer vision [12]. Digitized game moves could be assessed and processed automatically in a computer, but the participants would not be affected by the technology. However, reliable digitalization of game states through computer vision is susceptible to lighting conditions and occlusions, requiring optimal conditions and making it difficult to use in regular class room situations.

In this paper we thus explore the technology for yet another approach: we hide the required technology for digitalization and automated testing inside a physical game device. Inspired by the Porteus Maze test, a digital wooden maze device was developed that resembles those standard maze toys being used by children aged between 4 and 7. This digital wooden tabletop maze device is shown in Fig. 1(A). Inside the maze device, touch screen technology is hidden. The child moves a metal ball inside the wooden maze with a magnetic pen as shown in Fig. 1(C) without realizing that the pen and ball movements are automatically recorded, making it possible to do these tests in a less formal, child-oriented setting. In this paper we compare and analyze recordings automatically obtained by the wooden maze with recordings obtained from computer vision. For this, an overhead camera was installed as shown in Fig. 1(B).

From tests with children we show that the wooden maze can combine the advantages of both computer-based testing and classical standardized testing with physical objects. The digital wooden maze features automated data recording in real-time with high temporal and spatial resolution. Automated data analysis is performed offline on a standard PC. The maze is a physical object that fits on a table and is easy to use by young children who treat it like a standard toy without facing technological boundaries.

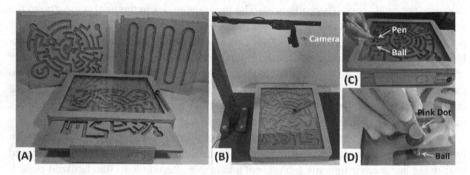

Fig. 1. (**A**): Digital Wooden Maze device with the different interchangeable maze structures. (**B**): Digital Maze setup with overhead camera for computer vision experiments; (**C**): Digital maze with custom-made pen. (**D**): Custom-made pen for controlling the magnetic ball. (Color figure online)

The remaining sections of this paper are organized as follows. Section 1 describes the digital wooden maze and data recording. Section 2 discusses the alternative approach of digitizing maze usage through computer vision. Section 3 and Sect. 4 present and discuss experimental results, respectively.

2   Digital Wooden Maze – Hardware and Data Processing

The digital wooden tabletop maze device (shown in Fig. 1(A)) weighs about 6.1 kg. Its material costs less than 600€. In low-volume fabrication a total price of less than 2500€ can be achieved. The maze device contains two separate touch screens placed back-to-back on top of each other. Screens are integrated into a wooden case as shown in the side view in Fig. 2(E). The wooden case and maze elements have been produced from sheets of Plywood that have been shaped through laser cutting and glued together. Inside the case and beneath the screens, the device contains a chamber that hosts the actual wooden maze structure. To allow for a variety of test items, we made the maze structures interchangeable. Figure 2(B–D) shows three existing wooden maze structures. The motor control structure (Fig. 2(D)) contains a single trace and was designed to gain insight into the base line (fine) motor capabilities of children. The assignment maze structure (Fig. 2(B)) allows testing children with three different maze solving tasks of increasing complexity. The exploration maze structure (shown in Fig. 2(C)) contains a free exploration maze pattern with which we want to gain insights into unstructured play behavior of children. The maze device contains four contact switches (Fig. 2(A)) that allow for automatic detection of the inserted maze structure due to different patterns milled into the top left corners of each maze structure (marked in red in Fig. 2(B–D)).

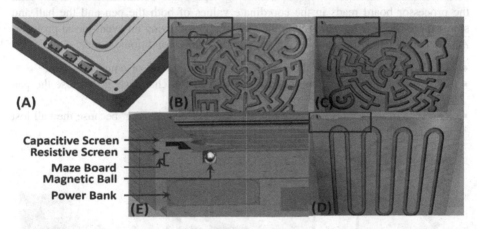

Fig. 2. (A): Contact switches inside the digital wooden maze device allow the automatic detection of inserted maze structures: (B): a maze structure with different assignments, (C): a maze structure for free exploration, (D): a maze structure for motor control tasks. (E): CAD picture of a cross-section of the digital wooden maze device.

A magnetic ball is inserted into the maze structures when sliding the maze structures into the digital wooden maze device. Once the maze structure is inserted, this magnetic ball can move freely inside the maze structure underneath the bottom screen but cannot accidentally be removed from the device.

Children move the magnetic ball within the maze structure with the help of a custom-made conductive pen (shown in Fig. 1(C) and (D)). The pen was made from an anodized aluminum pipe of 12 cm height with conductive tip and designed, so that it activates the capacitive multi-touch screen (BI-TFT19-PCAP10-4-USB from A1touch with an active area of 376.32 mm × 301.06 mm and a touch resolution of 4096 × 4096 pixels) on top of the maze device. As a result, when touching the top screen, the pen position can be continuously recorded by the maze device. In addition, the pen contains a magnetic tip that when close enough to the magnetic ball, pulls the magnetic ball against the resistive screen (5WR1902FA5 from A1touch with an active area of 376 mm × 301 mm and a touch resolution of 4096 × 4096 pixels) beneath the capacitive screen. As a result, the resistive screen can record the ball position. A combination of a capacitive and a resistive screen was chosen, so that pen and ball position can be detected independently without affecting each other.

When calibrated correctly, by fusing the knowledge about the layout of the inserted maze structure with the pen and ball positions recorded by the capacitive and resistive screen, respectively, the position of the pen and ball with respect to each other and within the maze can be determined. In addition, it can be detected when the ball and pen are connected to each other and when a child moves the pen without the ball.

Figure 3 provides an overview of the main electronics of the digital wooden maze device: Data obtained from the capacitive and resistive touch screen is recorded and processed by an embedded STM32F429 processor board. For ease of use, this processor board can be controlled from a custom-made app via a Bluetooth wireless communication interface. To save data storage space and communication bandwidth, the processor board reads in the coordinate values of both the pen and the ball and stores these in a text file along with the time stamp following an event-based protocol. A new coordinate is registered if any of the following conditions is met:

- The X or Y coordinate of the pen changes by more than or equal to 2 mm.
- The state of the connection between pen and screen changes e.g. because the pen was disconnected from the screen.
- The state of the connection between pen and ball changes e.g. because the ball lost contact with the pen.

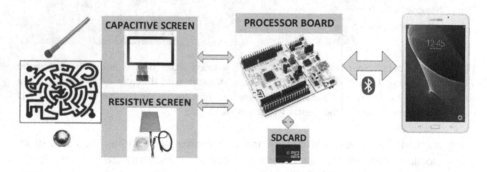

Fig. 3. Overview of main electronics inside the digital wooden maze.

Recorded data is stored in the following format: time since the startup of the maze in ms; id of the registered touch [0..10]; X coordinate of pen in mm; Y coordinate of pen in mm; a binary value that indicates if the pen touches the screen [0,1]; a binary value that indicates if ball and pen are connected [0,1]; the id of the inserted maze structure [0..3]; X coordinate of ball in mm; Y coordinate of ball in mm.

To avoid any loss of data e.g. during a loss of communication, all recorded data is stored on an SD memory card inside the maze device. All electronics are powered by a 10400 mAh power bank allowing for more than 7 h of continuous autonomous operation. The power bank is interchangeable so that the maze device can be kept operational during the charging process.

After recording, data is transferred to a PC for automated post-processing, feature extraction, and visualization. Figure 4 provides an overview of the processing steps. After the data acquisition step, we remove all data points that are not of interest to us. Such recorded points e.g. can be caused by the touch screen detecting contact by the hand or elbow of a child. Filtering of points consists of 3 steps:

(1) First, we remove all data points for which the ball and pen are not connected since for now we are only interested in movements where pen and ball move together.
(2) Secondly, we remove those data points where the distance between the consecutive x and y coordinates is above a given threshold. This step allows for removing data points caused by other touch events than the pen. The ideal threshold was found heuristically through extensive experimentation.
(3) Finally, we assign points according to the given tasks based on pre-defined start and end position on the maze as explained to the participating child.

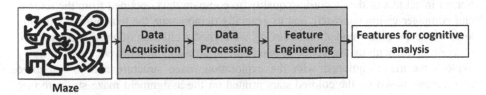

Fig. 4. Overview of data processing stages.

From the filtered valid points, we can extract a variety of features. This includes both those features required by the Porteus maze test (like crossing maze lines or going into dead ends) but also features that would be difficult to extract with a pencil-and-paper test like the position and duration that a child used to plan and rethink the applied maze-solving strategy. However, the evaluation and effect of these additional features for assessing cognitive abilities is beyond the scope of this paper. Here we focus on the presentation and evaluation of the new maze device mechatronics.

3   Digitalization of Pen Positions Through Computer Vision

We track the position of the pen with a camera to compare the processed outputs of the digital wooden maze device against data from camera tracking. The experimental setup for the tracking process is shown in Fig. 1(B). Tracking was accomplished through a HD720p webcam running at 30fps and an open-source object detection algorithm in OpenCV [13]. For ease of tracking the pen, a pink dot was added to the tip of the custom-made pen (see Fig. 1(D)) that is tracked during the experiments. Camera images are converted into HSV color space for better detection performance. The tracking algorithm detects the presence of the colored dot in the HSV camera images and saves the position to a text file. During the tracking process, the algorithm: (1) pre-processes the image frames (This step involves downsizing the image frame size and blurring the image to reduce high frequency noise.), (2) localizes all the regions in the image frame within the specified HSV range, (3) searches for the radii size of the pink dot in the localized regions found in the previous step, and (4) saves the coordinates along with a time stamp to a text file.

We adjusted color threshold parameters by hand to achieve a good detection performance. Still during experiments as expected from past studies [12] we experienced that detection performance was highly dependent on lighting conditions. To remove invalid point coordinates, we removed those data points where the distance between the consecutive x and y coordinates were above a given distance threshold. This step allows for removing falsely detected pen coordinates, similarly as for the data points directly obtained from the digital wooden maze device. Tracking ball positions was not possible with the camera setup due to occlusions and light reflections on the screen.

4   Experiments and Results

For an initial test of data recording quality, to compare data obtained from the screens and computer vision approach, and to generally demonstrate the feasibility of running tests with the digital wooden maze device, we invited 3 children of age 5 and one child of age 6 to test with us the device in two configurations. Children were asked to freely explore the maze equipped with the exploration maze structure and to run three assignments based on the colored stars printed on the assignment maze structure (see Fig. 5): Children always started at the center of the assignments maze structure and then got asked (1) to go to the yellow star and back, (2) to go to the green star and back, and (3) to go to the blue star and back.

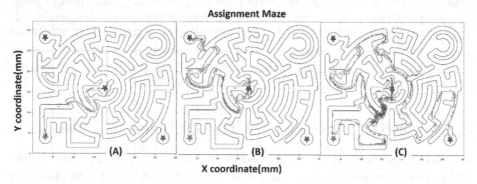

Fig. 5. Drawing of assignment maze structure overlayed with extracted data points for the three different assignments: **(A)** Assignment 1 (Go from red star int the middle to yellow star at the bottom left corner and back); **(B)** – Assignment 2 (Go from red star to green star in the top left corner and back); **(C)** – Assignment 3 (Go from red star to blue star in the bottom right corner and back). (Color figure online)

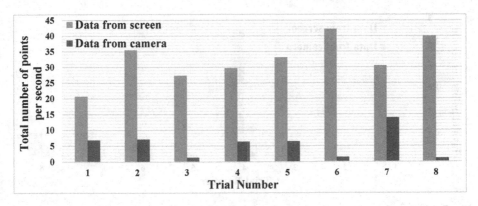

Fig. 6. Temporal resolution of screen and camera approach: total number of recorded points per second.

Table 1 presents the total number of collected and filtered (invalid) data points for the four individual participants and maze structure experiments. Numbers are given for both the data obtained through the maze's screen and through computer vision (camera). For the computer vision experiments we tried to create the best possible light conditions.

Table 1. Total number of data points collected and the invalid points from both Maze screen and Camera.

Trial No.	Maze structure	Participant No.	Maze screen			Camera		
			Total No. of points	No. of invalid points	Time (s)	Total No. of points	No. of invalid points	Time (s)
1	**Assignment**	1	9609	39	464.166	3232	27	473.677
2		2	4589	52	129.238	852	32	119.599
3		3	3326	37	121.65	145	25	105.327
4		4	3349	44	112.623	769	334	120.841
5	**Exploration**	1	7419	18	223.667	1365	19	211.976
6		2	2062	17	48.888	85	25	59.055
7		3	3930	24	128.831	1620	63	116.593
8		4	5935	48	148.261	169	80	149.499

To compare the performance of our approach (screen approach) with the camera approach, we plot for each trial and approach: in Fig. 6, the total number of points divided by the trial duration in seconds, in Fig. 7, the number of invalid points divided by the duration of the respective trial in seconds, and in Fig. 8, the number of invalid points divided by the total number of points in percent. The screen approach provides on average 82.79% more points per second, in the best case 96.58%, in the worst case

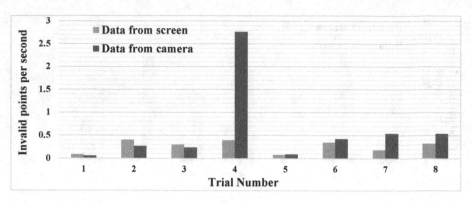

Fig. 7. Temporal resolution of screen and camera approach: number of invalid points per second

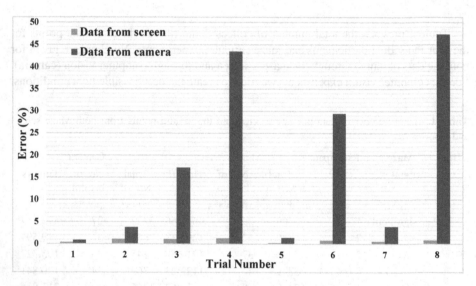

Fig. 8. Screen resolution of screen and camera approach: percentage of invalid (filtered) points with regard to total number of points.

54.45% and thus overall allows for a better temporal resolution. A reason is that the camera approach in contrast to the screen approach suffers from occlusions. So overall less points are detected in the camera images. In the screen method, inaccuracies are mostly generated when the pen loses contact with the ball. These usually occur if the pen is not held properly. As shown in Fig. 7, in three out of eight trials, the screen approach produced higher number of invalid points per second, on average 33.88%, and in the worst case 38.46%. This is partially caused by our definition of invalid points where we also filter situations where the ball is disconnected from the pen as invalid. This can also be caused by the fact that children sometimes rest their hands on the screen while playing, causing the top screen to detect both the hand and the pen. In the camera approach, the ball cannot even be detected. Thus, the data points being classified as valid in the screen approach are to be considered more reliable. The better screen resolution in terms of valid detected points also becomes visible when calculating an error value by normalizing the number of invalid points with regard to the total number of points as displayed in Fig. 8. On average the camera approach produces 95.62% more error than the screen approach, in the worst case 98.29% and in the best case 51.42%.

5   Discussion and Future Work

This paper presents a proof of concept for a digital wooden tabletop maze device designed for assessing cognitive abilities of young children. The novelty of the presented material lies in the approach and hardware. The maze device allows for stealth assessments inheriting advantages of computer-based testing like automated data acquisition and analysis but with a key advantage: The maze device looks like a normal wooden maze. Children can interact with the maze device in the way they are used to do with other tangible physical devices like toys. To proof the value of the maze device as a cognitive assessment tool, we are currently conducting a representative study with more children. So far, this paper presents only a pre-study with four children. However, the fact that the maze device allows for an extraction of similar features as the well-known Porteus maze test and mazes subtest from the WPPSI-R test is promising. Also, initial feedback from the four children who tested the device is very promising: all children showed great excitement when playing with the device and had no problems in handling the device. Also, their parents showed strong interest, making us hopeful that the maze device will be well-accepted by a general population.

Inspired by our experience with our camera-based digitalization approach of a board game for cognitive assessments, we compared the results obtained from the screens that have been integrated into the maze device with a camera-based tracking approach. Even under well-adjusted lighting conditions, the screen approach outperforms the camera-based approach. Due to its screen technology combining capacitive and resistance sensing, the digital maze is not susceptible to lighting conditions at all but can operate robustly in less-structured environments.

References

1. Blair, C., Razza, R.P.: Relating effortful control, executive function, and false belief understanding to emerging math and literacy ability in kindergarten. Child Dev. **78**(2), 647–663 (2007)
2. Borella, E., Carretti, B., Pelegrina, S.: The specific role of inhibition in reading comprehension in good and poor comprehenders. J. Learn. Disabil. **43**(6), 541–552 (2010)
3. Porteus, S.D.: The Porteus Maze Test and Intelligence. Pacific Books 1950 (1950)
4. Kirsch, P., et al.: Brain activation during mental maze solving. Neuropsychobiology **54**(1), 51–58 (2006)
5. Kaufman, A.S., Lichtenberger, E.O.: Essentials of WISC-III and WPPSI-R Assessment. Essentials of WISC-III and WPPSI-R Assessment. Wiley, Hoboken (2000)

6. Carlson, S.M.: Developmentally sensitive measures of executive function in preschool children. Dev. Neuropsychol. **28**(2), 595–616 (2005)
7. Kaufman, A.S.: The WPPSI-R: you can't judge a test by its colors. J. Sch. Psychol. **28**(4), 387–394 (1990). https://doi.org/10.1016/0022-4405(90)90027-5
8. Fleege, P.O., Charlesworth, R., Burts, D.C., Hart, C.H.: Stress begins in kindergarten: a look at behavior during standardized testing. J. Res. Child. Educ. **7**(1), 20–26 (1992). https://doi.org/10.1080/02568549209594836
9. Borghans, L., Meijers, H., Ter Weel, B.: The role of noncognitive skills in explaining cognitive test scores. Econ. Inq. **46**(1), 2–12 (2008)
10. Pillay, H.: An investigation of cognitive processes engaged in by recreational computer game players. J. Res. Technol. Educ. **34**(3), 336–350 (2002)
11. Wang, D., Zhang, C., Wang, H.: T-Maze: a tangible programming tool for children. In: Proceedings of the 10th International Conference on Interaction Design and Children, Ann Arbor, Michigan 2011 (2011)
12. Schmitt, F., Christopher, S.M., Tumanov, K., Weiss, G., Möckel, R.: Evaluating the adoption of the physical board game ludo for automated assessments of cognitive abilities. In: Göbel, S., et al. (eds.) JCSG 2018. LNCS, vol. 11243, pp. 30–42. Springer, Cham (2018). https://doi.org/10.1007/978-3-030-02762-9_5
13. https://www.pyimagesearch.com/2015/09/14/ball-tracking-with-opencv/. Accessed 19 Mar 2019

Interactive Robot Learning
for Multimodal Emotion Recognition

Chuang Yu and Adriana Tapus[✉]

Autonomous System and Robotics Lab, U2IS, ENSTA Paris Institut Polytechnique
de Paris, 828 boulevard des Maréchaux, 91120 Palaiseau, France
{chuang.yu,adriana.tapus}@ensta-paristech.fr

Abstract. Interaction plays a critical role in skills learning for
natural communication. In human-robot interaction (HRI), robots can
get feedback during the interaction to improve their social abilities. In
this context, we propose an interactive robot learning framework using
multimodal data from thermal facial images and human gait data for
online emotion recognition. We also propose a new decision-level fusion
method for the multimodal classification using Random Forest (RF)
model. Our hybrid online emotion recognition model focuses on the
detection of four human emotions (i.e., neutral, happiness, angry, and
sadness). After conducting offline training and testing with the hybrid
model, the accuracy of the online emotion recognition system is more
than 10% lower than the offline one. In order to improve our system,
the human verbal feedback is injected into the robot interactive learning. With the new online emotion recognition system, a 12.5% accuracy increase compared with the online system without interactive robot
learning is obtained.

Keywords: Interactive robot learning · Multimodal emotion
recognition · Human-robot interaction

1 Introduction

In the past decade, emotion detection during social interaction attracted more
and more attention with the rapid advances in the field of robotics. Research
studies have found human emotion perception as a fundamental component of
communication that plays a significant role in successful human-human interaction [8]. Emotion recognition during human-robot interaction can help robots to
understand user's state and exhibit a natural social interaction. However, human
emotion recognition is challenging. Many researchers use multimodal information to address emotion recognition [13]. In our paper, we also use a multimodal
system combining the information from thermal face images and gait information
during human-robot interaction. Even though many researchers study emotion
recognition models for robots, it is very expensive and time-consuming to label

Supported by ENSTA Paris.

and annotate large databases by hand. Interactive Robot Learning (IRL) can address this problem. During human-robot interaction, robots can get verbal feedback from humans to label or relabel the data extracted from the interaction [7]. IRL is very useful in the long-life learning situation where there is no large-scale data for emotion recognition. Robots can record the emotion-related features and obtain its label from the interaction with humans. Currently, most of the researches focus on offline emotion analysis. However, the online recognition capability is more challenging. The robot interactive learning can also improve flexibility of emotion recognition model in human-robot interaction.

In the last decades, numerous studies attempted the multimodal method with the visual, verbal, and physiological signals and the natural language in order to get a better ability of emotion recognition. Caridakis et al. [2] made use of the multimodal Bayesian classifier with features extracted from face images, gestures, body action, and speech information to classify 8 emotions namely anger, despair, interest, pleasure, sadness, irritation, joy, and pride. In addition, they employed the fusion methods at feature-level and decision-level. Regarding IRL, authors in [6] described what was IRL with mixed-initiative and how the memory-based human-robot interaction strategies worked in the learning environment. Lutkebohle et al. [9] developed an IRL system with the human speech feedback in the dialog loops to help a curious robot learn skills in the grasping task. The human feedback from the human-robot interaction was proved significantly useful during robot learning.

Moreover, to the best of our knowledge, no studies focus on the fusion of gait and thermal facial features together to detect human emotion in social robotics context. A very common scenario is when the human walks towards the social robot and stops in front of it to interact with it. In our work, we developed a multimodal emotion recognition method by using thermal facial images during human-robot interaction and gait data during walking towards the robot to recognize four emotional states (i.e., neutral, happy, angry, and sad). The offline emotion recognition is widely developed by researchers. However, the online testing of emotion recognition model is challenging in real-time HRI context. In this paper, we developed a new method based on Random Forest (RF) model and confusion matrices of two individual Random Forest models by using the data from the face thermal images and gait. In addition, the IRL method is used with the verbal human feedback in the learning loops in order to improve the performance of real-time emotion recognition. The experiment results shows the effectiveness of IRL in multimodal emotion recognition.

The rest of the paper is structured as follows: Sect. 2 describes the methodology; Sect. 3 shows the experimental setup. The experimental results are summarized in Sect. 4. The conclusions and discussions are part of Sect. 5.

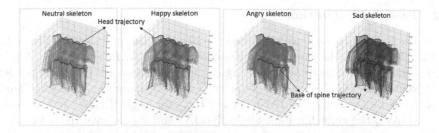

Fig. 1. The trajectories of skeleton

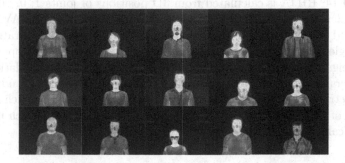

Fig. 2. Examples of thermal images from the database

2   Methodology

2.1   Multimodal Database

In our study, we collected the data (i.e., the thermal facial images and gait data) from multiple modalities. The database was built up with the data from the human-robot interaction experiments. Here, we use it for the training of the offline emotion recognition model. Many multimodal databases for affective computing exist in the literature. However, to the best of our knowledge, there are no open multimodal databases with face thermal images and gait data. In our past research, we conducted 300 human-robot interaction experiments with 15 participants to build up our database. During the experiments, each participant run 20 experiments (i.e., 5 times each emotion). The gait data was extracted from the RGB-D camera during human walking towards the robot and included 3D skeleton data with the positions of 25 joints and related timestamps of each frame. The trajectories of 3D skeletons are shown in Fig. 1. The thermal images with the human upper body were recorded from the thermal camera Optris Pi during human-robot interaction for 10 s. Then, we selected the suitable data where the participants' heads did not move much. The time duration of all data in the thermal database is from 5 s to 10 s. The examples of the thermal database are shown in Fig. 2.

636   C. Yu and A. Tapus

2.2 Features Extraction

From the RGB-D camera, we extracted the 3D positions of 25 joints. The index of the 25 joints in the human body is shown in Fig. 3. In this paper, 4 joint angles and 4 joint angular velocities are calculated as features including the left knee joint angle (LKJA) and its velocity (LKJAV), the right knee joint angle (RKJA) and its velocity (RKJAV), the left hip joint angle (LHJA) and its velocity (LHJAV), the right hip joint angle (RHJA) and its velocity (RHJAV). The definition of the joint angles is shown in Fig. 3(a). LHJA is calculated from 3D positions of joints 1, 0, 12, and 13. LKJA is calculated from 3D positions of joints 12, 13, and 14. RHJA is calculated from 3D positions of joints 1, 0, 16, and 17. RKJA is calculated from 3D positions of joints 16, 17, and 18. LHJAV, LKJAV, RHJAV, and RKJAV are just calculated through a subtraction operation of the current angle and the previous angle and the following division operation on the sampling time gap. The more detailed description of the calculation of the 8 parameters was presented in one of our past work [3]. In this study, we use Power Spectral Density (PSD) as the feature of the gait data, which describes the energy of the specific frequency or frequency range. Then, Welch method is applied to calculate PSD features [11].

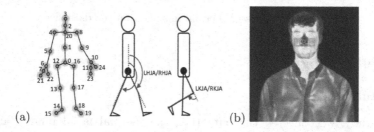

Fig. 3. Data: (a) Joint index and joint angle definition and (b) 3 facial ROIs

Many researchers have found that human emotions are correlated to the facial areas (e.g., left cheek, right cheek, and nose [10,14]). In this paper, we use these 3 facial Region of Interest (ROI) for human emotion detection [1] (see Fig. 3(b)). The average value and variance of these 3 facial regions are used as thermal facial features.

2.3 Fusion of Multimodal Classifiers

Previously, we have tested many machine learning models for offline emotion recognition including Hidden Markov Model (HMM) with thermal data, HMM model with gait data, and Random Forest (RF) model with thermal data, RF model with gait data, Controversial Neural Network (CNN) model with gait data, Support Vector Machine (SVM) model with thermal data, SVM model with gait data. In addition, CNN model with gait feature has only an offline testing accuracy of 55%. The offline accuracy of HMM, SVM and RF with gait data are 65%, 65% and 70%, respectively. SVM and RF have the accuracy of 55% and 60%, respectively. SVM and RF with both features obtain 70% and 80%, respectively. Hence, we found that RF had the best emotion recognition performance with the highest accuracy with respect to the other models. So, this paper applies RF as the basic machine learning model for emotion recognition.

The individual emotion classifier only with gait data and the one only with thermal face data have different recognition abilities for the 4 different emotions. During online testing, we found that the two individual models show distinct emotion recognition performance with different accuracy in each emotion situation. Hence, the decision-level fusion of the two individual models is necessary to make a better recognition accuracy. In this paper, we developed a new decision-level fusion method with twp RF classifiers for online emotion recognition and the framework is as shown in Fig. 4. The integration method is based on the modified confusion matrix and the probability vector of each emotion class.

We use the confusion matrix information to build up the decision-level hybrid model for emotion recognition. In the confusion matrix all the elements represent probabilities. The row of the confusion matrix represents the instances in a predicted class while the column represents the instances in the real class. Then, the elements of each column in the confusion matrix is divided by the total amount of instances in each column, respectively to get the modified confusion matrix. In the modified one, each column shows the probability of each real class in the predicted class situation. An example of our modified confusion matrix for the thermal emotion recognition model is shown in Fig. 5. For example, in column two corresponding to the predicted class "angry" in Fig. 5, TC_{02}, TC_{12}, TC_{22}, and TC_{32} represent the probabilities of neutral, happy, angry, and sad emotions, respectively when the predicted class is the angry emotion.

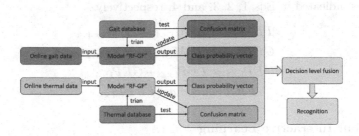

Fig. 4. The fusion framework of multimodal classifiers

During every online testing, the class probabilities of the thermal model make up the vector $TPM_{1\times4}$, as shown in Fig. 6. For example, the thermal emotion recognition model gets the prediction result "happy". From the above matrix, the predicted "happy" is "neutral" with probability TC_{01}, "happy" with probability TC_{11}, "angry" with probability TC_{21}, and "sad" with probability TC_{31}. Therefore, in the "happy" prediction situation, the probability vector of

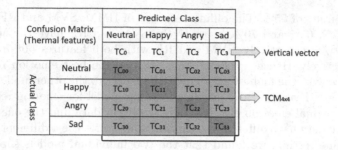

Fig. 5. Modified confusion matrix of thermal emotion recognition model

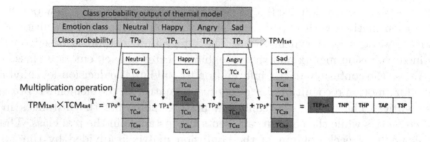

Fig. 6. Class probability calculation with modified confusion matrix

the 4 emotions is equal to $TP_1 \times TC_1$. Similarly, we can get the probability vectors of the 4 emotions in other 3 prediction situations. The process is as shown in Fig. 6.

The calculation of $TEP_{1\times4}$ for the thermal model, of $GEP_{1\times4}$ for the gait model, of $FUEP_{1\times4}$ for the two new vectors, and of FRR for the final recognition result is as indicated in Eqs. 1, 2, 3, and 4, respectively.

$$TEP_{1\times4} = TPM_{1\times4} \times TCM_{4\times4} \qquad (1)$$

$$GEP_{1\times4} = GPM_{1\times4} \times GCM_{4\times4} \qquad (2)$$

$$FUEP_{1\times4} = TEP_{1\times4} + GEP_{1\times4} \qquad (3)$$

$$FRR = argmax(FUEP_{1\times4}) \qquad (4)$$

2.4 Robot Interactive Learning

We apply an interactive learning method during the interaction in order to boost the emotion recognition performance of the robot. An overview of IRL system architecture is illustrated in Fig. 7. During the IRL experiments, if the predicted emotion does not match the real one, the gait and the thermal facial features are restored to retrain the emotion recognition models. The updated thermal and gait models will test the saved features again to get the new predicted results, respectively. The new predicted results will help update the two confusion matrices. If the predicted emotion is equal to the real one, we only update the two confusion matrices and the models are not retrained.

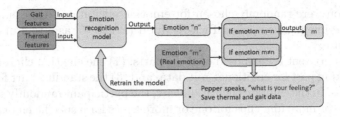

Fig. 7. Overview of the IRL architecture

3   Experimental Design

In our work, we use Kinect camera to detect the human gait information and the Optris thermal camera to obtain the thermal facial images for emotion recognition. In our experiments, we used Pepper robot. The experimental setup is as shown in Fig. 8. Our experiment is composed of three parts: the online testing, the IRL, and the online testing after IRL. 8 participants took part 8 times in each part. Hence, 64 experiments in every condition and 192 experiments in total were conducted for one month. The participants are students with different major backgrounds, with ages from 20 to 32, half women and half men. All the experiments were conducted in our robotics lab, with all the windows closed and the air conditioning turned on in order to keep the indoor temperature ranging from 20 to 28 °c.

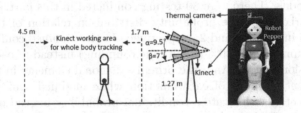

Fig. 8. Experimental setup

For the emotion elicitation methods, static images and films clips are considered extensively as stimuli to elicit different emotions in the laboratory and films are one of the most effective ways to elicit emotions [4]. In our experiments, for emotion elicitation, we used open film clips database-FilmStim [12], in which there are English and French videos that can elicit emotional states including amusement, anger, sadness, tenderness, fear, disgust, and neutral state. In our research, we only focus on 4 emotions: neutral, amusement, anger, and sadness. Hence, the film clips of 4 emotions in the database are used in our research, and more precisely: 6 clips for neutral emotion (3 English, 3 French), 13 clips for happy emotion (3 English, 10 French), 16 clips for angry emotion (9 English, 7 French), and 17 clips for sad emotion (7 English, 10 French). The film clips for

each emotion were randomly chosen for emotion elicitation. After emotion elicitation experiments, we applied Pick-A-Mood (PAM) [5] as a tool of emotional
state measure.

Each experiment is composed of three parts: (1) the emotion elicitation part,
(2) the walking part for emotional gait data, and (3) the standing part for thermal
facial images. In the emotion elicitation part, the participant randomly selects and
watches one or more film clips for one or more times for a specific emotion. Then,
the participant walks towards the robot with that specific emotion and stops
before the robot to start the interaction. The details of IRL part are described in
the following steps. For the other two parts, before and after IRL, there is no step
(6). The steps are as described below: (1) The participant completes EPQ to determine his/her personality traits (one time); (2) The participant randomly selects
and watches the film clips from FilmStim for a specific emotion; (3) The participant selects the emotional state from PAM for mood measurement; (4) The robot
instructs the participant to walk towards it with the specific emotional gait; (5)
The participant walks towards the robot and stops before it for 5 s; (6) The robot
asks, how do you feel? The robot records the emotion result and gait/thermal data
into a database for retraining the emotion recognition model; (7) Repeat steps
from 2 to 6 to complete eight or more experiments.

4   Experimental Results

Before online testing for emotion recognition, the offline RF models were tested
in order to get modified confusion matrix, which is used for fusion of our emotion
recognition models. There were 80 testing conducted in this part. The modified
confusion matrix shows the probability distribution relation of the four emotions as shown in Tables 1 and 2, respectively. In the modified confusion matrix,
each column sums up to 100% (if without rounding) instead of each row in the
original confusion matrix. And, the primary diagonal elements in the confusion
matrix represent accuracy of each emotion while modified confusion matrix's
diagonal elements just indicate a conditional probability instead of accuracy of
each emotion. In Table 2, the ratio with 91.67% is significantly high when the
real class and the predicted class both are sad one. That ratio in the modified
confusion matrix only represents the probability of "sad" when predicted class
is "sad", instead of the accuracy of "sad" (only 55%) in the confusion matrix.

Table 1. Modified confusion matrix of offline testing of gait model

Gait model (Offline testing)		Predicted class			
		Neutral	Happy	Angry	Sad
Real class	Neutral	75%	16%	0%	6.67%
	Happy	0%	52%	30%	6.67%
	Angry	10%	20%	65%	0%
	Sad	15%	12%	5%	86.67%

Table 2. Modified confusion matrix of offline testing of thermal models

Thermal model (Offline testing)		Predicted class			
		Neutral	Happy	Angry	Sad
Real class	Neutral	52%	25%	5.26%	0%
	Happy	12%	50%	21.05%	8.33%
	Angry	16%	20.83%	57.89%	0%
	Sad	20%	4.17%	15.79%	91.67%

For the integration of the model with gait features and the one with thermal facial features, we applied a decision-level method with the modified confusion matrix. Before IRL experiments, we conducted the online testing experiments with the decision-level model. The paper compared the recognition performance of the single models with gait features or thermal facial features and the multimodal model with both, which are with the accuracy of 54.6875% (gait model), 59.375% (thermal model), and 65.625% (fusion model), respectively. The results indicate a higher accuracy for the hybrid model than for any single models.

During IRL, when hybrid model recognition result does not match the real one, the data are saved for model retraining. The confusion matrices are updated with the testing results on the two individual classification models, which are retrained. After IRL, the online testing was conducted again with the updated hybrid model. At last, an online testing accuracy of 78.125% is obtained after IRL, which is an increase of more than 10% than the one before interactive learning (i.e., 65.625%), which demonstrates that the IRL method is useful for emotion recognition with gait and thermal facial data.

5   Conclusion and Discussion

In our paper, we developed a multimodal emotion recognition model with gait and thermal facial data, which is based on RF model and the modified confusion matrices of two individual models. Through comparison between the individual RF models and the decision-level hybrid model, we found that our integration method is useful to classify the emotion during human-robot interaction. In addition, we have conducted 192 experiments including three parts, namely online testing experiments before IRL, IRL experiments, and online testing after IRL. In these experiments, we compared the emotion recognition performance before and after IRL to find out that the interactive robot learning is useful, with an increase of more than 10% of the accuracy of multimodal emotion recognition with gait and thermal data. Our IRL architecture could potentially be used in robot long life learning in human-robot interaction scenarios.

References

1. Agrigoroaie, R., Tapus, A.: Physiological parameters variation based on the sensory stimuli used by a robot in a news reading task. In: 2018 27th IEEE International Symposium on Robot and Human Interactive Communication (RO-MAN), pp. 618–625. IEEE (2018)
2. Caridakis, G., et al.: Multimodal emotion recognition from expressive faces, body gestures and speech. In: Boukis, C., Pnevmatikakis, A., Polymenakos, L. (eds.) AIAI 2007. ITIFIP, vol. 247, pp. 375–388. Springer, Boston, MA (2007). https://doi.org/10.1007/978-0-387-74161-1_41
3. Chuang, Y., Adriana, T.: Multimodal emotion recognition with thermal and RGB-D cameras for human-robot interaction. In: 2019 19th International Conference on Advanced Robotics (ICAR). IEEE (2019, Under review)
4. Deng, Y., Yang, M., Zhou, R.: A new standardized emotional film database for Asian culture. Front. Psychol. **8**, 1941 (2017)
5. Desmet, P.M., Vastenburg, M., Romero, N.: Mood measurement with Pick-A-Mood: review of current methods and design of a pictorial self-report scale. J. Des. Res. **14**(3), 241–279 (2016)
6. Hanheide, M., Sagerer, G.: Active memory-based interaction strategies for learning-enabling behaviors. In: RO-MAN 2008-The 17th IEEE International Symposium on Robot and Human Interactive Communication, pp. 101–106. IEEE (2008)
7. Katagami, D., Yamada, S.: Interactive classifier system for real robot learning. In: Proceedings 9th IEEE International Workshop on Robot and Human Interactive Communication. IEEE RO-MAN 2000 (Cat. No. 00TH8499), pp. 258–263. IEEE (2000)
8. Keltner, D., Haidt, J.: Social functions of emotions at four levels of analysis. Cogn. Emot. **13**(5), 505–521 (1999)
9. Lutkebohle, I., et al.: The curious robot-structuring interactive robot learning. In: 2009 IEEE International Conference on Robotics and Automation, pp. 4156–4162. IEEE (2009)
10. Nakanishi, R., Imai-Matsumura, K.: Facial skin temperature decreases in infants with joyful expression. Infant Behav. Devel. **31**(1), 137–144 (2008)
11. Rahi, P., Mehra, R.: Analysis of power spectrum estimation using Welch method for various window techniques. Int. J. Emerg. Technol. Eng. **2**(6), 106–109 (2014)
12. Schaefer, A., Nils, F., Sanchez, X., Philippot, P.: Assessing the effectiveness of a large database of emotion-eliciting films: a new tool for emotion researchers. Cogn. Emot. **24**(7), 1153–1172 (2010)
13. Sebe, N., Cohen, I., Gevers, T., Huang, T., et al.: Multimodal approaches for emotion recognition: a survey (2005)
14. Sugimoto, Y., Yoshitomi, Y., Tomita, S.: A method for detecting transitions of emotional states using a thermal facial image based on a synthesis of facial expressions. Robot. Auton. Syst. **31**(3), 147–160 (2000)

Technical Innovations in Social Robotics

Teaching Commonsense and Dynamic Knowledge to Service Robots

Stephan Opfer[(✉)], Stefan Jakob, and Kurt Geihs

University of Kassel, Wilhelmshöher Allee 73, 34121 Kassel, Germany
{opfer,s.jakob,geihs}@uni-kassel.de

Abstract. Incorporating commonsense and coping with dynamic knowledge are key capabilities of service robots to efficiently interact with humans. In the presented system, we demonstrate how to equip service robots with commonsense knowledge and the dynamic reasoning capabilities of Answer Set Programming (ASP). We investigated the response of our system to basic human needs and evaluated the viability and scalability of the combination of the commonsense knowledge database ConceptNet 5 and the ASP solver Clingo. Our results show the flexibility and versatility of our approach. Further, we identified the need for research on scalability in case of environments that are abundant with objects.

Keywords: Commonsense reasoning · Dynamic knowledge · Answer Set Programming · Service robots · Cognitive Robotics · Human-robot interaction

1 Introduction

The research area of Cognitive Robotics is concerned with high-level control of robots and endowing robots with cognitive capabilities like learning and reasoning. In the context of human-robot interaction [12], these capabilities are key ingredients, to create elaborated dialogues that humans find pleasant to partake. In dialogue systems these capabilities, if present at all, are implemented by submodules of the dialogue manager that controls the state and flow of the conversation.

In this paper, we propose a reasoning system that allows humans to teach robots and to dynamically adapt the knowledge of the robots. Additionally, it provides a vast amount of commonsense knowledge (CK) for even understanding implicit service requests. Our approach utilises the database ConceptNet 5 (CN5) [15] as a source of CK and the Answer Set Programming (ASP) solver Clingo [6] as the underlying reasoner. For a detailed specification of ASP, the interested reader is referred to [3,7]. One reason for choosing ASP is its non-monotonic reasoning capability that makes it flexible regarding dynamic knowledge and helps to keep the knowledge base consistent. Furthermore, Clingo provides an easy-to-use and efficient implementation for ASP reasoning and the expressiveness of ASP outperforms many other decidable logical formalisms [13].

© Springer Nature Switzerland AG 2019
M. A. Salichs et al. (Eds.): ICSR 2019, LNAI 11876, pp. 645–654, 2019.
https://doi.org/10.1007/978-3-030-35888-4_60

The application domain considered in this paper is domestic service robots, where humans assign tasks or have implicit requests for the robots. The following short dialogue describes the vision of this paper. *Alice: "I am tired." Robot: "Do you want to sit down?"* The service robot should be able to understand the needs of a human. This has to be done without a priori knowledge specifically provided for this kind of situations and thus rely on a general CK database.

The main contribution in this paper is the improved flexibility and expressiveness of service robots by combining non-monotonic reasoning, dynamic teaching, human-robot interaction, and a vast amount of CK.

In the next section, we summarize related research that was conducted with a similar setup of tools or tackle related problems. Afterwards, in Sect. 3, we present dynamic reasoning with ASP and CN5 needed to understand the remaining paper. In Sect. 4, we explain the extraction of CK followed by its translation into ASP, necessary for utilising CK in domestic service robot scenarios. For evaluating the applicability of our approach, we investigate the runtime performance of CN5 and Clingo in Sect. 5 for different scenarios. In Sect. 6, we conclude the paper with a critical discussion, identifying potential improvements.

2   Related Work

In the following, we discuss state-of-the-art approaches and frameworks for utilising general knowledge in the field of autonomous service robots and emphasize the differences to our approach.

Erdem et al. present in [5] a hybrid planning approach utilizing ASP, Prolog, ConceptNet 4 (CN4), and a continuous motion planner. Their example scenario, tidying a house, is modelled in ASP, while the necessary CK about usual object locations and object properties are extracted from CN4 and represented within Prolog. In order to avoid inconsistencies, Erdem et al. rely on only two CK relations (*AtLocation* and *HasProperty*) and restrict their queries to a sufficiently small number of answers.

The work of Erdem et al. and our approach have a lot in common in general. However, apart from more current versions of ConceptNet and the ASP solver Clingo, we represent the CK directly in ASP, instead of external Prolog predicates. Furthermore, our approach allows retracting the CK from the ASP knowledge base, in case it causes inconsistencies or is overwritten by temporary exceptions from human input. As a result, our approach is much more suitable for the dynamic knowledge of long-term human-robot interaction.

In contrast to Erdem et al., Chen et al. [4] explicitly address human-robot interaction by processing limited segments of natural language (LSNL). For the automatic translation into ASP, the LSNL are restricted to if-then sentences. In contrast to our approach, other forms of CK cannot be added at runtime. In order to avoid inconsistencies during long-term human-robot interaction, the truth values of all ASP rules depend on a monotonically increasing and discrete time step.

In Lemaignan et al. [11] a framework for an autonomous robot with sophisticated human-robot interaction capabilities is described. The core reasoning formalism is ontology-based and utilises the Pellet reasoner. As a consequence new knowledge can only be added at runtime, by reclassifying the whole knowledge base. However, the knowledge base of the robot is enlarged by databases like WordNet and DBPedia that are also part of CN5. The dialogue management component Dialogs [10] intensively exploits the knowledge base for semantic resolution of nouns, pronouns, anaphors, and verbal phrases. In our opinion, an ASP-based approach would avoid several disadvantages of ontology-based reasoning [13].

As we explicitly address dynamic knowledge, the concepts and principles of truth maintenance systems [2], techniques for intentional forgetting [8], and the research in the field of Ambient Assisted Living [1] are therefore of interest for our approach, too. In order to retract CK from our knowledge base, we utilise the *External Statement* feature of the ASP solver Clingo.

3   Foundations

This section introduces the necessary basics for this paper, divided into two parts: Dynamic reasoning with Answer Set Programming in Sect. 3.1, and in Sect. 3.2 we introduce the CK database CN5.

3.1   Dynamic Reasoning with Answer Set Programming

ASP is a declarative logic programming approach, tackling NP-search problems. ASP can be seen as the result of research in the areas of knowledge representation, logic programming, and constraint satisfaction [3]. ASP is non-monotonic and thus allows to invalidate conclusions if contrary knowledge has been derived. For additional information, the interested reader is referred to [3,7].

The ASP solver Clingo [6] can be used in a multi-shot fashion, which means that a single solver instance can be used multiple times and derived knowledge can be reused. Furthermore, Clingo makes it possible to dynamically change knowledge by dividing an ASP program into *Program Sections* and changing the truth value of *External Statements*. An example of the usage of *External Statements* is presented in Listing 1.1.

```
1 #program birds.
2 #external -flies(tweety).
3 bird(tweety).
4 flies(X) :- bird(X), not -flies(X).
```

Listing 1.1. Example for the usage of *External Statements*.

This example contains the *Program Section* birds in Line 1, which can be used to explicitly address this program. The *External Statement* in Line 2 expresses the capability of tweety to fly, depending on the truth value of the *External Statement*. Initially, Clingo assumes that all *External Statements* are false unless they are assigned otherwise. Solving this program results in the Stable Model [7]: {bird(tweety), flies(tweety)}. Afterwards, the truth value of -flies(tweety) can be changed to true, resulting in a new Stable Model that contains the following atoms: {bird(tweety), -flies(tweety)}.

3.2   ConceptNet 5

ConceptNet 5 (CN5) is a multi-language knowledge database. Its structure is a semantic hypergraph that contains CK expressed in triples containing natural language The knowledge which has been collected from different sources like the Open Mind Common Sense project, Wiktionary, WordNet 3.0, DBPedia, and Wikipedia [15]. A node in the CN5 hypergraph is denoted as a concept, which is a combination of a natural language term, a language tag, and a sense label. The sense label distinguishes between nouns, verbs, adjectives, and adverbs. Edges between concepts contain the sources used to create it, e.g., WordNet, its weight, and the concepts connected to it. The weight is a sum of the weights of each source. A weight greater than 1.0 indicates that the edge has been extracted from a verified source like WordNet. Furthermore, each edge contains a relation denoting its meaning. The relations are either automatically extracted from sources like Wikipedia, which can be in any language or are part of a handmade set of English base relations. Table 1 is an excerpt from these base relations and their meaning.

Table 1. 14 from 40 CN5 base relations [15].

Relation	Meaning	Relation	Meaning
IsA	A is a kind of B	SymbolOf	A represents B
UsedFor	A is used for B	HasContext	A is in the context of B
CapableOf	A is able to B	MotivatedByGoal	Doing A to achieve B
RelatedTo	A and B are related	CausesDesire	A would make you want B
Desires	A wants to B	MadeOf	A is made of B
Causes	The effect of A is B	AtLocation	A is located at B
HasProperty	A is B	PartOf	A is part of B

In order to demonstrate the utility of CN5, let us consider the following utterance: "I'm tired!". Understanding the utterance as an implicit service request requires CK that is represented within CN5. For example, CN5 suggests to *rest*, which is *MotivatedByGoal tired* and that *going to sleep* is *UsedFor rest*.

4   A CK Course for Robots

Our automated approach of providing a service robot with CK includes several steps. In Sect. 4.1, we describe the retrieval of new knowledge from human-robot interaction, knowledge databases, or robotic sensory input. The knowledge is then automatically translated into ASP rules and made available on demand to, e.g., reason about the environment (see Sect. 4.2). The application example in Sect. 4.3 explains how the robot applies CK with or without further human interference.

4.1 Knowledge for Interactive Service Robots

We allow humans to teach service robots through informative utterances like "Cups are located in kitchens.". Therefore, the knowledge should be representable as n-ary predicates, in this case atLocation(cup, kitchen). If the service robot does not know anything about the things or concepts mentioned by the human, our approach fills the lack of knowledge by querying a knowledge database like CN5. A third source of knowledge is the sensory input of the robot. Frameworks like YOLO or the Google Vision API recognise objects in the video stream of the robot. Therefore, it is possible to identify a room, for example, as a kitchen, because of the recognised stove.

The knowledge from the different sources is either commonsense or situational knowledge. While CK is concerned with knowledge that can be considered to hold in general and seldom changes, situational knowledge is concerned with knowledge that is specific for the current situation and changes frequently, e.g., "The blue cup is located on the table in room R1405.". Sensory input always provides situational knowledge, while informative human utterances can include both, situational and CK. Knowledge databases like CN5 only include CK. Please note that, although with different frequencies, we consider both types of knowledge to be subject of change.

4.2 Modelling Knowledge in ASP

Translating the n-ary predicates, representing the relevant knowledge, into ASP is done as shown in Line 1 to 6 of Listing 1.2, for the example of CN5. Summarized in an extra program section, each edge corresponds to one ASP fact including the reliability of the sources of the predicates. Utilising the cs_AtLocation edges, e.g., a service robot is already capable of searching for items, without a human that needs to tell it where to start searching.

```
1 #program commonsenseKnowledge.
2 cs_CapableOf(cup,hold_liquids,7).
3 cs_AtLocation(cup,table,4).
4 cs_AtLocation(cup,shelf,3).
5 cs_UsedFor(cup,drinking,3).
6 cs_AtLocation(coffee,cup,2).
7 ...
8 #program situationalKnowledge(n,m).
9 #external -atLocation(n,m).
10 atLocation(n,m,W):- not -atLocation(n,m), typeOf(n,cup),
        typeOf(m,table), cs_AtLocation(cup,table,W).
```

```
11  atLocation(n,m,W):- not -atLocation(n,m), typeOf(n,cup),
        typeOf(m,shelf), cs_AtLocation(cup,shelf,W).
12  ...
13  #program sensorInput.
14  typeOf(blueCup,cup).
15  typeOf(kitchenTable,table).
16  typeOf(kitchenShelf,shelf).
17  ...
```

Listing 1.2. Extract from commonsense and situational knowledge about cups.

The *Program Section* situationalKnowledge(n,m), starting in Line 8, is necessary to apply the CK of the former section to objects and concepts encountered through object recognition or human-robot interaction. n and m are parameters used for grounding the *Program Section* with objects from the environment of the robot. The rule in Line 10, e.g., informally means that as long as there is no proof that n is not located at m, n is of type cup, m is of type table, and it is commonsense that a cup is usually located at a table with a reliability of W, it is assumed that n is located at m with the corresponding reliability. The *External Statement* in Line 9 can be set to true, e.g., via human-robot interaction, in order to give proof that a certain object n is not located at m.

4.3 Synergy of Commonsense and Situational Knowledge

The following example scenario clarifies how our approach helps to achieve the aforementioned vision (see Sect. 1) and illustrates how the presented components intertwine. Imagine a service robot able to extract knowledge from its environment. Therefore, the robot labels specific objects in its environment with categories from its CK, which is shown in Line 14 to 16 of Listing 1.2. Additional CK, for example, the possible locations of a cup, is integrated into the knowledge base on demand and is partially retracted from it according to the current situation. Relying on this knowledge, the robot would search for a cup on the kitchenTable, but the human asking for the cup already told it that currently there is no cup on the kitchenTable and thereby sets the *External Statement* -atLocation(blueCup, kitchenTable) to true. The robot does not know about any other table and therefore is searching for a cup in the kitchenShelf, instead.

5 Evaluation

The evaluation has been performed on a Desktop PC equipped with an Intel Core i7-8700K@3.7 GHz Hexa-Core, 64 GB DDR4-2133 MHz RAM, and Ubuntu 18.04 64 Bit as its operating system. The version of CN5 is 5.7 and the ASP solver Clingo 5.3.1 was used, which incorporates the grounder Gringo with version 5.3.1 and the solver Clasp with version 3.3.4. We conducted three experiments, as explained in the next sections. The first two evaluate how effective our approach is regarding performance and scalability. The last experiment investigates the understanding of implicit human requests by using ASP and CN5, only.

5.1   System Performance

The most essential step is to teach new concepts to service robots. We measured the runtime of the two included substeps, namely querying CN5 and translating the results into ASP. As the runtime depends on the size of the taught concept, we chose three exemplary concepts water (2425 edges), dog (1144 edges), and cup (333 edges), since they are a large, medium, and small-sized concept, respectively. The runtime for querying CN5 and translating the results into ASP was measured 2000 times. Both scale linearly with the number of edges (see Table 2), while the runtime for translating the query results into ASP is neglectable compared to the query process itself.

Table 2. Runtime evaluation of knowledge extraction and translation.

Concept	CN5 extraction	CN5 SD	ASP translation	ASP SD
Water	702.529 ms	15.322 ms	64.412 ms	1.335 ms
Dog	391.238 ms	21.164 ms	30.483 ms	1.389 ms
Cup	174.783 ms	5.985 ms	9.034 ms	0.305 ms

Another important aspect is the scalability of the knowledge base. Typically thousands of relations between objects need to be taught to service robots operating in an average household scenario. For the following experiment, we engineered a scenario consisting of 102 objects and rooms represented by 39 different concepts. The service robot is supposed to tidy up the household and therefore needs to know the usual locations of the objects. This experiment evaluates the initialization process of the knowledge base of a robot and consists of three main parts. The first part, like before, is the integration of sensor inputs into the knowledge base. Afterwards, the 39 different concepts stemming from the perceived objects are queried from CN5. Finally, 84 typical object locations are extracted from the situational knowledge. We consider the size of the scenario suitable for investigating the scalability of our approach inside small household environments. The runtime of the three consecutive steps was measured 1000 times, resulting in an average runtime of 68.2 s (SD: 0.46 s).

5.2   Implicit Human Service Requests

Within this experiment we approach the vision stated in the introduction of this paper, i. e. making service robots understand implicitly formulated desires of human beings. Therefore, the service robot was equipped with an algorithm to recognise basic human needs and their edges to other concepts within CN5. Our implementation utilises several CN5 base relations for finding solutions to basic human needs. At first, the *MotivatedByGoal* and *CausesDesire* relations identify activities that help to remedy the needs and further the *UsedFor* relation suggests objects and actions that are necessary for executing these activities.

Additionally, possible activities are expanded via synonym like relations, which include *SimilarTo*, *InstanceOf*, and *Synonym*.

Table 3. Excerpt from suggested actions for basic human needs.

Issue	Activity	Used objects or actions
Tired	Rest, sleep	Sitting down, sleeping at night, going to sleep, bed, hotel
Thirsty	Drink, drink water	Water, ice, beer mug, faucet, glass
Hungry	Cook, eat food, cook meal	Fork, forks, indian restaurant, stove, kitchen
Hot	Cool off, swim	Fan, pool, river, stream, ocean
Cold	Light fire, start fire	Match, matches, flint, kindling, lighter
Bored	Watch television, play games	Living room, playroom, computer, family room, basketball court
Ill	Go to doctor, lie down	Illness, bed
Smell	Take shower, take bath	Shower head, shower stall, portable shower head, bathtub, tub
Stink	Bathe	Bars of soap, bathtub, wash cloth, separate shower
Lonely	Call friend	Telephone

Table 3 lists an excerpt from the investigated basic needs and the actions found through the *MotivatedByGoal* relation. A tired human, e.g., is suggested to sleep. Making the robot a real assistant, instead of only a clever advice machine, it further analyses objects that are typically used for the suggested actions. A human that should sleep, e.g., needs a bed or a hotel. Although these results for fulfilling implicit human desires by service robots are very promising, further possible improvements are discussed in the next section.

6   Discussion and Conclusion

In this paper, we introduce our approach to assist humans in teaching service robots CK, while keeping the taught knowledge changeable. Furthermore, we show that a service robot utilising the CK database CN5 is capable of appropriately replying to implicit service requests of humans.

Through the performance evaluation of the teaching algorithm, the runtime for CN5 queries is identified as the most time-consuming step, often taking ten times longer than the translation into ASP. Therefore, caching mechanisms, as provided by web servers like *nginx*, would significantly reduce the runtime. However, the low runtime already allows the application in human-robot interaction, since answers are not noticeably delayed.

The reason for choosing ASP as knowledge representation language is its capability of non-monotonic reasoning and dynamically retracting knowledge via *External Statements* (see Sect. 4.3). Please note that the number of *External Statements* substantially influences the runtime of the reasoning process as shown in our preliminary work [14] and therefore limits the applicability for environments abundant with objects. Furthermore, to the best of our knowledge, it is open how *External Statements* relate to the research of intentional forgetting in ASP [9]. Although current results regarding forgetting knowledge [8] are discouraging from a theoretical point of view, we see a need for further research regarding this issue from a more practical point of view. A reason for retracting knowledge, apart from its invalidity, is to keep the knowledge base syntactically and semantically consistent.

Regarding the semantic consistency of our knowledge base, we plan to further utilise additional CN5 base relations like *Antonym, Synonym, IsA, DefinedAs,* and *PartOf* in order to detect inconsistent concept descriptions induced by the *HasProperty, HasContext,* or *RelatedTo* relations. An example is the concept of a plant, because it is connected to the concepts evergreen and deciduous, whose contradiction is represented by their *Antonym* relation. A service robot could conclude that both properties hold and introduce a semantic inconsistency to its knowledge base.

In our opinion, the results of solving implicit human requests are already encouraging (see Table 3) but can be improved by utilising the full potential of CN5. While the suggested activities for *tired* or *thirsty* are suitable, starting a fire in case the human user stated that it is *cold*, is not a feasible solution in a house. In order to improve the answer quality of the service robot and increase the number of recognised human needs, adopting additional features of CN5 like Relatedness, optimizing the average edge weight of extracted concept graphs, and considering the optional sense label of concepts are our most promising ideas. Especially the Relatedness feature could improve the results since they rely on word embeddings [15] and thus can be used to either merge closely related concepts like *fork* and *forks* or to make answers more suitable to the context of the conversation.

Finally, we conclude that teaching CK with the help of existing databases like CN5 should supersede the approach of learning everything from scratch because we have already achieved encouraging results without learning at all. Furthermore, in our opinion, ASP is the only knowledge representation and reasoning technology whose expressiveness and performance scales with our scenarios and at the same time provides ready to use implementations, like Clingo. Nevertheless, further research is deemed necessary concerning the capabilities of ASP regarding the handling of dynamic knowledge.

References

1. Ayari, N., Chibani, A., Amirat, Y., Matson, E.T.: A novel approach based on commonsense knowledge representation and reasoning in open world for intelligent ambient assisted living services. In: IROS - IEEE/RSJ International Conference on Intelligent Robots and Systems, pp. 6007–6013 (2015)

2. Beck, H.: Reviewing Justification-based Truth Maintenance Systems from a Logic Programming Perspective. Technical Report INFSYS RR-1843-17-02, Institute of Information Systems, TU Vienna, July 2017
3. Brewka, G., Eiter, T., Truszczyński, M.: Answer set programming at a glance. Commun. ACM **54**(12), 92–103 (2011)
4. Chen, X., Ji, J., Jiang, J., Jin, G., Wang, F., Xie, J.: Developing high-level cognitive functions for service robots. In: Proceedings of the 9th International Conference on Autonomous Agents and Multiagent Systems AAMAS 2010, Richland, SC, vol. 1, pp. 989–996 (2010)
5. Erdem, E., Aker, E., Patoglu, V.: Answer set programming for collaborative housekeeping robotics: representation, reasoning, and execution. Intell. Serv. Robot. **5**(4), 275–291 (2012)
6. Gebser, M., Kaminski, R., Kaufmann, B., Schaub, T.: Clingo=ASP+Control: Extended Report. Technical report, Knowledge Processing and Information Systems (2014)
7. Gelfond, M., Kahl, Y.: Knowledge Representation, Reasoning, and the Design of Intelligent Agents: The Answer-Set Programming Approach. Cambridge University Press, Cambridge (2014)
8. Gonçalves, R., Knorr, M., Leite, J.: You can't always forget what you want: on the limits of forgetting in answer set programming. In: European Conference on Artificial Intelligence (ECAI), pp. 957–965. Frontiers in Artificial Intelligence and Applications (2016)
9. Leite, J.: A bird's-eye view of forgetting in answer-set programming. In: Balduccini, M., Janhunen, T. (eds.) LPNMR 2017. LNCS (LNAI), vol. 10377, pp. 10–22. Springer, Cham (2017). https://doi.org/10.1007/978-3-319-61660-5_2
10. Lemaignan, S., Ros, R., Sisbot, E.A., Alami, R., Beetz, M.: Grounding the interaction: anchoring situated discourse in everyday human-robot interaction. Int. J. Soc. Robot. **4**(2), 181–199 (2012)
11. Lemaignan, S., Warnier, M., Sisbot, E.A., Clodic, A., Alami, R.: Artificial cognition for social human-robot interaction: an implementation. Artif. Intell. **247**, 45–69 (2017)
12. Matamoros, M., Harbusch, K., Paulus, D.: From commands to goal-based dialogs: a roadmap to achieve natural language interaction in RoboCup@Home. In: Holz, D., Genter, K., Saad, M., von Stryk, O. (eds.) RoboCup 2018. LNCS (LNAI), vol. 11374, pp. 217–229. Springer, Cham (2019). https://doi.org/10.1007/978-3-030-27544-0_18
13. Motik, B., Horrocks, I., Rosati, R., Sattler, U.: Can OWL and logic programming live together happily ever after? In: Cruz, I., et al. (eds.) ISWC 2006. LNCS, vol. 4273, pp. 501–514. Springer, Heidelberg (2006). https://doi.org/10.1007/11926078_36
14. Opfer, S., Jakob, S., Geihs, K.: Reasoning for autonomous agents in dynamic domains: towards automatic satisfaction of the module property. In: van den Herik, J., Rocha, A.P., Filipe, J. (eds.) ICAART 2017. LNCS (LNAI), vol. 10839, pp. 22–47. Springer, Cham (2018). https://doi.org/10.1007/978-3-319-93581-2_2
15. Speer, R., Chin, J., Havasi, C.: ConceptNet 5.5: an open multilingual graph of general knowledge. In: Proceedings of the Thirty-First AAAI Conference on Artificial Intelligence (AAAI-17), pp. 4444–4451 (2017)

Teaching Persian Sign Language to a Social Robot via the Learning from Demonstrations Approach

Seyed Ramezan Hosseini[1], Alireza Taheri[1(✉)], Ali Meghdari[1], and Minoo Alemi[1,2]

[1] Social and Cognitive Robotics Laboratory,
Sharif University of Technology, Tehran, Iran
{artaheri,meghdari}@sharif.edu
[2] Department of Humanities,
Islamic Azad University-West Tehran Branch, Tehran, Iran

Abstract. This paper proposes a novel framework for teaching sign language to RASA, a humanoid teaching assistant social robot. The ultimate goal was to design a user-friendly process by which the RASA robot could learn new signs from non-expert users. In the proposed method, the user would wear a motion capture suit and perform a sign multiple times to train a set of parallel Hidden Markov Models to encode each sign. Then, collision avoidance and the sign's comprehensibility were ensured by utilizing special mapping from the user's workspace to the robot's joint space. Lastly, the system's performance was assessed by teaching 10 Persian Sign Language (PSL) signs to the robot by a teacher and involving some participants familiar with PSL to investigate how distinguishable were the performed signs for them. We observed quite noticeable distinguish rate of –80% and 100% in their first and second guesses for the selected signs, respectively. Moreover, alongside those subjects, a group of participants unfamiliar with PSL was also asked to fill in a questionnaire in order to get all of the participants' viewpoints regarding the using of social robots in teaching sign languages. We indicated that with the mean score of 4.1 (out of 5), the subjects familiar with PSL believed that the performed signs generated by the robot were very close to being natural.

Keywords: Learning from demonstration · Sign language · Social robot · Hidden Markov Model

1 Introduction

Despite the recent growth in robotics [1–3], most robots still need to utilize complex processes to learn and perform each new task. These processes (usually including a vast amount of programming or reprogramming) are normally beyond the capabilities of non-expert users. This can be seen as a barrier in the expansion of domestic applications for robots. A practical solution for this weakness is implementing "Learning from Demonstration" (LfD) methods. These include methods in which robots learn new tasks by observing a teacher's performance of the tasks [4–6]. Addressing this

© Springer Nature Switzerland AG 2019
M. A. Salichs et al. (Eds.): ICSR 2019, LNAI 11876, pp. 655–665, 2019.
https://doi.org/10.1007/978-3-030-35888-4_61

definition, one can learn that the process consists of two phases: (1) data acquisition and (2) deriving new policies with regard to this data.

LfD, as an academic field, has a rich background with some original works dating back to the 1990s [6]. Some related works with similarities and common concerns with the current study are presented in the following. In 2002, Schaal [7] used a motion capture suit to teach "movement primitives" to a humanoid robot. In this work, the author used his previously proposed framework (i.e. Dynamic Movement Primitives (DMP)) alongside LfD to teach complex movements such as drumming and a tennis swing to the robot. Since then, using DMP alongside with LfD becomes a common method utilized in many of the later researches in this field. Matsubara et al. in 2010 [8] used this method to teach constrained object manipulation and a table tennis swing to a robotic arm. By adding a "style" parameter, they extended DMP to learn and regenerate different styles of a motion. In both the mentioned studies, the robot learned to generalize the initial instructions to other unobserved situations (i.e. different goal positions). In 2012, Pastor et al. [9] trained a Sarcos robotic arm to pour water into cups and accomplish pick-and-place operations. They moved the robot manually and used the robot's own sensors for data acquisition. In another research in 2012, Akgun et al. [10] taught a Simon Robot to write letters. They also moved the robot manually to teach it; however, instead of robot's sensors, data acquisition was done by special software that saved the hand positions over time. They further used their proposed methods to teach the robot some spatial tasks such as pouring, placing and scooping. Calinon et al. implemented different imitation-based algorithms to teach gestures to robots in various studies [11–14]. They used different types of robots (including humanoids and robotic arms), tasks (e.g. writing, collaboration, pick and place, feeding, clapping, etc.), and algorithms (Hidden Markov Models, Gaussian Mixture Regression, Riemannian manifolds, etc.).

In a follow up of our previous researches in using a social robot to educate children with hearing problems [15–17], this paper endeavors to propose and implement a "Learning from Demonstration" approach to empower our robot (called RASA) with active fingers to learn new vocabularies/signs of Persian Sign Language (PSL) from users/teachers who are not necessarily familiar with robotic technology. To the best of our knowledge, there is no similar applications in the field of LfD in the literature. Reaching this goal would enable us to systematically/easily improve the vocabulary of the robot with the help of sign language teachers. As the research questions of this study, we would like to investigate (1) how distinguishable are the performed PSL signs by the robot for participants familiar with PSL?, and (2) what are the subjects' viewpoints on the appropriateness and quality of the robot's sign reproduction ability? To this end, we first present our strategy to map the user's gestures to the robot's joint space. Then, after collecting a dataset from a person who is familiar with PSL, a Hidden Markov Model (HMM)-based algorithm is introduced/used to do the learning process and teach the robot some new PSL signs. Finally, a questionnaire is used to collect twenty one users' viewpoints (both familiar and unfamiliar with PSL) on the appropriateness and quality of RASA's sign reproduction ability. Moreover, for the participants who were familiar with PSL, we investigate the preliminary estimate of the signs distinguishability performed by the RASA robot.

2 Methodology

2.1 Data Acquisition Method

After reviewing the related works in this field [4–14, 18], one can see that there are many methods for gathering data. In this study, we chose using a full body motion capture suit on the teacher side. We used a Perception Neuron V2 suit from Noitom Ltd. [19]. It utilizes 32 IMU and gyro sensors to capture whole body movements. The suit comes with a proprietary software called Axis Neuron. The software can either save motions offline or broadcast them online via TCP/IP in a BVH format. Using C# code, we are able to read the broadcasted data and process them as the user's joint positions in space. We will later use these joint positions to keep/save the user's motions to teach our robot different signs. It should be mentioned that in this study, we only used the gloves of the motion capture suit.

2.2 RASA Robot

RASA is a social robotic platform designed to facilitate teaching PSL to deaf and hard of hearing Iranian children (Fig. 1). It was designed and constructed in the Social and Cognitive Robotics Lab., Sharif University of Technology, Iran. For this study, the most important feature of RASA is its Degrees of Freedom (DoF). RASA has thirteen DoF in each arm: seven in its active fingers, one in the wrist, one for forearm rotation, one in the elbow, and three for each shoulder joint [15, 20, 21]. Considering the required and various degrees of freedom as well as its animated face's ability to move the lips to comply with the robot's dialogue, RASA can perform comprehensible PSL signs [16]. It should be noted that in Persian Sign Language, in addition to the arm/finger movements, the dynamic movement of the lips is also essential to perform a sign correctly and completely.

Fig. 1. The RASA robot with active fingers.

2.3   Mapping User's Gestures to the Robot's Joint Space

Finding an appropriate mapping between the user and robot movements is one of the key factors in this study. An appropriate mapping is one which addresses the robot's kinematics, ensure collision avoidance, and make the robot's movement more distinguishable.

In order to achieve proper mapping, we divided each of the kinematic chains (i.e. the robots' arms) into two separate groups and then used different strategies for each group. The first group includes the 4 motors in the chain (for actuating/controlling the shoulder, arm, and elbow) and determines the end effector's position (i.e. the palm position). We used an interpolation method to map the user's arm position to the actuators' positions. In a preliminary step, a dataset of the user's hand positions' vectors (p_i) and the corresponding robot's actuators' positions ($m_{i,j}, i = 1, \cdots, 8, j = 1, \cdots, 4$) should be created. The dataset used in the current study had more than 150 entries covering the whole workspace of the robot with an acceptable resolution. In each iteration, we first searched inside the dataset to locate the nearest eight points ($p_i, i = 1, \cdots, 8$) around the current position of the user's hand position (p_0). Then we calculated the weighted mean of the corresponding motor positions ($m_{i,j}, i = 1, \cdots, 8, j = 1, \cdots, 4$) of these points. We used the inverse of the Euclidian distance between the current position and the points as the weight:

$$w_i = \frac{1}{|p_i - p_0|}, i = 1, \cdots, 8 \tag{1}$$

$$m_{0,j} = \frac{\sum_{i=1}^{8} w_i m_{i,j}}{\sum_{i=1}^{8} w_i}, j = 1, \cdots, 4 \tag{2}$$

This method ensures collision avoidance since the outputs remain in the region between the dataset points which are in the robot's workspace. It also reconcile the problems of complex Inverse Kinematics (IK) and redundancy of the robot's arm.

The second group includes the forearm, wrist, and finger motors which determine the palm orientation and the hand shape. These parts have simpler kinematics and do not cause collisions so we used a direct method to solve their kinematics and map the user's motion. At the end of the process, the output data was filtered using a moving average filter to avoid possible discontinuities in the course.

2.4   Learning Process

For each user, the data capturing process starts with wearing the gloves of the motion capture suit, connecting it to the PC, and starting the Data Acquisition Windows program written in C#. The Windows program asks a few questions about the sign (such as what is the sign's name?, which arms are included in the performance?, etc.) then it is ready to save the user's demonstrations. Later, the app allows the user to manage the recorded demonstrations: deleting bad demonstrations, adding new ones, or reviewing them by forcing the robot to executing a specific demonstration. When the user is satisfied with the collected demonstrations, the mathematical modeling of the training process starts. We have used Hidden Markov Models (HMM) as the core of the learning process. For each arm, the system trains three independent parallel HMMs:

- One model with three features (x, y, z) for hand position relative to the shoulder normalized by the user's height;
- One model with two features (i.e. the forearm and wrist motors' positions) for palm orientation; and
- One model for hand shape consisting of all the fingers motors' positions.

These independence assumptions help to reach a satisfying quality level with less data. The models are based on Calinon et al.'s works [22] on combining Gaussian Mixture Models (GMM) with HMMs. In this version, instead of using matrices, the hidden state generating probability is encoded by a GMM:

$$B_i(x) = \frac{\exp\left(-0.5(x - \mu_i)^T \sum_i^{-1} (x - \mu_i)\right)}{\sqrt{(2\pi)^k |\sum_i|}} \tag{3}$$

In Eq. (3), $B_i(x)$ is the probability of output x being generated by state i. μ_i and $\sum_i$ are the mean and covariance of the i-th state, respectively.

By the end of the training process, the user can see the results on the robot and if it was not satisfactory he/she can modify the collected demonstrations and retrain the models. After finalizing the training process, the models are sent to the robot's PC using a websocket client (Fig. 2).

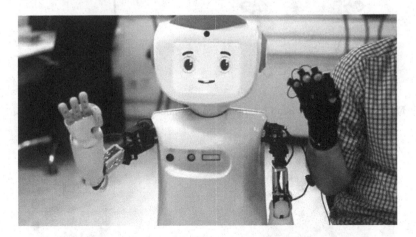

Fig. 2. The RASA robot during the learning process.

The following plots in Fig. 3 represents the HMMs for the hand position encoded models of 4 out of the 10 selected PSL signs which the robot performed in front of the participants of this study. Each circle represents a state and each arrow (and its color) represents the transition between them. The number of states are dependent on the sign's complexity. The GMMs cannot be shown because their dimensions are higher than the simple 2D graphs. Applying the mentioned HMM-based algorithm, our robot was empowered to reproduce the 10 signs from the dataset captured via a sign language teacher. The next step was collecting the viewpoints of the participants regarding the robot's performance. Figure 4 shows snapshots of RASA performing some signs.

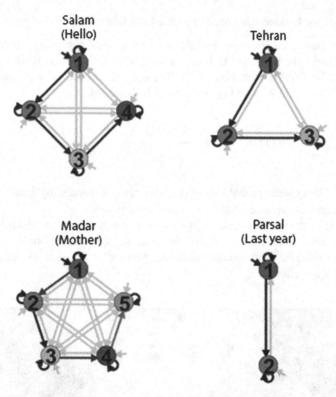

Fig. 3. HMMs for the hand position encoded models of four selected PSL signs.

Fig. 4. Snapshots of the RASA robot performing PSL signs.

2.5   Participants and Assessment of the Robot's Performance

21 students including 17 males and 4 females; mean age: 25 years, standard deviation: 3 years were recruited in this study for the assessment of the robot's performance.

A questionnaire was also developed (Table 1) and filled in by the participants to evaluate how acceptable and/or distinguishable the robot's performance is in reproducing signs learned (via the LfD algorithm) from a PSL teacher. The questionnaire consisted of two kinds of questions: (1) Part A: Sign Recognition and (2) Part B: the subject's overall viewpoint on the robot. It should be noted that if the participant scored equal to or above 3 on PSL familiarization, they were then asked to complete Part A of the questionnaire. On the other hand, Part B is filled by all of the participants.

Table 1. The questionnaire developed/used in this study to assess RASA's performance in reproducing signs learned via the LfD algorithm.

Part A: Sign Recognition for participants familiar with PSL			
Please rate your level of familiarity with PSL: *Answers: 1 2 3 4 5*			
If your answer is equal to or greater than 3, please fill in Part A in the questionnaire.			
No.	*Word*	*First Guess (individually)*	*Second Guess (provided multiple choices)*
A1	Word 1		
A2	Word 2		
...	...		
A10	Word 10		
Part B: Overall Viewpoints of the participants			
No.	*Questions*		*Answers: 1 2 3 4 5*
B1	How understandable were the movements of the RASA robot in signs' reproduction?		
B2	How natural were the movements of the RASA robot in signs' reproduction?		
B3	I think it's a good idea to use a social robot to teach sign language to typically developing people and individuals with hearing problem		
B4	I find the robot pleasant to interact with users via PSL		
B5	I find the robot enjoyable		

RASA performed 10 different PSL signs in order for all of the subjects. The selected words were "'Salam' (hello), 'Hatman' (Sure), 'Talash' (Try), 'Tehran' (Tehran), 'Pooshidan' (Put on), 'Shostan' (Wash), 'Ehsas' (Feeling), 'Doost Dashtan' (Love), 'Parsal' (Last year), 'Madar' (mother)". These signs are among the common signs taught during the first levels of PSL classes. The robot performed the words in the presence of the participants during a 30-min session.

For each sign, participants who were "familiar with PSL" were asked if they recognized each sign in the First Guess. Next, the subjects were given 5 choices (including the correct answer) to see if they can recognize the sign in their Second Guess with the aid of the given choices. We observed that from the 21 total participants, 7 were appropriately familiar with PSL and rated the robot's performance by answering the questions of Part A. These 7 participants had passed at least one level of PSL classes. The rest of the subjects did not have received any systematic education regarding PSL, but might have some general information about some PSL signs.

In addition, alongside the signs' recognition, all 21 participants were asked to rate the robot's overall performance of each sign/word on a 5-point Likert scale (i.e. Part B of the questionnaire). As seen in Table 1, they answered some questions regarding their overall viewpoints on the possibility/efficiency of using a social robot in the context of teaching sign language.

3   Results and Discussion

As it is mentioned, according to the completed questionnaires, 7 out of 21 participants were familiar with PSL (i.e. participants entered scores equal to or greater than 3). After RASA performed the 10 selected signs, we collected those 7 participants' answers of Part A to investigate the recognition rate of the robot's signs. The results of the First and Second guesses for those subjects are presented in Table 2. The overall performance of the participants for these signs were 80.2% and 100% for the first and second guesses, respectively. Moreover, the mean and standard deviation of the scores of Question B1 extracted from the questionnaires filled by the 7 participants were 4.14 (out of 5) and 0.69, respectively (The results of all 21 subjects regarding this question were 3.76 and 0.62, respectively). Therefore, considering these observations we can conclude that the proposed HMMs have reproduced understandable movements for signs, which makes the performance of the learning from demonstrations' approach fairly promising. It should be noted that due to limitations in the fingers' movements, we tended to choose signs which the robot would be able to perform. Although it is clear that involving more participants familiar with PSL would make the experiments and the results stronger, the reported result could be considered as a preliminary estimate of the algorithm's performance in teaching robots new signs by non-expert users.

Table 2. The success percentage of the sign recognition test for the participants who were familiar with PSL.

Word #	1	2	3	4	5	6	7	8	9	10	Mean (SD)
1st Guess	100	72	86	100	57	43	100	100	72	72	**80.2 (20.3)**
2nd Guess	100	100	100	100	100	100	100	100	100	100	**100 (0.0)**

The mean and standard deviation of Questions B2 to B5 answered by all 21 participants are presented in Table 3. Based on the results, the participants believed that the actions generated by the robot (i.e. the HMM outputs) were very close to being natural. Moreover, the overall opinions of the subjects indicated that the robot's attractiveness is quite high; and they are somewhat agree with the usefulness and success of a social robot in teaching and/or communicating via PSL. Due to the nature of such exploratory studies with small number of participants, it is difficult to say strong conclusions and the reported observations could be only considered as an estimate of the general viewpoints about the system's attractiveness and usefulness. We conducted paired T-tests on the data as an estimate of a possible significant difference between the two group's (those familiar and unfamiliar with PSL) viewpoints regarding the usefulness of social robots in teaching PSL. We observed that all of the p-values of our data are greater than 0.05, which did not show any significant difference between the scores of the two groups. It should be noted that such an analysis should be done with caution due to the small number of subjects (especially the number of the participants who were familiar with PSL) and the probable low reliability of the results. However, it may be reasonable that after observing the robot's performance and the subjects' general knowledge of PSL, both of the groups have the similar idea of using social robots in teaching and/or interacting via PSL. This particular finding agrees with findings of prior researches on effectiveness of using social robots in education [23]. Involving sign language teachers in such studies could give us more reliable information about the appropriateness of using robots in teaching and/or communication via sign language.

Table 3. The results of the questionnaires for all 21 participants (The scores are out of 5).

Question #	B2 - Natural	B3 - Usage	B4 - Pleasant	B5 - Enjoyable
Mean *(SD)*	**3.76** *(0.77)*	**3.62** *(1.24)*	**3.62** *(1.28)*	**3.86** *(1.11)*

4   Conclusion

We proposed a learning from demonstration framework to eliminate the need for expert operators to teach new PSL signs to our SL performing robot, RASA. The proposed framework facilitates the teaching process by utilizing a motion capture suit and wizard-like software to capture the user's performance of signs. The software will then encode the captured performance using hidden Markov models and Gaussian mixture models. After teaching 10 signs to the robot by a teacher, a questionnaire was used to assess the framework's proficiency. Participants who were familiar with sign language evaluated the robot's performance and were able to distinguish the signs with about 80% accuracy in their first guess and showed a 100% recognition rate in their second guess. The main limitations of this study were accessing adequate number of participants who are familiar with Persian Sign Language. In addition, considering RASA's actuators' limitations as well as its vague lip movements while performing some of the words, prevented us from being able to perform all PSL signs.

As a future work, it is recommended to study the teachers' experience instead of the robot's audiences by allowing non-expert users to use the framework to try and teach signs to the robot and then analyzing the robot's performance from the teachers' viewpoints.

Acknowledgement. This research was partially funded by the Iran Telecommunication Research Center (ITRC) (http://en.itrc.ac.ir/). We would also like to appreciate the Iranian National Science Foundation (INSF) for their complementary support of the Social & Cognitive Robotics Laboratory (http://en.insf.org/).

References

1. Yang, G.Z., McNutt, M.: Robotics takes off. Science **352**(6291), 1255 (2016)
2. Pratt, G.A.: Is a Cambrian explosion coming for robotics? J. Econ. Perspect. **29**(3), 51–60 (2015)
3. Shukla, M., Shukla, A.N.: Growth of robotics industry early in 21st century. Int. J. Comput. Eng. Res. (IJCER) **2**(5), 1554–1558 (2012)
4. Argall, B.D., Chernova, S., Veloso, M., Browning, B.: A survey of robot learning from demonstration. Robot. Auton. Syst. **57**(5), 469–483 (2009)
5. Chernova, S., Thomaz, A.L.: Robot learning from human teachers. Synth. Lect. Artif. Intell. Mach. Learn. **8**(3), 1–121 (2014)
6. Atkeson, C.G., Schaal, S.: Robot learning from demonstration. In: ICML, vol. 97, pp. 12–20, July 1997
7. Schaal, S.: Dynamic movement primitives -a framework for motor control in humans and humanoid robotics. In: Kimura, H., Tsuchiya, K., Ishiguro, A., Witte, H. (eds.) Adaptive Motion of Animals and Machines, pp. 261–280. Springer, Tokyo (2006). https://doi.org/10.1007/4-431-31381-8_23
8. Matsubara, T., Hyon, S.H., Morimoto, J.: Learning stylistic dynamic movement primitives from multiple demonstrations. In: 2010 IEEE/RSJ International Conference on Intelligent Robots and Systems, pp. 1277–1283. IEEE, October 2010
9. Pastor, P., Hoffmann, H., Asfour, T., Schaal, S.: Learning and generalization of motor skills by learning from demonstration. In: 2009 IEEE International Conference on Robotics and Automation, pp. 763–768. IEEE, May 2009
10. Akgun, B., Cakmak, M., Jiang, K., Thomaz, A.L.: Keyframe-based learning from demonstration. Int. J. Soc. Robot. **4**(4), 343–355 (2012)
11. Calinon, S., Billard, A.: Stochastic gesture production and recognition model for a humanoid robot. In: 2004 IEEE/RSJ International Conference on Intelligent Robots and Systems (IROS) (IEEE Cat. No. 04CH37566), vol. 3, pp. 2769–2774. IEEE, September 2004
12. Calinon, S., Billard, A.: Incremental learning of gestures by imitation in a humanoid robot. In: Proceedings of the ACM/IEEE International Conference on Human-Robot Interaction, pp. 255–262. ACM, March 2007
13. Zeestraten, M.J., Havoutis, I., Silvério, J., Calinon, S., Caldwell, D.G.: An approach for imitation learning on Riemannian manifolds. IEEE Robot. Autom. Lett. **2**(3), 1240–1247 (2017)
14. Silvério, J., Calinon, S., Rozo, L., Caldwell, D.G.: Learning task priorities from demonstrations. IEEE Trans. Robot. **35**(1), 78–94 (2018)
15. Zakipour, M., Meghdari, A., Alemi, M.: RASA: a low-cost upper-torso social robot acting as a sign language teaching assistant. In: Agah, A., Cabibihan, J.J., Howard, A., Salichs, M., He, H. (eds.) Social Robotics. ICSR 2016. LNCS, vol. 9979, pp. 630–639. Springer, Cham (2016). https://doi.org/10.1007/978-3-319-47437-3_62
16. Meghdari, A., Alemi, M., Zakipour, M., Kashanian, S.A.: Design and realization of a sign language educational humanoid robot. J. Intell. Robot. Syst. **95**(1), 3–17 (2019)
17. Hosseini, S.R., Taheri, A., Meghdari, A., Alemi, M.: "Let there be intelligence!"- a novel cognitive architecture for teaching assistant social robots. In: Ge, S. et al. (eds.) Social Robotics. ICSR 2018. LNCS, vol. 11357, pp. 275–285. Springer, Cham (2018). https://doi.org/10.1007/978-3-030-05204-1_27
18. Dillmann, R.: Teaching and learning of robot tasks via observation of human performance. Robot. Auton. Syst. **47**(2–3), 109–116 (2004)
19. Perception Neuron Motion Capture, July 2018. https://neuronmocap.com

20. Meghdari, A., Arefi, M., Mahmoudian, M.: Geometric adaptability: a novel mechanical design in the Sharif artificial hand. Int. J. Robot. Autom. **7**(2), 80–85 (1992)
21. Meghdari, A., Sayyaadi, H.: Optimizing motion trajectories of dexterous fingers by dynamic programming technique. Robotica Int. J. **10**(5), 419–426 (1992)
22. Calinon, S.: A tutorial on task-parameterized movement learning and retrieval. Intell. Serv. Robot. **9**(1), 1–29 (2016)
23. Belpaeme, T., Kennedy, J., Ramachandran, A., Scassellati, B., Tanaka, F.: Social robots for education: a review. Sci. Robot. **3**(21), eaat5954 (2018)

Learning to Gesticulate by Observation Using a Deep Generative Approach

Unai Zabala[iD], Igor Rodriguez[✉][iD], José María Martínez-Otzeta[iD],
and Elena Lazkano[iD]

Computer Science and Artificial Intelligence, Faculty of Informatics,
UPV/EHU, Manuel Lardizabal 1, 20018 Donostia, Spain
`igor.rodriguez@ehu.eus`
`http://www.sc.ehu.es/ccwrobot`

Abstract. The goal of the system presented in this paper is to develop
a natural talking gesture generation behavior for a humanoid robot, by
feeding a Generative Adversarial Network (GAN) with human talking
gestures recorded by a Kinect. A direct kinematic approach is used to
translate from human poses to robot joint positions. The provided videos
show that the robot is able to use a wide variety of gestures, offering a
non-dreary, natural expression level.

Keywords: Social robots · Motion capturing and imitation ·
Generative Adversarial Networks · Talking movements

1 Introduction

Social robotics [4] aims to provide robots with artificial social intelligence to
improve human-machine interaction and to introduce them in complex human
contexts. The demand for sophisticated robot behaviors requires to model and
implement human-like capabilities to sense, to process, and to act/interact naturally by taking into account emotions, intentions, motivations, and other related
cognitive functions.

Talking involves spontaneous gesticulation; postures and movements are relevant for social interactions even if they are subjective and culture dependent.
Aiming at building trust and making people feel confident when interacting
with them, socially acting humanoid robots should show human-like talking gesticulation. Therefore, they need a mechanism that generates movements that
resembles humans' in terms of naturalness. A previous work [24] made use of
gestures selected from a set of movements previously compiled. Those gestures

This work has been partially supported by the Basque Government (IT900-16 and
Elkartek 2018/00114) and the Spanish Ministry of Economy and Competitiveness
MINECO/FEDER (RTI 2018-093337-B-100, MINECO/FEDER, EU). We gratefully
acknowledge the support of NVIDIA Corporation with the donation of the Titan Xp
GPU used for this research.

M. A. Salichs et al. (Eds.): ICSR 2019, LNAI 11876, pp. 666–675, 2019.
https://doi.org/10.1007/978-3-030-35888-4_62

were then randomly concatenated and reproduced according to the duration of the speech. That approach was prone to produce repetitive movements and resulted in unnatural jerky expression.

The goal of the system presented in this paper is to develop a natural talking gesture generation behavior for a humanoid robot. At this step we aim to give a step forward by training a Generative Adversarial Network (GAN) gesture generation system with movements captured directly from humans. A Kinect sensor is used to track the skeleton of the talking person and a GAN is trained to generate a richer and more natural talking gesticulation.

Gestures (head, hands and arms movements) are used both to reinforce the meaning of the words and to express feelings through non-verbal signs. Among the different types of conversational movement of arms and hands synchronised with the flow of the speech, beats are those not associated with particular meaning [18]. References to talking gestures of the present work will be limited to beats.

The robotic platform employed in the performed experiments is a Softbank Robotics Pepper robot[1]. Currently, our robot is controlled using the *naoqi_driver*[2] package that wraps the needed parts of NAOqi[3] API and makes them available in ROS[4].

2   Related Work

According to Beck et al. [3], there are three main robot motion generation approaches: manually creating motion, motion capturing, and motion planning; for manual creation, it is required to set each joint position of the humanoid robot for each key frame (time step); the motion capture-based approach tries to mimic human gestures, recording human movements and mapping these data to a humanoid robot [22]; and motion planning approach relies on kinematics and/or dynamics equations to solve a geometric task. They found that the motion capturing approach produces the most realistic results, because the robot reproduces previously captured human movements.

Motion capturing and imitation is a challenge because humans and robots have different kinematic and dynamic structures. Motion capture (MoCap) is the process of recording motion data through any type of sensor. Applications of MoCap systems range from animation, bio-mechanics, medicine to sports science, entertainment, robotics [21,31] or even study of animal behavior [27]. MoCap systems rely on optical technologies, and can be marker-based (e.g. Vicon[5]) or markerless like RGB-D cameras. While the former ones provide more accurate results, the latter ones are less prone to produce gaps (missing values) that need

---

[1] https://www.ald.softbankrobotics.com/en/robots/pepper.

[2] http://wiki.ros.org/naoqi_driver.

[3] http://doc.aldebaran.com/2-5/naoqi/index.html.

[4] http://www.ros.org.

[5] https://www.vicon.com/.

to be estimated [19,29]. Many approaches make use of the Kinect sensors due to its availability [1,9,20].

No matter the motion capture system being used, there is a need to transfer human motion to the robot joints. This can be done by direct kinematics, adapting captured human joint angles to the robot. Or alternatively, inverse kinematics calculates the necessary joint positions given a desired end effector's pose.

On the other hand, generative models are probabilistic models capable of generating all the values for a phenomenon. Unlike discriminative models, they are able to generate not only the target variables but also the observable ones [28]. They are used in machine learning to (implicitly or explicitly) acquire the distribution of the data for generating new samples. There are many types of generative models. For instance, Bayesian Networks (BNs) [7], Gaussian Mixture Models (GMMs) [8] and Hidden Markov Models (HMMs) [23] are well known probability density estimators.

Focusing on generative models used for motion generation, in [14] the authors propose the combination of Principal Component Analysis (PCA) [30] and HMMs for encoding different movement primitives to generate humanoid motion. Tanwani [28] uses HSMM (Hidden Semi-Markov Models) for learning robot manipulation skills from humans. Regarding on social robotics, some generative approaches are being applied with different objectives. In [17] Manfrè et al. use HMMs for dance creation and in a later work they try variational auto-encoders again for the same purpose [2].

Deep learning techniques have also been applied to generative models, giving rise to deep generative models. A taxonomy of such models can be found in [10]. In particular Generative Adversarial Networks (GANs) [11] are semi-supervised emerging models that basically learn how to generate synthetic data from the given training data. GANs are deep generative models capable to implicitly acquire the probability density function in the training data, being able to automatically discover the internal structure of datasets by learning multiple levels of abstraction [15]. Gupta et al. [12] extend the use of GANs to generate socially acceptable motion trajectories in crowded scenes in the scope of self-driving cars. In [26] GANs showed to overcome other generative approaches such as HMM and GMM when confronted to the task of motion generation. In that work, movements produced synthetically (using choregraph) were used to train the different generative approaches. Instead, in this paper we feed the GAN with movements obtained by observing and capturing human talking gestures.

3   Developed Approach to Enhance Robot Spontaneity

The GAN used in the current approach takes as input only proprioceptive joint position information. In order to feed the GAN with natural motion data, a motion capturing approach is employed. Thus, these two aspects are exhaustively described here on.

3.1   Human Motion Capture and Imitation

In [25], direct kinematics was used to teleoperate a NAO robot. Human skeleton obtained with a Kinect was tracked and arm movements were replicated by the robot, while walking motions were commanded by using different spatial key movements. As the goal was to teleoperate the robot, there was no need for subtle and continuous motion since the arms only required to reach single poses when demanded by the operator. On the contrary, gesticulation requires continuous arm motion and involves also hands, head and fingers. Although the present work makes use of a similar motion capture and mapping system, the presented system has been enriched to cover all the aspects involved.

The Kinect uses structured light (depth map) and machine learning to infer body position [16]. The OpenNI based `skeleton_markers`[6] ROS package is able to extract in real time the 15 joints associated to the human skeleton.

Mapping Human's Arms into Robot's Space
Human arms have 7 degrees of freedom (DoF): a spherical joint at the shoulder, a revolute joint at the elbow and a spherical joint at the wrist. On the contrary, our humanoid's arms have 5 DoF: two at the shoulder (pitch and yaw) and elbow (yaw and roll), and one at the wrist (yaw) (Fig. 1). Thereby, the movement configurations of human and robot arms differ.

To transform the Cartesian coordinates obtained from the Kinect into *Pepper*'s coordinate space a joint control approach was employed. Note that the transformations are performed to the reference system of each individual joint, not to a robot's global reference frame. On the following explanation we will focus on the left arm. The analysis of the right arm is similar and it will be omitted here.

Pepper's left arm has five joints[7] (see Fig. 1): shoulder roll (LS_α) and pitch (LS_β), elbow roll (LE_α) and yaw (LE_γ) and wrist yaw (LW_γ). The `skeleton_markers` package can not detect the operator's hands' yaw motion and thus, LW_γ joints cannot be reproduced using the skeleton information. We chose another approach for LW_γ, that will be explained later on.

In order to calculate the shoulder's roll angle (LS_α) we use the dot product of the distance vector between both shoulders $(\overline{LRS})$ and the length vector between the shoulder and the elbow $(\overline{LSE})$. Note that, before computing that product, $\overline{LRS}$ and $\overline{LSE}$ vectors must be normalized. The LS_α angle is calculated in the Kinect's coordinate space, therefore, it must be transformed into the robot's coordinate space by rotating it $\frac{-\pi}{2}$ radians (Eq. 1).

$$LS_\alpha = \arccos\left(\overline{LRS} \cdot \overline{LSE}\right)$$
$$LS_\alpha^{robot} = LS_\alpha - \frac{\pi}{2} \tag{1}$$

---

[6] http://wiki.ros.org/skeleton_markers.
[7] http://doc.aldebaran.com/2-8/family/pepper_technical/joints_pep.html.

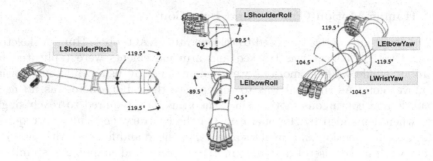

Fig. 1. Pepper's left arm joints and actuators (from Softbanks official Pepper's user guide (see Footnote 7)).

Elbow's roll (LE_α) angle is calculated in the same way as shoulder's roll angle (LS_α) but the length vector between the shoulder and the elbow ($\overline{LSE}$) and the length vector between the elbow and the hand ($\overline{LEH}$) are used instead. Again, those vectors need to be normalized and transformed to the robot's space, in this case by rotating it $-\pi$ radians.

With respect to elbow's yaw angle (LE_γ) calculation we use only the y and z components of the $\overline{LEH}$ vector. After normalizing $\overline{LEH}$, Eq. 2 is applied to obtain the LE_γ. Lastly, a range conversion is needed to get LE_γ^{robot} (from $[\frac{\pi}{2}, \pi]$ to $[-\frac{\pi}{2}, 0]$ and from $[-\pi, -\frac{\pi}{2}]$ to $[0, \pi]$).

$$LE_\gamma = \arctan \frac{LEH_z}{LEH_y}$$
$$LE_\gamma^{robot} = rangeConv(LE_\gamma) \tag{2}$$

To conclude with the joints, the shoulder pitch angle (LS_β) is calculated by measuring the angle between the shoulder to elbow vector and the z axis. $z = 0$ occurs with the arm extended at 90° with respect to the torso. Thus, lowering the arm produces negative pitch angle while raising it above the shoulder produces positive angular values.

The LS_β can be defined as:

$$\|A\| = LSE_z \quad \text{(by definition)}$$
$$\sin(LS_\beta) = \frac{\|A\|}{\|\overline{LSE}\|} = \frac{\|A\|}{1} \tag{3}$$
$$LS_\beta^{robot} = \arcsin(LSE_z)$$

where LSE_z is the Z coordinate of the shoulder to elbow vector.

Mapping Human's Hands into Robot's Space

Hands movements are common in humans while talking. We do rotate wrist and open and close hands, move fingers constantly. Unfortunately, the skeleton capturing system we are using does not allow to detect such movements. It is possible though to capture the state of the hands using a different approach.

The developed solution forces the user to wear coloured gloves, green in the palm of the hand and red in the back (Fig. 2). While the human talks, hands coordinates are tracked and those positions are mapped into the image space and a subimage is obtained for each hand. Angular information is afterwards calculated by measuring the number of pixels (max) of the outstanding color in a subimage. Equation 4 shows the procedure for the left hand. N is a normalizing constant and $maxW_\gamma$ stands for the maximum wrist yaw angle of the robot.

$$\begin{cases} LW_\gamma^{robot} = max/N \times maxW_\gamma & \text{if } max \text{ is palm} \\ LW_\gamma^{robot} = \frac{max-N}{N} \times maxW_\gamma & \text{otherwise} \end{cases} \tag{4}$$

Fig. 2. Snapshot of a data capture session.

In addition LE_γ is modified when humans palms are up (subimage has only green pixels) to easy the movement of the robot.

Regarding the fingers, as they cannot be tracked, their position is randomly set at each skeleton frame.

Mapping Human's Head into Robot's Space

Humans move the head while talking and thus, head motion should also be captured and mapped. The robot's head has 2 DoFs that allow the head to move left to right (yaw) and up and down (pitch) as shown in Fig. 3.

The Kinect skeleton tracking program gives us the (neck and) head 3D positions. The approach taken for mapping the yaw angle to the robot's head consists of applying a gain K_1 to the human's yaw value, once transformed into the robot space by a $-\frac{\pi}{2}$ rotation (Eq. 5).

$$H_\gamma^{robot} = K_1 \times H_\beta \tag{5}$$

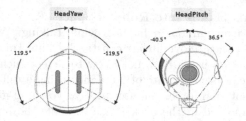

Fig. 3. Pepper's head joints and actuators (from Softbanks official Pepper's user guide (see Footnote 7)).

In order to approximate head's pitch angle, the head to neck vector ($\overline{HN}$) is calculated and rotated $-\frac{\pi}{2}$ and then, its angle is obtained (Eq. 6). Note that robot's head is an ellipsoid instead of an sphere. To avoid unwanted head movements a lineal gain is applied to the final value.

$$H_\beta^{robot} = \arctan\left(rotate(\overline{HN}, -\frac{\pi}{2})\right) + |K_2 * H_\gamma| \qquad (6)$$

3.2 Generative Model

GAN networks are composed by two different interconnected networks. The *Generator* (G) network generates possible candidates so that they are as similar as possible to the training set. The second network, known as *Discriminator* (D), judges the output of the first network to discriminate whether its input data are "real", namely equal to the input data set, or if they are "fake", that is, generated to trick with false data.

The training dataset given to the D network contained 2018 unit of movements (UM), being each UM is a sequence of 4 consecutive poses, and each pose 14 float numbers corresponding to joint values of head, arms, wrists and hands (finger opening). These samples were recorded by registering 5 different persons talking, about 9 min overall.

The D network is thus trained using that data to learn its distribution space and its input dimension is 56. On the other hand, the G network is seeded through a random input with a uniform distribution in the range $[-1, 1]$ and with a dimension of 100. The G intends to produce as output gestures that belong to the real data distribution and that the D network would not be able to correctly pick out as generated. Figure 4 depicts the architecture the generator and discriminator networks.

GAN has been trained for 2000 epochs and its hyper-parameter have been tuned experimentally; we set up a batch size of 16, a learning rate of 0.0002, Adam [13] as optimization method, and $\beta_1 = 0.5$ and $\beta_2 = 0.999$ as its parameters.

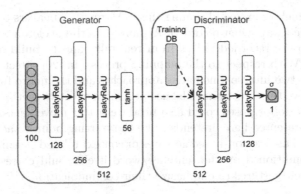

Fig. 4. GAN setup for talking gesture generation.

4   Results

The obtained robot performance can be appreciated in the following videos:

1. The first video[8] shows some instants recorded during the process of generating the database of movements captured through the motion capturing and imitation mechanisms. On the left side the participant talking and gesticulating is displayed, while the simulated robot mimicking the movements in real time (without GAN) is shown in the right side.
2. A second video[9] shows the evolution of the robot behavior during different steps of the training process. The final number of epochs was empirically set to 2000 for the model that has been integrated into the gesture generation system.

Notice that the temporal length of the audio intended to be pronounced by the robot determines the number of units of movement required to the generative model. Thus, the execution of those units of movements, one after the other, defines the whole movement displayed by the robot.

5   Conclusions and Further Work

In this work a talking gesture generation system has been developed using a GAN fed with natural motion data obtained through a motion capturing and imitation system. The suitability of the approach is demonstrated with a real robot. Results show that the obtained robot behavior is appropriate, and thanks to the movement variability the robot expresses itself with naturalness.

As further work, we intend to improve the skeleton capture process by using more robust systems, such as OpenPose [5,6] or wrnchAI[10] that allow to capture more detailed movements. In this way, the speakers would not need to wear the

---

[8] https://www.youtube.com/watch?v=iW1566ozbdg.

[9] https://www.youtube.com/watch?v=1It_Y_AEnts.

[10] https://wrnch.ai/.

gloves, that somehow are conditioning them. Moreover, speakers tend to behave in an constricted way when recorded. A more powerful skeleton tracker system would allow to use recorded videos from real talks and to build a more objective database. With respect to the mapping process, in [20] direct kinematics is compared with two inverse kinematics approaches and the neuro fuzzy approach seems to improve the direct one. The use of a more effective method to translate human poses to robot poses could also produce better movements.

The work presented here pretends to be the starting point to acquire a richer gesture set, such as emotion-based gestures or context related gestures. Moreover, a generator conditioned on the sentence/word itself would correspond to how humans use their gestures to emphasize their communication.

References

1. Alibeigi, M., Rabiee, S., Ahmadabadi, M.N.: Inverse kinematics based human mimicking system using skeletal tracking technology. J. Intell. Robotic Syst. **85**(1), 27–45 (2017)
2. Augello, A., Cipolla, E., Infantino, I., Manfrè, A., Pilato, G., Vella, F.: Creative robot dance with variational encoder. CoRR abs/1707.01489 (2017)
3. Beck, A., Yumak, Z., Magnenat-Thalmann, N.: Body movements generation for virtual characters and social robots. In: Judee, K.B., Nadia, M.-T., Maja, P., Alessandro, V. (eds.) Social Signal Processing, pp. 273–286. Cambridge University Press, Cambridge (2017)
4. Breazeal, C.: Designing sociable robots. In: Intelligent Robotics and Autonomous Agents. MIT Press, Cambridge (2004)
5. Cao, Z., Hidalgo, G., Simon, T., Wei, S.E., Sheikh, Y.: OpenPose: realtime multi-person 2D pose estimation using part affinity fields. arXiv preprint arXiv:1812.08008 (2018)
6. Cao, Z., Simon, T., Wei, S.E., Sheikh, Y.: Realtime multi-person 2D pose estimation using part affinity fields. In: CVPR (2017)
7. Castillo, E., Gutiérrez, J.M., Hadi, A.S.: Learning Bayesian networks. In: Expert Systems and Probabilistic Network Models. Monographs in computer science. Springer-Verlag, New York (1997). https://doi.org/10.1007/978-1-4612-2270-5_11
8. Everitt, B., Hand, D.: Finite Mixture Distributions. Chapman and Hall, New York (1981)
9. Fadli, H., Machbub, C., Hidayat, E.: Human gesture imitation on NAO humanoid robot using kinect based on inverse kinematics method. In: International Conference on Advanced Mechatronics, Intelligent Manufacture, and Industrial Automation (ICAMIMIA). IEEE (2015)
10. Goodfellow, I.: NIPS tutorial: generative adversarial networks. ArXiv e-prints, December 2017
11. Goodfellow, I., et al.: Generative adversarial nets. In: Advances in Neural Information Processing Systems, pp. 2672–2680 (2014)
12. Gupta, A., Johnson, J., Fei-Fei, L., Savarese, S., Alahi, A.: Social GAN: socially acceptable trajectories with generative adversarial networks. CoRR abs/1803.10892 (2018). http://arxiv.org/abs/1803.10892
13. Kingma, D.P., Ba, J.: Adam: a method for stochastic optimization. arXiv preprint arXiv:1412.6980 (2014)

14. Kwon, J., Park, F.C.: Using hidden markov models to generate natural humanoid movement. In: International Conference on Intelligent Robots and Systems (IROS). IEEE/RSJ (2006)
15. LeCun, Y., Bengio, Y., Hinton, G.: Deep learning. Nature **521**(7553), 436–444 (2015)
16. MacCormick, J.: How does the kinect work?. http://pages.cs.wisc.edu/ahmad/kinect.pdf. Accessed 3 June 2019
17. Manfrè, A., Infantino, I., Vella, F., Gaglio, S.: An automatic system for humanoid dance creation. Biologically Inspired Cogn. Architect. **15**, 1–9 (2016)
18. McNeill, D.: Hand and Mind: What Gestures Reveal About Thought. University of Chicago press (1992)
19. Mehta, D., et al.: VNect: real-time 3D human pose estimation with a single RGB camera. ACM Trans. Graph. **36**(4), 44:1–44:14 (2017)
20. Mukherjee, S., Paramkusam, D., Dwivedy, S.K.: Inverse kinematics of a NAO humanoid robot using Kinect to track and imitate human motion. In: International Conference on Robotics, Automation, Control and Embedded Systems (RACE). IEEE (2015)
21. Okamoto, T., Shiratori, T., Kudoh, S., Nakaoka, S., Ikeuchi, K.: Toward a dancing robot with listening capability: keypose-based integration of lower-, middle-, and upper-body motions for varying music tempos. IEEE Trans. Robot. **30**, 771–778 (2014). https://doi.org/10.1109/TRO.2014.2300212
22. Poubel, L.P.: Whole-body online human motion imitation by a humanoid robot using task specification. Master's thesis, Ecole Centrale de Nantes-Warsaw University of Technology (2013)
23. Rabiner, L.R.: A tutorial on hidden Markov models and selected applications in speech recognition. Proc. IEEE. **77**, 257–286 (1989)
24. Rodriguez, I., Astigarraga, A., Ruiz, T., Lazkano, E.: Singing minstrel robots, a means for improving social behaviors. In: IEEE International Conference on Robotics and Automation (ICRA), pp. 2902–2907 (2016)
25. Rodriguez, I., Astigarraga, A., Jauregi, E., Ruiz, T., Lazkano, E.: Humanizing NAO robot teleoperation using ROS. In: International Conference on Humanoid Robots (Humanoids) (2014)
26. Rodriguez, I., Martínez-Otzeta, J.M., Irigoien, I., Lazkano, E.: Spontaneous talking gestures using generative adversarial networks. Robot. Auton. Syst. **114**, 57–65 (2019)
27. Schubert, T., Eggensperger, K., Gkogkidis, A., Hutter, F., Ball, T., Burgard, W.: Automatic bone parameter estimation for skeleton tracking in optical motion capture. In: International Conference on Robotics and Automation (ICRA). IEEE (2016)
28. Tanwani, A.K.: Generative models for learning robot manipulation. Ph.D. thesis, École Polytechnique Fédéral de Laussane (EPFL) (2018)
29. Tits, M., Tilmanne, J., Dutoit, T.: Robust and automatic motion-capture data recovery using soft skeleton constraints and model averaging. PLOS One **13**(7), 1–21 (2018)
30. Wold, S., Esbensen, K., Geladi, P.: Principal component analysis. Chemometr. Intell. Lab. Syst. **2**(1–3), 37–52 (1987)
31. Zhang, Z., Niu, Y., Yan, Z., Lin, S.: Real-time whole-body imitation by humanoid robots and task-oriented teleoperation using an analytical mapping method and quantitative evaluation. Appl. Sci. **8**(10), 2005 (2018). https://www.mdpi.com/2076-3417/8/10/2005

Combining Static and Dynamic Predictions of Transfer Points for Human Initiated Handovers

Janneke Simmering[1], Sebastian Meyer zu Borgsen[1,2](✉) (iD), Sven Wachsmuth[1,2], and Ayoub Al-Hamadi[3]

[1] Bielefeld University, 33594 Bielefeld, Germany
{jsimmering,semeyerz,swachsmu}@techfak.uni-bielefeld.de
[2] CITEC, Bielefeld University, 33594 Bielefeld, Germany
[3] IIKT, University of Magdeburg, Magdeburg, Germany
ayoub.al-hamadi@ovgu.de
https://www.cit-ec.de, http://www.iikt.ovgu.de/nit.html

Abstract. In many scenarios where robots could assist humans, handover situations are essential. But they are still challenging for robots, especially if these are initiated by the human interaction partner. Human-human handover studies report average reaction times of 0.4 s, which is only achievable for robots, if they are able to predict the object transfer point (OTP) sufficiently early and then adapt to the human movement. In this paper, we propose a hand tracking system that can be used in the context of human initiated handover as a basis for human reaching motion prediction. The OTP prediction implemented is based on the minimum jerk model and combines a static estimation utilizing the human's initial pose and a dynamic estimation from the current hand trajectory. Results are generated and analyzed for a broad spectrum of human initiated scenarios. For these cases we examine the dynamics of different variants of the proposed prediction algorithm, i.e., how early is a robot's prediction of the OTP within a certain error range? The tracking delivers results with an average delay, after the initialization, of 0.07 s. We show that the OTP prediction delivers results after 75 % of the movement within a 10 cm precision box.

1 Introduction

Object handovers take place everywhere in our daily lives. With robots becoming more and more present in our common working or living environment, this is an essential part of the socially accepted interaction with them. Such close interactions demand a collaborative and precise synchronization of both partners in

S. Meyer zu Borgsen and S. Wachsmuth—This research/work was supported by the Cluster of Excellence Cognitive Interaction Technology 'CITEC' (EXC 277) at Bielefeld University, which is funded by the German Research Foundation (DFG).

© Springer Nature Switzerland AG 2019
M. A. Salichs et al. (Eds.): ICSR 2019, LNAI 11876, pp. 676–686, 2019.
https://doi.org/10.1007/978-3-030-35888-4_63

space and time. Previous handover studies provided evidence that an improved reactivity of the robot increases the acceptance of such systems [11]. This requires an early prediction of the object transfer point (OTP), which defines the object's position in 3d space where the actual object transfer event takes place (see marked coordinate system in Fig. 1(b)). This point can be inferred from the tracking of the hand position. Existing approaches can be distinguished by several factors. These include the number of cameras used, whether color, depth images or a combination of both is used and if the output is only one point describing the hand center position or if the hand's articulation is tracked. The proposed system should enable a robot to react to a handover considering a human-like timing. From human-human handover studies an average handover duration of about 1.24 s was reported [1]. The average reaction time was found to be about 0.4 s [12]. Therefore, the processing of the hand tracking and the planning of the robot's motion should only induce a minimal delay below 0.4 s. Approaches with a high processing time (e.g., Bray et al. [2]) do not fulfill these requirements. Hackenberg et al. [6] report a rate of more than 50 fps and rely only on depth images. But they assume strong visibility constraints, e.g., the palm always facing the camera with visible fingers, which are not always met in handover scenarios with occluding objects. Predicting human reaching motions in a handover scenario is a very recent research topic. OTP predictions have been tackled by [7, 8, 14]. Most approaches learn human motions and need many human demonstrations or use imitation learning [10, 13]. In order to generalize different handover scenarios and individuals large data sets are needed. Li and Hauser present a number of different models to predict human reaching motions, but only present preliminary results for two of them [9]. Nemlekar et al. combine a modified version of the Probabilistic Movement Primitives approach from Maeda et al. with an offline component in order to predict an estimated OTP as soon as a handover intent is detected [10, 12]. Our proposed system is based on Nemlekar's approach but substitutes the Probabilistic Movement Primitives component with the minimum jerk model, which is the first model presented by Li and Hauser [9]. The minimum jerk model was originally proposed by Flash and Hogan as a mathematical model for describing human arm movements [5]. Our approach is inspired by Chen et al. [4] who report a rate of more than 300 fps. As the robot should interact autonomously, our method relies only on one depth camera which is mounted in the robot's chest. Similar to Chen et al., we segment the hand and estimate the hand center based on the boundary points of the segmented region providing an input for a mean-shift based tracking. For the OTP prediction, we apply a model-based approach utilizing the minimum jerk model combined with the basic idea of Nemlekar et al. [5, 9, 12]. Instead of optimizing the approach for a minimal displacement at the end of the tracking, we examine the effects of different combination schemes of static and dynamic OTP prediction in the early reaching phase.

2   Approach

Similar to Nemlekar et al. [12], our system combines an offline and online component for the OTP prediction, but we examine the combination schemes in a more
sophisticated manner. The minimum jerk model is a simple method for trajectory generation minimizing a cost criterion based on the trajectory's jerk [5]. It
is used in the online component and predicts the human hand motions based on
the current hand position, the handover start time, and the estimated end time
[9]. The current hand position is provided by a hand tracking system (Sect. 2.1
that is used to continuously update the OTP prediction. The initialization of
the tracking system is given by a hand detection on a color image based on
OpenPose [3]. This provides accurate results but takes up some processing time
which leads to an initial delay of the tracking results of between 0.3 s and 0.4 s.
This 2D position is then converted, based on the corresponding depth image,
into a 3D position which is further used for low-latency tracking. Point clouds
are buffered in order to deal with the initial delay and to provide a continuous
tracking input. The hand tracking relies only on point clouds. The camera used
is an Intel RealSense D435, which has a wider opening angle for the depth sensor
than for the color image and, therefore supports a larger interaction space during the tracking after the initialization. The OTP is defined as the 3D position
at which the object will be handed over. With the approach from Nemlekar et
al. [12] a prediction for this point is available as soon as the intent for a handover
is detected.

2.1   Hand Tracking with Point Clouds

The hand tracking system, adapted from Chen et al. [4], purely relies on point
clouds. It determines the hand position (x_{hand}) in the current frame, as well as
the current velocity of the hand, given the hand position from the previous frame.
In each frame, the point x closest to the previous hand position, in the point
cloud, is found as a seed for the current hand hypothesis. Chen et al. use the
geodesic distance of points to avoid including other body parts in the segmented
hand region [4]. A similar effect can be achieved by removing points from the
point cloud whose distance to x is greater than a certain distance. This region
is used as hand region (r_{hand}). The points at the edge of the region r_{hand} are
found as boundary points. The hand position is then approximated as the point
(x_{approx}) with the most boundary points within a radius d_{ms}, i.e., assuming it
at the end of the arm [4]. A mean-shift step then refines the hand position [4]:

$$x_{hand} = \frac{\sum_{p \in r_{hand}} p * 1_{d(p,x_{approx}) < d_{ms}}}{\sum_{p \in r_{hand}} 1_{d(p,x_{approx}) < d_{ms}}} \tag{1}$$

The calculated position x_{hand} is the result of the current hand tracking and
serves as the input for the next tracking step.

2.2 Object Transfer Point Prediction

For the OTP prediction a static and a dynamic OTP are used (see [12]). The weighted sum of these two points, the integrated OTP, is the actual output that is sent to the robot as a grasp position goal. During the handover the static OTP is calculated once based on the initial position of the human partner as half-way between robot and human. The dynamic OTP is calculated based on the model defined below utilizing the reaching motion of the human partner, so far observed. The static OTP is instantly available at the start of a handover, so that the robot can start to reach out as soon as the handover intent is detected. On the one hand, it is also a relatively safe prediction, that typically is not too far away from the actual OTP. Therefore, it can reduce the prediction error that the dynamic OTP initially might have because it is missing a sufficient motion history. On the other hand, the dynamic OTP can adapt the prediction to the current situation and is supposed to provide a more accurate position than the static OTP, once a certain amount of the movement was observed. The difference in the movement speed of humans and robots allows the dynamic OTP to become more accurate early during the robot's movement, because the human's motion will proceed faster than the robot's motion. Thus, the key objective is to weight these OTP predictions accordingly, so that a robot is able to react fast and accurately to human initiated handovers.

The utilization of the minimum jerk model for the dynamic OTP prediction is based on the assumption that human motions are smooth, which means, that the jerk of the motion is as small as possible. To predict the OTP, the end time of the movement is needed in order to resolve the minimum-jerk equation for the end position x_f [5]. Here an average handover time can be used. Basili et al. found that the time between the initiation of the handover and the actual handover is $1.24\,\text{s} \pm 0.28\,\text{s}$ [1]. Due to the bell shaped velocity profile the end time can be updated during the hand over at the velocity extremum, which can be detected. It is reached when 50 % of the complete movement is executed. Consequently, the end time can be predicted at this point by adding the time that already passed since the handover started $(t_c - t_0)$ to the current time. Thus, the minimum jerk model for x_f, which is the predicted end position of the movement and therefore the dynamic OTP, is:

$$x_f = \frac{x_c - x_0}{10 * (\frac{t_c-t_0}{t_f-t_0})^3 - 15 * (\frac{t_c-t_0}{t_f-t_0})^4 + 6 * (\frac{t_c-t_0}{t_f-t_0})^5} + x_0 \qquad (2)$$

The error of the model should decrease over the observation time.

The static and dynamic OTP are interpolated to calculate the integrated OTP as the result of the prediction. This interpolation can either be applied to the whole time period, or only when the dynamic OTP is reasonably stable. Otherwise, the static OTP can be used solely, until the dynamic OTP is continuously in a reasonable range, i.e. within the space between human and robot. For the weight calculation there are two possible functions. It can either be calculated as ratio of the movement executed – where t_s is the time at which the dynamic OTP delivers usable results – or with a parable function that has its maximum in the origin and goes through the point (1,1) [12]:

$$W_{lin} = \frac{t_c - t_s}{t_f - t_s}, \quad W_{quad} = 0.2 * (\frac{t_c - t_s}{t_f - t_s}) + 0.8 * (\frac{t_c - t_s}{t_f - t_s})^2 \qquad (3)$$

The integrated OTP is calculated as formulated in Eq. 4 [12].

$$OTP_{integrated} = W * OTP_{dynamic} + (1 - W) * OTP_{static} \qquad (4)$$

In the context of mobile robots that autonomously perform safe movements, there are some traits the prediction should have. First the overall error of the prediction should be as small as possible to avoid that the robot moves in unpredictable directions which would confuse the human partner. The prediction should also be as good as possible early during the handover and be able to deal with different users. We implemented three different features that are supposed to provide these traits and can be combined for an improved prediction:

Feature 1 (Initial fixation). *Fixate static prediction until the dynamic prediction reaches the interaction space estimated.*

Feature 2 (Linear interpolation). *Use linear interpolation instead of quadratic.*

Feature 3 (Update end time). *Update end time after peak velocity detection (extremum of bell shaped profile).*

3   Evaluation

In the evaluation we assess the precision of the estimated OTP over time and analyze the influence of the integration scheme (Eq. 4) including Features 1–3. Therefore, we recorded several handover scenarios from the robot's perspective (see Fig. 1(c)–(e)). This data was used to evaluate the success rate of the hand tracking, the time delay of the tracking data, as well as the quality of the OTP prediction.

Test Cases and Evaluation Procedure: In the test cases considered, we systematically vary several aspects of handover configurations in order to test the generality of the model: (i) initial position relative to the robot, (ii) giver vs. receiver, (iii) small vs. large objects, (iv) direct handover vs. pre-grasp/hand change, (v) normal vs. tall person, (vi) posture with hands closer vs. farther away from the body. The general process of the test cases is given in Fig. 1. The human interaction partner approaches the robot from a distance of about 2 m and moves his/her arm to the handover position in front of the robot (see coordinate system in Fig. 1(b)). The case where the human stands straight in front of the robot and acts as a receiver was recorded seven times in total. Five of these recordings are from a person that is 1.7 m tall and, additionally, vary the postures by keeping the hands closer or farther away from the body. The other two are conducted

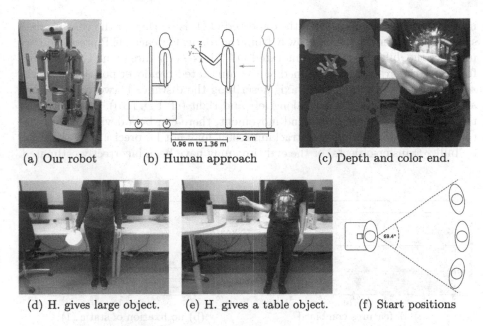

(a) Our robot   (b) Human approach   (c) Depth and color end.

(d) H. gives large object.   (e) H. gives a table object.   (f) Start positions

Fig. 1. Experiment Setup: A participant receives or gives an object from/to the Meka M1 Mobile Manipulator robot (a). Starting 2 m away the human approaches the robot and reaches the object transfer point (coordinate system in (b), red X in (f)). The final position in the interaction with the annotation of the reference position is shown as depth and color image (f). Start position (c) and start configurations (d, e) are varied. (Color figure online)

with a person who is 1.9 m tall. A similar situation with the human acting as giver was recorded for four different objects (two smaller bottles and two bulky objects, a bowl and a box of cereals). In another case one of the bottles was held with both hands in the beginning; in three cases the object was moved into the hand before the handover either by taking the object from a table next to the human or by passing it from the left to the right hand. The start position was varied in three cases where the human stands at the edge of the robot's field of view; in one of them the human acted as giver in the other two as receiver. The last scenario recorded a longer interaction in which the human approached the robot and waved his/her right hand around before performing a reaching motion. Altogether, 19 recordings of handover scenarios were used for the evaluation.

For each scenario, the camera stream of the robot and the tracking result was recorded; the reference handover position was manually annotated (see Fig. 1(c)). Then, the OTP prediction was performed multiple times on the same hand-tracking data using different configurations of activated algorithmic features: *initial fixation* (1), *linear vs. quadratic interpolation* (2), and *update end-time* (3). The prediction starts once a handover intent is detected which is defined as significant increase of the velocity towards the robot while the velocity to the left and right and height are relatively small. The OTP is continuously predicted

682   J. Simmering et al.

until the estimated end time of the expected OTP is reached or the velocity data
shows a movement of the hand away from the robot. For each OTP prediction, we
measure the difference to the annotated OTP in x-/y-/z-direction. The reference
frame for the evaluation is defined as the annotated handover position with the
z-axis pointing upwards, the y-axis describing the distance between the human
and the robot, and the x-axis along left and right (cf. Fig. 1(b)). Thus, even for
the end point of the tracked hand movement, there can be a deviation from the
reference position because the tracking result may not be precise (e.g. occlusion
by bulky transfer-objects) or the end time may have been incorrectly estimated.

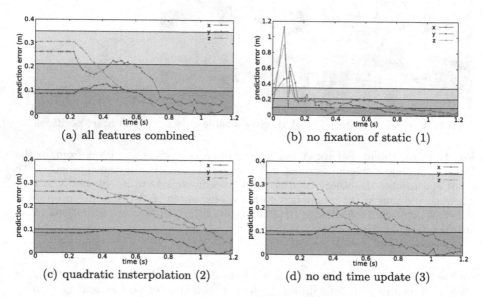

(a) all features combined

(b) no fixation of static (1)

(c) quadratic insterpolation (2)

(d) no end time update (3)

Fig. 2. Absolute error of the OTP prediction over time for four different feature combinations on the example of a vis-à-vis handover as the most common example. Error
ranges that contain most test cases when all features are activated: light gray 0.35 m
for overall error y and z direction, gray 0.2 m for overall error x direction and dark gray
0.1 m end time error range for all directions

Overall Results: In Fig. 2 results of different system configurations are shown. It
can be seen that (i) without fixation (Fig. 2(b)) the OTP prediction in the first
0.2 s is unstable; (ii) with quadratic interpolation (Fig. 2(c)) the prediction error
shrinks slower; a similar effect shows up (iii) without end time update (Fig. 2(d)).
Thus, each algorithmic feature enhances the prediction either by reducing the
overall error or by reaching a smaller deviation earlier in time. The initialization
of the tracking, i.e. the initial hand pose estimation on the rgb frame, takes
between 0.3 s and 0.4 s. During this phase, the system buffers about 10 depth
frames, which are processed afterwards by the tracking. In the following, this
delay is decreased to 0.07 s on average leading to very short reaction times of
the robot (see Fig. 3).

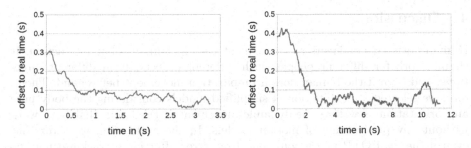

Fig. 3. Delay of the hand tracking for a normal and the long test case.

In order to provide an evaluation over all test cases, we define different error ranges and report how many test cases are within these error ranges for different system configurations. First we measure the error ranges of the configuration with all features activated. The maximal error in 17 of 19 test cases (over the complete time interval) is below 35 cm for the y- and z-axes and in 18 of 19 test cases it is below 20 cm for the x-axis. Thus, we define [20 cm × 35 cm × 35 cm] as a first coarse precision box. Considering the *end-time error* at the detected OTP, 11 of the 19 test cases are below 10 cm in $[x/y/z]$. This defines a second more restrictive precision box (the error ranges of both precision boxes – the coarse:[20 × 35 × 35] and fine:[10 × 10 × 10] – are visualized in Fig. 2). If the fine precision box is relaxed from a 10 cm to a 15 cm range, 15 of 19 cases are finally within it. Ideally, the OTP prediction should stay in the coarse precision box during the complete movement. Here a low deviation along the x-axis (<20 cm) is important because a larger deviation would trigger the robot to turn away. In the different test cases, we noticed a single case where the x-corridor was slightly missed (max. x-error 20.4 cm). This has been one of cases where the human initially stands at the edge of the robot's field of view. A larger deviation along the y-axis would trigger the robot to adjust to a wrong distance to the human. This has been missed only two times, where the end-point has been wrongly estimated.

Considering the influence of the algorithmic features, we measured that only 13 instead of 17 cases stay inside the coarse precision box [20 × 35 × 35] along the y- and z-axes, if no end time update is performed. On the downside, in two cases an update of the end-time lead to a slight miss of the 10 × 10 × 10 precision box. In the case where all features are activated, the OTP predictions converge to the fine precision box (<10 cm) after 75 % of the movement. This increases to 82 %, if there is no end-time update. The 15 cm-precision box converges after 64 % of the movement, if all algorithmic features are activated. For the quadratic interpolation, the OTP prediction reaches the fine 10 cm-precision box after 90 % of the movement in only 9 of 19 test cases.

4   Discussion

Human-initiated handovers are a frequent case in human-robot interaction. It should work for different people, with different objects, from different directions, and even if the human does a preparation movement beforehand. Therefore, we selected a combination of simplified models considering the body pose and orientation as well as the dynamic movement of the hand, that both work without any pre-learning of motion models. In the evaluation, we show that even if the final OTP predictions (end-time error after hand tracking) may be similar, there are large differences between OTP predictions during the movement of the human's hand. These early predictions are most important, when the robot should smoothly react on the human-initiated handover. However, these are rarely analyzed systematically. Thus, we take a deeper look at the impact of different algorithmic combination schemes on these prediction dynamics. The results show that the motion-based OTP prediction is quite poor in the beginning. Therefore, Feature 1 (Initial fixation) improves the prediction by limiting the OTP prediction error. This leads to a smoother interaction with the robot, because its movements are more predictable and human-like. The quadratic interpolation does not exploit the fast improvement of the dynamic prediction, thus the end error range is reached for fewer cases and later during the handover. The end-time update (Feature 3) together with the dynamic prediction is responsible for adjusting the prediction to the partially observed handover. This manifests itself in an earlier convergence to the fine precision box defined by the error range for the end-time. Overall, the features described in Sect. 2.2 enhance the prediction results and reach a smaller error range early during the handover while maintaining a limited maximal error over the complete movement. This fulfills the requirement, that the robot is able to move in the right direction early during a handover.

Limitations of the system were found for large objects, like bowls. These were already hard to see for the depth sensor due to shadows which resulted in a poor hand tracking and prediction since in this case the end error range was not reached in any of the directions. Furthermore, seven other cases did not reach the end-time error range in at least one direction, which is mostly due to the noisy velocity data which can lead to an early termination of the prediction process, because the end of the handover movement is wrongly detected. Therefore, the method still can be improved by less noisy velocity data and more advanced detection methods for the start and end-time of the handover.

5   Conclusion

We presented an object transfer point (OTP) prediction which combines a static and a dynamic prediction of an OTP for human initiated object handover from and to a robot. This approach is integrated with our low-latency handtracking algorithm, for which we combined state-of-the-art techniques to estimate the position of a human hand in a color image and track it on depth clouds. This way we achieved a tracking performance of on average 0.07 s delay after the initialization phase. The whole system was able to run on off-the-shelf hardware on a mobile humanoid service robot. We could show that the combination of a static and dynamic OTP for predicting the handover position is useful for an early estimation that becomes more accurate over time, allowing the robot to start its movement early and adapt over time, decreasing wait times and allowing precise adaption to the human interaction partner. As we build upon the minimum-jerk-model, we do not need to train the system with lots of data and are independent of retraining for a different kind of robot. Evaluation on a wide range of situations showed validity of this approach. This leads to robots that adapt to the human and, thus facilitate socially accepted human-robot interactions.

References

1. Basili, P., Huber, M., Brandt, T., Hirche, S., Glasauer, S.: Investigating human-human approach and hand-over. In: Vernon, D., et al. (eds.) Human Centered Robot Systems, vol. 6. Springer, Heidelberg (2009). https://doi.org/10.1007/978-3-642-10403-9_16
2. Bray, M., Koller-Meier, E., Van Gool, L.: Smart particle filtering for 3D hand tracking. In: Proceedings of Sixth IEEE International Conference on Automatic Face and Gesture Recognition. IEEE, Seoul, Korea (2004)
3. Cao, Z., Hidalgo, G., Simon, T., Wei, S.E., Sheikh, Y.: OpenPose: Realtime Multi-Person 2D Pose Estimation using Part Affinity Fields. arXiv:1812.08008 (2018)
4. Chen, C., Chen, Y., Lee, P., Tsai, Y., Lei, S.: Real-time hand tracking on depth images. In: 2011 Visual Communications and Image Processing (VCIP), November 2011
5. Flash, T., Hogan, N.: The coordination of arm movements: an experimentally confirmed mathematical model. J. Neurosci. 5(7), 1688–1703 (1985)
6. Hackenberg, G., McCall, R., Broll, W.: Lightweight palm and finger tracking for real-time 3D gesture control. In: 2011 IEEE Virtual Reality Conference, March 2011
7. Huber, M., et al.: Evaluation of a novel biologically inspired trajectory generator in human-robot interaction. In: RO-MAN 2009 - The 18th IEEE International Symposium on Robot and Human Interactive Communication, September 2009
8. Kajikawa, S., Ishikawa, E.: Trajectory planning for hand-over between human and robot. In: Proceedings 9th IEEE International Workshop on Robot and Human Interactive Communication. IEEE RO-MAN 2000 (Cat. No. 00TH8499), September 2000
9. Li, Z., Hauser, K.: Predicting object transfer position and timing in human-robot handover tasks. In: Science and Systems (2015)
10. Maeda, G.J., Neumann, G., Ewerton, M., Lioutikov, R., Kroemer, O., Peters, J.: Probabilistic movement primitives for coordination of multiple human-robot collaborative tasks. Auton. Robots 41(3), 593–612 (2017)
11. Meyer zu Borgsen, S., Bernotat, J., Wachsmuth, S.: Hand in hand with robots: differences between experienced and naive users in human-robot handover scenarios. In: Kheddar, A., et al. (eds.) Social Robotics. ICSR 2017. LNCS, vol. 10652. Springer, Cham (2017). https://doi.org/10.1007/978-3-319-70022-9_58

12. Nemlekar, H., Dutia, D., Li, Z.: Object transfer point estimation for fluent human-robot handovers. In: International Conference on Robotics and Automation (ICRA). Montreal, Canada (2019)
13. Perez-D'Arpino, C., Shah, J.A.: Fast target prediction of human reaching motion for cooperative human-robot manipulation tasks using time series classification. In: 2015 IEEE International Conference on Robotics and Automation (ICRA). IEEE, Seattle, WA, USA, May 2015
14. Shibata, S., Sahbi, B.M., Tanaka, K., Shimizu, A.: An analysis of the process of handing over an object and its application to robot motions. In: Computational Cybernetics and Simulation 1997 IEEE International Conference on Systems, Man, and Cybernetics, vol. 1, October 1997

Monitoring Blind Regions with Prior Knowledge Based Sound Localization

Jani Even[1,2(✉)], Satoru Satake[2], and Takayuki Kanda[1,2]

[1] Kyoto University, Kyoto, Japan
even@robot.soc.i.kyoto-u.ac.jp
[2] Advanced Telecommunications Research Institute International, Kyoto, Japan

Abstract. This paper presents a sound localization method designed for dealing with blind regions. The proposed approach mimics Human's ability of guessing what is happening in the blind regions by using prior knowledge. A user study was conducted to demonstrate the usefulness of the proposed method for human-robot interaction in environments with blind regions. The subjects participated in a shoplifting scenario during which the shop clerk was a robot that has to rely on its hearing to monitor a blind region. The participants understood the enhanced capability of the robot and it favorably affected the rating of the robot using the proposed method.

Keywords: Robot audition · Sound localization · User study

1 Introduction

In human-made environments, our field of view is often occluded creating blind regions as illustrated in Fig. 1. When confronted to a blind region, we cannot rely on our vision to gather information, but we are able to make some informed guesses using our hearing. Moreover, we are still able to pinpoint with a relatively good accuracy the origin of some of the sounds we hear because of the large amount of prior knowledge at our disposal.

For example, considering a shop like the one depicted in Fig. 1, a shop clerk could somehow guess where a customer is in the blind region if the customer makes a recognisable sound by touching an item and the clerk knows where such an item is likely to be. If there are several such items, the crude spatial information contained in the reflected and diffracted sounds leaking from the blind region may be enough to reduce some ambiguities. However, in the same situation, a robot clerk would be clueless as conventional sound source localization methods used in robot audition are not designed to handle blind regions.

In this paper, we first briefly introduce a sound source localization method that exploits prior knowledge in order to localize sound sources in blind regions.

This research was supported by JST CREST Grant Number JPMJCR17A2, Japan.

M. A. Salichs et al. (Eds.): ICSR 2019, LNAI 11876, pp. 687–696, 2019.
https://doi.org/10.1007/978-3-030-35888-4_64

Fig. 1. Robot in an environment where occlusion creates a blind region.

We call the new approach "Localization by Knowledge" because the main difference between the proposed approach and the conventional sound source localization methods is the use of the prior knowledge.

We believe that a robot displaying a good level of understanding of what is happening in the blind regions would induce a feeling of being monitored for the users even when they are out of its sight. To confirm our intuition, we designed a user study to prove that participants notice the enhanced localization capability of the robot and that replacing conventional sound source localization by the proposed localization by knowledge has an influence on the interaction when dealing with blind regions.

2   Related Work

2.1   Study of Human Hearing

The association of sound producing objects with acoustics events that is at the heart of our "localization by knowledge" is motivated by the ecological approach to hearing presented by Gaver in [7]. Gaver defines everyday listening as "the experience of listening to events rather than sounds" (p. 1). The work of Gaver stresses the importance of relating the sound to the object and take into account the location for human perception of acoustic events. This is also what we are trying to achieve with the "localization by knowledge" (with less emphasis on the physics of sound production).

2.2   Sound Source Localization

Sound source localization has been addressed by many studies in the fields of acoustic signal processing and robotics [1]. In particular, there is large body of work on sound source localization using microphone array [5]. However, most of the research is dealing with cases where the line-of-sight is not occluded. A few exceptions are the works by Mak and Furukawa [10], Even et al. [6] and Takami et al. [12]. However, in any of these works, there is no notion of acoustic events associated to objects or any use of acoustic event classification.

2.3 Sound Source Localization and Human Robot Interaction

Although many of Human Robot Interaction (HRI) research would assume that robots and users verbally communicate, very few research considers blind region. A notable exception is the work by Cha et al. where the participants rely on hearing to localize a robot moving out of their field of view [3]. But, there is no perception from the robot point of view.

Moreover, to the knowledge of the authors, there is currently no research in HRI that investigated how a robot showing its sound source localization capability is perceived by the users. We believe that our study, by introducing a robot that exhibits sound source localization capability for blind regions, addresses one of the ways for robots to challenge users' perception.

3 Localization by Knowledge

The proposed method first generates a set of candidate locations for sounds that stand out of the background. Then, the true origin of the detected sounds is pinpointed by combining these candidates with an estimation of the direction of arrival of the perceived sound.

3.1 Candidate Locations

In order to develop an acoustic event classifier with a limited number of training data, we used the "VGGish" feature extractor to convert sound to embedding vectors [9]. "VGGish" is designed to take as input a block of 960 ms of audio data and transform it into a feature vector of size 128. As a consequence, localization by knowledge also works on audio blocks of 960 ms. To have a more reactive system, a half block overlap is performed. Then, the front-end produces a 128-dimensional feature vector that describes the last 960 ms of audio data every 480 ms.

The detector decides if a feature vector represents a meaningful acoustic event or just background noise to be discarded. To build the detector, a 128 dimensions Gaussian Mixture Model (GMM) with a full covariance matrix was used to model the feature vectors extracted from recorded background noise. The feature vectors that have a low probability according to that GMM are considered meaningful acoustic events.

The meaningful acoustic events that are not part of the background are assigned classes by the classifier. The classes define the "types of sound" we are expecting to hear from the blind regions (See Sect. 4).

The prior knowledge used in our approach is the locations of the objects that are likely to produce these sounds. Consequently, the class assigned by the classifier directly corresponds to one or several candidate locations.

]
Figure 2 shows the different steps of the localization by knowledge in the context of the mock-up shop depicted in Fig. 1. Let assume that the acoustic event in Fig. 2-a is detected and successfully classified. Each of the shelves

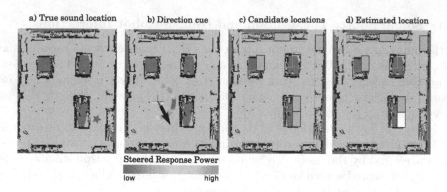

a) True sound location   b) Direction cue   c) Candidate locations   d) Estimated location

Steered Response Power

low   high

Fig. 2. Fusion (d) of candidate locations (c) and SRP (b) for a given sound source (a). (Color figure online)

(green boxes) in Fig. 2-c is associated to a type of sound (This is the prior knowledge). The shelves in blue are the subset of the shelves that have the same sound type as the detected sound. These are the candidate locations for the detected sound.

3.2 Sound Source Localization and Fusion

We use an implementation of the steered response power (SRP) [2] to estimate the direction of arrival of the sound impinging a microphone array mounted on the robot. The colored arcs in front of the robot in Fig. 2-b represents the estimated powers coming from all the directions in front of the robot. There is a peak of power in the direction of the incoming sound. The problem is that conventional sound localization algorithm like SRP do not reliably indicate the sound direction when there is no line-of-sight. The sound is coming from around the structure occluding the direct propagation path, either by diffraction or reflection. However, for relatively small occluding structures, these methods give a rough estimate of the direction as in Fig. 2-b.

Given a set of candidate locations and an estimated direction of sound, the fusion step determines which of these candidate locations is the true origin of the detected sound. The current set of candidate locations Fig. 2-c is combined with the SRP Fig. 2-b to estimate the location of the acoustic event Fig. 2-d. The shelf in white is selected as the estimated location because it is the candidate location that is the closest to the SRP direction.

An experiment was conducted in the mock-up store depicted in Fig. 1 to quantify the improvement of the estimated sound direction when using the prior knowledge. For the sound emitted in the blind regions, the ratio of direction estimates within 3° of the true direction jumped from 0.28 to 0.91.

4 Environment and Training Data

The evaluation was conducted in a convenience store mock-up built in our facility (see Fig. 1).

The robot was a Robovie2 which is a humanoid robot. The audio acquisition device was the microphone array of a Kinect v2 (see Fig. 1). The robot was also equipped with laser range finders in the front and the back for self-localization and safety during autonomous navigation.

Before any interaction took place, the robot was driven through the environment to gather odometry and range data to create a 2D map of the room [8]. Afterward, the robot was able to determine precisely its position and orientation in the room [4] and navigate safely in the environment.

We recorded around 96 min of background noise (approx. 12,000 feature vectors) when the robot is powered on but not moving to create the GMM based detector.

The classifier used in the experiments presented in this paper was a fully connected neural network with one hidden layer (100 units) and rectified linear unit activations. It is a relatively simple classifier because it is applied on the feature vectors that are already processed by the VGGish feature extractor. The complete neural network including the VGGish feature extractor has 14 hidden layers.

To train the classifier, in addition to the background noise, we recorded the sound when an experimenter was handling different items at different locations in the store. The items producing similar sounds when handled were associated to the same sound class. For example, all items wrapped in a plastic bag are of class "bag". We defined 4 sound classes: "bag", "can", "box" and "background" and we created a balanced training set with 788 acoustic event feature vectors per class (the overall precision and recall were around 93%).

In a shop environment, it is reasonable to assume that there is a record of which items are on which shelves. Consequently, we created an overlay on the 2D map that represents the shelves geometry. This overlay is associated with a structure that contains the type of the items and their associated sound classes. This prior knowledge map is the one that appeared in Fig. 2-c.

5   User Study

5.1   Scenario

The experiment took place in the store mock-up we built in our facility. The robot was introduced to the participants as the store clerk. The participants were told to pretend to steal some items while the robot cannot see them. At the beginning, the robot stood close to the cashier, while the participant was in the blind region with a shopping bag (Fig. 3-a). Then, the participant shoved one item in the shopping bag (Fig. 3-b). When the sound of this action was detected, first the robot said something and then it moved to the blind region. There, the robot stopped and displayed a specific gaze pattern (Fig. 3-c). Then, it went back close to the cashier.

Fig. 3. Experiment setting and experiment phases.

5.2   Hypothesis

Using localization by knowledge, the robot should be able to pinpoint the precise location from where a sound was emitted in the blind region. It should also know what type of sound it is and relate the acoustic event to an item. Thus, we expect the participants to notice this sound localization capability. Moreover, we expect the participants to understand that localization by knowledge enables the robot to better monitor what is happening in the blind regions. Consequently, we also expect the participants to think that a robot using localization by knowledge is a good deterrent for shoplifting. Thus, we made the following prediction:

Prediction 1: A robot that uses localization by knowledge rather than conventional sound localization will be rated higher for sound localization accuracy in the blind region.

Prediction 2: A robot that uses localization by knowledge rather than conventional sound localization will induce a stronger feeling of being monitored.

Prediction 3: A robot that uses localization by knowledge rather than conventional sound localization will be judged fitter for preventing shoplifting.

5.3   Method

Participants. We recruited 17 participants (10 females and 7 males, average age 34.8 years old, standard deviation 10.3 years) that were paid for their participation. All participants had normal hearings.

Conditions. To test the impact of the localization by knowledge on the participants in this scenario, two different behaviors were designed. One using the localization by knowledge (proposed method) and one using a baseline method. Both the sentence the robot told before moving and the gaze pattern it displayed in the blind region were condition dependent.

Proposed method: The robot used localization by knowledge to understand from which of the shelf in the blind region the acoustic event was emitted. The prior knowledge also provided the type of the items on that shelf. When the sound was detected, before moving the robot said, "I wonder if it was in the X shelf?" where X was the name of the items. After the robot reached to the blind region, it looked at the selected shelf.

Baseline method: The robot used SRP to obtain the sound direction. The shelves in the blind region that were close enough to the direction given by SRP were selected. When the sound was detected, before moving the robot said, "I wonder what it is?" After it reached to the blind region, it looked at all the shelves.

Both methods used SRP for estimating the direction of arrival of the sound but only the proposed method fuses this information with the prior knowledge. Consequently, only the robot using the proposed method is able to look at the shelf from which the sound was emitted. Namely, for the proposed method the robot showed that it recognizes the sound (voice) but also the precise location (gaze).

Procedure. The study had a within-participant design. Each of the participants experienced the scenario for the two conditions: one session with a robot using the baseline method and one session with the robot using the proposed condition. The order of the conditions was counter-balanced.

For each session, the participant was asked to be in the blind region and hold the shopping bag. Then, while the robot was standing close to the cashier, we asked the participants to pretend to steal (shove in the shopping bag) any of the chocolate bags from the shelves on the right (Fig. 3-b). Then, the participant had to step back and observe the behavior of the robot (Fig. 3-c). Finally, the robot was going back to its initial position. These steps were repeated three times for each conditions. The participants were notified of the change of conditions (we used the terms "robot 1" and "robot 2" to refer to the conditions). After the two sessions, the participants were asked to fill a questionnaire about each of the sessions. Finally, a short interview was conducted. The experimental protocol was approved by our Institutional Review Board.

Measurement. The questionnaire (in Japanese) consisted of three items that we asked the participants to rate on 7-point Likert scale. The items were:

Perceived listening capability: "This robot understands precisely from where the sound originated." (1-strongly disagree to 7-strongly agree)

Perceived monitoring capability: "I felt that this robot was monitoring me." (1-strongly disagree to 7-strongly agree)

Overall evaluation: "Fitness of the robot as a shoplifting prevention" (1-Bad to 7-Good)

5.4 Results

Observations. The participants understood the instructions and the experiment went smoothly. After the robot came one time, some of the participants were trying to handle the items without doing noise (which is difficult with the chocolate bags). When stepping back to observe the robot, some of the participants went farther away than others as if they were afraid of the robot or felt guilty (some of these observations were confirmed by the short interviews).

Technical Evaluation. For each of the conditions there was 51 pretended shoplifting attempts. Both of the conditions were affected by the false alarms of the GMM based detector. Namely, a sound not related to the pretended shoplifting that triggered the behavior. There was five such cases for the baseline method and two for the proposed method. These numbers are of the same order of magnitude and this type of error was mainly overlooked by the participants. Otherwise the robot came in a timely manner for all the other pretended shoplifting attempts.

For the proposed method, there were four classification errors resulting in the robot talking of unrelated items (e.g. talking about soda can whereas the participant was handling a chocolate bag). These errors were noticed every time they occurred. Unfortunately, two of these four errors happened for the same participant.

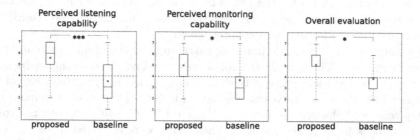

Fig. 4. Results of the questionnaire.

Verification of Predictions. To check the statistical significance of the results, we used the Wilcoxon signed-rank test. The statistics t and the p values are reported. In addition, to account for the effect size, Cohen's d values are also reported.

Verification of prediction 1: Fig. 4 (left) shows the results of the questionnaire for the perceived listening capability. There is a statistically significant difference $t = 20.0$, $p < .0127$ and a very large effect $d = 1.33$. The robot with the proposed method is perceived to have more listening capability than the one with the baseline method. We conclude that our prediction 1 is verified.

Verification of prediction 2: The results for the perceived monitoring capability are given in Fig. 4 (center). There is a statistically significant difference $t = 14.5$, $p < .028$ and a large effect $d = 0.81$. The robot with the proposed method is perceived to have more monitoring capability than the one with the baseline method. The prediction 2 is also verified.

Verification of prediction 3: The overall evaluation results are given in Fig. 4 (right). The proposed method was evaluated significantly higher than the baseline method $t = 19.5$, $p < .036$ and the effect was large $d = 0.92$. Thus, prediction 3 is also verified.

6   Discussion

6.1   Findings and Implications

In the user study, the participants understood very well that the proposed method had a better understanding of the sound origin. The robot was showing its understanding from the start by telling about the items it heard. When in the blind region, the robot gazed at the estimated location to convey to the participants the information that it knew the precise location. Several participants reported during the interview that the proposed robot checked for the missing items. They even assumed that there was some active vision process going on. Humans routinely confirm sound related information using vision [11]. On the contrary the gaze pattern displayed by the baseline robot made the participants think it was clueless about what happened. The participants felt that with the proposed method, the robot was checking the right shelf. But, they did not think that the robot looked directly at the place missing an item. The reason is that the robot had only a "shelf level knowledge".

There is a trade-off between the number of classes and the partition of the space. With few classes, locations are likely to be larger. For example, a shelf displaying chocolate bags and a neighboring shelf displaying candy bags are merged together as a large location of "bag" class. But if the classifier differentiates chocolate bags from candy bags then the shelves are not merged into a single location. Thus, it is possible to tune localization by knowledge for a given environment or a given application by playing with this number of class versus resolution trade-off.

6.2   Limitations

The proposed method relies on acoustic event classification to exploit the prior knowledge. In the user study, a classification error results in a very noticeable failure of the proposed method. Both the speech and the gaze pattern of the robot are pointing to the wrong item and location. Each of these errors were mentioned by the participants during the short interviews. In this experiment, the number of classes was small and consequently the classifier had a high accuracy. To extend this approach to a situation where a larger number of classes has to be recognized, it is likely necessary to record a large dataset. However, by using pre-trained features (embedding) as we did sufficient performance may be attainable with a moderately large dataset. Moreover, in this age of big data, it is likely that more powerful embedding networks will become available.

7   Conclusion

This paper introduced "localization by knowledge" which is a new approach to sound source localization specifically designed to deal with blind regions. We conducted a user study to evaluate the impact of the proposed method during human-robot interaction involving a blind region. The participants were asked to pretend stealing an item in the blind region of a mock-up store that was monitored by a clerk robot. The sound localization capability of the clerk robot using the proposed method was highly evaluated compared to a clerk robot using a baseline method. The participants also rated the monitoring capability of that clerk robot higher and estimated it was better fit for preventing shoplifting. In future studies, we would to investigate if the participants understand that the robot uses prior knowledge about the location of the objects.

References

1. Argentieri, S., Danès, P., Souères, P.: A survey on sound source localization in robotics: from binaural to array processing methods. Comput. Speech Lang. **34**(1), 87–112 (2015)
2. Brandstein, M., Silverman, H.: A robust method for speech signal time-delay estimation in reverberant rooms. IEEE Conference on Acoustics, Speech, and Signal Processing, ICASSP 1997, pp. 375–378 (1997)
3. Cha, E., Fitter, N.T., Kim, Y., Fong, T., Matarić, M.J.: Effects of robot sound on auditory localization in human-robot collaboration. In: Proceedings of the 2018 ACM/IEEE International Conference on Human-Robot Interaction HRI 2018, pp. 434–442 (2018)
4. Dellaert, F., Fox, D., Burgard, W., Thrun, S.: Monte carlo localization for mobile robots. In: IEEE International Conference on Robotics and Automation (ICRA99), May 1999
5. DiBiase, J., Silverman, H., Brandstein, M.: Microphone Arrays : Signal Processing Techniques and Applications. Springer, Heidelberg (2007). https://doi.org/10.1007/978-3-662-04619-7
6. Even, J., Morales, Y., Kallakuri, N., Ishi, C., Hagita, N.: Audio ray tracing for position estimation of entities in blind regions. In: Proceedings of IEEE/RSJ International Conference on Intelligent Robots and Systems, IROS 2014, pp. 1920–1925 (2014)
7. Gaver, W.W.: What in the world do we hear?: an ecological approach to auditory event perception. Ecol. Psychol. **5**(1), 1–29 (1993)
8. Grisetti, G., Stachniss, C., Burgard, W.: Improved techniques for grid mapping with rao-blackwellized particle filters. IEEE Trans. Rob. **23**(1), 34–46 (2007)
9. Hershey, S., et al.: CNN architectures for large-scale audio classification. In: 2017 IEEE International Conference on Acoustics, Speech and Signal Processing (ICASSP), pp. 131–135 (2017)
10. Mak, L.C., Furukawa, T.: Non-line-of-sight localization of a controlled sound source. In: 2009 IEEE/ASME International Conference on Advanced Intelligent Mechatronics, pp. 475–480 (2009)
11. Shelton, B.R., Searle, C.L.: The influence of vision on the absolute identification of sound-source position. Percept. Psychophysics **28**(6), 589–596 (1980)
12. Takami, K., Liu, H., Furukawa, T., Kumon, M., Dissanayake, G.: Non-field-of-view sound source localization using diffraction and reflection signals. In: 2016 IEEE/RSJ International Conference on Intelligent Robots and Systems (IROS), pp. 157–162 (2016)

Improving the Visual Comfort of Virtual Reality Telepresence for Robotics

Harvey Cash and Tony J. Prescott[✉]

Department of Computer Science and Sheffield Robotics,
The University of Sheffield, Sheffield, UK
{hcash1,t.j.prescott}@sheffield.ac.uk
https://www.sheffield.ac.uk/dcs

Abstract. Telepresence technologies enable users to exhibit a presence in a remote location, through the use of sensors, networks and robotics. State-of-the-art telepresence research swaps conventional desktop monitors for Virtual Reality (VR) headsets, in order to increase the user's immersion in the remote environment, though often at the cost of increased nausea and oculomotor discomfort. We describe a novel method for telepresence via VR, aimed at improving comfort, by accounting for discrepancies between robot and user head pose. This is achieved through a "decoupled" image projection technique, whereby the user is able to look across captured imagery rendered to a virtual display plane. Evaluated against conventional projection techniques, in a controlled study involving 19 participants, decoupled image projection significantly reduced mean perceived nausea and oculomotor discomfort while also improving immersiveness and the perceived sensation of presence.

Keywords: Robot telepresence · Virtual reality · Visual comfort

1 Introduction

Telepresence encompasses a broad field of research, characterised by two main technological challenges: allowing users to *perceive* a remote environment, and allowing users to *affect* that remote environment. Modern state-of-the-art telepresence research often employs Virtual Reality (VR) headsets and robotics (see, e.g. Martinez et al. [6]). While the feeling of remote presence is enhanced by the immersive nature of perception through a VR headset, the user's actions are measured by some manner of input method (from keyboards and controllers, through to more sophisticated motion tracking techniques). The obtained information is then used to control mechanical actuators in the remote location. With this technology, a user might hope to perceive and affect remote objects in as intuitive a manner as would be possible were they directly present themselves. Telepresence at this level would have wide reaching applications: from enabling specialists to perform work where they are needed most, regardless of distance (e.g. remote surgery), to enabling workers to operate safely in hazardous conditions as of yet too complex for completely autonomous solutions (e.g. search and

© Springer Nature Switzerland AG 2019
M. A. Salichs et al. (Eds.): ICSR 2019, LNAI 11876, pp. 697–706, 2019.
https://doi.org/10.1007/978-3-030-35888-4_65

rescue), to supporting variable autonomy where human operators take control of otherwise autonomous robot systems for short periods. The latter application could be particularly significant for social robotics, allowing human operators to augment the currently limited interaction capabilities of robots.

As modern telepresence systems seek to incorporate VR headsets, in order to enhance the sensation of being remotely present, they trade away the comfort of conventional desktop monitors. While merely frustrating when observed on a desktop monitor, the technical limitations of telepresence (robot DoF, video frame rate, network latency, etc.) also contribute to nausea and oculomotor discomfort (e.g. eye strain) [2,5] and reduced presence [4] in VR users (see [8] for a recent review). Increased discomfort effectively limits the length of time a user can spend telepresent. These limitations become especially crippling when considered in the commercial space, where the use of high quality robotics and cameras may be prohibited by cost. Nausea and oculomotor discomfort in VR systems are caused primarily by discrepancies between what the user *should* see, given the position and orientation of their eyes, and what they are *actually* shown by their Head Mounted Display (HMD). We therefore sought to design and develop an image projection technique that could reduce this view discrepancy, circumventing those hardware limitations contributing to it, and thereby improving the visual comfort of VR telepresence.

2 Approach

2.1 Decoupled Image Projection

The discrepancies noted above are most often caused by the limited DoF and range of motion available to the robot, network latency, and frame rate of camera imagery. One strategy to reduce visual discomfort, then, is to circumvent these hardware limitations in software - transforming received camera imagery based on known pose information in order to reduce the discrepancy between head pose and view pose (i.e. position and orientation of perspective shown by the VR headset). Thus, a *decoupled* image projection technique may be appropriate. Figure 1 illustrates the difference between conventional 'coupled' image projection and the 'decoupled' technique. Rather than feeding camera imagery immediately to a user's VR Headset, images are first rendered to a virtual display plane, which exists some distance in front of the user.

Decoupled image projection transforms the display plane by the head pose of the robot, allowing the user's perspective to move freely across the image, entirely independent of any robot hardware limitations. This is illustrated at times t1 and t2 of Fig. 1, wherein the user's vision moves synchronously with the user's head direction, without remaining anchored to the robot imagery. Responsibility for bringing camera imagery to the centre of the user's view therefore falls to the head tracking system. If the user looks to the right but the robot fails to move accordingly, they are nonetheless shown a corresponding change in perspective.

Decoupling increases the orientation-time accuracy of imagery rendered to the headset. In this way, head motion occurring between frames rendered to the

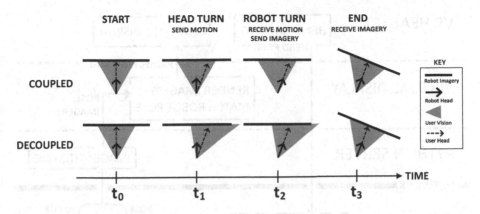

Fig. 1. Comparison of coupled and decoupled image projection

virtual display is limited only to the refresh rate of the VR Headset itself (typically 90 Hz), which is significantly smoother than the 15 fps frame rate typically supplied by commercially available robot cameras. This technique has been used by Aykut et al. [1] as a means of tackling network latency through recording wide angle camera imagery in excess of the field of view of the user. While success in that study was evaluated through the proportion of the headset display that remained filled with pixel data, here we evaluated the technique against its capacity for improving the comfort of telepresence, specifically our study addressed two questions: (i) To what degree does decoupled image projection improve the visual comfort of VR telepresence, over conventional coupled projection? (ii) How does the immersiveness of the experience vary between these scenarios?

2.2   Implementation

Figure 2 depicts a robot and client (local desktop computer) separated by a network and the *Decoupled Image Projection Pipeline* we designed to improve user comfort. The position and texture of the virtual display is updated whenever frames are available from the robot's cameras thus depending on robot specifications. Movement of the user's head occurring within the 3D environment, decoupled from the robot's hardware limitations (i.e. frame rate, DoF), executes at a typical refresh rate of 90 Hz. Sampling imagery from the Virtual Display and projecting it to the VR Headset thus provides a smooth correspondence between user head orientation and the perspective they are shown.

The developed technique was designed with commercially available robots and robotic avatars in mind. The Consequential Robotics MIRO robot [7] was selected as a testbed in part due to its limitations: (i) the robot has 2 DoF of head movement, yaw and pitch, where each axis has an angular range less than that of a human; (ii) head position varies with orientation differently than in humans, due to differing neck physiology; (iii) MIRO has two stereo-separated

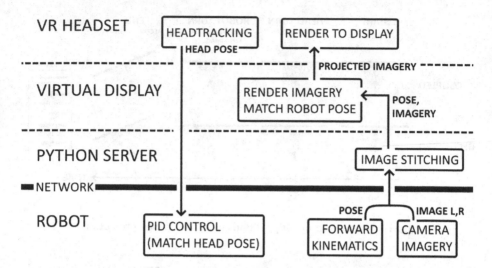

Fig. 2. Decoupled Image Projection Pipeline. The pose of the robot's head is calculated through forward kinematics, and passed together with the left and right eye images over the network to the client. The client performs image stitching to combine the left and right imagery within a local Python server, before passing the robot head pose and combined imagery on to the 3D software environment. A virtual display plane is transformed to match the robot pose, and the combined imagery rendered onto it.

eye cameras, with an effective Inter-Pupillary Distance different to humans'; (iv) MIRO cameras are limited to a maximum of 1280×720 pixel resolution at 15 frames per second. These limitations are similar to those of other commercially available social robot platforms, making MIRO suitably representative. Initial development and evaluation has taken place on a simulated robot within Unity3D with the aim of transferring the VR telepresence system to the physical robot platform for further evaluation and testing in the near future.

2.3 Experimental Hypothesis

In addition to the issues of discrepant head pose as just discussed, telepresence systems typically suffer from time-lags that can increase discomfort and reduce the experience of immersiveness. In the current study we therefore compared coupled and decoupled projection in two settings, one with zero time-lag (fast) and a second with a 400 ms (slow). The experimental hypothesis was that decoupled projection would lead to improved comfort and a greater sense of immersiveness than conventional projection, and that these effects would be more pronounced when the system responsiveness was slow.

3   Methods

3.1   Participants

19 participants were recruited for the evaluation experiment, age range 20–35 (mean 23, s.d. 3.9), gender ratio 13:6 (male:female), all were students or researchers at the University of Sheffield recruited by personal contact. All participants reported having normal vision. All participants signed a consent form and had access to bottled water during the experiment (to minimise any discomfort arising from dehydration), participants were not paid.

3.2   Apparatus

Care was taken to design the simulated robot (see Fig. 3) such that interfacing with it presented the same challenges involved in interfacing with a physical robot: including limited DoF, limited ranges of motion, and network latency. A single virtual eye camera, centrally located, was used as a surrogate for panoramic stitched imagery from the MiRo robot's stereo cameras.

In order to ensure that participants attended visually during telepresence immersion, they were presented with a number of Mahjong tiles, and were asked to find the two that match. Participants controlled which tiles are selected using an XBOX controller. Sets of tiles were generated randomly within the constraints that exactly two tiles matched on each trial.

The experiment took place within a bespoke human-robot interaction laboratory at the University of Sheffield. The room was set up such that participants were unable to see the software being used to run the experiment (see Fig. 4).

Fig. 3. Simulated MiRo robot and environment in Unity3D (left: robot, right: user perspective)

3.3   Design and Procedure

The experiment followed a within-subjects design with four conditions as shown in Table 1. Participants were informed that the study would be to compare the

Fig. 4. Room setup for final evaluation experiment

relative comfort of different virtual reality experiences, but were not given any information as to exactly what would be varied between tests. Condition order was randomised for each participant, and tile permutations were randomised within each condition. The time spent in each condition (see Table 1) was 3 min, and the rest time between conditions was 6 min - in order to reduce carried-over discomfort from previous conditions.

Table 1. Table of experimental conditions

Condition name	Vision method	Simulated network delay (round trip)
COUPLED-FAST	Coupled	0 ms
COUPLED-SLOW	Coupled	400 ms
DECOUPLED-FAST	Decoupled	0 ms
DECOUPLED-SLOW	Decoupled	400 ms

At the start of the experiment, and after each condition, participants were asked to self-assess their experience of nausea and oculomotor discomfort through the Simulator Sickness Questionnaire (SSQ) shown in Table 2, based on the original by Kennedy [3]. Each question was answered on a 0–3 linear scale (none to severe) and results combined to produce nausea (sum of items 1, 6–8, 12–16) and oculomotor (sum of 2–5, 9–11) scores at the start of the experiment (baseline) and after each condition (post-test). This allowed adjusted nausea and oculomotor scores to be calculated for each condition by subtracting the baseline from the post-test score. Participants were also asked to rate their feelings of immersion (described as "If fully immersed, you would be so engaged that you forget you are wearing the [VR] headset.") and presence (described as "If fully present, you would feel as though you were *actually* there with the tiles, in that world.") as either none, slight, moderate, or high (questions 0a and 0b in Table 2). These were also mapped into a linear score of 0–3, and a combined 'quality' score of Immersion * Presence calculated (Fig. 8).

After all conditions had been completed participants were debriefed and given an opportunity to provide feedback.

Table 2. Table of immersion and simulator sickness questions

0a. How Immersive was the experience?	0b. How Present did you feel?
1. General Discomfort	2. Fatigue
3. Headache	4. Eye Strain
5. Difficulty Focusing	6. Salivation Increasing
7. Sweating	8. Nausea
9. Difficulty Concentrating	10. Fullness of the Head
11. Blurred Vision	12. Dizziness with eyes open
13. Dizziness with eyes closed	14. Vertigo
15. Stomach Awareness	16. Burping

4   Results

All participants completed the experiment. Figure 5 shows the means and standard deviations for SSQ scores by condition. Across both nausea and oculomotor scores, and for both zero and 400 ms delays, there is a clear trend for decoupled image projection to be perceived as more comfortable than coupled.

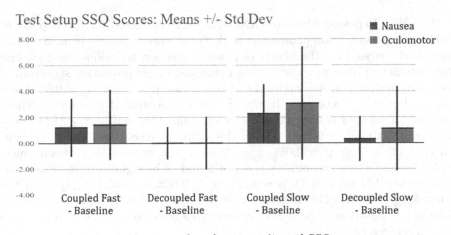

Fig. 5. Nausea and oculomotor adjusted SSQ scores

In order to further compare the coupled and decoupled display techniques, we subtract coupled from decoupled for each participant's nausea and oculomotor scores. If the result is positive, the discomfort caused by coupled can be considered to be higher than that caused by decoupled. These comparisons are shown in Figs. 6 and 7 for the fast and slow conditions respectively. Each dot shows the score of one or more participants, as indicated by the participant number. That all but two (of nineteen) participants are in the upper right quadrant indicates that this difference is neutral or positive for both oculomotor and nausea and therefore that the decoupled condition was largely experienced as more comfortable than coupled."

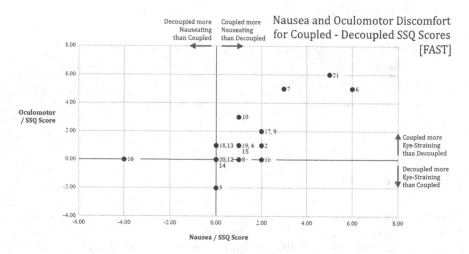

Fig. 6. Zero delay coupled minus decoupled comparison

Two-Way Repeated Measures ANOVAs were conducted for the dependent variables of per-condition nausea and oculomotor score (adjusted by initial baselines) and analysed for the effects of image projection technique, latency, and their interaction. Results indicate that decoupled image projection significantly decreased oculomotor discomfort ($F(1,18) = 23.31$, $p < 0.000$, $\eta_p^2 = 0.564$) and nausea ($F(1,18) = 18.09$, $p < 0.000$, $\eta_p^2 = 0.501$) compared to coupled. There was also an effect of latency (fast better than slow) for oculomotor ($F(1,18) = 5.48$, $p = 0.031$, $\eta_p^2 = 0.233$) though this failed to reach significance for nausea ($F(1,18) = 3.29$, $p = 0.086$, $\eta_p^2 = 0.155$). The interaction between image projection technique and latency was not found to be significant in either case (oculomotor: $F(1,18) = 0.43$, $p = 0.521$, $\eta_p^2 = 0.023$; nausea: $F(1,18) = 1.72$, $p = 0.206$, $\eta_p^2 = 0.087$). This indicates that the effect of decoupled as an improvement over coupled may be relatively independent of time delay in relation to these measures.

Figure 8 shows the combined Immersion * Presence score by condition. In both latency conditions the decoupled system was, on average, rated as more

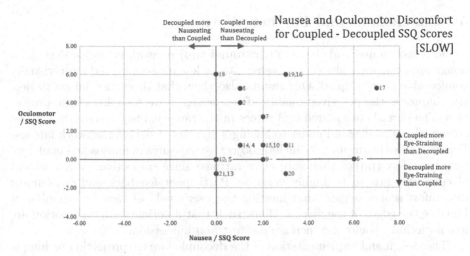

Fig. 7. 400 ms delay coupled minus decoupled comparison

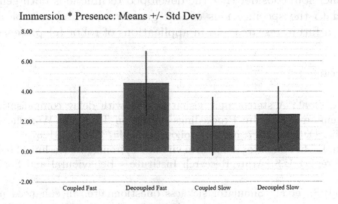

Fig. 8. Combined immersion and presence scores

immersive than the coupled one. Two way repeated measures ANOVA showed significant main effects due to both technique (F(1,18) = 8.39, p = 0.01, η_p^2 = 0.318) and latency (F(1,18) = 15.76, p = 0.001, η_p^2 = 0.467) and a significant technique*latency interaction (F(1,18) = 5.48, p = 0.031, η_p^2 = 0.233).

From feedback collected during and following the experiment, many participants reported feeling that their field of view had been constricted in the decoupled/slow condition, and that they felt distracted by the movement of the virtual display. We suggest that this perceived distraction, made worse by increased network latency, could reduce oculomotor comfort.

5   Conclusions and Further Work

At both fast (0 ms) and slow (400 ms round trip) network latencies, decoupled image projection was shown, on average, to be less nauseating and more visually comfortable than coupled. Our results also show that decoupled image projection improves the perceived quality of telepresence over coupled image projection. The partial eta squared (η_p^2) values in the range 0.3 to 0.5 show these to be strong effects similar in impact to having a significant delay in network latency. Future studies might usefully include objective measures of nausea and oculomotor discomfort (rather than subjective ratings) since subjective self-assessment of comfort tends to be highly variable. Participant feedback and oculomotor discomfort scores suggest that limiting the user's field of view by cropping or blurring the edges of the display plane, such that its orientation and motion are less noticeable, could also increase comfort and immersion.

The design and implementation of the decoupled image projection technique proceeded with the limitations of commercially available robotics in mind at all times. We therefore consider that the developed technique is both generalisable (not limited to the specifications of any given robot) and suitable for broad application in future research and in applications of robot telepresence.

References

1. Aykut, T., et al.: A stereoscopic vision system with delay compensation for 360 [degree] remote reality. In: Proceedings of the on Thematic Workshops of ACM Multimedia, October 2017. https://doi.org/10.1145/3126686.3126751
2. Kolasinski, E.M.: Simulator sickness in virtual environments (technical report 1027). Technical report U.S. Army Research Institute - Behavioural and Social Science (1995)
3. Kennedy, R.S., et al.: Simulator sickness questionnaire: an enhanced method for quantifying simulator sickness. Int. J. Aviat. Psychol. **3**, 203–220 (1993)
4. Slater, M., Usoh, M.: An experimental exploration of presence in virtual environments. Technical report 689. University College London, Department of Computer Science, pp. 3–4 (1993)
5. Marc, L., et al.: Visual discomfort and visual fatigue of stereoscopic displays: a review. J. Imaging Sci. Tech. **53**, 30201-1–30201-14 (2009)
6. Martinez-Hernandez, U., Boorman, L.W., Prescott, T.J.: Telepresence: immersion with the iCub humanoid robot and the oculus rift. In: Wilson, S.P., Verschure, P.F.M.J., Mura, A., Prescott, T.J. (eds.) LIVINGMACHINES 2015. LNCS (LNAI), vol. 9222, pp. 461–464. Springer, Cham (2015). https://doi.org/10.1007/978-3-319-22979-9_46
7. Consequential Robotics. MiRo Project. http://consequentialrobotics.com/miro/. Accessed 12 Feb 2018
8. Weech, S., Barnett-Cowan, M., Kenny, S.: Presence and cybersickness in virtual reality are negatively related: a review. Front. Psychol. **10**, 158 (2019). https://www.frontiersin.org/article/10.3389/fpsyg.2019.00158. https://doi.org/10.3389/fpsyg.2019.00158

Third Eye: Exploring the Affordances of Third-Person View in Telepresence Robots

Aneesh P. Tarun[1]([⊠]) [iD], Nauman M. Baig[1],
Jack (Shen-Kuen) Chang[1,2], Rabia Tanvir[1],
Sumaiyah Shihipar[1], and Ali Mazalek[1]

[1] Ryerson University, Toronto, ON, Canada
{aneesh, nauman.m.baig, rabia.tanvir, sumaiyah.shihipar,
mazalek}@ryerson.ca, jackskchang@gmail.com
[2] ChoroPhronesis, Pennsylvania State University, University Park, PA, USA

Abstract. Social interaction through telepresence robots can be challenging for a robot operator due to lack of spatial awareness caused by limited idiothetic cues and narrow field of view of a robot's camera. We explore the use of a third-person perspective, popular in video game design, to provide missing spatial cues to remote robot operators. We present the design and implementation of Third Eye, a system that enables controlling telepresence robots through a third-person view. Third Eye comprises a controllable third-person camera with a wide field of view, attached to a robot, and bimanual controls for remote operation. Observations from a user study show that Third Eye enabled the robot operators to have a better awareness of the robot 'bodies' they controlled. This, in turn, afforded new behavior for operators. In addition, the camera design supported ecologically valid interaction for social telepresence. Quantitative data shows that Third Eye has comparable navigation efficiency to existing systems.

Keywords: Telepresence robots · Third-person perspective · MRP

1 Introduction

The use of telepresence robots, or Mobile Remote Presence Systems (MRPs), in social contexts is increasing with their adoption by offices, schools, museums, hospitals, etc. This increasing use is largely due to the mobility of MRPs, the increase in geographically distributed families and workers [1], and the availability of relatively affordable commercial MRPs such as Double, Beam, vGo, Giraff, etc. [2]. Such MRPs provide a first-person view of the local ecology (home or office space, where the robot is located) to a robot operator (remotely located) as they move the robot and interact with collaborators (people in the local ecology).

The quality of social interactions offered by an MRP is dependent on the nature and quality of bidirectional audio and video of the MRP. While an MRP's visual point of view is modeled on our own egocentric view—a camera looking outward from the front of the robot body—it does not replicate the human eye's wider field of view (FoV) and stereoscopic vision, or the human body's idiothetic cues, such as those from

© Springer Nature Switzerland AG 2019
M. A. Salichs et al. (Eds.): ICSR 2019, LNAI 11876, pp. 707–716, 2019.
https://doi.org/10.1007/978-3-030-35888-4_66

the vestibular system and proprioception. Lack of such cues adds to the challenge of navigating MRPs [3] and limits a robot operator's awareness of the MRP's local ecology, including the robot's physical state and the collaborators' actions. The problem of limited awareness is further amplified in situations where a robot is stuck, is navigating unknown environments, or when the collaborators are moving around. Earlier works incorporated various strategies: providing spatial information to the operator using overview maps [4], sensor-based mapping and alerting systems [5], and navigation assistance [6].

We suggest that a diegetic visual representation of MRP within a robot operator's view can provide better awareness of the navigable space. We propose to implement the third-person camera model for MRPs thereby making the robot's body visible within the view of the navigable ecology. Such an approach has been used successfully to present a player's character in video games [7] and in virtual reality contexts [8]. The use of an overhead view in controlling robots has also yielded better situational awareness [8–11]. However, their use has not been explored in social contexts. We explore this neglected design space with Third Eye, examining the affordances and potential benefits of making the robot's body visible to the operator.

In this paper, we present the design, implementation, and evaluation of Third Eye, a system for supporting third-person view in MRPs. Third Eye is designed as a physical augmentation to existing MRPs. This is achieved by attaching a third-person camera— a physical rig that mounts a motorized camera, with 180° fish-eye view—above and behind an MRP. Third Eye shows a controllable third-person view of an MRP to a robot operator. An operator can pan the third-person view while simultaneously controlling the robot's movement. This supports an operator to look and move around a local ecology using visual cues from the robot and the navigation space.

Quantitative results from our study show that the third-person view has comparable navigation efficiency to that of traditional MRPs, although participants tended to bump into obstacles less often in the third-person view. Qualitative feedback (including our observations) indicate that Third Eye provided a better awareness of the robot's physical state. Participants were able to notice the state and speed of the robot. The view also afforded varied and ecologically valid strategies for navigation and communication. Results indicate that supporting both these views in appropriate contexts can be beneficial for social telepresence. We conclude the paper with a summary of our observations and note emergent design themes when incorporating third-person views.

2   Related Work

Chen et al. [3] outlined the challenges of effectively navigating telepresence systems. They also surveyed different solutions by researchers to these challenges. On one end of the solution space for this problem, researchers have proposed wider FoV cameras [12–14], stereoscopic cameras [14], overview maps [4], sensor-based alerts and maps [5], and better robot control systems.

On the other end of the solution space, researchers are negotiating the role of MRPs in decision making through autonomous driving systems [6, 15]. However, Takayama et al. [6] show that, for people with a high locus of control, autonomous systems may introduce more time and effort for navigation. This indicates that there is a need for striking a balance between autonomy and control when designing control systems for MRPs. With Third Eye, we explore the benefits of visual cues afforded by alternative visual representation of MRPs for navigation.

Video game designers have widely used first-person view to immerse players into the game world with a familiar point of view. However, the third-person view is preferred in several action and simulation games (e.g. Fortnite, Tomb Raider series). Game designers note that this view, where the camera perspective is fixed to and trailing a game character, provides: better visibility of character actions; wider FoV; easier judgement of distances in game worlds; ability to see clothing and body language of the player's character [7].

However, Chesher [16] observes that such a view is more detached from the game world than the first-person view and threatens a player's sense of self within these simulated worlds. In contrast, Black [17] notes that the relationship between the player and the game body is more nuanced. He argues that the third-person view is no less engaging than the first-person view owing to the fluidity of the boundaries of our experiential selves.

Saakes et al. [10] reported that third-person perspective provided by pole-mounted cameras or drones led to fewer collisions and more success in search and rescue tasks. With Monocle, researchers explored multiple ways to integrate third-person view and first-person view in telepresence robots [11]. Hughes et al. [8] experimented with different camera configurations in robots using interactive virtual environments (IVEs) where virtual cameras were attached to virtual robots. They found that cameras with controllable orientation, independent of the robot, were beneficial for navigation and search tasks but were less efficient in inspection activities up close.

Participants in Robocup competitions noted that they have had better success when controlling their robots through a camera view that showed some or all of a robot's chassis [9]. Above studies excluded social interaction/communication in evaluations. We think that there are unexplored affordances and benefits of third-person views in such less-formal contexts.

3   Third Person-Perspective Design

We designed and built Third Eye as an augmentation to commercial MRPs. Third Eye modifies a robot operator's live view with a controllable third-person view of the robot within the navigating environment. Third Eye includes a controllable camera fixed to the robot body such that the view follows the robot's position and orientation. Operators drive the MRP with the dominant hand (the arrow keys on a keyboard, typical to commercial MRPs). Simultaneously, they can use their non-dominant hand (radial controller) to rotate the camera independent of the robot's movements. Here, we outline our design choices and interaction techniques.

The visibility of a robot's chassis and back is beneficial in situational awareness when controlling the robot [5]. We mounted a camera to the back of an MRP to provide a tightly coupled third-person view. The entirety of the robot's body, including the region surrounding the wheels, was visible.

Independent camera control and rotation can increase functional presence for remote operators [8]. We designed the Third Eye camera to rotate (pan) independently of the robot's orientation. Third Eye pans quicker than the robot body supporting high interface fidelity [15]. In addition, we ensured that the panning of the third-person view is visible, and obvious to collaborators. This design enabled us to support better awareness of an operator's attention and gaze [18, 19].

We added bimanual interaction [20] to allow simultaneous control of robot movements (finer control using the dominant hand) and camera rotation (coarse actions using the non-dominant hand). This is also an ecologically valid design mimicking how a person looks around while walking in a physical space.

Navigating with misaligned camera views or remembering to realign the two camera views frequently may add more mental load to an operator [8]. We included two interaction techniques where a user can choose to either align the Third Eye view with the robot view, or turn the entire robot to the Third Eye view direction. This reinforces a user's intent when they wish to 'go' in a certain direction where they are 'looking'.

3.1   Implementation

We built Third Eye (Fig. 1(a)) as an augmentation to a first-generation Double robot. We designed and built it through an iterative design process.

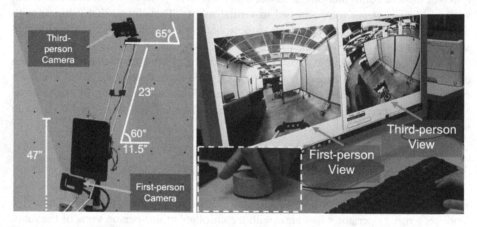

Fig. 1. (a) Third Eye System with dimensions for the camera mount. (b) Pilot moving the MRP using keyboard commands. Both the camera views are shown here for illustration purposes. (inset) Radial controller used by the pilot for rotating Third Eye with their non-dominant hand.

Hardware. A Nexus 5 smartphone with an attached 180° FoV fish-eye lens, mounted on a stepper motor, acts as the controllable camera. Increase in FoV has shown to improve interaction quality for the operators [21], lead to better task efficiency [12], and improve search and navigation tasks [22]. In addition, the fish-eye lens allows the camera to be mounted not too far from the robot body while enabling a full view of the robot with a small occluded region ahead [7]. The center of the camera vertically aligns with the center of the motor axis of rotation. The rig is mounted on the back of a Double robot using custom mounts and thin hollow aluminum rods. The stepper motor is driven by an ESP8266 Wi-Fi module and powered by Lithium-Polymer batteries.

Software and Controls. A custom android application transmits the Third Eye camera (audio and video) stream, as well as the first-person stream, to the robot operator's computer over the network. We used WebRTC protocol to transmit the video feed over a local Wi-Fi network. With this setup, we kept the live video stream lag to under 200 ms. The two camera streams, motor commands, and robot commands are managed by a server running on the robot operator's computer. A web-based user interface allows a robot operator to view the camera streams and control the robot and Third Eye. Keyboard commands drive the robot while a radial controller (Microsoft Surface Dial) is used for rotating and centering Third Eye (Fig. 1(b)).

4 Evaluation

Prior studies in telepresence systems have evaluated the task efficiencies of third-person perspectives in search and rescue contexts [10, 11]. However, with respect to social context, user behavior and communication are also important. We added tasks that included navigation and communication in an office setting. We were also keen on observing and reflecting on the emergent operator behavior and design opportunities with Third Eye. We conducted a mixed-methods study to compare Third Eye with a traditional MRP for navigation, search, and communication tasks. We recruited 15 participants (mean age 24.2 years, 5 females, 10 males) from the local community who had prior experience using at least one audio-video communication system (e.g., Skype, Google Hangouts, Facetime). All of the participants were right-handed.

Experiment Setup. We designed a within-subject study where participants were asked to perform navigation and communication tasks in two conditions: commercial MRP condition (MRP) and Third Eye condition (TE). The order of the conditions was counterbalanced and randomly assigned to participants. The two task conditions were our independent variables. User input, time to completion, and user errors were the dependent variables. We gathered quantitative data to compare the efficiencies of using the Third Eye system and a commercial MRP in search tasks. We gathered qualitative input and observations to understand the navigation and communication strategies in a social telepresence context. A (first generation) Double robot was mounted with Third Eye for TE condition. The same robot was mounted with a Nexus 5 smartphone and a 180° fish-eye lens to provide a first-person view for the MRP condition. This setup allowed us to ensure consistent video quality between TE and MRP.

In the MRP condition, participants were able to control the robot and see the first-person view as well as the robot's built-in downward view (looking down at the wheel). In the TE condition, participants could control the robot and Third Eye bimanually. Camera height was different between the two conditions (as expected). We factored this into our final discussion and analysis. Our goal was to compare Third Eye and its associated interaction techniques in its entirety to a commercial MRP with minimal modifications (modified FoV).

Participants were seated comfortably in front of a 27" monitor displaying the camera feed (first-person view or the third-person view). A keyboard and a radial controller were placed in front of the user for controlling the system.

Training Task. Participants spent 5 min, on average, before each task condition to get comfortable with the controls and with navigation.

Study Task. For each condition, the actual task involved navigating an office space (33.5' × 20') and searching for three different 4" × 3" white cards that were posted at pre-determined locations on the office walls. Each card had generic symbols printed on it. The participant could interact with a collaborator (an actor in the local ecology) if they needed help. After the search task was completed, the participant had to locate a unique object (a bag, a microphone) and guide the collaborator to that object and provide instructions for keeping the object safe. Lastly, the participants had to map the location of the symbols on a paper map of the office space to see how well they recalled locations. The office space, the location of the note cards, and the symbols were changed between conditions. We designed two unique office space setups that had similar complexity of navigation. Each office space setup was of the same size, and they all had four narrow pathways, four dead ends, and four workspaces to navigate through. We hypothesized that the participants in the TE condition would have the least amount of errors and faster task completion times.

Data Collection. We captured user input (keystrokes, dial actions); time taken for task and sub-task completion; and general observations. Participants completed a questionnaire on their preferred system, and answered open-ended questions about the system and their experience with the system.

4.1 Results

All the participants completed each task condition in under 20 min. Participants completed the task a little faster in TE (M = 9.07 min, SD = 3.99 min) than in MRP (M = 9.80 min, SD = 5.70 min) however, this difference was not significant (t (14) = 0.408, ns).

User Error. Two types of errors were recorded: (1) hitting/crashing of the robot against an obstacle; and (2) error in marking the search locations on a paper map. Participants in the TE condition crashed the robot a total of 20 times (total over all participants) whereas participants in the MRP condition crashed the robot a total of 26 times. However, the difference (MRP M = 1.73, SD = 1.33; TE M = 1.33, SD = 1.80) was not significant (t(14) = 0.692, ns). Total number of location-marking errors were the same between MRP and TE conditions with a total of 6 errors across all participants per condition.

Participant Preference. 7 participants preferred TE, 5 participants wanted the ability to use both the systems with their unique viewpoints, and only 3 participants showed preference for MRP. Participants noted several reasons for their preference for TE: the ability to see the robot's wheels and its surroundings; ability to look around while driving; ability to turn to where they are looking. P10 noted that TE's unique view allowed them to move more fluidly and confidently than when in MRP condition. Participants who wanted to be able to use both views indicated that both views had their inherent benefits and flaws. Participants who sided with MRP chose it noting that the view felt "natural" and the detail of the video stream quality was better than the TE stream which was much farther from the scene ahead.

Navigation. The amount of time spent by participants in moving forward and backward tended to be more in the TE condition. Participants also tended to turn left and right more in the MRP condition. However, the data showed a lot of variance and we found no significant difference between the two conditions for different movements.

Awareness of the Robot. When guiding the collaborators to located objects in the office space, participants tended to associate themselves with the robot body in the MRP condition. They asked the collaborator to "follow me" and pick up an object that is "right in front of me" or "to my left". In the TE condition, participants tended to be more aware of the robot body. They referred to the robot both in the first person and in the third person. They would ask the collaborators to "follow me" and pick up an object that is "in front of my robot" or "in front of my device." P7, when facing the collaborator, rotated the Third Eye camera away and asked them to look "where I am pointing towards" referring to the rotated camera's direction of sight. P13 and P15 used the camera rotation for pointing at objects as well. P4, P5, and P7 were conscious of Third Eye jutting out at the back of the robot. Three participants noticed the robot's wobbling when in the TE condition. P4 accurately noted how slowly the robot backs up. Some participants commented on the visibility of the robot's wheels. P2 mentioned "it was more realistic because it felt like I was seeing my feet." P4 noted "I liked how I was able to relax a bit and not worrying [sic] if the robot will hit the wall as I could see the robot's wheel." When they bumped the robot against an obstacle, P15 noted "Hitting the robot at that strength actually felt like an accident…I felt discomfort." P15 also indicated that this reaction was based on a personal experience.

Interaction with Collaborators. All participants noted that interacting with collaborators was comparable to an audio-video (Skype) chat for both the MRP and TE conditions. More participants preferred the first-person view for a natural face-to-face interaction. But there were no negative concerns around communicating when using Third Eye. In line with our original design goal, participants used Third Eye's rotations as a way of communicating gaze and intent.

5 Discussion and Conclusion

The quantitative measures trended towards the outcomes we expected: faster task completion and lower crashes were observed in the TE condition. However, these were not statistically significant differences and therefore did not support our hypotheses (faster task completion times, and fewer errors in TE). We think that tasks of longer duration may yield further insights quantitatively. While the TE and MRP conditions have comparable task performance, qualitative feedback and our observations yielded interesting results and emergent user behavior along several themes. We summarize our findings and note emergent design themes.

Navigation in Local Ecology. There were differences in search strategies and driving techniques that may explain why neither MRP nor TE showed a clear advantage. First, participants tended to "look around" more in the TE than in the MRP condition. In addition, the lack of close-up view in TE led to an increase in maneuvering around found objects. Awareness of the robot's wobbling also made a few participants very cautious in TE. Lack of information about the surroundings made some participants more confident when driving the robot forward in the MRP condition.

The navigation strategies observed in TE closely resembled people's movements in physical space and game character movements. Participants used Third Eye to look around the space and choose where to move the robot. They also pointed at objects using the camera orientation (deictic cues) when interacting with collaborators in the local ecology.

Interacting with Collaborators. Participants noted the ability to move and/or look around as leading to a "more natural" way of interacting with remote collaborators. P9 and P11 mentioned that the interaction was too short to gauge the quality of conversations in the tasks. P5 noted that a lack of spatial awareness (in MRP) affected their ability to locate and interact with the collaborator. P7 indicated that MRP was less expressive than TE, where they could rotate Third Eye, for communicating eye gaze. Participants utilized camera rotation in TE to 'look at' the collaborator and guide them where to go using gaze pointing. Participants in MRP were more likely to ask collaborators to follow them to a location. Collaborators in the space noted that they were better able to understand user intent in TE condition as they could see the participants' gaze and follow directional cues.

Robot Body. The perceived wobbling of the robot negatively affected the participants' speed of navigation. However, participants' awareness of the robot body's state and its speed, observed with Third Eye, presents a design opportunity. The larger FoV and the visibility of the robot's body and immediate environment provided the participants with diegetic information of the robot's state. One participant felt discomfort when the robot forcefully hit an obstacle, comparing it to the feeling of being in an accident. Participants tended to back up the robot more while navigating in the third-person view than in the first-person view. We observed that participants referred to the robot both in the first-person and third-person when using Third Eye. This parallels the ambiguous relationship gamers can have with their game characters [23]. P10 summarized the ambiguity like this: "Even though I was distancing myself from becoming that robot [in TE], I still felt, because everything was a lot more fluid in looking, moving, interacting, it actually felt more like human interaction."

Controls. Overall, the camera controls were well received and used as intended, but only three participants chose to look around simultaneously while driving the robot. This indicates that the use of camera controls while driving was perceived to be cognitively taxing. The differences in the search strategies between the two views, combined with the ease of camera panning, hint that the participants used the panning as an epistemic action [24] for scanning the 'problem space' prior to locating the target artifacts. We think that there is opportunity for seamlessly switching between the two views based on actions (e.g., looking around) or context (e.g., obstacle nearby).

Future Directions. We think that a longer user study could shed more light on other aspects of telepresence with Third Eye such as our sense of presence and how to support richer social interactions and collaborative tasks. The participants' awareness of the robot body's state and its speed, observed with Third Eye, presents design opportunities that we hope to explore. For example, subtle movements or actuations on the robot body could be designed to convey meaningful cues to both the operator and the collaborators.

Conclusion. We presented the design, implementation, and evaluation of Third Eye, a system for supporting third-person view in MRPs. We focus on exploring the affordances of a third-person view in social telepresence systems. We conducted a comparative evaluation of Third Eye with a commercial MRP for search and communication tasks. We observed emergent behaviors emphasizing social context of use: use of camera orientation to express intent; awareness of (robot) body in space; variety and complexity in robot movements; using physical body navigation behaviors when using MRPs. Quantitative results from our two studies show that the third-person view has comparable navigation efficiency to that of traditional MRPs.

Acknowledgements. We thank Dr. Jason Nolan for his insights and for lending his equipment for research. We also thank Tamara Mahbubani, Syeda Zahra, Nabeel Ahmed, Farisa Hossain, Victor Alexandru, and Ronak Maru for their collaboration. This research was supported through grants from the Social Sciences and Humanities Research Council of Canada, the Canada Research Chairs Program, the Canada Foundation for Innovation, and the Ontario Ministry for Research and Innovation.

References

1. United Nations. Department of Economic and Social Affairs - Population Division: International Migration Report 2017 (ST/ESA/SER.A/403) (2017)
2. Kristoffersson, A., Coradeschi, S., Loutfi, A.: A review of mobile robotic telepresence. Adv. Hum.-Comput. Interact. **2013**, 1–17 (2013). https://doi.org/10.1155/2013/902316
3. Chen, J.Y.C., Haas, E.C., Barnes, M.J.: Human performance issues and user interface design for teleoperated robots. IEEE Trans. Syst. Man Cybern. Part C (Appl. Rev.) **37**, 1231–1245 (2007). https://doi.org/10.1109/TSMCC.2007.905819
4. Coltin, B., Biswas, J., Pomerleau, D., Veloso, M.: Effective semi-autonomous telepresence. In: Röfer, T., Mayer, N.M., Savage, J., Saranlı, U. (eds.) RoboCup 2011. LNCS (LNAI), vol. 7416, pp. 365–376. Springer, Heidelberg (2012). https://doi.org/10.1007/978-3-642-32060-6_31
5. Keyes, B., Casey, R., Yanco, H.A., Maxwell, B.A., Georgiev, Y.: Camera placement and multi-camera fusion for remote robot operation. In: IEEE International Workshop Safety, Security Rescue Robotics, pp. 22–24 (2006)
6. Takayama, L., Marder-Eppstein, E., Harris, H., Beer, J.M.: Assisted driving of a mobile remote presence system: system design and controlled user evaluation. In: IEEE International Conference on Robotics and Automation. pp. 1883–1889. IEEE (2011). https://doi.org/10.1109/ICRA.2011.5979637

7. Adams, E.: Fundamentals of Game Design (2013). https://doi.org/10.1017/CBO9781107 415324.004

8. Hughes, S., Manojlovich, J., Lewis, M., Gennari, J.: Camera control and decoupled motion for teleoperation. In: IEEE International Conference on Systems, Man and Cybernetics, pp. 1339–1344. IEEE (2003). https://doi.org/10.1109/ICSMC.2003.1244597

9. Lima, P., et al.: RoboCup 2004 competitions and symposium: a small kick for robots, a giant score for science. AI Mag. **26**, 36–61 (2005). https://doi.org/10.1609/AIMAG.V26I2.1812

10. Saakes, D., Choudhary, V., Sakamoto, D., Inami, M., Lgarashi, T., Igarashi, T.: A teleoperating interface for ground vehicles using autonomous flying cameras. In: International Conference on Artificial Reality Telexistence (2013). https://doi.org/10.1109/ICAT.2013.6728900

11. Seo, S.H., Rea, D.J., Wiebe, J., Young, J.E.: Monocle: interactive detail-in-context using two pan-and-tilt cameras to improve teleoperation effectiveness. In: RO-MAN 2017 - 26th IEEE International Symposium on Robot and Human Interactive Communication (2017). https://doi.org/10.1109/ROMAN.2017.8172419

12. Johnson, S., Rae, I., Mutlu, B., Takayama, L.: Can you see me now?: how field of view affects collaboration in robotic telepresence. In: Proceedings of the 33rd Annual ACM Conference on Human Factors in Computing Systems - CHI 2015, pp. 2397–2406. ACM Press, New York (2015). https://doi.org/10.1145/2702123.2702526

13. Kress, G., Almaula, H.: Sensorimotor requirements for teleoperation. FMC Corporation, San Diego, CA, Report R-6279 (1988)

14. Scribner, D.R., Gombash, J.W.: The Effect of Stereoscopic and Wide Field of View Conditions on Teleoperator Performance (1998). http://www.dtic.mil/docs/citations/ADA341218

15. Giudice, N.A., Tietz, J.D.: Learning with virtual verbal displays: effects of interface fidelity on cognitive map development. In: Freksa, C., Newcombe, N.S., Gärdenfors, P., Wölfl, S. (eds.) Spatial Cognition 2008. LNCS (LNAI), vol. 5248, pp. 121–137. Springer, Heidelberg (2008). https://doi.org/10.1007/978-3-540-87601-4_11

16. Chesher, C.: Neither gaze nor glance, but glaze: relating to console game screens. SCAN J. Media Arts Cult. **1**, 98–117 (2004)

17. Black, D.: Why can i see my avatar? embodied visual engagement in the third-person video game. Games Cult. **12**, 179–199 (2015). https://doi.org/10.1177/1555412015589175

18. Luff, P., Heath, C., Kuzuoka, H., Hindmarsh, J., Yamazaki, K., Oyama, S.: Fractured ecologies: creating environments for collaboration. Hum. Comput. Interact. **18**, 51–84 (2003). https://doi.org/10.1207/S15327051HCI1812_3

19. Morita, T., Mase, K., Hirano, Y., Kajita, S.: Reciprocal attentive communication in remote meeting with a humanoid robot. In: Proceedings of the Ninth International Conference on Multimodal Interfaces - ICMI 2007, pp. 228–235. ACM Press, New York (2007). https://doi.org/10.1145/1322192.1322232

20. Guiard, Y.: Asymmetric division of labor in human skilled bimanual action: the kinematic chain as a model. J. Mot. Behav. **19**, 486–517 (1987)

21. Kiselev, A., Kristoffersson, A., Loutfi, A.: The effect of field of view on social interaction in mobile robotic telepresence systems. In: ACM/IEEE International Conference on Human-Robot Interaction, pp. 214–215. ACM (2014)

22. Arthur, K.W.: Effects of field of view on performance with head-mounted displays (2000). http://wwwx.cs.unc.edu/Research/eve/dissertations/2000-Arthur.pdf

23. Newman, J.: The myth of the ergodic videogame. Game Stud. **2**, 1–17 (2002)

24. Kirsh, D., Maglio, P.: On distinguishing epistemic from pragmatic action. Cogn. Sci. **18**, 513–549 (1994). https://doi.org/10.1207/s15516709cog1804_1

Privacy and Safety of the Social Robots

Privacy Concerns in Robot Teleoperation: Does Personality Influence What Should Be Hidden?

Sogol Balali[1], Ross T. Sowell[2][✉], William D. Smart[1], and Cindy M. Grimm[1]

[1] Oregon State University, Corvallis, OR 97331, USA
[2] Rhodes College, Memphis, TN 38112, USA
sowellr@rhodes.edu

Abstract. Advances in robotics technology will bring more teleoperated robots into homes to perform a variety of household tasks. This raises new privacy concerns as the remote operator can control the robot and its camera, and record its sensor data. One way to provide some privacy protection is through on-board processing of the data to filter out sensitive visual information. But what do people want hidden, and how should we hide it? Do the personality traits of a particular user influence that choice?

We designed an 85-question survey to help answer these questions and analyzed the data from 81 respondents. We found that people are most concerned about hiding identifiable personal or financial information and valuables from a household robot, and we found that they prefer stronger filters to hide such items. We also found some evidence of the existence of correlations between a person's familiarity with technology, sociability, and trust and their privacy concerns.

Keywords: Teleoperation · Privacy · GenderMag · Remote viewing

1 Introduction

Domestic robots bring the promise of reducing the burden of mundane household chores, but they also threaten our privacy because a robot is essentially a remotely movable camera platform. A remote user teleoperating a robot can "snoop"—intentionally or not—and even record data for later viewing.

Previous work [6,9,11] has proposed a variety of filters that can be applied to the robot's video feed to provide different types of privacy protection. These studies have shown that such filters can be used to protect privacy while not adversely affecting basic task performance. While this is essential work in demonstrating the feasibility of the approach, it makes many assumptions about people's privacy expectations and how they would like those expectations to be upheld.

In this paper we take a step back and seek to better understand how members of the general public actually *think* about privacy. What are people's privacy

© Springer Nature Switzerland AG 2019
M. A. Salichs et al. (Eds.): ICSR 2019, LNAI 11876, pp. 719–729, 2019.
https://doi.org/10.1007/978-3-030-35888-4_67

concerns? What kinds of filters would people want to use in practice and what kinds of things would they want to protect? By examining these questions, we gain a deeper understanding of how to categorize objects for filtering, the relationship between a concern to hide something and the desired filtering type, and how personality may affect those concerns.

We designed a survey to identify privacy-sensitive items in the home and to match those items with specific filter choices. We also aimed to understand how people's personality traits might influence their privacy choices. More subtly, we want to know the *granularity* of these concerns—are there categories we can group items into? Specifically, this study considered three research questions: (1) What items do people consider privacy-sensitive in their homes?; (2) What filters do people want to utilize in order to hide their privacy-sensitive items?; and (3) Can personality traits be used to predict people's privacy preferences?

2   Related Work

"Privacy" is a very broad term, with various social sciences—anthropology, sociology, psychology, economics—studying it from different angles. For example, Marshall [15] proposes a Personal Preference Scale which assesses different subjective states of privacy that were derived from a theory first outlined by Westin [20]. These psychological states include: (a) intimacy, (b) solitude, (c) anonymity, (d) reserve, (e) seclusion, and (f) not neighboring, which can be thought of as withdrawal from one's community. Other theories (e.g., Altman [4]) emphasize the determinants of privacy with respect to behavioral and interpersonal management and control. Researchers working from this theory have been more concerned with manipulating physical and interpersonal environments and have used assessment tools from other theories (e.g., self-disclosure, self-consciousness, etc.) to measure various specific psychological outcomes [14].

While there are intuitive qualitative measures of privacy, we were unable to find any quantitative measures in the literature. Moreover, most of the work on privacy in a technological context centers on data privacy, rather than on physical privacy. Acquisti et al. [3] conducted a series of studies that attempted to determine the monetary value people were willing to attach to their personal data. Surprisingly, they found that the cost that people would tolerate to buy extra protections was different from the price they would charge for selling that same data. They concluded that what people perceive data privacy to be worth is very dependent on context, and on how the question is framed. They caution against single measures of privacy, and claim that all valuations of privacy should be "interpreted with extreme caution." Moreover, they offer evidence that people are highly inconsistent in their privacy-related decisions, and raise the question of whether or not people can rationally navigate issues related to data privacy. John et al. [10] offer additional evidence that data privacy preferences are very subject to context and framing.

Privacy in social robotics remains a nascent research space, but a few studies have been published in this area. Syrdal et al. [19] studied disclosure of personal information and Caine et al. [7] studied privacy-enhancing behaviors. Wong and Mulligan [21] studied the concepts that videos can communicate to potential users about privacy. Denning et al. [8] demonstrated security vulnerabilities in commercially available robots. Lee et al. [13] studied users' perceptions of privacy with a social robot in the workplace. Hubers et al. [9], Butler et al. [6], and Klow et al. [11] studied the trade-off between filtering the robot's video feed to protect user privacy and keeping it unfiltered so the remote operator can use the robot effectively. Rueben et al. [17] compiled a taxonomy of privacy types and concerns, and Krupp et al. [12] ran focus groups which indicated that this taxonomy lines up well with the concerns of members of the public. Rueben et al. [16] also investigated how the framing of these systems—and how they are described to the people who will interact with them—affects how they are perceived. The more "friendly" framing evoked far weaker privacy concerns.

Our study builds on this work by bridging the gap between abstract definitions of visual privacy and a concrete realization on a physical robot, essentially asking "What do you want to hide and how?" This answer will obviously vary from person to person. For this reason, we also draw on existing work that characterizes how personality traits influence the way people interact with software (GenderMag [5]). Preliminary work [18] suggests that the GenderMag characterizations carry over to a teleoperation task.

The GenderMag Method [5] defines personality traits along five facets (motivation, information processing styles, computer self-efficacy, risk aversion, and tinkering). We know social measures and culture play a big role in terms of privacy as it relates to physical spaces and social interactions [17] but, to our knowledge, there is no standardized set of questions for measuring this. Therefore—in addition to the GenderMag questions—we include a set of questions broadly related to the areas of trust, control, sociability, and fear of judgment. To our knowledge, our study is the first to examine personality traits as a predictor of concerns for privacy in robotics.

3 Methods

Our approach is a survey[1] that includes both quantitative questions (filter choice, privacy concerns) and additional open-ended questions to capture missing items and participant reasoning. The first third of the survey consists of demographic and personality questions, the second third asked questions about how comfortable participants were with letting a remote operator view specific items, and the last third asked questions about what filters participants would use, both by item and by category. For the comfort and filter questions we asked participants to mark N/A for items they did not use. We distributed the survey using Amazon Mechanical Turk in order to reach a relatively broad audience that was familiar with technology.

[1] Complete copy of the survey: https://bit.ly/2Xg30Pn.

3.1   Survey Design

Before asking the privacy and personality trait questions we introduced a household robot framing context [16] where we show a video of a Fetch robot (see Fig. 1) cleaning up a cup of coffee, wiping the counter, and then waving goodbye. Participants were given the following scenario, "You are holding an event at your home soon, that you need to clean up for. However, your home is not clean, and you will not be able to clean it alone by that time. Therefore, you asked a cleaning service company for help and they promised to send Fetch, a very capable cleaning robot to your home." Participants were also told that "Fetch will work mostly by itself but for some messes it needs to be controlled remotely by the staff at the cleaning service company."

We proposed 5 filtering techniques, (a) no filter, (b) blurring, (c) line drawing plus blurring, (d) black box, and (e) object elimination, presented with image examples (see Fig. 2). No filter is considered to be the lowest level of concealment and object elimination the highest.

Fig. 1. Fetch, the housekeeping robot, used in our video framing.

An initial pilot study (MTurk survey) was conducted that used standard informational privacy questions, a photo of a robotic plumber, and a small set of items and filters and open-ended questions about what participants would like to hide. This study identified messes as a novel category. We combined the survey results with previous work [9,17] to select the 67 items, 9 categories (see Table 1), and filters (see Fig. 2).

The proposed categories are defined as follows: **Pictures:** all types of paintings or photos at home like family pictures (8 items), **EPT:** electronics, paper, TV; any surface like TVs, tablets, papers that can reveal personal information (5 items), **Financial:** documents that contain information about one's financial or identification records like tax information (9 items), **Hygiene:** any item that helps humans maintain their personal hygiene like deodorants (9 items), **Expensive:** any financially valuable item like jewelry (7 items), **Sentimental:** any item of high value to someone because of personal or emotional association rather than material worth like a gift from a beloved person (3 items), **Messes:** any item that can make a place look untidy like dirty clothes (12 items), **Health:** any item that convey information about someone's health status like health test results (5 items), **Humans** any human who lives in a home or visits the residence of the home like friends (9 items).

We conducted 4 pilot studies with 4 graduate students. Our pilot participants took the entire survey and provided feedback about the flow of the survey questions. We initially distributed the survey to 21 MTurk participants in order to perform an initial analysis and check for data validity. We then distributed the survey to an additional 80 participants. Survey length was, on average, 23.37 min.

3.2   Participants

We had 78 unique participants who completed the full survey (three were identified as re-taking the survey; we kept only their first response). We also had 6
participants who quit the survey just before answering the filter questions. This
resulted in 84 participants (57 males, 26 females and 1 other) who answered the
privacy comfort questions and 78 participants (52 males, 25 females and 1 other)
who answered the filtering questions. Ages were: 31% 18–30, 44% 30–40, 14%
40–50, 11% over 50. 56% of the participants were highly familiar with robots,
41% medium, 3% no familiarity. 44% had bachelor degrees, 7% had a masters
or PhD, and the rest had no college degree.

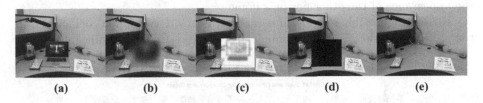

Fig. 2. (a) No filter (b) Blurring filter (c) Line drawing plus blurring filter (d) Black
box filter (e) Object elimination filter

3.3   Data Analysis

We used a 7-point Likert scale (1 - high-level to 7 - low-level) for our comfort
questions. For the plots shown here we condensed this into 3 groups (1–2 comfortable, 3–4 neutral, 6–7 uncomfortable). We ignored answers marked as N/A.
To create a comfort level score for each category we averaged the comfort level
for the items (we did not explicitly ask for a comfort score for the category, only
items).

For the filter questions, we converted the filters to a linear scale (1 for no
filter, 5 for object elimination) based on their information-hiding abilities. We
ignored answers marked as N/A.

We show four data summaries in Fig. 3: (1) **comfort (cat)**: average percentage of people who fall into each level of comfort across all the items inside a
category, (2) **comfort (obj)**: percentage of people whose average comfort score
for all of the items inside a category fall into each level of comfort, (3) **filter
(cat)**: percentage of participants that choose each filtering technique for each
category of items, and (4) **filter (obj)**: overall percentage of participants who
chose each filtering technique for selected items from each category of items.

Comparing category averages to item ones shows the level of agreement
between the two. We plot the comfort questions next to the filters to show
comfort-filter agreement.

Our demographic questions consist of traditional ones (e.g. age, gender, education level) and ones specific to our study (e.g. trust, sociability, GenderMag).

We group the specific demographic questions into six traits, and again we reduce the 7-point Likert scale to 3 levels (low, medium, high) for discussion.

Trust is the "firm belief in the reliability, truth, ability, or strength of someone or something" [1]. *Willingness of being in control* is "the power to influence or direct people's behavior or the course of events" [1]. *Sociability* is "the quality of being inclined to seek or enjoy companionship" [2]. *Familiarity with technology* is the state of being "well informed about or proficient in the use of modern technology, especially computers." [1]. *GenderMag*: We used four GenderMag [5] facets: (1) information processing style, (2) computer self-efficacy, (3) attitude toward risk, and (4) willingness to explore or tinker. *Being afraid of other people's judgment* refers to an unpleasant emotion caused by the belief that someone makes considered decisions or comes to sensible conclusions about the appearance of the other person's home.

To identify possible relationships we used Pearson correlation coefficients. In the following section, coefficients above 0.4^2 were considered significant.

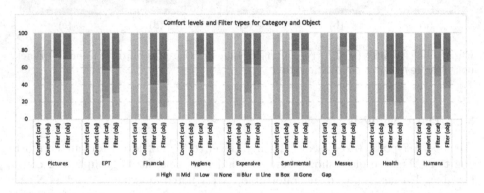

Fig. 3. Summary of Comfort Levels (columns 1&2) and Filter choices (columns 3&4), for each category. We show scores calculated in two methods (per category and per item) as outlined in Sect. 3.3.

4   Results

RQ1. What items do people consider privacy sensitive in their homes? (see Fig. 3): For comfort level, the financial category was ranked as "not comfortable" by 70% of the participants. The electronics and expensive categories ranked second and third respectively (32% and 25%).

---

^{2} Above 0.4 is considered to be significant when studying social data due to its complex nature.

Table 1. Participants' suggested items for each category

Category name	Items suggested by participants
Pictures	Collectibles, pictures of coworker, naughty posters, valuable objets d'art
EPT	Personal contacts, Google calendar, video games, computer showing visited websites and personal email
Financial	Social security card, birth certificate, life insurance, bank statements, check stubs, blank checks or credit cards, incorporation documents, business related documents
Hygiene	Sunscreen, bathing supplies, household cleaners, specialty cleaners, pest control items
Expensive	Collectibles, games, books, vinyl records, expensive luggage, expensive appliances, credit and debit cards, guns
Sentimental	Gifts from family, family hand down items, personal photos, flowers
Messes	Full garbage bins, uncleaned toilets and bathtubs, dog poop, loose accessories, toiletries, random home accessories scattered about, power tools during DIY projects, broken furnishings, bed not made, family portraits, tech area
Health	Bandages, splints, casts, nebulizar, underwear
Humans	Co-workers, maintenance personnel, utility service personnel, friends to friends

The sentimental category was of the least concern, with 71% of participants choosing the "comfortable" scores. Participants were also largely comfortable with the messes (69%), personal hygiene (64%) humans (60%) and photos (58%) categories.

While items mostly tracked with their categories (compare first two bars of each category in Fig. 3), there were a few exceptions. Paintings of political parties and religious beliefs were ranked "not comfortable" more often than wall paintings and favorite artist posters. Similarly, elder care, baby hygiene, and sexual health products were more sensitive than other hygiene products.

Table 1 lists items that participants thought were missing from our categories.

RQ2. What filters do people want to utilize in order to hide their privacy sensitive items? Not surprisingly, filter choice varied with category (see Fig. 4). In general, "no filter" tracked with categories that people ranked "comfortable". The "black box" filter similarly tracked with "uncomfortable" scores, especially for the financial documents. The "line" filter was rarely chosen (3%), perhaps because it was unfamiliar to participants.

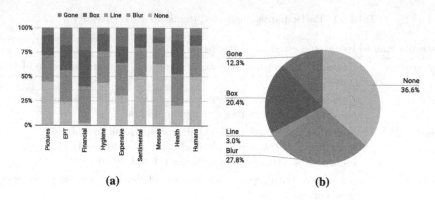

Fig. 4. (a) Filter popularity by category. (b) Filter popularity across all categories.

The filter/comfort scores were strongly correlated in the following categories: Pictures, EPT, Expensive, Messes, and Humans. This implies that an increasing level of discomfort was correlated with an increase in the strength of the filter. There was no strong correlation in the Health, Sentimental, or Financial categories, although the *trend* was the same. In these three cases the full range of the filters was not used, just the two end points (no filter—Health and Sentimental) or box/elimination filters (financial documents).

Filter choice also interacted with task. One of our participants commented "I would let them [robot's operator] see anything. If the point is for them to clean up the mess I would not have an issue with them seeing it [items in messes category] in the first place or I would not have called them."

RQ3. Can personality traits be used to predict people's privacy preferences? There were no significant correlations with age, gender, educational level, and familiarity with robots. There are very few correlations with our 6 personality traits either; we summarize the personality traits distributions in Fig. 5 and list correlations with filters and comfort level (both at the item and the category level) where they exist.

Trust: While we found no correlation between overall Trust score and privacy concerns, we did identify the following specific correlations. Trusting a worker not to break things at home by accident was inversely correlated with comfort level for tax information. Trusting the people who are known as well-behaved was inversely correlated with comfort level for pictures of pets.

Willingness of Being in Control: There were no Control-related correlations.

Sociability: While we found no correlation between overall Sociability score and privacy concerns, we did identify the following specific correlations. Hosting formal events was inversely correlated with comfort level for the Human's category. Fewer strangers (technicians) in the house was also correlated with being comfortable with the robot operator seeing a handmade gift from friends.

Familiarity with Technology: Positive correlations were found with (1) Paintings or images that indicate your religious beliefs, (2) Nail care products, (3) Handmade gifts from friends, and (4) Home cleaning products/ tools. The Skype/ Video chat question within this demographic trait was correlated with 2 categories (Paintings and Messes) and 12 specific items (1) Posters of favorite

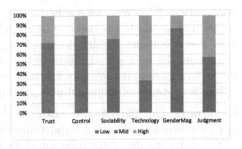

Fig. 5. Personality trait distributions

singers/artists/movies, (2) Paintings, (3) Pet pictures, (4) Religious belief paintings/images, (5) Face, hair and body care products, (6) Nail care products, (7) Expensive electronics, (8) Handmade gifts from friends, (9) Unorganized clean dishes, (10) Dirty dishes, (11) Dietary health products/supplements, and (12) Walkers/wheelchairs/walking aids.

GenderMag: In Fig. 5, Low represents the "Abby" personality, whose facet values are most frequently seen in females [5], High represents "Tim" (facet values mostly seen in males), and Mid is "Pat" (mixed facets). While we found no correlation between overall GenderMag personality and privacy concerns, we did identify the following specific correlations. Computer self-efficacy was correlated with comfort for strangers who knock on the door. Being afraid of messing things up when trying new settings of the robot was inversely correlated with comfort for home cleaning, products. Lastly, blaming the robot manufacturer when incapable of setting up the robot was correlated with the filter for jewelry and inversely correlated with comfort for unfinished home projects.

Being Afraid of Other People's Judgment: There were no Judgment-related correlations.

In addition to the above correlations, we identified a handful of correlations that appear spurious; we include them for completeness: the number of purposes for which people use their cell phones was correlated with comfort for posters of favorite singers, artists, and movies. Adapting to new technology was correlated with comfort level for nail care products. Being concerned about a worker breaking something was correlated with comfort level for tax returns. Becoming more trusting towards people who behave well in their homes was correlated with comfort level for viewing pets.

5   Discussion

We discuss our findings and limitations from the point of view of three stakeholders.

Home Robot Manufacturers: This study confirms that people are uncomfortable with some items being observable by a home robot teleoperator, specifically items that are financially valuable or can convey identifiable personal or financial information. Moreover, we learned that people do have different filtering preferences, and as the items become more privacy-sensitive, people choose a higher level of concealment. Identifying the items that people find privacy-sensitive and employing the best suited filters to hide them is vital for home robot manufacturers to ensure that they gain the trust of their users which ultimately increases public acceptance of home robots and improves human-robot social interaction.

Designers: Our participants not only chose different filters for different items, but also commented on the importance of having multiple filtering options. One of the participants (P46) mentioned "I like to have different options for controlling my privacy. Blurring and Black Box give me options for my privacy." Another participant (P64) commented "It [having different filtering techniques] would give me more comfort in my privacy, especially if I can edit what can be filtered or not." Thus, interface designers should be aware that what a robot can see or do will influence how comfortable people are, and it is vital for them to allow users to choose their own filter settings.

Researchers: As can be seen from RQ3 in Sect. 4, there are many unanswered questions about the personality traits that can help us predict humans privacy concerns (i.e., what they find privacy-sensitive and the level of concealment they wish to have to hide the items in their home). Future work will build upon the findings of this paper to focus on exploring techniques to predict privacy concerns and how to best employ them in the design of home robots.

Limitations: MTurk provides access to a variety of people, but it is still a biased population. We mitigated this by recruiting 81 participants. We attempted to cover the most common categories of items that exist in homes, but we may have missed some categories. We also employed 5 filtering techniques that demonstrate a range of levels of concealment, but many more filtering techniques may be proposed. It is possible that other personality traits (or combinations of the ones we used) would produce better correlations. However, many of our distributions were skewed to one side or the other, indicating that another explanation for lack of correlation is lack of variation in response.

6   Conclusions

We conducted a study to identify the items that people consider to be privacy-sensitive and the filters they would like to use to address their privacy concerns. Moreover, this study examined the correlation between personality traits and privacy concerns. We found correlations between comfort levels and filter choices, and these were similar for items within a category. If the categories are highly privacy-sensitive then the choice of filter skews to the higher levels of concealment. We found some correlations between personality traits and privacy concerns, and more research is warranted to efficiently predict privacy preferences.

Acknowledgment. We would like to thank Abrar Fallatah for her insights and supports.

References

1. Oxford Advanced Learner's Dictionary. Oxford University Press, Oxford (2013)
2. Merriam-Webster's Advanced Learner's English Dictionary: Merriam-Webster. Inc (2016)
3. Acquisti, A., John, L., Loewenstein, G.: What is privacy worth? In: Future of Privacy Forum's Best "Privacy Papers for Policy Makers" Competition (2010)
4. Altman, I.: Privacy regulation: culturally universal or culturally specific? J. Soc. Issues **33**(3), 66–84 (1977)
5. Burnett, M., et al.: GenderMag: a method for evaluating software's gender inclusiveness. Interact. Comput. **28**(6), 760–787 (2016)
6. Butler, D., Huang, J., Roesner, F., Cakmak, M.: The privacy-utility tradeoff for remotely teleoperated robots. In: Human-Robot Interaction. ACM, Portland, OR (2015)
7. Caine, K., Sabanovic, S., Carter, M.: The effect of monitoring by cameras and robots on the privacy enhancing behaviors of older adults. In: Human-Robot Interaction, pp. 343–350. ACM, March 2012
8. Denning, T., Matuszek, C., Koscher, K., Smith, J.R., Kohno, T.: A spotlight on security and privacy risks with future household robots: attacks and lessons. In: Ubiquitous Computing, pp. 105–114. ACM (2009)
9. Hubers, A., et al.: Using video manipulation to protect privacy in remote presence systems. Social Robotics. LNCS (LNAI), vol. 9388, pp. 245–254. Springer, Cham (2015). https://doi.org/10.1007/978-3-319-25554-5_25
10. John, L.K., Acquisti, A., Loewenstein, G.: The best of strangers: Context dependent willingness to divulge personal information (2009)
11. Klow, J., Proby, J., Rueben, M., Sowell, R.T., Grimm, C.M., Smart, W.D.: Privacy, utility, and cognitive load in remote presence systems. In: Human-Robot Interaction, pp. 167–168. ACM (2017)
12. Krupp, M.M., Rueben, M., Grimm, C.M., Smart, W.D.: A focus group study of privacy concerns about telepresence robots. In: Symposium on Robot and Human Interactive Communication, pp. 1451–1458, August 2017
13. Lee, M.K., Takayama, L.: "Now, i have a body": uses and social norms for mobile remote presence in the workplace. In: SIGCHI, pp. 33–42. ACM (2011)
14. Margulis, S.T.: On the status and contributions of Westin's and Altman's theories of privacy. J. Soc. Issues **59**(2), 411–429 (2003)
15. Marshall, N.J.: Dimensions of privacy preferences. Multivariate Behav. Res. **9**(3), 255–272 (1974)
16. Rueben, M., Bernieri, F.J., Grimm, C.M., Smart, W.D.: Framing effects on privacy concerns about a home telepresence robot. In: Human-Robot Interaction, pp. 435–444. ACM (2017)
17. Rueben, M., Grimm, C.M., Bernieri, F.J., Smart, W.D.: A taxonomy of privacy constructs for privacy-sensitive robotics. CoRR abs/1701.00841 (2017)
18. Showkat, D., Grimm, C.: Identifying gender differences in information processing style, self-efficacy, and tinkering for robot tele-operation. In: Ubiquitous Robots, pp. 443–448, June 2018
19. Syrdal, D.S., Walters, M.L., Otero, N., Koay, K.L., Dautenhahn, K.: "He knows when you are sleeping" : Privacy and the personal robot companion (2007)
20. Westin, A.F.: Privacy and Freedom. Athenaeum, New York (1967)
21. Wong, R.Y., Mulligan, D.K.: These aren't the autonomous drones you're looking for: investigating privacy concerns through concept videos. J. Hum.-Robot Interact. **5**(3), 26–54 (2016)

Privacy, Utility, and Cognitive Load in Remote Presence Systems

Jeffrey Klow[1], Jordan Proby[2], Matthew Rueben[3], Ross T. Sowell[4]($\boxtimes$),
Cindy M. Grimm[1], and William D. Smart[1]

[1] Oregon State University, Corvallis, OR 97331, USA
[2] Cornell College, Mount Vernon, IA 52314, USA
[3] University of Southern California, Los Angeles, CA 90089, USA
[4] Rhodes College, Memphis, TN 38112, USA
sowellr@rhodes.edu

Abstract. As robotics technology improves, remotely-operated telepresence robots will become more prevalent in homes and businesses, allowing guests, business partners, and contractors to visit and accomplish tasks without being physically present. These devices raise new privacy concerns: a telepresence robot may be used by a remote operator to spy on the local area, or recorded video may be viewed by a third party. Video filtering is one method of reducing spying ability while still allowing the remote operator to perform their task. In this paper, we examine the effects of three different visual conditions (filters) on the remote operator's ability to discern details while completing a navigation task. We found that applying such filters protected privacy without significantly affecting the operator's ability to perform the task, and that a depth image filter was the most effective privacy protector. We also found that the cognitive load of driving the robot has a slight privacy-protecting effect.

Keywords: Privacy-sensitive robotics · Privacy interfaces · Remote presence systems · Image filters

1 Introduction

As robotics technology improves, robots in the home and workplace will become much more common. In particular, we are already seeing advances in remote presence technologies, such as the Double 2 [3], VGo [13], and Beam [12]. These systems go beyond basic phone and video calling to allow someone to not just see, hear, and talk, but to also move around and explore a remote environment as if they were there. While early applications have been focused on telecommuting, education, and health care, remotely teleoperated robots are now being developed for many different purposes including package delivery, construction surveying, and janitorial tasks.

Along with exciting new capabilities, these systems also raise new privacy concerns. In traditional voice and video calling, the local user has some inherent

© Springer Nature Switzerland AG 2019
M. A. Salichs et al. (Eds.): ICSR 2019, LNAI 11876, pp. 730–739, 2019.
https://doi.org/10.1007/978-3-030-35888-4_68

control over their own privacy because the remote person can only see what the local user points their camera at. In remote presence systems, the remote person is in control of the camera, can move the robot around, and, depending on the capabilities of the robot, manipulate the environment. Many of the potential benefits of having a remotely operated robot are lost if the local user must be present to make sure that the robot only sees and touches the things that it is supposed to see and touch.

In this paper we explore a "privacy by design" [2] approach where we restrict the viewing capabilities of the remote user *at the local end*. In contrast to previous work that relies on object detection and tracking (which may fail) to obscure selected objects, our goal is to record video in only as much detail as is necessary to accomplish the task, and no more.

One potential drawback to this approach is that our efforts to protect privacy might diminish the utility of our robot. There is a natural trade-off between privacy and utility [1]. At one extreme we could blindfold our robot and not allow it to move. This would maximize privacy protection, but the robot would be prevented from accomplishing many useful tasks. On the other hand, we could permit the robot to freely move and share data from all of its sensors with the robot operator. This may maximize utility—but would offer no privacy protections.

Fig. 1. Four visual conditions, from left to right: No filter, Depth image, standard Sobel, Combined (Combo) Sobel. Note the features of the book and ease of determining where the box is in each case.

To explore the trade-offs of this approach, we present a user study that examines the effects of data filtering on both teleoperated robot utility and privacy protections afforded by such filters. Our specific contributions are: (1) A user study evaluating the effects of data filtering on both privacy protection *and* the ability to perform a navigation task; and (2) An examination of the privacy-protecting effects of cognitive load for drivers of remotely-operated robots.

2   Related Work

The construct of privacy has been examined from a number of different disciplines ranging from anthropology to sociology [8]. No universal definition or operational-ization for privacy exists. For this paper, we exclusively refer to informational pri-vacy, as outlined in the privacy taxonomy proposed by Rueben et al. [11]. We are concerned only with obscuring text, images, and similar sensitive information from the remote operator of the robot. Certain filters may additionally protect social privacy by preventing identification of nearby individuals, thereby providing a degree of anonymity, but we do not focus on this effect.

There is a small, but growing, body of work on implementing and evaluating tools for protecting visual privacy by obscuring things in the robot's video feed. Jana et al. [6] present a privacy tool for simplifying videos to only the necessary information. Although no user study is conducted, the tool is shown to preserve utility and protect privacy through a simple analysis. Raval et al. [9] present two more video privacy tools. One uses markers to specify private areas, and the other uses hand gestures for the same purpose. Rueben et al. [10] report on a user study comparing three different interfaces for specifying visual privacy preferences to a robot. Butler et al. [1] coin the term "privacy-utility tradeoff" and test a pick-and-place task with the PR2 robot; Hubers et al. [5] did similar tests for a patrol surveillance task with the Turtlebot 2 robot. Both studies found it feasible to complete the tasks with effective privacy filters in place.

One of the difficulties with many of the previous approaches is that the privacy protections that they provide rely on accurate object detection and tracking, and on robot localization. Failure to detect an object or correctly estimate its size results in insufficient (or wholly absent) privacy protections. Further, drawing on the recording concerns noted by Lee et al. [7], the robot's owner may assume that the robot is always recording. In such a case, even a single-frame object detection or localization error would reveal the entirety of the private object.

In contrast, our approach applies data filtering by default to the entire image rather than a selected object. Butler et al. [1] also filter the entire transmitted image but only evaluate it on a simple remote manipulation task with a stationary robot. The study presented in this paper is the first to evaluate the effects of live, real-time data filtering on a remote operator's ability to perform a navigation task with a mobile robot.

We are also interested in exploring the effects of cognitive load on privacy protection. Wickens et al. [14] indicate that, as an individual's cognitive load increases beyond a certain point, their performance on the tasks making up that load decreases. It follows that the difficulty of driving an unfamiliar robot, with or without visual modifications, may have some effect on the driver's ability to notice or identify objects near the robot.

3   Experiment

The focus of this study is on the influence of various visual conditions on the remote operator's ability to perform a navigation task while noticing (and potentially identifying) items in their surroundings.

3.1 Hypotheses

We make the following hypotheses:

- H1: Data filters can be applied to the video feed of a robot in real time while still allowing the operator to complete an assigned navigation task.
- H2: Data filters are capable of protecting the privacy of the robot owner's local area by reducing the operator's ability to notice or identify objects in that area.
- H3: The increased cognitive load of driving the robot will protect privacy by rendering the operator "too busy" to notice or identify objects in the area.

3.2 Task and Environment

Participants completed a navigation task that asked them to: (1) locate two landmarks (beach balls) in an unfamiliar environment; (2) remotely drive a robot to each of these positions in turn; and (3) return to the starting position. The experimental space was set up as an "obstacle course", cluttered with objects such as toys and computer accessories. While navigating through the course, the participant was asked to talk about what they were seeing and thinking. Immediately afterward, the participant was shown a recording of their most recent drive and again asked to comment in the same manner. This was repeated for a total of four drive-review pairs, each with one of the four visual conditions described in Sect. 3.3.

Four layouts were created to help mitigate any learning effect. Each measured approximately 3 m by 5 m and contained several cardboard boxes to act as obstacles. The boxes were placed such that the drivable space was an "X" or "H" shape, ensuring that the distance driven was approximately equal in both layouts. Two beach balls were placed in opposite corners within each layout such that the robot did not have line-of-sight to either of them from its starting position in a third corner.

As a substitute for sensitive information such as credit cards or legal documents, we chose to place books throughout the space. Five books were used, placed in each layout such that the robot was nearly certain to see all five while completing the task.

3.3 Visual Conditions

We evaluated three visual filters, illustrated in Fig. 1 and the supplementary video,[1] chosen for their simplicity and for their potential to hide details while still providing spatial context.

1. Unfiltered (**Control**): A grayscale video stream. This condition represents the maximum utility side of the privacy-utility tradeoff. Grayscale was used instead of color to match the other conditions, which lacked color.

---

[1] https://youtu.be/7WMVzb1h1DA.

2. Depth image (**Depth**): The Kinect's depth camera value, mapped to grayscale. Closer objects appear darker. This preserves spatial structure but hides texture, such as text.
3. Sobel filter (**Sobel**): A standard Sobel operator was applied to the video feed. Strong edges appear as dark lines while flat areas appear white. This preserves both spatial structure *and* texture, reducing privacy protections.
4. Combined Sobel (**Combo**): The Sobel operator combined with the Depth filter. The lighter pixel from both is kept. This refines the Sobel filter by largely removing texture from the video feed.

3.4   Apparatus and Implementation

A Turtlebot 2 robot running the Robot Operating System (ROS) [4] was used for this study. Video filters were coded as standalone ROS nodes, written in C++ and using the OpenCV library. During the study, the user was provided with a second laptop connected via private wifi network to the Turtlebot computer.

3.5   Design

Each participant experienced all four layouts and all four filters. The order in which the filters were presented was counterbalanced with each possible permutation of the four filters being assigned at most once. The order of layouts was counterbalanced in the same manner. For each participant, the specific filter and layout permutations were selected independently and at random from the pool of the ones not yet used.

3.6   Procedure

Participants were greeted in the hallway outside the testing space. After the consent process, they completed an optional demographic survey which included two questions asking about frequency of video game playing and prior experience with remote-controlled robots. While these were completed, the experimenter entered the testing room to fetch the robot for a short driving practice. At this point, it was verbally explained that driving a robot was the primary activity of the study, and that the video from each drive is recorded.

Next, the participant was given the opportunity to examine the robot and drive it around in the hallway to practice. Users were additionally asked to drive into the testing room and run into a beach ball. This was intended to improve spatial awareness of the robot and its surroundings prior to actual testing. After colliding with the beach ball, the user was allowed to drive about until they felt confident enough to proceed. Most users spent approximately 5 min on this practice (which used the Control visual condition).

Following the test drive, a short video of the various visual conditions was shown, with an explanation of the basic features of each being given. After that the participant was given a brief introduction to the talk-aloud protocol used during the study, along with a short example video of what a typical trial might look like. In particular, we asked participants to comment on everything they saw. The participant was also informed that the robot always begins a trial looking at a corner, and that their task is to locate two beach balls, bump into them, and return to their starting position.

The participant was then given control of the robot and asked to begin the first trial. If the participant stopped talking for approximately five seconds, the experimenter prompted them to resume with "What do you see?" or "Tell me about what's happening."

Upon finishing the first task, the participant was shown a recording of their drive and asked to again talk-aloud as they watched it. This was repeated for the remaining three trials.

3.7 Measures

For the driving component, we recorded whether or not the participant completed the task successfully, how long it took for them to complete the task, how many times they collided with other objects, and how many books they noticed or could identify. The user is considered to have succeeded at the task if they were able to bump into both of the beach balls and navigate back to within 0.5 m of their starting position. During the review phase, we recorded how many books the participant was able to notice or identify.

For the purposes of this study, we define "notice" to mean that the user has commented on the object and was able to recognize it as a member of a broad class of objects, such as books or toys. We define "identify" to mean that the user commented on the object and correctly labeled it as some specific object or entity, such as a toy elephant or reading a book's title. We consider identification of a book to be a breach of privacy, as the visual modifications of the data filters were unable to prevent the driver from reading potentially-sensitive text. On the other hand, we do not consider simply noticing that an object is a book to be a breach of privacy, as awareness of an object's general type and location is likely to be helpful in preventing collisions and completing the navigation task.

3.8 Participants

We recruited 21 participants from the Mount Vernon, Iowa area via recruitment fliers in public spaces, postings in a local Facebook group, and the Cornell College email newsletter. Participants were compensated $10. The mean age was 40 years old (S.D. 16). 62% of respondents identified as female and 62% identified as male. With regards to familiarity with robots and other remotely-operated devices, 57% reported "Not at all familiar," while 38% reported "slightly familiar" and only one reported "very familiar." In reporting the frequency with which they played video games, 76% reported "hardly ever." Of the remainder, two reported "a few times per week," two reported "a few times per month," and only one reported "daily." We found no evidence that these factors correlated with any of our recorded metrics.

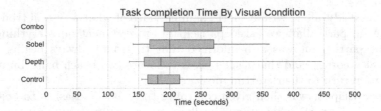

Fig. 2. Time Required for Task Completion. The increase in time taken over the control condition is only statistically significant for the Combo filter.

4   Results

4.1   H1: Utility

85.5% of users successfully completed the task, with no statistically significant difference between the control and any of the filtered visual conditions (as measured by a 1-sample t-test against the control mean). Collision rates were also not statistically significantly different across all three filter conditions, averaging 1.3 collisions per drive. The average time to complete the trial in the control condition was 198 s. In the three filter conditions, completion took longer, as shown in Fig. 2, but this difference was only statistically significant in the case of the Combo filter, at an average of 238 s per trial ($d = .656$, $p = .023$).

4.2   H2: Privacy

In the control condition, participants noticed an average of 3.29 books and identified an average of 1.10 (see Fig. 3). Participants noticed and identified fewer books in all filter conditions, averaging 1.61 fewer books noticed and 0.93 fewer identified. This effect was more pronounced during the review video talk-aloud; in the control condition participants noticed an average 3.80 books and identified 1.20 (presumably due to the decreased cognitive load of not having to drive the robot). In the filter conditions, they noticed an average of 1.75 fewer books and identified 1.07 fewer. All of these differences were statistically significantly different (all $d > 1.1$, all $p < .001$).

Evaluating the individual visual conditions, the Depth image condition had the most dramatic effect on performance, with 2.38 fewer objects noticed on average during the drive and 2.60 fewer noticed upon review. The Combo condition resulted in 1.75 fewer objects noticed on average during the drive and 1.84 fewer upon review. Both showed similar reduced identification rates, with 1.1 fewer identifications on average during the drive and 1.2 fewer during review (all $p < .001$). The Sobel filter showed weakest performance in all areas, with an average of 0.91 fewer notices during the drive ($p = .057$) and 0.80 fewer notices upon review ($p = .028$). Identification rates were similarly lower at 0.62 fewer during driving ($p = .023$) and 0.75 fewer upon review ($p = .005$).

All results in this section were obtained using a paired t-test comparing, on a per-participant basis, notice and identification rates during the drives and reviews of each condition against the corresponding rates in the control trial.

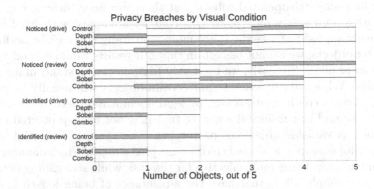

Fig. 3. Privacy Results. Note the effectiveness of the Depth image across all metrics. Also note the differences between the Noticed drive and review and the similarity between Identification drive and review.

4.3 H3: Cognitive Load

The cognitive load imposed by having to drive the robot only resulted in 0.5 fewer objects being noticed compared to the review video, averaged across all conditions ($p < .001$). Identification rates were virtually identical, with only 0.01 additional objects identified, on average, during review.

With respect to individual visual conditions, the greatest cognitive load effect was seen in the control condition, with 0.55 additional books noticed during the review compared to the drive ($p = .012$). The only other significant effect was seen in the Combo condition, an increase of 0.4 books ($p = .028$). The differences in notice rates with respect to the other two visual conditions were not statistically significant, nor were any effects on the identification rates from any individual filter.

These results were calculated using a paired t-test comparing each user's notice and identification rates during each drive against the rates for the corresponding review.

5 Discussion

Our first finding is that using visual filters did not affect task performance, but did increase task time. This was most pronounced in the Combo filter, possibly because it was unfamiliar. The filters were effective at reducing privacy violations with the depth image performing the best.

Threats to Generalizability: It is possible that our task and/or environment were too "simple" to tease out task performance differences. We tested a single navigation task, useful for determining the operator's ability to construct a mental map of the space and move through it without collisions. This is an essential task in mobile teleoperated robots, but there are many others, e.g., object manipulation. Our study took place in a constructed space with fixed layouts. While we attempted to make the space more "naturally chaotic" by adding various clutter objects, we cannot be certain that our results would extend to a real living room or office. Similarly, we used only textbooks as a stand-in for private information. While we can assume that certain objects will usually be privacy-sensitive, such as credit cards, books, or legal documents, there are many other objects that could be considered sensitive that may not be as protected by these filters, such as valuable objects or prototypes. The space of potential filters is also large—for example, a blurred color image plus a depth edge enhancer—with some combinations being more effective for the task while still eliding detail. We chose to test simple filters that have the advantages of being low-cost, easy to implement, require low battery usage, etc., but we expect that many additional filters exist or can be developed that would potentially be more effective for particular tasks.

We observed a difference in task completion time between the user's first trial and all subsequent trials, indicating that our initial training was insufficient (first: 252 s, second: 214, $p = .003$). The third and fourth trial times were not statistically different from the second.

There is a small, but noticeable, decrease in detection rates while driving the robot versus reviewing the video. This has implications for conducting tasks via telepresence; we hypothesize that the cognitive load of driving the robot reduced the participant's ability to observe items not related to the driving task.

We only considered benign operators and "accidental" breaches of privacy. Further work—and a different study design—would be needed to determine if these filters are sufficient to protect against "snooping" during the task.

6   Conclusion

We conducted a user study to examine the effects of data filtering on a remote operator's ability to perform a navigation task and discern details about the robot's surroundings. We found that, when the user's view is filtered, they were slightly slower to complete their assigned task but no more likely to collide with objects or fail the task. The applied filters all reduced the operator's ability to notice nearby objects or correctly identify them when compared to an unfiltered drive. Of the three visual conditions, the depth image filter best protected privacy. Additionally, when users watched recordings of their own previous driving trials, they noticed slightly more objects but were no more or less likely to correctly identify them.

Acknowledgements. This work was supported by the US National Science Foundation, under award CNS 1359480.

References

1. Butler, D., Huang, J., Roesner, F., Cakmak, M.: The privacy-utility tradeoff for remotely teleoperated robots. In: Proceedings of the 10th ACM/IEEE International Conference on Human-Robot Interaction (HRI). Portland, OR (2015)
2. Cavoukian, A.: Privacy by design: The 7 foundational principles (2016). http://www.privacybydesign.ca/index.php/about-pbd/7-foundational-principles/. Information and Privacy Commissioner of Ontario
3. Double Robotics: Double robotics - telepresence robot for telecommuters (2019). http://www.doublerobotics.com/
4. Foundation OSR: indigo - ros wiki (2014). http://wiki.ros.org/indigo
5. Hubers, A., et al.: Using video manipulation to protect privacy in remote presence systems. Social Robotics. LNCS (LNAI), vol. 9388, pp. 245–254. Springer, Cham (2015). https://doi.org/10.1007/978-3-319-25554-5_25
6. Jana, S., Narayanan, A., Shmatikov, V.: A scanner darkly: protecting user privacy from perceptual applications. In: Proceedings of the 2013 IEEE Symposium on Security and Privacy SP 2013, pp. 349–363. IEEE Computer Society, Washington (2013). https://doi.org/10.1109/SP.2013.31, http://dx.doi.org/10.1109/SP.2013.31
7. Lee, M.K., Tang, K.P., Forlizzi, J., Kiesler, S.: Understanding users' perception of privacy in human-robot interaction. In: 2011 6th ACM/IEEE International Conference on Human-Robot Interaction (HRI), pp. 181–182. IEEE (2011)
8. Newell, P.B.: Perspectives on privacy. J. Environ. Psychol. **15**, 87–104 (1995)
9. Raval, N., Srivastava, A., Lebeck, K., Cox, L., Machanavajjhala, A.: Markit: privacy markers for protecting visual secrets. In: UbiComp 2014 - Adjunct Proceedings of the 2014 ACM International Joint Conference on Pervasive and Ubiquitous Computing, pp. 1289–1295 (2014). https://doi.org/10.1145/2638728.2641707
10. Rueben, M., Bernieri, F.J., Grimm, C.M., Smart, W.D.: Evaluation of physical marker interfaces for protecting visual privacy from mobile robots. In: 2016 25th IEEE International Symposium on Robot and Human Interactive Communication (RO-MAN), pp. 787–794, August 2016. https://doi.org/10.1109/ROMAN.2016.7745209
11. Rueben, M., Grimm, C.M., Bernieri, F.J., Smart, W.D.: A taxonomy of privacy constructs for privacy-sensitive robotics. CoRR abs/1701.00841 (2017). http://arxiv.org/abs/1701.00841
12. Suitable Technologies Inc.: We're transforming human interaction in an increasingly virtual world (2019). https://suitabletech.com/
13. VGo: Vgo robotic telepresence for healthcare, education, and business (2019). http://www.vgocom.com/
14. Wickens, C., Hollands, J., Banbury, S., Parasuraman, R.: Engineering Psychology and Human Performance. Pearson, London (2013)

How a Robot's Social Credibility Affects Safety Performance

Patrick Holthaus$^{(\boxtimes)}$ ⓘ, Catherine Menon ⓘ, and Farshid Amirabdollahian ⓘ

Adaptive Systems Research Group, School of Engineering and Computer Science,
University of Hertfordshire, Hatfield AL10 9AB, UK
{p.holthaus,c.menon,f.amirabdollahian2}@herts.ac.uk

Abstract. This paper connects the two domains of Human-Robot Interaction (HRI) and safety engineering to ensure that the design of interactive robots considers the effect of social behaviours on safety functionality. We conducted a preliminary user study with a social robot that alerts participants during a puzzle-solving task to a safety hazard. Our study findings show an indicative trend where users who were interrupted by a socially credible robot were more likely to act to mitigate the hazard than users interrupted by a robot lacking social credibility.

Keywords: Human-robot interaction · Social credibility · Robot safety

1 Introduction

In HRI, the social capabilities of interactive robots are of primary interest due to their impact on acceptability. Social capabilities such as proxemics, gestures, head orientation and gaze direction have been shown to improve a robot's interaction quality [4], to lead to a better user understanding of their behaviours [17], and to facilitate the ways in which robots can learn from humans [5]. Similarly, lack of appropriate social capabilities can cause end-users to resist or minimise engagement with the robot [14]. An ongoing research challenge in this area is to identify appropriate domain-specific social behaviours that meet the user expectations for a robot. Such social behaviours need to be consistent with the environment, the robot's other functionality, and the intended course of the interaction. We refer to robots which demonstrate a well integrated compilation of such social behaviours as being socially *credible* [19].

As well as social behaviours, another area of concern is the safety performance of interactive robots. Within the UK, the Health and Safety Executive requires that the risk posed by such systems should be reduced "As Low As Reasonably Practicable" [11]. This requires a consideration of the risks that an interactive robot might pose, as well as functions that it can perform safely [13]. In a domestic context,

Supported by the Assuring Autonomy International Programme and the University of Hertfordshire's Robot House.

M. A. Salichs et al. (Eds.): ICSR 2019, LNAI 11876, pp. 740–749, 2019.
https://doi.org/10.1007/978-3-030-35888-4_69

one of the primary safety functions performed by an interactive assistive robot is alerting the user to potential hazards. For example, the robot might remind the user to take necessary medication if this is overdue, or alert the user to an oven which has been left on. In this way, the robot and human act together to mitigate hazards which arise externally. Identifying safety functionality is an ongoing research area in robotics, as is identification of the ways in which robots might mitigate hazards present in the environment.

Our work brings together the two domains of HRI and safety engineering to ensure that the design of interactive robots considers both safety functionality and social behaviours. Both of these must be *designed into* the robot, and safety and social requirements can interact in complex ways.

Current assistive robots are being designed with both safety and social considerations in mind. For example, the Care-O-Bot 4 has been constructed to take account of both end-user acceptability and safety considerations [10]. In addition, international safety standards such as ISO 13482 [13] consider the hazards presented by such robots when undertaking their specified behaviour (which may include social actions). However, owing to the comparative rarity and novelty of domestic interactive robots, there has not yet been significant academic work looking specifically at how safety and social behaviours might interact with each other. Safety standards promote a design-for-safety approach which, if considered in isolation, may negatively influence the possible social behaviours which the robot can demonstrate. Similarly, designing for social behaviours alone may not adequately consider the safety requirements of these robots and the behaviours needed to fulfill them.

It is our position that both safety and social considerations can have an effect on each other, with the social behaviours of the robot affecting its safety performance and vice versa [19]. In this paper, we seek to identify a connection between a robot's social actions and the effectiveness of its safety performance. Specifically, we hypothesise that social deficiencies in a robot can undermine its perceived authority when alerting a user to hazards in the domestic environment, and consequently reduce its fitness to serve as a safety monitoring device in the home. As a first approach, we present a preliminary study that investigates user responses when notified of a safety hazard by either a socially credible robot, or a robot that lacks social credibility. The study aims to provide an initial link between a robot's social credibility and user willingness to act on its safety-related alert functions. Our study findings show an indicative trend that users who were alerted to an environmental hazard by a socially credible robot are more likely to act on this alert and mitigate the hazard than users alerted to it by a robot lacking social credibility.

2   Related Work

This section introduces concepts we rely on and explore in the conducted experiment. We discuss socially appropriate and credible behaviours as well as safety in HRI and related domains. Existing research that connects both areas has historically been limited to the phenomenon of trust in social robots. [7]

explores the relation of robot performance and behavioural style on a user's trust. Likewise, [24] shows that the task-type has an influence on whether a person follows robot orders. Standards such as ISO 13482 [13] do consider the need to build safety into social robots from the beginning, but are still relatively new.

2.1 Socially Appropriate Behaviours

Interactive robots are often equipped with social behaviours to improve various performance aspects in their respective domain [6]. Verbal and non-verbal behaviours can have a positive effect on people's perceived interaction quality when they are easy to comprehend [17] and meet expectations [2].

People have, for example, personal preferences when asked about comfortable interaction distances and angles [28]. Yet, they apply similar metrics to robots as to humans [16]. It has been further shown that human-like body orientations before and during face-to-face interaction have a positive effect on the perceived interaction quality [12]. Robot navigation that respects human personal space [15] and employs appropriate passing distances is also believed to increase the acceptance of robots in the home and public [23]. Head orientation and gaze can be used to demonstrate a robot's current focus of attention [22] and facilitate social bonds with humans [1]. Differences in robot politeness are easily detected by humans but are not necessarily influencing the interaction quality [25]. However, a positive effect of polite utterances on user engagement can be identified [9].

2.2 Safety and Human Interactions

Although not looking specifically at interactive robots, much work exists on the efficacy of safety-critical (partially) autonomous systems which alert users to hazards or act in coordination with users to mitigate hazards. Such systems include sat-navs, speed monitoring systems, cockpit monitoring systems, automated vehicle operational alerts and medical devices. For all of these systems a known risk is user disengagement: if the user ceases to engage with or pay attention to the system, they are unable to mitigate hazards identified by the system.

Studies have shown that the method of alert or interruption used by the system has significant implications for user disengagement. In [29], users chose to switch off a speed monitoring and sat-nav system that they found "irritating", even while acknowledging that the speed warnings improved safety. Still in the automotive domain, there have been a number of accidents involving automated vehicles which are in part due to user disengagement with the systems. [20] discusses the case of a Tesla crash in automated mode, in which the user had failed to engage with the system despite repeated warnings and [21] discusses a similar case, where repeated warnings were ignored. In [26], it was found that when a cockpit alert was given, pilots would attempt to debug the automation instead of acting on the alert. This was attributed to the fact that the pilots were monitoring status via the flight control unit (which shows commanded paths, rather than actual) instead of the automation. The alert contradicted their perspective of the system, and was judged to be a failure of automation.

3 Method

We conducted a preliminary study with 30 participants that investigates their responses when notified of different safety hazards by either a socially credible robot, or a robot that explicitly violates these social norms. The study aims to establish a link between a robot's social credibility and its authority regarding safety-related functions. We thereby hypothesise a negative effect of a lack of social credibility on the willingness of humans to follow safety-related alerts and the thoroughness of their actions. The experiment was approved by the University of Hertfordshire's Health, Science, Engineering and Technology Ethics Committee under protocol number COM/SF/UH/03714.

3.1 Experimental Design

We manipulated two independent variables of which one varied in two and the other in three dimensions so that we ended up with a 2×3 experiment design. As we assume an effect of the manipulation on thoroughness regarding safety warnings given by the robot, we used a combination of questionnaires as well as response types and timings to hazard warnings as measurements.

Independent Variables. The first variable describes the character of the robot's social behaviour, which was either *According to social Norms (AN)* as described in Sect. 2.1 or *Violating social Norms (VN)*. This variable is designed as two conditions between subjects (15 participants per condition). In total, we altered the robot behaviour in the following characteristics: (a) its distance during greeting (appropriate vs too far) (b) its passing distance during puzzle solving (appropriate vs too close) (c) its position during interruption (frontal vs from behind) (d) its head position during interruption (up vs down) (e) its verbal interruptions and confirmations (impolite vs polite, cf. Table 1). All other behaviour, including verbal hazard alerts were unanimous in both conditions to ensure a proper understanding of the alert.

Table 1. Robot utterances by condition

Utterance	According (AN)	Violating (VN)
Interrupt	Excuse me?	Hey!
Greet	Hello and welcome to Robot House	Another one, then
Begin	Please sit down and begin your puzzle now	You can sit down and begin your puzzle now
Action	Thank you	Good
No Action	–	Good
Ending	Please wait for the experimenter now	They are coming to see you now

Fig. 1. Participant manipulation areas. The *oven*, switchable *power plugs* with appliances and the *Pepper* with its information display are depicted left to right.

We further assumed a difference in the perceived severity of various hazards (cf. Sect. 2.2). Accordingly, we introduced a second independent variable as three successive experiment phases, with each participant experiencing all phases. During each phase (cf. Sect. 3.2), the robot notified the participant of one of the following safety hazards: (*severe*) The *oven* in the kitchen has been left on; (*minor*) Some *power plugs* in the kitchen have been left on; and (*moderate*) The *Pepper* robot in the bedroom is overheating. Figure 1 depicts the three manipulation areas for the participants.

Dependent Variables. We measured the following dependent variables for each participant to investigate our hypothesis: (1) their assessment of severity for each hazard (2) their perception of the robot as a social agent (3) their willingness and thoroughness to react to robot warnings.

The questionnaire that was given to each participant after the experiment was composed of multiple parts: Firstly, demographic information of age, gender and prior experience with robots was gathered. Following were semantic-differential questions (safe-dangerous) that assessed the physical safety of the three different hazards *oven*, *power plugs*, or *Pepper* overheating to measure the first dependent variable (1). We then included two questionnaires to verify our experimental conditions and investigate dependent variable (2): The Robotic Social Attributes Scale (RoSAS) [8] and the *GodSpeed* questionnaire [3] followed by individual Likert-style questions [18] about the robot's sociability. We added further Likert-style questions to verify people attributed the robot an understanding of safety-relevant situations. Lastly, we asked participants open questions about reasons why they decided to act or not to act to investigate variable (3).

Besides using subjective questionnaires, we measured dependent variable (3) with objective criteria, i.e. (I) whether participants actively responded to the utterance by standing up and (II) the amount of time spent to perform an action that eliminates the hazard. Criterium (I) was observed and annotated using the live video feed while (II) was measured using the robot house sensory infrastructure. In case of the *oven*, no timings were available. The *power plugs* timings were measured four times (cf. Sect. 3.2) and averaged.

3.2   Experimental Procedure

Environment. The study was carried out in the Robot House, a four-bedroom home near the university campus used for human-robot experiments. Besides standard furniture and appliances found in a typical house, it is also equipped with smart home sensors and actuators. In the current experiment, we used an omni-directional ceiling camera to monitor and record the interaction. We also manipulated and recorded the kitchen's power plugs to measure participants' responses to robot prompts. As the main interaction medium we opted to use a *Fetch Mobile Manipulator* (*Fetch*) robot [30]. In addition, *Pepper* [27] serves as a secondary robot that poses a potential safety hazard (cf. Sect. 3.1). It remains non-interactive in a standing posture throughout the experiment. It displays pseudo sensory data and a shutdown button that triggers a resting position on its screen. We tasked the participants with doing cognitive puzzles (Sudoku) to keep them occupied and give them a valid reason for ignoring the robot.

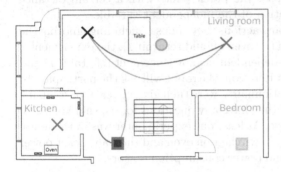

Fig. 2. Overview of experimentation area. Participants solved the task and filled out the questionnaire at the position of the green circle. The (initial) robot positions are indicated with blue squares. Brown crosses indicate searching locations for the robot. The *oven* and switchable *power plugs* are also marked inside the kitchen. (Color figure online)

Course of Action. Participants were given the information sheet and were asked if they had any queries or questions. They could begin the experiment upon consent to participate.

We then introduced each participant to the house (cf. Fig. 2) starting with the kitchen. We pointed them towards all visible appliances, mentioning the oven and switchable power sockets amongst others. We explained that the robot has remote access to the sensors and knows about their state, for example whether the oven and power sockets are on. We also pointed at the *Pepper* robot in the bedroom from afar and mentioned that it was plugged in and currently charging.

Following this, we showed participants the *Fetch* robot that would be used for the experiment, and ran through basic safety information. We explained that the participant should sit at the living room table, completing as many cognitive tasks (i.e., Sudoku puzzles) as possible in the allotted time. We told them that the robot may interrupt them at times, and that should they wish to, they may choose to perform an action in response to this interruption. We told them that it was up to them to decide whether to perform an action or not, but that if they did perform an action, then when this was completed they should return to their position sitting at the table again.

We then left the room and the *Fetch* robot performed its initial greeting behaviour for the participant using the utterance according to the current condition (cf. Table 1). The robot told the participant to sit and begin with their Sudoku puzzles, and then followed the procedure below for each phase (*oven*, *power plugs* x2, *Pepper*):

1. Go to parking position in the living room and wait 30 s.
2. Inspect the area by turning around and moving the camera head around.
3. Navigate to the location in which the robot finds a possible threat (kitchen in case of *oven* and *power plugs*, looking towards bedroom in case of *Pepper*)
4. Inspect the area with the head again.
5. Navigate to participant, interrupt and alert them about the item in question.

As part of its behaviour the robot navigates to an alternative position behind the participant before the second interruption (*power plugs* 1). We do this for two reasons: Firstly, all participants experience a robot that moves behind their back. Secondly, the robot has to pass the participants with a certain distance which contributes to the manipulation of the independent variable.

After the participant has taken any actions they choose (including ignoring the robot or leaving the room to switch the oven off and returning), the experimenter will trigger a condition- and action-dependent acknowledgement (cf. Table 1) and the next phase begins. After the last iteration, the robot will ask the participant to wait for the experimenter. The questionnaires were then given to each participant. Finally, we asked the participant if they have any questions for us, thanked them for their time, and helped them leave. At least one experimenter was in the house at all times, to monitor the robot, the switched-on oven and the wall socket power switches with the help of cameras and power consumption sensors.

4   Results

As this study was a preliminary study, and thus low participant numbers, no statistical significance between conditions was expected for the evaluation of the questionnaires. In this section, we instead report tendencies and trends we can identify in the collected data.

Participant's Assessment of Severity. While there is no apparent difference between the two social conditions, variances for *power plugs* are higher for *AN* and variances for *Pepper* are higher for *VN*. Across conditions, ratings regarding the danger differ between the types of hazards, see Fig. 3. Distinct differences are noticable between *oven* and *power plugs*. Potential danger is also rated high for *Pepper*.

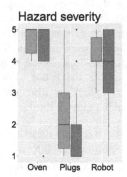

Fig. 3. Safety ratings per condition (*AN* left, *VN* right) for every warning. The boxes display scores on a 5-point scale (1: safe; 5: dangerous) for each device (*oven*, *power plugs*, *Pepper*).

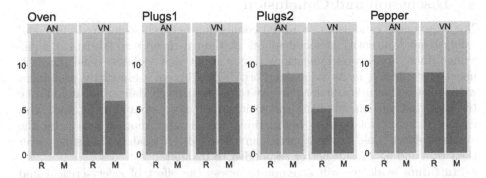

Fig. 4. Participant responses to hazard warnings. The bars depict absolute response rates for each warning (*oven, power plugs* x2, *Pepper*) grouped by condition (*AN/VN*). The first column gives the number of people who responded [R] to the utterance by standing up and exploring the area. The second column denotes whether participants carried out the intended physical manipulation [M] at the target object.

Perception of the Robot as a Social Agent.

Although we do not observe significant differences between the two social conditions, tendencies indicate that *AN* is performing better in every item of the *GodSpeed* and RoSAS questionnaire. The following mean values and standard deviation have been recorded: Anthropomorphism *AN*: 3 (0.87) *VN*: 2.75 (0.64), Animacy *AN*: 3.23 (0.78) *VN*: 2.98 (0.77), Likeability *AN*: 3.96 (0.55) *VN*: 3.58 (0.67), Perceived Intelligence *AN*: 4.23 (0.45) *VN*: 3.96 (0.46), Warmth *AN*: 2.7 (1.07) *VN*: 2.79 (1.22), Competence *AN*: 4.57 (1.02) *VN*: 4.34 (1.22), Discomfort *AN*: 1.8 (0.75) *VN*: 2.29 (0.97).

Willingness and Thoroughness to React to Robot Warnings.

Results show a general tendency for people in the *AN* condition to respond better to the robot's hazard warnings (cf. Fig. 4), in particular at the second *power plugs* phase. Furthermore, there is a noticeable decline in response rate compared to the first *power plugs* warning. In the *AN* condition it seems that participants almost always performed an action whenever they showed a reaction as opposed to the *VN* condition where they sometimes reacted but decided against the manipulation of objects. Participants in the *VN* condition additionally took longer on average before switching off any *power plugs* if they did (cf. Fig. 5). *Pepper* was switched off after approximately the same time period.

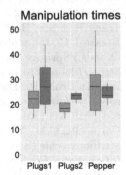

Manipulation times

Fig. 5. Manipulation times per condition (*AN* left, *VN* right) for each hazard warning. The boxes display the time in seconds people needed to shut off a device (*power plugs* x2 and *Pepper*) if they manipulated the object.

5 Discussion and Conclusion

The experiment establishes an initial connection between social credibility and safety-related authority of social robots. Although there is no statistical significance, there are several indications that a robot that violates social norms is negatively affected in its safety authority. This becomes especially prominent with hazards that users do not perceive to be particularly dangerous. It could be the case that participants liked the social robot more, wanted to interact with it, and therefore followed its instructions accordingly. Another reason for the observed effect could be that participants trusted AN's safety assessment over their own and as a result better responded to its alerts.

In future work, we will attempt to assess the effect of safety-critical and safety-related alerts on the rated sociability of the robot with a full fledged study, where current results provide size-effect calculations for the next study's sample-size needed to achieve a reasonable power.

References

1. Admoni, H., Scassellati, B.: Social eye gaze in human-robot interaction: a review. J. Hum.-Robot Interact. **6**(1), 25–63 (2017)
2. Bartneck, C., Forlizzi, J.: A design-centred framework for social human-robot interaction. In: RO-MAN 2004. 13th IEEE International Workshop on Robot and Human Interactive Communication, pp. 591–594. IEEE (2004)
3. Bartneck, C., Kulić, D., Croft, E., Zoghbi, S.: Measurement instruments for the anthropomorphism, animacy, likeability, perceived intelligence, and perceived safety of robots. Int. J. Soc. Robot. **1**(1), 71–81 (2009)
4. Bensch, S., Jevtić, A., Hellström, T.: On Interaction Quality in Human-Robot Interaction, February 2017
5. Breazeal, C.: Role of expressive behaviour for robots that learn from people. Philos. Trans. Roy. Soc. B: Biol. Sci. **364**(1535), 3527–3538 (2009)
6. Breazeal, C., Dautenhahn, K., Kanda, T.: Social robotics. In: Siciliano, B., Khatib, O. (eds.) Springer Handbook of Robotics, pp. 1935–1972. Springer, Cham (2016). https://doi.org/10.1007/978-3-319-32552-1_72
7. van den Brule, R., Dotsch, R., Bijlstra, G., Wigboldus, D.H.J., Haselager, P.: Do robot performance and behavioral style affect human trust? Int. J. Soc. Robot. **6**(4), 519–531 (2014)
8. Carpinella, C.M., Wyman, A.B., Perez, M.A., Stroessner, S.J.: The robotic social attributes scale (RoSAS): development and validation. In: Proceedings of the 2017 International Conference on Human-Robot Interaction, pp. 254–262. ACM (2017)
9. Castro-González, Á., et al.: The effects of an impolite vs. a polite robot playing rock-paper-scissors. In: Agah, A., Cabibihan, J.-J., Howard, A.M., Salichs, M.A., He, H. (eds.) ICSR 2016. LNCS (LNAI), vol. 9979, pp. 306–316. Springer, Cham (2016). https://doi.org/10.1007/978-3-319-47437-3_30
10. Fraunhofer IPA: Care-o-bot data sheet (2018). https://www.care-o-bot.de/en/care-o-bot-4/technical-data.html
11. Health and Safety Executive: Health and Safety At Work Act (1974)
12. Holthaus, P., Pitsch, K., Wachsmuth, S.: How can i help? Int. J. Soc. Robot. **3**(4), 383–393 (2011)
13. International Organization for Standardization: ISO/IEC 13482:2014: Robots and robotic devices – Safety requirements for personal care robots (2014)

14. Klamer, T., Ben Allouch, S., Heylen, D.: "Adventures of harvey" – use, acceptance of and relationship building with a social robot in a domestic environment. In: Lamers, M.H., Verbeek, F.J. (eds.) HRPR 2010. LNICST, vol. 59, pp. 74–82. Springer, Heidelberg (2011). https://doi.org/10.1007/978-3-642-19385-9_10

15. Koay, K.L., Syrdal, D., Bormann, R., Saunders, J., Walters, M.L., Dautenhahn, K.: Initial design, implementation and technical evaluation of a context-aware proxemics planner for a social robot. In: Kheddar, A. et al. (eds.) Social Robotics. ICSR 2017. LNCS, vol. 10652, pp. 12–22. Springer, Cham (2017). https://doi.org/10.1007/978-3-319-70022-9_2

16. Koay, K.L., Syrdal, D.S., Ashgari-Oskoei, M., Walters, M.L., Dautenhahn, K.: Social roles and baseline proxemic preferences for a domestic service robot. Int. J. Soc. Robot. **6**(4), 469–488 (2014)

17. Lichtenthäler, C., Kirsch, A.: Legibility of robot behavior: a literature review (2016)

18. Likert, R.: A technique for the measurement of attitudes. Arch. Psychol. **22**, 1–55 (1932)

19. Menon, C., Holthaus, P.: Does a loss of social credibility impact robot safety? balancing social and safety behaviours of assistive robots. In: International Conference on Performance. Safety and Robustness in Complex Systems and Applications (PESARO 2019), pp. 18–24. IARIA, Valencia, Spain (2019)

20. National Transportation Safety Board: Collision Between a Car Operating with Automated Vehicle Control Systems and a Tractor Semitrailer Truck Near Williston, Florida, May 7 2016. Technical Report HAR1702 (2016)

21. National Transportation Safety Board: Preliminary Report Highway HWY18FH011. Technical Report HWYFH011 (2018)

22. Renner, P., Pfeiffer, T., Wachsmuth, I.: Spatial references with gaze and pointing in shared space of humans and robots. In: Freksa, C., Nebel, B., Hegarty, M., Barkowsky, T. (eds.) Spatial Cognition 2014. LNCS (LNAI), vol. 8684, pp. 121–136. Springer, Cham (2014). https://doi.org/10.1007/978-3-319-11215-2_9

23. Rios-Martinez, J., Spalanzani, A., Laugier, C.: From proxemics theory to socially-aware navigation: a survey. Int. J. Soc. Robot. **7**(2), 137–153 (2015)

24. Salem, M., Lakatos, G., Amirabdollahian, F., Dautenhahn, K.: Would you trust a (faulty) robot?: effects of error, task type and personality on human-robot cooperation and trust. In: Proceedings of the Tenth Annual ACM/IEEE International Conference on Human-Robot Interaction HRI 2015, pp. 141–148. ACM, New York (2015)

25. Salem, M., Ziadee, M., Sakr, M.: Effects of politeness and interaction context on perception and experience of HRI. In: Herrmann, G., Pearson, M.J., Lenz, A., Bremner, P., Spiers, A., Leonards, U. (eds.) ICSR 2013. LNCS (LNAI), vol. 8239, pp. 531–541. Springer, Cham (2013). https://doi.org/10.1007/978-3-319-02675-6_53

26. Sarter, N.B., Woods, D.D.: Team play with a powerful and independent agent: operational experiences and automation surprises on the airbus A-20. Hum. Factors **39**(4), 553–569 (1997)

27. Softbank Robotics: Pepper. https://www.softbankrobotics.com/emea/en/pepper

28. Syrdal, D.S., Koay, K.L., Walters, M.L., Dautenhahn, K.: A personalized robot companion?-the role of individual differences on spatial preferences in HRI scenarios. In: RO-MAN 2007-The 16th IEEE International Symposium on Robot and Human Interactive Communication, pp. 1143–1148. IEEE (2007)

29. Wall, J., Cuenca, V., Creef, K., Barnes, B.: Attitudes and opinions towards intelligent speed adaptation. In: 2013 IEEE Intelligent Vehicles Symposium Workshops (IV Workshops), pp. 37–42. IEEE (2013)

30. Wise, M., Ferguson, M., King, D., Diehr, E., Dymesich, D.: Fetch & Freight: Standard Platforms for Service Robot Applications (2016)

Correction to: More Than You Expect: Priors Influence on the Adoption of Intentional Stance Toward Humanoid Robots

Jairo Perez-Osorio, Serena Marchesi, Davide Ghiglino, Melis Ince, and Agnieszka Wykowska

Correction to:
Chapter "More Than You Expect: Priors Influence
on the Adoption of Intentional Stance Toward Humanoid
Robots" in: M. A. Salichs et al. (Eds.): *Social Robotics*,
LNAI 11876, https://doi.org/10.1007/978-3-030-35888-4_12

Unfortunately, the authors of this article had failed to add an acknowledgement to their contribution. This missing acknowledgement was added to the article and reads as follows:

Acknowledgement:
This work received support from the European Research Council (ERC) under the European Union's Horizon 2020 research and innovation program (grant awarded to AW, titled "InStance: Intentional Stance for Social Attunement." G.A. No: ERC-2016-StG-715058).

The updated version of this chapter can be found at
https://doi.org/10.1007/978-3-030-35888-4_12

Author Index

Printed in the United States
By Bookmasters